First Course in Fundamentals of
MATHEMATICS

Allyn and Bacon, Inc.
Boston • Rockleigh, N.J. • Atlanta • Dallas • San Jose
London • Sydney • Toronto

First Course
in Fundamentals of
MATHEMATICS

Edwin I. Stein

Editor: Andrew P. Mastronardi
Designers: L. Christopher Valente
                 Dorothy R. Spence
Preparation Services Manager: Martha E. Ballentine
Senior Buyer: Roger E. Powers

Photo Research: Portfolio/Mary Ruzila
Cover Design: John Martucci Studios
Technical Art: ANCO Art Services
Photo Credits: The Picture Cube/David Strickler, p. 5
                   The Picture Cube/Richard Wood, p. 41
                   Frank Siteman, p. 81
                   The Picture Cube/Eric Roth, p. 87
                   The Picture Cube/Richard Wood, p. 133
                   The Picture Cube/Sharon A. Bazarian, p. 177
                   The Picture Cube/Eric Roth, p. 215
                   Andrew Brilliant, p. 227
                   Stock, Boston/Donald Dietz, p. 273
                   Andrew Brilliant, p. 281
                   The Picture Cube/Richard Wood, p. 383
                   Stock, Boston/Peter Vandermark, p. 453

ISBN 0-205-08711-6

Printed in the United States of America.

2   3   4   5   6   7   8   9   93   92   91   90   89   88   87

Preface

First Course in Fundamentals of Mathematics is the introductory textbook of a comprehensive general mathematics program for the junior and senior high schools.

This edition contains a wealth of material in all the basic topics of arithmetic, providing computational practice for the development and maintainance of skills. Problem Solving sections throughout apply these skills to the everyday world. Opening inventory tests assess arithmetic and problem solving skills taught in earlier grades. These inventory tests are keyed to sections or pages where explanatory material and practice exercises may be found. This makes the book adaptable to the specific needs of each individual student.

First Course in Fundamentals of Mathematics also includes a strategy for solving word problems, a comprehensive study of the metric system, customary and metric geometry with a specific strategy for solving word problems involving geometry, an introduction to algebra and statistics, and consumer applications of mathematics. It contains a complete study of integers and rational numbers and their properties, and geometric measurement and constructions covering a wide range of geometric relationships and facts. Spending and managing money applications, including unit pricing and writing checks are also featured in this text. Estimating Answers and Check by Calculator sections provide practice in checking arithmetic processes.

Featured in the arithmetic sections are a new way of writing shortened names for large whole numbers, scientific notation, number theory and enrichment materials such as the Sieve of Eratosthenes, Goldbach's conjecture, Euclid's algorithm, Euler's formula, and the Russian peasant and lattice methods of multiplication.

The practice material is varied and carefully graded by difficulty. Keyed Chapter Reviews and Achievement Tests are provided throughout the text. Important explanatory material and sample problems are emphasized by color screens and boxes.

A Competency Check Test ends the book. It also is keyed to specific sections where the students can go for remedial help.

First Course in Fundamentals of Mathematics meets the many and varied requirements of today's programs in mathematics for all students.

EDWIN I. STEIN

Contents

3 NUMBER SENTENCES—EQUALITIES AND INEQUALITIES 81

4 COMMON FRACTIONS 87

Contents

5 DECIMAL FRACTIONS

6 PERCENT

7   SQUARE ROOTS—IRRATIONAL NUMBERS   215

8   UNITS OF MEASURE AND MEASUREMENT   227

11 INFORMAL GEOMETRY   383

12 APPLICATIONS OF MATHEMATICS —PROBLEM SOLVING

453

INVENTORY TEST   *Skills of Previous Grades*

The numeral at the end of each of the following problems indicates the sections where explanatory material may be found.

1. Read the numeral 8,047,516 or write it as a word statement.   (1–7)

2. Write a numeral naming: Nine hundred five thousand, seventy-six.   (1–8)

3. Rearrange the digits of 629,308 so that the numeral names the greatest possible number.   (1–6)

4. Round 679,815 to the nearest thousand.   (1–10)

5. Add:
   26,848
   5,985
   97,879
   78,507
   4,399   (2–9)

6. Subtract:
   194,256
   87,309   (2–10)

7. Multiply:
   947
   806   (2–11)

8. Divide:
   $694\overline{)352{,}552}$
   (2–16)

9. Is 864,000 divisible by 10? by 5? by 2? by 4? by 9? by 8? by 3? by 6?   (2–17)

10. What is the greatest common factor of 54 and 81?   (1–21)

11. Find the least common multiple of 16 and 10.   (1–24)

12. Factor 24 as the product of prime numbers.   (1–19)

13. Express $\frac{40}{72}$ in lowest terms.   (4–2)

14. Express $\frac{3}{4}$ as 20ths.   (4–3)

15. Express $\frac{21}{6}$ as a mixed number.   (4–5)

16. Express $8\frac{7}{3}$ in simplest form.   (4–5)

17. Express $9\frac{4}{5}$ as an improper fraction.   (4–5)

18. Find the lowest common denominator of the following fractions: $\frac{5}{6}$ and $\frac{7}{8}$.   (4–6)

19. Are $\frac{15}{27}$ and $\frac{35}{63}$ equivalent fractions?   (4–4)

20. Which of the following are true: **a.** $\frac{1}{2} < \frac{3}{5}$? **b.** $\frac{5}{8} > \frac{7}{10}$?   (4–8)

21. Add: **22.** Subtract: **23.** Multiply: **24.** Divide:

$5\frac{3}{4}$ $4\frac{1}{2}$ $1\frac{1}{5} \times 3\frac{3}{4}$ (4–13) $6 \div 7\frac{1}{3}$

$7\frac{2}{3}$ (4–11) $3\frac{5}{8}$ (4–12)   (4–15)

25. Find $\frac{1}{4}$ of $2\frac{7}{8}$.   (4–16)

26. 49 is what fractional part of 63?   (4–17)

27. $\frac{2}{3}$ of what number is 18?   (4–18)

28. Read the numeral 14.078 or write it as a word statement.   (5–2)

29. Write the decimal numeral naming: Eighty and six hundredths.   (5–3)

30. Round 538.6394 to the nearest hundredth.   (5–5)

31. Which of the following are true:

     a. 0.47 = .047?   **b.** 1.9 > .275?   **c.** .8 < .799?   (5–6)

32. Add: **33.** Subtract:

     9.34 + 40.8   (5–7)   8.7 − .59   (5–8)

34. Multiply: **35.** Divide:

     .008 × 2.5   (5–9) $.02\overline{)1.2}$ (5–11)

36. Find .6 of 15.9.   (5–19)

37. 32 is what decimal part of 48?   (5–20)

38. .25 of what number is 16?   (5–21)

39. Multiply 25.6 by 100. (5–10)   **40.** Divide 68.47 by 10. (5–12)

41. Write in scientific notation: 7,200,000.   (5–14)

42. Express $\frac{3}{4}$ as a decimal numeral.   (5–15)

43. Express 0.8 as a numeral naming a common fraction.   (5–17)

44. Express 23% as a decimal numeral.   (6–2)

45. Express 70% as a numeral naming a common fraction.   (6–3)

46. Express 0.67 as a percent.   (6–4)

47. Express $\frac{5}{8}$ as a percent.   (6–5)

48. Find 9% of 75.   (6–6)

49. What percent of 60 is 24?   (6–7)

50. 15% of what number is 105?   (6–8)

In each of the following, answer only what is asked. Do not solve the entire problem unless required. Also see pages 74 and 75.

1. **Problem:** Tom has $125.00 in his savings account. When he withdraws $8.65, how much money will be left in his account?
   a. What facts are given?
   b. What is the question asked?

2. **Problem:** Nancy's mother, who is 42 years old, bought a new refrigerator, paying $50 down and the balance in 12 monthly payments. What is the amount of each payment?
   a. What facts are given?
   b. What is the question asked?
   c. Which fact is not necessary?
   d. Are enough facts given? If not, which fact is missing?

3. **Problem:** What is the average speed of an airplane when it flies a distance of 1,250 miles in $2\frac{1}{2}$ hours?
   a. What facts are given?
   b. What is the question asked?
   c. Which operation should be used with the given facts?
   d. Write a mathematical sentence (or equation) that relates the given facts to what is asked.

4. **Problem:** Multiply as indicated: 71×49
   a. First estimate your answer by using rounded numbers.
   b. Then find the actual answer by using given numbers.

5. **Problem:** If your dinner bill at a restaurant came to $9.75 and a 4% sales tax is added, what is your total bill?
   a. What facts are given?
   b. What is the question asked?
   c. Which given facts should be used with which operation?
   d. In what order should the operations be used?
   e. Write a mathematical sentence (or equation) that relates the given facts to what is asked.
   f. First estimate your answers. Then perform the operations accurately to find your answer.
   g. Write your answer. Compare it with the estimated answer for reasonableness.

INVENTORY TEST
PROBLEM SOLVING SKILLS OF PREVIOUS GRADES

Solve each of the following problems. Then turn to the pages indicated by the colored numerals for more practice. Also see pages 74 and 75.

1. The population of Boston increased from 18,320 in 1790 to 597,254 recently. Find the amount of increase. (76)

2. A ribbon, 4 feet long, is cut into two pieces. If one piece measures $19\frac{3}{4}$ inches, what is the length of the second piece of ribbon? (125)

3. If a train travels at the average speed of 55.8 miles per hour, how long will it take to go from New York City to Miami, a distance of 1,323 miles? (168)

4. How many problems out of 40 must a student get right to earn a grade of 75%? (211)

5. A small computer that regularly sells for $699 is reduced 15%. What is the sale price? (458)

6. Find the interest a person owes at the end of a year if $3,000 is borrowed at $14\frac{1}{2}$%. (208)

7. At a sale you can buy two tires, the first at regular price and the second at half price. How much will the two tires cost if the regular price of a tire is $55? (458)

8. Which is the better buy: 6 donuts for 77¢ or 8 donuts for $1.01? (459)

9. If you sleep from 10:20 P.M. to 7:15 A.M. the next morning, how long are you asleep? (256)

10. The postage rate for first class mail is $.20 for the first ounce and $.17 for each additional ounce. How much postage is needed to send a package weighing 8 ounces by first class mail? (168)

11. If the Super Bowl XVI football game was telecast nationwide from Pontiac, Michigan at 4 P.M. (EST), what time was it seen in Los Angeles (PST)? (262)

12. Who has the higher average score (arithmetic mean): Maria with scores of 91; 76; 85 or Pedro with scores of 78; 89; 88? How much higher? (278)

13. How much change should you get if you purchase 2 shirts at $14.97 each and give a $50 bill in payment? (464)

14. What are the actual dimensions of a living room floor if plans drawn to scale 1 inch = 4 feet show dimensions of $4\frac{1}{2}$ inches by $3\frac{3}{4}$ inches? (404)

15. Which is longer: the circumference of a circular table top measuring 28 inches in diameter or the perimeter of a square table top measuring 25 inches on each side? How much longer? (Use $\frac{22}{7}$ for π). (430, 432)

16. A rug, 9 feet by 12 feet, is placed on a rectangular floor 13 feet by 15 feet. How many square feet of floor space is not covered by the rug? (434)

CHAPTER 1
Number and Decimal System of Numeration

1-1 NUMBER AND NUMERAL

Number is an abstract or mental idea. The number symbols we write and see are not numbers but names for numbers which we call *numerals*. Although 19 is commonly called a number, actually it is a numeral or group of number symbols which represent the number named *nineteen*. However, number symbols are generally used to denote both numbers and numerals as "Add the numbers 27 and 36" and "Write the numeral 594."

Word names for any specific number differ because of differences in languages, although the same number symbols are used. In Spanish nineteen is *diez y nueve*; in French, *dix-neuf*; in Italian, *diciannove*; in German, *neunzehn*. A number may have many names; it may be represented by symbols in many ways.

> The number named *nineteen* may be represented by any one of the following numerals:
>
> 19   XIX   12 + 7   32 − 13   19 × 1 $\frac{38}{2}$
>
> However, 19 is considered the simplest numeral.

Each of the number symbols 0, 1, 2, 3, 4, 5, 6, 7, 8, and 9 is called a *digit* or figure. The numeral 5 contains one digit; the numeral 46 contains two digits; 979 contains three digits; etc.

EXERCISES

1. Which is larger, numeral 7 or numeral 9?
2. Which is larger, number 7 or number 9?
3. Write the numeral 5,273; rewrite the numeral but replace the digit 3 with the digit 8.

4. How many digits are in the numeral 7,003,498?
5. Write a two-digit numeral using the digits:
   a. 8 and 4   **b.** 2 and 5   **c.** 7 and 1   **d.** 0 and 6
6. **a.** Write a 3-digit numeral containing the digits 5, 4, and 7.
   b. Write a 4-digit numeral containing the digits 3, 8, 9, and 6.
7. Write four different number names for each of the following numbers:
   a. six   **b.** twenty   **c.** fourteen   **d.** fifty   **e.** eleven
8. Write the simplest numeral that names the number expressed by:
   a. $11 - 3$ **b.** 5×6 **c.** $30 + 9$ **d.** $25 \div 5$

1–2 ONE-TO-ONE CORRESPONDENCE

We see at the right that the number of □'s is exactly the same as the number of ○'s. When they are paired off, we find

□   □   □   □
↕   ↕   ↕   ↕
○   ○   ○   ○

there is one □ for every ○ and one ○ for every □, no more no less. This kind of exact pairing or matching or mapping is called *one-to-one correspondence* and is indicated by a two-headed arrow since the matching is done in both directions. In counting there is a one-to-one correspondence between the objects being counted and each of the counting numbers.

EXERCISES

1. Copy, then pair off the objects in the following groups, placing them in one-to-one correspondence by using the two-headed arrow.

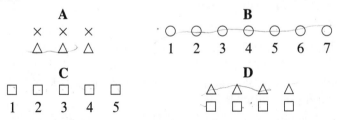

2. If two groups of objects are in one-to-one correspondence, is it true that they are equal in number?

3. In which of the following may the objects be paired so that there is one-to-one correspondence?

A
× × × × × × × ×

B
△ △ △ △ △ △

C
□ □ □ □ □ □

D
1 2 3 4 5 6 7 8

4. Copy, then match, this collection of dots in a one-to-one correspondence with the numerals naming the counting numbers, beginning with 1.

● ● ● ● ● ● ● ● ● ● ● ●

1–3 CARDINAL NUMBER AND ORDINAL NUMBER

Number answers the questions of "How many?" and "Which one?". The number that tells how many things are in a collection or its size is called a *cardinal number*. When we count, we match each object to a corresponding number belonging to a standard group of counting numbers and the last number named tells how many objects there are in all. The number that tells the position or order of an object in a collection such as first, second, third, fourth, and so on is called an *ordinal number*. The same number symbols are used to represent both cardinal and ordinal numbers.

EXERCISES

1. Which of the following are cardinal numbers? Which are ordinal numbers?

   a. The class read page 5 of a book containing 360 pages.
   b. Scott spent fifty cents for the third day in succession.
   c. Stephen had 10 examples to do for homework but had only example number 9 incorrect.
   d. The classroom contained 5 rows of 8 seats in each row; Carmela sat in seat 7 in row 3.
   e. Marilyn ranked number 6 in her class of 130 pupils.

2. Write the numeral that names the cardinal number for this group of objects:

△ △ △ △ △ △ △ △ △

3. Write the numeral that names the ordinal number representing the position of the ● from the left side of this group of objects:

4. Does the following sentence contain a cardinal number? If so, name it. Does the following sentence contain an ordinal number? If so, name it.

The month of September has 30 days, and this year September 15 is a Friday.

1–4 NATURAL NUMBERS—WHOLE NUMBERS

The numbers 0, 1, 2, 3, 4, 5, 6, 7, 8, 9, 10, 11, 12, 13, 14, etc. are called *whole numbers*. The whole numbers beginning with 1 that are used in counting are called counting or *natural numbers*. Zero is generally not considered to be a natural number.

Instead of the "etc." at the end of the numbers, three dots may be used to indicate that the group of numbers is unlimited.

> 1, 2, 3, 4, . . . means "one, two, three, four, and so on endlessly."
>
> 1, 2, 3, . . . , 20 means "one, two, three, and so on up to and including twenty."

EXERCISES

1. Can you name the greatest whole number? Is there a greatest whole number?
2. Is there a last whole number? If so, what is it?
3. Is there a first whole number? If so, what is it?

4. Whole numbers have order; each is followed by another whole number, called the *successor*, which is one (1) greater. The whole number preceding another whole number is called the *predecessor*.

   a. In 1, 2, 3, 4, 5, 6, 7, 8, 9, 10, 11, 12, . . ., what is the successor of 6? The predecessor of 9?

   b. Arrange the following numbers in order of size, smallest first:

   ~~14~~ ~~8~~ ~~6~~ ~~11~~ ~~3~~ ~~13~~ 26 ~~19~~ ~~5~~ 31 ~~15~~ 28 ~~20~~ 37 ~~18~~

5. What whole numbers are between 8 and 11? Between 13 and 21?

6. Write in order the numerals for the next five whole numbers that follow these numbers:

   a. 8   **b.** 89   **c.** 102   **d.** 325

1–5 THE NUMBER LINE

A straight line that has its points labeled with numerals so that each point is associated with a number is called a *number line*.

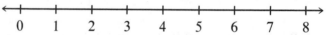

To draw a number line, two points are chosen with the one on the left labeled 0 and the other point labeled 1. With the interval between these points as the unit of measure, points are located to the right of the point marked 1, equally spaced along the line. Each point is assigned a corresponding whole number (*coordinate*) in consecutive order. There is a one-to-one correspondence between these numbers and the points on the line.

We may compare numbers by the number line. The number corresponding to the point on the line farther to the right is the larger number.

EXERCISES

D	H	A	P	Z	I	W	C	M	V	F	Y	Q	B	N	X
0	1	2	3	4	5	6	7	8	9	10	11	12	13	14	15

1. What number corresponds to the point marked:

   A? B? C? D? F? M? N? V? W? X? Y? Z?

2. What letter labels the point corresponding to each of the following numbers:

5? 1? 13? 12? 3? 7? 0? 15? 8? 4? 9? 2?

3. Which corresponding point is farther to the right on the number line:

a. 6 or 9?   **c.** 14 or 8?   **e.** 0 or 10?
b. 15 or 12?   **d.** 12 or 5?   **f.** 2 or 11?

4. Draw a number line showing whole numbers 0–10. Label each point corresponding to a number with a letter of the alphabet.

SYSTEMS OF NUMERATION

A *system of numeration* is a method of naming numbers by writing numerals. Basic number symbols of varying values are arranged according to the principles of grouping used in the specific system.

Although some ancient systems of numeration used different grouping symbols instead of place value, repeating them when necessary, others used the principle of place value where the total value of each number symbol was determined by its position or place in the numeral. In our modern numeration systems we use place value along with the principles of addition and multiplication which were also used in some of the ancient systems.

The *base* of a numeration system is the number it takes in any one place to make *one* (1) in the next higher place; it is the unit of grouping.

1–6 DECIMAL SYSTEM OF NUMERATION

In our system of notation, called the *decimal system,* ten number symbols 0, 1, 2, 3, 4, 5, 6, 7, 8, and 9 are used to represent all numbers. These number symbols are of Hindu-Arabic origin. They were introduced in Europe during the 12th century and are now used generally throughout the world. They were brought to the United States by the colonists.

There is no single number symbol in our numeration system to represent ten or numbers greater than ten. Numerals representing numbers greater than nine are formed by writing two or more number symbols next to each other in different positions or places.

Our system of writing numerals is built on the base ten. It takes ten in any one place to make one in the next higher place. It takes 10 ones to make 1 ten, 10 tens to make 1 hundred, 10 hundreds to make 1 thousand, and so forth.

	Trillions			Billions			Millions			Thousands			Ones		
quadrillions	hundred trillions	ten trillions	trillions	hundred billions	ten billions	billions	hundred millions	ten millions	millions	hundred thousands	ten thousands	thousands	hundreds	tens	ones
3,	3	3	3,	3	3	3,	3	3	3,	3	3	3,	3	3	3

In the number scale the ones (sometimes called units) are located on the right. One place to the left of the ones position is the tens place; one place to the left of the tens position is the hundreds place. These three places form a group or period.

The scale illustrates that the periods in increasing order are: ones, thousands, millions, billions, trillions, and quadrillions. The names of other periods in increasing order are quintillion, sextillion, septillion, octillion, nonillion, and decillion. A decillion is written as:

$$1,000,000,000,000,000,000,000,000,000,000,000$$

The decimal system is a positional system. It uses place value to represent each power of ten instead of a special symbol. The value of each place in the decimal numeral is ten times the value of the next place to the right.

Thus, in the numeral the value of each digit depends not only on the symbol but also on its position in the numeral. The digit 8 in the decimal numeral 86 means 8 tens but in the decimal numeral 865 it means 8 hundreds.

The zero symbol indicates "not any" and, when used as a placeholder, it indicates no ones, no tens, etc. A four-digit numeral such as 2,694 indicates 2 thousands, 6 hundreds, 9 tens, 4 ones; or 26 hundreds, 9 tens, 4 ones; or 269 tens, 4 ones; or 2,694 ones.

1. In the numeral 5,863,295,482,716 what digit is in the:
   a. ones place
   b. thousands place
   c. tens place
   d. millions place
   e. hundreds place
   f. hundred thousands place
   g. ten thousands place
   h. billions place
   i. ten millions place
   j. trillions place
   k. ten billions place
   l. hundred millions place

2. What place does the zero hold in each of the following numerals:
   a. 98,027
   b. 406,928
   c. 3,425,103
   d. 80,215,896

3. Complete the following:
   a. 4,862,357 = ... millions ...... hundred thousands ...... ten thousands ...... thousands ...... hundreds ...... tens ...... ones
   b. 7,864 = ... thousands ...... hundreds ...... tens ...... ones
      or = ... hundreds ...... tens ...... ones
      or = ... tens ...... ones
      or = ... ones

4. Write the numeral naming the number:
   3 *millions* 4 *hundred thousands* 9 *ten thousands* 0 *thousands* 5 *hundreds* 8 *tens* 2 *ones*

5. What new group does 1 more than 99,999 make? 1 more than 9,999,999?

6. Which number is greater?
   a. 4,862,917 or 4,862,971
   b. 12,689,754 or 12,698,457

7. Which number is smaller?
   a. 975,062 or 975,026
   b. 5,748,841 or 5,784,148

8. Name the greatest possible:
   a. 4-place number
   b. 7-place number

9. Name the smallest possible:
   a. 6-place number
   b. 9-place number

10. Write the numeral that names the greatest number possible using the digits:
    a. 9, 1, 8
    b. 4, 7, 2, 5
    c. 3, 4, 0, 8, 2, 5
    d. 7, 0, 9, 1, 4, 9, 3

11. Write the numeral that names the smallest number possible using the digits:
    a. 7, 6, 2
    b. 9, 3, 0, 6
    c. 5, 3, 4, 7, 9, 1
    d. 8, 0, 5, 0, 3, 1, 6

12. Rearrange the digits in each of the following numerals so that it names the greatest possible number:

    a. 204,913   **b.** 46,986   **c.** 4,306,072   **d.** 17,553,421

13. Rearrange the digits in each of the following numerals so that it names the smallest possible number:

    a. 7,146   **b.** 670,392   **c.** 8,680,407   **d.** 51,866,924

14. Arrange the following numbers according to size, writing the numeral for the greatest first:

    437,218   437,128   437,812   437,182

15. Arrange the following numbers according to size, writing the numeral for the smallest first:

    5,986,752   5,986,725   5,698,527   5,869,257

1–7 READING NUMERALS NAMING WHOLE NUMBERS

Before reading a numeral containing four digits or more, it is advisable to separate it by commas into as many groups (or periods) of three digits as possible, starting from the ones place and counting to the left. Sometimes spaces are used instead of commas to separate these groups. With the exception of this section and section 1–8, only commas will be used in this book.

To read a numeral, we begin at the left and read each period of digits separately, applying the name of the period indicated by each comma or space as it is reached. The word "and" is not used between names of the periods.

The numeral 78,356,912,405 is read: *Seventy-eight billion, three hundred fifty-six million, nine hundred twelve thousand, four hundred five.*

The numeral 9 468 300 is read: *Nine million, four hundred sixty-eight thousand, three hundred.*

A 4-digit numeral may appear without a comma or space.

8900 is read either as: *Eighty-nine hundred*
or as: *Eight thousand, nine hundred.*

---

1. Separate each of the following numerals into proper groups (periods) by using commas:

   a. 63041
   b. 58162840
   c. 3913596804
   d. 8150270000000
   e. 10319473285206
   f. 2403920000038675

2. Separate each of the following numerals into proper periods by using spaces:

   a. 86450
   b. 6154269803
   c. 40000000000
   d. 90476813254088
   e. 790333386415580
   f. 3440025169728350

3. Read, or write in words, each of the following:

   a. 908
   b. 5,046
   c. 46,867
   d. 800,075
   e. 3,729,681
   f. 20,005,998
   g. 86,418,134
   h. 6,359,722,018
   i. 78,404,015,263
   j. 814,875,000,000
   k. 4,394,481,356,672
   l. 19,006,507,093,855

4. Read, or write in words, each of the following:

   a. 1 529
   b. 36 803
   c. 470 054
   d. 2 978 005
   e. 608 500 025
   f. 7 900 000 000
   g. 53 847 926 010
   h. 94 703 514
   i. 833 400 207 000
   j. 7 553 899 000 462
   k. 65 478 206 953 071
   l. 416 003 050 900 000

5. Read each of the following in two ways:

   a. 4300   **b.** 9200   **c.** 7800   **d.** 6750   **e.** 3175

6. Read, or write in words, each of the numerals that appear in the following:

   a. The final presidential election returns showed that one candidate received 42,797,153 votes, the second, 34,434,100 votes, and the third, 5,533,927 votes.
   b. The area of the earth's surface is approximately 196,938,800 square miles.
   c. There are 2,730,242 farms in the United States covering 1,006,218,650 acres of land.
   d. The public debt of the United States in 1890 was $1,132,396,584 and recently was $907,701,290,900.
   e. The Pacific Ocean has a surface area of 64,186,300 square miles and an average depth of 13,739 feet.

Number and Decimal System of Numeration   15

1–8 WRITING NUMERALS NAMING WHOLE NUMBERS

We write each period of digits and use commas (or sometimes spaces) to represent the names of the periods.

> Sixty-nine million, four hundred twenty-five thousand, nine hundred eighty-six written as a numeral is 69,425,986 (or sometimes 69 425 986).

EXERCISES

1. Write, using commas, the numeral that names each of the following:

   a. Fifty-four million.
   b. Seven hundred forty-nine thousand.
   c. Nine trillion.
   d. Six hundred eighty-five billion.
   e. Twenty-seven thousand, two hundred thirty-two.
   f. Three hundred eight thousand, seven hundred eighty-nine.
   g. Fifty-four million, six hundred forty-one thousand.
   h. Nine million, seven hundred fifty thousand, three hundred twenty-five.
   i. Eight hundred thirty-four million, five hundred thousand, seventy-six.
   j. Two billion, four hundred eleven million, two hundred eighteen thousand.
   k. Forty-five billion, eight hundred thirty thousand, ten.
   l. Twenty trillion, fifty-nine billion, four hundred million, one hundred fifty-nine.

2. Write, using spaces, the numeral that names each of the following:

   a. Five hundred twenty-eight thousand.
   b. Seven billion.
   c. Eight hundred sixty-five million.

d. 43 trillion.

e. Seven hundred six thousand, twenty-nine.

f. Sixty million, four hundred seven thousand, one hundred ninety-five.

g. Three billion, five hundred nineteen million, forty thousand, eight hundred.

h. Fifty-one trillion, seven hundred million, thirty thousand.

1–9 SHORTENED NAMES FOR LARGE WHOLE NUMBERS

Shortened names are sometimes used to indicate large whole numbers whose numerals end in a series of zeros.

> 52 *billion* is the shortened name for 52,000,000,000.

Here we see that the period name *billion* is used to replace the 9 zeros holding places in the numeral. Similarly, the period name *thousand* is used to replace 000 (3 zeros); *million* to replace 000,000 (6 zeros); *trillion* to replace 000,000,000,000 (12 zeros); and so on.

Thus, to write the complete numeral for the shortened name, we replace the period name by annexing the appropriate number of zeros to the given numeral prefix.

> 745 *million* is 745,000,000.

To write the shortened name for a numeral that ends in a series of zeros, we replace the required number of zeros by the equivalent period name.

> 30,000 becomes 30 *thousand*.
> 9,000,000,000,000 becomes 9 *trillion*.

Also see section 5–13.

1. Write the complete numeral for each of the following:

    a. 7 thousand; 63 thousand; 325 thousand; 40 thousand
    b. 58 billion; 104 billion; 6 billion; 800 billion
    c. 4 million; 79 million; 100 million; 967 million
    d. 89 trillion; 3 trillion; 241 trillion; 50 trillion
    e. The Treasury sold $12 billion of 52-week bills.

2. Write the shortened name for each of the following:

    a. In millions: 89,000,000; 2,000,000; 155,000,000; 20,000,000
    b. In billions: 18,000,000,000; 734,000,000,000;
                        300,000,000,000; 5,000,000,000
    c. In thousands: 6,000; 99,000; 806,000; 100,000
    d. In trillions: 63,000,000,000,000; 825,000,000,000,000
    e. In millions: yesterday over 49,000,000 shares of stock were sold.

1–10 ROUNDING WHOLE NUMBERS

Newspapers often use round numbers in their story leads. An increase in population of 36,927 may be reported as "an increase of almost 37,000" and a bridge costing $2,163,875 may be reported as one "costing more than $2,000,000."

Using the number line to round numbers, we consider a point (which corresponds to the number to be rounded) that is located halfway or more than halfway between two points of reference to be closer to the point corresponding to the larger number.

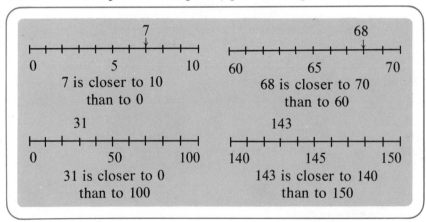

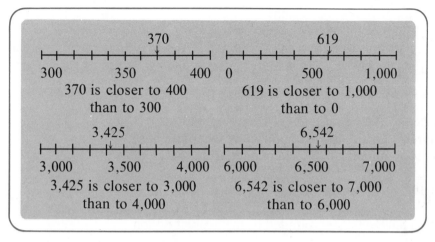

370 is closer to 400
than to 300

619 is closer to 1,000
than to 0

3,425 is closer to 3,000
than to 4,000

6,542 is closer to 7,000
than to 6,000

Numbers may be rounded to the nearest ten, hundred, thousand, etc. depending on what is required.

To round a whole number without using the number line, we find the place in the numeral to which the number is to be rounded (the nearest ten, hundred, thousand, etc.). We then rewrite the given digits to the left of the required place and we write a zero in place of each digit to the right of the required place. If the first digit dropped is 5 or more, we increase the given digit in the required place by 1, otherwise we write the same digit as given.

However, as many digits to the left are changed as necessary when the given digit in the required place is 9 and one (1) is added.

4,691,826 rounded to the nearest:

hundred is:	4,691,800
thousand is:	4,692,000
million is:	5,000,000

EXERCISES

1. Select the numbers that are nearer to:

a. 0 than 10:	3	7	4	6	8
b. 10 than 0:	1	6	2	9	4
c. 70 than 80:	78	74	71	77	72
d. 400 than 300:	317	385	353	348	306

e. 8,000 than 9,000:	8,600	8,125	8,499	8,703	8,514
f. 60,000 than 50,000:	53,000	57,300	54,736	55,002	59,487
g. 300,000 than 400,000:	375,000	304,000	351,003	338,785	349,999
h. 7,000,000 than 6,000,000:	6,225,000	6,630,000	6,409,786	6,745,261	6,300,078

2. Any number from:

   a. 45 to 54 rounded to the nearest ten is what number?
   b. 650 to 749 rounded to the nearest hundred is what number?
   c. 12,500 to 13,499 rounded to the nearest thousand is what number?
   d. 9,500,000 to 10,499,999 rounded to the nearest million is what number?
   e. 7,500,000,000 to 8,499,999,999 rounded to the nearest billion is what number?

3. Round each of the following numbers to the nearest:

   a. Ten:

48	74	26	483	7,965

   b. Hundred:

320	592	6,278	1,506	24,814

   c. Thousand:

4,750	8,341	15,539	47,852	63,267

   d. Ten thousand:

36,000	94,729	71,987	423,275	786,498

   e. Hundred thousand:

910,000	252,495	664,019	3,180,531	29,349,653

   f. Million:

4,700,000	7,328,000	15,445,625	916,503,064	8,432,198,572

   g. Billion:

6,824,000,000	1,050,900,000	8,496,570,000	39,975,201,750	121,263,000,000

4. Round the numbers that appear in the following to the nearest:

   a. Thousand: The recent census showed there were 98,912,192 males and 104,299,734 females living in the United States.
   b. Million: Fire losses for a recent year amounted to $3,264,800,000.
   c. Billion: $87,476,798,000 was spent by the Defense Department in 1975.
   d. Thousand: The Mediterranean Sea has an area of 969,100 square miles.
   e. Million: Motor vehicle registrations for a recent year reached 129,943,087.

1–11 EXPONENTS

When we use two equal factors in multiplication like 3×3, we may write it in exponential form as 3^2, which is read "three to the second power" or "the second power of three" or "three squared" or the "square of three."

$5 \times 5 \times 5$ may be written as 5^3, which is read "five to the third power" or "five cubed" or "the cube of five."

2^4 represents $2 \times 2 \times 2 \times 2$ or the product 16 and is read "two to the fourth power."

10^5 represents $10 \times 10 \times 10 \times 10 \times 10$ or the product 100,000 and is read "ten to the fifth power."

The small numeral written to the upper right (superscript) of the repeated factor is called an *exponent*. When it names a natural number, it tells how many times the factor is being used in multiplication. The factor that is being repeated is called the *base*. The number 2^4 uses 2 as the base and 4 as the exponent. Numbers such as 2^3, 2^4, 2^5, 2^6, etc. are called *powers* of 2.

EXERCISES

1. Read, or write in words, each of the following:

   a. 6^5 **b.** 10^7 **c.** 4^{15} **d.** 2^1 **e.** 14^{10} **f.** 8^3 **g.** 25^8 **h.** 100^2

2. Write as a numeral:

   a. Three to the fourth power   **d.** Four cubed
   b. Nine to the eighth power   **e.** Twelve to the sixth power
   c. Seven squared   **f.** Twenty to the tenth power

3. What is the exponent in: **a.** 5^9?   **b.** 10^{11}?   **c.** 3^5?   **d.** 8^1?   **e.** 15^{18}?

4. What is the base in: **a.** 7^8?   **b.** 4^3?   **c.** 19^6?   **d.** 24^{15}?   **e.** 50^9?

5. How many times is the base being used as a factor in:

   a. 3^7?   **b.** 8^3?   **c.** 4^{10}?   **d.** 6^2?   **e.** 10^{13}?

6. Use the exponential form to write:

   a. $5 \times 5 \times 5$ **e.** $7 \times 7 \times 7 \times 7 \times 7 \times 7 \times 7 \times 7$
   b. $9 \times 9 \times 9 \times 9$ **f.** $3 \times 3 \times 3 \times 3 \times 3 \times 3 \times 3$
   c. 6×6 **g.** $4 \times 4 \times 4 \times 4 \times 4 \times 4 \times 4 \times 4 \times 4 \times 4$
   d. $8 \times 8 \times 8 \times 8 \times 8$ **h.** $2 \times 2 \times 2 \times 2 \times 2 \times 2 \times 2 \times 2 \times 2 \times 2 \times 2$

7. Express each of the following as a product of a repeated factor:

    a. $6^3 = 6 \times 6 \times 6$ **b.** 7^6 **c.** 12^4 **d.** 9^{10} **e.** 2^8 **f.** 3^{15} **g.** 5^9 **h.** 8^{12}

8. a. Express 8 as a power of 2.   **d.** Express 32 as a power of 2.
    b. Express 36 as a power of 6.   **e.** Express 64 as a power of 4.
    c. Express 125 as a power of 5.   **f.** Express 81 as a power of 3.

9. First express each of the following as a product of a repeated factor, then in exponent form:

    a. $49 = 7 \times 7 = 7^2$ **b.** 27 **c.** 16 **d.** 121 **e.** 625 **f.** 64 **g.** 144 **h.** 128

10. Find the value of each of the following:

    a. 15^2 **b.** 5^3 **c.** 2^7 **d.** 3^5 **e.** 6^3 **f.** 7^4 **g.** 4^6 **h.** 2^{10}

1–12 POWERS OF TEN

Using 10 as a repeated factor, we develop the following table of powers of 10:

$$
\begin{aligned}
10 &= 10 &&= 10^1 \\
100 &= 10 \times 10 &&= 10^2 \\
1{,}000 &= 10 \times 10 \times 10 &&= 10^3 \\
10{,}000 &= 10 \times 10 \times 10 \times 10 &&= 10^4 \\
100{,}000 &= 10 \times 10 \times 10 \times 10 \times 10 &&= 10^5 \\
1{,}000{,}000 &= 10 \times 10 \times 10 \times 10 \times 10 \times 10 &&= 10^6
\end{aligned}
$$

Observe in the above table:

(1) 10 used one time as a factor may be written with the exponent 1, although the exponent 1 usually is omitted.

(2) The number of zeros found after the digit 1 in the product (first column above) corresponds in each case to the exponent of 10 (third column above). For example, in $1{,}000 = 10^3$ there are 3 zeros in the product (1,000) and the exponent of 10^3 is 3.

Any numeral having all digits zeros except the first digit, such as 20 or 500 or 6,000, may be expressed as a product of a digit and a power of ten.

$$6{,}000 = 6 \times 1{,}000 = 6 \times 10^3$$

1. Express each of the following as a power of ten:
   a. 100
   b. 100,000
   c. 10,000,000
   d. 1,000,000,000
   e. 100,000,000,000
   f. 1,000,000,000,000

2. Express each of the following as a product of a digit and a power
   of ten:
   a. 30
   b. 400
   c. 90,000
   d. 5,000
   e. 3,000,000
   f. 700,000
   g. 400,000,000
   h. 60,000,000
   i. 2,000,000,000
   j. 70,000,000,000
   k. 900,000,000,000
   l. 8,000,000,000
   m. 4,000,000,000,000
   n. 50,000,000,000,000
   o. 600,000,000,000,000
   p. 3,000,000,000,000,000
   q. 70,000,000,000,000
   r. 20,000,000,000,000,000

1–13 WRITING DECIMAL NUMERALS AS POLYNOMIALS—EXPANDED NOTATION

The value of each place in a decimal numeral may be expressed as a power of ten.

> The digit 7 in 79 means 7 tens or 7×10.
> The digit 5 in 579 means 5 hundreds
> $$\text{or } 5 \times 100 = 5 \times 10^2.$$
> The digit 8 in 8,579 means 8 thousands
> $$\text{or } 8 \times 1,000 = 8 \times 10^3.$$

The complete value of each digit in a decimal numeral is equal to the value of the digit itself times its place value.

A decimal numeral may be written as the sum of the products of each digit in the numeral and its place value expressed as a power of ten.

> The decimal numeral 8,579
>
> $= 8$ thousands $+ 5$ hundreds $+ 7$ tens $+ 9$ ones
> $= (8 \times 1,000) + (5 \times 100) + (7 \times 10) + (9 \times 1)$
> $= (8 \times 10^3) + (5 \times 10^2) + (7 \times 10^1) + (9 \times 1)$

Writing a numeral in this expanded form as an indicated sum (*polynomial*) is sometimes called *expanded notation*. Observe that the place values are powers of ten arranged in a decreasing order from left to right.

1. Express each of the following polynomials as a decimal numeral:

    a. $(5 \times 10^4) + (3 \times 10^3) + (7 \times 10^2) + (6 \times 10^1) + (8 \times 1)$
    b. $(7 \times 10^5) + (9 \times 10^4) + (2 \times 10^3) + (1 \times 10^2) + (4 \times 10^1) + (3 \times 1)$

2. Write each of the following numerals in expanded form as a polynomial:

a. 96	**e.** 8,209	**i.** 459,284	**m.** 6,529,104,249
b. 358	**f.** 617,932	**j.** 8,293,456	**n.** 23,865,200,684
c. 2,927	**g.** 3,248,766	**k.** 93,045,327	**o.** 475,218,836,095
d. 41,965	**h.** 72,543	**l.** 205,699,182	**p.** 92,783,556,104

1–14 ROMAN SYSTEM OF NUMERATION

The Romans used the following number symbols in their system of numeration:

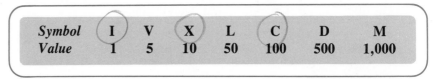

Symbol	I	V	X	L	C	D	M
Value	1	5	10	50	100	500	1,000

They formed Roman numerals by writing from left to right as a sum, first the symbol for the greatest possible value, with symbols I, X, C, and M used as many as three times when necessary, then the symbol for the next smaller value, etc.

When symbols I, X, or C preceded a Roman number symbol of greater value, its value was subtracted from the larger value.

$$IV = 5 - 1 = 4 \qquad\qquad XL = 50 - 10 = 40$$
$$IX = 10 - 1 = 9 \qquad\qquad XC = 100 - 10 = 90$$
$$CD = 500 - 100 = 400$$
$$CM = 1,000 - 100 = 900$$

$$MDCXLVII = \ ?$$

Since	M =	1,000
	D =	500
	C =	100
	XL =	40
	V =	5
	II =	2
		1,647

$$MDCXLVII = 1,647$$

$$178 = 100 + 50 + 20 + 5 + 3$$
$$= \ C + L + XX + V + III$$
$$= CLXXVIII$$

The symbols V, L, and D never preceded a Roman number symbol of greater value and were never used in succession. A bar above the symbol indicated that the value of the symbol was multiplied by 1,000.

EXERCISES

1. What number does each of the following Roman numerals represent?

III	VIII	IV	XI	XV	IX	XVII	XIX
XXV	XXIV	XXVIII	XXX	XXXVI	XXXIX	XXXII	XXXIV
XL	XLVI	LXII	LXXXIX	XC	XCVIII	LIV	XLIX
CXXVI	CCXLI	CDXLIV	DCCLVI	CMVIII	MCXLV	MDCCXI	MCMLIV

2. Write the Roman numeral for each of the following numbers:

2	6	9	13	18	19	14	16
20	31	24	36	29	34	27	35
43	45	56	69	73	84	99	96
104	289	462	596	947	1335	1651	1969

3. What time is indicated on the clock face?

4. A cornerstone is marked MCMXXIV.

What date does it represent?

5. What number is represented by the Roman numeral in each of the following:

    a. Page XVII   **b.** Paragraph XXIX   **c.** Chapter LXVI
    d. Item XLIV   **e.** Page XCIII   **f.** Item CCXC

6. In making an outline what Roman numeral should you use following:

    a. VIII   **b.** XIV   **c.** XIX   **d.** XXIII   **e.** XXXIX   **f.** XLIX

1–15 EVEN AND ODD NUMBERS

Whole numbers may be separated into even and odd numbers. An *even number* is a whole number that can be divided exactly (divisible) by two (2). Zero is considered an even whole number. An *odd number* is a whole number that cannot be divided exactly by two (2).

Numbers whose numerals end with a 0, 2, 4, 6, or 8 are even numbers.
Numbers whose numerals end with a 1, 3, 5, 7, or 9 are odd numbers.

EXERCISES

1. Which of the following are odd numbers? Which are even numbers?

    18   25   63   70   47   100   709   942   1,836   23,861

2. Does 1 more than any even number make an odd number? Does 1 more than any odd number make an even number?

3. Write the numerals of all one-digit odd numbers. Write the numerals of all the even numbers greater than 11 but less than 23.

4. Select any two odd numbers. Is their sum an odd number or an even number? Is their product an odd number or an even number?

5. Select any two even numbers. Is their sum an odd number or an even number? Is their product an odd number or an even number?

6. Select any odd and any even number. Is their sum an odd number or an even number? Is their product an odd number or an even number?

1–16 PRIME AND COMPOSITE NUMBERS

Whole numbers other than 0 and 1 may be separated into prime and composite numbers.

A *prime number* is a whole number other than 0 and 1 which is divisible (is divided exactly) only by itself and by 1 and by no other whole number. It is any whole number greater than 1 whose only factors are 1 and itself. See page 31.

> 17 is a prime number; it can be divided exactly only by 17 and by 1.

A *composite number* is any whole number greater than 1 which is divisible by any whole number other than 1 and itself.

> 10 is a composite number; it can be divided exactly not only by 10 and by 1 but also by 2 and by 5.

A composite number can be expressed as a product of prime numbers. Each composite number has only one set of prime factors but the factors may be arranged in different orders. See page 31.

> 10 may be expressed as 2×5 or 5×2.

The *Sieve of Eratosthenes,* a method discovered by the Greek mathematician Eratosthenes, may be used to find primes less than a given number.

To find all prime numbers less than 36 by this method, we write the numerals 2 to 35 inclusive (1 is excluded; it is not a prime number) as follows:

2 3 ~~4~~ 5 ~~6~~ 7 ~~8~~ ~~9~~ ~~10~~ 11 ~~12~~ 13 ~~14~~ ~~15~~ ~~16~~ 17 ~~18~~
19 ~~20~~ ~~21~~ ~~22~~ 23 ~~24~~ ~~25~~ ~~26~~ ~~27~~ ~~28~~ 29 ~~30~~ 31 ~~32~~ ~~33~~ ~~34~~ ~~35~~

We cross out numerals representing numbers which are not primes by the following procedure:

(1) 2 is a prime number. We retain numeral 2 but we cross out every second numeral after 2.

(2) 3 is a prime number. We retain numeral 3 but we cross out every third numeral after 3. Some of the numerals are already crossed out but they are included in the count.

(3) Numeral 4 is already crossed out.

(4) 5 is a prime number. We retain numeral 5 but we cross out every fifth numeral after five.

(5) We continue this process until all numerals for numbers other than prime numbers are crossed out.

> The prime numbers less than 36 are:
> 2, 3, 5, 7, 11, 13, 17, 19, 23, 29, 31.

Two prime numbers are called *twin primes* if one number is two more than the other number. 29 and 31 are a pair of twin primes.

Two numbers are said to be *relatively prime* to each other when they have no common factors other than 1. The numbers do not necessarily have to be prime numbers. The numbers 14 and 25 are relatively prime to each other because 1 is the only whole number that will divide into both 14 and 25 exactly.

EXERCISES

1. Which of the following are prime numbers?

   45   59   1   101   78   97   87   73   65   51

2. Which of the following are composite numbers?

   84   27   79   111   0   53   61   57   91   47

3. Name five composite numbers that are greater than 88 but less than 95.

4. Are there any even prime numbers? If so, what are they?

5. Name all the one-digit prime numbers.

6. Name all the one-digit odd prime numbers.

7. Use the Sieve of Eratosthenes to find all the prime numbers less than 200.

8. What twin primes may be found among numbers less than 100? Between 100 and 200?

9. Goldbach, a German mathematician, conjectured that "any even number greater than 4 can be expressed as the sum of two odd prime numbers." For example:

$$6 = 3 + 3$$

$$10 = 5 + 5 \text{ or } 7 + 3$$

$$24 = 5 + 19 \text{ or } 7 + 17 \text{ or } 11 + 13$$

This conjecture has never been proved.

Choose any even number between the following given numbers and find a pair of odd prime numbers that has your chosen even number as their sum.

a. 31 and 41   **c.** 61 and 81
b. 41 and 61   **d.** 81 and 101

10. Which of the following are relatively prime?

a. 9 and 21   **c.** 24 and 35   **e.** 28 and 63
b. 72 and 13   **d.** 54 and 45   **f.** 38 and 57

FACTORS AND FACTORING

1–17 FACTORS

When we multiply four by five to get the answer twenty (in symbols $4 \times 5 = 20$), the numbers 4 and 5 are called *factors* and the number in the answer is called the *product*.

A *factor* is any one of the numbers used in multiplication to form a product. Thus, one factor × another factor = product.

EXERCISES

Name the factors and the product in each of the following:

a. $7 \times 3 = 21$ **d.** $11 \times 6 = 66$ **g.** $12 \times 9 = 108$
b. $5 \times 9 = 45$ **e.** $5 \times 0 = 0$ **h.** $25 \times 5 = 125$
c. $1 \times 8 = 8$ **f.** $15 \times 15 = 225$ **i.** $4 \times 13 = 52$

We see from $4 \times 5 = 20$, $20 \div 4 = 5$, and $20 \div 5 = 4$, that 20 is divided exactly by factor 4 and by factor 5; from $10 \times 2 = 20$, $20 \div 2 = 10$, and $20 \div 10 = 2$, that 20 is divided exactly by factor 2 and by factor 10; from $20 \times 1 = 20$, and $20 \div 1 = 20$ and

$20 \div 20 = 1$ that 20 is divided exactly by factor 1 and by factor 20.

The factors of 20 are: 1, 2, 4, 5, 10, and 20.

A factor of a number divides the number exactly with *no* remainder. Every natural number has as factors 1 and the given number itself. The other factors are whole numbers which divide the given number exactly. Knowledge of the multiplication facts will help determine factors by inspection. Or we may select small numbers and test whether they divide the given number exactly. If any number does, both the divisor and the quotient are factors.

Other pairs of factors of a given number may be found from a known pair of factors, whose product is the given number, by dividing one factor by a number that makes it divisible and then multiplying the other factor by this number. For example, using 8 and 9, a pair of factors of 72, we divide factor 8 by 2 and multiply factor 9 by 2 to get factors 4 and 18; if we divide factor 18 by 3 and multiply factor 4 by 3, we get factors 6 and 12, etc.

EXERCISES

1. Can 24 be divided exactly by 2? by 12? by 3? by 4? by 5? by 6? by 8? by 10? by 18? by 24? Write the factors of 24.

2. Is 4 a factor of 36? Is 12 a factor of 60? Is 18 a factor of 54? Is 7 a factor of 54?

3. What is the other factor when:

   a. 5 is one factor of 30?   **d.** 12 is one factor of 96?

   b. 9 is one factor of 63?   **e.** 10 is one factor of 1,000?

   c. 8 is one factor of 56?   **f.** 100 is one factor of 100,000?

4. Write all the factors of each of the following numbers:

a. 8	**d.** 32	**g.** 56	**j.** 125	**m.** 80	**p.** 360
b. 19	**e.** 54	**h.** 84	**k.** 120	**n.** 92	**q.** 240
c. 14	**f.** 90	**i.** 60	**l.** 64	**o.** 100	**r.** 75

1–18 FACTORING A NATURAL NUMBER

To factor a natural number means to replace the number by its whole-number factors expressed as an indicated product. This indicated product may contain two or more whole-number factors. A prime number may be expressed only as the product of the given number and 1. The prime number 29 is expressed as 29×1.

> To factor 20 means to replace 20 by any one of the following indicated products of:
>
> (1) Two whole-number factors: 1×20 or 2×10 or 4×5 or 5×4 or 10×2 or 20×1.
> (2) Three whole-number factors: $2 \times 2 \times 5$ or $1 \times 2 \times 10$ or $1 \times 4 \times 5$ arranged in different orders.
> (3) More than three whole-number factors since the factor 1 may be repeated: $20 \times 1 \times 1 \times 1$ or $4 \times 5 \times 1 \times 1 \times 1 \times 1 \times 1$ or $2 \times 2 \times 5 \times 1 \times 1 \times 1 \times 1 \times 1$ etc. However, the factor 1 is usually excluded when there are more than two whole-number factors in the indicated product.

EXERCISES

1. Factor as the product of two whole-number factors in as many ways as possible:

   a. 16   **b.** 11   **c.** 42   **d.** 64   **e.** 80   **f.** 100   **g.** 52   **h.** 110

2. Factor as the product of three whole-number factors in as many ways as possible:

   a. 30   **b.** 66   **c.** 70   **d.** 18   **e.** 98   **f.** 75   **g.** 63   **h.** 242

3. Factor as the product of four whole-number factors in as many ways as possible:

   a. 36   **b.** 90   **c.** 56   **d.** 150   **e.** 132   **f.** 210   **g.** 330   **h.** 441

1–19 COMPLETE FACTORIZATION

A composite number may be expressed as a product of prime numbers. The number is said to be *completely factored* only if the factors are all prime numbers (prime factors).

When 20 is factored as 4×5 or 10×2, it is not completely factored since the 4 and 10 are not prime numbers. However 4×5 may be expressed as $2 \times 2 \times 5$ by factoring the 4; and 10×2 may be expressed as $5 \times 2 \times 2$ or $2 \times 5 \times 2$ by factoring the 10.

Complete factoring of 20 produces $2 \times 2 \times 5$ or $5 \times 2 \times 2$ or $2 \times 5 \times 2$. Observe that the factors are the same 2, 2, and 5 but they appear in different orders. Thus, each composite number has only one set of prime factors but the prime factors may be arranged in different orders.

To factor completely, we first find two factors of the given number and then continue factoring any of the factors which are composite numbers until only prime factors result. For example:

$$20 = 4 \times 5 = 2 \times 2 \times 5 \quad \text{or} \quad 20 = 2 \times 10 = 2 \times 2 \times 5$$

Each of these may be arranged as a factor tree:

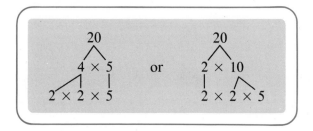

Or we divide the given number and the resulting quotients successively by prime numbers that divide these numbers exactly until a quotient of 1 is obtained. The divisors are the prime factors. Observe in the model example at the right how the quotients are brought down in each row.

$$
\begin{array}{r}
2)\overline{20} \\
2)\overline{10} \\
5)\underline{5} \\
1
\end{array}
$$

$$20 = 2 \times 2 \times 5$$

1. Factor each of the following numbers as a product of prime numbers, using a factor tree:

   a. 42   **c.** 24   **e.** 90   **g.** 100
   b. 27   **d.** 64   **f.** 72   **h.** 320

2. Factor each of the following numbers as a product of prime numbers:

   a. 56   **d.** 60   **g.** 105   **j.** 132   **m.** 300
   b. 32   **e.** 36   **h.** 200   **k.** 180   **n.** 480
   c. 75   **f.** 144   **i.** 54   **l.** 225   **o.** 720

1–20 COMMON FACTORS

> 3 is a factor of 6. Factors of 6 are: 1, 2, 3, 6
> 3 is a factor of 15. Factors of 15 are: 1, 3, 5, 15
> Therefore, 3 is a common factor of 6 and 15.
> 1 is also a common factor of 6 and 15.

Any number that is a factor of each of two or more given whole numbers is called a *common factor* of the numbers (sometimes called *common divisor* of the numbers).

Observe that 1 is a common factor of any two or more numbers. Some given numbers like 2 and 3 have no common factor except 1; other numbers like 4 and 10 have one common factor (2) other than 1; still other numbers like 18 and 24 have many common factors (2, 3, and 6) other than 1.

1. What are the factors of 16? What are the factors of 24? What are the common factors of 16 and 24?
2. What are the factors of 8? What are the factors of 12? What are the factors of 20? What are the common factors of 8, 12, and 20?

3. For each of the following groups of numbers, first find the factors of each number, then find their common factors:

   a. 6 and 8   **c.** 36 and 60   **e.** 32 and 72
   b. 9 and 15   **d.** 18, 24, and 30   **f.** 48, 96, and 120

4. For each of the following groups of numbers write the common factors:

   a. 4 and 10   **c.** 35 and 63   **e.** 10, 12, and 16
   b. 24 and 32   **d.** 18 and 27   **f.** 54, 72, and 90

1–21 GREATEST COMMON FACTOR

> The factors of 18 are: 1, 2, 3, 6, 9, 18
> The factors of 24 are: 1, 2, 3, 4, 6, 8, 12, 24
> The common factors of 18 and 24 are 1, 2, 3, and 6.
> The greatest common factor is 6.

The *greatest common factor* of two or more whole numbers is the greatest whole number that will divide all the given numbers exactly.

To determine the greatest common factor (GCF), or greatest common divisor, of two or more given numbers, we factor each given number completely as a product of prime numbers. Then we select all the prime factors that are common to all the given numbers and find their product.

> Find the GCF of 24 and 18:
> $$24 = 2 \cdot 2 \cdot 2 \cdot 3$$
> $$18 = 2 \cdot 3 \cdot 3$$
>
> Prime factors 2 and 3 are common.
> Therefore the GCF = $2 \cdot 3$ or 6.
>
> Find the GCF of 36 and 90:
> $$36 = 2 \cdot 2 \cdot 3 \cdot 3$$
> $$90 = 2 \cdot 3 \cdot 3 \cdot 5$$
>
> Prime factors 2, 3, and 3 are common.
> Therefore the GCF = $2 \cdot 3 \cdot 3$ or 18.

Or we may use Euclid's method of finding the GCF of two given numbers as follows:

We divide the larger given number by the smaller number. Then we divide the divisor by the remainder, then we divide the next divisor by the next remainder, continuing in this way until the remainder is zero. The *last non-zero remainder* is the greatest common factor (GCF).

Find the GCF of 24 and 18:

$$18) \overline{24} \quad (1 \quad R6$$
$$6) \overline{18} \quad (3 \quad R0$$

Answer, GCF = 6

EXERCISES

1. What are the factors of 64? What are the factors of 96? What are the common factors of 64 and 96? What is the greatest common factor of 64 and 96?
2. What are the common factors of 45, 75, and 120? What is the greatest common factor of 45, 75, and 120?
3. Find the greatest common factor of each of the following groups of numbers:
   a. 5 and 6   d. 8 and 28   g. 6, 8, and 10
   b. 36 and 42   e. 65 and 91   h. 8, 12, and 18
   c. 24 and 40   f. 87 and 58   i. 24, 36, and 108
4. Use Euclid's method to find the greatest common factor of:
   a. 24 and 60   c. 35 and 84   e. 108 and 132
   b. 45 and 100   d. 63 and 90   f. 306 and 414

NUMBER MULTIPLES

1–22 MULTIPLES

A *multiple* of a given whole number is a product of the given number and another whole number factor. Since $0 \times 7 = 0$; $1 \times 7 = 7$; $2 \times 7 = 14$; $3 \times 7 = 21$; $4 \times 7 = 28$; and $5 \times 7 = 35$, the products 0, 7, 14, 21, 28, and 35 are multiples of 7. Each is a product of 7 and another number. A multiple of a given number is divisible by the given number. The above multiples of 7 (0, 7, 14, 21, 28, and 35) are divisible by 7.

> All multiples of 7 may be expressed as:
>
> 0, 7, 14, 21, 28, 35, 42, . . .

EXERCISES

1. Name four different multiples of each of the following numbers:
   a. 3   **b.** 2   **c.** 9   **d.** 15   **e.** 4   **f.** 20   **g.** 48   **h.** 100
2. Which of the following numbers are multiples of 6?
   52   72   28   48   32   36   90   86   100   102
3. Are all whole numbers multiples of 1?
4. Are all even whole numbers multiples of 2?
5. 5 is a factor of 15. Is 15 a multiple of 5? 9 is a factor of 72. Is 72 a multiple of 9? If a number is a factor of a second number, is the second number a multiple of the first number?
6. What are the factors of 32? Is 32 a multiple of each of its factors?
7. Write all the multiples of each of the following, listing the first five:

a. 4	**d.** 12	**g.** 18	**j.** 72	**m.** 200
b. 6	**e.** 11	**h.** 13	**k.** 36	**n.** 125
c. 5	**f.** 30	**i.** 25	**l.** 50	**o.** 320

1–23   COMMON MULTIPLES

Any number which is a multiple of two or more numbers is called the *common multiple* of the numbers. Numbers may have many common multiples.

> 15 is a multiple of 3; 15 is a multiple of 5; 15 is a common multiple of 3 and 5. Some of the other common multiples of 3 and 5 include 30, 45, 60, 75, and 90. All common multiples of 3 and 5 are 0, 15, 30, 45, 60, . . .

1. Is 24 a multiple of 6? Is 24 a multiple of 8? Is 24 a common multiple of 6 and 8? Is 24 divisible by 6 and by 8? Is the common multiple of two or more given numbers divisible by each of the given numbers?

2. What are the first 15 multiples of 2? of 3? What are the first 5 common multiples of 2 and 3?

3. Write all common multiples of each of the following, listing the first four multiples:

   a. 2 and 5   **e.** 5 and 4   **i.** 2, 3, and 4
   b. 6 and 4   **f.** 3 and 9   **j.** 2, 4, and 8
   c. 3 and 7   **g.** 18 and 22   **k.** 6, 8, and 12
   d. 8 and 10   **h.** 15 and 25   **l.** 10, 25, and 100

4. Is the product of 8 and 3 a common multiple of 8 and 3? Is the product of two whole numbers a common multiple of the two numbers?

5. Is the product of 6 and 10 a common multiple of 6 and 10? Is it the smallest common multiple? If not, what is the smallest natural number that can be divided exactly by both 6 and 10?

1–24   LEAST COMMON MULTIPLE

The *least common multiple* (LCM) of two or more numbers is the smallest natural number which is the multiple of all of them. It is the smallest possible natural number that can be divided exactly by all the given numbers.

Zero (0) is excluded when determining the least common multiple, although it is a common multiple of any group of numbers.

The LCM may be found by factoring the given numbers as primes and forming a product of these primes using each the greatest number of times it appears in the factored form of any one number.

The LCM of 8 and 10 is found as follows:

Since $8 = 2 \cdot 2 \cdot 2$
and $10 = 2 \cdot 5$

Therefore, LCM $= \overset{8}{\overbrace{2 \cdot 2 \cdot 2} \cdot 5}$

Answer, LCM $= 40$ 10

1. Find the least common multiple for each of the following:

a. 12 and 16	**e.** 20 and 24	**i.** 96 and 108	**m.** 6, 10, and 12
b. 3 and 4	**f.** 50 and 100	**j.** 84 and 144	**n.** 2, 3, and 5
c. 10 and 15	**g.** 32 and 56	**k.** 39 and 65	**o.** 4, 12, and 20
d. 14 and 21	**h.** 54 and 72	**l.** 90 and 135	**p.** 18, 27, and 45

2. Find the greatest common factor and the least common multiple of each of the following pairs of numbers. For each pair of numbers compare the product of the GCF and LCM with the product of the two given numbers. What do you find in each case?

a. 10 and 15	**b.** 32 and 20	**c.** 9 and 8	**d.** 72 and 96

CHAPTER REVIEW

1. Write three different numerals naming the number twelve. (1–1)
2. In which of the following groups may the objects be paired so that there is one-to-one correspondence? (1–2)

   x △ △ △ △ △ y ☐ ☐ ☐ ☐ ☐ ☐ z ○ ○ ○ ○ ○

3. Does the sentence "Of the 25 players on the softball team, Lisa ranked number 3 in batting" contain a cardinal number? If so, name it. Does it contain an ordinal number? If so, name it. (1–3)
4. Are there any natural numbers between 18 and 23? If so, name them. (1–4)
5. On the number line what point corresponds to 5? to 3? (1–5)

   A C G E F B H D
   ←•—•—•—•—•—•—•—•→
   0 1 2 3 4 5 6 7

6. a. Write the numeral that names the smallest number possible using the digits 8, 1, 5, 2, 4, 1. (1–6)

    b. Which number is greater: 698,898 or 698,988? (1–6)

7. Read, or write in words: 2,875,306,014,009. (1–7)

8. Write the numeral that names:

    a. Forty-three billion, two hundred thirty-six thousand, nineteen. (1–8)

    b. 369 million. (1–9)

9. Round: (1–10)

    a. 483,498,627 to the nearest million.

    b. 50,176,038 to the nearest ten thousand.

10. What is the numeral 6 called in 3^6? What is the numeral 3 called? Find the value of 3^6. (1–11)

11. Use exponential notation to write:
$7 \cdot 7 \cdot 7 \cdot 7 \cdot 7 \cdot 7 \cdot 7 \cdot 7 \cdot 7$. (1–11)

12. Express 600,000 as a product of a digit and a power of ten. (1–12)

13. Express 4,583,219 in expanded form as a polynomial. (1–13)

14. Which of the following are odd numbers? Which are even numbers?

    221   972   1,050   694   409 (1–15)

15. Use the Sieve of Eratosthenes to find all the prime numbers less than 48. (1–16)

16. Name four composite numbers that are greater than 28 but less than 35. (1–16)

17. Are 15 and 36 relatively prime? (1–16)

18. Write all the factors of 96. (1–17)

19. What are the common factors of 24 and 36? (1–20)

20. What is the greatest common factor of 75 and 105? (1–21)

21. Write 60 as a product of two whole-number factors in as many ways as possible. (1–18)

22. Factor 48 as the product of prime numbers. (1–19)

23. Write all the multiples of 8, listing the first six. (1–22)

24. Write all the common multiples of 6 and 9, listing the first five. (1–23)

25. What is the least common multiple of 8, 12, and 18? (1–24)

ACHIEVEMENT TEST

1. On the number line, what number corresponds to the point marked B? the point marked D? (1–5)

```
      E   D   G   A   C   I   H   B   J   F
  <---•---•---•---•---•---•---•---•---•---•--->
      0   1   2   3   4   5   6   7   8   9
```

2. Read, or write in words: 96,845,007,503. (1–7)
3. Write the numeral that names:

   a. Seventeen million, nine hundred twenty-four thousand, six hundred. (1–8)
   b. 74 billion. (1–9)

4. Which number is greater: 1,267,686 or 1,267,668? (1–6)
5. Round 29,999,741 to the nearest thousand. (1–10)
6. Which of the following are odd numbers? Which are even numbers? (1–15)

   618 843 704 5,900 4,265

7. Which of the following are prime numbers: 17, 27, 37, 47, 57? (1–16)
8. a. Write all the factors of 42. (1–17)
   b. Write all the common factors of 12, 16, and 18. (1–20)
   c. What is the greatest common factor of 54, 72, and 90? (1–21)

9. Factor 108 as a product of prime numbers. (1–19)
10. a. Which of the following are multiples of 9? (1–22)
       27 49 72 63 108
    b. Write the common multiples of 20 and 25, listing the first three numbers. (1–23)
    c. What is the least common multiple of 24, 36, and 60? (1–24)

2

CHAPTER 2
Properties–Operations with Whole Numbers

2–1 BINARY OPERATIONS

When we add 8 and 5 or subtract 19 from 107 or multiply 18 by 62 or divide 72 by 6, we are operating with two numbers to get a third number. We call this a *binary operation*.

In arithmetic we use the binary operations of addition, subtraction, multiplication and division. When we use any one of these operations, the resulting answer is said to be *unique* because it is the "one and only number" that may result from that operation on the given two numbers.

There are certain characteristics or properties that the operations have. A property is not true unless it holds in all cases. Therefore to determine whether a property is not true it is sufficient to show that it does not hold in one case.

2–2 INVERSE OPERATIONS

Operations that undo each other are called *inverse operations*. If we first add 3 to 5 and then subtract 3 from the answer, we return to the 5.

$$(5 + 3) - 3 = 5$$
Subtraction undoes addition.

If we first subtract 6 from 8 and then add 6 to the answer, we return to the 8.

$$(8 - 6) + 6 = 8$$
Addition undoes subtraction.

Thus addition and subtraction are inverse operations, they undo each other. If we first multiply 5 by 4 and then divide the answer by 4, we return to the 5.

$$(5 \times 4) \div 4 = 5$$
Division undoes multiplication.

If we first divide 30 by 6 and then multiply the answer by 6, we return to 30.

$$(30 \div 6) \times 6 = 30$$
Multiplication undoes division.

Thus multiplication and division are inverse operations, they undo each other.

EXERCISES

1. Find the missing numbers or symbols of operation as indicated:

a. $(10 \times 3) \div 3 = \square$ **i.** $(11 + \square) - 3 = 11$ **q.** $(12 \times 4) ? 4 = 12$

b. $(8 + 7) - 7 = ?$ **j.** $(20 \div n) \times 4 = 20$ **r.** $(15 + 12) ? 12 = 15$

c. $(15 - 9) + 9 = n$ **k.** $(16 - ?) + 8 = 16$ **s.** $(48 \div 6) ? 6 = 48$

d. $(24 \div 8) \times 8 = \square$ **l.** $(6 \times n) \div 5 = 6$ **t.** $(50 - 1) ? 1 = 50$

e. $(17 - 5) + ? = 17$ **m.** $(\square \div 2) \times 2 = 40$ **u.** $(32 ? 8) - 8 = 32$

f. $(9 \times 6) \div \square = 9$ **n.** $(? - 7) + 7 = 21$ **v.** $(13 ? 5) + 5 = 13$

g. $(28 \div 7) \times \square = 28$ **o.** $(n + 6) - 6 = 37$ **w.** $(4 ? 3) \div 3 = 4$

h. $(14 + 3) - n = 14$ **p.** $(? \times 10) \div 10 = 60$ **x.** $(56 ? 8) \times 8 = 56$

2. a. Is division the inverse operation of subtraction?
b. Is subtraction the inverse operation of addition?
c. Is multiplication the inverse operation of division?
d. Is addition the inverse operation of multiplication?

Properties—Operations with Whole Numbers   **43**

2-3 COMMUTATIVE PROPERTY

Of Addition

Adding 2 and 3 gives the same sum as adding 3 and 2. That is: 2 + 3 = 3 + 2. When we add one number to a second number, we get the same sum as when we add the second number to the first number. *The commutative property of addition permits us to change the order of adding two numbers without affecting the sum.*

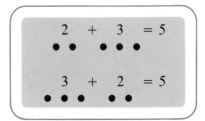

Of Multiplication

Multiplying 2 and 3 gives the same product as multiplying 3 and 2. That is: 2 × 3 = 3 × 2. See the arrays at the right. They are arrangements of dots in rows and columns. When we multiply one number by a second number, we get the same product as when we multiply the second number by the first number. *The commutative property of multiplication permits us to change the order of multiplying two factors without affecting the product.*

EXERCISES

---

1. a. Add:

    (1) 6   5   (2) 9   4
           5   6   4   9

b. Subtract:

    (1) 13   8   (2) 17   9
          8   13   9   17

c. Multiply:

    (1) 8   4   (2) 3   6
          4   8   6   3

d. Divide:

    (1) 12 ÷ 4   (2) 36 ÷ 9
         4 ÷ 12   9 ÷ 36

e. Does interchanging addends (numbers that are added) affect the sum?

f. Does interchanging the minuend and subtrahend affect the answer when we subtract?

g. Does interchanging factors affect the product?

h. Does interchanging the dividend and divisor affect the quotient?

i. Does the commutative property hold for subtraction? For division?

2. Which of the following statements are true?

a. $15 - 19 = 19 - 15$ **d.** $49 \div 7 = 7 \div 49$ **g.** $90 \div 15 = 15 \div 90$
b. $34 + 10 = 10 + 34$ **e.** $158 + 25 = 25 + 158$ **h.** $75 - 39 = 39 - 75$
c. $24 \times 6 = 6 \times 24$ **f.** $35 \times 87 = 87 \times 35$ **i.** $63 + 54 = 54 + 63$

3. Find the numbers that will make the following statements true:

a. $67 + 34 = ? + 67$ **c.** $45 \times ? = 36 \times 45$
b. $59 \times 61 = 61 \times ?$ **d.** $? + 60 = 60 + 85$

2–4   ASSOCIATIVE PROPERTY

Of Addition

Since addition is a binary operation, only two numbers may be added at any one time. When there are three addends, we must first select two addends, find their sum, and then add the third addend to this sum.

> $2 + 4 + 6$ may be thought of as either:
> $(2 + 4) + 6$ which is $6 + 6 = 12$
> or $2 + (4 + 6)$ which is $2 + 10 = 12$
> Thus, $(2 + 4) + 6 = 2 + (4 + 6)$

The associative property of addition permits us to group or associate the first and second numbers and add their sum to the third number or to group or associate the second and third numbers and add their sum to the first number. Either way we get the same final sum.

Of Multiplication

Since multiplication is a binary operation, only two factors may be multiplied at any one time. When there are three factors, we must first select two factors, find their product, and then multiply this product by the third factor.

Properties—Operations with Whole Numbers   **45**

$$2 \times 4 \times 6 \text{ may be thought of as either:}$$
$$(2 \times 4) \times 6 \text{ which is } 8 \times 6 = 48$$
$$\text{or} \quad 2 \times (4 \times 6) \text{ which is } 2 \times 24 = 48$$
$$\text{Thus,} \quad (2 \times 4) \times 6 = 2 \times (4 \times 6)$$

The associative property of multiplication permits us to group or associate the first and second numbers and multiply their product by the third number or to group or associate the second and third numbers and multiply their product by the first number. We get the same final product in each case.

EXERCISES

1. Find the value of $(12 + 6) + 4$. Find the value of $12 + (6 + 4)$. Is the statement $(12 + 6) + 4 = 12 + (6 + 4)$ true? Select any three numbers. Check whether the associative property holds for the addition of these numbers.

2. Find the value of $(18 - 5) - 2$. Find the value of $18 - (5 - 2)$. Is the statement $(18 - 5) - 2 = 18 - (5 - 2)$ true? Does the associative property hold for subtraction?

3. Find the value of $(20 \times 5) \times 3$. Find the value of $20 \times (5 \times 3)$. Is the statement $(20 \times 5) \times 3 = 20 \times (5 \times 3)$ true? Select any three numbers. Check whether the associative property holds for multiplication of these numbers.

4. Find the value of $(16 \div 8) \div 2$. Find the value of $16 \div (8 \div 2)$. Is the statement $(16 \div 8) \div 2 = 16 \div (8 \div 2)$ true? Does the associative property hold for division?

5. When we add a column of three addends in a down direction and check by adding in an up direction, what property are we using?

6. Which of the following statements are true?

   a. $(9 \times 7) \times 4 = 9 \times (7 \times 4)$
   b. $(75 \div 15) \div 5 = 75 \div (15 \div 5)$
   c. $(47 - 12) - 10 = 47 - (12 - 10)$
   d. $(82 + 35) + 15 = 82 + (35 + 15)$
   e. $(24 + 16) + 32 = 24 + (16 + 32)$
   f. $(51 \times 8) \times 19 = 51 \times (8 \times 19)$

7. Find the numbers that will make the following statements true:

   a. $(6 + 8) + 9 = 6 + (? + 9)$
   b. $(12 \times 4) \times ? = 12 \times (4 \times 7)$
   c. $(? \times 10) \times 5 = 20 \times (10 \times 5)$
   d. $(22 + ?) + 16 = 22 + (8 + 16)$
   e. $(36 + 9) + 25 = 36 + (9 + ?)$
   f. $(20 \times 50) \times 30 = ? \times (50 \times 30)$

8. Show by using the commutative and associative properties that:

a. $3 + 8 + 7 = (3 + 7) + 8$ **c.** $9 + 6 + 11 = 6 + (9 + 11)$
b. $5 \times 9 \times 2 = (5 \times 2) \times 9$ **d.** $4 \times 7 \times 2 = 7 \times (4 \times 2)$

2–5 DISTRIBUTIVE PROPERTY OF MULTIPLICATION OVER ADDITION

To find the product of $3 \times (2 + 6)$ we may find the sum of 2 and 6 and then multiply this sum (8) by 3.

$$\text{That is: } 3 \times (2 + 6) = 3 \times 8 = 24$$

Or we may multiply the 2 by 3 and the 6 by 3 and add the products.

$$\text{That is: } 3 \times (2 + 6) = (3 \times 2) + (3 \times 6) = 6 + 18 = 24$$

Either way we get the same final result.

The distributive property of multiplication over addition tells us that when we multiply one number by the sum of a second and a third number we get the same result as when we add the product of the first and second numbers to the product of the first and third numbers. Multiplication is being distributed over addition.

We use the distributive property in computation such as 2×43.

$$2 \times 43 = 2 \times (40 + 3)$$
$$= (2 \times 40) + (2 \times 3)$$
$$= 80 + 6 = 86$$

$$\text{or} \quad \begin{array}{r} 43 \\ \times\ 2 \\ \hline \end{array} = \begin{array}{r} 40 + 3 \\ \times\ 2 \\ \hline \end{array} = \begin{array}{r} 40 \\ \times\ 2 \\ \hline \end{array} + \begin{array}{r} 3 \\ \times\ 2 \\ \hline \end{array}$$

Properties—Operations with Whole Numbers

We also use the distributive property in the following:

$$(7 \times 4) + (7 \times 8) = 7 \times (4 + 8)$$
$$\text{or} \quad (4 \times 7) + (8 \times 7) = (4 + 8) \times 7$$

EXERCISES

1. Find the value of $6 \times (3 + 4)$. Find the value of $(6 \times 3) + (6 \times 4)$. Is the statement $6 \times (3 + 4) = (6 \times 3) + (6 \times 4)$ true? What property is used here?

2. Show how the distributive property is used in computing 3×23.

3. Find the numbers that will make the following statements true:

   a. $7 \times (4 + ?) = 7 \times 4 + 7 \times 5$
   b. $8 \times (3 + 9) = 8 \times ? + 8 \times 9$
   c. $4 \times (12 + 7) = ? \times 12 + ? \times 7$
   d. $10 \times 8 + 10 \times 6 = ? \times (8 + 6)$
   e. $15 \times 14 + 15 \times ? = 15 \times (14 + 11)$

   f. $5 \times (1 + 4) = 5 \times ? + 5 \times ?$
   g. $16 \times (3 + 7) = 16 \times ? + ? \times 7$
   h. $21 \times (? + ?) = 21 \times 10 + 21 \times 8$
   i. $32 \times 9 + 32 \times 6 = ? \times (? + ?)$
   j. $50 \times (11 + 17) = ? \times ? + ? \times ?$

4. Find the value of $6 + (3 \times 4)$. Find the value of $(6 + 3)(6 + 4)$. Is the statement $6 + (3 \times 4) = (6 + 3)(6 + 4)$ true? Is addition distributed over multiplication?

5. Is the statement $4 \times (8 - 5) = (4 \times 8) - (4 \times 5)$ true? Is multiplication distributed over subtraction?

2-6 CLOSURE

When we add two whole numbers such as 4 and 6, is the sum a whole number? Yes, it is 10. Can you find two whole numbers whose sum is not a whole number?

When we multiply the two whole numbers 8 and 5, is the product a whole number? Yes, it is 40. Can you find two whole numbers whose product is not a whole number?

When we subtract the whole number 9 from the whole number

12, is the result a whole number? Can you find two whole numbers whose difference is not a whole number? Try to subtract 8 from 6.

When we divide the whole number 12 by the whole number 4, is the quotient a whole number? Can you find two whole numbers whose quotient is not a whole number? Try to divide 8 by 6.

If we, using all numbers in a given group, add any two numbers (or subtract or multiply or divide) and get as our answer in every case one of the numbers described in the given group, we say the group is closed under that operation. This property is called *closure*.

Not all groups of numbers are closed under all operations. We have seen that the whole numbers are closed under addition and multiplication because the answers in *every* case are whole numbers but are not closed under subtraction and division because the answers in *some* cases are not whole numbers. A property must hold for *all* cases.

EXERCISES

1. Are the prime numbers closed under the operation of addition? Subtraction? Multiplication? Division?
2. Are the even natural numbers closed under the operation of addition? Subtraction? Multiplication? Division?
3. Are 5, 10, 15, 20, 25, . . . closed under the operation of addition? Subtraction? Multiplication? Division?
4. Is zero (0) closed under the operation of addition? Subtraction? Multiplication? Division?
5. Is the pair of numbers 0 and 1 closed under the operation of addition? Subtraction? Multiplication? Division?
6. Are 10, 20, 30, 40, 50, . . . closed under the operation of addition? Subtraction? Multiplication? Division?
7. Which of the groups of numbers at the right are closed under:

   a. Addition?   2, 4, and 8

   b. Subtraction?   0, 1, 2, 3, and 4
                          10, 100, 1000, . . .

   c. Multiplication?   3, 6, 9, 12, . . .
                          1, 3, 5, 7, . . .

   d. Division?   4, 8, 12, 16, . . .

2–7 PROPERTIES OF ZERO

When we add zero (0) to any number, the number remains unchanged. This addition property of zero is illustrated by the following:

The sum of 6 and 0 is 6. $6 + 0 = 6$
The sum of 0 and 9 is 9. $0 + 9 = 9$

A number which, when added to a given number, does not change the given number is called the *additive identity* (or identity element for addition). Therefore zero (0) is the additive identity. The following are other important properties of zero:

(1) Zero subtracted from any number is the number. $8 - 0 = 8$

(2) The difference between any number and itself is zero. $12 - 12 = 0$

(3) When a non-zero number is multiplied by zero, the product is zero. $0 \times 7 = 0$

(4) When 0 is multiplied by a non-zero number, the product is zero. $8 \times 0 = 0$

(5) When zero is multiplied by zero, the product is zero. $0 \times 0 = 0$
Thus, the product of any number and zero is zero.

(6) If the product of two numbers is 0, then one of the factors is zero or both factors are zero.

(7) If zero is divided by any number other than zero, the quotient is zero. $0 \div 5 = 0$

(8) In arithmetic the division by 0 is excluded.

Since multiplication and division are inverse operations, $6 \div 2 = 3$ may be thought of as $3 \times 2 = 6$.

Thus $6 \div 0 = ?$ may be thought of as $? \times 0 = 6$. Since the product of any number and zero is zero and not 6, the statement $6 \div 0$ is meaningless; there is no answer.

Also $0 \div 0 = ?$ may be thought of as $? \times 0 = 0$. Since the product of *any* number and zero is zero, then the answer could be any number and so is indeterminate.

Therefore divisions like $6 \div 0$ written also as $0\overline{)6}$ or $\dfrac{6}{0}$ and $0 \div 0$ written also as $0\overline{)0}$ or $\dfrac{0}{0}$ are excluded.

1. Determine the value of each of the following:

a. $7 - 0$ d. 50×0 g. $0 \div 12$ j. 0×18

b. $0 + 11$ e. $34 + 0$ h. $\frac{16}{16}$ k. $8 \times 6 \times 4 \times 0 \times 9$

c. $25 - 25$ f. 0×0 i. $\dfrac{9 - 9}{15 + 14}$ l. $\dfrac{25 - 5}{17 - 17}$

2. Which of the following represent the number zero?

a. $\frac{8}{8}$ b. $8 - 8$ c. $0 \div 10$ d. $\dfrac{14 - 14}{21}$ e. $\dfrac{27 - 15}{5 - 5}$

3. Which of the following are meaningless or indeterminate?

a. $9 \div 0$ b. $0 \div 4$ c. $0 \div 0$ d. $\dfrac{23 - 23}{16 - 15}$ e. $\dfrac{6 - 2}{48 - 48}$

2–8 PROPERTIES OF ONE

When we multiply any number by one (1), the number remains unchanged. This multiplicative property of one is illustrated by the following:

1 times 4 is 4. $1 \times 4 = 4$
9 times 1 is 9. $9 \times 1 = 9$

A number which, when multiplied by a given number, does not change the given number is called the *multiplicative identity* (or the identity element for multiplication). Therefore one (1) is the multiplicative identity.

We shall see that the multiplicative identity, one, is used when changing fractions to lower and higher terms, when dividing fractions, and when dividing by a decimal.

The following are other important properties of one:

(1) When any number, except zero, is divided by itself, the quotient is one. Since the fraction bar indicates division, one may be expressed in symbols as follows:

$\frac{1}{1}$, $\frac{2}{2}$, $\frac{3}{3}$, $\frac{4}{4}$, $\frac{5}{5}$, $\frac{6}{6}$, $\frac{7}{7}$, $\frac{8}{8}$, $\frac{9}{9}$, $\frac{10}{10}$, $\frac{11}{11}$, etc.

(2) One raised to any power is one. For example:

$$1^6 = 1 \times 1 \times 1 \times 1 \times 1 \times 1 = 1$$

(3) When one is added to any whole number, we get the next higher whole number.

(4) When one is added to any even number, we get an odd number. When one is added to any odd number, we get an even number.

1. Determine the value of each of the following:

   a. $\frac{6}{6}$ **f.** 7×1^{12}

   b. 18×1 **g.** $1^{15} \times 1^{24}$

   c. 1^4 **h.** $\dfrac{24 - 15}{4 + 5}$

   d. 1×53

   e. $30 \times 1 \times 1 \times 1$ **i.** $1 \times 1 \times 1 \times 1 \times 2 \times 1 \times 1 \times 1$

2. Which of the following represent the number 1?

   a. $4 - 4$ **b.** $\frac{4}{4}$ **c.** 5^1 **d.** 1^5 **e.** $\dfrac{28 - 13}{3 \times 5}$

2–9 COMPUTATION—ADDITION

We use addition to put together or combine quantities to find the total number. Only like quantities may be added: ones with ones, tens with tens, hundreds with hundreds, etc. The numbers we add are called the *addends* and the answer is called the *sum*. The symbol used to indicate addition is the *plus* sign ($+$).

To add whole numbers, we add each column, beginning with the ones column. If the sum of any column is ten or more, we write the last digit of the sum in the answer and carry the other digits to the next column to the left. We check by adding the columns in the opposite direction.

$$
\begin{array}{r}
356 \\
89 \\
\underline{293} \\
738 \\
\end{array}
$$
356 ↖
89 ← Addends
293 ↙
738 ← Sum
Answer, 738

1. Add and check:

   a.

1	7	3	4	6	2	8	3	5	1	0
4	2	3	5	1	0	4	6	9	7	8

b.	3	1	6	0	5	7	4	1	7	0	5
	4	1	2	4	3	1	6	2	7	2	4

c.	5	9	3	8	4	2	5	9	4	0	6
	1	0	7	1	4	5	7	9	2	5	3

d.	7	9	5	0	6	2	8	2	8	4	6
	3	6	5	9	5	4	3	1	7	3	0

e.	4	6	2	4	1	6	5	3	7	0	8
	9	4	3	7	5	7	0	8	9	6	2

f.	2	4	3	7	1	3	1	6	0	2	8
	6	8	1	4	9	0	8	6	3	8	6

g.	8	0	5	7	6	8	5	9	2	9	8
	8	7	8	5	8	0	2	1	7	7	5

h.	9	4	1	3	5	0	9	2	1	7	2
	5	1	3	9	6	1	4	2	6	0	9

i.	3	6	0	9	7	9	7	4	3	8	9
	2	9	0	8	8	2	6	0	5	9	3

2. Find the missing numbers:

a. $5 + 7 = ?$ d. $? - 9 = 7$ g. $? - 3 = 11$ j. $\square + \square = 18$

b. $9 + 8 = \square$ e. $5 + 6 = n$ h. $8 + 7 = n$ k. $n - 4 = 13$

c. $n - 3 = 6$ f. $\square - 2 = 1$ i. $6 + n = 8$ l. $9 - n = 9$

3. Add each of the following:

a.	2	12	22	52	82
	7	7	7	7	7

c.	9	29	39	69	89
	4	4	4	4	4

b.	53	64	6	1	74
	5	2	93	38	4

d.	27	79	4	5	38
	8	9	67	49	6

4. Add and check:

a.	426	682	29	491	528
	7	43	8	238	325
	983	9	537	475	846
	6	95	86	289	587

b.	3,582	9,734	6,359	2,187	4,139
	165	859	4,869	5,854	8,267
	2,859	26	3,687	3,895	5,918
	406	4,583	5,948	4,669	7,656

c.				
9	638	217	82,152	487
286	46	59	75	2,849
58	9	4,895	3,946	86,296
7	28	684	820	908
526	253	8	1,639	4,356

d.				
396	3,688	49,962	62,835	29,157
9,274	42,916	90,556	91,684	45,209
833	259	77,385	26,893	63,982
409	59,837	82,597	80,795	42,867
84,582	9,479	29,481	39,886	50,786

e.				
825	1,369	9,408	38,257	51,863
4,932	58,473	35,765	989	7,156
526	257	89,159	8,192	8,399
39,688	45,164	849	77,266	70,565
5,897	3,828	98,267	6,097	49,284

f.				
92,868	46,556	21,684	74,396	48,395
57,859	80,908	89,299	58,795	64,857
65,967	58,385	67,588	26,888	39,848
42,686	61,579	92,907	41,479	99,059
78,679	83,438	81,554	78,393	68,586

g.				
6,584	4,593	82,584	14,688	89,765
923	688	93,635	69,526	48,489
78	46	6,987	83,989	69,473
92,654	239	5,279	59,675	53,269
7,369	58,427	38,096	65,114	95,786
827	948	96,887	82,879	28,698

h.				
853,264	4,672	684,597	563,875	486,554
96,587	635,967	483,698	285,973	560,893
9,467	72,584	599,569	864,798	915,921
658	9,593	367,475	975,687	357,865
17,425	298,449	952,388	869,506	831,479
8,269	587,976	876,959	372,452	699,837

5. Add horizontally:

a. 68 + 29 + 64   c. 8354 + 918 + 6239   e. 615 + 98 + 9 + 968

b. 306 + 85 + 747   d. 40 + 56 + 8 + 99   f. 9057 + 2892 + 4688 + 5145

6. Arrange in columns, then find the sum of each of the following:

a. 25; 47; 82   c. 4,075; 5,385; 1,625   e. 8,000; 60; 900; 40

b. 349; 876; 946   d. 867; 9; 16; 218   f. 563; 89; 7; 6,475; 44

2-10 COMPUTATION—SUBTRACTION

In subtraction a quantity is taken away from another given quantity and the number left over (called the *remainder*) is found. Sometimes subtraction is used to compare two quantities. Here we are finding the difference between two numbers or finding how much more or less one number is than the other. Subtraction is also used in situations where we are required to find how much more is needed. Here we know the sum and one addend and we are required to find the other addend.

The terms that we generally use in subtraction are: *minuend*, the number from which we subtract; *subtrahend*, the number we subtract; and *remainder* or *difference*, the answer in subtraction. Instead of these terms, to simplify the language we can use *sum* as the number from which we subtract, *addend* as the number we subtract and the *missing addend* as the answer. $8 - 5 = ?$ is thought of as $5 + ? = 8$. Subtraction is not considered a principle operation but as an *inverse operation of addition*. The minus sign $(-)$ is the symbol used to indicate subtraction. We can subtract only like quantities: ones from ones, tens from tens, hundreds from hundreds, etc.

To subtract whole numbers, we subtract the digits in the subtrahend from the corresponding digits in the minuend, starting from the ones place. When any digit in the subtrahend is greater than the corresponding digit in the minuend, we increase this digit in the minuend by 10 by taking 1 from the preceding digit in the next higher place and changing it to 10 of the next lower place. This is called *regrouping*. Some people call it *borrowing*.

$$
\begin{array}{ll}
728 \leftarrow \text{Minuend} & 728 \leftarrow \text{Sum} \\
\underline{-453} \leftarrow \text{Subtrahend} & \underline{-453} \leftarrow \text{Addend} \\
275 \leftarrow \text{Remainder or} & 275 \leftarrow \text{Addend} \\
\qquad\quad \text{Difference} & \\
\end{array}
$$

$$\textit{Answer, } 275$$

728 = 7 hundreds 2 tens 8 ones = 6 hundreds 12 tens 8 ones
453 = 4 hundreds 5 tens 3 ones = <u>4 hundreds   5 tens 3 ones</u>
                                       2 hundreds   7 tens 5 ones = 275

We check by adding the remainder to the subtrahend. Their sum should equal the minuend.

1. Subtract and check:

a.

2	9	8	3	10	11	4	9	13	6	8
0	5	8	2	4	8	1	8	6	5	6

b.

7	9	12	6	7	10	11	14	5	6	10
7	6	5	4	6	7	9	7	3	1	9

c.

10	5	15	8	12	16	9	7	16	10	8
1	2	7	1	8	7	2	3	8	6	2

d.

1	6	7	6	9	17	0	11	12	17	12
1	3	4	6	4	8	0	5	3	9	7

e.

11	9	4	5	11	9	10	8	13	10	16
2	1	2	4	4	3	5	3	4	2	9

f.

12	10	13	14	5	12	15	14	11	18	14
9	8	7	9	1	6	8	5	6	9	6

g.

10	7	4	14	11	9	7	11	4	8	13
3	1	3	8	7	9	2	3	4	5	8

h.

15	7	6	8	13	12	8	13	5	9	15
6	5	2	4	5	4	7	9	0	7	9

2. Find the missing numbers:

a. $16 - 9 = \square$ **d.** $4 + \square = 8$ **g.** $8 + n = 13$ **j.** $? + 3 = 4$

b. $13 - 5 = n$ **e.** $n + 7 = 15$ **h.** $10 - \square = \square$ **k.** $n + 5 = 11$

c. $? + 6 = 14$ **f.** $12 - 7 = ?$ **i.** $\square + 9 = 17$ **l.** $7 + \square = 12$

3. Subtract and check:

a.

59	63	88	95	82	47	86	70
7	8	23	78	57	27	83	24

b.

347	984	825	617	500	902	316	603
26	565	179	598	344	496	85	405

c.

5,238	9,386	3,752	8,126	5,174	9,145	6,000	7,594
4,125	2,931	57	4,077	1,886	9	5,842	3,748

d.

9,285	1,527	8,467	7,418	8,641	4,529	8,506	2,016
6	49	2,053	3,156	7,936	1,780	4,748	860

e.	62,874	84,592	89,327	46,285	90,526	30,000
	11,562	63,870	639	32,189	64,865	8,503

f.	98,463	35,862	25,174	85,000	91,052	32,067
	72,340	17,927	87	6,958	80,389	15,938

g.	874,506	297,506	619,385	720,094	982,050
	391,275	8,617	253,419	510,638	875

h.	4,669,857	6,984,506	4,930,807	8,914,050	4,000,000
	2,179,427	2,893,715	25,040	5,806,973	3,806,796

i.	586	4,052	1,537	64,828	891,060	3,101,953
	298	3,987	68	56,179	859,184	9,478

j.	925	3,840	8,545	42,516	650,000	7,430,467
	786	2,761	3,987	27,899	559,077	6,629,408

4. Subtract horizontally:

a. 48 − 29   153 − 78   324 − 169   5,000 − 525   2,800 − 15
b. 85 − 56   247 − 187   900 − 287   8,160 − 5,296   67,000 − 6,700

5. a. From 800 subtract 279.   **d.** From 4,267 take 1,098.
b. Take 517 from 603.   **e.** Subtract 43,963 from 51,825.
c. Subtract 3,809 from 7,000.   **f.** From 70,688 take 9,878.

6. Find the difference between: **a.** 1,680 and 494   **b.** 20,000 and 2,000.

2–11   COMPUTATION—MULTIPLICATION

Multiplication is a short way of adding two or more quantities of the same size. 5 + 5 becomes 2 fives or 2 × 5. 8 + 8 + 8 becomes 3 eights or 3 × 8. We may think of multiplication as successive addition or repeated addition of equal or identical numbers.

Multiplication is a method of combining groups of equal size or groups containing the same number of things to find how many there are altogether. In order to multiply we must know the number of equal groups and the size or how many things there are in each group.

The terms we generally use in multiplication are: *multiplicand,* the number that we multiply; *multiplier,* the number by which we multiply; *product,* the answer in multiplication; *partial product,* the product obtained by multiplying the multiplicand by any figure in the multiplier containing two or more figures; and *factor,* any number that is multiplied. Since both the multiplicand and multiplier are factors, we could say:

factor × factor = product
                  instead of multiplier × multiplicand = product.

The times sign (×) or the raised dot (·) indicate multiplication.

One-Digit Multipliers

To multiply by a one-digit multiplier, we multiply each digit in the multiplicand by the one-digit multiplier, starting from the right. If the product or total for any place is ten or more, we write the last digit in the answer and add the other digit to the next product.

$$
\begin{array}{r}
48 \leftarrow \text{Multiplicand or Factor} \\
\times 2 \leftarrow \text{Multiplier or Factor} \\
\hline
96 \leftarrow \text{Product}
\end{array}
$$

Answer, 96

Multipliers of Two or More Digits

To multiply by a multiplier containing two or more digits, we multiply all the digits in the multiplicand by each digit in the multiplier, starting from the right, to find the partial products. The partial products are written under each other with the numerals placed so that the right-hand digit of each partial product is directly under its corresponding digit in the multiplier. Then we add the partial products. Observe that the distributive principle is used in the model problem. We check by interchanging the multiplier and multiplicand and multiplying again or by division if it has been studied.

$$
\begin{array}{r}
12 \\
\times 23 \\
\end{array}
=
\begin{array}{r}
12 \\
\times \ 20 \\
\hline
240 \\
\end{array}
+
\begin{array}{r}
12 \\
\times \ 3 \\
\hline
36 \\
\end{array}
\qquad
\begin{array}{r}
12 \\
\times 23 \\
\hline
36 \\
240 \\
\hline
276 \\
\end{array}
\text{ or }
\begin{array}{r}
12 \\
23 \\
\hline
36 \leftarrow \text{Partial} \\
24 \leftarrow \text{Products} \\
\hline
276 \\
\end{array}
$$

Answer, 276

1. Multiply and check:

a.	8	3	4	3	9	5	2	1	4	5	6
	1	6	0	4	6	7	4	2	3	9	1
b.	6	5	7	2	8	9	4	7	4	3	1
	2	3	4	8	4	3	6	7	5	0	5
c.	7	3	1	7	2	8	7	6	2	4	6
	3	2	1	6	5	3	0	3	7	2	4
d.	8	1	2	0	7	5	4	0	3	1	7
	8	7	3	0	9	1	7	6	8	9	2
e.	3	4	9	7	2	9	8	9	1	6	3
	1	8	4	5	6	7	2	8	6	7	5
f.	2	8	9	0	5	9	8	6	5	7	8
	9	7	1	8	6	5	6	9	8	1	9
g.	3	4	2	1	6	5	1	3	0	1	9
	7	9	2	4	6	2	8	3	9	3	9
h.	8	4	6	5	9	7	0	4	6	5	3
	5	4	5	4	2	8	5	1	8	5	9

2. Find the answer to each of the following:

a. 3 times 2, then add 1.	**f.** 5 times 3, then add 2.
b. 5 times 7, then add 6.	**g.** 8 times 6, then add 5.
c. 9 times 8, then add 8.	**h.** 9 times 9, then add 6.
d. 4 times 3, then add 1.	**i.** 0 times 8, then add 7.
e. 6 times 8, then add 4.	**j.** 7 times 5, then add 3.

3. Multiply and check:

a.	32	72	13	78	197	856	380	703
	2	4	6	8	4	7	9	8
b.	8,016	6,080	9,354	8,005	59,687	94,758	80,103	25,914
	5	7	2	4	8	9	7	6

Properties—Operations with Whole Numbers

4. Multiply and check:

a.
21	69	51	92	56	60	86	70	8	91
43	35	87	26	75	97	50	70	69	10

b.
231	937	452	750	409	54	805	954	400	568
24	85	69	48	36	983	90	99	25	87

c.
3,825	1,728	9,076	6,080	14,243	78,049	65,874	50,904
79	81	90	96	12	67	56	38

d.
196	468	259	892	784	969	501	640	793	607
217	349	783	495	597	829	467	800	108	906

e.
1,728	8,936	4,800	5,280	26,569	40,706	80,020	89,978
456	659	307	178	827	905	204	698

f.
2,347	4,339	8,476	7,845	4,018	6,738	3,050	6,159
3,157	4,856	7,288	9,387	5,009	7,654	3,050	4,000

g.
95,468	43,560	80,070	90,406	29,783	89,612	93,654	70,500
7,986	2,895	3,004	5,634	49,976	27,064	85,917	90,010

h.
98	56	497	89	854	325	6,080	2,586	3,928	26,541
7	83	96	320	479	958	306	144	5,196	9,085

5. Do as directed in each of the following:

a. 12 times 90   144 times 65   507 times 704

b. 36 × 75   320 × 100   728 × 897

c. 24 × 16 × 8   35 × 42 × 19   46 × 301 × 69

d. Multiply 85 by 72.   Multiply 349 by 60.   Multiply 144 by 700.

e. Find the product of 40 and 70.   Find the product of 624 and 89.   Find the product of 5,280 and 405.

2–12   FACTORIAL

The product of all natural numbers up to and including a given number is called the *factorial* of the given number.

> Four factorial, written as 4!, means
> 1 × 2 × 3 × 4 or the product 24.
>
> One factorial, written as 1!, is equal to 1.

Find the products represented by the following:

1. 3!	**5.** 8!	**9.** 9!	**13.** 5!3!
2. 5!	**6** 1!	**10.** 12!	**14.** 2!4!6!
3. 2!	**7.** 7!	**11.** 2!3!	**15.** 2!3!4!
4. 6!	**8.** 10!	**12.** 6!4!	**16.** 3!5!6!

2–13 SQUARING A NUMBER

The *square* of a number is the product obtained when a given number is multiplied by itself.

Thus to square a number we multiply the given number by itself.

> Square 9:
>
> $9 \times 9 = 81$
>
> *Answer*, 81

Square each of the following numbers:

1. 7	**5.** 39	**9.** 100	**13.** 1,250
2. 12	**6.** 40	**10.** 206	**14.** 3,847
3. 28	**7.** 75	**11.** 584	**15.** 1,760
4. 53	**8.** 89	**12.** 800	**16.** 9,003

2–14 RUSSIAN PEASANT METHOD OF MULTIPLICATION

In the Russian Peasant method of multiplication one factor is multiplied by 2 (or doubled) and the corresponding other factor is divided by 2 (or halved). The resulting factors are doubled and halved respectively until the halved number 1 is reached. Any fraction associated with the halved number is dropped.

To find the answer, all the doubles corresponding to even halves are first crossed out. Then the remaining doubles are added. The sum, thus found, is the desired answer.

Properties—Operations with Whole Numbers

To multiply 125 by 59 using the Russian Peasant method, we first write the given factors 125 and 59 in two columns as shown. We double one factor and halve the other, continuing in this way until 1 is reached in the column of halves. The number 500 is crossed out in the column of doubles since the corresponding halved number is 14, an even number. The sum of the remaining doubles

Doubles	Halves
125	59
250	29
500̶	14
1,000	7
2,000	3
4,000	1
7,375	

$$(125 + 250 + 1,000 + 2,000 + 4,000)$$

is found to be 7,375 which is the product of 125 and 59.

EXERCISES

Multiply by the Russian Peasant method:

1. 28×65
2. 97×83
3. 149×92
4. 51×367
5. 434×250
6. 893×475
7. 629×564
8. 700×803
9. 295×389
10. 366×508
11. 481×969
12. 108×630

2–15 LATTICE METHOD OF MULTIPLICATION

The Gelosia or lattice method of multiplication was used late in the 15th century. John Napier (1550–1617) used a similar idea to invent a system of rods, called Napier Bones, to multiply numbers.

The lattice is a frame of squares. Each square has a diagonal line drawn through it.

To multiply 9,564 by 287 by the lattice method, one factor (9,564) is written above the frame and the other factor (287) is written at the right, with one digit of each used for each square.

Each digit at the top is used as a factor for each corresponding square in the column below it and each digit at the right is used as a factor for each corresponding square in the row to the left of it. For each square, the corresponding digit at the top and at the right are used as factors and the product is written in the squares (units under the diagonal and tens above the diagonal). If a product consists only of units, then a zero is written in the tens place.

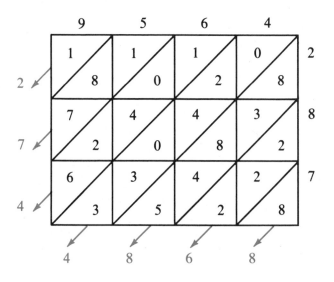

Answer, 2,744,868

Notice in the:

Top row: 9 × 2 = 18; 5 × 2 = 10; 6 × 2 = 12; 4 × 2 = 8
Middle row: 9 × 8 = 72; 5 × 8 = 40; 6 × 8 = 48; 4 × 8 = 32
Bottom row: 9 × 7 = 63; 5 × 7 = 35; 6 × 7 = 42; 4 × 7 = 28

We then add along the diagonals from right to left as we do in ordinary addition, carrying when necessary to the next diagonal.

EXERCISES

Multiply by the lattice method:

1. 67 × 85	**4.** 926 × 755	**7.** 875 × 6,429	**10.** 83,496 × 4,009
2. 326 × 49	**5.** 604 × 907	**8.** 3,508 × 2,706	**11.** 62,051 × 95,902
3. 858 × 203	**6.** 4,318 × 524	**9.** 7,325 × 4,277	**12.** 59,898 × 83,465

2–16 COMPUTATION—DIVISION

Division is a method of finding how many equal groups can be formed when we know the total number of things and the number of things it takes (sometimes called the size) to make a group. Division is also used to find the number of things in (or the size of) one

Properties—Operations with Whole Numbers

of the equal groups when we know the number of equal groups and the total number of things. Sometimes division is used to compare one number with another.

In division we generally use the following terms: *dividend,* the number that we divide: *divisor,* the number by which we divide; *quotient,* the answer in division; *remainder,* the number left over when the division is not exact; and *partial dividend,* the first part of the given dividend or digits of the dividend annexed to the remainder. The symbols ÷ and ⌐ and the fraction bar (—) are used to indicate division.

Division is not considered a principle operation but as an *inverse operation of multiplication.* Thus division is sometimes thought of as the process of finding the factor which multiplied by a given factor is equal to the given product.

$18 \div 3 = ?$ is considered either as $3 \times ? = 18$ or $? \times 3 = 18$.

Thus, dividend ÷ divisor = quotient
means: divisor × quotient = dividend
or: factor × factor = product

Dividing a Whole Number by a Whole Number

(1) *To divide a whole number by a whole number,* we first find the *quotient digit* by dividing the one-digit divisor or the trial divisor, when the divisor contains more than one digit, into the first digit of the dividend. When the divisor contains two or more digits, we use as the trial divisor the first digit of the divisor if the next digit on the right is 0, 1, 2, 3, 4, or 5 and increase the first digit of the divisor by one (1) if the next digit on the right is 6, 7, 8, or 9. The greatest digit that can be used in the quotient at any time is 9.

(2) We multiply the divisor by the quotient digit and write this product under the corresponding digits in the dividend. This product must be the same or less than the partial dividend. If it is greater, then we use as the trial quotient digit one (1) less than the digit first tried.

(*1*) Divide:

$$\frac{2}{32)896}$$

(*2*) Multiply:

$$\frac{2}{32)896}$$
$$64$$

(3) We subtract this product from the corresponding numbers in the dividend. The remainder must be less than the whole divisor. If it is not, then we use as the trial quotient digit one (1) more than the digit tried.

(4) We bring down the next digit of the dividend and annex it to the remainder, if any.

(5) (6) (7) Then using the remainder and annexed numbers as partial dividends, we repeat the above steps for each partial dividend.

We check by multiplying the quotient by the divisor and adding the remainder, if any, to the product. The result should equal the dividend.

(3) Subtract:

$$\begin{array}{r} 2 \\ 32\overline{)896} \\ 64 \\ \hline 25 \end{array}$$

(4) Bring down digit:

$$\begin{array}{r} 2 \\ 32\overline{)896} \\ 64 \\ \hline 256 \end{array}$$

(5) Divide:

$$\begin{array}{r} 28 \\ 32\overline{)896} \\ 64 \\ \hline 256 \end{array}$$

(6) Multiply:

$$\begin{array}{r} 28 \\ 32\overline{)896} \\ 64 \\ \hline 256 \\ 256 \end{array}$$

(7) Subtract:

$$\begin{array}{r} 28 \\ 32\overline{)896} \\ 64 \\ \hline 256 \\ 256 \\ \hline \end{array}$$

Answer, 28

Writing Remainders

When a division is not exact, the remainder may be written in the answer using the letter R to indicate it or it may be written as a fraction in lowest terms or it may be indicated (when the divisor is a large number) by a + sign in the answer. In certain social situations remainders are sometimes dropped. For example, the answer when determining how many pieces of ribbon each 5 inches long may be cut from a piece 36 inches long is 7 pieces not $7\frac{1}{5}$ pieces.

$$\begin{array}{r} 3 \\ 5\overline{)17} \\ 15 \\ \hline 2 \end{array}$$

Answer, 3 R 2

or $3\frac{2}{5}$

$$\begin{array}{r} 2 \\ 1{,}760\overline{)3{,}617} \\ 3\ 520 \\ \hline 97 \end{array}$$

Answer, 2+

$$\begin{array}{r} 7 \\ 5\overline{)36} \\ 35 \\ \hline 1 \end{array}$$

Answer, 7 pieces

Properties—Operations with Whole Numbers

1. Divide and check:

   a. 2)18   8)16   3)15   1)7   5)35   7)21   4)32   8)72   9)54

   b. 6)48   3)6   8)40   2)14   1)2   5)40   7)35   3)3   6)24

   c. 1)4   4)28   2)6   3)27   4)20   2)2   3)18   7)49   2)12

   d. 9)18   1)9   5)45   8)8   7)14   5)10   2)4   7)42   5)15

   e. 7)56   4)16   6)18   9)0   5)20   8)64   1)1   2)10   7)28

   f. 2)8   5)5   9)45   6)12   1)5   3)12   8)32   7)63   1)3

   g. 5)30   6)36   4)8   9)72   8)48   5)25   9)9   7)7   3)24

   h. 9)81   4)12   9)36   4)36   6)54   3)21   9)63   3)9   6)30

   i. 2)16   8)56   4)4   8)24   1)6   6)6   9)27   6)42   4)24

2. Find the missing numbers:

   a. $4 \times ? = 28$

   b. $8 \times \square = 32$

   c. $7 \times n = 63$

   d. $\square \times \square = 81$

   e. $? \times 6 = 54$

   f. $n \times 7 = 42$

   g. $72 \div 9 = \square$

   h. $\square \div 4 = 9$

   i. $25 \div \square = \square$

   j. $? \times 3 = 12$

   k. $n \times 9 = 45$

   l. $\frac{\square}{5} = 8$

3. Divide and check:

   2)84   8)96   4)872   5)810   7)9,247   6)9,468   3)75,693   8)99,984

4. Divide each of the following. Be careful where you put the first quotient digit:

   7)427   4)368   3)1,029   9)8,568

   8)6,992   6)49,266   3)26,517   4)13,968

5. Watch the zeros in each of the following division problems:

   2)60   6)720   5)4,000   3)6,906

   5)510   9)9,045   4)80,120   7)73,542

6. Divide each of the following:

   a. By 2:   58;   614;   1,706;   73,592;   96,510

   b. By 6:   84;   738;   5,442;   42,480;   23,676

   c. By 3:   57;   291;   4,215;   26,928;   50,007

   d. By 8:   96;   840;   7,648;   56,736;   31,448

e.	By 5:	70;	625;	4,300;	81,975;	60,125
f.	By 7:	98;	392;	2,695;	56,049;	69,314
g.	By 9:	90;	711;	5,682;	27,000;	10,422
h.	By 4:	72;	668;	3,160;	97,876;	72,160

7. Find the quotient and the remainder in each of the following:

   $8\overline{)59}$ $4\overline{)95}$ $5\overline{)726}$ $6\overline{)8,755}$ $8\overline{)6,727}$ $3\overline{)44,698}$ $8\overline{)56,095}$ $6\overline{)91,577}$

8. Divide. Write the remainder as a fraction in lowest terms:

   $5\overline{)48}$ $6\overline{)46}$ $3\overline{)31}$ $8\overline{)986}$ $6\overline{)8,195}$ $9\overline{)31,980}$ $7\overline{)84,356}$ $4\overline{)33,962}$

9. Do as indicated:

   a. $3,425 \div 5$ c. $3,628 \div 4$ e. $39,704 \div 8$ g. $81,675 \div 9$
   b. $8,991 \div 9$ d. $1,770 \div 6$ f. $41,972 \div 7$ h. $32,072 \div 8$

10. Divide and check:

   a. $10\overline{)40}$ $14\overline{)28}$ $19\overline{)76}$ $63\overline{)189}$ $48\overline{)336}$ $50\overline{)500}$ $96\overline{)864}$ $59\overline{)354}$

   b. $18\overline{)612}$ $97\overline{)4,462}$ $89\overline{)5,162}$ $32\overline{)7,648}$ $76\overline{)69,768}$

   c. $90\overline{)34,110}$ $79\overline{)32,232}$ $94\overline{)131,130}$ $65\overline{)520,585}$ $48\overline{)415,584}$

   d. $31\overline{)722}$ $76\overline{)6,565}$ $88\overline{)9,039}$ $64\overline{)45,467}$ $90\overline{)34,733}$

11. Write the remainder as a fraction in the following:

   $80\overline{)290}$ $48\overline{)3,488}$ $56\overline{)32,662}$ $81\overline{)96,215}$ $31\overline{)42,810}$

12. Divide and check:

   a. $298\overline{)894}$ $132\overline{)3,696}$ $344\overline{)60,200}$ $978\overline{)644,502}$ $546\overline{)221,130}$

   b. $600\overline{)491,400}$ $607\overline{)549,942}$ $380\overline{)189,240}$ $672\overline{)565,152}$ $293\overline{)830,655}$

   c. $2,240\overline{)64,960}$ $6,080\overline{)1,270,720}$ $9,006\overline{)81,108,036}$ $7,657\overline{)6,003,088}$

13. Find the quotient and the remainder in each of the following:

   $144\overline{)1,368}$ $875\overline{)42,375}$ $752\overline{)696,935}$ $1,728\overline{)39,450}$ $3,600\overline{)20,000}$

14. Do as indicated:

   a. $17,856 \div 48$ c. $355,118 \div 503$ e. $144,342 \div 297$
   b. $522,291 \div 969$ d. $776,640 \div 96$ f. $1,400,000 \div 2,240$

15. Divide and check:

   a. $29\overline{)2,107}$ $144\overline{)38,629}$ $759\overline{)685,436}$ $918\overline{)776,899}$ $9,455\overline{)595,688}$

   b. $84\overline{)5,628}$ $52\overline{)49,192}$ $792\overline{)331,056}$ $307\overline{)303,009}$ $4,298\overline{)154,728}$

2–17 TESTS FOR DIVISIBILITY

A number is said to be *divisible* by another number if it can be divided exactly by the second number with no remainder.

The following are some quick tests to determine whether a number is divisible by 2, 3, 4, 5, 6, 8, 9, 10.

(1) A number is divisible by 2 only if it ends in 0, 2, 4, 6, or 8. All even numbers are divisible by 2.

(2) A number is divisible by 3 only if the sum of its digits is divisible by 3.

> 2,541 is divisible by 3.
> 2 + 5 + 4 + 1 = 12 and 12 is divisible by 3.
>
> 1,526 is not divisible by 3.
> 1 + 5 + 2 + 6 = 14 and 14 is not divisible by 3.

(3) A number is divisible by 4 only if it is an even number and the number represented by the last two digits (tens and units digits) is divisible by 4. Numbers ending in two zeros are divisible by 4.

> 58,2*64* is divisible by 4 because *64* is divisible by 4.

(4) A number is divisible by 5 only if it ends in 5 or 0.

> 8,325 ends in 5, thus it is divisible by 5.
> 59,740 ends in 0, thus it is divisible by 5.

(5) A number is divisible by 6 only if it is an even number and the sum of its digits is divisible by 3.

> The *even* number 8,244 is divisible by 6.
> 8 + 2 + 4 + 4 = 18 and 18 is divisible by 3.

(6) A number is divisible by 8 only if it is an even number and the number represented by the last three digits (hundreds, tens, and units digits) is divisible by 8. Numbers ending in three zeros are divisible by 8. Use this test only when the number is 1,000 or larger.

> The *even* number 258,496 is divisible by 8 because 496 is divisible by 8.

(7) A number is divisible by 9 only if the sum of its digits is divisible by 9.

> 86,355 is divisible by 9.
> 8 + 6 + 3 + 5 + 5 = 27 and 27 is divisible by 9.

(8) A number is divisible by 10 only if it ends in 0.

> 6,320 is divisible by 10 because it ends in 0.

EXERCISES

1. a. Is 83,592 divisible by 3?   by 2?   by 6?   by 9?
   b. Is 578,976 divisible by 4?   by 2?   by 8?   by 6?
   c. Is 67,500 divisible by 2?   by 5?   by 10?   by 4?
   d. Is 956,000 divisible by 5?   by 10?   by 6?   by 8?
   e. Is 468,765 divisible by 9?   by 6?   by 2?   by 3?

Properties—Operations with Whole Numbers   **69**

2. Determine whether the following numbers are divisible:

a. by 4:	832;	6,794;	8,500;	71,676;	924,635
b. by 3:	558;	7,213;	6,087;	46,881;	483,754
c. by 5:	678;	9,000;	5,265;	28,206;	571,525
d. by 2:	742;	8,504;	7,988;	80,593;	920,000
e. by 6:	285;	9,726;	2,073;	53,262;	727,824
f. by 9:	531;	4,699;	28,386;	47,979;	869,463
g. by 8:	5,952;	8,217;	52,678;	61,000;	644,862
h. by 10:	890;	4,000;	63,505;	80,640;	278,130

2–18 CHECKING BY CASTING OUT NINES

The operations of addition, subtraction, multiplication, and division may be checked by a method called *casting out nines*. This method is not perfect since an incorrect answer sometimes will check.

In this checking process each given number is divided by nine, the nines (quotient) are then cast out (discarded) and only the remainder called the *excess* is used.

Suppose 4,728 is divided by 9. We find there are 525 nines and 3 ones. The remainder 3 indicates there are 3 ones in excess of an exact number of nines (525 nines).

$$\begin{array}{r} 525 \\ 9\overline{)4,728} \\ 4\ 5 \\ \hline 22 \\ 18 \\ \hline 48 \\ 45 \\ \hline 3 \end{array}$$

This excess in a number may be found by an easier method than dividing the given number by 9.

Suppose we add the digits in 4,728; we find the sum is 21. If we add the digits in 21, we find the sum is 3. This sum is the same as the remainder we found when we divided.

$$4 + 7 + 2 + 8 = 21$$
$$2 + 1 = 3$$

Thus we may find the excess ones with respect to the number of groups of nine a number possesses by adding the digits in a given number, then adding the digits in the sum, continuing in this way until the final sum is a one-digit number less than 9. If the sum is 9, it is replaced by a zero since the original number is divisible by 9 and 0 is the remainder. This final sum is the *excess*.

To Check Addition

We find the excess in each addend and in the sum. The sum of the excesses in the addends should equal the excess in the sum of the addends.[1]

$$
\begin{array}{ll}
238 \; (4) & (4) + (6) + (3) \\
591 \; (6) & \quad = (13) = (4) \\
+426 \; (3) & \\
\hline
1{,}255 \; (4) &
\end{array}
$$

Addition:

To Check Subtraction

We find the excess in the minuend, subtrahend, and answer. The sum of the excesses in the subtrahend and answer should equal the excess in the minuend. When the excess in the minuend is 0, use 9.

Subtraction:

$$
\begin{array}{ll}
7{,}523 \; (8) & (8) - (7) = (1) \\
-2{,}941 \; (7) & \\
\hline
4{,}582 \; (1) & \text{or } (7) + (1) = 8
\end{array}
$$

To Check Multiplication

We find the excess in the multiplicand, multiplier, and product. The product of the excess in the factors should equal the excess in the product.[1]

Multiplication:

$$
\begin{array}{ll}
46 \; (1) & \\
\times 57 \; (3) & (1) \times (3) = (3) \\
\hline
322 & \\
2\;30 & \\
\hline
2{,}622 \; (3) &
\end{array}
$$

---

[1] If the sum or product of the excesses is a two-digit number, simplify and express as a single digit excess.

Properties—Operations with Whole Numbers

To Check Division

We find the excess in the divisor, dividend, quotient, and remainder if any. The product of the excesses in the divisor and quotient increased by the excess in the remainder should equal the excess in the dividend.[1] When the excess in the divisor is 0, use 9.

Division:

$$
\begin{array}{r}
68 \\
32\overline{)2{,}176} \\
192 \\
\overline{256} \\
256
\end{array}
\qquad
\begin{array}{l}
(5) \\
(5)\overline{)(7)} \\
\\
(5) \times (5) = (25) = (7)
\end{array}
$$

EXERCISES

Compute each of the following as directed and check by casting out nines.

1. Add:

654	2,668	78,350	42,837	96,258
8,327	7,157	4,767	95,143	67,442
259	3,826	83,208	88,375	31,597
3,671	5,593	9,315	61,086	87,646
462	8,714	25,785	49,878	32,899

2. Subtract:

6,825	31,057	78,459	387,052	962,584
4,786	2,658	52,847	193,728	638,796

3. Multiply:

325	678	5,687	2,974	83,060
413	745	357	6,758	50,721

4. Divide:

$76\overline{)61{,}028}$ $132\overline{)3{,}696}$ $569\overline{)49{,}503}$ $380\overline{)189{,}240}$ $918\overline{)776{,}899}$

---

[1] If the sum or product of the excesses is a two-digit number, simplify and express as a single digit excess.

2–19 PATTERNS

(1) *Fibonacci Sequence*

This is a sequence of natural numbers in which every number after the second number is equal to the sum of the two preceding numbers. What are the next five numbers after 21?

1, 1, 2, 3, 5, 8, 13, 21, . . .

(2) *Pascal's Triangle*

This is a triangular arrangement of rows of numbers, each row increasing by one number. Each row, except the first, begins and ends in a 1 written diagonally. Beginning with the second row, each number is the sum of the numbers just to the left and right of it in the row above. Note that the numbers are placed midway between the numbers of the row directly above it. Find the numbers that belong in the next four rows.

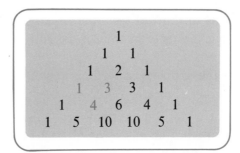

2–20 FRAME ARITHMETIC

Find the whole numbers that belong in each frame. Use the same number when the same frame appears more than once.

1. $\square + 6 = 15$ **4.** $\square \div 5 = 4$ **7.** $\square + \square = \square$ **10.** $\square \div \square = \square$

2. $\square - 3 = 8$ **5.** $\square + \square = 28$ **8.** $\square \times \square = \square$ **11.** $\square \times 8 = 56$

3. $4 \times \square = 24$ **6.** $\square \times \square = 36$ **9.** $\square - \square = \square$ **12.** $17 - \square = 10$

13. For which of the above problems can you find more than one correct answer?

14. $\triangle + \square = 10$ **17.** $\triangle \times \square = 12$ **20.** $\square \div \triangle = 3$ **23.** $\square \div \triangle = \square$

15. $\square - \triangle = 2$ **18.** $\square \times \square = \triangle$ **21.** $\triangle - \square = \square$ **24.** $\square - \square = \triangle$

16. $\square + \square = \triangle$ **19.** $\square \times \triangle = 18$ **22.** $\triangle \times \square = \triangle$ **25.** $\square \div \square = \triangle$

26. For which problems 14 to 25 inclusive can you find more than one pair of correct answers?

PROBLEM SOLVING STRATEGY

Use the following procedure in solving problems:

1 Read the problem carefully to find:
   a. The facts that are given.
   b. What is being asked.

2 Decide what to do to solve the problem.
   a. Which given facts should be used with which operations?
   b. If more than one step is needed, in what order should the operations be used?
   c. Select only the facts you need. Sometimes more facts than are needed are given. Other times not enough facts are given.
   d. Write or think of a mathematical sentence (or equation) that relates the given facts to what is asked.

3 Solve the problem according to your plan. Perform the operation or operations accurately:
   a. First with rounded numbers to estimate your answer.
   b. Then with the actual numbers to find your answer.
   c. Use a diagram or drawing when necessary.

4 Answer
   a. Write your answer.
   b. Check your answer. Compare it with your estimated answer for reasonableness.

Problem: How much change should you get from $20 when you purchase an electronic game costing $15.89?

1 Read and find:
   Given facts   Game costs $15.89; $20 given in payment.
   Question asked How much change should you get?

2 Decide on Plan: Subtract the cost of the game ($15.89) from the amount given in payment ($20).
   Think $20.00 − $15.89 = amount of change

3 Solve:

Estimate $20 - $16 = $4

Actual $20.00 amount given in payment
         $15.89 cost of game
          $4.11 amount of change

4 Answer:

Write answer   Answer, $4.11 amount of change
Compare answer   The answer $4.11 compares reasonably with the $4 estimate.

Problem: If it costs $1.95 to develop a roll of film and $.29 for each print, how much will it cost to develop the film and make 12 prints?

1 Read and find:

Given facts   Developing the film cost $1.95; each print costs $.29.

Question asked   What is the total cost to develop the film and make 12 prints?

2 Decide on plan: Multiply the cost of a print ($.29) by the number of prints (12) to find the cost of the prints and to this product add the cost of developing the film ($1.95).

Think   (12 × $.29 + $1.95) = total cost

3 Solve:

Estimate   (12 × $.30) + $2.00 = total cost
            $3.60   + $2.00 = $5.60

Actual $.29 cost per print $3.48 cost of prints
          12 prints   1.95 cost of developing
           58                  $5.43 total cost
           29
         $3.48 cost of prints

4 Answer:

Write answer   Answer, $5.43 total cost
Compare answer   The answer $5.43 compares reasonably with the $5.60 estimate.

First study pages 74–75. Then solve each problem.

1. A recent count showed that in the United States there were 4,710 national banks, 1,072 state banks, 479 mutual savings banks, and 8,675 other banks. Find the total number of banks in the United States.

2. The area of Greenland is 840,000 square miles. If the area of Australia is 2,968,000 square miles, how much larger is Australia than Greenland?

3. At the school athletic field there are 28 sections each seating 76 persons. What is the total seating capacity?

4. If 1 kilogram (kg) of grass seed covers 35 square meters (m²), how many kilograms are needed for a lawn with an area of 665 square meters?

5. In 1492 there were about 846,000 American Indians in what is now the United States. Recently a census revealed there are 763,594 American Indians. Find the decrease in population.

6. What is the perimeter of the United States, excluding Alaska and Hawaii, if the northern boundary is 3,987 miles long, eastern boundary 5,565 miles long, southern boundary 5,654 miles long, and western boundary 2,730 miles long?

7. At an average speed of 475 m.p.h. how far can an airplane fly in 15 hours?

8. In Jacques Cartier High School there are 5 classes with 39 pupils on roll, 13 classes with 38 pupils, and 12 classes with 37 pupils. Find the total enrollment of the school.

9. Mr. Johnson can buy an automobile for $7,850 cash or $400 down and $270 a month for 30 months. How much can he save by paying cash?

10. Ms. Martinez plans to drive from New York to Chicago, a distance of 840 miles. If she averages 40 m.p.h., how long will it take to make the trip? How many gallons of gasoline will be required if her car averages 14 miles per gallon?

11. During a recent year the mints of the United States manufactured a total of 754,317,384 nickels and 1,100,512,100 dimes. How many more dimes than nickels were manufactured?

12. Tom's father earns $450 per week. John's mother earns $1,870 per month. Who earns more per year? How much more?

To estimate a sum, a difference, a product, or a quotient, first round the given numbers to convenient place values (see page 18) and then perform the operation or operations.

For each of the following select your nearest estimate:

1. 979 + 448 + 890 is approximately:	2,500	2,100	2,300
2. 7,013 − 3,962 is approximately:	4,000	3,000	10,000
3. 53 × 49 is approximately:	2,000	2,500	3,000
4. 760 ÷ 25 is approximately:	30	3	300
5. 10,000 − 4,959 is approximately:	4,000	5,000	6,000
6. 625,946 + 878,091 is approximately:	1,500,000	1,600,000	1,400,000
7. 812 × 97 is approximately:	70,000	80,000	90,000
8. 4,210 ÷ 42 is approximately:	10	1,000	100
9. 399 × 704 is approximately:	280,000	210,000	300,000
10. 9,285 + 3,192 + 5,886 is approximately:	18,000	17,000	19,000
11. 41,307 − 38,296 is approximately:	300	3,000	30,000
12. 409,345 ÷ 506 is approximately:	800	80	8,000

Indicate which answers are incorrect by using your calculator. If a calculator is not available, check by computation.
Compute as indicated.

1. a.	**b.**	**c.**	**2. a.**	**b.**
3,575	58,167	876,849	43,208	59,043
9,683	64,839	45,799	− 7,109	− 49,658
4,839	71,095	386,587	36,099	9,485
6,597	57,330	3,478	**c.** 683,008	**d.** 835,172
+ 7,036	+ 38,596	+ 698,986	− 394,937	− 676,384
31,830	291,027	2,011,699	289,071	168,788

3. a. 837 × 514 = 430,218
   b. 4,768 × 875 = 4,072,000

4. a. 23,368 ÷ 46 = 508
   b. 396,372 ÷ 804 = 483

5. a. 23 + 16,412 + 109 = 16,644
   b. 551,640 + 2,089 + 410 = 554,149

6. a. 4,800 − 480 = 4,220
   b. 62,936 − 32,852 = 30,084

7. a. 36 × 15 × 12 = 6,580
   b. 5,415 × 8,623 = 46,693,545

8. a. 661,941 ÷ 1,659 = 399
   b. 11,537,000 ÷ 4,150 = 2,880

CHAPTER REVIEW

1. Find the missing numbers: (2–2)

   a. $(12 \times 7) \div 7 = \square$ b. $(14 - 8) + 8 = \square$

   c. What operation is the inverse operation to addition?

2. Which of the following statements are true? (2–3, 2–4)

   a. $16 + 8 = 8 + 16$ e. $(16 + 4) + 2 = 16 + (4 + 2)$
   b. $16 - 8 = 8 - 16$ f. $(16 - 4) - 2 = 16 - (4 - 2)$
   c. $16 \times 8 = 8 \times 16$ g. $(16 \times 4) \times 2 = 16 \times (4 \times 2)$
   d. $16 \div 8 = 8 \div 16$ h. $(16 \div 4) \div 2 = 16 \div (4 \div 2)$

3. What do we mean by the commutative property of addition? (2–3)
4. What do we mean by the associative property of multiplication? (2–4)
5. Find the numbers that will make the following statement true: (2–5)

   a. $6 \times (3 + 5) = ? \times 3 + ? \times 5$
   b. $4 \times (8 + 2) = ? \times ? + ? \times ?$

6. Are the even whole numbers closed under the operation of addition? Subtraction? Multiplication? Division? (2–6)
7. Determine the value of each of the following: (2–7, 2–8)

   a. $6 + 0$ d. $\dfrac{13 - 5}{6 + 2}$ g. 0×2 j. $\dfrac{11 - 11}{10}$

   b. $17 - 17$ e. 1^7 h. $0 \div 5$ k. $18 - 0$

   c. 0×0 f. $\dfrac{16 + 4}{5 - 5}$ i. 20×1 l. $\frac{17}{17}$

8. Add: 9. Add: (2–9)

   45,584   43
   96,137   82,514
   30,598   567,827
   58,943   9,549
   76,456   493,875

10. Subtract:

596,138
489,046

11. Subtract:

7,040,603
6,989,594

(2–10)

12. Multiply:

8,359
9,678

13. Multiply:

90,506
807

(2–11)

14. Square each of the following numbers: **a.** 81   **b.** 420   (2–13)

15. Multiply 562 by 87 using the Russian Peasant method.   (2–14)
16. Multiply 3,695 by 418 using the lattice method.   (2–15)

17. Divide:

$$904)\overline{289,280}$$

18. Divide:

$$3,691)\overline{25,191,075}$$

(2–16)

19. **a.** Is 71,586 divisible by 2? by 3? by 6? by 9?   (2–17)
    b. Is 293,000 divisible by 10? by 8? by 5? by 4?

20. Compute each of the following as directed, then check by casting out nines: (2–18)

    a. Add:

    63,594
    2,855
    19,768
    329
    54,887

    b. Subtract:

    685,104
    638,695

    c. Multiply:

    735
    984

    d. Divide:

    $$196)\overline{64,288}$$

ACHIEVEMENT TEST

1. Write 460 billion as a complete numeral. (1–9)
2. Round 47,309,571,006 to the nearest million. (1–10)
3. Write 499 as a Roman numeral. (1–14)
4. What is the greatest common factor of 84 and 63? (1–21)
5. Factor 120 as the product of prime factors. (1–19)
6. What is the least common multiple of 50, 100, and 125? (1–24)
7. Find the missing numbers: (2–2 to 2–5)

   a. $(8 - 3) + 3 = \square$ d. $(6 \times 7) \times 3 = 6 \times (? \times 3)$
   b. $11 + 10 = ? + 11$ e. $(8 + 4) + 5 = 8 + (4 + ?)$
   c. $15 \times 9 = 9 \times ?$ f. $2 \times (3 + 4) = ? \times 3 + ? \times 4$

8. Is 1 closed under addition? Multiplication? Division? Subtraction? (2–6)

9. Add: 10. Subtract: 11. Multiply: (2–9 to 2–11)

   85,876   613,002   798
   76,988   158,075   869
   59,649
   60,795
   98,489

12. Divide: 13. Divide: (2–16)

   886)792,084   1,052)325,068

14. Is 23,954 divisible by 3? by 2? by 4? by 6? (2–17)

15. Multiply 875 by 268. Check by casting out nines. (2–18)

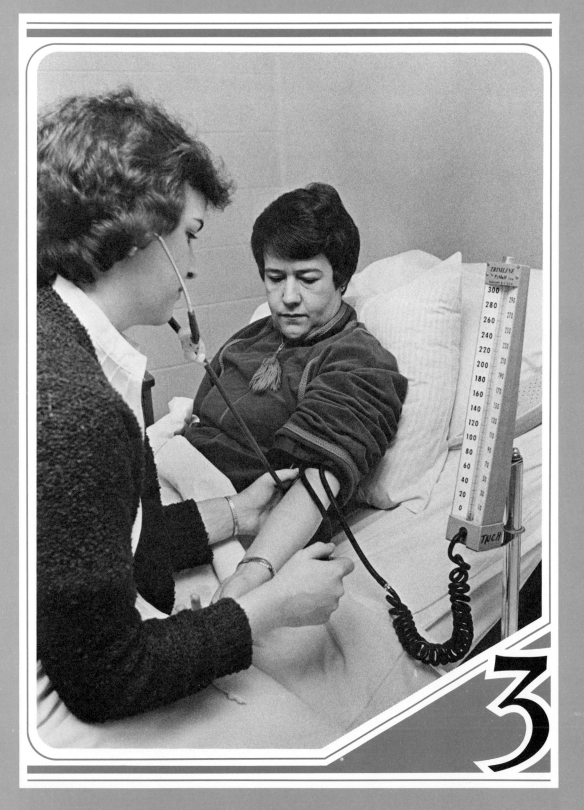

CHAPTER 3
Number Sentences–Equalities and Inequalities

3–1 NUMBER SENTENCES

Sentences that deal with numbers are called *number sentences* or *mathematical sentences*. The *equality* $4 + 8 = 12$ is a number sentence. It reads "Four plus eight is equal to twelve." The symbol $=$ is the equality sign. It means "is equal to" and is the verb in the sentence. The expressions on both sides of the equality sign designate the same number.

Number sentences may be true or they may be false. The number sentence $4 + 8 = 12$ is true but the sentence $9 - 5 = 6$ is false. A sentence that is either true or false is called a *statement*. A sentence cannot be both true and false at one time.

When two numbers are compared, one number may be:

(1) Equal to the other.
(2) Greater than the other.
(3) Less than the other.

In any specific case only one of these three possibilities is true.

When one number is greater than or less than a second number, an *inequality* exists. An inequality is a number sentence. It may be true or false. Symbols of inequality include: $\neq$, $>$, $<$, $\not>$, and $\not<$. Each symbol is a verb in a number sentence.

> The symbol $\neq$ means "is not equal to."
> $8 - 3 \neq 6$ is read
> "Eight minus three is not equal to six."
>
> The symbol $>$ means "is greater than."
> $10 > 4$ is read "Ten is greater than four."
>
> The symbol $<$ means "is less than."
> $3 < 7$ is read "Three is less than seven."

The symbol $\not>$ means "is not greater than."
$5 \times 6 \not> 40$ is read
"Five times six is not greater than forty."

The symbol $\not<$ means "is not less than."
$2 + 1 \not< 0$ is read
"Two plus one is not less than zero."

EXERCISES

1. Read, or write in words, each of the following:

  a. $16 > 9$ **h.** $20 \div 4 \not< 3$ **o.** $6 \times 0 \not< 15 - 15$
  b. $12 \not< 11$ **i.** $16 - 9 \neq 8$ **p.** $72 \div 8 \not> 1 \times 12$
  c. $8 \neq 4 + 2$ **j.** $30 \times 4 > 100$ **q.** $20 - 3 \neq 48 \div 3$
  d. $4 < 6$ **k.** $8 \times 3 \neq 48 \div 4$ **r.** $4 - 4 < 4 \div 4$
  e. $11 \not> 15$ **l.** $18 + 5 \not< 7 \times 6$ **s.** $97 + 3 \not< 10^2$
  f. $6 - 3 < 7$ **m.** $10 \times 9 = 9 \times 10$ **t.** $42 - 7 > 42 \div 7$
  g. $9 \times 6 \not> 54$ **n.** $35 \div 7 > 11 - 8$ **u.** $14 \times 2 = 56 \div 2$

2. Write each of the following sentences symbolically:

  a. The sum of four and twelve is not equal to fifteen.
  b. Sixty-four is less than nine times eight.
  c. The product of seven and six is not greater than fifty.
  d. Ten is equal to thirty divided by three.
  e. Eleven times five is greater than forty plus fourteen.
  f. Eighty divided by five is not less than ninety minus seventy-five.

3. Determine which of the following sentences are true and which are false:

  a. $9 = 6$ **k.** $8 + 4 = 4 + 8$
  b. $8 > 3$ **l.** $12 \div 12 \not< 12 - 12$
  c. $5 < 1$ **m.** $0 \div 5 > 24 \times 0$
  d. $4 \neq 8$ **n.** $8 \times 12 > 100 - 5$
  e. $1 > 0$ **o.** $3 + 5 + 7 < 7 + 5 + 3$
  f. $6 + 4 \not< 14 - 4$ **p.** $8 \times (9 - 1) > 9 \times (8 - 1)$
  g. $12 + 5 < 20 - 5$ **q.** $20 \times 18 = 18 \times 20$
  h. $7 \times 6 \neq 100 \div 2$ **r.** $8 \times 7 \not< 81 - 28$
  i. $28 \div 7 \not> 2^2$ **s.** $2^3 < 3^2$
  j. $9 \times 4 > 54 - 19$ **t.** $4 \times (2 + 8) \neq (4 \cdot 2) + (2 \cdot 8)$

3-2 REFLEXIVE, SYMMETRIC, AND TRANSITIVE PROPERTIES

Equality has a *reflexive* property. That is, any number is equal to itself. $a = a$. Inequality has no reflexive property because a number cannot be greater or smaller than itself.

Equality has a *symmetric* property. That is, if one number is equal to a second number, then the second number is equal to the first number. If $a = b$, then $b = a$. Inequality does not have this property. If one number is greater than a second number, the second number cannot be greater than the first number. If one number is smaller than a second number, the second number cannot be smaller than the first number.

Equality and inequality both have the *transitive* property. That is, if one number is equal to a second number and the second number is equal to a third number, then the first number is equal to the third number.

> If $a = b$ and $b = c$, then $a = c$.

If one number is greater than a second number and the second number is greater than a third number, then the first number is greater than the third number.

> If $a > b$ and $b > c$, then $a > c$.
> Similarly if $a < b$ and $b < c$, then $a < c$.

EXERCISES

1. **a.** Can 8 be greater than itself? Can any number be greater than itself?
   b. Can 3 be less than itself? Can any number be less than itself?
   c. What property does the sentence $9 = 9$ illustrate? State it.

    d. Which one of the following sentences is true: $6 > 6$; $6 = 6$; $6 < 6$?

    e. Do inequalities have a reflexive property?

2. Which of the following are symmetric?

    a. $8 = 6 + 2$ and $6 + 2 = 8$

    b. $12 > 7 + 4$ and $7 + 4 > 12$

    c. $10 \div 2 < 6$ and $6 < 10 \div 2$

    d. $2 \times 2 = 2 + 2$ and $2 + 2 = 2 \times 2$

    e. $8 \times 5 < 6 \times 7$ and $6 \times 7 < 8 \times 5$

    f. $21 - 8 > 4 \times 3$ and $4 \times 3 > 21 - 8$

    g. What is the symmetric property of equalities?

    h. Do inequalities have a symmetric property?

3. Complete by using the transitive property:

    a. $8 > 6$ and $6 > 4$, then $8 > ?$.

    b. $3 < 51$ and $51 < 70$, then $3 < ?$.

    c. $4 \times 5 = 10 + 10$ and $10 + 10 = 20$, then $4 \times 5 = ?$.

    d. $2^3 < 4^2$ and $4^2 < 3^4$, then $2^3 < ?$.

    e. $12 + 3 > 2 \times 5$ and $2 \times 5 > 8 \div 2$, then $12 + 3 > ?$.

    f. $35 - 5 = 27 + 3$ and $27 + 3 = 10 \times 3$ then, $35 - 5 = ?$.

    g. State the transitive property. Do equalities have the transitive property? Do inequalities have the transitive property?

CHAPTER REVIEW

1. Read, or write in words, each of the following: (3–1)

    a. $18 < 25$ **c.** $6 > 1$ **e.** $2 \not> 8$

    b. $4 \times 7 = 28$ **d.** $5 \neq 6 - 3$ **f.** $4 \not< 9$

2. Write each of the following sentences symbolically: (3–1)

    a. Two times six is greater than ten.

    b. Eleven is not less than the sum of four and five.

3. Which of the following sentences are true and which are false?   (3–1)

    a. $0 > 1$ **c.** $3 < 9$ **e.** $6 \not< 2$

    b. $8 \neq 8$ **d.** $12 \not> 4$ **f.** $7 = 5$

4. Illustrate the transitive property of an inequality.   (3–2)

5. Illustrate the symmetric property of an equality.   (3–2)

ACHIEVEMENT TEST

1. Read the numeral 46,518,003 or write it as a word statement. (1–7)
2. Write 36 trillion as a complete numeral. (1–9)
3. Rearrange the digits of 718,505 so that the numeral names the smallest possible number. (1–6)
4. Round 329,608,470,500 to nearest billion. (1–10)
5. Are all prime numbers odd numbers? Name an even prime number. (1–15, 1–16)
6. Are all composite numbers even numbers? Name an odd composite number. (1–15, 1–16)

7. Add: 9,459   (2–9)
        46,783
         8,276
        39,925
        57,578

8. Subtract: 1,506,002   (2–10)
              595,087

9. Multiply: 4,685   (2–11)
                739

10. Divide: 586)368,594   (2–16)

11. a. Write all the factors of 70. (1–17)
    b. Write all the common factors of 18 and 81. (1–20)
    c. What is the greatest common factor of 45, 16, and 105? (1–21)

12. a. Write the multiples of 8, listing the first five numbers. (1–22)
    b. Write the common multiples of 10, 16, and 40. (1–23)
    c. What is the least common multiple of 12 and 18? (1–24)

13. Which property is illustrated by each of the following? (2–3, 2–4, 2–5)
    a. $(14 + 17) + 9 = 14 + (17 + 9)$
    b. $81 \times 36 = 36 \times 81$
    c. $110 + 69 = 69 + 110$
    d. $(56 \times 18) \times 27 = 56 \times (18 \times 27)$
    e. $43 \times (24 + 15) = (43 \times 24) + (43 \times 15)$

14. Which of the following name zero? Which name one? (2–7, 2–8)
    a. $16 - 16$ b. $0 \div 30$ c. $42 \div 42$ d. 0×0 e. 1^8

15. Which of the following sentences are true and which are false? (3–1)
    a. $2 \neq 3$ b. $8 < 11$ c. $5 > 0$ d. $9 \not< 9$ e. $12 \not> 6$

CHAPTER 4
Common Fractions

4–1 MEANING OF A FRACTION

When a thing or unit is divided into equal parts, the number expressing the relation of one or more of the equal parts to the total number of equal parts is called a *fraction*.

If a strip of paper is divided into three equal parts, each part is *one-third* of the whole strip and is represented by the fraction symbol $\frac{1}{3}$.

If the strip of paper is divided into two equal parts, each part is called *one-half* $\left(\frac{1}{2}\right)$; four equal parts, each part is called *one-fourth* $\left(\frac{1}{4}\right)$, five equal parts, each part is called *one-fifth* $\left(\frac{1}{5}\right)$; etc.

Although "fraction" is generally used to mean both the fractional number and the numeral written for the number, some mathematicians use the term "fraction" to mean the symbol or fractional numeral and "rational number" to mean the fractional number. We shall use the term "fraction" to mean both the number and the numeral except in situations where it may be misunderstood.

The symbol for a *common fraction* consists of a pair of numerals, one written above the other, with a horizontal bar between them. The number represented below the fraction bar cannot be zero. In the fraction $\frac{3}{8}$, the numbers 3 and 8 are the *terms* of the fraction. The number above the fraction bar is called the *numerator*. The number below the fraction bar is called the *denominator*. In the fraction $\frac{3}{8}$, 3 is the numerator and 8 is the denominator. The denominator tells us the number of equal parts into which the object is divided. The numerator tells us how many equal parts are being used. The fraction $\frac{3}{8}$ means 3 parts of 8 equal parts.

$$\frac{3}{8}$$

Sometimes a group of things is divided into equal parts. The number expressing the relation of one or more of the equal parts of a group to the total number of equal parts is considered to be a fraction.

> A class of 20 pupils is divided into 2 teams of 10 pupils each.
> Each team is one-half ($\frac{1}{2}$) of the class.

Observe in the following that the *larger* the denominator, the *smaller* the *size* of the *part*.

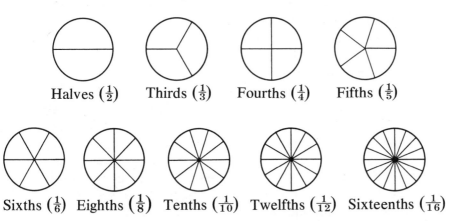

Halves ($\frac{1}{2}$)　　Thirds ($\frac{1}{3}$)　　Fourths ($\frac{1}{4}$)　　Fifths ($\frac{1}{5}$)

Sixths ($\frac{1}{6}$)　Eighths ($\frac{1}{8}$)　Tenths ($\frac{1}{10}$)　Twelfths ($\frac{1}{12}$)　Sixteenths ($\frac{1}{16}$)

Since the counting numbers and whole numbers are not adequate in making measurements, fractions were invented to meet this need.

Observe in the following that the *smaller the size* of the part (subdivision of the unit), the *more precise* is the measurement.

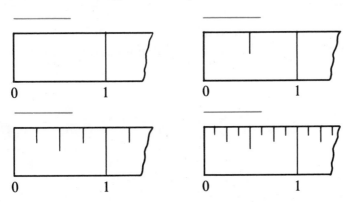

A fraction is used to indicate that one number is divided by another number. Some mathematicians call the number they get when they divide a whole number by any whole number, except zero, a *rational number*.

> 8 divided by 4 usually written as 8 ÷ 4 or 4)8 becomes $\frac{8}{4}$, read "eight over four"; the horizontal bar means "divided by."
>
> 7 divided by 4 becomes $\frac{7}{4}$.   3 divided by 4 becomes $\frac{3}{4}$. The whole number 2 may be considered $\frac{2}{1}$; 3 as $\frac{3}{1}$; 4 as $\frac{4}{1}$, etc.

Thus, if a fraction is an indicated division, the numerator is the number that is divided and the denominator is the number by which you divide.

A fraction may be used to compare two things or two groups of things. For example: a foot is $\frac{1}{3}$ of a yard.

Some mathematicians think of a fraction as an ordered number pair represented by a pair of numerals written within parentheses in a specific order. (7, 8) is an ordered pair of numbers with 7 called the first number and 8 the second number. (8, 7) is a different ordered number pair since 8 is first and 7 is second.

> (7, 8) would be associated with the fraction $\frac{7}{8}$ and (8, 7) would be associated with the fraction $\frac{8}{7}$.

The fraction $\frac{7}{8}$ may also mean $7 \times \frac{1}{8}$ or $\frac{1}{8}$ of 7. Generalizing, if a represents the numerator and b the denominator, then the fraction $\frac{a}{b}$ may also mean $a \times \frac{1}{b}$ or $\frac{1}{b} \times a$.

EXERCISES

1. Read, or write in words, each of the following fractions:

a. $\frac{1}{3}$; $\frac{1}{6}$; $\frac{1}{7}$; $\frac{1}{10}$; $\frac{1}{24}$; $\frac{1}{72}$; $\frac{1}{50}$; $\frac{1}{48}$; $\frac{1}{75}$; $\frac{1}{100}$

b. $\frac{5}{8}$; $\frac{4}{5}$; $\frac{3}{4}$; $\frac{11}{16}$; $\frac{5}{12}$; $\frac{9}{10}$; $\frac{8}{6}$; $\frac{3}{100}$; $\frac{17}{20}$; $\frac{15}{8}$

2. Write each of the following as a numeral:

   a. one-fifth   **c.** one ninety-third   **e.** fifty-nine hundredths
   b. one-eighth   **d.** five-sixths   **f.** thirty-one fourths

3. Into how many equal parts is the following figure divided?
Write as a numeral the size of one of the equal parts.

4. Each of the following figures is divided into equal parts. In
each case, write what the size of each part is called, then write
it as a numeral.

5. Write the numeral that represents the shaded part in each of
the following figures:

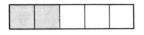

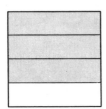

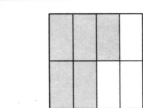

6. Write as a numeral how full each of the following containers is:

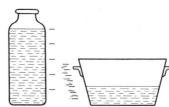

7. Write the numeral naming the fraction indicated in each of the
following measuring devices or gauges.

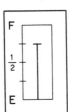  

8. Draw figures like each of the following, then divide them into the required number of parts:

    a. Divide into eighths   **d.** Divide into thirds
    b. Divide into halves   **e.** Divide into sixths
    c. Divide into twelfths

    a.   **b.**   **c.**   **d.**   **e.**

9. Draw figures like each of the following, then shade the part that represents the given fraction:

a. $\frac{1}{2}$

b. $\frac{5}{6}$

c. $\frac{1}{3}$

d. $\frac{3}{4}$

e. $\frac{7}{10}$

f. $\frac{1}{2}$

g. $\frac{2}{3}$

h. $\frac{3}{4}$

i. $\frac{5}{8}$

j. $\frac{4}{5}$

10. **a.** What part of the pie is left?
      b. What fractional part of a dozen eggs was used?

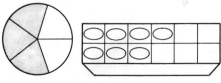

11. What fractional part of the hour past 12 o'clock is indicated on each clock?

12. a. Write the numeral naming the fraction using 4 as the numerator and 5 as the denominator.
   b. Write the numeral naming the fraction using 32 as the denominator and 11 as the numerator.

13. Express each of the following as a numeral naming a fraction:
   a. 7 divided by 10   f. 3 ÷ 8   k. $2\overline{)1}$
   b. 3 divided by 5   g. 13 ÷ 16   l. $5\overline{)4}$
   c. 2 divided by 3   h. 1 ÷ 6   m. $10\overline{)3}$
   d. 11 divided by 25   i. 25 ÷ 32   n. $24\overline{)19}$
   e. 6 divided by 3   j. 22 ÷ 7   o. $32\overline{)27}$

14. a. What does $\frac{5}{6}$ mean? Express $\frac{5}{6}$ in two other ways.

   b. What does $\frac{1}{5}$ mean? Express $\frac{1}{5}$ in two other ways.

   c. What does $\frac{4}{9}$ mean? Express $\frac{4}{9}$ in two other ways.

15. a. Compare an inch to a foot. An inch is what part of a foot?
   b. Compare a quart to a gallon. A quart is what part of a gallon?
   c. Compare a nickel to a dime. A nickel is what part of a dime?
   d. Compare a day to a week. A day is what part of a week?
   e. Compare a centimeter to a meter. A centimeter is what part of a meter?

16. Write each of the following ordered pairs of numbers as a numeral naming a fraction:
   a. (5, 7)   c. (6, 25)   e. (17, 24)   g. (23, 60)
   b. (9, 4)   d. (11, 100)   f. (12, 5)   h. (37, 100)

17. Write each of the following fractions as an ordered pair:
   a. $\frac{6}{11}$ c. $\frac{5}{16}$ e. $\frac{19}{6}$ g. $\frac{25}{16}$
   b. $\frac{10}{7}$ d. $\frac{11}{40}$ f. $\frac{59}{100}$ h. $\frac{31}{35}$

18. Which of the following:

   a. Name $\frac{3}{4}$: $\frac{1}{4} \times 3$; $\frac{1}{3} \times 4$; $3 \times \frac{1}{4}$; $4 \times \frac{1}{3}$?

   b. Name $\frac{12}{7}$: $\frac{1}{12} \times 7$; $12 \times \frac{1}{7}$; $\frac{1}{7} \times 12$; $7 \times \frac{1}{12}$?

   c. Name $\frac{5}{9}$: $9 \times \frac{1}{5}$; $\frac{1}{9} \times 5$; $5 \times \frac{1}{9}$; $\frac{1}{5} \times 9$?

EQUIVALENT FRACTIONS

Fractions that name the same number are called *equivalent fractions*.

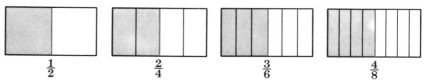

$$\frac{1}{2} \qquad \frac{2}{4} \qquad \frac{3}{6} \qquad \frac{4}{8}$$

The fractions $\frac{1}{2}$, $\frac{2}{4}$, $\frac{3}{6}$, and $\frac{4}{8}$ are equivalent fractions. They name the same number which in simplest form is $\frac{1}{2}$. This group of equivalent fractions may be written as follows:

$$\frac{1}{2}, \frac{2}{3}, \frac{3}{6}, \frac{4}{8}, \frac{5}{10}, \frac{6}{12}, \cdots$$

The fraction listed first is the name of the fractional number in simplest form.

4–2 EXPRESSING FRACTIONS IN LOWEST TERMS

When the numerator and denominator have no common factor except 1, the fraction is in *simplest form* or in *lowest terms*. When the 4 and 8 of the fraction $\frac{4}{8}$ are each:

(1) Divided by 2, we get the equivalent fraction $\frac{2}{4}$.

(2) Divided by 4, we get the equivalent fraction $\frac{1}{2}$.

$$\frac{4}{8} = \frac{4 \div 2}{8 \div 2} = \frac{2}{4}$$

$$\frac{4}{8} = \frac{4 \div 4}{8 \div 4} = \frac{1}{2}$$

Thus when the numerator and denominator of any fraction are each divided by the same number, except by zero, the result is an equivalent fraction. Therefore to express a fraction in lowest terms:

(a) We factor the numerator and denominator, using as one of the factors the greatest factor common to both. (Use whole numbers other than 1 or 0.)

(b) Then we divide both the numerator and denominator by this common factor.

The multiplicative identity one (1) may be used as shown:

Express $\frac{30}{48}$ in lowest terms:

$$\frac{30}{48} = \frac{5 \cdot 6}{8 \cdot 6} = \frac{5}{8} \quad \text{or}$$

$$\frac{30}{48} = \frac{5 \cdot 6}{8 \cdot 6} = \frac{5}{8} \times 1 = \frac{5}{8}$$

EXERCISES

1. Use the section of the ruler to obtain answers to the following:[1]

   a. $\frac{2''}{4} = \frac{''}{2}$ $\frac{4''}{16} = \frac{''}{4}$ $\frac{6''}{8} = \frac{''}{4}$

   b. $\frac{8''}{16} = \frac{''}{2}$ $\frac{4''}{8} = \frac{''}{2}$ $\frac{10''}{16} = \frac{''}{8}$

   c. $\frac{2''}{8} = \frac{''}{4}$ $\frac{14''}{16} = \frac{''}{8}$ $\frac{2''}{16} = \frac{''}{8}$

2. Express each of the following in lowest terms:

   a. $\frac{5}{10}$ $\frac{3}{24}$ $\frac{2}{32}$ $\frac{3}{15}$ $\frac{5}{60}$ $\frac{11}{77}$ $\frac{2}{12}$ $\frac{7}{56}$ $\frac{6}{42}$ $\frac{9}{90}$

   b. $\frac{6}{12}$ $\frac{5}{20}$ $\frac{8}{64}$ $\frac{9}{45}$ $\frac{12}{36}$ $\frac{14}{42}$ $\frac{25}{100}$ $\frac{32}{96}$ $\frac{15}{75}$ $\frac{16}{80}$

   c. $\frac{4}{18}$ $\frac{14}{16}$ $\frac{12}{15}$ $\frac{20}{32}$ $\frac{36}{48}$ $\frac{50}{75}$ $\frac{56}{64}$ $\frac{54}{72}$ $\frac{28}{42}$ $\frac{36}{54}$

   d. $\frac{10}{50}$ $\frac{30}{90}$ $\frac{60}{100}$ $\frac{210}{700}$ $\frac{400}{1000}$, $\frac{4500}{5000}$ $\frac{6000}{7500}$ $\frac{960}{3600}$ $\frac{5400}{7200}$ $\frac{150}{2400}$

   e. $\frac{54}{144}$ $\frac{96}{160}$ $\frac{80}{112}$ $\frac{105}{140}$ $\frac{225}{400}$ $\frac{252}{324}$ $\frac{294}{336}$ $\frac{576}{648}$ $\frac{204}{228}$ $\frac{273}{315}$

3. Which fractions are not expressed in lowest terms?

   a. $\frac{4}{7}$ $\frac{5}{8}$ $\frac{4}{9}$ $\frac{6}{9}$ c. $\frac{5}{8}$ $\frac{11}{12}$ $\frac{21}{28}$ $\frac{25}{32}$ e. $\frac{8}{15}$ $\frac{12}{35}$ $\frac{9}{45}$ $\frac{17}{20}$

   b. $\frac{9}{10}$ $\frac{7}{10}$ $\frac{5}{10}$ $\frac{3}{10}$ d. $\frac{3}{4}$ $\frac{3}{5}$ $\frac{3}{6}$ $\frac{3}{8}$ f. $\frac{27}{36}$ $\frac{21}{32}$ $\frac{25}{34}$ $\frac{24}{39}$

4. Find which fractions are equivalent in each group:

   a. $\frac{6}{8}$ $\frac{12}{15}$ $\frac{18}{24}$ $\frac{9}{12}$ c. $\frac{15}{25}$ $\frac{6}{9}$ $\frac{4}{6}$ $\frac{14}{21}$ e. $\frac{40}{48}$ $\frac{8}{16}$ $\frac{10}{12}$ $\frac{15}{18}$

   b. $\frac{16}{32}$ $\frac{4}{8}$ $\frac{32}{64}$ $\frac{8}{16}$ d. $\frac{10}{32}$ $\frac{9}{24}$ $\frac{21}{56}$ $\frac{6}{16}$ f. $\frac{28}{35}$ $\frac{35}{50}$ $\frac{20}{25}$ $\frac{9}{15}$

---

[1] The symbol ″ represents "inch."

Common Fractions   95

4-3 EXPRESSING FRACTIONS IN HIGHER TERMS

If we multiply both the 1 and 2 of the fraction $\frac{1}{2}$:

(1) By 2, we get the equivalent fraction $\frac{2}{4}$.
(2) By 4, we get the equivalent fraction $\frac{4}{8}$.

Thus, when the numerator and denominator of any fraction are each multiplied by the same number, except by zero, the result is an equivalent fraction.

Therefore, to express a fraction in higher terms where the new denominator is specified:

(1) We divide the *new* denominator by the denominator of the given fraction.
(2) Then we multiply *both* the numerator and denominator of the given fraction by the quotient. This is the same as multiplying the fraction by the multiplicative identity one (1).

Change $\frac{2}{3}$ to 12ths:

$$\frac{2}{3} = \frac{2 \times 4}{3 \times 4} = \frac{8}{12} \quad \text{or} \quad \frac{2}{3} = \frac{2}{3} \times 1 = \frac{2 \times 4}{3 \times 4} = \frac{8}{12}$$

EXERCISES

1. Use the chart, on the following page, to express fractions in higher terms:

a. $\frac{1}{2} = \frac{}{4}$	$\frac{1}{4} = \frac{}{16}$	$\frac{1}{6} = \frac{}{12}$	$\frac{1}{2} = \frac{}{10}$	$\frac{1}{3} = \frac{}{6}$
b. $\frac{1}{8} = \frac{}{16}$	$\frac{1}{5} = \frac{}{10}$	$\frac{1}{3} = \frac{}{12}$	$\frac{1}{2} = \frac{}{6}$	$\frac{1}{4} = \frac{}{12}$
c. $\frac{1}{2} = \frac{}{12}$	$\frac{1}{2} = \frac{}{8}$	$\frac{1}{4} = \frac{}{8}$	$\frac{1}{2} = \frac{}{16}$	$\frac{3}{4} = \frac{}{8}$
d. $\frac{3}{4} = \frac{}{16}$	$\frac{2}{3} = \frac{}{6}$	$\frac{7}{8} = \frac{}{16}$	$\frac{5}{6} = \frac{}{12}$	$\frac{5}{8} = \frac{}{16}$
e. $\frac{2}{5} = \frac{}{10}$	$\frac{3}{4} = \frac{}{12}$	$\frac{4}{5} = \frac{}{10}$	$\frac{3}{8} = \frac{}{16}$	$\frac{2}{3} = \frac{}{12}$

1															
$\frac{1}{2}$								$\frac{1}{2}$							
$\frac{1}{4}$				$\frac{1}{4}$				$\frac{1}{4}$				$\frac{1}{4}$			
$\frac{1}{8}$		$\frac{1}{8}$		$\frac{1}{8}$		$\frac{1}{8}$		$\frac{1}{8}$		$\frac{1}{8}$		$\frac{1}{8}$		$\frac{1}{8}$	
$\frac{1}{16}$	$\frac{1}{16}$	$\frac{1}{16}$	$\frac{1}{16}$	$\frac{1}{16}$	$\frac{1}{16}$	$\frac{1}{16}$	$\frac{1}{16}$	$\frac{1}{16}$	$\frac{1}{16}$	$\frac{1}{16}$	$\frac{1}{16}$	$\frac{1}{16}$	$\frac{1}{16}$	$\frac{1}{16}$	$\frac{1}{16}$

$\frac{1}{3}$				$\frac{1}{3}$				$\frac{1}{3}$			
$\frac{1}{6}$		$\frac{1}{6}$		$\frac{1}{6}$		$\frac{1}{6}$		$\frac{1}{6}$		$\frac{1}{6}$	
$\frac{1}{12}$	$\frac{1}{12}$	$\frac{1}{12}$	$\frac{1}{12}$	$\frac{1}{12}$	$\frac{1}{12}$	$\frac{1}{12}$	$\frac{1}{12}$	$\frac{1}{12}$	$\frac{1}{12}$	$\frac{1}{12}$	$\frac{1}{12}$

$\frac{1}{5}$		$\frac{1}{5}$		$\frac{1}{5}$		$\frac{1}{5}$		$\frac{1}{5}$	
$\frac{1}{10}$	$\frac{1}{10}$	$\frac{1}{10}$	$\frac{1}{10}$	$\frac{1}{10}$	$\frac{1}{10}$	$\frac{1}{10}$	$\frac{1}{10}$	$\frac{1}{10}$	$\frac{1}{10}$

2. Express as fractions in the indicated higher terms:

a. $\frac{1}{2} = \frac{}{24}$ $\frac{1}{8} = \frac{}{32}$ $\frac{1}{10} = \frac{}{50}$ $\frac{1}{6} = \frac{}{48}$ $\frac{1}{5} = \frac{}{20}$ $\frac{1}{16} = \frac{}{32}$ $\frac{1}{3} = \frac{}{15}$

b. $\frac{4}{5} = \frac{}{10}$ $\frac{2}{3} = \frac{}{24}$ $\frac{3}{5} = \frac{}{25}$ $\frac{3}{4} = \frac{}{36}$ $\frac{7}{8} = \frac{}{56}$ $\frac{21}{32} = \frac{}{64}$ $\frac{13}{16} = \frac{}{80}$

c. $\frac{9}{10} = \frac{}{100}$ $\frac{1}{4} = \frac{}{100}$ $\frac{1}{2} = \frac{}{100}$ $\frac{2}{5} = \frac{}{100}$ $\frac{3}{4} = \frac{}{100}$ $\frac{17}{20} = \frac{}{100}$ $\frac{21}{25} = \frac{}{100}$

3. Express:

a. $\frac{1}{6}$ as 24ths   d. $\frac{15}{16}$ as 80ths   g. $\frac{4}{5}$ as 20ths   j. $\frac{7}{10}$ as 60ths

b. $\frac{2}{3}$ as 36ths   e. $\frac{3}{4}$ as 32nds   h. $\frac{11}{12}$ as 72nds   k. $\frac{19}{32}$ as 64ths

c. $\frac{1}{2}$ as 16ths   f. $\frac{23}{25}$ as 100ths   i. $\frac{3}{8}$ as 40ths   l. $\frac{4}{15}$ as 30ths

4. Equivalent fractions may be developed from the name of the fractional number in simplest form by expressing it successively in higher terms. Examples are:

$$\frac{1}{5}, \frac{2}{10}, \frac{3}{15}, \frac{4}{20}, \cdots \quad \text{and} \quad \frac{2}{3}, \frac{4}{6}, \frac{6}{9}, \frac{8}{12}, \cdots$$

Write the group of fractions equivalent to:

a. $\frac{1}{4}$ d. $\frac{3}{8}$ g. $\frac{3}{4}$ j. $\frac{5}{6}$ m. $\frac{4}{7}$ p. $\frac{9}{13}$ s. $\frac{17}{50}$

b. $\frac{1}{7}$ e. $\frac{1}{6}$ h. $\frac{1}{16}$ k. $\frac{1}{3}$ n. $\frac{1}{15}$ q. $\frac{1}{20}$ t. $\frac{23}{30}$

c. $\frac{2}{5}$ f. $\frac{5}{9}$ i. $\frac{7}{12}$ l. $\frac{3}{10}$ o. $\frac{2}{11}$ r. $\frac{8}{25}$ u. $\frac{31}{40}$

5. For each of the following fractions, write the simplest form and three other equivalent fractions:

a. $\frac{8}{12}$ c. $\frac{49}{56}$ e. $\frac{35}{84}$ g. $\frac{18}{63}$ i. $\frac{99}{144}$

b. $\frac{24}{32}$ d. $\frac{6}{22}$ f. $\frac{45}{72}$ h. $\frac{6}{27}$ j. $\frac{70}{100}$

Common Fractions

97

4-4 TESTING FOR EQUIVALENT FRACTIONS

We can tell that one fraction is equivalent to another fraction by expressing each given fraction in lowest terms. If the resulting fractions are the same, then the given fractions are equivalent.

> Are $\frac{6}{8}$ and $\frac{9}{12}$ equivalent fractions?
>
> Yes, $\frac{6}{8} = \frac{9}{12}$ since $\frac{6}{8} = \frac{3}{4}$ and $\frac{9}{12} = \frac{3}{4}$.

Examination of $\frac{6}{8} = \frac{9}{12}$ will show that the product of the numerator of the first fraction and the denominator of the second fraction (6×12) is equal to the product of the numerator of the second fraction and the denominator of the first fraction (9×8). Since $6 \times 12 = 72$ and $9 \times 8 = 72$, then $6 \times 12 = 9 \times 8$.

Thus, we may say that:

When two fractions are equivalent, the cross products are equal.
When the cross products are equal, the two fractions are equivalent.

> Are $\frac{10}{15}$ and $\frac{6}{9}$ equivalent fractions?
>
> $\frac{10}{15} = \frac{6}{9}$ is true if $10 \times 9 = 6 \times 15$.
>
> Since $10 \times 9 = 90$ and $6 \times 15 = 90$, then
> $10 \times 9 = 6 \times 15$.
>
> Thus, $\frac{10}{15}$ and $\frac{6}{9}$ are equivalent fractions.

EXERCISES

Test whether each of the following pairs of fractions are equivalent by using the method of:

1. Lowest terms:

  a. $\frac{3}{6}$ and $\frac{8}{12}$ **c.** $\frac{6}{10}$ and $\frac{12}{15}$ **e.** $\frac{2}{4}$ and $\frac{3}{9}$ **g.** $\frac{10}{12}$ and $\frac{15}{18}$ **i.** $\frac{21}{27}$ and $\frac{35}{45}$

  b. $\frac{10}{16}$ and $\frac{15}{24}$ **d.** $\frac{6}{8}$ and $\frac{12}{18}$ **f.** $\frac{15}{25}$ and $\frac{6}{10}$ **h.** $\frac{16}{24}$ and $\frac{26}{39}$ **j.** $\frac{18}{42}$ and $\frac{14}{35}$

2. Equal cross products:

a. $\frac{3}{4}$ and $\frac{7}{12}$ c. $\frac{10}{15}$ and $\frac{12}{18}$ e. $\frac{8}{20}$ and $\frac{9}{24}$ g. $\frac{4}{6}$ and $\frac{11}{22}$ i. $\frac{48}{54}$ and $\frac{14}{16}$

b. $\frac{10}{16}$ and $\frac{15}{24}$ d. $\frac{42}{48}$ and $\frac{30}{35}$ f. $\frac{13}{26}$ and $\frac{4}{8}$ h. $\frac{14}{21}$ and $\frac{6}{10}$ j. $\frac{35}{63}$ and $\frac{10}{18}$

3. Either method:

a. $\frac{4}{5}$ and $\frac{9}{12}$ c. $\frac{8}{12}$ and $\frac{6}{9}$ e. $\frac{6}{12}$ and $\frac{8}{14}$ g. $\frac{7}{16}$ and $\frac{3}{8}$ i. $\frac{35}{60}$ and $\frac{27}{48}$

b. $\frac{6}{8}$ and $\frac{10}{15}$ d. $\frac{8}{10}$ and $\frac{20}{25}$ f. $\frac{9}{24}$ and $\frac{6}{16}$ h. $\frac{20}{35}$ and $\frac{28}{49}$ j. $\frac{15}{40}$ and $\frac{70}{80}$

4–5 PROPER FRACTIONS, IMPROPER FRACTIONS, MIXED NUMBERS

We sometimes use the same number of parts as there are in the whole unit such as: $\frac{3}{3} = 1$ $\frac{6}{6} = 1$ or a number of parts greater than the number of parts in the whole unit such as:

$\frac{7}{4} = 1\frac{3}{4}$ $\frac{6}{3} = 2$

A fraction whose numerator is smaller than its denominator such as $\frac{3}{4}$ is called a *proper fraction*. The value of a proper fraction is always less than one.

A fraction whose numerator is equal to or greater than its denominator such as $\frac{6}{6}$ or $\frac{7}{4}$ is called an *improper fraction*. The value of an improper fraction is one or more than one.

A *mixed number* consists of a whole number and a fraction such as $3\frac{1}{4}$.

EXERCISES

1. Read or write in words:

$4\frac{3}{10}$; $1\frac{6}{7}$; $2\frac{5}{8}$; $10\frac{1}{2}$; $3\frac{2}{3}$; $5\frac{29}{32}$; $8\frac{9}{14}$; $12\frac{13}{25}$; $17\frac{11}{12}$; $9\frac{7}{16}$

2. Write as a numeral:

Fourteen and three-fourths; Three and one-seventh; Forty and five-sixteenths.

3. Which name a whole number?

$\frac{3}{5}$; 4; $5\frac{1}{2}$; 9; $\frac{7}{8}$; $2\frac{3}{4}$; $6\frac{2}{3}$; $\frac{11}{16}$; 1; $\frac{5}{6}$

4. Which name a common fraction?

$\frac{9}{10};$ 6; $8\frac{1}{4};$ $2\frac{3}{8};$ $\frac{1}{3};$ 3; $4\frac{5}{16};$ $\frac{5}{8};$ 10; $\frac{2}{5}$

5. Which name a mixed number?

4; $2\frac{2}{3};$ $\frac{5}{7};$ $4\frac{1}{5};$ 6; $\frac{3}{4};$ 8; $1\frac{9}{16};$ 1; $12\frac{1}{2}$

6. Which name a proper fraction?

$\frac{2}{5};$ $\frac{7}{4};$ $\frac{8}{8};$ $\frac{1}{3};$ $\frac{7}{8};$ $\frac{3}{2};$ $\frac{6}{5};$ $\frac{9}{10};$ $\frac{5}{6};$ $\frac{21}{12}$

7. Which name an improper fraction?

$\frac{1}{2};$ $\frac{10}{10};$ $\frac{18}{6};$ $\frac{5}{8};$ $\frac{8}{5};$ $\frac{2}{3};$ $\frac{22}{7};$ $\frac{9}{4};$ $\frac{15}{20};$ $\frac{32}{32}$

8. Select the numerator of each fraction:

$\frac{2}{3};$ $\frac{11}{8};$ $\frac{1}{2};$ $\frac{13}{16};$ $\frac{5}{6};$ $\frac{7}{12};$ $\frac{19}{20};$ $\frac{37}{100};$ $\frac{5}{10};$ $\frac{14}{5}$

9. Select the denominator of each fraction:

$\frac{3}{4};$ $\frac{7}{10};$ $\frac{1}{8};$ $\frac{22}{7};$ $\frac{11}{16};$ $\frac{8}{3};$ $\frac{25}{32};$ $\frac{5}{6};$ $\frac{49}{100};$ $\frac{43}{64}$

10. a. What measurement is indicated on the ruler by:

  A? B? C? D? E? F? G? H?

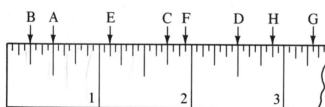

  b. What reading on the thermometer is indicated by:

  A? B? C? D? E? F? G? H?

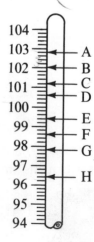

To express an improper fraction as a whole or mixed number, we divide the numerator by the denominator and write the remainder, if any, as a fraction expressed in lowest terms.

Change $\frac{5}{3}$ to a mixed number:
$$\frac{5}{3} = 5 \div 3 = 1\frac{2}{3}$$
Answer, $1\frac{2}{3}$

To express a mixed number in simplest form, we simplify the fraction of the given mixed number and add the result to the given whole number wherever possible.

Express $5\frac{11}{4}$ in simplest form.
Since $\frac{11}{4} = 2\frac{3}{4}$, then
$$5\frac{11}{4} = 5 + 2\frac{3}{4} = 7\frac{3}{4}$$
Answer, $7\frac{3}{4}$

EXERCISES

1. Use a ruler to determine the equivalent whole number or mixed number:

   a. $\frac{2''}{2}$ $\frac{4''}{4}$ $\frac{16''}{16}$ $\frac{8''}{8}$ $\frac{4''}{2}$ $\frac{8''}{2}$ $\frac{32''}{16}$ $\frac{24''}{8}$

   b. $\frac{5''}{4}$ $\frac{5''}{2}$ $\frac{13''}{8}$ $\frac{25''}{16}$ $\frac{7''}{2}$ $\frac{23''}{8}$ $\frac{13''}{4}$ $\frac{37''}{16}$

   c. $\frac{6''}{4}$ $\frac{10''}{8}$ $\frac{28''}{16}$ $\frac{20''}{8}$ $\frac{14''}{4}$ $\frac{42''}{16}$ $\frac{14''}{8}$ $\frac{36''}{16}$

2. Express each of the following as a numeral for a whole number or a mixed number:

   a. $\frac{6}{6}$ $\frac{10}{10}$ $\frac{5}{5}$ $\frac{12}{12}$ $\frac{12}{6}$ $\frac{10}{2}$ $\frac{48}{8}$ $\frac{32}{4}$ $\frac{56}{7}$ $\frac{75}{15}$

   b. $\frac{4}{3}$ $\frac{16}{9}$ $\frac{11}{6}$ $\frac{23}{16}$ $\frac{9}{2}$ $\frac{18}{5}$ $\frac{35}{8}$ $\frac{27}{10}$ $\frac{22}{7}$ $\frac{35}{18}$

   c. $\frac{10}{6}$ $\frac{21}{12}$ $\frac{12}{9}$ $\frac{40}{32}$ $\frac{26}{4}$ $\frac{35}{10}$ $\frac{42}{30}$ $\frac{44}{16}$ $\frac{15}{9}$ $\frac{65}{25}$

3. Express each of the following in simplest form:

   a. $5\frac{2}{2}$ $9\frac{6}{6}$ $3\frac{5}{5}$ $14\frac{8}{8}$ $1\frac{10}{10}$ $6\frac{8}{4}$ $4\frac{12}{3}$ $7\frac{18}{6}$ $13\frac{14}{2}$ $9\frac{60}{12}$

   b. $3\frac{6}{8}$ $1\frac{16}{24}$ $9\frac{24}{32}$ $8\frac{5}{20}$ $6\frac{85}{100}$ $29\frac{6}{9}$ $14\frac{9}{12}$ $24\frac{8}{14}$ $15\frac{21}{30}$ $18\frac{35}{50}$

   c. $7\frac{5}{3}$ $6\frac{9}{2}$ $8\frac{17}{5}$ $5\frac{21}{8}$ $19\frac{15}{4}$ $3\frac{14}{8}$ $6\frac{25}{10}$ $8\frac{40}{12}$ $11\frac{75}{60}$ $10\frac{425}{100}$

To express a whole number as a fraction with a specified denominator, we multiply the whole number by the fraction equivalent to *one (1)* that has the specified denominator as both the numerator and denominator. Also see page 116.

EXERCISES

1. Express 1 as:

   a. twelfths   **b.** sixteenths   **c.** hundredths   **d.** twenty-fourths

2. How many sixths are in 8?

3. How many tenths are in 3?

4. How many:

   a. half inches are in 4 inches?   **c.** quarter inches are in 12 inches?
   b. eighth inches are in 6 inches?   **d.** sixteenth inches are in 9 inches?

5. Find the missing numbers:

   a. $1 = \frac{?}{20}$ **b.** $4 = \frac{?}{8}$ **c.** $2 = \frac{?}{12}$ **d.** $7 = \frac{?}{16}$ **e.** $9 = \frac{?}{5}$

To express a mixed number as an improper fraction, we multiply the whole number by the denominator of the fraction and add the numerator of the fraction to this product. Then we write this sum over the denominator of the fraction.

Express $2\frac{3}{4}$ as an improper fraction:

Briefly: $2\frac{3}{4} = \frac{11}{4}$

or $2\frac{3}{4} = 2 + \frac{3}{4} = \frac{8}{4} + \frac{3}{4} = \frac{11}{4}$

Answer, $\frac{11}{4}$

1. Use a ruler to determine how many:

   a. Halves of an inch are in: $2\frac{1}{2}''$; $1\frac{1}{2}''$; $3\frac{1}{2}''$; $5\frac{1}{2}''$

   b. Quarters of an inch are in: $\frac{3}{4}''$; $3\frac{1}{4}''$; $2\frac{3}{4}''$; $6\frac{1}{2}''$

   c. Eighths of an inch are in: $3\frac{1}{8}''$; $1\frac{7}{8}''$; $2\frac{5}{8}''$; $4\frac{3}{4}''$; $7\frac{1}{2}''$

   d. Sixteenths of an inch are in: $\frac{11}{16}''$; $2\frac{13}{16}''$; $3\frac{3}{8}''$; $4\frac{1}{2}''$; $5\frac{3}{4}''$

2. Express each of the following as an improper fraction:

a.	$1\frac{1}{5}$	$1\frac{1}{3}$	$1\frac{1}{6}$	$1\frac{1}{7}$	$1\frac{1}{12}$
b.	$1\frac{1}{10}$	$1\frac{1}{8}$	$1\frac{1}{32}$	$1\frac{1}{15}$	$1\frac{1}{18}$
c.	$1\frac{5}{8}$	$1\frac{7}{10}$	$1\frac{11}{12}$	$1\frac{5}{6}$	$1\frac{13}{23}$
d.	$1\frac{11}{16}$	$1\frac{7}{9}$	$1\frac{19}{24}$	$1\frac{13}{18}$	$1\frac{23}{50}$
e.	$3\frac{1}{7}$	$4\frac{1}{2}$	$3\frac{1}{3}$	$2\frac{1}{10}$	$9\frac{1}{4}$
f.	$6\frac{1}{8}$	$3\frac{1}{5}$	$7\frac{1}{6}$	$10\frac{1}{9}$	$12\frac{1}{3}$
g.	$4\frac{5}{6}$	$5\frac{9}{10}$	$7\frac{3}{5}$	$8\frac{15}{16}$	$4\frac{7}{9}$
h.	$12\frac{3}{4}$	$4\frac{5}{8}$	$6\frac{15}{32}$	$15\frac{11}{12}$	$20\frac{5}{7}$

4–6 EXPRESSING FRACTIONS AS EQUIVALENT FRACTIONS WITH COMMON DENOMINATOR

   A *common denominator* is a number that can be divided exactly by the denominators of all the given fractions. It is a multiple of the denominators of the given fractions.

   The *lowest common denominator* (LCD) is the smallest natural number that can be divided exactly by the denominators of all the given fractions. It is the least common multiple of the given denominators.

   The LCD may be found by inspection:

   (1) When the LCD is a denominator of one of the given fractions. LCD of $\frac{1}{2}$ and $\frac{1}{8}$ is 8.

   (2) When the LCD is the product of the denominators of the given fractions. LCD of $\frac{1}{3}$ and $\frac{1}{5}$ is 15.

When the LCD is greater than any given denominator but smaller than the product of all the denominators, we use the method used in finding the least common multiple (see page 37).

Find the LCD of $\frac{7}{12}$, $\frac{5}{6}$ and $\frac{2}{8}$:

$12 = 2 \cdot 2 \cdot 3$ $LCD = 2 \cdot 2 \cdot 3 \cdot 2$
$6 = 2 \cdot 3$ $LCD = 24$
$8 = 2 \cdot 2 \cdot 2$

Answer, 24

To express each given fraction as an equivalent fraction having the lowest common denominator as its denominator, we first find the LCD, then we express each fraction as an *equivalent* fraction with the LCD as its denominator.

EXERCISES

First find the lowest common denominator (LCD) of the given fractions in each of the following, then change each fraction to an equivalent fraction with the LCD as its denominator:

1. a. $\frac{1}{4}$ and $\frac{1}{16}$ **c.** $\frac{3}{8}$ and $\frac{3}{4}$ **e.** $\frac{5}{6}$ and $\frac{5}{12}$ **g.** $\frac{13}{16}$ and $\frac{1}{2}$ **i.** $\frac{5}{6}$ and $\frac{13}{24}$

b. $\frac{1}{2}$ and $\frac{5}{6}$ **d.** $\frac{7}{12}$ and $\frac{2}{3}$ **f.** $\frac{7}{8}$ and $\frac{11}{24}$ **h.** $\frac{9}{20}$ and $\frac{3}{5}$ **j.** $\frac{18}{25}$ and $\frac{37}{100}$

2. a. $\frac{1}{3}$ and $\frac{1}{4}$ **c.** $\frac{1}{2}$ and $\frac{4}{5}$ **e.** $\frac{3}{5}$ and $\frac{5}{6}$ **g.** $\frac{7}{9}$ and $\frac{1}{2}$ **i.** $\frac{7}{16}$ and $\frac{2}{3}$

b. $\frac{1}{5}$ and $\frac{1}{8}$ **d.** $\frac{3}{8}$ and $\frac{2}{3}$ **f.** $\frac{1}{3}$ and $\frac{4}{5}$ **h.** $\frac{2}{5}$ and $\frac{11}{12}$ **j.** $\frac{5}{6}$ and $\frac{4}{7}$

3. a. $\frac{1}{8}$ and $\frac{1}{6}$ **c.** $\frac{5}{8}$ and $\frac{9}{10}$ **e.** $\frac{5}{6}$ and $\frac{3}{10}$ **g.** $\frac{15}{16}$ and $\frac{11}{12}$ **i.** $\frac{11}{24}$ and $\frac{13}{18}$

b. $\frac{7}{10}$ and $\frac{3}{4}$ **d.** $\frac{3}{8}$ and $\frac{7}{12}$ **f.** $\frac{5}{12}$ and $\frac{9}{10}$ **h.** $\frac{5}{6}$ and $\frac{7}{16}$ **j.** $\frac{19}{20}$ and $\frac{7}{16}$

4. a. $\frac{1}{2}$, $\frac{1}{4}$ and $\frac{1}{8}$ **e.** $\frac{1}{3}$, $\frac{1}{2}$ and $\frac{1}{5}$ **i.** $\frac{1}{4}$, $\frac{1}{8}$ and $\frac{1}{6}$ **m.** $\frac{1}{10}$, $\frac{1}{8}$ and $\frac{1}{12}$

b. $\frac{1}{3}$, $\frac{1}{6}$ and $\frac{1}{2}$ **f.** $\frac{3}{4}$, $\frac{2}{3}$ and $\frac{2}{5}$ **j.** $\frac{11}{12}$, $\frac{5}{6}$ and $\frac{3}{8}$ **n.** $\frac{2}{3}$, $\frac{5}{8}$ and $\frac{1}{6}$

c. $\frac{3}{4}$, $\frac{5}{6}$ and $\frac{7}{12}$ **g.** $\frac{1}{2}$, $\frac{2}{3}$ and $\frac{1}{4}$ **k.** $\frac{9}{16}$, $\frac{7}{8}$ and $\frac{19}{24}$ **o.** $\frac{7}{10}$, $\frac{15}{16}$ and $\frac{11}{12}$

d. $\frac{11}{16}$, $\frac{5}{8}$ and $\frac{1}{4}$ **h.** $\frac{2}{3}$, $\frac{5}{6}$ and $\frac{3}{5}$ **l.** $\frac{4}{5}$, $\frac{1}{4}$ and $\frac{9}{10}$ **p.** $\frac{3}{8}$, $\frac{3}{10}$ and $\frac{7}{16}$

4–7 NUMBER LINE

There is a point on the number line corresponding to each fraction and mixed number.

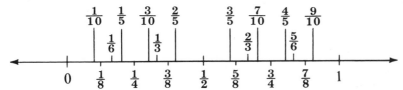

The interval between each whole number on the number line may be divided into halves, thirds, fourths, fifths, etc. so that there is a point on the number line corresponding to each fraction and mixed number. The number of points corresponding to the fractions are *unlimited* or *infinite* because there is always another fraction between any two fractions we select. All we have to do is find the fraction midway between the two given fractions by adding the fractions and dividing the sum by two. We usually say that the *order is dense* if between any two numbers there is an unlimited number of numbers. Thus the order of fractions is said to be dense.

EXERCISES

1. Copy this line segment. Label each point of division with its corresponding fraction in simplest form.

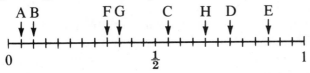

2. What fraction corresponds to point *A*? *B*? *C*? *D*? *E*? *F*? *G*? *H*?
3. Find the midpoint between *A* and *B*. Label it *M*. What fraction is associated with point *M*?
4. Find the midpoint between *A* and *M*. Label it *N*. What fraction is associated with point *N*? What fraction is associated with the midpoint between *N* and *M*?
5. As the parts of the line get smaller and smaller, is there a midpoint for each part? Will this continue endlessly? Do all these points have fractions which correspond? Do you see that there is always another fraction between any two fractions?
6. Under each fraction you used to label the given points on the number line write names of two other equivalent fractions.

4-8 COMPARING FRACTIONS

If two fractions have the same (like) denominator, the fraction with the greater numerator is obviously the greater fraction. $\frac{4}{5}$ is greater than $\frac{2}{5}$.

However, to compare two fractions with different (unlike) denominators, we first express the given fractions as fractions with a common denominator and then take the given fraction that is equivalent to the fraction having the greater numerator and *common denominator* as the greater fraction.

Which is greater $\frac{3}{4}$ or $\frac{2}{3}$?

Since $\frac{3}{4} = \frac{9}{12}$ and $\frac{2}{3} = \frac{8}{12}$,

$\frac{3}{4}$ is greater than $\frac{2}{3}$ or $\frac{3}{4} > \frac{2}{3}$.

Examination of the sentence $\frac{3}{4} > \frac{2}{3}$ will show that the product of the numerator of the first fraction and the denominator of the second fraction (3×3) is greater than the product of the numerator of the second fraction and the denominator of the first fraction (2×4). If this condition is true when we compare two fractions, we may say that the first fraction is greater than the second fraction.

Examination of the sentence $\frac{2}{3} < \frac{3}{4}$ meaning "$\frac{2}{3}$ is less than $\frac{3}{4}$" will show that the product of the numerator of the first fraction and the denominator of the second fraction (2×4) is less than the product of the numerator of the second fraction and the denominator of the first fraction (3×3). If this condition is true when we compare two fractions, we may say that the first fraction is less than the second fraction.

Whether $\frac{3}{4} > \frac{2}{3}$ is true depends on whether

$3 \times 3 > 2 \times 4$ is true.

Since $3 \times 3 = 9$ and $2 \times 4 = 8$ and $9 > 8$,

then $3 \times 3 > 2 \times 4$ and $\frac{3}{4} > \frac{2}{3}$.

Whether $\frac{2}{3} < \frac{3}{4}$ is true depends on whether

$2 \times 4 < 3 \times 3$ is true.

Since $2 \times 4 = 8$ and $3 \times 3 = 9$ and $8 < 9$,

then $2 \times 4 < 3 \times 3$ and $\frac{2}{3} < \frac{3}{4}$.

Summarizing:

If a represents the numerator of the first fraction; b, the denominator of the first fraction; c, the numerator of the second fraction; and d, the denominator of the second fraction, then:

(1) $\frac{a}{b} = \frac{c}{d}$ if $a \times d = c \times b$ Two fractions are equivalent.

(2) $\frac{a}{b} > \frac{c}{d}$ if $a \times d > c \times b$ First fraction is greater.

(3) $\frac{a}{b} < \frac{c}{d}$ if $a \times d < c \times b$ First fraction is smaller.

EXERCISES

1. Use the common denominator method to determine which of the following statements are true:

a. $\frac{1}{5} > \frac{1}{4}$ e. $\frac{2}{3} > \frac{7}{12}$ i. $\frac{7}{10} < \frac{2}{3}$ m. $\frac{13}{16} > \frac{19}{24}$ q. $\frac{11}{20} < \frac{9}{16}$

b. $\frac{1}{8} > \frac{1}{10}$ f. $\frac{2}{5} > \frac{3}{8}$ j. $\frac{11}{12} < \frac{9}{10}$ n. $\frac{5}{9} < \frac{6}{7}$ r. $\frac{17}{18} > \frac{19}{20}$

c. $\frac{4}{5} > \frac{9}{10}$ g. $\frac{5}{6} < \frac{7}{8}$ k. $\frac{2}{3} < \frac{5}{8}$ o. $\frac{19}{25} < \frac{73}{100}$ s. $\frac{9}{25} < \frac{3}{8}$

d. $\frac{11}{16} > \frac{1}{2}$ h. $\frac{3}{4} < \frac{5}{6}$ l. $\frac{1}{2} < \frac{3}{5}$ p. $\frac{30}{45} > \frac{20}{30}$ t. $\frac{7}{12} > \frac{9}{16}$

2. Use the cross product test to determine which of the following statements are true:

a. $\frac{1}{5} > \frac{1}{4}$ e. $\frac{11}{16} > \frac{2}{3}$ i. $\frac{4}{5} < \frac{7}{8}$ m. $\frac{19}{25} > \frac{3}{4}$ q. $\frac{5}{11} > \frac{2}{5}$

b. $\frac{1}{9} > \frac{1}{7}$ f. $\frac{7}{9} > \frac{17}{24}$ j. $\frac{11}{12} < \frac{5}{6}$ n. $\frac{5}{12} > \frac{7}{18}$ r. $\frac{36}{48} < \frac{15}{20}$

c. $\frac{5}{8} > \frac{7}{12}$ g. $\frac{3}{4} < \frac{5}{8}$ k. $\frac{3}{4} < \frac{4}{5}$ o. $\frac{11}{15} < \frac{13}{20}$ s. $\frac{9}{25} > \frac{26}{75}$

d. $\frac{1}{2} > \frac{5}{8}$ h. $\frac{8}{15} < \frac{9}{16}$ l. $\frac{13}{16} < \frac{21}{25}$ p. $\frac{3}{10} < \frac{7}{16}$ t. $\frac{5}{16} < \frac{19}{64}$

Common Fractions

3. Arrange each of the following groups of fractions according to size, greatest first:

a. $\frac{5}{12}$, $\frac{11}{12}$, and $\frac{7}{12}$ c. $\frac{9}{10}$, $\frac{5}{6}$, and $\frac{4}{5}$ e. $\frac{7}{16}$, $\frac{1}{4}$, and $\frac{3}{8}$

b. $\frac{5}{16}$, $\frac{5}{8}$, and $\frac{5}{12}$ d. $\frac{3}{5}$, $\frac{5}{8}$, and $\frac{2}{3}$ f. $\frac{4}{7}$, $\frac{5}{8}$, and $\frac{9}{14}$

4. Arrange each of the following groups of fractions according to size, smallest first:

a. $\frac{4}{5}$, $\frac{2}{5}$, and $\frac{3}{5}$ c. $\frac{5}{12}$, $\frac{3}{10}$, and $\frac{7}{16}$ e. $\frac{7}{8}$, $\frac{3}{4}$, and $\frac{5}{6}$

b. $\frac{3}{4}$, $\frac{3}{16}$, and $\frac{3}{8}$ d. $\frac{2}{3}$, $\frac{1}{2}$, and $\frac{3}{4}$ f. $\frac{3}{8}$, $\frac{2}{5}$, and $\frac{7}{20}$

4–9 COMPARING PARTS OF UNITS OF DIFFERENT SIZES

EXERCISES

1. Which is larger:
$\frac{1}{2}$ of figure A or $\frac{1}{2}$ of figure B?

2. Which is larger:
$\frac{3}{4}$ of figure C or $\frac{3}{4}$ of figure D?

3. Which is larger:

a. $\frac{1}{2}$ minute or $\frac{1}{2}$ hour?   d. $\frac{2}{3}$ gallon or $\frac{2}{3}$ quart?

b. $\frac{1}{4}$ ton or $\frac{1}{4}$ pound?   e. $\frac{1}{10}$ meter or $\frac{1}{10}$ centimeter?

c. $\frac{3}{4}$ foot or $\frac{3}{4}$ inch?   f. $\frac{7}{10}$ kilogram or $\frac{7}{10}$ gram?

4. Is $\frac{1}{6}$ of [figure] larger, the same as, or smaller than $\frac{1}{3}$ of [figure] ?

5. Is $\frac{2}{5}$ of [figure] larger, the same as, or smaller than $\frac{3}{4}$ of [figure] ?

6. Is $\frac{2}{3}$ of [figure] larger, the same as, or smaller than $\frac{1}{2}$ of [figure] ?

4–10 ROUNDING MIXED NUMBERS

To round a mixed number to the nearest whole number like $3\frac{5}{8}$ or $7\frac{2}{5}$, we drop the fraction but add 1 to the whole number when the fraction is one-half or more. We do not add anything when the fraction is less than one-half.

> $3\frac{5}{8}$ rounded to nearest whole number is 4.
>
> $7\frac{2}{5}$ rounded to nearest whole number is 7.

EXERCISES

Round each of the following mixed numbers to the nearest whole number:

1. a. $2\frac{3}{4}$ **b.** $8\frac{2}{3}$ **c.** $7\frac{5}{6}$ **d.** $1\frac{7}{12}$ **e.** $3\frac{9}{16}$ **f.** $4\frac{8}{15}$ **g.** $12\frac{7}{10}$ **h.** $11\frac{1}{2}$

2. a. $5\frac{1}{3}$ **b.** $4\frac{3}{8}$ **c.** $9\frac{2}{5}$ **d.** $6\frac{7}{16}$ **e.** $1\frac{3}{10}$ **f.** $8\frac{3}{7}$ **g.** $14\frac{4}{9}$ **h.** $32\frac{12}{25}$

3. a. $9\frac{1}{4}$ **b.** $7\frac{1}{2}$ **c.** $2\frac{11}{16}$ **d.** $14\frac{3}{5}$ **e.** $25\frac{15}{32}$ **f.** $9\frac{5}{11}$ **g.** $16\frac{13}{24}$ **h.** $10\frac{29}{39}$

4–11 COMPUTATION—ADDITION OF FRACTIONS AND MIXED NUMBERS

(1) *To add fractions with like denominators,* we add the numerators and write the sum over the common denominator. We express the answer in simplest form.

> (1) Vertically:
>
> $$\begin{array}{r} \frac{5}{16} \\ +\frac{7}{16} \\ \hline \frac{12}{16} = \frac{3}{4} \end{array}$$
>
> or
>
> Horizontally:
>
> $$\frac{5}{16} + \frac{7}{16}$$
> $$= \frac{5+7}{16}$$
> $$= \frac{12}{16} = \frac{3}{4}$$
>
> *Answer,* $\frac{3}{4}$

Observe that the distributive property is used here.

$$\frac{5}{16} = 5 \times \frac{1}{16} \text{ and } \frac{7}{16} = 7 \times \frac{1}{16}$$

Therefore $\frac{5}{16} + \frac{7}{16} = 5 \times \frac{1}{16} + 7 \times \frac{1}{16} = (5 + 7)\frac{1}{16} = 12 \times \frac{1}{16} = \frac{12}{16}$.

(2) *To add fractions with unlike denominators,* we express the given fractions as equivalent fractions having a common denominator and add as we do with like denominators.

(2) Add:

$$\frac{1}{2} = \frac{3}{6}$$
$$\frac{2}{3} = \frac{4}{6}$$
$$\overline{\qquad\qquad \frac{7}{6} = 1\frac{1}{6}}$$

Answer, $1\frac{1}{6}$

(3) *To add a fraction and a whole number,* we annex the fraction to the whole number.

(3) $4 + \frac{2}{3} = 4\frac{2}{3}$

Answer, $4\frac{2}{3}$

(4) *To add a mixed number and a whole number,* we add the whole numbers and annex the fraction to this sum.

(4) $2\frac{1}{2} + 3 = 5\frac{1}{2}$

Answer, $5\frac{1}{2}$

(5) *To add a mixed number and a fraction,* we add the fractions and annex their sum to the whole number.

(5) Add:

$$2\frac{2}{5} = 2\frac{4}{10}$$
$$\frac{1}{2} = \frac{5}{10}$$
$$\overline{\qquad\qquad 2\frac{9}{10}}$$

Answer, $2\frac{9}{10}$

(6) *To add mixed numbers,* we first add the fractions and then add this sum to the sum of the whole numbers. We express answers in simplest form.

(6) Add:

$$4\frac{3}{4} = 4\frac{6}{8}$$
$$2\frac{5}{8} = 2\frac{5}{8}$$
$$\overline{\qquad\qquad 6\frac{11}{8} = 7\frac{3}{8}}$$

Answer, $7\frac{3}{8}$

1. Use a ruler to determine the sum of each of the following:

a. $\frac{3}{4}''$ $\frac{9}{16}''$ $\frac{1}{8}''$ $\frac{6}{16}''$ $\frac{1}{4}''$ $\frac{1}{8}''$ $\frac{5}{16}''$ $\frac{3}{4}''$ $\frac{15}{16}''$ $\frac{7}{8}''$ $\frac{7}{16}''$

  $\frac{1}{4}''$ $\frac{7}{16}''$ $\frac{2}{8}''$ $\frac{7}{16}''$ $\frac{1}{4}''$ $\frac{5}{8}''$ $\frac{7}{16}''$ $\frac{3}{4}''$ $\frac{9}{16}''$ $\frac{7}{8}''$ $\frac{13}{16}''$

b. $\frac{1}{2}''$ $\frac{1}{4}''$ $\frac{5}{8}''$ $\frac{1}{2}''$ $\frac{3}{4}''$ $\frac{1}{2}''$ $\frac{7}{8}''$ $\frac{3}{8}''$ $\frac{5}{16}''$ $\frac{1}{2}''$ $\frac{5}{8}''$

  $\frac{1}{8}''$ $\frac{1}{2}''$ $\frac{1}{4}''$ $\frac{7}{16}''$ $\frac{3}{16}''$ $\frac{3}{4}''$ $\frac{1}{4}''$ $\frac{11}{16}''$ $\frac{3}{4}''$ $\frac{13}{16}''$ $\frac{3}{4}''$

2. Add on a number line or by use of the fraction chart (see page 97) to determine which of the following statements are true:

a. $\frac{1}{10} + \frac{3}{10} = \frac{2}{5}$ c. $\frac{1}{3} + \frac{1}{6} = \frac{1}{2}$ e. $\frac{1}{2} + \frac{1}{6} = \frac{2}{3}$

b. $\frac{5}{12} + \frac{7}{12} = 1$ d. $\frac{3}{10} + \frac{1}{2} = \frac{4}{5}$ f. $\frac{2}{3} + \frac{1}{4} = \frac{5}{6}$

Add:

3. $\frac{1}{5}$ $\frac{4}{7}$ $\frac{2}{3}$ $\frac{15}{32}$ $\frac{9}{20}$ $\frac{8}{16}$ $\frac{1}{6}$ $\frac{3}{10}$ $\frac{5}{12}$
  $\frac{2}{5}$ $\frac{2}{7}$ $\frac{1}{3}$ $\frac{17}{32}$ $\frac{11}{20}$ $\frac{5}{16}$ $\frac{1}{6}$ $\frac{2}{10}$ $\frac{3}{12}$

4. $\frac{4}{5}$ $\frac{2}{3}$ $\frac{7}{9}$ $\frac{6}{12}$ $\frac{3}{4}$ $\frac{12}{16}$ $\frac{9}{16}$ $\frac{3}{4}$ $\frac{9}{10}$
  $\frac{3}{5}$ $\frac{2}{3}$ $\frac{7}{9}$ $\frac{11}{12}$ $\frac{2}{4}$ $\frac{13}{16}$ $\frac{11}{16}$ $\frac{3}{4}$ $\frac{7}{10}$

5. $\frac{1}{8}$ $\frac{2}{5}$ $\frac{11}{16}$ $\frac{1}{6}$ $\frac{5}{12}$ $\frac{1}{2}$ $\frac{27}{60}$ $\frac{3}{20}$ $\frac{19}{32}$
  $\frac{1}{2}$ $\frac{3}{10}$ $\frac{1}{4}$ $\frac{2}{3}$ $\frac{5}{24}$ $\frac{1}{6}$ $\frac{7}{15}$ $\frac{41}{100}$ $\frac{5}{8}$

6. $\frac{1}{2}$ $\frac{3}{4}$ $\frac{1}{4}$ $\frac{3}{5}$ $\frac{3}{8}$ $\frac{2}{3}$ $\frac{4}{5}$ $\frac{2}{3}$ $\frac{7}{8}$
  $\frac{1}{3}$ $\frac{1}{5}$ $\frac{2}{3}$ $\frac{1}{6}$ $\frac{2}{5}$ $\frac{1}{10}$ $\frac{1}{2}$ $\frac{3}{4}$ $\frac{1}{3}$

7. $\frac{1}{4}$ $\frac{1}{10}$ $\frac{5}{6}$ $\frac{3}{16}$ $\frac{3}{8}$ $\frac{7}{12}$ $\frac{5}{8}$ $\frac{3}{4}$ $\frac{3}{10}$
  $\frac{1}{6}$ $\frac{3}{4}$ $\frac{1}{8}$ $\frac{7}{10}$ $\frac{5}{12}$ $\frac{5}{16}$ $\frac{7}{10}$ $\frac{5}{6}$ $\frac{11}{16}$

8.

$\frac{1}{4}$	$\frac{5}{6}$	$\frac{12}{16}$	$\frac{4}{5}$	$\frac{3}{10}$	$\frac{11}{24}$	$\frac{3}{8}$	$\frac{5}{12}$	$\frac{1}{2}$
$\frac{1}{4}$	$\frac{1}{6}$	$\frac{9}{16}$	$\frac{2}{5}$	$\frac{9}{10}$	$\frac{13}{24}$	$\frac{1}{2}$	$\frac{2}{3}$	$\frac{3}{4}$
$\frac{1}{4}$	$\frac{5}{6}$	$\frac{13}{16}$	$\frac{4}{5}$	$\frac{7}{10}$	$\frac{17}{24}$	$\frac{3}{16}$	$\frac{1}{6}$	$\frac{2}{3}$

9.

$\frac{13}{24}$	$\frac{11}{32}$	$\frac{15}{64}$	$\frac{7}{8}$	$\frac{9}{20}$	$\frac{14}{15}$	$\frac{3}{4}$	$\frac{5}{6}$	$\frac{4}{5}$
$\frac{7}{24}$	$\frac{13}{32}$	$\frac{25}{64}$	$\frac{5}{8}$	$\frac{19}{20}$	$\frac{11}{15}$	$\frac{11}{16}$	$\frac{1}{2}$	$\frac{7}{10}$

10.

$\frac{5}{8}$	$\frac{1}{3}$	$\frac{4}{7}$	$\frac{13}{15}$	$\frac{15}{16}$	$\frac{17}{24}$	$\frac{5}{6}$	$\frac{3}{10}$	$\frac{7}{8}$
$\frac{4}{5}$	$\frac{9}{10}$	$\frac{8}{9}$	$\frac{9}{10}$	$\frac{11}{12}$	$\frac{9}{16}$	$\frac{7}{8}$	$\frac{2}{5}$	$\frac{7}{12}$
						$\frac{3}{4}$	$\frac{19}{100}$	$\frac{13}{16}$

11. $\frac{1}{8} + \frac{5}{8}$ $\frac{7}{16} + \frac{9}{16}$ $\frac{1}{3} + \frac{1}{5}$ $\frac{3}{8} + \frac{5}{6}$ $\frac{11}{16} + \frac{7}{8}$ $\frac{3}{4} + \frac{2}{3} + \frac{5}{6}$ $\frac{7}{8} + \frac{9}{16} + \frac{1}{2}$

12.

4	$\frac{5}{8}$	$5\frac{3}{4}$	9	$4\frac{2}{5}$	$\frac{2}{3}$	$\frac{5}{12}$	$6\frac{3}{4}$
$\frac{2}{5}$	3	2	$5\frac{13}{16}$	$\frac{1}{5}$	$1\frac{1}{2}$	$5\frac{1}{4}$	$\frac{1}{4}$

13. $5 + \frac{3}{4}$ $3\frac{2}{3} + 4$ $\frac{7}{8} + 10$ $9 + 2\frac{13}{16}$ $\frac{7}{12} + 3\frac{5}{12}$ $\frac{11}{16} + 3 + 6\frac{1}{2}$

14.

$2\frac{1}{3}$	$6\frac{4}{9}$	$5\frac{3}{8}$	$3\frac{1}{10}$	$7\frac{1}{4}$	$17\frac{5}{12}$	$2\frac{4}{5}$	$7\frac{2}{3}$
$5\frac{1}{3}$	$2\frac{1}{9}$	$1\frac{3}{8}$	$8\frac{3}{10}$	$3\frac{3}{4}$	$10\frac{7}{12}$	$3\frac{2}{5}$	$1\frac{2}{3}$

15.

$4\frac{2}{5}$	$3\frac{5}{8}$	$5\frac{1}{4}$	$2\frac{1}{2}$	$1\frac{3}{4}$	$2\frac{7}{12}$	$2\frac{1}{6}$	$12\frac{1}{4}$
$9\frac{3}{10}$	$1\frac{13}{16}$	$8\frac{1}{3}$	$7\frac{2}{5}$	$4\frac{1}{10}$	$8\frac{3}{8}$	$5\frac{1}{3}$	$13\frac{7}{12}$

16.

$5\frac{12}{16}$	$4\frac{3}{8}$	$2\frac{7}{10}$	$12\frac{3}{4}$	$7\frac{2}{3}$	$3\frac{5}{6}$	$8\frac{1}{2}$	$12\frac{9}{10}$
$4\frac{9}{16}$	$1\frac{7}{8}$	$5\frac{9}{10}$	$11\frac{3}{4}$	$8\frac{4}{5}$	$5\frac{3}{8}$	$3\frac{5}{6}$	$9\frac{1}{2}$

17.

$3\frac{1}{8}$	$4\frac{2}{5}$	$1\frac{9}{10}$	$1\frac{1}{2}$	$2\frac{1}{10}$	$3\frac{2}{3}$
$2\frac{3}{8}$	$3\frac{1}{5}$	$6\frac{3}{10}$	$3\frac{3}{16}$	$7\frac{1}{2}$	$1\frac{3}{4}$
$1\frac{1}{8}$	$7\frac{2}{5}$	$2\frac{7}{10}$	$5\frac{1}{4}$	$4\frac{1}{5}$	$4\frac{5}{6}$

18.

$6\frac{7}{8}$	$2\frac{2}{3}$	$8\frac{3}{4}$	$7\frac{13}{16}$	$\frac{5}{8}$	$3\frac{3}{4}$
$3\frac{1}{6}$	$6\frac{1}{2}$	$4\frac{7}{8}$	$2\frac{1}{4}$	$9\frac{2}{3}$	$\frac{1}{2}$
$8\frac{7}{10}$	$7\frac{4}{5}$	$5\frac{5}{6}$	$1\frac{5}{8}$	$\frac{11}{12}$	$5\frac{2}{3}$

19. $3\frac{19}{32} + 1\frac{11}{16} + 5\frac{3}{4}$ $2\frac{1}{6} + 4\frac{7}{8} + 3\frac{5}{16}$ $6\frac{3}{4} + 5\frac{5}{8} + 1\frac{1}{6}$ $7\frac{11}{12} + 2\frac{11}{15} + 3\frac{13}{24}$

20. Which of the following statements are true?

   a. $\frac{5}{8} + \frac{2}{8} = \frac{2}{8} + \frac{5}{8}$

   b. $\left(\frac{1}{16} + \frac{3}{16}\right) + \frac{5}{16} = \frac{1}{16} + \left(\frac{3}{16} + \frac{5}{16}\right)$

   c. $1\frac{2}{3} + 4\frac{1}{2} = 4\frac{1}{2} + 1\frac{2}{3}$

21. **a.** Does the commutative property hold for the addition of fractions?

   b. Does the associative property hold for the addition of fractions?

4–12 COMPUTATION—SUBTRACTION OF FRACTIONS AND MIXED NUMBERS

(1) *To subtract fractions with like denominators,* we subtract the numerators and write the difference over the common denominator. We express the answer in lowest terms.

(1) Vertically: Horizontally:

$$\frac{4}{5}$$
$$-\frac{3}{5}$$
$$\frac{1}{5}$$

or

$$\frac{4}{5} - \frac{3}{5}$$

$$= \frac{4 - 3}{5}$$

$$= \frac{1}{5}$$

Answer, $\frac{1}{5}$

(2) *To subtract fractions with unlike denominators,* we express the fractions as equivalent fractions having a common denominator and subtract as we do with like denominators.

(3) *To subtract a fraction or mixed number from a whole number,* we regroup by taking one (1) from the whole number and express it as a fraction making the numerator and denominator the same. Then we subtract the fractions and we subtract the whole numbers.

(2) Subtract:

$$\frac{11}{12} = \frac{11}{12}$$

$$\frac{1}{4} = \frac{3}{12}$$

$$\frac{8}{12} = \frac{2}{3}$$

Answer, $\frac{2}{3}$

(3) Subtract:

$$4 = 3\frac{8}{8}$$

$$1\frac{5}{8} = 1\frac{5}{8}$$

$$2\frac{3}{8}$$

Answer, $2\frac{3}{8}$

(4) *To subtract a whole number from a mixed number,* we find the difference between the whole numbers and annex the fraction to this difference.

(5) *To subtract a fraction or a mixed number from a mixed number,* first we subtract the fractions then the whole numbers. If the fraction in the subtrahend is greater than the fraction in the minuend, we regroup by taking one (1) from the whole number in the minuend to increase the fraction of the minuend, then we subtract. We express answers in simplest form.

(4) Subtract:

$$6\frac{3}{5} - 2 = 4\frac{3}{5}$$

Answer, $4\frac{3}{5}$

(5) Subtract:

$$6\frac{1}{3} = 6\frac{2}{6} = 5\frac{8}{6}$$

$$2\frac{1}{2} = 2\frac{3}{6} = 2\frac{3}{6}$$

$$3\frac{5}{6}$$

Answer, $3\frac{5}{6}$

1. Subtract on a ruler:

$\frac{3}{4}''$	$\frac{9}{16}''$	$\frac{5}{8}''$	$\frac{13}{16}''$	$\frac{7}{8}''$	$\frac{11}{16}''$	$\frac{5}{8}''$	$\frac{1}{2}''$	$\frac{13}{16}''$
$\frac{2}{4}''$	$\frac{2}{16}''$	$\frac{1}{8}''$	$\frac{5}{16}''$	$\frac{5}{8}''$	$\frac{5}{16}''$	$\frac{1}{4}''$	$\frac{3}{16}''$	$\frac{3}{4}''$

2. Subtract on a number line or by use of the fraction chart (see page 97) to determine which of the following statements are true:

a. $\frac{5}{6} - \frac{1}{6} = \frac{1}{2}$ **c.** $\frac{9}{10} - \frac{3}{10} = \frac{3}{5}$ **e.** $\frac{11}{12} - \frac{1}{4} = \frac{2}{3}$

b. $\frac{11}{12} - \frac{7}{12} = \frac{1}{3}$ **d.** $\frac{1}{2} - \frac{2}{5} = \frac{1}{10}$ **f.** $\frac{7}{8} - \frac{5}{6} = \frac{1}{12}$

Subtract:

3.

$\frac{4}{5}$	$\frac{6}{7}$	$\frac{15}{16}$	$\frac{9}{10}$	$\frac{7}{12}$	$\frac{1}{2}$	$\frac{29}{32}$	$\frac{5}{6}$	$\frac{7}{9}$
$\frac{2}{5}$	$\frac{4}{7}$	$\frac{5}{16}$	$\frac{3}{10}$	$\frac{5}{12}$	$\frac{1}{2}$	$\frac{17}{32}$	$\frac{5}{6}$	$\frac{4}{9}$

4.

$\frac{1}{3}$	$\frac{11}{12}$	$\frac{3}{5}$	$\frac{1}{2}$	$\frac{9}{10}$	$\frac{5}{6}$	$\frac{3}{4}$	$\frac{7}{8}$	$\frac{2}{3}$
$\frac{1}{6}$	$\frac{2}{3}$	$\frac{1}{10}$	$\frac{3}{8}$	$\frac{3}{4}$	$\frac{11}{24}$	$\frac{2}{3}$	$\frac{3}{10}$	$\frac{5}{8}$

5.

$6\frac{5}{8}$	$8\frac{1}{2}$	$4\frac{11}{16}$	$9\frac{4}{5}$	$12\frac{9}{20}$	$20\frac{5}{24}$	$5\frac{2}{3}$	$6\frac{7}{8}$	$2\frac{1}{4}$
3	4	1	7	8	15	5	6	2

6.

$\frac{9}{10}$	$\frac{13}{15}$	$\frac{17}{20}$	$\frac{15}{16}$	$\frac{5}{6}$	$\frac{11}{12}$	$1\frac{13}{16}$	$9\frac{5}{12}$	$25\frac{1}{6}$
$\frac{9}{10}$	$\frac{7}{15}$	$\frac{9}{20}$	$\frac{5}{6}$	$\frac{7}{10}$	$\frac{5}{16}$	1	9	25

7.

$3\frac{4}{5}$	$7\frac{5}{6}$	$2\frac{3}{8}$	$1\frac{9}{10}$	$9\frac{11}{12}$	$10\frac{7}{12}$	$6\frac{1}{2}$	$3\frac{4}{5}$	$9\frac{3}{4}$
$\frac{1}{5}$	$1\frac{1}{6}$	$\frac{3}{8}$	$\frac{3}{10}$	$9\frac{11}{12}$	$10\frac{5}{12}$	$\frac{3}{8}$	$\frac{2}{3}$	$2\frac{1}{6}$

8.

1	1	8	9	4	6	8	12	8
$\frac{7}{8}$	$\frac{1}{3}$	$\frac{3}{4}$	$3\frac{1}{8}$	$1\frac{5}{6}$	$5\frac{1}{2}$	$6\frac{9}{16}$	$2\frac{3}{5}$	$7\frac{3}{8}$

9. $6\frac{1}{5}$ $\qquad$ $7\frac{3}{8}$ $\qquad$ $4\frac{1}{6}$ $\qquad$ $5\frac{1}{2}$ $\qquad$ $4\frac{2}{5}$ $\qquad$ $8\frac{3}{10}$ $\qquad$ $1\frac{3}{16}$ $\qquad$ $13\frac{7}{8}$ $\qquad$ $9\frac{5}{12}$
$\underline{3\frac{3}{5}}$ $\qquad$ $\underline{2\frac{7}{8}}$ $\qquad$ $\underline{1\frac{5}{6}}$ $\qquad$ $\underline{2\frac{5}{8}}$ $\qquad$ $\underline{3\frac{3}{4}}$ $\qquad$ $\underline{2\frac{5}{6}}$ $\qquad$ $\underline{\frac{9}{16}}$ $\qquad$ $\underline{9\frac{11}{12}}$ $\qquad$ $\underline{\frac{2}{3}}$

10. $8\frac{7}{10}$ $\qquad$ $15\frac{2}{3}$ $\qquad$ $20\frac{9}{10}$ $\qquad$ 15 $\qquad$ 10 $\qquad$ 14 $\qquad$ $10\frac{5}{8}$ $\qquad$ $4\frac{1}{4}$ $\qquad$ $7\frac{3}{8}$
$\underline{4\frac{1}{2}}$ $\qquad$ $\underline{9\frac{1}{4}}$ $\qquad$ $\underline{8\frac{3}{8}}$ $\qquad$ $\underline{8\frac{15}{32}}$ $\qquad$ $\underline{9\frac{1}{3}}$ $\qquad$ $\underline{10\frac{2}{3}}$ $\qquad$ $\underline{1\frac{4}{5}}$ $\qquad$ $\underline{3\frac{1}{3}}$ $\qquad$ $\underline{6\frac{11}{16}}$

11. a. $\frac{5}{6} - \frac{3}{8}$ $\qquad$ **b.** $7\frac{5}{8} - 7$ $\qquad$ **c.** $10\frac{3}{4} - \frac{2}{3}$ $\qquad$ **d.** $5 - 4\frac{4}{5}$ $\qquad$ **e.** $14\frac{3}{8} - 6\frac{9}{10}$

4–13 COMPUTATION—MULTIPLICATION OF FRACTIONS AND MIXED NUMBERS

To multiply fractions and mixed numbers, we first express each mixed number, if any, as an improper fraction and each whole number, if any, as a fraction by writing the whole number over 1. Then where possible we divide any numerator and denominator by the greatest possible number that is exactly contained in both (greatest common factor). This reduction simplifies computation. Finally we multiply the resulting numerators and multiply the resulting denominators, expressing the answer in simplest form.

$$\frac{1}{5} \times 7 = \frac{1}{5} \times \frac{7}{1} = \frac{7}{5} = 1\frac{2}{5}$$

Answer, $1\frac{2}{5}$

$$10 \times \frac{3}{4} = \frac{\overset{5}{\cancel{10}}}{1} \times \frac{3}{\underset{2}{\cancel{4}}} = \frac{15}{2} = 7\frac{1}{2}$$

Answer, $7\frac{1}{2}$

$$\frac{4}{5} \times \frac{2}{3} = \frac{8}{15}$$

Answer, $\frac{8}{15}$

$$1\frac{9}{16} \times 3\frac{3}{5} = \frac{\overset{5}{\cancel{25}}}{\underset{8}{\cancel{16}}} \times \frac{\overset{9}{\cancel{18}}}{\underset{1}{\cancel{5}}} = \frac{45}{8} = 5\frac{5}{8}$$

Answer, $5\frac{5}{8}$

When we multiply a mixed number and a whole number, the vertical form may also be used.

$$\begin{array}{r} 15 \\ \times 2\frac{1}{4} \\ \hline 30 \\ 3\frac{3}{4} \\ \hline 33\frac{3}{4} \end{array} \qquad \frac{1}{4} \times 15 = \frac{15}{4} = 3\frac{3}{4}$$

Answer, $33\frac{3}{4}$

EXERCISES

Multiply:

1. $\frac{1}{3} \times 3$ $\frac{5}{8} \times 8$ $\frac{1}{12} \times 60$ $\frac{7}{10} \times 100$ $\frac{1}{16} \times 2$

    $\frac{5}{12} \times 3$ $\frac{1}{10} \times 6$ $\frac{7}{16} \times 12$ $\frac{1}{16} \times 36$ $\frac{7}{8} \times 28$

2. $6 \times \frac{1}{6}$ $10 \times \frac{7}{10}$ $18 \times \frac{1}{6}$ $16 \times \frac{3}{4}$ $3 \times \frac{1}{12}$

    $2 \times \frac{7}{8}$ $14 \times \frac{1}{16}$ $6 \times \frac{5}{8}$ $35 \times \frac{1}{10}$ $45 \times \frac{5}{6}$

3. $\frac{1}{8} \times 5$ $\frac{3}{16} \times 1$ $\frac{1}{4} \times 9$ $\frac{2}{3} \times 2$ $\frac{13}{6} \times 5$

    $7 \times \frac{1}{12}$ $3 \times \frac{2}{7}$ $17 \times \frac{1}{6}$ $21 \times \frac{13}{16}$ $12 \times \frac{51}{16}$

4. $\frac{1}{2} \times \frac{1}{4}$ $\frac{7}{8} \times \frac{5}{6}$ $\frac{1}{3} \times \frac{3}{16}$ $\frac{2}{5} \times \frac{1}{8}$ $\frac{3}{4} \times \frac{5}{24}$

    $\frac{4}{5} \times \frac{15}{16}$ $\frac{21}{32} \times \frac{8}{9}$ $\frac{12}{5} \times \frac{5}{12}$ $\frac{25}{18} \times \frac{9}{10}$ $\frac{22}{7} \times \frac{35}{16}$

5. $4 \times 2\frac{3}{4}$ $48 \times 3\frac{11}{16}$ $5 \times 3\frac{7}{10}$ $12 \times 2\frac{13}{32}$ $8 \times 5\frac{2}{3}$

    $2\frac{1}{2} \times 2$ $1\frac{1}{3} \times 6$ $6\frac{7}{12} \times 4$ $1\frac{7}{16} \times 20$ $4\frac{3}{8} \times 7$

6. $\frac{5}{8} \times 3\frac{3}{4}$ $\frac{3}{10} \times 2\frac{1}{6}$ $\frac{9}{16} \times 4\frac{5}{6}$ $\frac{2}{3} \times 1\frac{7}{20}$ $\frac{7}{8} \times 3\frac{1}{7}$

    $2\frac{7}{8} \times \frac{5}{6}$ $1\frac{1}{2} \times \frac{1}{4}$ $2\frac{5}{12} \times \frac{3}{16}$ $5\frac{3}{5} \times \frac{7}{8}$ $6\frac{1}{4} \times \frac{2}{25}$

7. $2\frac{1}{2} \times 3\frac{1}{2}$ $3\frac{7}{8} \times 1\frac{4}{5}$ $8\frac{1}{3} \times 4\frac{7}{10}$ $2\frac{5}{8} \times 1\frac{5}{6}$ $3\frac{1}{7} \times 6\frac{1}{8}$

    $9\frac{1}{3} \times 1\frac{7}{8}$ $4\frac{4}{5} \times 2\frac{13}{16}$ $1\frac{1}{2} \times 4\frac{2}{3}$ $4\frac{1}{6} \times 1\frac{11}{25}$ $8\frac{1}{10} \times 2\frac{2}{9}$

8. $\frac{22}{7} \times \frac{9}{16} \times \frac{7}{8}$　　　　　　　$6 \times 2\frac{3}{16} \times \frac{4}{5}$　　　　　　$1\frac{3}{4} \times 2\frac{1}{2} \times 3\frac{1}{7}$

　　$2\frac{5}{6} \times 5\frac{1}{2} \times 3\frac{2}{3}$　　　　　　　$3\frac{3}{8} \times 2\frac{2}{3} \times 4\frac{1}{2}$　　　　　　$3\frac{1}{7} \times \frac{3}{4} \times 6\frac{1}{8}$

9. Multiply vertically:

$17\frac{2}{3}$	$41\frac{5}{8}$	$5\frac{1}{2}$	$9\frac{5}{6}$	$26\frac{13}{16}$	21	56	8	19	45
9	24	3	14	37	$3\frac{1}{7}$	$73\frac{7}{8}$	$2\frac{1}{3}$	$6\frac{1}{4}$	$89\frac{11}{12}$

10. Which of these statements are true?

a. $\frac{3}{5} \times \frac{7}{8} = \frac{7}{8} \times \frac{3}{5}$

b. $\left(\frac{9}{10} = 2\frac{1}{2}\right) \times 3\frac{3}{4} = \frac{9}{10} \times \left(2\frac{1}{2} \times 3\frac{3}{4}\right)$

c. $1\frac{2}{3} \times 6\frac{4}{5} = 6\frac{4}{5} \times 1\frac{2}{3}$

11. a. Does the commutative property hold for the multiplication of fractions?

b. Does the associative property hold for the multiplication of fractions?

c. Is $\frac{3}{4} \times (8 + 12) = \frac{3}{4} \times 8 + \frac{3}{4} + 12$ true? Does the distribution property of multiplication over addition hold when fractions are used?

12. Square each of the following:

a. $\frac{2}{3}$　**b.** $\frac{1}{2}$　**c.** $\frac{4}{5}$　**d.** $\frac{5}{8}$　**e.** $\frac{7}{12}$　**f.** $1\frac{1}{4}$　**g.** $3\frac{7}{8}$　**h.** $2\frac{1}{6}$　**i.** $4\frac{3}{5}$　**j.** $5\frac{9}{16}$

4–14　MULTIPLICATIVE INVERSE

If the product of two numbers is one (1), then each factor is called the *multiplicative inverse* or *reciprocal* of the other.

> 4 and $\frac{1}{4}$ are multiplicative inverses of each other because $4 \times \frac{1}{4} = 1$.
>
> $\frac{3}{2}$ and $\frac{2}{3}$ are multiplicative inverses of each other because $\frac{3}{2} \times \frac{2}{3} = 1$.

Observe that the numerator of one fraction becomes the denominator of its reciprocal and its denominator becomes the numerator of its reciprocal. Zero has no inverse for multiplication.

Write the multiplicative inverse or reciprocal of each of the following:

1. a. 3   **b.** 5   **c.** 12   **d.** 0   **e.** 6   **f.** 1   **g.** 25   **h.** 100

2. a. $\frac{1}{5}$ **b.** $\frac{1}{7}$ **c.** $\frac{1}{10}$ **d.** $\frac{2}{9}$ **e.** $\frac{22}{7}$ **f.** $\frac{25}{32}$ **g.** $\frac{15}{16}$ **h.** $\frac{11}{5}$

3. Find the missing numbers.

a. $6 \times ? = 1$ **d.** $? \times 7 = 1$ **g.** $\frac{4}{7} \times ? = 1$ **j.** $8 \times \frac{1}{8} = ?$

b. $9 = ? = 1$ **e.** $\frac{1}{3} \times ? = 1$ **h.** $? \times \frac{9}{5} = 1$ **k.** $\frac{3}{4} \times \frac{4}{3} = ?$

c. $? \times 4 = 1$ **f.** $? \times \frac{1}{2} = 1$ **i.** $\frac{3}{4} \times ? = 1$ **l.** $\frac{1}{5} \times 5 = ?$

4–15 COMPUTATION—DIVISION OF FRACTIONS AND MIXED NUMBERS

Division is the inverse operation of multiplication.

> When we divide 20 by 5, the quotient is 4. $20 \div 5 = 4$
> When we multiply 20 by $\frac{1}{5}$, the product is 4. $20 \times \frac{1}{5} = 4$

Dividing a given number by 5 gives the same answer as multiplying the given number by its multiplicative inverse (or reciprocal) $\frac{1}{5}$.

When we divide 4 by $\frac{1}{3}$, written as $4 \div \frac{1}{3}$, we are finding how many thirds are in four whole units. In each whole unit there are 3 thirds; in 4 units there are 4×3 thirds or 12 thirds. $4 \div \frac{1}{3}$ and 4×3 are both names for the number 12.

Thus to divide a number by another number, we may instead multiply the first number by the reciprocal of the divisor. Usually this idea is stated briefly as "invert the divisor and multiply."

This principle may be developed by using a complex fraction, the multiplicative inverse and the multiplicative identity one (1) as shown on the following page.

A *complex fraction* is a fraction in which the numerator or denominator or both have a fraction as a term. The complex fraction $\dfrac{\frac{3}{5}}{\frac{2}{3}}$ may be expressed as $\frac{3}{5} \div \frac{2}{3}$ since they represent the same number. (The fraction bar means division.)

$$\frac{3}{5} \div \frac{2}{3} = \frac{\frac{3}{5}}{\frac{2}{3}} = \frac{\frac{3}{5}}{\frac{2}{3}} \times 1 = \frac{\frac{3}{5} \times \frac{3}{2}}{\frac{2}{3} \times \frac{3}{2}} = \frac{\frac{3}{5} \times \frac{3}{2}}{1} = \frac{3}{5} \times \frac{3}{2} = \frac{9}{10}$$

We multiply both numerator and denominator by $\frac{3}{2}$, the multiplicative inverse of the denominator $\frac{2}{3}$, to get 1 as our denominator.

To divide fractions and mixed numbers by the reciprocal method:

(1) We express each mixed number, if any, as an improper fraction and each whole number, if any, as a fraction by writing the whole number over 1.
(2) We invert the divisor (number after the division sign) to find the reciprocal and multiply as in the multiplication of fractions, using reduction where possible.

$$12 \div \frac{15}{16} = \frac{\overset{4}{\cancel{12}}}{1} \times \frac{16}{\underset{5}{\cancel{15}}} = \frac{64}{5} = 12\frac{4}{5}$$

Answer, $12\frac{4}{5}$

$$1\frac{1}{3} \div 2\frac{1}{4} = \frac{4}{3} \div \frac{9}{4} = \frac{4}{3} \times \frac{4}{9} = \frac{16}{27}$$

Answer, $\dfrac{16}{27}$

Sometimes the given fractions are expressed as equivalent fractions having a common denominator and the numerator of the first fraction is divided by the numerator of the second fraction to obtain the answer.

$\frac{3}{5} \div \frac{2}{3} = \frac{9}{15} \div \frac{10}{15} = 9 \div 10 = \frac{9}{10}$

9 fifteenths divided by 10 fifteenths is 9 divided by 10.

Answer, $\frac{9}{10}$

To simplify a complex fraction, we divide the numerator of the complex fraction by its denominator.

$$\frac{\frac{15}{16}}{\frac{5}{6}} = \frac{15}{16} \div \frac{5}{6} = \frac{\overset{3}{\cancel{15}}}{\underset{8}{\cancel{16}}} \times \frac{\overset{3}{\cancel{6}}}{\underset{1}{\cancel{5}}} = \frac{9}{8} = 1\frac{1}{8}$$

Answer, $1\frac{1}{8}$

Observe that when a number is divided by a fraction less than 1, the quotient is always greater than the given number. When a number is divided by 1, the quotient is always equal to the given number. When a number is divided by a mixed number or a whole number greater than 1, the quotient is always less than the given number.

EXERCISES

Divide:

1. $\frac{3}{5} \div 3$ $\frac{15}{16} \div 5$ $\frac{27}{32} \div 3$ $\frac{1}{2} \div 4$ $\frac{1}{3} \div 8$

    $\frac{5}{6} \div 2$ $\frac{3}{4} \div 8$ $\frac{5}{8} \div 10$ $\frac{15}{16} \div 60$ $\frac{21}{32} \div 28$

2. $2\frac{1}{2} \div 5$ $10\frac{1}{8} \div 9$ $6\frac{2}{3} \div 4$ $13\frac{1}{3} \div 16$ $4\frac{4}{5} \div 20$

    $7\frac{1}{3} \div 4$ $1\frac{7}{8} \div 4$ $2\frac{11}{16} \div 8$ $5\frac{3}{4} \div 2$ $7\frac{7}{8} \div 5$

3. $\frac{7}{8} \div \frac{1}{8}$ $\frac{1}{3} \div \frac{2}{3}$ $\frac{5}{6} \div \frac{5}{6}$ $\frac{1}{5} \div \frac{1}{2}$ $\frac{3}{4} \div \frac{2}{3}$

    $\frac{5}{8} \div \frac{5}{32}$ $\frac{2}{3} \div \frac{4}{5}$ $\frac{15}{16} \div \frac{9}{10}$ $\frac{25}{32} \div \frac{15}{16}$ $\frac{3}{4} \div \frac{9}{16}$

4. $8 \div \frac{1}{4}$ $5 \div \frac{5}{6}$ $12 \div \frac{2}{3}$ $2 \div \frac{4}{5}$ $15 \div \frac{9}{10}$

    $7 \div \frac{2}{3}$ $1 \div \frac{1}{6}$ $9 \div \frac{7}{16}$ $1 \div \frac{5}{8}$ $7 \div \frac{21}{32}$

5. $6\frac{3}{5} \div \frac{1}{5}$ $8\frac{2}{3} \div \frac{2}{3}$ $4\frac{1}{5} \div \frac{7}{8}$ $3\frac{3}{4} \div \frac{1}{2}$ $1\frac{1}{8} \div \frac{3}{4}$

     $2\frac{11}{12} \div \frac{15}{16}$ $3\frac{1}{3} \div \frac{5}{6}$ $2\frac{4}{5} \div \frac{7}{10}$ $2\frac{1}{2} \div \frac{2}{3}$ $5\frac{1}{3} \div \frac{11}{16}$

6. $\frac{1}{4} \div 1\frac{1}{4}$ $\frac{1}{6} \div 2\frac{5}{6}$ $\frac{7}{12} \div 1\frac{2}{3}$ $\frac{15}{16} \div 3\frac{1}{2}$ $\frac{5}{8} \div 3\frac{3}{4}$

     $\frac{21}{32} \div 4\frac{3}{8}$ $\frac{9}{10} \div 2\frac{2}{5}$ $\frac{2}{3} \div 1\frac{3}{8}$ $\frac{5}{8} \div 2\frac{2}{3}$ $\frac{3}{4} \div 1\frac{3}{5}$

7. $11 \div 2\frac{3}{4}$ $58 \div 3\frac{5}{8}$ $7 \div 8\frac{3}{4}$ $4 \div 18\frac{2}{3}$ $6 \div 4\frac{1}{2}$

     $18 \div 2\frac{7}{10}$ $4 \div 8\frac{2}{3}$ $9 \div 1\frac{2}{3}$ $12 \div 12\frac{4}{5}$ $1 \div 1\frac{3}{4}$

8. $3\frac{3}{8} \div 4\frac{2}{5}$ $5\frac{1}{2} \div 2\frac{2}{3}$ $24\frac{1}{2} \div 3\frac{1}{2}$ $18\frac{3}{4} \div 1\frac{9}{16}$ $1\frac{5}{6} \div 2\frac{7}{8}$

     $2\frac{1}{2} \div 3\frac{3}{4}$ $4\frac{1}{4} \div 4\frac{1}{4}$ $5\frac{11}{16} \div 4\frac{1}{2}$ $12\frac{1}{4} \div 1\frac{5}{16}$ $19\frac{1}{3} \div 2\frac{5}{12}$

9. $\left(\frac{7}{8} \div \frac{3}{16}\right) \div \frac{2}{3}$ $\left(8\frac{2}{3} \div 1\frac{5}{8}\right) \div 1\frac{1}{2}$ $7\frac{1}{2} \div \left(2\frac{3}{4} \div \frac{2}{3}\right)$ $1\frac{7}{8} \div \left(2\frac{5}{6} \div 2\frac{2}{5}\right)$

10. Simplify:

$\dfrac{\frac{9}{16}}{\frac{3}{8}}$ $\dfrac{\frac{4}{5}}{\frac{5}{12}}$ $\dfrac{\frac{8}{49}}{\frac{22}{7}}$ $\dfrac{2\frac{5}{8}}{3\frac{3}{4}}$ $\dfrac{3\frac{3}{5}}{\frac{7}{10}}$

$\dfrac{\frac{14}{15}}{7}$ $\dfrac{1\frac{1}{2}}{9}$ $\dfrac{37\frac{1}{2}}{100}$ $\dfrac{8}{\frac{4}{5}}$ $\dfrac{9}{2\frac{1}{4}}$

FRACTIONAL RELATIONSHIPS BETWEEN NUMBERS

Fractions are used to express relationships between numbers. There are 3 types of relationships: (1) finding a fractional part of a number; (2) finding what fractional part one number is of another; and (3) finding a number when a fractional part of it is known.

4–16 FRACTIONAL PART OF A NUMBER

We often find a fractional part of a quantity like $\frac{2}{3}$ of a dozen ($\frac{2}{3}$ of 12). Here we use the process of multiplication, $\frac{2}{3}$ of 12 means $\frac{2}{3} \times 12$. The word "of" used in this way means "times."

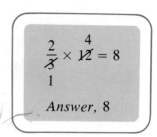

$$\frac{2}{\cancel{3}} \times \cancel{12}^{4} = 8$$

Answer, 8

Find the following:

1. a. $\frac{1}{2}$ of 8   **b.** $\frac{1}{3}$ of 17   **c.** $\frac{1}{4}$ of $\frac{4}{5}$ **d.** $\frac{1}{5}$ of 120   **e.** $\frac{1}{6}$ of 3

2. a. $\frac{1}{8}$ of 34   **b.** $\frac{1}{10}$ of $8\frac{1}{3}$ **c.** $\frac{1}{12}$ of 96   **d.** $\frac{1}{9}$ of 72   **e.** $\frac{1}{36}$ of 25

3. a. $\frac{2}{3}$ of 48   **b.** $\frac{3}{4}$ of 24   **c.** $\frac{7}{8}$ of 6   **d.** $\frac{5}{6}$ of 178   **e.** $\frac{2}{5}$ of 80

4. a. $\frac{9}{10}$ of 35   **b.** $\frac{9}{100}$ of 700   **c.** $\frac{5}{12}$ of 60   **d.** $\frac{5}{8}$ of $7\frac{1}{2}$ **e.** $\frac{4}{5}$ of 175

5. a. $\frac{3}{8}$ of 50   **b.** $\frac{7}{10}$ of 19   **c.** $\frac{11}{12}$ of 9   **d.** $\frac{3}{5}$ of 2   **e.** $\frac{3}{10}$ of $\frac{7}{8}$

6. a. $\frac{7}{12}$ of 360   **b.** $\frac{1}{16}$ of 24   **c.** $\frac{5}{12}$ of $7\frac{1}{5}$ **d.** $\frac{11}{16}$ of 80   **e.** $\frac{5}{6}$ of 4

4–17 WHAT FRACTIONAL PART ONE NUMBER IS OF ANOTHER

A fraction is used to express what part one number is of another. When we find what part of a dozen 8 things are, we are using 8 things out of 12 or $\frac{8}{12}$ of a dozen which, expressed in lowest terms, is $\frac{2}{3}$ of a dozen.

$$\frac{8}{12} = \frac{2 \cdot 4}{3 \cdot 4} = \frac{2}{3}$$

Answer, $\frac{2}{3}$

To find what fractional part one number is of another, we write a numeral naming a fraction with the number of parts used as the numerator and the number of parts in the whole unit or group as the denominator. Where necessary, we express the fraction in lowest terms.

Find the following:

1. a. What part of 8 is 3?   **b.** What part of 5 is 2?   **c.** What part of 16 is 9?

2. a. 1 is what part of 6?   **b.** 7 is what part of 8?   **c.** 3 is what part of 10?

3. a. What part of 12 is 9?   **b.** What part of 20 is 16?   **c.** What part of 54 is 42?

4. a. 2 is what part of 14?   **b.** 36 is what part of 40?   **c.** 65 is what part of 100?

5. a. What part of 56 is 35?   **b.** 108 is what part of 144?   **c.** What part of 60 is 45?

4-18 FINDING THE NUMBER WHEN A FRACTIONAL PART OF IT IS KNOWN

Suppose we are required to find the number when $\frac{2}{3}$ of it is 8:

Since $\frac{2}{3}$ of the number = 8

$\frac{1}{3}$ of the number = $8 \div 2 = 4$

$\frac{3}{3}$ of the number = $3 \times 4 = 12$

Therefore the number = 12

Note: We divide by 2 $\left(\text{which is the numerator of } \frac{2}{3}\right)$ and we multiply by 3 $\left(\text{which is the denominator of } \frac{2}{3}\right)$. We are doing the same thing when we multiply by the multiplicative inverse $\frac{3}{2}$.

$$\overset{4}{\cancel{8}} \times \frac{3}{\underset{1}{\cancel{2}}} = 12$$

Answer, 12

Therefore to find the number when a fractional part of it is known, we multiply the given number that represents the fractional part of the unknown number by the multiplicative inverse (reciprocal) of the given fraction (or divide the given number by the given fraction as shown below).

$$8 \div \frac{2}{3}$$
$$8 \times \frac{3}{2} = 12$$

Find the following:

1. a. $\frac{1}{2}$ of what number is 12?   c. $\frac{1}{8}$ of what number is 7?

   b. $\frac{1}{5}$ of what number is 20?

2. a. 5 is $\frac{1}{4}$ of what number?   c. 30 is $\frac{1}{10}$ of what number?

   b. 6 is $\frac{1}{12}$ of what number?

3. a. $\frac{3}{4}$ of what number is 27?   c. $\frac{5}{6}$ of what number is 60?

   b. $\frac{2}{3}$ of what number is 48?

4. a. 56 is $\frac{7}{8}$ of what number?   c. 27 is $\frac{9}{10}$ of what number?

   b. 40 is $\frac{2}{5}$ of what number?

5. a. $\frac{5}{12}$ of what number is 100?   c. $\frac{3}{8}$ of what number is 12?

   b. $\frac{4}{5}$ of what number is 72?

6. a. 85 is $\frac{17}{20}$ of what number?   c. 54 is $\frac{9}{100}$ of what number?

   b. 60 is $\frac{15}{16}$ of what number?

4–19   PROBLEM SOLVING

First study pages 74–75. Then solve each problem.

1. Joan's mother bought two chickens, one weighing $3\frac{7}{8}$ lb. and the other $4\frac{3}{4}$ lb. What was the total weight of the chickens?

2. How many degrees above normal is a temperature of $101\frac{2}{5}$ degrees Fahrenheit if normal body temperature is $98\frac{3}{5}$ degrees?

3. If $1\frac{7}{10}$ meters of goods are needed to make a chair cover, how many meters of goods are needed to make 6 covers?

4. An airplane flew 920 kilometers (km) in $2\frac{1}{4}$ hours. What was its average ground speed?

5. A merchant cut $4\frac{2}{3}$ yards of cloth from a bolt containing $34\frac{1}{4}$ yards. What length remained in the bolt?

6. A house worth $39,200 was assessed for $\frac{3}{4}$ of its value. What is the assessed value of the house?

7. A stock which closed on Monday at $42\frac{5}{8}$ gained $1\frac{3}{4}$ points on the following day. At what price did it close on Tuesday?

8. How many floor boards $2\frac{1}{4}$ inches wide are needed to cover a floor 15 feet wide?

9. How many miles do $8\frac{3}{16}$ inches represent if the scale 1 inch = 80 miles is used?

10. If you can walk $\frac{3}{4}$ mile in $\frac{2}{5}$ hour, at this rate how far can you walk in one hour?

11. What is the outside diameter of a tube $\frac{3}{8}$ inch thick if the inside diameter is $2\frac{11}{16}$ inches?

12. Ann delivers papers after school each day and on Saturdays, spending $1\frac{1}{4}$ hours for each delivery. How many hours each week does she use to deliver papers?

13. A closed box measuring $9\frac{11}{16}$ inches by $8\frac{7}{8}$ inches by $5\frac{3}{4}$ inches is made of wood $\frac{3}{16}$ inch thick. Find the inside dimensions.

14. Joe built a book case with 3 shelves each $3\frac{1}{2}$ feet long. He also used 2 pieces of wood each $3\frac{3}{4}$ feet long and two side pieces each $4\frac{1}{2}$ feet long. How many feet of wood were required?

15. A family plans to spend $\frac{1}{4}$ of its annual income of $21,600 for shelter, $\frac{1}{3}$ for food and clothing, $\frac{1}{6}$ for general expenses, and $\frac{3}{20}$ for miscellaneous expenses. What fractional part is left for savings? How much is allowed annually for each item?

16. If a car was driven 98 kilometers in $1\frac{3}{4}$ hours, what was its average speed?

17. How many pieces of wood each $1\frac{1}{3}$ feet long can be cut from a board 16 feet long?

18. Find the perimeter of a triangle if its sides measure $2\frac{5}{8}$ inches, $1\frac{11}{16}$ inches, and $1\frac{3}{4}$ inches.

19. Find the weight of 19 pieces of metal rod each $2\frac{1}{2}$ feet long if the rods weigh $1\frac{7}{8}$ lb. per foot.

20. Which weighs more and how much more, 3 large candy bars each weighing $8\frac{3}{4}$ oz. or 24 small ones each weighing $\frac{7}{8}$ oz.?

ESTIMATING ANSWERS

To estimate a sum, a difference, a product, or a quotient, first round the given fractions to the nearest whole numbers and the given whole numbers to convenient place values and then perform the operation or operations.

For each of the following select your nearest estimate:

1. $8\frac{7}{8} + 4\frac{1}{4}$ is approximately:	12	13	14
2. $9\frac{3}{8} - 4\frac{1}{3}$ is approximately:	4	5	6
3. $6\frac{3}{4} \times 5\frac{1}{8}$ is approximately:	30	35	40
4. $8 \div 3\frac{3}{4}$ is approximately:	3	2	4
5. $11\frac{3}{4} + 9\frac{1}{8}$ is approximately:	19	20	21
6. $\frac{2}{3}$ of 97 is approximately:	65	60	70
7. $10\frac{4}{5} - 2\frac{5}{6}$ is approximately:	8	9	10
8. $11\frac{7}{8} \div 3$ is approximately	4	5	3
9. $1\frac{1}{2} \times 6\frac{5}{6}$ is approximately:	6	8	10
10. $7\frac{9}{10} - 1\frac{1}{4}$ is approximately:	5	6	7
11. $4\frac{1}{2} + 2\frac{5}{6} + 3\frac{5}{8}$ is approximately:	9	10	11
12. $7\frac{1}{2} \div 1\frac{1}{8}$ is approximately:	7	8	6
13. $14\frac{7}{8} - 5\frac{1}{16}$ is approximately:	9	10	11
14. $\frac{9}{10}$ of 159 is approximately:	140	120	160
15. $15\frac{3}{8} + 7\frac{3}{4} + 2\frac{2}{3}$ is approximately:	28	26	24
16. $22 \div \frac{3}{4}$ is approximately:	22	24	30
17. $7\frac{1}{8} + 10\frac{2}{3} + 4\frac{1}{5}$ is approximately:	21	22	23
18. $9 - 3\frac{1}{5}$ is approximately:	4	5	6
19. $2\frac{1}{4} \div 9\frac{5}{8}$ is approximately:	4	$\frac{1}{4}$	40
20. $9\frac{7}{8} \times 4\frac{1}{5}$ is approximately:	36	40	48
21. $\frac{5}{6}$ of 608 is approximately:	500	550	600
22. $11\frac{1}{4} \div \frac{1}{2}$ is approximately:	20	24	22
23. $7\frac{4}{5} \times 3\frac{1}{8}$ is approximately:	21	25	29
24. $\frac{3}{8}$ of 475 is approximately:	160	170	180

Common Fractions 127

CHAPTER REVIEW

1. Write (8, 11) as a numeral naming a fraction. (4–1)
2. Express $\frac{56}{72}$ in lowest terms. (4–2)
3. Which of the following are not in lowest terms: $\frac{8}{19}, \frac{34}{51}, \frac{27}{75}, \frac{16}{81}$? (4–2)
4. Express $\frac{7}{12}$ as 60ths. (4–3)
5. Are $\frac{54}{90}$ and $\frac{21}{35}$ equivalent fractions? (4–4)
6. Which of the following fractions is not equivalent to the other three fractions: $\frac{14}{21}, \frac{38}{57}, \frac{18}{28}, \frac{24}{36}$? (4–4)
7. Write the group of fractions equivalent to $\frac{5}{8}$. (4–3)
8. Write the group of equivalent fractions of which $\frac{16}{20}$ is a member. (4–3)
9. Write a numeral naming: (4–5)

    a. a common fraction   **c.** a mixed number
    b. an improper fraction   **d.** a proper fraction

10. Express $\frac{39}{16}$ as a mixed number. (4–5)
11. Express $4\frac{7}{9}$ as an improper fraction. (4–5)
12. What is the lowest common denominator (LCD) of the fractions $\frac{5}{6}, \frac{5}{8}$, and $\frac{3}{4}$? (4–6)
13. Which of the following statements are true? (4–8)

    a. $\frac{3}{7} < \frac{4}{9}$ **b.** $\frac{42}{48} = \frac{54}{64}$ **c.** $\frac{7}{12} > \frac{9}{16}$ **d.** $\frac{15}{36} < \frac{11}{24}$ **e.** $\frac{24}{33} > \frac{49}{63}$

14. Arrange $\frac{2}{3}, \frac{7}{11}$, and $\frac{5}{8}$ by size, smallest first. (4–8)
15. Round $3\frac{5}{9}$ to the nearest whole number. (4–10)
16. Add: **17.** Add: (4–11)

$$4\frac{3}{5}$$

$$2\frac{1}{2}$$

$$5\frac{7}{10}$$

                               $1\frac{1}{4} + \frac{2}{3} + 3\frac{5}{6}$

18. Subtract:

$5\frac{1}{3}$

$2\frac{7}{8}$

19. Subtract: (4–12)

$12 - 6\frac{9}{16}$

20. Multiply:

$6 \times 3\frac{3}{4}$

21. Multiply: (4–13)

$8\frac{1}{3} \times \frac{4}{5} \times 1\frac{1}{2}$

22. Is the product *greater than*, *equal to*, or *less than* a given number when the given number is multiplied by: (4–13)

  a. 1?
  b. A number greater than 1?
  c. A number less than 1?

23. Write the multiplicative inverse of: **a.** 9 **b.** $\frac{1}{8}$ **c.** $\frac{11}{16}$. (4–14)

24. Divide: **25.** Divide: **26.** $\dfrac{\frac{5}{6}}{\frac{7}{12}}$ (4–15)

$15 \div 3\frac{1}{3}$ $6\frac{1}{8} \div 3\frac{1}{7}$

27. Is the quotient *greater than*, *equal to*, or *less than* a given number when the given number is divided by: (4–15)

  a. 1?
  b. A number greater than 1?
  c. A number less than 1 (zero excluded)?

28. Find $\frac{3}{8}$ of 75. (4–16)

29. What part of 90 is 54? (4–17)

30. $\frac{7}{12}$ of what number is 56? (4–18)

REVIEW EXERCISES

1. Add:

968	2,597	89,628	82,165	34,079
4,592	8,465	35,977	25,997	88,926
89	3,879	2,849	34,458	81,798
1,649	5,983	93,626	47,429	96,654
7,287	2,654	8,705	93,976	57,973

2. Subtract:

8,591	38,654	48,265	697,000	821,062
6,846	729	9,897	498,915	368,798

3. Multiply:

46	593	608	957	8,529
89	64	700	986	731

4. Divide:

$42\overline{)2,814}$ $85\overline{)81,005}$ $761\overline{)660,548}$ $309\overline{)279,954}$ $2,240\overline{)860,160}$

5. Add:

$\dfrac{3}{16}$ $1\dfrac{1}{4}$ $4\dfrac{11}{12}$ $3\dfrac{7}{8}$ $6\dfrac{5}{6}$

$\dfrac{3}{4}$ $\dfrac{2}{3}$ $2\dfrac{5}{12}$ $5\dfrac{1}{2}$ $1\dfrac{3}{8}$

6. Subtract:

$\dfrac{5}{8}$ $6\dfrac{13}{16}$ $1\dfrac{3}{4}$ $7\dfrac{1}{2}$ $5\dfrac{7}{10}$

$\dfrac{1}{3}$ $2\dfrac{5}{16}$ $\dfrac{7}{8}$ $1\dfrac{2}{3}$ $4\dfrac{1}{6}$

7. Multiply:

$\dfrac{3}{4} \times \dfrac{5}{6}$ $5\dfrac{1}{2} \times 8$ $\dfrac{7}{12} \times 4\dfrac{2}{3}$ $2\dfrac{5}{8} \times 3\dfrac{1}{7}$ $3\dfrac{1}{3} \times 1\dfrac{3}{5}$

8. Divide:

$\dfrac{7}{8} \div \dfrac{1}{4}$ $4\dfrac{1}{2} \div \dfrac{5}{16}$ $9 \div 2\dfrac{3}{4}$ $3\dfrac{3}{16} \div 5\dfrac{2}{3}$ $4\dfrac{5}{6} \div 1\dfrac{1}{5}$

ACHIEVEMENT TEST

1. Write 83 trillion as a complete numeral. (1–9)
2. Round 835,482,503,069 to the nearest billion. (1–10)
3. Write MCMLXIX as a decimal numeral. (1–14)
4. What is the greatest common factor of 27, 81, and 108? (1–21)
5. Factor 360 as the product of prime factors. (1–19)
6. What is the least common multiple of 40, 64, and 80? (1–24)
7. Find the missing numbers: (2–2 to 2–5)

   a. $1\frac{1}{2} + \frac{7}{8} = ? + 1\frac{1}{2}$ d. $\left(\frac{2}{3} \times \frac{5}{6}\right) \times \frac{7}{8} = ? \times \left(\frac{5}{6} \times \frac{7}{8}\right)$

   b. $\left(\frac{4}{5} \times 9\right) \div 9 = \square$ e. $\left(2\frac{1}{4} + \frac{1}{8}\right) + ? = 2\frac{1}{4} + \left(\frac{1}{8} + \frac{9}{10}\right)$

   c. $\frac{3}{4} \times 6 = 6 \times ?$ f. $\frac{1}{2} \times \left(\frac{3}{4} + \frac{1}{4}\right) = ? \times \frac{3}{4} + ? \times \frac{1}{4}$

8. Is the group of all odd natural numbers closed under addition?
   Multiplication? (2–6)

9. Add: 10. Subtract: 11. Multiply: (2–9 to 2–11)

   43,938   400,703   4,908
   95,677   906   5,007
   29,856
   86,969
   91,238

12. Square each of the following numbers: (2–13)

    a. 73
    b. 209

13. Divide: 14. Divide: (2–16)

    918)451,656   1,058)313,168

15. Is 635,000 divisible by 4? by 2? by 8? by 10? by 5? (2–17)
16. Write in words each of the following: (3–1)

    a. $15 > 10$ c. $5 - 5 < 5 \div 5$
    b. $8 \times 5 > 45$ d. $9 \neq 5 + 3$

17. Complete by using the transitive property: $\hspace{2cm}$ (3–2)

$\quad$ **a.** $9 > 5$ and $5 > 3$, then $9 > ?$

$\quad$ **b.** $2^4 < 5^2$ and $5^2 < 3^3$, then $2^4 < ?$

18. Express $\frac{108}{144}$ in lowest terms. $\hspace{3cm}$ (4–8)

19. Express $\frac{3}{5}$ as 40ths. $\hspace{4cm}$ (4–3)

20. Write the group of equivalent fractions of which $\frac{28}{49}$ is a member. $\hspace{6cm}$ (4–3)

21. Which of the following statements are true? $\hspace{1.5cm}$ (4–8)

$\quad$ **a.** $\frac{3}{4} < \frac{5}{8}$ $\hspace{2cm}$ **c.** $\frac{26}{29} = \frac{32}{48}$ $\hspace{2cm}$ **e.** $\frac{11}{23} < \frac{3}{7}$

$\quad$ **b.** $\frac{7}{12} > \frac{6}{11}$ $\hspace{2cm}$ **d.** $\frac{8}{13} < \frac{9}{15}$

22. Arrange $\frac{1}{3}$, $\frac{2}{5}$, and $\frac{3}{8}$ by size, greatest first. $\hspace{1.5cm}$ (4–8)

23. Add: $\hspace{1.5cm}$ **24.** Subtract: $\hspace{1.5cm}$ **25.** Multiply: (4–11 to 4–13)

$\quad 4\frac{5}{6}$ $\hspace{2.5cm}$ $11 - 5\frac{3}{8}$ $\hspace{2.5cm}$ $5\frac{1}{3} \times 4\frac{5}{8}$

$\quad 9\frac{3}{4}$

$\quad 2\frac{1}{2}$

$\quad \overline{\hspace{1.5cm}}$

26. Write the multiplicative inverse of: $\hspace{2cm}$ (4–14)

$\quad$ **a.** 6

$\quad$ **b.** $\frac{1}{2}$

$\quad$ **c.** $\frac{5}{8}$

27. Divide: $\hspace{5cm}$ (4–15)

$\quad 3\frac{3}{4} \div \frac{4}{5}$

28. Find $\frac{5}{16}$ of 128. $\hspace{4cm}$ (4–16)

29. What part of 84 is 63? $\hspace{3cm}$ (4–17)

30. $\frac{9}{10}$ of what number is 153? $\hspace{2.5cm}$ (4–18)

CHAPTER 5
Decimal Fractions

5–1 PLACE VALUE

On the decimal number scale each place has one tenth the value of the next place to the left. By extending the scale to the right of the ones place, we express parts of one. When one whole unit is divided into ten (10) equal parts, the size of each equal part is one tenth $\left(\frac{1}{10}\right)$.

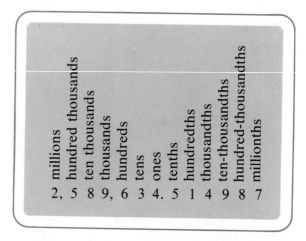

Following the arrangement that each place has one tenth the value of the next place to the left, we express $\frac{1}{10}$ of one whole unit on the number scale by using the next place on the right of the ones place. This place is called "tenths." To separate the whole number from the parts or fraction we use a dot which is called a "decimal point." Thus the numeral for the common fraction $\frac{1}{10}$ and the numeral for the decimal fraction .1 name the same number. Both represent the size of one of the equal parts when a whole unit is divided into 10 equal parts.

$\frac{1}{10}$	$\frac{1}{10}$	$\frac{1}{10}$	$\frac{1}{10}$	$\frac{1}{10}$	$\frac{1}{10}$	$\frac{1}{10}$	$\frac{1}{10}$	$\frac{1}{10}$	$\frac{1}{10}$
.1	.1	.1	.1	.1	.1	.1	.1	.1	.1

When a whole unit is divided into 100 equal parts, the size of each equal part is $\frac{1}{100}$. Since each place on the number scale has one tenth the value of the next place to the left, the second place to the right of the decimal point has $\frac{1}{10}$ the value of tenths. But $\frac{1}{10}$ of a tenth is one hundredth $\left(\frac{1}{10} \times \frac{1}{10} = \frac{1}{100}\right)$. Therefore, the value of the second place to the right of the decimal point is "hundredths." Both $\frac{1}{100}$ and .01 name the same number.

The third place to the right of the decimal point expresses thousandths $\left(.001 = \frac{1}{1000}\right)$, the fourth place expresses ten-thousandths $\left(.0001 = \frac{1}{10,000}\right)$, the fifth place expresses hundred-thousandths $\left(.00001 = \frac{1}{100,000}\right)$, the sixth place expresses millionths $\left(.000001 = \frac{1}{1,000,000}\right)$, etc.

A *decimal fraction* is a fractional number having as its denominator some power of ten (10; 100; 1,000; etc.) and is named by a numeral in which the denominator is not written as it is in a common fraction but is expressed by place value. Only numerators appear in decimal notation.

A *mixed decimal* is a number containing a whole number and a decimal fraction. The numeral in the scale on the opposite page names a mixed decimal.

Since multiples of one are expressed in the places to the left of the ones place and parts of one are expressed in the places to the right of the ones place, the ones place is the center of the numeration system and not the decimal point.

The word "decimal" is derived from the Latin word "decem" meaning ten. Our money system is a decimal system. 10 mills = 1 cent ($.01); 10 cents = 1 dime ($.10); 10 dimes = 1 dollar ($1.00 or $1).

EXERCISES

1. Write each of the following as a decimal numeral:

a. $\frac{3}{10}$, $\frac{7}{10}$, $\frac{8}{10}$, $\frac{1}{10}$, $\frac{9}{10}$

b. $\frac{25}{100}$, $\frac{9}{100}$, $\frac{87}{100}$, $\frac{60}{100}$, $\frac{43}{100}$

c. $\frac{563}{1000}$, $\frac{71}{1000}$, $\frac{4}{1000}$, $\frac{350}{1000}$, $\frac{400}{1000}$

2. Write the decimal numeral that corresponds to the shaded part of each of the following:

a. 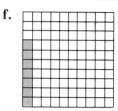   b. 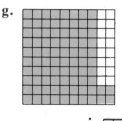   c.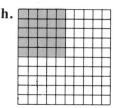

d. 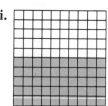   e.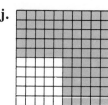

f.   g.   h.

i.   j.

3. The last digit on the right in the following odometer readings registers tenths of a mile. Write the mileage indicated by these readings using decimal numerals.

| 1 | 2 | 6 | 5 | 8 | 3 | | 2 | 4 | 5 | 0 | 3 | 7 | | 4 | 7 | 0 | 9 | 6 | 4 |

| 3 | 9 | 4 | 8 | 9 | 9 | | 5 | 0 | 0 | 2 | 0 | 8 |

4. Some rulers have each inch subdivided into tenths of an inch. Write as decimal numerals the measurements indicated by A, B, C, D, E, F, G, and H.

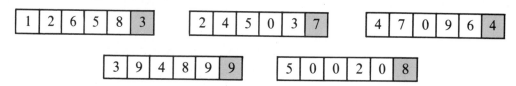

5. Find the missing values:

   a.   .25 = __ tenths ____ hundredths or ____ hundredths.
   b.   .08 = __ tenths ____ hundredths or ____ hundredths.

c. .746 = __ tenths ____ hundredths _____ thousandths or
_____ thousandths.

d. .590 = __ tenths ____ hundredths _____ thousandths or
_____ thousandths or ____ hundredths.

e. .204 = __ tenths ____ hundredths _____ thousandths or
_____ thousandths.

6. In the metric system of measurement, 10 millimeters (mm) =
   1 centimeter (cm). Write each of the following measurements
   as a decimal numeral in terms of centimeters:

   a. 2 mm, 7 mm, 5 mm, 9 mm, 1 mm
   b. 14 mm, 21 mm, 39 mm, 43 mm, 17 mm

7. Express each of the following as a decimal numeral:

   a. 3 dimes   **c.** 8 dimes 4 pennies   **e.** 9 dollars 6 dimes 7 pennies
   b. 6 pennies   **d.** 4 dollars 5 dimes   **f.** 5 dollars 9 dimes 2 pennies

8. Write each of the following as a decimal numeral:

   a. $\frac{17}{10}$, $\frac{36}{10}$, $\frac{278}{100}$, $\frac{906}{100}$, $\frac{1254}{1000}$ **b.** $\frac{10}{10}$, $\frac{100}{100}$, $\frac{1000}{1000}$, $\frac{20}{10}$, $\frac{300}{100}$

9. Change each of the following to:

   Tenths   Hundredths   Thousandths
   a. .60, .20, .30, .80   **a.** .7, .9, .4, .1, .5   **a.** .4, .1, .6, .8, .3
   b. .700, .800, .400, .600   **b.** .500, .800, .100, .300   **b.** .90, .50, .60, .20, .80
   c. 5, 9, 6, 3, 8   **c.** 1, 6, 3, 9, 4   **c.** 2, 8, 1, 7, 6

10. Write the decimal numeral that represents each of the follow-
    ing:

    a. 4 tenths 5 hundredths
    b. 9 tenths 0 hundredths 4 thousandths
    c. 0 tenths 0 hundredths 8 thousandths 7 hundred-thousandths
    d. 3 ones 2 tenths
    e. 6 hundreds 9 tens 0 ones 5 tenths 1 hundredth

11. What decimal corresponds to point *A*? *B*? *C*? *D*? *E*? *F*? *G*? *H*?

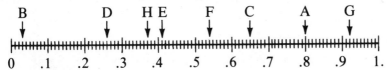

5–2 READING NUMERALS NAMING DECIMAL FRACTIONS

To read a numeral naming a decimal fraction, we read the numeral to the right of the decimal point as we would a numeral for a whole number and use the name that applies to the place value of the last digit on the right. The numeral may have a zero written in the one place just preceding the decimal point.

> .497 or 0.497 is read:
> Four hundred ninety-seven thousandths.

To read a numeral naming a mixed decimal, we first read the numeral for the whole number to the left of the decimal point, then the numeral for the decimal fraction, using the word "and" to mark the position of the decimal point.

> 16.52 is read:
> Sixteen *and* fifty-two hundredths.

EXERCISES

Read, or write in words, each of the following:

1. **a.** .6; .8; .1; .4; .9   **b.** 0.5; 0.2; 0.7; 0.3; 0.6
2. **a.** .04; .07; .02; .08; 0.01   **b.** .37; 0.19; .70; 0.46; .85
3. **a.** 3.5; 8.2; 16.7; 79.3; 210.8   **b.** 1.42; 5.09; 24.75; 98.16; 356.64
4. **a.** .003; .006; 0.004; .008; .005   **c.** .375; 0.667; .908; .625; .132
   b. .017; .082; 0.054; .090; 0.025   **d.** 2.016; 9.503; 14.281; 56.875; 400.064
5. **a.** .0004; .0097; .8603; 0.9375; 9.0841
   b. .00005; 0.04173; .15625; 1.00048; 3.84129
   c. .000007; .050932; 0.998998; 4.000533; 4.000533; 8.014006

5–3 WRITING NUMERALS NAMING DECIMAL FRACTIONS

To write a numeral naming a decimal fraction, we write the digits as we do a numeral naming a whole number and prefix it with a decimal point so that the name of the part corresponds to the place value of the last digit. We insert (prefix) as many zeros as are required between the decimal point and the first digit when it is necessary to make the name of the part and the place value of the last digit correspond.

> Thirty-six thousandths is written as .036 or 0.036

To write a numeral naming a mixed decimal, we first write the numeral for the whole number followed by a decimal point (to indicate the word "and" and to separate the numeral for the whole number from the numeral for the decimal fraction), then we write the numeral naming the decimal fraction.

> One hundred and five tenths is written as 100.5

EXERCISES

Write each of the following as a decimal fraction or mixed decimal:

1. **a.** Seven tenths; five tenths; one tenth
   b. Two and three tenths; three hundred forty-nine and two tenths
2. **a.** Three hundredths; ninety-six hundredths; forty hundredths
   b. One and seven hundredths; twelve and fourteen hundredths; six hundred and fifty-one hundredths
3. **a.** Eight and four thousandths; three hundred and eighteen thousandths; one hundred forty and three hundred sixty-two thousandths
4. **a.** Ninety-seven ten-thousandths; two hundred-thousandths; eighty thousand twenty-four millionths
   b. Four and five ten-thousandths; sixty and thirty-seven millionths; forty-nine and four thousand eight hundred seventy-six hundred-thousandths

5–4 WRITING DECIMALS AS POLYNOMIALS— EXPANDED NOTATION

The value of each place in a decimal numeral may be expressed as a power of ten.

$\frac{1}{10}$ may be written as $\frac{1}{10^1}$; $\frac{1}{100}$ as $\frac{1}{10 \times 10}$ or $\frac{1}{10^2}$;

$\frac{1}{1,000}$ as $\frac{1}{10 \times 10 \times 10} = \frac{1}{10^3}$;

$\frac{1}{10,000}$ as $\frac{1}{10 \times 10 \times 10 \times 10}$ or $\frac{1}{10^4}$; etc.

It can be shown that $\frac{1}{10} = 10^{-1}$; $\frac{1}{10^2} = 10^{-2}$;

$\frac{1}{10^3} = 10^{-3}$; $\frac{1}{10^4} = 10^{-4}$; etc. and that $10^0 = 1$.

A decimal numeral may be expressed as the sum of the products of each digit in the numeral and its place value expressed as a power of ten.

$.4358 = 4$ tenths $+ 3$ hundredths $+ 5$ thousandths $+ 8$ ten-thousandths

$$= 4 \times \frac{1}{10} + 3 \times \frac{1}{100} + 5 \times \frac{1}{1,000} + 8 \times \frac{1}{10,000}$$

$$= 4 \times \frac{1}{10^1} + 3 \times \frac{1}{10^2} + 5 \times \frac{1}{10^3} + 8 \times \frac{1}{10^4}$$

$$= (4 \times 10^{-1}) + (3 \times 10^{-2}) + (5 \times 10^{-3}) + (8 \times 10^{-4})$$

The numeral 532.896 is written in expanded form as:
$$(5 \times 10^2) + (3 \times 10^1) + (2 \times 10^0) + (8 \times 10^{-1}) + (9 \times 10^{-2}) + (6 \times 10^{-3})$$

Observe that the place values are powers of ten arranged in a decreasing order from left to right.

1. Express each of the following as a decimal numeral:

   a. $(6 \times 10^{-1}) + (4 \times 10^{-2}) + (9 \times 10^{-3})$
   b. $(4 \times 10^{-1}) + (5 \times 10^{-2}) + (8 \times 10^{-3}) + (7 \times 10^{-4})$
   c. $(3 \times 10^2) + (5 \times 10^1) + (6 \times 10^0) + (2 \times 10^{-1}) + (4 \times 10^{-2})$
   d. $(2 \times 10^4) + (8 \times 10^3) + (0 \times 10^2) + (5 \times 10^1) + (9 \times 10^0) + (7 \times 10^{-1}) +$
   $\quad (6 \times 10^{-2}) + (1 \times 10^{-3})$

2. Write each of the following numerals in expanded form as a polynomial:

a. .75	**c.** 0.6041	**e.** 4.7	**g.** 517.26	**i.** 1,256.38
b. .832	**d.** .34952	**f.** 28.39	**h.** 805.934	**j.** 6,492.973

5–5 ROUNDING DECIMALS

Often there is need both in measurement and in money situations for rounding decimals.

To round a decimal, we find the place to which the number is to be rounded, rewriting the given digits to the left of the required place and dropping all the digits to the right of the required place. If the first digit dropped is 5 or more, we increase the given digit in the required place by 1; otherwise, we write the same digit as given. However, as many digits to the left are changed as necessary when the given digit in the required place is 9 and one (1) is added.

.32 rounded to the nearest tenth is .3 because .32 is closer to .30 than it is to .40. Note that .3 and .30 are names for the same number.

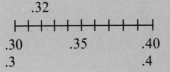

.807 rounded to the nearest hundredth is .81 because .807 is closer to .810 than it is to .800. Note that .81 and .810 are names for the same number.

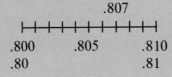

1. Select the numbers that are nearer to:

a. .5 than .6	.52	.57	.54	.59	.58
b. 0.1 than 0.2	0.16	0.13	0.19	0.11	0.17
c. .87 than .88	.871	.878	.874	.873	.879
d. .90 than .91	.903	.906	.904	.907	.901
e. .246 than .247	.2468	.2460	.2466	.2463	.2467
f. 8 than 9	8.2	8.709	8.49	8.51	8.634

2. Any number from:

   a. .35 to .44 rounded to the nearest tenth is what number?

   b. .615 to .624 rounded to the nearest hundredth is what number?

   c. .8275 to .8284 rounded to the nearest thousandth is what number?

   d. 13.5 to 14.4 rounded to the nearest whole number is what number?

3. Round each of the following numbers to the nearest:

a. Tenth:	0.56	1.42	6.93	4.07	23.25
	.47	.86	0.745	2.33	5.962
b. Hundredth:	0.619	6.544	14.238	23.6253	9.4709
	.936	.693	0.1925	7.395	16.0694
c. Thousandth:	.1728	4.8273	9.1065	56.83945	18.0507
	0.4362	0.0546	.38526	9.4384	48.19688
d. Ten-thousandth:	.31625	0.49353	7.54196	13.680506	6.58927
e. Hundred-thousandth:	.000047	.000382	0.050604	1.350365	4.0906096
f. Millionth:	0.0000084	.0093255	.0000049	1.0384563	2.1938427
g. Whole number:	4.6	11.4	29.16	8.09	99.501
	41.3	9.81	64.56	4.475	1.399

4. When required to find an amount correct to the nearest cent or nearest dollar, we follow the same procedure as with decimals. When the amount contains a fractional part of a cent, we drop the fraction but add one cent when the fraction is $\frac{1}{2}$ or more.

   > $1.574 rounded to nearest cent is $1.57
   >
   > $.68$\frac{3}{4}$ rounded to nearest cent is $.69

Round each of the following amounts to the nearest:

a. Cent: $.582 $.098 $1.264 $29.807 $7.5962

             $.48$\frac{1}{2}$ $.56$\frac{2}{5}$ 8.18\frac{2}{3}$ 5.47\frac{3}{8}$ 36.53\frac{5}{6}$

             $.354 $.079 1.45\frac{3}{5}$ 82.86\frac{5}{12}$ $34.0649

b. Dollar: $3.48 $2.37 $8.69 $75.18 $237.75

             $5.25 $9.82 $57.49 $66.98 $540.87

5–6 COMPARING DECIMALS

When necessary, we express the given numbers as numerals containing the same number of decimal places and take the greater number as the greater decimal.

> Which is greater .6 or .58?
>
> .6 = .60
> .58 = .58
>
> *Answer,* .6 is greater.

A mixed decimal or whole number is greater than a decimal fraction.

EXERCISES

1. Which is greater:

  a. .4 or .39?   **d.** .249 or .25?   **g.** .195 or .1949?   **j.** 2.45 or .253?
  b. .72 or .597?   **e.** 3.8 or .38?   **h.** 1.68 or .307?   **k.** 5.009 or 5.0101?
  c. .9 or .084?   **f.** .862 or 8.42?   **i.** 7.921 or 7.9209?   **l.** .06 or .009?

2. Which is smaller:

  a. .3 or .31?   **d.** .8 or .799?   **g.** 4.3 or 4.29?   **j.** 5.0846 or 5.08461?
  b. .60 or .06?   **e.** .0073 or .008?   **h.** 7.99 or 8.3?   **k.** 3.8 or .39?
  c. .48 or .5?   **f.** 6.92 or .692?   **i.** 3.67 or 3.067?   **l.** .989 or .9889?

Arrange the following numbers according to size, writing the numeral for:

3. Greatest number first:

    a. 5.93, 59.7, .598, .0599
    b. .07, .007, .7, .0007
    c. 4.78, .0978, .529, .6
    d. 1.5, .03, .069, .19
    e. 2.02, 1.989, 1.9895, 2.009

4. Smallest number first:

    a. 8.5, 85, .85, .085
    b. .78, .933, 6.84, .6841
    c. 9.06, .91, .9059, 8.95
    d. .34, .342, .3401, .3398
    e. 1.03, 0.998, 0.9989, 1.016

5. Which of the following are true statements?

    a. .14 < .2   **c.** .9 = 0.9   **e.** .048 > .05   **g.** .299 < .3   **i.** .0004 > .039
    b. .80 > .8   **d.** 3.4 < .34   **f.** .238 < .2381   **h.** 16.5 = 1.65   **j.** .999 < 1

5–7 COMPUTATION— ADDITION OF DECIMALS

Since $.5 = \frac{5}{10}$ and $.3 = \frac{3}{10}$, then $.5 + .3$ and $\frac{5}{10} + \frac{3}{10}$ both name the same number, *eight tenths.*

Decimal Fraction:	Common Fraction:
$.5$	$\frac{5}{10}$
$+.3$	$+\frac{3}{10}$
$.8$	$\frac{8}{10}$

To add decimals:

When it is necessary to write the numerals in columns, we write each addend so that the decimal points are under each other. Zeros may be annexed to the numerals naming decimal fractions so that the addends have the same number of decimal places.

Then we add as in the addition of whole numbers, placing the decimal point in the sum directly under the decimal points in the addends.

When an answer ends in one or more zeros to the right of the decimal point, the zeros may be dropped unless it is necessary to show the exact degree of measurement. We check by adding the columns in the opposite direction.

Add: Add:

6.8 + .47   .26
                               .19
  6.80   .35
   .47   .80 = .8
 ─────   ─────
  7.27

Answer, 7.27   *Answer, .8*

EXERCISES

1. Use this section of the metric ruler to find the sum of each of the
following:

| 0.3 cm | 0.1 cm | 0.4 cm | 6.2 cm | 2.4 cm | 2.8 cm | 0.7 cm | 3.5 cm |
| 0.2 cm | 0.8 cm | 0.6 cm | 1.5 cm | 0.9 cm | 3.6 cm | 5.9 cm | 4.5 cm |

2. In each of the following first add the common fractions or mixed
numbers, then the decimals. Compare answers.

a. $\frac{1}{10}$ .1   **b.** $\frac{24}{100}$ .24   **c.** $2\frac{7}{10}$ 2.7

$+\frac{2}{10}$ $+.2$ $+\frac{19}{100}$ $+.19$ $+3\frac{51}{100}$ $+3.51$

3. Add:

a.   .2   0.5   .09   .25   3.05   1.2   .48
         .4   0.7   .03   .82   4.09   .9   7.
         .1   0.8   .06   .53   1.06   .36   .6

b.   .9   .34   .98   9.23   1.4   8.403   43.28
         .6   .17   .31   8.42   .82   6.248   36.93
         .7   .46   .42   9.71   3.57   1.352   59.84
         .6   .08   .59   2.83   .6   7.189   20.87

Decimal Fractions   145

c.	.3	.06	8.3	4.47	6.527	.5684	491.32
	.8	.47	9.8	9.06	2.157	.9748	322.85
	.6	.57	3.5	1.59	3.008	.5327	403.26
	.5	.28	2.7	3.85	1.282	.7046	915.83
	.7	.15	4.8	5.23	5.309	.8195	226.06

d.	0.9	.53	6.4	.3	85.09	.16928	812.97
	0.3	.68	9.5	4.91	19.44	.51107	966.32
	0.4	.71	2.8	2.	6.84	.2355	801.49
	0.7	.27	4.6	.524	27.75	.83214	602.33
	0.5	.54	2.5	3.14	46.81	.5030	579.25
	0.6	.98	8.2	.32	.96	.17159	914.08

e.	$.96	$1.75	$83.25	$129.75	$ 2.64	$ 54.03	$806.57
	.88	.56	96.71	7.46	14.79	39.29	7.62
	.09	3.19	9.48	11.09	.59	615.86	95.26
	.76	4.79	.56	347.85	6.08	49.63	136.48
	.97	.16	91.43	2.17	548.67	263.52	345.03

f.	$.38	$9.84	$23.37	$445.76	$616.35	$520.88	$268.31
	.85	3.68	9.75	386.07	897.42	17.46	985.67
	.92	4.25	8.99	91.50	58.09	391.50	29.35
	.79	9.93	54.78	9.86	145.27	69.21	840.58
	.08	5.88	3.26	407.96	9.69	458.68	706.43
	.53	4.26	75.58	85.67	207.34	6.74	149.99

4. Add as indicated:

a. .6 + .2
.07 + 1.3
4.9 + 3.7
18 + .25
.34 + .8

b. 1.84 + 9
.1 + .059
6 + .04
.951 + .24
1.408 + .27

c. .47 + .52 + .85
.35 + 4.2 + 91
2.54 + 83.5 + .927
.005 + .05 + .5
.106 + .9 + .23

d. .35 + .7
.08 + 1.2
9.6 + .58
.4 + .05
.19 + 3

e. 2.84 + .45
1.6 + .397
7.32 + .3
54.9 + .518
40.2 + 8.65

f. 4.23 + .75 + .386
1.69 + .582 + 60.7
85.5 + 9.14 + 208
.756 + .82 + .5
.07 + .017 + .7

g. $.26 + $.57 + $.84
$32.75 + $22.94 + $87.63
$.63 + $5.67 + $23.75
$9.99 + $3.48 + $17.06
$28.85 + $10.39 + $63.97

h. $.86 + $5.28 + $.63
$4.49 + $3.87 + $51.29
$.28 + $15.61 + $7.86
$6.79 + $23.75 + $.57
$50.32 + $84.09 + $65.48

5–8 COMPUTATION—
SUBTRACTION OF DECIMALS

Since $.36 = \frac{36}{100}$ and $.15 = \frac{15}{100}$, then $.36 - .15$ and $\frac{36}{100} - \frac{15}{100}$ both name the same number, twenty-one hundredths.

Decimal Fraction:	Common Fraction:
$.36$	$\frac{36}{100}$
$-.15$	$-\frac{15}{100}$
$.21$	$\frac{21}{100}$

To subtract decimals:

When it is necessary to write the numerals, we write the subtrahend under the minuend so that the decimal points are directly under each other. Zeros may be annexed to the decimal fraction or a decimal point and zeros to a whole number in the minuend so that the minuend and subtrahend will have the same number of decimal places.

We subtract as in the subtraction of whole numbers, placing the decimal point in the remainder (or difference) directly under the decimal points of the subtrahend and minuend. When an answer ends in one or more zeros to the right of the decimal point, the zeros may be dropped unless it is necessary to show the exact degree of measurement. We check by adding the remainder to the subtrahend. Their sum should equal the minuend.

Subtract:

$.56 - .47$	$25 - 1.64$	$25.83 - 6.73$
$.56$	25.00	25.83
$.47$	1.64	6.73
$.09$	23.36	$19.10 = 19.1$

Answer, .09   *Answer, 23.36*   *Answer, 19.1*

1. Subtract, using the section of the metric ruler on page 145.

0.9 cm	0.8 cm	1.0 cm	3.5 cm
−0.2 cm	−0.3 cm	−0.8 cm	−3.1 cm

7.2 cm	4.0 cm	8.7 cm	6.3 cm
−4.9 cm	−2.5 cm	−7.8 cm	−0.7 cm

2. In each of the following first subtract the common fractions or mixed number, then the decimals. Compare answers.

a. $\frac{7}{10}$ .7   b. $8\frac{3}{10}$ 8.3   c. $4\frac{9}{10}$ 4.9

$-\frac{4}{10}$ −.4 $-3\frac{6}{10}$ −3.6 $-1\frac{53}{100}$ −1.53

3. Subtract:

a.

.8	.37	0.84	.09	8.7	9.2	6.1	5.4	.75	.62	8.7	0.15
.5	.14	0.29	.03	1.2	3.8	4.7	1.9	.68	.22	3.7	0.12

b.

.28	.36	9.4	.432	5.17	.416	.604	53.5	86.54	65.1
.08	.29	8.4	.257	1.69	.387	.066	8.2	43.95	7.4

c.

4.026	.9685	56.17	8.523	0.9608	4.43	.59325	.8624
1.548	.7949	27.89	6.681	0.1599	3.55	.28963	.8619

d.

397.26	61.864	.05693	805.41	9.4257	5.000	8.0000
178.79	53.879	.05598	319.87	2.4248	3.817	6.0593

e.

9.47	0.3	8.	4.1	.05	5.8	7.	1.032
.6	0.154	2.68	.39	.0485	.704	3.002	.28

f.

$6.35	$2.08	$50.00	$58.15	$248.31	$643.06	$300.00	$4,000.00
4.67	.59	27.36	49.65	209.54	88.97	149.60	2,708.21

4. Subtract as indicated:

a. .51 − .27
.048 − .039
.207 − .087
.4100 − .3608
8.038 − 4.168

b. .64 − .6
.845 − .84
.407 − .38
.36 − .178
.005 − .0001

c. 5.8 − .32
9 − .625
2 − 1.964
3 − .002
8.81 − 1.9009

d. $.70 − $.56
$8.32 − $4.63
$19.60 − $6.85
$22.86 − $19.57
$118.50 − $23.76

e. $3.82 − $.95
$7.50 − $.75
$9.69 − $2
$106.23 − $99
$6.05 − $.87

f. $5 − $.62
$10 − $.74
$4 − $1.25
$9 − $3.06
$7 − $5.91

g. Subtract .67 from .8
Take $.43 from $5

From .071 take .06
From $6.80 subtract $5

Subtract 2.125 from 3
From $3.17 take $.98

5–9 COMPUTATION— MULTIPLICATION OF DECIMALS

The product of the common fractions $\frac{3}{10}$ and $\frac{7}{10}$ is $\frac{21}{100}$.

Decimally this is written

$$.3 \times .7 = .21$$

The product of $\frac{2}{10}$ and $\frac{4}{100}$ is $\frac{8}{1000}$.

Decimally this is written

$$.2 \times .04 = .008$$

Observe that the number of decimal places in the product is equal to the sum of the number of decimal places in the factors.

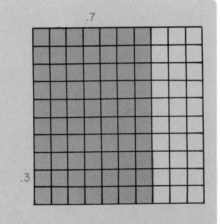

Each square = .01

.7 of the large square is shaded. .3 of the shaded squares are shaded □. A count of the squares shaded □ illustrates that .3 × .7 = .21

To multiply decimals:

We write the given numerals and multiply as in the multiplication of whole numbers. The decimal point in one factor does not necessarily have to be directly under the decimal point in the second factor. We point off in the product, counting from right to

Decimal Fractions

left, as many decimal places as there are in *both* factors together. When the product contains fewer digits than the required number of decimal places, we prefix as many zeros as are necessary.

When a decimal answer ends in one or more zeros to the right of the decimal point, the zeros may be dropped unless it is necessary to show the exact degree of measurement. We check by interchanging the two factors and multiplying again.

Multiply:	Multiply:
.6	.14
.3	0.5
.18	.070 = .07
Answer, .18	*Answer,* .07
Multiply:	Multiply:
.04	2.3
.02	.005
.0008	.0115
Answer, .0008	*Answer,* .0115

EXERCISES

1. In each of the following first multiply the common fractions or mixed numbers, then multiply the decimals. Compare answers.

   a. $\frac{4}{10} \times \frac{9}{10}$ b. $\frac{5}{10} \times \frac{6}{10}$ c. $\frac{8}{10} \times \frac{3}{100}$ d. $\frac{19}{100} \times \frac{47}{100}$ e. $3\frac{1}{10} \times 1\frac{7}{10}$

$$\begin{array}{r} .4 \\ \times .9 \\ \hline \end{array} \qquad \begin{array}{r} .5 \\ \times .6 \\ \hline \end{array} \qquad \begin{array}{r} .8 \\ \times .03 \\ \hline \end{array} \qquad \begin{array}{r} .19 \\ \times .47 \\ \hline \end{array} \qquad \begin{array}{r} 3.1 \\ \times 1.7 \\ \hline \end{array}$$

2. Multiply:

   a.
.2	3	8	.6	24	.4	9.5	100	0.5	144
3	.3	.9	5	0.7	90	56	.6	35	.8

   b.
.12	.29	9	.07	3.14	.165	25	.0105	800	6.0075
6	81	.01	15	6	910	.008	45	.0003	40

c.	.4	0.3	.4	.29	.13	.1	.925	.2063	8.92	9.7
	.6	0.2	.5	.7	.6	.09	0.8	.4	.7	3.8

d.	3.87	4.91	.05	7.28	10.54	2.693	4.107	9.0681	6.823	1.0509
	.5	.6	8.2	5.8	3.9	0.5	8.6	2.8	.4	2.7

e.	.46	.32	.14	.01	.8	.068	.004	12.75	2.03	.006
	.53	.33	.07	.01	.50	.75	.02	.06	2.03	.09

f.	3.8	4.7	0.5	9.3	15.6	3.084	5.469	6.318	.007	2.9051
	.25	.39	1.75	.87	2.76	0.12	.04	5.16	7.83	12.06

g.	.587	.008	.116	0.6	14.75	7.004	.0028	1.875
	.625	.014	.129	3.849	2.125	.1055	1.529	1.875

h.	.3937	3.1416	1.0936	.6214	478.3	50.75	6.4516	4.875
	0.9	8.5	20.4	.93	.7646	.9144	800.9	2.2046

i.	.003	29.8	.01	84.96	3.005	93.04	462.50	798.36
	.3	7.68	.0009	2.172	540	26.7	.875	.0585

3. In examples involving money, find products correct to nearest cent:

a.	$.87	$6.59	$18.25	$208.40	$856	$9,000	$328.20
	12	60	.03	.29	.625	.045	.007

b.	$20	$4,000	$5.26	$.95	$280	$69.25	$57.90
	$.37\frac{1}{2}$	$.05\frac{1}{2}$	$.66\frac{2}{3}$	$.83\frac{1}{3}$	$.04\frac{3}{4}$	$.03\frac{1}{4}$	$.16\frac{2}{3}$

4. Multiply as indicated:

a. .6 × .4   b. $\frac{1}{2}$ × $.78   c. $\frac{1}{2}$ × $.59   d. .75 × $4

8 × .005 $\frac{3}{4}$ × $.92 $\frac{5}{6}$ × $3.45   .6 × $.50

14 × .03 $\frac{7}{8}$ × $1.52 $\frac{2}{3}$ × $38   .02 × $8

.07 × 20 $1\frac{2}{3}$ × $10.47 $2\frac{3}{4}$ × $10.50 $.87\frac{1}{2}$ × $24

.01 × .018 $1\frac{5}{12}$ × $4.08 $3\frac{5}{8}$ × $7.31   .04 × $9.50

5. Square each of the following:

a. .3	c. .02	e. .48	g. 3.14	i. 73.8	k. 39.37
b. .9	d. .001	f. 2.37	h. .989	j. 15.26	l. 3.2808

5–10 MULTIPLYING BY POWERS OF TEN

To multiply a decimal by 10; 100; 1,000 or larger powers of ten quickly, we first write the digits of the given numeral, then we move the decimal point as many places to the right of the original position as there are zeros in the given multiplier. Where the product requires them, we use zeros as placeholders.

$$10 \times 4.82 = 48.2$$
$$100 \times .06 = 6$$
$$1,000 \times 7.5 = 7,500$$

EXERCISES

1. Multiply each of the following numbers by 10:

.7;	.16;	.945;	.08;	6.5;	4.27;
0.1;	.075;	.003;	7.50;	41.6;	6.048

2. Multiply each of the following numbers by 100:

.53;	.06;	.3;	.478;	.009;	6.48;
1.7;	44.1;	9.225;	0.15;	0.4;	.29

3. Multiply each of the following numbers by 1,000:

.864;	.25;	.8;	.9018;	6.376;	4.61;
.0006;	17.1;	39.37:	.0045;	0.5;	.04

4. Multiply by short method:

a. $100,000 \times 8.6$

b. $9.7 \times 1,000,000$

c. $10,000,000 \times 12.1$

d. $36.9 \times 1,000,000$

e. $100,000,000 \times 1.8$

f. $3.4 \times 1,000,000,000$

g. $48.5 \times 10,000,000,000$

h. $1,000,000,000 \times 27.3$

5–11 COMPUTATION—DIVISION OF DECIMALS

(1) (2) *To divide a decimal fraction or mixed decimal by a whole number,* we divide as in the division of whole numbers, placing the decimal point in the quotient directly above the decimal point in the dividend.

(1)
$$\begin{array}{r} 1.6 \\ 4\overline{)6.4} \end{array}$$

Answer, 1.6

(2)
$$\begin{array}{r} .06 \\ 7\overline{).42} \end{array}$$

Answer, .06

(3) *To divide a whole number by a whole number where the division is not exact,* this division may be carried out to as many decimal places as are required in the quotient by annexing a decimal point and the required zeros to the dividend.

(3)
$$4\overline{)11} = 4\overline{)11.00}$$
$$2.75$$

Answer, 2.75

(4) *To divide a decimal fraction or mixed decimal by a decimal fraction or mixed decimal,* we make the divisor a whole number by multiplying it by the proper power of ten so that its decimal point is moved to the right of the last digit indicating its new position by a caret (∧). We multiply the dividend by the same power of ten so that its decimal point is moved to the right as many places as we moved the decimal point in the divisor and indicate its new position by a caret (∧). The following illustrates this:

(4)
$$.03\overline{)\,.645} = \frac{.645}{.03} = \frac{.645}{.03} \times 1$$
$$= \frac{.645 \times 100}{.03 \times 100} = \frac{64.5}{3} = 3\overline{)64.5}$$

Note that the multiplicative identity 1 is used here.

Thus, $.03\overline{)\,.645}$ becomes $3\overline{)64.5}$

Instead of doing all the work shown above, we may move decimal points directly in the given problem and indicate the new positions by carets.

Then we divide as in the division of whole numbers, placing the decimal point in the quotient directly above the caret (∧) in the dividend.

$$21.5$$
$.03\overline{)\,.645}$ becomes $.03_{\wedge}\overline{)\,.64_{\wedge}5}$

When the dividend contains fewer decimal places than required, we annex as many zeros as are necessary to a decimal fraction dividend, and a decimal point and the required zeros to a dividend containing a whole number.

Decimal Fractions

Divide 119.1 by .003:

$$\begin{array}{r} 39\ 700. \\ .003\overline{)119.100_\wedge} \end{array}$$

Answer, 39,700

Divide $5 by $1.25:

$$\begin{array}{r} 4 \\ \$1.25_\wedge\overline{)\$5.00_\wedge} \end{array}$$

Answer, 4

We check by multiplying the quotient by the divisor and adding the remainder, if any, to the product. The result should be equal to the dividend.

To find the quotient correct to the nearest required decimal place:

(1)		(2)
We find the quotient to one more than the required number of decimal places, then round it off.	**or**	We find the quotient to the required number of decimal places, adding 1 to the last digit of the quotient if the remainder is equal to one-half or more of the divisor.

(1) We find the quotient to one more than the required number of decimal places, then round it off.

Find quotient to nearest hundredth:

$$\begin{array}{r} 2.883 \\ 3\overline{)8.650} \end{array}$$

2.883 rounded to nearest hundredth is 2.88

Answer, 2.88

or

(2) We find the quotient to the required number of decimal places, adding 1 to the last digit of the quotient if the remainder is equal to one-half or more of the divisor.

Find quotient to nearest tenth:

$$\begin{array}{r} 1.5 \\ 12\overline{)19.1} \\ \underline{12} \\ 7\ 1 \\ \underline{6\ 0} \\ 1\ 1 \end{array}$$

$\frac{1}{2}$ of the divisor 12 is 6. The remainder 11 is greater than 6. So, the digit 5 of the quotient is increased to 6.

Answer, 1.6

1. In each of the following annex zeros to the dividend until the division is exact:

$12\overline{)9}$ $80\overline{)52}$ $25\overline{)37}$ $56\overline{)49}$ $125\overline{)1}$

2. Divide:

a.	$3\overline{)6.3}$	$6\overline{).852}$	$8\overline{).0056}$	$38\overline{).266}$	$87\overline{)520.26}$
b.	$8\overline{)40.56}$	$7\overline{)6.013}$	$75\overline{)697.5}$	$48\overline{)36.00}$	$16\overline{)1.0000}$
c.	$8.5\overline{)399.5}$	$.9\overline{)53.01}$	$1.8\overline{).432}$	$6.4\overline{).0512}$	$4.5\overline{).009}$
d.	$.2\overline{)8.18}$	$.5\overline{).004}$	$.9\overline{).0054}$	$7.5\overline{)65.325}$	$3.4\overline{)17.0}$
e.	$.53\overline{).424}$	$.77\overline{)1.9558}$	$6.29\overline{)54.094}$	$.05\overline{).01}$	$.35\overline{)10.5}$
f.	$.03\overline{).00021}$	$.96\overline{)24.00}$	$.88\overline{)2.068}$	$39.37\overline{)338.582}$	$3.14\overline{)20.41}$
g.	$.005\overline{).745}$	$.618\overline{).4944}$	$1.025\overline{)4.1}$	$.134\overline{).67}$	$2.349\overline{)14.094}$
h.	$.006\overline{)19.236}$	$.043\overline{)1.29}$	$.375\overline{)150.000}$	$1.125\overline{)16.875}$	$.018\overline{).01674}$
i.	$.7\overline{)49}$	$9.6\overline{)24}$	$.04\overline{)6}$	$2.75\overline{)22}$	$6.058\overline{)3029}$

3. Find quotient correct to nearest tenth:

$15\overline{)13}$ $25.4\overline{)54.96}$ $.875\overline{).6}$ $.62\overline{)5.9}$ $1.1\overline{)20}$

4. Find quotient correct to nearest hundredth:

$9\overline{)4}$ $.7\overline{)3}$ $.625\overline{).52}$ $.87\overline{)63.5}$ $16.39\overline{)3.94}$

5. Find quotient correct to nearest thousandth:

$12\overline{)85}$ $2.2\overline{)3,000}$ $.039\overline{)4.75}$ $7.5\overline{).896}$ $1.47\overline{)5.04}$

6. Find answer correct to nearest cent:

$8\overline{)\$.56}$ $144\overline{)\$291.62}$ $96\overline{)\$79.25}$ $72\overline{)\$8.43}$ $108\overline{)\$5,126.03}$

7. Divide:

$\$.06\overline{)\$30}$ $\$.10\overline{)\$9.70}$ $\$1.75\overline{)\$46}$ $\$.59\overline{)\$18.91}$ $\$2.47\overline{)\$253.36}$

8. Divide as indicated:

a. $71.68 \div 100$ d. $.9 \div .009$ g. $\$29.25 \div \$2.25$
b. $.0141 \div 4.7$ e. $21 \div .375$ h. $\$3 \div \$.05$
c. $62.5 \div .25$ f. $\$115.74 \div 18$ i. $\$18 \div \$.24$

5-12   DIVIDING BY POWERS OF TEN

We divide whole numbers and decimals by powers of ten (10; 100; 1,000; etc.) quickly by first writing the digits of the given numeral, then we move the decimal point as many places to the left of its original position as there are zeros in the given divisor.

$$600 \div 10 = 60 \qquad 284.1 \div 100 = 2.841$$
$$9 \div 100 = .09 \qquad 825.4 \div 1,000 = .8254$$

EXERCISES

1. Divide each of the following numbers by 10:

   40;   56;   8;   .3;   2.7;   579;   .42;   .385;   36.9;   800;   6.27;   93.54

2. Divide each of the following numbers by 100:

   600;   8,000;   415;   89;   2;   .7;   .626;   70.4;   831.97;   530;   9.63;   40

3. Divide each of the following numbers by 1,000:

   3,000;   8,375;   486;   57;   .281;   .5;   868.4;   6;   250,000;   1,230;   .01;   4,000.5

4. Divide by the short method:

   a. $3,900,000 \div 100,000$ **d.** $437,580,000 \div 1,000,000$

   b. $7,800,000 \div 10,000$ **e.** $2,400,000,000 \div 1,000,000,000$

   c. $15,200,000 \div 1,000,000$ **f.** $225,000,000,000 \div 100,000,000$

5-13   SHORTENED NAMES FOR LARGE WHOLE NUMBERS

To name a large whole number whose numeral ends in a series of zeros, newspapers and periodicals are now using a numeral followed by the name of the appropriate period of the number scale.

14.9 *million* is the shortened name for 14,900,000.
3.28 *billion* is the shortened name for 3,280,000,000.

To write the complete numeral for the shortened name, we multiply the number named by the given numeral prefix by the power of ten that is equivalent to the value of the period name (or place value) used. See section 5-10 for short method.

> 14.9 million = 14.9 × 1,000,000 = 14,900,000
> 3.28 billion = 3.28 × 1,000,000,000 = 3,280,000,000

To write the shortened name for the numeral ending in zeros, we divide the given number by the power of ten that is equivalent to the value of the period name (or place value) that we use. See section 5-12 for short method.

> 14,900,000 = 14.9 million since
> $\qquad\qquad$ 14,900,000 ÷ 1,000,000 = 14.9
> 3,280,000,000 = 3.28 billion since
> $\qquad\qquad$ 3,280,000,000 ÷ 1,000,000,000 = 3.28

EXERCISES

1. Write the complete numeral for each of the following:
   a. 57.4 million; 9.25 million; 125.6 million; 6.598 million
   b. 2.3 thousand; 46.59 thousand; 8.827 thousand; 496.4 thousand
   c. 19.9 billion; 105.2 billion; 3.94 billion; 94.703 billion
   d. 8.7 trillion; 17.6 trillion; 6.65 trillion; 254.741 trillion
   e. Money market fund assets increased by $3.57 billion to reach a total of $179.99 billion.

2. Write the shortened name for each of the following:
   a. In billions: 8,500,000,000; 42,900,000,000; 255,840,000,000; 6,967,000,000
   b. In millions: 76,400,000; 5,770,000; 349,300,000; 36,828,000
   c. In hundreds: 3,910; 2,584; 19,650; 97,437
   d. In thousands: 50,700; 9,120; 783,400; 4,236,960
   e. In trillions: 9,600,000,000,000; 86,500,000,000,000; 705,900,000,000,000

Decimal Fractions

5-14 SCIENTIFIC NOTATION

A brief form of writing numerals usually for very large or very small numbers is known as *scientific notation*. A number is expressed in scientific notation when it is greater than 1 but less than 10 multiplied by some power of ten.

> 6,700,000 is 6.7 million, which may be expressed in scientific notation as 6.7×10^6

To write a numeral in scientific notation, we rewrite the significant digits:

(1) As a numeral for a whole number if there is only one significant digit, as in 6,000,000.

(2) As a numeral for a mixed decimal if there are two or more significant digits, as in 6,700,000 or 6,780,000, using the first digit as a numeral for a whole number and for all other digits as the numeral for a decimal fraction.

Then we indicate that this numeral is multiplied by the required power of ten.

The required power of ten may be determined as follows:

By dividing the whole number or mixed decimal into the given number and changing the quotient into a power of ten or by counting the number of places the decimal point is being moved.

When the given number is 10 or greater, a positive integer[1] is used for the exponent.

> Write 73,400,000 in scientific notation:
>
> $73,400,000 = 7.34 \times ?$
>
> $$\text{Divide } 7.34 \overline{)73,400,000.00_\wedge} \; \dfrac{10,000,000}{}$$
>
> However $10,000,000 = 10^7$
>
> $73,400,000 = 7.34 \times 10^7$
>
> *Answer,* 7.34×10^7

---

[1] See page 283.

Thus $73,400,000 = 7.34 \times 10^7$. Note that the decimal point is moved 7 places to the left.

When the given number is between 0 and 1, a negative integer[1] is used for the exponent.

Write .000048 in scientific notation:
$$.000048 = 4.8 \times ?$$

$$\begin{array}{r} .00001 \\ \hline 4.8 \overline{)\,.0\,00048} \end{array}$$

Divide: $4.8 \overline{)\,.0\,00048}$

However $.00001 = 10^{-5}$
$$.000048 = 4.8 \times 10^{-5}$$

Answer, 4.8×10^{-5}

Thus $.000048 = 4.8 \times 10^{-5}$. Note that the decimal point is moved 5 places to the right.

EXERCISES

1. Express each of the following numbers in scienic notation:

   a. 40   65   900   387   7,000   4,830   6,090
   b. 30,000   84,000   460,000   75,000,000   3,274,000
   c. 5,000,000,000   6,700,000   198,000,000,000   59,306,000,000,000
   d. 860000000000   45200000000000   7000000000000000   38000000000000000
   e. 18.5   396.1   27.92   87.017   934.82   6,528.7   3,928.36

2. Express each of the following numbers in scientific notation:

   a. .6   .8   .4   .27   .03   .54   .95
   b. .076   .004   .591   .0623   .3006   .0058   .9214
   c. .00037   .00196   .08285   .000694   .0000075
   d. .0000021   .00000583   .000000035   .000000106   .0000000294
   e. .000000000064   .0000000000408   .00000000005   .000000000000719

3. Express each of the following numbers in scientific notation:

   a. Light travels at a speed of 300,000 kilometers per second.

---
[1] See page 283.

Decimal Fractions   **159**

b. The earth is 239,000 miles from the moon and 93,000,000 miles from the sun.

c. The weight of the earth is 6,594,000,000,000,000,000,000 tons and its volume is 259,900,000,000 cubic miles.

d. Our Milky Way is about 966,000,000,000,000,000,000 kilometers in diameter.

e. A millimicron is .00000003927 inch and an inch is about .000016 mile.

5–15 EXPRESSING NUMERALS NAMING COMMON FRACTIONS AS DECIMAL NUMERALS

Since a common fraction indicates division (for example, $\frac{3}{4}$ means 3 divided by 4), to express a numeral naming a common fraction as a decimal numeral we divide the numerator by the denominator.

$$\frac{3}{4} = 3 \div 4 = 4\overline{)3.00}\,^{.75}$$

Answer, .75

When the common fraction has as its denominator some power of ten (10; 100; 1,000; etc.), we drop the denominator and rewrite the numerator, placing the decimal point so that the name of the part and the place value of the last digit correspond.

$$\frac{489}{1,000} = .489$$

To express a numeral naming a mixed number as a decimal numeral, we express the numeral for the common fraction as a numeral for a decimal fraction and annex it to the numeral for the whole number.

$$3\frac{1}{2} = 3.5$$
since $\frac{1}{2} = .5$

EXERCISES

1. Express each of the following as a 1-digit numeral naming a decimal fraction:

$$\frac{7}{10}, \qquad \frac{9}{10}, \qquad \frac{1}{10}, \qquad \frac{3}{10}, \qquad \frac{4}{10}, \qquad \frac{1}{2}, \qquad \frac{2}{5}, \qquad \frac{9}{15}, \qquad \frac{1}{5}, \qquad \frac{4}{5}$$

2. Express each of the following as a 2-digit numeral naming a decimal fraction:

$$\frac{21}{100}, \qquad \frac{7}{100}, \qquad \frac{59}{100}, \qquad \frac{1}{4}, \qquad \frac{3}{4}, \qquad \frac{4}{25}, \qquad \frac{9}{50}, \qquad \frac{17}{20}, \qquad \frac{27}{36}, \qquad \frac{14}{56}$$

3. Express each of the following as a 3-digit numeral naming a decimal fraction:

$$\frac{728}{1000}, \quad \frac{3}{8}, \quad \frac{1}{8}, \quad \frac{5}{8}, \quad \frac{7}{8}, \quad \frac{45}{72}, \quad \frac{7}{56}, \quad \frac{18}{48}, \quad \frac{84}{96}, \quad \frac{61}{1000}$$

4. Express each of the following as a 2-digit numeral naming a decimal fraction. Retain the remainder as a common fraction.

$$\frac{1}{3}, \quad \frac{1}{6}, \quad \frac{2}{3}, \quad \frac{5}{6}, \quad \frac{7}{12}, \quad \frac{35}{42}, \quad \frac{14}{32}, \quad \frac{33}{36}, \quad \frac{9}{48}, \quad \frac{10}{24}$$

5. Express each of the following as a numeral naming a mixed decimal:

$$1\frac{1}{2}, \quad 2\frac{3}{4}, \quad 5\frac{9}{10}, \quad 3\frac{5}{8}, \quad 9\frac{7}{8}, \quad \frac{8}{5}, \quad \frac{9}{2}, \quad \frac{11}{8}, \quad \frac{15}{4}, \quad \frac{23}{10}$$

5–16 REPEATING DECIMALS

To change the fraction $\frac{2}{3}$ to a decimal we divide 2 by 3. However, we can see in the example that the division is not exact. The remainder at each step is the same (2). Examination of the quotient will show that the digit 6 repeats and will keep repeating endlessly as we extend the division.

When we change $\frac{3}{11}$ to a decimal, we observe that this division also is not exact. The remainder at each second step is the same (3). Examination of the quotient will show that the pair of digits 27 repeats and will keep repeating endlessly as we extend the division.

$$
\begin{array}{ll}
\begin{array}{r}
.666 \\
3\overline{)2.000} \\
\underline{1\,8} \\
20 \\
\underline{18} \\
20 \\
\underline{18} \\
2
\end{array}
&
\begin{array}{r}
.2727 \\
11\overline{)3.0000} \\
\underline{2\,2} \\
80 \\
\underline{77} \\
30 \\
\underline{22} \\
80 \\
\underline{77} \\
3
\end{array}
\end{array}
$$

We call these decimals which have a digit or group of digits repeating endlessly *repeating decimals*. The first quotient above is written as .66$\overline{6}$ . . . (or .$\overline{6}$ . . . or simply .$\overline{6}$) and the second quotient as .2727 . . . (or .27̄ . . . or simply .2̄7̄). The bar indicates the repeating sequence (period) and the dots indicate that the sequence repeats endlessly.

When we change $\frac{3}{4}$ to a decimal, the exact quotient is .75 which could be written as .750 or .7500 or .75000̄ . . . . The decimal form .75 is called a *terminating decimal*. However, since it may also be written in the repeating form .750̄ . . . or .7500̄ . . . or .75000̄ . . . , we see that the terminating decimals are repeating decimals.

Summarizing, observe that if a remainder of 0 occurs in the division, the quotient is a terminating decimal. If, however, after a series of divisions, a remainder other than 0 repeats, then the sequence of digits obtained in the quotient between occurrences of this remainder will repeat endlessly.

Since we consider a terminating decimal to be a repeating decimal, then it is possible to express every common fraction as a repeating decimal.

EXERCISES

Express each of the following as a numeral naming a repeating decimal. Indicate the repeating sequence by a horizontal bar.

a. $\frac{1}{3}$	f. $\frac{4}{9}$	k. $\frac{11}{15}$	p. $\frac{8}{9}$	u. $\frac{8}{17}$
b. $\frac{1}{8}$	g. $\frac{7}{12}$	l. $\frac{5}{23}$	q. $\frac{9}{11}$	v. $\frac{7}{13}$
c. $\frac{1}{6}$	h. $\frac{8}{11}$	m. $\frac{19}{21}$	r. $\frac{2}{5}$	w. $\frac{19}{24}$
d. $\frac{4}{7}$	i. $\frac{6}{13}$	n. $\frac{7}{18}$	s. $\frac{13}{15}$	x. $\frac{4}{27}$
e. $\frac{5}{16}$	j. $\frac{15}{33}$	o. $\frac{14}{17}$	t. $\frac{12}{19}$	y. $\frac{13}{18}$

5–17 EXPRESSING NUMERALS NAMING DECIMAL FRACTIONS AS NUMERALS NAMING COMMON FRACTIONS

To express a numeral naming a decimal fraction as a numeral naming a common fraction, we write the numeral for a common fraction so that:

The digits of the decimal numeral are the numerator, and a power of ten (10; 100; 1,000; etc.) corresponding to the place value of the last digit of the decimal numeral is the denominator. The fraction is then expressed in lowest terms.

$$.45 = \frac{45}{100} = \frac{9}{20}$$

Answer, $\frac{9}{20}$

To express a numeral naming a mixed decimal as a numeral naming a mixed number, we write the numeral naming the decimal fraction as a numeral naming a common fraction and annex it to the numeral for the whole number.

$$2.5 = 2\frac{5}{10} = 2\frac{1}{2}$$

Answer, $2\frac{1}{2}$

EXERCISES

1. Express each of the following as a numeral naming a common fraction:

   a. .3, .4, .6, .2, .8, .57, .25, 0.85, 0.75, 0.68

   b. .60, .05, .70, .04, .90, .193, .625, 0.375, 0.125, 0.875

   c. $.12\frac{1}{2}$, $.87\frac{1}{2}$, $.06\frac{1}{4}$, $.62\frac{1}{2}$, $.37\frac{1}{2}$, $.16\frac{2}{3}$, $.33\frac{1}{3}$, $.66\frac{2}{3}$, $0.83\frac{1}{3}$, $0.08\frac{1}{3}$

2. Express each of the following as a numeral naming a mixed number:

   1.2, 3.5, 4.25, 9.875, 6.08, $2.87\frac{1}{2}$, $7.66\frac{2}{3}$, $8.12\frac{1}{2}$, $10.33\frac{1}{3}$, $5.06\frac{1}{4}$

5–18 EXPRESSING A REPEATING DECIMAL AS A NUMERAL NAMING A COMMON FRACTION

To change a repeating decimal to a common fraction:

We multiply the given repeating decimal by some power of 10 so that there is a whole number to the left of the decimal point and the repeating sequence begins to the right of the decimal point. If the repeating sequence has 1 digit, we multiply by 10; if 2 digits, we multiply by 100, etc. We subtract the given number from this product to get a whole number for the difference. (1) (2)

(When a repeating decimal begins with digits other than those used in the repeating sequence, another step is necessary as shown in (3).)

Then we solve the resulting equation (see page 362) to find the required common fraction.

Thus we see that every common fraction may be expressed as a repeating decimal and every repeating decimal may be expressed as a common fraction.

(1) $.55\overline{5} \ldots = ?$

$$\text{Let } n = .555 \ldots$$
$$10\,n = 5.555 \ldots$$
$$10\,n - n = 5$$
$$9\,n = 5$$
$$n = \frac{5}{9}$$

Answer, $\frac{5}{9}$

(2) $.1818\overline{18} \ldots = ?$

$$\text{Let } n = .181818 \ldots$$
$$100\,n = 18.181818 \ldots$$
$$100\,n - n = 18$$
$$99\,n = 18$$
$$n = \frac{18}{99}$$
$$n = \frac{2}{11}$$

Answer, $\frac{2}{11}$

(3) $.2666\overline{6} \ldots = ?$

$$\text{Let } n = .2666 \ldots$$
$$100\,n = 26.666 \ldots$$
$$\text{and } 10\,n = 2.666 \ldots$$
$$\text{then } 90\,n = 24$$
$$n = \frac{24}{90}$$
$$n = \frac{4}{15}$$

Answer, $\frac{4}{15}$

EXERCISES

Express each of the following as a numeral naming a common fraction:

a. $.22\overline{2} \ldots$ d. $.933\overline{3} \ldots$ g. $.\overline{81} \ldots$ j. $.\overline{153846}$

b. $.\overline{36} \ldots$ e. $.08\overline{3} \ldots$ h. $.458\overline{3} \ldots$ k. $.\overline{285714}$

c. $.\overline{8}$ f. $.041\overline{6}$ i. $.91\overline{6} \ldots$ l. $.\overline{095238}$

DECIMAL RELATIONSHIPS BETWEEN NUMBERS

Decimal fractions like common fractions are used to express relationships between numbers. Similarly there are 3 types of relationships: finding a decimal part of a number, finding what decimal part one number is of another, and finding a number when a decimal part of it is known.

5–19 DECIMAL PART OF A NUMBER

To find a decimal part of a number, we multiply the number by the given decimal.

Find .09 of 25:

$$\begin{array}{r} 25 \\ \times .09 \\ \hline 2.25 \end{array}$$

Answer, 2.25

EXERCISES

1. Find:
  a. .3 of 36
  b. .9 of 400
  c. .05 of 257
  d. .48 of 350
  e. .91 of 1,800
  f. .001 of 8
  g. .875 of 320
  h. .0625 of 6,400

2. Find:
  a. .2 of .9
  b. .1 of .46
  c. .7 of .012
  d. .05 of .4
  e. .38 of .97
  f. .82 of .509
  g. .625 of .86
  h. .004 of .6

3. Find:
  a. .4 of 7.3
  b. .08 of 2.99
  c. .7 of 9.25
  d. .6 of 80.41
  e. .08 of 12.93
  f. .25 of 5.37
  g. .01 of 183.26
  h. .009 of 400.08

5-20 WHAT DECIMAL PART ONE
NUMBER IS OF ANOTHER

Since a fraction expresses what part one number is of another and a common fraction may be expressed as an equivalent decimal fraction, to find what decimal part one number is of another, we write the numeral of a common fraction that expresses the fractional part one number is of the other, then we divide the numerator by the denominator.

What decimal part of 25 is 4?

$$\frac{4}{25} = 4 \div 25 = 25\overline{)4.00}$$

$$\begin{array}{r} .16 \\ 25\overline{)4.00} \\ \underline{2\ 5} \\ 1\ 50 \\ \underline{1\ 50} \\ \cdots \end{array}$$

Answer, .16

EXERCISES

Find the following:

1. **a.** What decimal part of 2 is 1? **b.** 2 is what decimal part of 5?
2. **a.** What decimal part of 4 is 3? **b.** 1 is what decimal part of 4?
3. **a.** 5 is what decimal part of 8? **b.** What decimal part of 8 is 7?
4. **a.** What decimal part of 16 is 1? **b.** 9 is what decimal part of 16?
5. **a.** What decimal part of 3 is 1? **b.** 5 is what decimal part of 6?
6. **a.** What decimal part of 15 is 6? **b.** What decimal part of 100 is 80?
7. **a.** 36 is what decimal part of 48? **b.** 49 is what decimal part of 56?
8. **a.** What decimal part of 27 is 18? **b.** 25 is what decimal part of 30?
9. **a.** 84 is what decimal part of 108? **b.** What decimal part of 24 is 10?
10. **a.** What decimal part of 0.8 is 0.4? **b.** 4.55 is what decimal part of 6.5?

5-21 FINDING THE NUMBER WHEN A DECIMAL PART OF IT IS KNOWN

We have found that to determine the number when a fractional part of it is known, we divide the given number that represents the fractional part of the unknown number by the given fraction. Similarly, to find the number when a decimal part of it is known, we divide the given number that represents the decimal part of the unknown number by the given decimal fraction.

.16 of what number is 4?

$$
\begin{array}{r}
25 \\
.16\overline{)4.00} \\
3\,2 \\
\hline
80 \\
80 \\
\hline
\end{array}
$$

Answer, 25

EXERCISES

Find the following:

1. **a.** .3 of what number is 9? **b.** .4 of what number is 28?
2. **a.** .8 of what number is 6? **b.** .2 of what number is 1?
3. **a.** .09 of what number is 540? **b.** 329 is .47 of what number?
4. **a.** .375 of what number is 900? **b.** .0625 of what number is 45?
5. **a.** .4 of what number is 5? **b.** .06 of what number is 78?
6. **a.** .75 of what number is 29? **b.** .9 of what number is 15?
7. **a.** 60 is .5 of what number? **b.** 2 is .6 of what number?
8. **a.** .25 of what number is 700? **b.** 2,072 is .518 of what number?
9. **a.** .125 of what number is 210? **b.** .875 of what number is 46?
10. **a.** 40 is .62$\frac{1}{2}$ of what number? **b.** 8.1 is .16$\frac{2}{3}$ of what number?

First study pages 74–75. Then solve each problem.

1. The length of the United States flag is 1.9 times its width. How long should a flag be if its width is 5 feet?

2. Find the total rainfall for a month during which 0.62 cm; 3.12 cm; 0.23 cm; 0.46 cm; 1.37 cm; 1.28 cm; and 2.81 cm of rain fell.

3. Normal atmospheric pressure is 29.92 inches of mercury. How much above normal is a barometric pressure of 30.30 inches?

4. The per capita public debt of the United States in 1860 was $2.06. How many times as great (to the nearest whole number) was the debt recently when it averaged $3,739.92 per person?

5. Steel weighs 7.7 times as much as an equal volume of water. If 1 cubic centimeter of water weighs 1 gram, how much does 25.2 cubic centimeters of steel weigh?

6. How much do you save on each can if you buy 1 dozen cans of corn for $3.60 instead of $.32 each?

7. Find the new bank balance if the previous monthly balance was $583.06, deposits during the month were $406.58, $93.89, $396.34, $157.95, and $268.43, and checks drawn and cash withdrawals were $309.25, $125.87, $436.81, and $75.64.

8. A television set costs $325 or $32.50 down and 24 monthly payments of $13.75 each. How much do you save by paying cash?

9. An object 50 feet high can be seen at sea for a distance of 8.1 nautical miles. If an object 800 feet high is visible for 32.4 nautical miles, how many times as far can the taller object be seen?

10. A record of 163.465 m.p.h. was set at the Indianapolis Speedway in 1972. How much slower than the record was the speed in a recent year when the winning speed was 142.862 m.p.h.?

11. An airplane flew 1,230.6 kilometers in 1.5 hours. What was its average ground speed?

12. What is the maximum length that is acceptable if a tolerance of .005 inch is permitted on a piece designed to be 1.625 inches?

13. Workers in manufacturing industries averaged 40.3 hours of work and earnings of $49.25 per week in 1947. During a recent year the work week averaged 39.4 hours and earnings increased to $280.53. Find the increase in average earnings per hour of work.

14. To find the batting average, divide the number of hits by the number of times at bat, finding the quotient to the nearest thousandth. Find the batting average of each player:

a. Peter, 3 hits out of 10 times at bat.
b. Jose, 6 hits out of 25 times at bat.
c. Todd, 15 hits out of 45 times at bat.
d. Carlos, 54 hits out of 186 times at bat.
e. Ed, 49 hits out of 165 times at bat.

15. To find the fielding average, divide the sum of the put-outs and assists by the sum of the errors, put-outs and assists, finding the quotient to the nearest thousandth. Find the fielding average of each of the following players:

a. Maria, 5 errors, 37 put-outs and 49 assists.
b. Debbie, 2 errors, 8 put-outs and 10 assists.
c. Janet, 3 errors, 41 put-outs and 108 assists.
d. Bridget, 6 errors, 198 put-outs and 26 assists.
e. Barbara, 12 errors, 290 put-outs and 425 assists.

ESTIMATING ANSWERS

To estimate a sum, a difference, a product or a quotient, first round the given numbers to convenient place values (see page 141) and then perform the operation or operations. For each of the following select your nearest estimate:

1. .84 + .47 + .79 is approximately:	.2	2	.25
2. .938 − .412 is approximately:	.005	.05	.5
3. 48 × .98 is approximately:	.47	4.7	47
4. 21 ÷ .4 is approximately:	5.2	52	.525
5. 6.23 − .198 is approximately:	.06	.6	6
6. .19 × 10.1 is approximately:	.2	2	.019
7. 2.7 + 5.1 + 9.3 is approximately:	17	1.7	170
8. .99 ÷ .05 is approximately:	.24	2.5	20
9. $8.58 + $3.74 + $2.71 is approximately:	$15	$19.40	$13.25
10. $43.95 ÷ 4 is approximately:	$9.75	$11	$10.25
11. .08 × $19.75 is approximately:	$1.60	$1.90	$1.97
12. $69.11 − $58.99 is approximately:	$12	$11	$10
13. .926 + .759 + .429 is approximately:	200	21.4	2

Decimal Fractions

14. 72 × $6.90 is approximately:	$50	$420	$500
15. .019 ÷ .2 is approximately:	.95	.1	1.05
16. 85 − 69.9 is approximately:	1.6	12.1	15
17. $9.29 + $17.38 + $6.43 is approximately:	$40	$33	$30.50
18. $100 − $74.06 is approximately:	$27	$26.94	$26
19. 2.93 × .004 is approximately:	.1	.01	1.01
20. $107.99 ÷ $.12 is approximately:	90	900	9

CHECK BY CALCULATOR

Use your calculator to check each of the following given answers. Indicate which answers are incorrect. If a calculator is not available, check by computation.

1. Add:

a.	**b.**	**c.**	**d.**	**e.**
57	8,376	39,968	78,925	496,326
964	9,847	29,396	62,398	839,945
8,592	4,096	48,803	85,166	407,638
39	5,858	96,869	60,597	751,895
398	7,926	74,187	87,269	678,946
10,150	36,103	289,223	373,355	3,174,750

2. Subtract:

a.	**b.**	**c.**	**d.**	**e.**
6,582	28,804	865,000	536,247	1,976,304
5,762	9,205	456,898	347,861	908,795
820	18,599	409,102	188,386	1,068,509

3. Multiply:

a. 86 × 93 = 7,988

b. 478 × 69 = 32,982

c. 964 × 538 = 518,632

d. 675 × 930 = 626,750

e. 429 × 905 = 388,245

f. 5,672 × 817 = 4,654,027

4. Divide:

a. 25,233 ÷ 39 = 657

b. 11,250 ÷ 525 = 18

c. 426,924 ÷ 708 = 603

d. 836,784 ÷ 894 = 926

e. 171,147 ÷ 267 = 641

f. 2,083,650 ÷ 870 = 2,495

5. Compute as indicated:

a.	b.	c.	d.	e.
437	75,834	69,644	468,509	1,006,023
9,586	66,957	82,798	−279,495	− 587,126
859	88,476	54,609	188,014	418,897
47,383	49,328	63,176		
+28,998	+58,695	+98,698		
87,263	338,290	369,925		

f. $5,396 \times 4,788 = 25,736,048$ **h.** $3,035,223 \div 6,207 = 489$

g. $7,809 \times 3,069 = 23,965,821$ **i.** $824,850 \div 975 = 856$

6. Add:

    a. $.608 + .540 + .725 = 1.883$ **c.** $.859 + 7 = .866$

    b. $.9 + .43 = .52$ **d.** $3.95 + 69.4 = 10.89$

           e. $\$.95 + \$6.89 + \$28.46 = \$36.30$

7. Subtract:

    a. $.463 - .393 = .070$ **c.** $90 - 79.6 = 10.4$

    b. $62.5 - 4 = 62.1$ **d.** $9.746 - 2.51 = 7.236$

           e. $\$35 - \$17.99 = \$18.01$

8. Multiply:

    a. $26 \times .97 = 24.22$ **c.** $18.3 \times 69.1 = 1,264.53$

    b. $3.8 \times .005 = .019$ **d.** $.012 \times .003 = .036$

           e. $.075 \times 9,000 = 675$

9. Divide:

    a. $.48 \div 16 = .03$ **c.** $8.47 \div .5 = 169.4$

    b. $30 \div .02 = .15$ **d.** $6 \div 80 = .075$

           e. $17.4 \div 4.35 = .4$

10. Compute as indicated:

    a. $.001 \times .001 = .002$ **e.** $.6 \times 4.2 = .252$

    b. $9.8 - .42 = .56$ **f.** $.694 + .54 + .3 = 1.034$

    c. $28 \div .04 = 700$ **g.** $8.1 \div .9 = .9$

    d. $.26 + 7.1 = 197$ **h.** $.7091 - .317 = .3921$

CHAPTER REVIEW

1. Write as a numeral: Three hundred and two thousandths. (5–1)
2. Read or write in words: .0584 (5–2) (5–3)
3. Write 5,807.439 as a polynomial. (5–4)
4. Round **a.** 26.4198 to the nearest thousandth. (5–5)
   b. $9.8949 to the nearest cent.
5. Arrange 6.6, .066, 66, and .66 by size, greatest number first. (5–6)
6. Which of the following are true statements? (5–6)

   a. .03 < .30   **c.** 5.0 = 0.5   **e.** .29 < .3
   b. 1 > .99   **d.** .806 > .8055

7. Add: 8. Add: $527.63 (5–7)
   3.69 + 58.2 + .197   93.59
                               4.76
                               839.97
                               789.58

9. Subtract: 10. Subtract: (5–8)

   .786 − .24 $63 − $1.28

11. Multiply: 12. Multiply to the nearest cent: (5–9)

   .23 × .004 $68.59
                            .62$\frac{1}{2}$

13. Multiply 58.9276 by 100. (5–10)
14. **a.** Divide: **b.** Divide to the nearest cent: (5–11)

   .125$\overline{).5}$ 60$\overline{)\$593.27}$

15. Divide 62.59 by 1,000. (5–12)
16. **a.** Write as a complete numeral: 24.7 billion (5–13)
    b. Write the shortened name in trillions: 836,540,000,000,000
17. Write by scientific notation: **a.** 370,000,000,000   **b.** .000046 (5–14)
18. Express $\frac{11}{25}$ as a decimal numeral. (5–15)

19. Express $\frac{7}{9}$ as a repeating decimal. (5–16)
20. Express .74 as a numeral naming a common fraction. (5–17)
21. Express .$\overline{64}$ . . . as a numeral naming a common fraction. (5–18)
22. Find .06 of 275. (5–19)
23. What decimal part of 72 is 56? (5–20)
24. .15 of what number is 90? (5–21)
25. A set of furniture for a dining-room can be purchased with cash for $1,095. If you purchase it on the installment plan, you are to make 12 monthly payments of $98.55 each. How much money in finance charges will you have paid at the end of the 12 months? (5–22)

REVIEW EXERCISES

1. Add:

66	5,198	28,107	69,428	83,045
527	93,456	9,689	85,274	19,249
4,852	825	57,843	67,855	56,963
9	6,218	18,936	96,589	40,586
275	58,324	2,559	38,417	58,879

2. Subtract:

6,159	84,206	92,345	291,500	580,604
2,949	9,185	87,258	69,809	391,786

3. Multiply:

24	879	307	725	5,280
57	93	409	916	184

4. Divide:

48)1,392   96)8,928   144)122,968   735)609,315   6,080)358,720

5. Add:

$\frac{1}{6}$ $\frac{7}{8}$ $5\frac{1}{3}$ $9\frac{3}{4}$ $7\frac{11}{12}$

$\frac{2}{3}$ $2\frac{13}{16}$ $6\frac{5}{8}$ $4\frac{9}{10}$ $3\frac{5}{6}$

6. Subtract:

$\frac{9}{10}$ $5\frac{3}{8}$ 10 $6\frac{3}{4}$ $8\frac{2}{3}$

$\frac{1}{2}$ 4 $8\frac{9}{16}$ $4\frac{29}{32}$ $3\frac{4}{5}$

7. Multiply:

$\frac{2}{3} \times \frac{9}{16}$ $\begin{array}{r} 24 \\ \times 4\frac{5}{8} \end{array}$ $3\frac{3}{4} \times 7\frac{1}{5}$ $\frac{7}{8} \times 2\frac{3}{5}$ $\frac{2}{3} \times 8\frac{1}{4}$

8. Divide:

$\frac{15}{16} \div \frac{5}{8}$ $4\frac{1}{2} \div \frac{3}{4}$ $12\frac{1}{4} \div 8$ $6\frac{2}{3} \div 5\frac{5}{6}$ $1\frac{3}{8} \div 2\frac{1}{3}$

9. Add:

$.605 + .250 + .105$ $.8 + .02$ $.432 + 8$ $6.49 + 23.1$

$\$.83 + \$5.94 + \$18.59$

10. Subtract:

$.825 - .775$ $34.29 - 3$ $80 - 29.4$ $5.854 - 1.63$ $\$25 - \$18.46$

11. Multiply:

$\begin{array}{r} 75 \\ .69 \end{array}$ $\begin{array}{r} 2.7 \\ .003 \end{array}$ $\begin{array}{r} 9.2 \\ 4.6 \end{array}$ $\begin{array}{r} 3.1416 \\ 8.5 \end{array}$ $\begin{array}{r} \$6,000 \\ .045 \end{array}$

12. Divide:

$13\overline{).52}$ $.05\overline{)70}$ $.62\overline{).1736}$ $40\overline{)2}$ $2.45\overline{)49}$

ACHIEVEMENT TEST

1. Factor 1,728 as the product of prime factors.   (1–19)
2. Round 43,980,514,306 to the nearest million.   (1–10)
3. Is 6, 12, 18, 24, . . . closed under addition? Subtraction? Multiplication? Division?   (2–6)

4. Add: 5. Subtract: 6. Multiply: (2–9 to 2–11)

$$
\begin{array}{rrr}
629,849 & 8,100,052 & 5,086 \\
74,987 & \underline{5,603,994} & \underline{9,070} \\
258,694 \\
9,038 \\
\underline{367,856}
\end{array}
$$

7. Divide: 8. Divide: (2–16)

$6,080)\overline{1,854,400}$ $7,096)\overline{745,080}$

9. Write in words each of the following: (3–1)

    a. $12 < 25$ c. $18 + 6 \not< 7 + 8$
    b. $12 > 10$ d. $20 - 4 \neq 20 \div 4$

10. Express $\frac{49}{196}$ in lowest terms.   (4–2)

11. Express $\frac{5}{6}$ as 72nds.   (4–3)

12. Write the group of equivalent fractions of which $\frac{6}{16}$ is a member.   (4–3)

13. Which of the following statements are true?   (4–8)

    a. $\frac{3}{5} < \frac{6}{11}$ b. $\frac{18}{24} = \frac{63}{84}$ c. $\frac{8}{17} > \frac{4}{9}$ d. $\frac{11}{13} \not> \frac{5}{6}$ e. $\frac{13}{15} < \frac{6}{7}$

14. Arrange $\frac{15}{24}$, $\frac{27}{48}$, and $\frac{7}{12}$ by size, smallest first.   (4–8)

15. Add: 16. Subtract: 17. Multiply: (4–11 to 4–13)

    $6\frac{7}{16} + 4\frac{3}{4} + 9\frac{5}{8}$ $10\frac{1}{4}$ $9\frac{3}{8} \times 2\frac{5}{6}$

                                $\underline{-4\frac{3}{5}}$

18. Divide: 19. Divide: (4–15)

    $24 \div 2\frac{2}{3}$ $3\frac{1}{2} \div 21$

20. What fractional part of 52 is 44? (4–17)

21. $\frac{4}{15}$ of what number is 140? (4–18)

22. Write 652.147 as a polynomial. (5–4)

23. Round: (5–5)

    a. 6.05024 to the nearest tenth.

    b. 18.61\frac{7}{12}$ to the nearest cent.

24. Arrange .41, 4.1, .041, and 41 by size, greatest first. (5–6)

25. Which of the following are true statements? (5–6)

    a. .0800 = .080   **b.** .02 > .012   **c.** 0.989 < 0.998

    d. .56 > .562   **e.** 1.2 $\not<$ .122

26. Add: **27.** Subtract: **28.** Multiply: (5–7 to 5–9)

    $.85 + $1.93 + $24.88   .6 − .509   .2003 × .001

29. Divide: **30.** Divide: (5–11)

    $.04)\overline{$12}$ $.011)\overline{.004048}$

31. **a.** Write 3.59 million as a complete numeral. (5–13)

    b. Write the shortened name for 64,800,000,000 in billions. (5–13)

32. Write in scientific notation: (5–14)

    a. 8,400,000,000,000   **b.** .00000027

33. Express $\frac{36}{80}$ as a decimal numeral. (5–15)

34. Express $\frac{5}{13}$ as a repeating decimal. (5–16)

35. Express .416 as a numeral naming a common fraction. (5–17)

36. Express .41$\overline{6}$ . . . as a numeral naming a common fraction. (5–18)

37. Find .625 of 9.36 (5–19)

38. What decimal part of 65 is 39? (5–20)

39. 1.05 of what number is 336? (5–21)

40. The telephone rate between two zones is $.42 for the first 3 minutes and $.12 for each additional minute. How long was a call for which the charge is $1.14? (5–22)

CHAPTER 6
Percent

6–1 MEANING OF PERCENT

Percent, represented by the symbol %, is used extensively in our daily affairs. It is the language of business. We experience the use of percent in situations like the following:

A bank pays 5% interest on deposits and charges 15% interest on loans. A girl pays 4% tax on telephone service for local and toll calls. A salesman earns 6% on what he sells. A department store advertises a 20% reduction on sales items. A working woman finds that an 18% withholding tax, 6.7% social security tax and 3% state income tax are deducted from her paycheck. A customer pays 14% carrying charges on a new refrigerator. A family receives a 1% discount for paying the real estate taxes on their home in advance. The label in a coat indicates that the material is 40% Dacron and 60% wool. The cost of living has increased 1.3%. A storekeeper makes a profit of 28% on all merchandise sold in the store. A student receives a mark of 86%. The average daily attendance of a class is 95%.

What does percent mean?

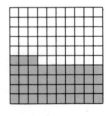

The large square on the right contains 100 small squares. We see that 43 small squares are shaded. But 43 out of a hundred is 43 hundredths. Therefore 43 hundredths of the large square is shaded. 43 hundredths written as a numeral naming a common fraction is $\frac{43}{100}$ and as a numeral naming a decimal fraction is .43. Both represent the part of the large square that is shaded.

There is still another way of indicating that 43 hundredths of the square is shaded. We may say that 43 percent, written 43%, of the square is shaded.

Thus, percent means hundredths.

Percent is a fraction in which the numeral preceding the % symbol is considered the numerator and the % symbol represents the denominator 100. It is equivalent to a two-place decimal fraction or to a common fraction having 100 as its denominator.

57 squares of the hundred squares are not shaded. Therefore 57 hundredths or 57% of the large square is not shaded. If 43% of the square is shaded and 57% of the square is not shaded, the whole square is the sum of the two or 100%.

100% of anything is $\frac{100}{100}$ of it or all of it.

Any percent less than 100% is equal to a fraction less than 1. 100% is equal to 1. Any percent more than 100% is equal to a number greater than 1.

A percent may also be considered a ratio. 85%, which is equivalent to $\frac{85}{100}$, is the ratio of 85 to 100.

EXERCISES

1. In each of the following first find how many small squares out of a hundred are shaded. Then express the answer as a percent.

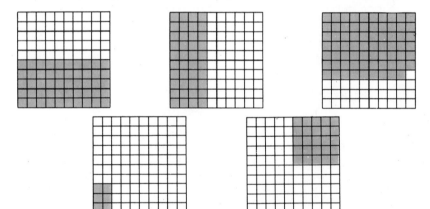

2. Illustrate the following percents. For each draw a 100-square, then shade the part corresponding to the given percent.

   a. 15%   **b.** 83%   **c.** 7%   **d.** 60%   **e.** 100%

3. Express each of the following as a percent:

a. 21 hundredths	49 hundredths	81 hundredths	70 hundredths
b. 8 hundredths	4 hundredths	9 hundredths	1 hundredth
c. $37\frac{1}{2}$ hundredths	$5\frac{1}{4}$ hundredths	$\frac{1}{2}$ hundredth	$\frac{3}{4}$ hundredth
d. 62.5 hundredths	3.8 hundredths	5.75 hundredths	0.5 hundredth
e. 200 hundredths	150 hundredths	$266\frac{2}{3}$ hundredths	300 hundredths

4. Express each of the following as a percent:

    a. 51 out of 100   **c.** 68 out of 100   **e.** 2 out of 100   **g.** 9 out of 100

    b. $12\frac{1}{2}$ out of 100 **d.** $6\frac{3}{4}$ out of 100 **f.** 37.5 out of 100 **h.** 4.25 out of 100

5. Find how many hundredths are in:

    a. 6%; 9%; 1%   **c.** $4\frac{3}{4}$%; $87\frac{1}{2}$%; $\frac{1}{4}$%

    b. 34%; 95%; 67%   **d.** 5.2%; 62.5%; 0.8%

6. Express each of the following as a percent:

    a. The ratio of 11 to 100   **c.** The ratio of 6 to 100

    b. The ratio of 93 to 100   **d.** The ratio of 59 to 100

PERCENTS, DECIMAL FRACTIONS, AND COMMON FRACTIONS

Since percent means hundredths, it may be expressed both as a numeral for an equivalent decimal fraction or as a numeral for an equivalent common fraction and vice-versa.

6–2 PERCENTS AS DECIMAL FRACTIONS

The % symbol represents 2 decimal places. When it is removed there should be 2 more decimal places than in the original numeral.

To express a percent as a numeral for a decimal fraction, we rewrite the digits of the given percent but drop the percent symbol. Then we move the decimal point two places to the left. A decimal point is understood after the ones digit in a numeral naming a whole number.

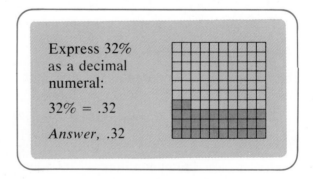

Express 32% as a decimal numeral:

32% = .32

Answer, .32

When the percent is a decimal percent such as 14.6%, the answer contains more than 2 decimal places.

$$14.6\% = .146$$

When the percent is 100% or more, the answer is a numeral naming a whole number or a mixed decimal.

$$400\% = 4$$
$$153\% = 1.53$$

When the percent is a common fraction less than one percent such as $\frac{1}{2}\%$, the answer may be written as a two-place decimal numeral $.00\frac{1}{2}$ (or as .005 since $\frac{1}{2}\% = .5\% = .005$).

When the percent is a mixed number percent such as $18\frac{3}{4}\%$, the answer may be written as a two-place decimal numeral $.18\frac{3}{4}$ (or as .1875 since $18\frac{3}{4}\% = 18.75\% = .1875$).

EXERCISES

1. Express each of the following percents as a decimal numeral:

   a. 28%   64%   75%   17%   42%
   b. 5%   3%   1%   6%   8%
   c. 30%   10%   80%   50%   40%
   d. 194%   125%   103%   269%   158%
   e. 160%   100%   110%   170%   220%
   f. $62\frac{1}{2}\%$ $3\frac{1}{4}\%$ $5\frac{3}{4}\%$ $33\frac{1}{3}\%$ $\frac{1}{8}\%$
   g. 23.8%   4.9%   137.51%   0.2%   0.875%
   h. 86%   7%   130% $8\frac{7}{8}\%$ 6.45%

2. Express each of the following percents as a numeral naming a whole number:

   500%   300%   200%   800%   100%

6–3 PERCENTS AS COMMON FRACTIONS

Since the % symbol is equivalent to the denominator 100, the denominator 100 may be used to replace the % symbol.

To express a percent as a numeral for a common fraction, we write the digits of the given percent as the numerator over 100 as the denominator. Then, if possible, we express the fraction in lowest terms.

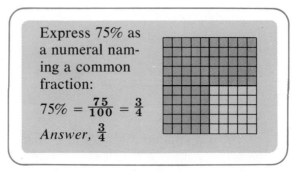

Express 75% as a numeral naming a common fraction:

$$75\% = \frac{75}{100} = \frac{3}{4}$$

Answer, $\frac{3}{4}$

When the percent is 100% or more, the answer is a numeral naming a whole number or a mixed number.

$$150\% = \frac{150}{100} = 1\frac{1}{2}$$

or

$$150\% = 100\% + 50\%$$
$$= 1 + \frac{1}{2} = 1\frac{1}{2}$$

When the percent is a mixed number percent, we express the percent as a decimal fraction, then as a common fraction in its lowest terms.

$$12\frac{1}{2}\% = .12\frac{1}{2} = .125 = \frac{125}{1,000} = \frac{1}{8}$$

or

$$12\frac{1}{2}\% = \frac{12\frac{1}{2}}{100} = 12\frac{1}{2} \div 100 = \frac{\overset{1}{\cancel{25}}}{2} \times \frac{1}{\underset{4}{\cancel{100}}} = \frac{1}{8}$$

1. What percent of each of the following squares is shaded?
What fractional part of each square is shaded?

 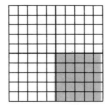 

 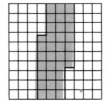

2. Express each of the following percents as a numeral naming a
common fraction in lowest terms:

a.   50%;   25%;   80%;   30%;   20%;   10%;   40%;   70%;   90%;   60%

b.   5%;   85%;   4%;   36%;   55%;   96%;   22%;   35%;   74%;   15%

c. $37\frac{1}{2}$%; $62\frac{1}{2}$%; $87\frac{1}{2}$%; $12\frac{1}{2}$%; $6\frac{1}{4}$%; $33\frac{1}{3}$%; $16\frac{2}{3}$%; $66\frac{2}{3}$%; $83\frac{1}{3}$%; $8\frac{1}{3}$%

3. Express each of the following percents as a numeral naming a
mixed number:

125%;   160%;   120%;   210%;   390%; $162\frac{1}{2}$%; $187\frac{1}{2}$%; $133\frac{1}{3}$%; $266\frac{2}{3}$%; $412\frac{1}{2}$%

6–4   DECIMAL FRACTIONS AS PERCENTS

Since the % symbol repre-
sents two decimal places (hundredths), we can use the symbol
to replace two decimal places.

*To express a decimal fraction
as a percent,* we write the digits
of the numeral naming the given
decimal. We move the decimal

Express .57 as a
percent:

.57 = 57%

Answer, 57%

point two places to the right and write the percent symbol after the numeral.

In a percent the decimal point is not written after the last digit. Observe that the percent has two less decimal places than the equivalent decimal fraction.

$$.0004 = .04\% \qquad .819 = 81.9\% \qquad .7 = .70 = 70\%$$

A mixed decimal is equal to more than 100%.

$$1.94 = 194\%$$

A whole number is equivalent to some multiple of 100%.

$$2 = 2.00 = 200\% \qquad 3 = 3.00 = 300\%, \text{ etc.}$$

EXERCISES

Express each of the following decimals as a percent:

1. .28	.51	.65	.40	.96
2. .06	.04	.01	.09	.05
3. .4	.8	.5	.2	.3
4. 5.00	3.00	9	7	4
5. 1.37	2.05	1.6	1.45	1.9
6. $.62\frac{1}{2}$	$.05\frac{1}{2}$	$.07\frac{3}{4}$	$.70\frac{5}{8}$	$1.16\frac{2}{3}$
7. .875	.0225	1.206	.004	.0005
8. $.00\frac{1}{2}$	$.00\frac{7}{8}$	$.00\frac{1}{4}$	$.00\frac{3}{4}$	$.00\frac{2}{5}$
9. .73	.08	.60	.9	8
10. 1.42	2.3	$.06\frac{1}{4}$	.0975	1.528

6-5 COMMON FRACTIONS AS PERCENTS

Since the % symbol is equivalent to the denominator 100, the % symbol may be used to replace the denominator 100.

$$\frac{5}{100} = 5\%$$

Sometimes the fraction has a denominator that can be changed quickly to the denominator 100.

$$\frac{7}{20} = \frac{7 \times 5}{20 \times 5} = \frac{35}{100} = 35\%; \frac{12}{200} = \frac{12 \div 2}{200 \div 2} = \frac{6}{100} = 6\%$$

Generally the fraction has a denominator which cannot be changed easily to the denominator 100. However, a common fraction may be expressed as a decimal fraction and a decimal fraction may be expressed as a percent.

To express a common fraction as a percent, we divide the numerator by the denominator, finding the quotient to two decimal places. We rewrite the digits in the quotient, drop the decimal point, and write the percent symbol % after the numeral.

Express $\frac{7}{8}$ as a percent:

$$\frac{7}{8} = 7 \div 8 = 8\overline{)7.00} \quad .87\tfrac{1}{2} = 87\tfrac{1}{2}\%$$

Answer, $87\tfrac{1}{2}\%$

If the decimal fraction equivalent is not exact hundredths, we can either write the remainder as a numeral naming a common fraction as shown above or round off the percent to the degree desired: nearest whole percent, tenth of a percent, hundredth of a percent, etc.

Percent

$$\frac{2}{3} = .66\frac{2}{3} = 66\frac{2}{3}\%$$

or

$$\frac{2}{3} = .666\frac{2}{3} = 66.7\%$$

or

$$\frac{2}{3} = .6666\frac{2}{3} = 66.67\%$$

A mixed number is equal to more than 100%.

$$1\frac{3}{4} = 175\% \quad \text{since} \quad 1 = 100\% \quad \text{and} \quad \frac{3}{4} = 75\%.$$

EXERCISES

1. Express each of the following fractions as a percent:

   a. $\frac{9}{100}, \frac{27}{100}, \frac{53}{100}, \frac{90}{100}, \frac{146}{100}$

   b. $\frac{1}{4}, \frac{1}{2}, \frac{3}{5}, \frac{3}{4}, \frac{1}{5}$

   c. $\frac{7}{10}, \frac{2}{5}, \frac{9}{10}, \frac{4}{5}, \frac{1}{10}$

   d. $\frac{9}{50}, \frac{3}{25}, \frac{19}{20}, \frac{11}{25}, \frac{17}{20}$

   e. $\frac{40}{200}, \frac{16}{400}, \frac{30}{600}, \frac{21}{700}, \frac{35}{500}$

   f. $\frac{1}{8}, \frac{1}{3}, \frac{1}{6}, \frac{5}{8}, \frac{2}{9}$

   g. $\frac{3}{8}, \frac{5}{6}, \frac{7}{8}, \frac{7}{12}, \frac{13}{16}$

   h. $\frac{9}{12}, \frac{21}{35}, \frac{48}{96}, \frac{14}{56}, \frac{63}{90}$

   i. $\frac{19}{57}, \frac{48}{56}, \frac{70}{112}, \frac{60}{72}, \frac{84}{126}$

   j. $\frac{12}{14}, \frac{21}{27}, \frac{20}{36}, \frac{15}{33}, \frac{27}{63}$

2. Express each of the following fractions as a percent:

   a. To nearest whole percent: $\frac{4}{7}, \frac{5}{9}, \frac{2}{3}, \frac{11}{16}, \frac{16}{18}$

   b. To nearest tenth of a percent: $\frac{2}{9}, \frac{6}{7}, \frac{5}{12}, \frac{1}{6}, \frac{52}{60}$

   c. To nearest hundredth of a percent: $\frac{5}{7}, \frac{11}{12}, \frac{7}{9}, \frac{19}{24}, \frac{14}{49}$

3. Express each of the following mixed numbers as a percent:
   $1\frac{1}{4}, 1\frac{5}{8}, 2\frac{1}{2}, 2\frac{3}{5}, 1\frac{1}{3}$

4. Express each of the following improper fractions as a percent:

   a. $\frac{34}{34}, \frac{41}{41}, \frac{112}{112}, \frac{16}{8}, \frac{27}{3}$

   b. $\frac{3}{2}, \frac{9}{5}, \frac{5}{4}, \frac{17}{8}, \frac{11}{3}$

TABLE OF EQUIVALENTS PERCENTS, DECIMALS, AND COMMON FRACTIONS

Percent	Decimal	Common Fraction
5%	.05	$\frac{1}{20}$
$6\frac{1}{4}\%$	$.06\frac{1}{4}$	$\frac{1}{16}$
$8\frac{1}{3}\%$	$.08\frac{1}{3}$	$\frac{1}{12}$
10%	.10 or .1	$\frac{1}{10}$
$12\frac{1}{2}\%$	$.12\frac{1}{2}$ or .125	$\frac{1}{8}$
$16\frac{2}{3}\%$	$.16\frac{2}{3}$	$\frac{1}{6}$
20%	.20 or .2	$\frac{1}{5}$
25%	.25	$\frac{1}{4}$
30%	.30 or .3	$\frac{3}{10}$
$33\frac{1}{3}\%$	$.33\frac{1}{3}$	$\frac{1}{3}$
$37\frac{1}{2}\%$	$.37\frac{1}{2}$ or .375	$\frac{3}{8}$
40%	.40 or .4	$\frac{2}{5}$
50%	.50 or .5	$\frac{1}{2}$
60%	.60 or .6	$\frac{3}{5}$
$62\frac{1}{2}\%$	$.62\frac{1}{2}$ or .625	$\frac{5}{8}$
$66\frac{2}{3}\%$	$.66\frac{2}{3}$	$\frac{2}{3}$
70%	.70 or .7	$\frac{7}{10}$
75%	.75	$\frac{3}{4}$
80%	.80 or .8	$\frac{4}{5}$
$83\frac{1}{3}\%$	$.83\frac{1}{3}$	$\frac{5}{6}$
$87\frac{1}{2}\%$	$.87\frac{1}{2}$ or .875	$\frac{7}{8}$
90%	.90 or .9	$\frac{9}{10}$
100%	1.00 or 1	

6-6 COMPUTATION—FINDING A PERCENT OF A NUMBER

In our work with common fractions we studied how to find a fractional part of a number like $\frac{4}{5}$ of 750. Since a percent is just another way of writing a numeral naming a common fraction, finding 80% of 750 is like finding $\frac{4}{5}$ of 750. When we multiplied decimals, we learned how to find a decimal part of a number like .12 of 67. Since a percent is another way of writing a numeral naming a decimal fraction, finding 12% of 67 is like finding .12 of 67.

Since a percent may be written either as a decimal or a common fraction, to find a percent of a number, we change the percent to its equivalent decimal fraction or common fraction. Then we multiply the given number by this fraction.

Find 12% of 67:

$12\% = .12$

$$\begin{array}{r} 67 \\ \times .12 \\ \hline 1\ 34 \\ 6\ 7 \\ \hline 8.04 \end{array}$$

Answer, 8.04

Find 80% of 750:

$80\% = \frac{4}{5}$

$$\frac{4}{\cancel{5}} \times \frac{\cancel{750}^{150}}{1} = 600$$

Answer, 600

When finding a mixed number or common fraction percent of a number, we may use the decimal percent form.

$18\frac{1}{2}\%$ of $500 = .18\frac{1}{2} \times 500$ or $.185 \times 500$
since $18\frac{1}{2}\% = 18.5\% = .185$

$\frac{3}{4}\%$ of $120 = .00\frac{3}{4} \times 120$ or $.0075 \times 120$
since $\frac{3}{4}\% = .75\% = .0075$

When finding a percent of an amount of money, we round the answers to the nearest cent.

4% of $1.28 = .04 \times \$1.28 = \$.0512 = \$.05$

Find:

1. a. 48% of 85   26% of 30   11% of 98   57% of 615   83% of 4,000

  b. 29% of 140   15% of 98   94% of 632   38% of 497   72% of 3,259

  c. 4% of 60   8% of 35   3% of 9   9% of 200   1% of 4,275

  d. 5% of 82   6% of 148   2% of 375   7% of 906   4% of 8,647

  e. 10% of 20   40% of 7   80% of 468   60% of 250   30% of 5,000

2. a. 6% of 6.8   13% of 7.4   9% of 8.18   36% of 4.25   91% of 8.60

  b. 18% of 14.56   4% of 91.05   63% of 42.96   1% of 483.29   88% of 907.43

3. a. $26\frac{1}{2}$% of 54 $94\frac{1}{2}$% of 300 $43\frac{1}{4}$% of 48 $18\frac{1}{4}$% of 964 $65\frac{3}{4}$% of 2,000

  b. $5\frac{1}{2}$% of 8 $6\frac{1}{4}$% of 24 $9\frac{3}{4}$% of 672 $1\frac{1}{2}$% of 1,287 $4\frac{3}{4}$% of 9,175

  c. $34\frac{3}{8}$% of 72 $7\frac{5}{8}$% of 400 $4\frac{2}{3}$% of 969 $25\frac{1}{6}$% of 4,200 $9\frac{7}{8}$% of 1,000

4. a. 20.6% of 81   17.9% of 650   36.1% of 8   83.2% of 4.75   61.4% of 3,400

  b. 8.3% of 40   2.5% of 3   4.9% of 2.91   1.6% of 92.83   7.8% of 5,000

  c. 19.28% of 300   80.05% of 2.000   94.62% of 750   57.81% of 6,450

5. a. 100% of 70   300% of 45   500% of 180   200% of 4.25   800% of 1,000

  b. 128% of 9   193% of 87   142% of 256   376% of 8.94   217% of 3,500

  c. 106% of 205   101% of 3,000   107% of 75   205% of 12.5   409% of 4,000

  d. 150% of 32   120% of 8   360% of 545   110% of 6.8   240% of 7,500

  e. 183.6% of 40   100.2% of 1,000   112.84% of 5   246.5% of 18.75

  f. $117\frac{1}{2}$% of 6 $232\frac{1}{4}$% of 480 $100\frac{1}{2}$% of 6,000 $104\frac{3}{4}$% of 47.4

6. a. $\frac{1}{2}$% of 500 $\frac{1}{4}$% of 32 $\frac{3}{4}$% of 2,000 $\frac{1}{2}$% of 28.46 $\frac{3}{4}$% of 105.23

  b. $\frac{3}{8}$% of 48 $\frac{7}{8}$% of 600 $\frac{2}{3}$% of 144 $\frac{5}{8}$% of 108.64 $\frac{1}{6}$% of 9,000

  c. .08% of 70   0.3% of 2,000   0.5% of 9   0.6% of 26.25   0.1% of 12,000

  d. 0.29% of 4   0.73% of 100   0.46% of 85   0.52% of 7.5   0.89% of 4,000

7. Use fractional equivalents for percents to find:

  a. 50% of: 8; 20; 56; 140; 392   **d.** 75% of: 4; 24; 76; 136; 860

  b. 25% of: 12; 36; 68; 124; 600   **e.** 20% of: 5; 40; 95; 225; 1,000

  c. 10% of: 50; 90; 140; 480; 1,250   **f.** 80% of: 10; 55; 175; 340; 1,425

g. $66\frac{2}{3}\%$ of: 6; 30; 72; 171; 807   o. 70% of: 10; 300; 450; 1,000; 5,600

h. $87\frac{1}{2}\%$ of: 16; 56; 144; 960; 2,400   p. $62\frac{1}{2}\%$ of: 80; 144; 400; 1,296; 7,200

i. $12\frac{1}{2}\%$ of: 32; 96; 80; 128; 264   q. $37\frac{1}{2}\%$ of: 32; 104; 800; 3,512; 4,000

j. $33\frac{1}{3}\%$ of: 3; 48; 120; 729; 1,500   r. $83\frac{1}{3}\%$ of: 18; 42; 132; 864; 2,406

k. $16\frac{2}{3}\%$ of: 24; 60; 96; 282; 2,094   s. 90% of: 60; 100; 250; 960; 8,000

l. 30% of: 20; 70; 130; 500; 1,700   t. $6\frac{1}{4}\%$ of 64; 112; 192; 1,600; 3,920

m. 40% of: 15; 50; 75; 325; 1,300   u. $8\frac{1}{3}\%$ of: 12; 96; 288; 1,728; 9,000

n. 60% of: 45; 65; 180; 740; 2,225   v. 5% of: 40; 100; 260; 500; 1,380

8. Use fractional equivalents for percents to find:

a. 10% of 70	40% of 65	50% of 92	80% of 200	30% of 450
b. 25% of 84	75% of 536	90% of 400	20% of 875	60% of 1,250
c. $87\frac{1}{2}\%$ of 72	$12\frac{1}{2}\%$ of 432	$37\frac{1}{2}\%$ of 960	$62\frac{1}{2}\%$ of 584	$6\frac{1}{4}\%$ of 800
d. $33\frac{1}{3}\%$ of 69	$66\frac{2}{3}\%$ of 360	$83\frac{1}{3}\%$ of 144	$16\frac{2}{3}\%$ of 300	$8\frac{1}{3}\%$ of 2,400
e. 50% of 35	10% of 123	$33\frac{1}{3}\%$ of 79	20% of 42	$16\frac{2}{3}\%$ of 21

9. Use mixed numbers for percents to find:

a. 125% of 28	150% of 354	275% of 260	160% of 800	190% of 1,000
b. $187\frac{1}{2}\%$ of 440	$133\frac{1}{3}\%$ of 960	$162\frac{1}{2}\%$ of 5,600	$183\frac{1}{3}\%$ of 630	$266\frac{2}{3}\%$ of 720

10. Find each of the following to the nearest cent:

a. 26% of $90	33% of $6	54% of $237	86% of $1,250	47% of $4,000
b. 5% of $7	1% of $23	6% of $508	4% of $9,500	3% of $649
c. 69% of $.40	42% of $.50	18% of $9.24	95% of $56.83	70% of $125.75
d. 3% of $.68	9% of $.80	7% of $5.67	6% of $71.09	2% of $482.91
e. $12\frac{1}{2}\%$ of $136	$66\frac{2}{3}\%$ of $.87	$1\frac{1}{2}\%$ of $96.82	$\frac{3}{4}\%$ of $600	
f. 5.2% of $70	0.7% of $360	16.52% of $40.06	0.1% of $52.87	
g. 120% of $56	136% of $1.20	$100\frac{1}{2}\%$ of $2,000	$287\frac{1}{2}\%$ of $480	

11. Use fractional equivalents for percents to find each of the following to the nearest cent:

a. 50% of $648	10% of $900	25% of $2,000	$16\frac{2}{3}\%$ of $1,800	$62\frac{1}{2}\%$ of $680
b. 60% of $.50	20% of $8.70	90% of $19.30	75% of $5.24	$33\frac{1}{3}\%$ of $9.54
c. 30% of $1.29	40% of $.63	$66\frac{2}{3}\%$ of $4.75	$83\frac{1}{3}\%$ of $10	70% of $63.89

6-7 COMPUTATION—FINDING WHAT PERCENT ONE NUMBER IS OF ANOTHER

Since percent is a fraction, the relationship "What fractional part of 8 is 2?" or "What decimal part of 8 is 2?" can also be stated as "What percent of 8 is 2?"

This relationship as a common fraction is $\frac{1}{4}$ since $\frac{2}{8} = \frac{1}{4}$; as a decimal fraction it is .25 since $\frac{2}{8} = \frac{1}{4} = .25$; and as a percent it is 25% since $\frac{2}{8} = \frac{1}{4} = .25 = 25\%$.

To find what percent one number is of another, we find what fractional part one number is of the other expressed in lowest terms. Then we change this fraction to a percent, using the percent equivalent if it is known, otherwise we change the fraction first to a 2-place decimal, then to a percent.

What percent of 40 is 26?

$$\frac{26}{40} = \frac{13}{20} = 20\overline{)13.00} \quad \begin{array}{r} .65 = 65\% \\ \hline \end{array}$$

$$\begin{array}{r} 12\ 0 \\ \hline 1\ 00 \\ 1\ 00 \\ \hline \cdot\ \cdot\ \cdot \end{array}$$

Answer, 65%

Sometimes the fraction has a denominator that can be changed easily to the denominator 100.

$$\frac{8}{25} = \frac{8 \times 4}{25 \times 4} = \frac{32}{100} = 32\%$$

$$\frac{24}{300} = \frac{24 \div 3}{300 \div 3} = \frac{8}{100} = 8\%$$

When the percent is not an exact whole number, we can either show the remainder as a common fraction or round off the percent to the degree desired: nearest whole percent, nearest tenth of a percent, nearest hundredth of a percent, etc.

Percent

9 is what percent of 32?

$$.28\tfrac{1}{8}$$
$$\frac{9}{32} = 32\overline{)9.00}$$
6 4
2 60
2 56
4

$$.2812\tfrac{1}{2}$$
$$\frac{9}{32} = 32\overline{)9.0000}$$
6 4
2 60
2 56
40
32
80
64
16

Answer, $28\frac{1}{8}\%$, or 28% when rounded to nearest whole percent, or 28.1% when rounded to nearest tenth of a percent, or 28.13% when rounded to nearest hundredth of a percent.

An improper fraction is equal to 100% or more.

What percent of 5 is 8?

$\frac{8}{5} = 1\frac{3}{5} = 160\%$

Answer, 160%

EXERCISES

Find the answer to each of the following:

1. a. What percent of 100 is 29?
   b. 18 is what percent of 25?
   c. 7 is what percent of 20?
   d. What percent of 4 is 3?
   e. 9 is what percent of 50?
   f. 3 is what percent of 10?
   g. 2 is what percent of 5?
   h. 1 is what percent of 2?

2. a. What percent of 3 is 1?
   b. What percent of 6 is 5?
   c. What percent of 8 is 7?
   d. 3 is what percent of 8?

3. a. What percent of 7 is 5?
   b. What percent of 12 is 11?
   c. 19 is what percent of 24?
   d. 4 is what percent of 9?
   e. 9 is what percent of 16?
   f. What percent of 15 is 13?

4. a. What percent of 100 is 75?
   b. 20 is what percent of 25?
   c. What percent of 20 is 8?
   d. 25 is what percent of 50?
   e. What percent of 10 is 4?
   f. 6 is what percent of 75?

5. a. What percent of 200 is 40?
  b. 48 is what percent of 300?
  c. What percent of 800 is 56?
  d. 15 is what percent of 500?
  e. What percent of 400 is 24?
  f. 12 is what percent of 600?

6. a. What percent of 12 is 6?
  b. 18 is what percent of 45?
  c. What percent of 80 is 32?
  d. 63 is what percent of 72?
  e. 9 is what percent of 36?
  f. What percent of 60 is 42?
  g. 45 is what percent of 75?
  h. What percent of 144 is 108?

7. a. What percent of 56 is 49?
  b. 18 is what percent of 48?
  c. What percent of 42 is 28?
  d. 50 is what percent of 80?
  e. What percent of 27 is 9?
  f. 45 is what percent of 54?

8. a. What percent of 43 is 43?
  b. What percent of 100 is 200?
  c. 25 is what percent of 5?
  d. 150 is what percent of 150?
  e. 54 is what percent of 18?
  f. What percent of 300 is 1,200?

9. a. What percent of 4 is 7?
  b. 12 is what percent of 5?
  c. What percent of 18 is 27?
  d. 44 is what percent of 24?
  e. 8 is what percent of 3?
  f. What percent of 8 is 15?
  g. 81 is what percent of 30?
  h. What percent of 75 is 105?

10. Round to the nearest whole percent:

  a. What percent of 9 is 5?
  b. 28 is what percent of 32?
  c. What percent of 72 is 15?
  d. 3 is what percent of 16?
  e. What percent of 12 is 11?
  f. 20 is what percent of 14?

11. Round to the nearest tenth of a percent:

  a. 5 is what percent of 6?
  b. What percent of 36 is 21?
  c. 55 is what percent of 102?
  d. What percent of 18 is 11?
  e. 10 is what percent of 45?
  f. What percent of 48 is 80?

12. Round to the nearest hundredth of a percent:

  a. What percent of 15 is 4?
  b. 3 is what percent of 9?
  c. What percent of 283 is 100?
  d. 17 is what percent of 32?
  e. What percent of 12 is 2?
  f. 50 is what percent of 38?

13. a. What percent of 3.6 is 2.7?
  b. .8 is what percent of 2?
  c. What percent of 4.5 is 9?
  d. .04 is what percent of .1?
  e. What percent of 10 is .5?
  f. 3.08 is what percent of 15.4?

14. a. What percent of 6 is $1\frac{1}{2}$?
  b. $\frac{1}{3}$ is what percent of $\frac{5}{6}$?
  c. What percent of $6\frac{7}{8}$ is $4\frac{1}{8}$?
  d. $2\frac{1}{4}$ is what percent of $3\frac{3}{4}$?
  e. What percent of $\frac{1}{4}$ is $\frac{7}{8}$?
  f. 5 is what percent of $1\frac{2}{3}$?

15. a. What percent of $48 is $12?
  b. $.16 is what percent of $.25?
  c. What percent of $2 is $.50?
  d. $18 is what percent of $22.50?
  e. What percent of $.60 is $.96?
  f. $8.70 is what percent of $108.75?

6-8 COMPUTATION—FINDING THE NUMBER WHEN A PERCENT OF IT IS KNOWN

When a fractional part or a decimal part of a number is known, the required number is found by dividing the given number by the common fraction or decimal fraction respectively (see pages 124 and 167).

$\frac{3}{4}$ of what number is 18?

$$18 \div \frac{3}{4} = \frac{\overset{6}{\cancel{18}}}{1} \times \frac{4}{\underset{1}{\cancel{3}}} = 24$$

Answer, 24

.75 of what number is 18?

$$.75_\wedge \overline{)18.00_\wedge}^{\,24.}$$

Answer, 24

Since a percent is a fraction, to find the number when a percent of it is known, we divide the given number by the common fraction or decimal fraction equivalent of the percent.

To find the answer to "75% of what number is 18?," we express 75% as $\frac{3}{4}$ or .75 and think of the problem as "$\frac{3}{4}$ of what number is 18?" or ".75 of what number is 18?"

75% of what number is 18?

$$75\% = \frac{3}{4} \qquad\qquad \text{or} \qquad\qquad 75\% = .75$$

$$18 \div \frac{3}{4} = \frac{\overset{6}{\cancel{18}}}{1} \times \frac{4}{\underset{1}{\cancel{3}}} = 24 \qquad\qquad .75_\wedge \overline{)18.00_\wedge}^{\,24.}$$

Answer, 24

1. Use decimal equivalents of the percents to find the following missing numbers:

   a. 18% of what number is 9?

   b. 6% of what number is 15?

   c. 54 is 2% of what number?

   d. 40% of what number is 200?

   e. 30.6 is 51% of what number?

   f. 96 is 32% of what number?

   g. 4 is 5% of what number?

   h. 75% of what number is 39?

   i. 72 is 90% of what number?

   j. 3% of what number is 85.29?

2. Use fractional equivalents of the percents to find the following missing numbers:

   a. 50% of what number is 97?

   b. 9 is 10% of what number?

   c. 75% of what number is 144?

   d. $37\frac{1}{2}$% of what number is 225?

   e. 408 is $66\frac{2}{3}$% of what number?

   f. 41 is 25% of what number?

   g. $33\frac{1}{3}$% of what number is 81?

   h. 900 is 60% of what number?

   i. 1,000 is $62\frac{1}{2}$% of what number?

   j. $83\frac{1}{3}$% of what number is 375?

Find the missing numbers:

3. a. 100% of what number is 8?

   b. 400% of what number is 36?

   c. 52 is 200% of what number?

   d. 149 is 100% of what number?

   e. 200 is 500% of what number?

   f. 300% of what number is 81?

4. a. 125% of what number is 60?

   b. 750 is $166\frac{2}{3}$% of what number?

   c. 108% of what number is 540?

   d. 189 is 150% of what number?

   e. $212\frac{1}{2}$% of what number is 34?

   f. 94.5 is 135% of what number?

5. a. 4.5% of what number is 36?

   b. 54 is 0.6% of what number?

   c. 101.2% of what number is 5,060?

   d. 283 is 28.3% of what number?

   e. 0.1% of what number is 20?

   f. 98.75% of what number is 11,850?

6. a. $5\frac{1}{2}$% of what number is 220?

   b. $\frac{3}{4}$% of what number is 6?

   c. 3,195 is $106\frac{1}{2}$% of what number?

   d. 3,740 is $93\frac{1}{2}$% of what number?

   e. 680 is $4\frac{1}{4}$% of what number?

   f. $\frac{1}{2}$% of what number is 90?

7. a. 4% of what amount is $100?

   b. $1.60 is $16\frac{2}{3}$% of what amount?

   c. 175% of what amount is $48.30?

   d. $\frac{1}{4}$% of what amount is $250?

   e. $45 is 18% of what amount?

   f. 90% of what amount is $.54?

   g. $27.65 is $3\frac{1}{2}$% of what amount?

   h. $6.85 is 0.5% of what amount?

6-9 PERCENT—SOLVING BY PROPORTIONS

The three basic types of percentage may be treated as one through the use of the proportion.

(1) Find 25% of 12.

25% is the ratio of 25 to 100 or $\frac{25}{100}$.

To find 25% of 12 means to determine the number (n) which compared to 12 is the same as 25 compared to 100.

(2) What percent of 12 is 3?

To find what percent of 12 is 3 means to find the number (n) per 100 or the ratio of a number to 100 which has the same ratio as 3 to 12. The proportion $\frac{n}{100} = \frac{3}{12}$ is formed and solved.

(3) 25% of what number is 3?

25% is the ratio of 25 to 100 or $\frac{25}{100}$.

To find the number of which 25% is 3 means to determine the number (n) such that 3 compared to this number is the same as 25 compared to 100. The proprotion $\frac{3}{n} = \frac{25}{100}$ is formed and solved.

(1)
$$\frac{n}{12} = \frac{25}{100}$$
$$100\,n = 300$$
$$n = 3$$
Answer, 3

(2)
$$\frac{n}{100} = \frac{3}{12}$$
$$12\,n = 300$$
$$n = 25$$
Answer, 25%

(3)
$$\frac{3}{n} = \frac{25}{100}$$
$$25\,n = 300$$
$$n = 12$$
Answer, 12

EXERCISES

1. Write each of the following as a ratio:

   a. 4%   **c.** 60%   **e.** 5%   **g.** 400%   **i.** $6\frac{3}{4}\%$ **k.** 4.8%   **m.** 0.4%

   b. 23%   **d.** 85%   **f.** 130%   **h.** $37\frac{1}{2}\%$ **j.** $\frac{1}{2}\%$ **l.** $83\frac{1}{3}\%$ **n.** 175%

2. Find:

   a. 6% of 50   **d.** $62\frac{1}{2}\%$ of 296   **g.** 2% of $59

   b. 80% of 105   **e.** 14% of 519   **h.** 163% of 1,000

   c. 75% of 96   **f.** 5% of 6.24   **i.** $3\frac{1}{4}\%$ of 2,400

3. Find each of the following:

   a. 7 is what percent of 28?

   b. What percent of 50 is 47?

   c. What percent of 120 is 36?

   d. 60 is what percent of 72?

   e. 12 is what percent of 8?

   f. What percent of $.76 is $.57

   g. 20 is what percent of 25?

   h. What percent of $3 is $.90?

4. Find each of the following:

   a. 35% of what number is 224?

   b. 85% of what number is 17?

   c. 75% of what number is 18?

   d. 52 is 4% of what number?

   e. 26 is 26% of what number?

   f. 3.2% of what number is 16?

   g. 5% of what amount is $65?

   h. $8.20 is 40% of what amount?

6–10 COMMON FRACTION, DECIMAL FRACTION, AND PERCENT NUMBER RELATIONSHIPS—SOLVING BY EQUATION

The equation[1] may be used to find:

(1) A fractional part or decimal part or percent of a number.

(2) What fractional part or decimal part or percent one number is of another.

(3) A number when a fractional part or decimal part or percent of it is known.

To use this method:

We read each problem carefully to find the facts which are related to the missing number. We represent this unknown number by a letter. We form an equation by translating two equal facts, with at least one containing the unknown, into algebraic expressions and writing one expression equal to the other. Where necessary, we change the percent to a common fraction or to a decimal equivalent.

Then we solve the equation and check.

---

[1] See page 362.

(1)	(2)	(3)
Find $\frac{1}{4}$ of 12:	What fractional part of 12 is 3?	$\frac{1}{4}$ of what number is 3?
$\frac{1}{4} \times 12 = n$ $3 = n$ $n = 3$ *Answer*, 3	$n \times 12 = 3$ $12\,n = 3$ $\dfrac{12\,n}{12} = \dfrac{3}{12}$ $n = \frac{1}{4}$ *Answer*, $\frac{1}{4}$	$\frac{1}{4} \times n = 3$ $\frac{1}{4}\,n = 3$ $4 \cdot \frac{1}{4}\,n = 4 \cdot 3$ $n = 12$ *Answer*, 12
Find .25 of 12:	What decimal part of 12 is 3?	.25 of what number is 3?
$.25 \times 12 = n$ $3 = n$ $n = 3$ *Answer*, 3	$n \times 12 = 3$ $12\,n = 3$ $n = \frac{1}{4}$ $n = .25$ *Answer*, .25	$.25 \times n = 3$ $.25\,n = 3$ $\dfrac{.25\,n}{.25} = \dfrac{3}{.25}$ $n = 12$ *Answer*, 12
Find 25% of 12:	What percent of 12 is 3?	25% of what number is 3?
$25\% \times 12 = n$ $.25 \times 12 = n$ $3 = n$ $n = 3$ *Answer*, 3	$n\% \times 12 = 3$ $\dfrac{n}{100} \times 12 = 3$ $\dfrac{12\,n}{100} = \dfrac{3}{1}$ $12\,n = 300$ $n = 25$ *Answer*, 25%	$25\% \times n = 3$ $.25\,n = 3$ $\dfrac{.25\,n}{.25} = \dfrac{3}{.25}$ $n = 12$ *Answer*, 12

EXERCISES

1. Find:

a. $\frac{1}{2}$ of 60   **c.** $\frac{7}{15}$ of 90   **e.** $\frac{2}{3}$ of 84   **g.** $\frac{5}{8}$ of 94

b. $\frac{2}{5}$ of 75   **d.** $\frac{11}{12}$ of 132   **f.** $\frac{3}{10}$ of 500   **h.** $\frac{3}{4}$ of 25

2. Find:

   a. .2 of 18   **c.** .04 of 95   **e.** .98 of 6   **g.** .065 of 8.3

   b. .75 of 26   **d.** .33 of 1.49   **f.** .475 of 840   **h.** .625 of 24

3. Find:

   a. 4% of 560   **c.** 6% of 3,000   **e.** $66\frac{2}{3}$ % of $.27   **g.** 200% of 39

   b. 29% of 700   **d.** 132% of 400   **f.** 75% of $12.68   **h.** $4\frac{1}{2}$ % of $5,000

4. Find:

   a. $\frac{5}{6}$ of 54   **c.** .8 of 59   **e.** $62\frac{1}{2}$ % of $5.76   **g.** $\frac{7}{8}$ of 144

   b. 3% of 750   **d.** $\frac{4}{9}$ of 72   **f.** .03 of 4.5   **h.** 125% of 800

5. Find each of the following:

   a. What fractional part of 5 is 3?   **d.** What fractional part of 70 is 42?

   b. 6 is what fractional part of 90?   **e.** What fractional part of 91 is 26?

   c. 16 is what fractional part of 24? **f.** 81 is what fractional part of 108?

6. Find each of the following:

   a. What decimal part of 12 is 9?   **d.** What decimal part of 40 is 36?

   b. 2 is what decimal part of 4?   **e.** 18 is what decimal part of 54?

   c. 16 is what decimal part of 25?   **f.** What decimal part of 60 is 50?

7. Find each of the following:

   a. 12 is what percent of 48?   **d.** What percent of $25 is $17?

   b. 9 is what percent of 50?   **e.** What percent of 39 is 39?

   c. What percent of 600 is 18?   **f.** 20 is what percent of 16?

8. Find each of the following:

   a. What fractional part of 48 is 32?   **d.** 84 is what fractional part of 108?

   b. What decimal part of 30 is 24?   **e.** $45 is what percent of $54?

   c. What percent of 900 is 63?   **f.** 120 is what decimal part of 160?

9. Find each of the following: **10.** Find each of the following:

   a. $\frac{1}{6}$ of what number is 37?   **a.** 270 is .75 of what number?

   b. $\frac{2}{3}$ of what number is 90?   **b.** 56 is .8 of what number?

   c. 125 is $\frac{5}{8}$ of what number?   **c.** .375 of what number is 75?

11. Find each of the following:

   a. 5 is 10% of what number?   **d.** 20% of what number is 9?

   b. 18 is 3% of what number?   **e.** $87\frac{1}{2}$% of what number is 49?

   c. 24 is 72% of what number?   **f.** 30 is 125% of what number?

12. Find each of the following:

    a. $\frac{4}{5}$ of what number is 40?   **d.** $\frac{3}{7}$ of what number is 84?

    b. .05 of what number is 6?   **e.** 17 is .125 of what number?

    c. 3% of what number is 9?   **f.** 1.28 is 32% of what number?

13. Find each of the following:

    a. 80% of what number is 20?   **d.** $24 is what percent of $72?

    b. 13 is what percent of 20?   **e.** $.97 is 25% of what amount?

    c. 5% of $207   **f.** 115% of 83

6–11 DISCOUNT

Discount is the amount that an article is reduced in price. The regular or full price of the article is called the *list price* or *marked price*. The price of the article after the discount is deducted is called the *net price* or *sale price*. The percent taken off is called the *rate of discount*. This rate is sometimes expressed as a common fraction. Manufacturers sometimes allow trade discounts.

Often when a bill is paid at the time of purchase or within a specified time thereafter, a reduction called *cash discount* is allowed. The terms of sale are usually stated on the bill. For example, the terms 3/10, *n*/30 mean that a 3% discount is allowed if the bill is paid within 10 days and the full amount is due by the 30th day. The *net amount* is the amount of the bill after the cash discount is deducted.

When two or more discounts are given, they are called *successive discounts*.

(1) *To find the discount* when the list price and rate of discount are given, we multiply the list price by the rate of discount.

(2) *To find the net price,* we subtract the discount from the list price.

(3) *To find the rate of discount,* we find what percent the discount is of the list price.

(4) *To find the list price* when the net price and rate of discount are given, we subtract the given rate from 100%, then divide the answer into the net price.

(5) *To find the net amount,* we subtract the cash discount from the original amount of the bill. When two or more successive discount rates are given, we do not add the rates but use them one at a time.

Find the discount and net price when the list price is $240 and the rate of discount is 18%:

$240 list price
×.18 rate
‾‾‾‾‾
1920
240
‾‾‾‾‾
$43.20 discount

$240.00 list price
−43.20 discount
‾‾‾‾‾‾‾‾‾
$196.80 net price

Answer, $43.20 discount; $196.80 net price

What is the rate of discount when the list price is $35 and the discount is $14?

$$\frac{\$14}{\$35} = \frac{2}{5} = 40\%$$

Answer, 40%

EXERCISES

1. A camera marked $35 was sold at a discount of 20%. How much discount was allowed? What was the net price?
2. Find the discount and the net price when:

   a. the list price is $96 and the rate of discount is 12%.
   b. the rate of discount is 4% and the list price is $8.59.
3. What rate of discount was given if a coat that regularly sells for $85 is sold for $51?
4. Find the discount and the rate of discount when:

   a. the list price is $60 and the net price is $55.
   b. the net price is $1.05 and the list price is $1.50.
5. Lisa saved $48 by buying a typewriter at a sale when prices were reduced 25%. What was the regular price of the type-writer?
6. Find the list price when:

   a. the net price is $6.40 and the rate of discount is 20%.
   b. the rate of discount is 6% and the net price is $211.50.
7. What is the net amount when the amount of a bill is $235 and the rate of cash discount is 3%?

8. Find the cash discount received and the net amount paid when:

   a. the amount, $450, of bill dated Nov. 25 is paid on Nov. 30. Terms of payment were 5/15, *n*/60.

   b. the amount, $829.75, of bill dated Feb. 1 is paid on Feb. 28. Terms of payment were: 2/10, *n*/30.

9. A dealer lists radios to sell at $59 each. If she allows a 15% trade discount and an additional 4% cash discount, what is the net cash price of a radio?

10. Find the net price when:

    a. the list price is $170 and the rates of discount are 15%, 5%.

    b. the list price is $395.50 and the rates of discount are 40%, 3%.

11. On which is the rate of discount greater and how much greater, a refrigerator reduced from $600 to $450 or one reduced from $840 to $630?

12. What is the net price of a dishwasher listed at $349 with a trade discount of 10% and an additional cash discount of 2%?

13. A bag marked $45 was sold for $36. What rate of discount was given?

14. Find the sale price of each of the following articles:

    a. Suit: regular price $125; reduced 25%.

    b. Coat: marked to sell for $98.75; reduced 40%.

    c. Lamp: regular price $87.20; $37\frac{1}{2}$% off.

    d. Television set: listed at $375; 15% off.

    e. Table: marked to sell for $99.95; reduced 8%.

15. Find the regular price of a clothes dryer that sold for $196 at a 30% reduction sale.

6–12 COMMISSION

A salesperson who sells goods for another person is usually paid a sum of money based on the value of the goods sold. This money which is received for the services is called *commission*. When it is expressed as a percent, it is called the *rate of commission*. The amount that remains after the commission is deducted from the total selling price is called *net proceeds*. When a buyer purchases goods for another person, the buyer also is usually paid a commission for the services based on the cost of the goods. Salespeople and buyers are sometimes called *agents*.

(1) Selling: *To find the commission when the amount of sales and rate of commission are given,* we multiply the amount of sales by the rate of commission. To find the net proceeds, we subtract the commission from the amount of sales.

(2) Buying: *To find the commission when the cost of goods purchased and rate of commission are given,* we multiply the cost of goods purchased by the rate of commission. To find the total cost, we add the commission to the cost of goods purchased.

(3) *To find the rate of commission,* we find what percent the commission is of the amount of sales (or cost of goods purchased).

(4) *To find the sales when the commission and rate of commission are given,* we divide the commission by the rate.

Find the commission and net proceeds when the sales are $86.98 and the rate of commission is 7%:

$86.98 sales
×.07 rate
$6.0886
= $6.09 commission

$86.98 sales
−6.09 commission
$80.89 net proceeds

Answer, $6.09 commission;
$80.89 net proceeds

Find the rate of commission if the commission is $19.20 on sales of $320:

$$\frac{\$19.20}{\$320} = \$320\overline{)\$19.20} \quad \frac{.06}{} = 6\%$$
$$\underline{19\ 20}$$

Answer, 6% commission

EXERCISES

1. A real estate agent sold a house for $66,500 and was paid a commission of 7%. What was the amount of the agent's commission? How much money did the owner receive?

2. Find the commission and net proceeds when:

   a. the sales are $140 and the rate of commission is 8%.
   b. the rate of commission is 25% on sales of $865.60.

3. A lawyer collected a debt of $900 for a client, charging $135 commission for her services. What rate of commission did she charge?

4. Find the rate of commission when:

   a. the sales are $90 and the commission is $15.
   b. the commission is $3.75 and the sales are $25.
   c. the sales are $640 and the net proceeds are $560.
   d. the net proceeds are $730.80 and the sales are $812.

5. How much must a salesperson sell each week to earn $270 weekly if she is paid 9% commission on sales?

6. Find the amount of sales when:

   a. the commission is $329 and the rate of commission is 14%.
   b. the rate of commission is $12\frac{1}{2}$% and the commission is $26.50.

7. If an agent charges 2% commission for purchasing goods, how much will he receive for buying 825 crates of berries at $10.40 a crate? What is the total cost of the berries?

6–13 PROFIT AND LOSS

Merchants are engaged in business to earn a profit. To determine the profit, each merchant must consider the cost of goods, the selling price of the same goods, and the operating expenses. The *cost* is the amount the merchant pays for the goods. The *selling price* is the amount the merchant receives for selling the goods. The *operating expenses* or *overhead* are expenses of running the business. They include wages, rent, heat, light, telephone, taxes, insurance, advertising, repairs, supplies, and delivery costs.

The difference between the selling price and the cost is called the *margin*. The terms *gross profit, spread,* and *markup* sometimes are also used. The margin is often erroneously thought of as the profit earned. Actually, the profit earned, called *net profit,* is the amount that remains after both the cost and the operating expenses are deducted from the selling price.

To earn a profit the merchant must sell the goods at a price which is greater than the sum of the cost of the goods and the operating expenses. If the selling price is less than the sum of the cost and operating expenses, the goods are sold at a *loss*.

The profit may be expressed as a percent of either the cost or the selling price. This percent is called the *rate of profit*. (The loss may also be expressed in a similar way.)

To determine the selling price of the articles they sell, some merchants use the percent markup (or gross profit) based on the cost while other merchants use the rate based on the selling price. This *percent markup* is an estimated rate large enough to cover the proportionate amount of overhead expenses to be borne by each article and the amount of profit desired. The percent markup (or gross profit) is the percent the margin is of the cost or of the selling price.

To find the selling price: (1) We add the cost, operating expenses, and net profit; or (2) add the cost and margin; or (3) multiply the cost by the percent markup on cost, then add the product to the cost.

If the rate of markup on cost is 34%, what is the selling price of an article that costs $25?

$25 cost
×.34 rate
100
75
$8.50 markup

$25.00 cost
+8.50 markup
$33.50 selling price

Answer, $33.50 selling price

To find the margin or gross profit or markup: (1) We subtract the cost from the selling price; or (2) multiply the cost by the percent markup on cost; or (3) add the operating expenses and net profit.

Find the rate of markup on cost if an article costs $40 and sells for $55:

$55 selling price
−40 cost
$15 markup

$$\frac{\$15}{\$40} = \frac{3}{8} = 37\tfrac{1}{2}\%$$

Answer, $37\tfrac{1}{2}\%$ markup on cost

To find the net profit: (1) We subtract the operating expenses from the margin; or (2) add the cost and the operating expenses, and subtract this sum from the selling price.

Find the net profit and rate of net profit on the selling price if an article costs $18.50, operating expenses are $1.50, and it sells for $24:

$18.50 cost $24 selling price
+1.50 operating expenses   −20
$20.00 total cost $4 net profit

$$\frac{\$4}{\$24} = \frac{1}{6} = 16\tfrac{2}{3}\%$$

Answer, $4 net profit; $16\tfrac{2}{3}\%$ net profit on selling price

To find the loss, we add the cost and the operating expenses, and subtract the selling price from this sum.

To find the percent markup (or gross profit) on cost, we find what percent the margin is of the cost. When based on selling price, we find what percent the margin is of the selling price.

To find the rate of net profit (or loss) on the selling price, we find what percent the net profit (or loss) is of the selling price. When based on the cost, we find what percent the profit (or loss) is of the cost.

To find the selling price when the cost and percent markup (or gross profit) on the selling price are given, we subtract the percent markup from 100%, then divide the answer into the cost.

Find the selling price of an article that costs $17 and the percent markup on the selling price is 32%:

100% = selling price
−32% = markup
68% = cost

$$\begin{array}{r} \$\ 25 \\ .68\ )\overline{\$17.00} \\ 13\ 6 \\ \hline 3\ 40 \\ 3\ 40 \end{array}$$

Answer, $25 selling price

1. What should the selling price of a camera be if it costs the dealer $35 and the rate of markup on cost is 30%?

2. Find the selling price when the rate of markup on cost is 28% and the cost is $49.50.

3. A freezer costing $172 was sold for $249. If the overhead expenses were $39, what was the net profit?

4. Find the net profit when the cost is $95.40, selling price is $154.75, and operating expenses are $16\frac{2}{3}\%$ of the cost.

5. A merchant purchases a kitchen sink for $102. His markup is 40% of the selling price. What is the selling price of the sink?

6. Find the selling price when the cost is $6.90 and the rate of markup on the selling price is 25%.

7. Find the rate of gross profit on the selling price of a gas range if it cost $190 and sold for $250.

8. Find the rate of gross profit on the selling price when the selling price is $107.25 and the cost is $85.80.

9. Find the rate of markup on the cost when the cost is $36 and the selling price is $48.

10. Find the rate of net profit on the selling price when the selling price is $360, cost is $275.25 and overhead is $36.75.

11. A dishwasher that cost $180 was sold for $144. What was the rate of loss on the cost?

12. Find the selling price of each of the following articles:

    a. Television set, costing $425 and 24% markup on cost.
    b. Watch, costing $39 and 30% markup on cost.
    c. Dress, costing $13 and 35% markup on selling price.
    d. Camera, costing $29.60 and 20% markup on selling price.
    e. CB radio, costing $165 and 25% markup on selling price.

13. How much would a table cost a dealer if she used a 32% rate or markup on the cost and sold the table for $66?

14. A refrigerator was purchased by a dealer for $275. He marked it to sell at a margin of 28% of the cost. It was sold at a discount of 10% on the marked price. What was the gross profit?

15. A merchant purchased video games at $282.24 a dozen. At what price each must she sell them to make a profit of $33\frac{1}{3}\%$ on the selling price?

6–14 SIMPLE INTEREST

Just as people pay rent for the use of a house belonging to someone else, people pay interest for the use of money belonging to others. *Interest* is money paid for the use of money. The money borrowed or invested on which interest is paid is called the *principal*. Interest paid on the principal only is called *simple interest*. The interest charged is generally expressed as a percent of the principal. This percent is called the *rate of interest*. Unless specified otherwise, the rate of interest is the rate per year. The sum of the principal and the interest is called the *amount*.

(1) *To find the interest,* we multiply the principal by the rate of interest per year. Then we multiply this product by the time expressed in years. (2 mo. = $\frac{1}{6}$ yr.; 120 da. = $\frac{1}{3}$ yr.; semi-annual = $\frac{1}{2}$ yr.; quarterly = $\frac{1}{4}$ yr.)

The interest (i) equals the principal (p) times the rate of interest per year (r) times the time expressed in years (t). This rule expressed as a formula is: $i = prt$.

Find the interest and the amount due on $375 borrowed for 4 years at 15%:

$375 principal	$375 principal
.15 rate	225 interest
1875	$600 amount
375 interest for 1 year	
56.25	
×4	
$225.00 interest for 4 years	

Answer, $225 interest: $600 amount

Find the interest on $500 for 2 yr. 8 mo. at 6%:

$p = \$500$ $i = prt$

$r = 6\% = \frac{6}{100}$ $i = 500 \times \frac{6}{100} \times 2\frac{2}{3}$

$t = 2$ yr. 8 mo. $= 2\frac{2}{3}$ yr. $i = \$80$

$i = ?$

Answer, $80 interest

---

(2) *To find the interest by the formula,* we write the interest formula, substitute the given quantities, then compute as

required. The rate is usually expressed as a decimal but a common fraction may be used.

(3) *To find the amount,* we add the interest and the principal.

(4) *Sixty-day or 6% method.*—To find the interest for 60 days at 6%, we move the decimal point in the principal two places to the left.

(5) *To find the annual rate of interest,* we find what percent the interest for one year is of the principal.

What is the annual rate of interest if the annual interest on a principal of $150 is $18?

$$\frac{\$18}{\$150} = \$18 \div \$150 = \$150)\overline{\$18.00}^{.12\ =\ 12\%}$$

Answer, 12%

---

(6) *To find the principal when the annual rate and annual interest are known,* we divide the interest by the rate.

EXERCISES

Find the interest on:

1. **a.** $600 for 1 yr. at 13%
   b. $875 for 1 yr. at 9%
   c. $1,500 for 1 yr. at $10\frac{1}{2}$%
   d. $2,400 for 1 yr. at $8\frac{3}{4}$%

2. **a.** $1,900 for 3 yr. at 6%
   b. $425 for 2 yr. at 14%
   c. $6,000 for 4 yr. at $7\frac{1}{2}$%
   d. $7,500 for 6 yr. at $11\frac{3}{4}$%

3. **a.** $1,000 for $\frac{3}{4}$ yr. at 10%
   b. $2,800 for $2\frac{1}{2}$ yr. at 4%
   c. $8,400 for $5\frac{2}{3}$ yr. at $9\frac{1}{2}$%
   d. $9,600 for $\frac{7}{12}$ yr. at $12\frac{3}{4}$%

4. **a.** $650 for 6 mo. at 5%
   b. $1,700 for 3 mo. at 16%
   c. $2,100 for 10 mo. at $11\frac{1}{2}$%
   d. $3,600 for 11 mo. at $4\frac{3}{4}$%

5. **a.** $375 for 1 yr. 8 mo. at 6%
   b. $480 for 3 yr. 4 mo. at 15%
   c. $10,000 for 4 yr. 7 mo. at $8\frac{1}{4}$%
   d. $20,000 for 8 yr. 2 mo. at $13\frac{1}{2}$%

6. Find the exact interest (1 yr. = 365 da.) on:

   a. $9,000 for 73 da. at 6%   **b.** $6,400 for 15 da. at 9%

7. Find the interest (1 yr. = 360 da.) on:

   a. $8,500 for 30 da. at 8%   **b.** $5,000 for 90 da. at 15%

8. Find the semi-annual interest on:

   a. $675 at 12%   **b.** $8,200 at 8.8%

9. Find the quarterly interest on:

   a. $3,250 at 20%   **b.** $10,500 at $8\frac{3}{4}$%

10. Use the 6%, 60-day method to find the interest on:

    a. $1,750 for 60 da. at 6%   **c.** $1,800 for 30 da. at 6%
    b. $867 for 60 da. at 6%   **d.** $900 for 30 da. at 3%

11. Marilyn borrowed $800 at 9% interest for 1 year. What was the total amount she paid back at the end of the year?

12. Find the interest and the amounts due on the following loans:

    a. $1,100 for 1 yr. at 18%   **b.** $950 for 5 yr. at $7\frac{1}{2}$%

13. What is the annual rate of interest if the principal is $360 and the annual interest is $54?

14. What is the annual rate of interest if the principal is $700 and the interest for 4 years is $84?

15. Find the annual rates of interest when the interest for:

    a. 1 yr. on $80 is $3.20   **b.** 6 yr. on $750 is $270.

16. Find the principal on which the annual interest is:

    a. $104 when the annual rate is 8%   **b.** $382.50 when the annual rate is 15%

17. How much money must be invested at 10% to earn $20,000 per year?

18. What is the amount due on a loan of $575 for 2 years at $15\frac{1}{2}$% interest?

19. Steve's father bought a house for $75,000. He paid 40% down and gave a mortgage bearing $13\frac{3}{4}$% interest for the remainder. How much interest does he pay semi-annually?

20. Charlotte's aunt receives $270 interest each year on an investment of $3,000. She also receives $190 semi-annual interest on an investment of $4,000. On which investment does she receive a higher rate of interest? How much higher?

First study pages 74–75. Then solve each problem.

1. How many examples out of 15 may a pupil get wrong and still earn a grade of 80%?

2. If 95% of a class of 40 students were promoted, how many students were left back?

3. Mr. Williams saved $2,304 from his annual income of $25,600. What percent of his income did he save?

4. During the school year Pierre was absent 9 days and was present 171 days. What percent of the time was he present?

5. What is the cost of a pair of shoes marked $38.50 if a discount of 6% is allowed?

6. Ms. Lee bought an oil burner for $900. She paid 30% in cash. If the balance is to be paid in 18 equal monthly installments, how much must she pay each month?

7. What percent was a piano reduced if it was marked $1,200 and sold for $1,050?

8. A salesperson receives $95 per week and 3% commission on sales. What are his total earnings if his weekly sales are $9,879?

9. A team won 18 games and lost 6 games. What percent of the games played did it lose?

10. Mrs. McBride saved $2.50 by buying a blanket at a reduction of 10%. What was the regular price?

11. A house worth $44,500 is insured for 80% of its value. If the house burned down, how much would the owner receive?

12. At what price each must a dealer sell shirts costing $43.20 a dozen to make a profit of 35% on the cost?

13. Mrs. Jones bought a building for $54,000 and sold it for $67,500. What percent of the cost did she gain?

14. A grocer purchased 24 cans of peas for $5.76. What percent of the cost did he gain if he sold them for $.30 a can?

15. A merchant bought a refrigerator for $375 and marked it to sell for a profit of 40% of the cost. She sold it for 15% less than the marked price. Find the selling price and the profit.

16. The price of eggs dropped from $.90 a dozen to $.81. Find the percent of decrease in price.

17. Mr. Rossi bought a house for $48,900. He paid $33\frac{1}{3}\%$ down and gave a mortgage bearing $12\frac{3}{4}\%$ interest for the balance. How much interest does he pay each year?

18. What is the sales tax on a lawn mower costing $65 if the tax rate is $3\frac{1}{4}\%$?

19. On January 1 a savings account showed a balance of $280. How much interest will be earned by the end of the year at the annual rate of $5\frac{1}{2}\%$?

ESTIMATING ANSWERS

To estimate a product or a quotient, first round the given fractions to nearest whole numbers and the given whole numbers to convenient place values and then perform the operations.

1. 4% of 98 is approximately:	498	.4	4
2. 69% of $6,050 is approximately:	$4,000	$4,800	$450
3. $5\frac{7}{8}\%$ of $39 is approximately:	$.23	$2.30	$23
4. $3\frac{1}{8}\%$ of 7,000 is approximately:	200	20	220
5. $9\frac{3}{4}\%$ of $550 is approximately:	$5.50	$55	$.55

6. 3 is approximately 25% or 60% or 6% of 51.

7. 8 is approximately 6% or 7% or 8% of 99.

8. 7 is approximately 30% or 35% or 40% of 24.

9. 15 is approximately 15% or 20% or 25% of 76.

10. 19 is approximately 30% or 25% or 20% of 102.

CHECK BY CALCULATOR

Indicate which answers are incorrect by using your calculator. If a calculator is not available, check by computation.

1. Add:
   a. 4,325 + 97 + 8,582 + 745 + 9,857 = 23,606
   b. 3,794 + 6,583 + 5,969 + 1,078 + 8,356 = 25,880
   c. 67,479 + 2,685 + 939 + 5,867 + 86,998 = 163,968
   d. 45,926 + 73,858 + 42,667 + 53,071 + 92,588 = 308,110
   e. 85,567 + 92,738 + 47,968 + 78,524 + 69,475 = 374,172

2. Subtract:

    a. $9,216 - 6,543 = 2,673$ **b.** $60,592 - 46,498 = 14,084$
    c. $125,000 - 67,054 = 57,946$ **d.** $826,431 - 755,940 = 70,491$
            e. $5,047,983 - 3,926,995 = 1,120,988$

3. Multiply:

    a. $75 \times 97 = 7,275$ **b.** $629 \times 56 = 35,224$
    c. $805 \times 640 = 525,200$ **d.** $7,839 \times 491 = 3,848,949$
            e. $9,308 \times 5,067 = 48,163,636$

4. Divide:

    a. $37,062 \div 87 = 436$ **b.** $53,044 \div 596 = 89$
    c. $252,730 \div 635 = 398$ **d.** $188,727 \div 903 = 209$
            e. $1,695,680 \div 2,240 = 747$

5. Add:

    a. $1.25 + 9.76 + 4.58 = 15.59$ **b.** $.985 + .572 + .443 = 2.000$
    c. $.526 + 2 = .528$ **d.** $7.3 + .684 = 7.984$

6. Subtract:

    a. $.86 - .79 = .7$ **b.** $40.9 - 2.63 = 38.27$
    c. $8.954 - 3.24 = 8.630$ **d.** $9 - 6.5 = 2.5$

7. Multiply:

    a. $.2 \times .38 = .76$ **b.** $.006 \times .075 = .045$
    c. $2,000 \times .0004 = 8.$ **d.** $3.1416 \times 15.07 = 47.343912$

8. Divide:

    a. $8.64 \div 18 = 4.8$ **b.** $78.85 \div 8.3 = 9.5$
    c. $.02 \div .05 = .04$ **d.** $.00028 \div .04 = .007$

9. Find:

    a. 3% of $85 = 2.55$ **b.** 9% of $20.56 = 18.504$
    c. 125% of $10 = 1.25$ **d.** 6.8% of $18.4 = 1.2512$

10. Find each of the following:

    a. 48 is what percent of 64?   75%   **b.** What percent of 25 is 19?   76%
    c. What percent of 144 is 36?   25%   **d.** 24 is what percent of 20?   120%

11. Find each of the following:

    a. 16% of what number is 24?   150   **b.** 2 is 5% of what number?   4
    c. 175% of what number is 63?   36   **d.** 6.5% of what number is 260?   400

CHAPTER REVIEW

1. Express each of the following as a percent: (6–1)
    a. 92 hundredths
    b. 63 out of 100
    c. The ratio of 17 to 100

2. Express each of the following percents as a decimal numeral: (6–2)
    a. 9%   b. 67%   c. 180%   d. $83\frac{1}{3}\%$ e. 4.7%

3. Express each of the following percents as a numeral naming a
    common fraction: (6–3)
    a. 25%   b. $16\frac{2}{3}\%$ c. 60%   d. $87\frac{1}{2}\%$ e. 48%

4. Express each of the following as a percent:

    a. .08   .31   1.4   .5793 $.00\frac{1}{2}$ (6–4)

    b. $\frac{1}{2}$ $\frac{51}{68}$ $\frac{36}{64}$ $\frac{13}{25}$ $\frac{88}{100}$ (6–5)

5. Find 39% of 462.   (6–6)
6. Find $4\frac{1}{4}\%$ of $95.87.   (6–6)
7. Find 243% of 918.   (6–6)
8. Find 5.9% of 8,000.   (6–6)
9. Find $\frac{3}{4}\%$ of $2,600.   (6–6)
10. What percent of $57 is $38?   (6–7)
11. 30 is what percent of 24?   (6–7)
12. What percent of 81 is 18?   (6–7)
13. 90% of what number is 72?   (6–8)
14. 120 is $62\frac{1}{2}\%$ of what number?   (6–8)
15. 5% of what amount is $1.25   (6–8)

CHAPTER 7
Square Roots–Irrational Numbers

The *square root* of a number is that number which when multiplied by itself produces the given number. It is one of the two equal factors of a product.

An *irrational number* is a number that cannot be expressed as a quotient of two whole numbers (with division by zero excluded). A number that is both a non-terminating and non-repeating decimal like the square root of any positive number other than perfect squares (numbers having an exact square root) is an irrational number.

There is a point on the number line that corresponds to each irrational number. To locate the point corresponding to $\sqrt{2}$ on the number line, we construct a square with the side measuring the unit length. By the Rule of Pythagoras we can show that the length of the diagonal of this square is $\sqrt{2}$. Thus, to locate the points corresponding to $\sqrt{2}$ and $-\sqrt{2}$* on the number line, we describe an arc using the diagonal as the radius. The points where the arc intersects the number line are the required points.

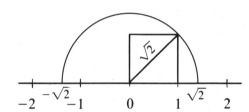

7–1 SQUARE ROOT BY ESTIMATION, DIVISION, AND AVERAGE

We may find the *approximate* square root of a number by:

(1) Estimating the square root of the given number.
(2) Dividing the given number by the estimated square root.
(3) Finding the average of the resulting quotient and the estimated square root.

---

* See page 285.

(4) Dividing the given number by the result of step (3).

(5) Finding the average of the divisor and quotient found in step (4).

(6) Continuing this process to obtain a greater degree of approximation as the divisor and quotient will eventually approximate each other.

Find the square root of 7:

To find the square root of 7 by this method, since the square root of 4 is 2 and the square root of 9 is 3, we estimate that the square root of 7 is between 2 and 3, perhaps 2.5*.

Dividing 7 by 2.5, we get the quotient 2.8. Averaging 2.5 and 2.8, we get 2.65.

Dividing 7 by 2.65, we get the quotient 2.64. Averaging 2.65 and 2.64, we get 2.645.

```
        2.8                    2.64
2.5 )7.0 0        2.65 )7.00 00
    5 0                 5 30
    2 0 0              1 70 0
    2 0 0              1 59 0
     ...                 11 00
                         10 60
                            40
```

```
   2.5              2.65
 + 2.8            + 2.64
2)5.3(2.65       2)5.29(2.645
```

Answer, 2.645

* 2.6 would be a better estimate and would result in the same answer.

EXERCISES

Find the square root of each of the following by estimation, division, and average:

a. 11	d. 54	g. 75	j. 87	m. 138	p. 200
b. 28	e. 39	h. 110	k. 19	n. 98	q. 160
c. 5	f. 91	i. 44	l. 185	o. 67	r. 320

7-2 SQUARE ROOT—ALTERNATE METHOD

To find the square root of a number, we write its numeral under the square root symbol $\sqrt{}$, and separate the numeral into groups of two digits each to the left and then to the right of the decimal point. If a numeral naming a whole number contains an odd number of digits, there will be one group with one digit on the left. If a numeral naming a decimal fraction contains an odd number of digits, a zero is annexed so that each group contains two digits.

(1) We find the largest square (49) which can be subtracted from the first group at the left (54) and write it under this group.

(2) We write the square root (7) of this largest square as the first digit in the answer. Each digit in the answer is written directly over its corresponding group.

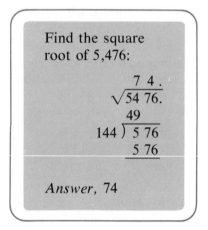

Find the square root of 5,476:

$$
\begin{array}{r}
7\ 4.\ \ \ \ \\
\sqrt{54\ 76.}\ \\
49\ \ \ \ \ \\
144\ )\ \overline{5\ 76}\ \\
5\ 76\ \\
\end{array}
$$

Answer, 74

(3) After we subtract the square, the next group (76) is annexed to the remainder (5).

(4) A trial divisor is formed by multiplying the root already found (7) by 2 and annexing a zero which is not written but used mentally.

(5) We divide the dividend (576) by this trial divisor (140) and annex the quotient (4) to the root already found. We also annex it to the trial divisor to form the complete divisor (144).

(6) We multiply the complete divisor by the new digit (4) of the root and subtract this product from the dividend.

(7) This process is continued until all groups are used or the required number of decimal places has been obtained. The decimal point in the answer is placed directly above the decimal point in the given numeral.

Find the square root of 66,049:

$$\begin{array}{r} 2\ 5\ 7 \\ \sqrt{6\ 60\ 49.} \\ \underline{4} \\ 45\overline{)2\ 60} \\ \underline{2\ 25} \\ 507\overline{)\quad 35\ 49} \\ \underline{35\ 49} \end{array}$$

Answer, 257

Find the square root of .09:

$$\begin{array}{r} .3 \\ \sqrt{.09} \end{array}$$

Answer, .3

Find the square root of 9.8:

$$\begin{array}{r} 3.1 \\ \sqrt{9.80} \\ \underline{9} \\ 61\overline{)\quad 80} \\ \underline{61} \\ 19 \end{array}$$

Answer, 3.1

EXERCISES

Find the square root of each of the following numbers. If there is a remainder, find answer correct to nearest hundredth:

1. a. 81
    b. 2,500
    c. .36
    d. .0004
    e. 6,400
    f. .000001

2. a. 324
    b. 961
    c. 4,624
    d. 8,649
    e. 9,409
    f. 4,096

3. a. 38,416
    b. 24,964
    c. 99,856
    d. 616,225
    e. 410,881
    f. 59,049

4. a. 71,824
    b. 350,464
    c. 900,601
    d. 227,529
    e. 703,921
    f. 484,416

5. a. 2,399,401
    b. 6,185,169
    c. 1,525,225
    d. 9,771,876
    e. 8,048,569
    f. 7,557,001

6. a. 70,107,129
    b. 15,952,036
    c. 35,188,624
    d. 93,837,969
    e. 43,454,464
    f. 73,874,025

7. a. 11,449
    b. 824,464
    c. 498,436
    d. 902,500
    e. 253,009
    f. 608,400

8. a. 49,070,025
    b. 8,427,409
    c. 9,072,144
    d. 64,080,025
    e. 36,844,900
    f. 24,068,836

9. a. .4624
    b. 3.61
    c. 8,172.16
    d. 8
    e. 1,000
    f. 675

10. a. 49.7
    b. 6.5
    c. 193.2
    d. .234
    e. 25.963
    f. 31.9

7-3 SQUARE ROOT BY USE OF TABLE

Using the table of squares and square roots (see page 489), we can find directly the square roots of whole numbers 1 to 99 inclusive and of the perfect squares (squares of whole numbers) given in the table.

To find the square root of any whole number from 1 to 99 inclusive, we first locate the given number in the "No." column and then move to the right to the corresponding "Square Root" column to obtain the required square root.

To find the square root of a perfect square given in the table, we first locate this number in the "Square" column and then move to the left to the corresponding "No." column to obtain the required square root.

EXERCISES

Find the square root of each of the following numbers:

1. a. 18   **c.** 94   **e.** 39   **g.** 61
    b. 53   **d.** 76   **f.** 87   **h.** 45

2. a. 26   **c.** 82   **e.** 71   **g.** 41
    b. 34   **d.** 63   **f.** 98   **h.** 57

3. a. 3,844   **c.** 5,929   **e.** 2,916
    b. 8,281   **d.** 764   **f.** 4,225

4. a. 6,561   **c.** 1,849   **e.** 841
    b. 9,025   **d.** 1,024   **f.** 7,569

7-4 PRINCIPAL SQUARE ROOT*

Since $(+5) \times (+5) = 25$ and $(-5) \times (-5) = 25$, it follows that 25 has two square roots: $+5$ and -5. Whole numbers, other than zero, each have two square roots, a positive square root and a negative square root. Zero has only one square root, which is zero (0). The positive square root of a number is called the *principal square root.*

---

* Take this section only if operations with positive and negative numbers have been studied.

1. Find the two square roots of each of the following numbers:

   a. 9   c. 36   e. 196   g. 576
   b. 100   d. 169   f. 256   h. 625

2. What is the principal square root of each of the following numbers?

   a. 81   c. 64   e. 225   g. 484
   b. 4   d. 121   f. 900   h. 529

CHAPTER REVIEW

1. Find the square root of each of the following numbers by estimation, division, and average: (7–1)

   a. 6   c. 30   e. 78
   b. 17   d. 45   f. 180

2. Find the square root of each of the following numbers by using the table: (7–3)

   a. 20   c. 89   e. 9,604
   b. 43   d. 961   f. 3,025

3. Find the square root of each of the following numbers. If there is a remainder, find answer correct to nearest hundredth: (7–2)

   a. 4,356   c. 6,544,810   e. 725.3
   b. 56,169   d. 97   f. 49.25

REVIEW EXERCISES

1. Add:

29	3,054	68,947	92,156	75,239
4,638	897	7,052	85,285	18,925
394	52,168	34,369	31,647	38,346
77	36	8,497	52,839	50,182
462	5,785	15,568	49,903	64,697

2. Subtract:

8,500	91,556	46,835	311,524	805,003
698	30,849	9,187	190,615	798,096

3. Multiply:

96	485	708	490	8,249
59	64	891	370	536

4. Divide:

$24\overline{)2,088}$ $36\overline{)23,004}$ $903\overline{)366,618}$ $365\overline{)21,535}$ $1,728\overline{)129,600}$

5. Add:

$4\frac{7}{16}$ $12\frac{2}{3}$ $8\frac{11}{12}$ $2\frac{3}{8}$ $8\frac{1}{2}$

$5\frac{3}{4}$ $6\frac{4}{5}$ $2\frac{5}{8}$ $4\frac{5}{6}$ $5\frac{7}{10}$

6. Subtract:

2 $8\frac{3}{4}$ $10\frac{1}{2}$ $5\frac{2}{3}$ $7\frac{3}{10}$

$1\frac{7}{12}$ $2\frac{13}{16}$ 7 $3\frac{1}{4}$ $4\frac{5}{6}$

7. Multiply:

$\frac{3}{10} \times \frac{5}{6}$ $\frac{5}{8} \times 2\frac{3}{4}$ $6 \times 5\frac{7}{8}$ $3\frac{1}{3} \times 2\frac{1}{4}$ $2\frac{11}{12} \times 1\frac{3}{5}$

8. Divide:

$\frac{2}{3} \div 3$ $14 \div 1\frac{5}{16}$ $\frac{4}{5} \div 1\frac{1}{3}$ $5\frac{3}{4} \div \frac{1}{2}$ $3\frac{3}{8} \div 3\frac{3}{5}$

9. Add:

.901 + .899	6.429 + 1.34	20 + 1.8 + 0.36
.004 + .4 + .04	$6.29 + $.78	

10. Subtract:

.403 − .095   6.9 − 0.42   500 − .235   7.54 − 1.8 $43 − $27.89

11. Multiply:

3.14	4,000	.075	$284.60	$3.84
50	0.049	.008	.05	$.62\frac{1}{2}$

12. Divide:

$24)\overline{.96}$ $6.1)\overline{.0427}$ $.08)\overline{48}$ $.043)\overline{3.01}$ $144)\overline{$83.52}$

13. Find each of the following:

    a. 2% of $39   **c.** $83\frac{1}{3}$% of $5.58   **e.** 5.9% of 160

    b. 53% of 495   **d.** 175% of $92   **f.** $6\frac{3}{4}$% of $254.20

14. **a.** What percent of $.12 is $.04?   **d.** 140 is what percent of 1,000?

      b. 72 is what percent of 90?   **e.** 12 is what percent of 5?

      c. 17 is what percent of 68?   **f.** What percent of $80 is $1.60?

15. **a.** 30% of what amount is $18   **d.** 120% of what number is 78?

      b. 35 is 5% of what number?   **e.** 7 is 56% of what number?

      c. 12% of what number is 16?   **f.** 4.8% of what number is 6?

16. Find the square root of each of the following numbers by estimation, division, and average:

    a. 3   **b.** 29   **c.** 13   **d.** 42   **e.** 130   **f.** 77

17. Find the square root of each of the following numbers using the table:

    a. 98   **b.** 47   **c.** 55   **d.** 3,969   **e.** 676   **f.** 7,921

18. Find the square root of each of the following numbers. If there is a remainder, find the answer correct to nearest hundredth:

    a. 274,576   **b.** 654,481   **c.** 58,644,964   **d.** 107   **e.** 9.3

ACHIEVEMENT TEST

1. What is the greatest common factor of 24, 90, and 42?   (1–21)
2. Factor 600 as the product of prime factors.   (1–19)
3. What is the least common multiple of 6, 8, and 30?   (1–24)
4. Write MCMXLVI as a decimal numeral.   (1–14)
5. Arrange by size, greatest first: (1–6)

   749,876   794,678   749,786   794,687

6. Write as a numeral:

   a. Sixty-four million, five hundred six thousand, twenty-nine.   (1–8)
   b. Seventeen and eleven twelfths.   (4–5)
   c. Forty and five hundredths.   (5–3)
   d. 62.7 billion   (5–13)

7. Round:

   a. 429,604,125 to the nearest million.   (1–10)
   b. $9\frac{11}{21}$ to the nearest whole number.   (4–10)
   c. .023509 to the nearest thousandth.   (5–5)
   d. $87.4068 to the nearest cent.   (5–5)

8. Expand each of the following as a polynomial: (1–13)

   a. 6,245,873   b. 834.507

9. Find the missing numbers: (2–2 to 2–5)

   a. $15 + 11 = ? + 15$ d. $(9 \times 17) \times 4 = ? \times (17 \times 4)$
   b. $\frac{3}{4} \times ? = 5 \times \frac{3}{4}$ e. $(.32 + 18) + 4.9 = .32 + (? + 4.9)$
   c. $(2.9 \times 6) \div 6 = ?$ f. $18 \times (6\frac{1}{2} + 7) = ? \times 6\frac{1}{2} + ? \times 7$

10. Is 9, 18, 27, . . . closed under addition? Subtraction? Multiplication? Division?   (2–6)

11. Add:	12. Subtract:	13. Multiply:	(2–9 to 2–11)
6,925	4,050,609	605	
87,694	929,819	897	
529			
98,977			
6,486			

14. Divide:

$941\overline{)5,951,825}$

15. Divide:

$3,007\overline{)24,065,021}$

(2–16)

16. Is 834,600 divisible by 3? by 2? by 6? by 9? by 4? (2–17)

17. Which of the following statements are true?

   a. $3 - 3 = \frac{3}{3}$; $8^2 > 9 \times 7$; $9 - 0 < 9 + 0$; $60 + 40 \not> 4 \times 25$ (3–1)

   b. $\frac{5}{8} < \frac{5}{9}$ $\frac{25}{60} = \frac{10}{24}$ $\frac{8}{11} > \frac{5}{7}$ $\frac{13}{18} \not< \frac{2}{3}$ (4–8)

   c. $.04 > .039$ $.1 < .10$ $.003 = .030$ $.62 \not> .619$ (5–6)

18. Express $\frac{34}{85}$ in lowest terms. (4–2)

19. Express $\frac{19}{24}$ as 96ths. (4–3)

20. Write the four fractions equivalent to $\frac{20}{32}$. (4–3)

21. Arrange by size, greatest first: (4–8)

$\frac{5}{8}, \quad \frac{3}{5}, \quad \frac{1}{2}, \quad \frac{7}{11}, \quad \frac{4}{9}, \quad \frac{2}{3}$

22. Add:

$4\frac{5}{6} + 2\frac{3}{8} + 3\frac{1}{2}$

23. Subtract:

$12\frac{1}{4} - \frac{2}{3}$

24. Multiply:

$3\frac{1}{7} \times 9\frac{4}{5}$

(4–11 to 4–13)

25. Divide:

$27 \div 3\frac{3}{4}$

26. Divide:

$4\frac{7}{8} \div 5\frac{1}{3}$

(4–15)

27. Find $\frac{5}{12}$ of 168. (4–16)

28. What fractional part of 90 is 36? (4–17)

29. 42 is $\frac{7}{8}$ of what number?   30. $\frac{3}{7}$ of what number is 81? (4–18)

31. Arrange by size, greatest first: (5–6)

   7.07,   .077,   .770,   7.70

32. Add:

.85 + 9.6 + 43

33. Subtract:

8.6 − .69

34. Multiply:

.015 × .008

(5–7 to 5–9)

35. Divide: **a.** $\$.06\overline{)\$9}$ **b.** $.023\overline{).000345}$ (5–11)

36. **a.** Write 8.91 trillion as a complete numeral. (5–13)
    b. Write the shortened name for 415,700,000 in millions.

37. Write in scientific notation: (5–14)
    a. 760,000,000,000,000   **b.** .00000000195

38. Express each of the following as a decimal numeral: (5–15)
    $\frac{3}{4}, \quad \frac{11}{25}, \quad \frac{12}{27}, \quad \frac{18}{48}, \quad \frac{84}{96}$

39. Write $\frac{13}{18}$ as a repeating decimal. (5–16)

40. Express each of the following as a numeral naming a common fraction: (5–17)

.02,   .40,   0.256,   .081,   .87$\frac{1}{2}$

41. Write .$\overline{72}$ . . . as a numeral naming a common fraction. (5–18)

42. Find 1.04 of $51. (5–19)

43. 28 is what decimal part of 70? (5–20)

44. 17 is .68 of what number? (5–21)

45. Express each of the following as a decimal numeral: (6–2)

87%,   6$\frac{1}{4}$%,   174.2%,   158%,   0.39%

46. Express each of the following as a numeral naming a common fraction: (6–3)

3%,   37$\frac{1}{2}$%,   76%,   62$\frac{1}{2}$%,   8$\frac{1}{3}$%

47. Express each of the following as a percent: (6–4 to 6–5)

.07,   1.325,   2.8, $\frac{5}{6}$, $\frac{13}{25}$, $\frac{57}{76}$

48. Find 5$\frac{1}{2}$% of 116.   **49.** Find 104% of $69.75 (6–6)

50. What percent of $84 is $63? (6–7)

51. 6% of what amount is $3,000? (6–8)

52. Todd bought a football for $12 less 35% discount. How much did he pay for it? (6–11)

53. A real estate agent received $2,070 commission for selling a house for $34,500. What rate of commission did she charge? (6–12)

54. At what price each must a merchant sell ties to realize a gross profit of 25% on the selling price if he buys them at $18 a dozen? (6–13)

55. How much money must be invested at 6% to earn $5,400 per year? (6–14)

56. Some time ago Mrs. Rojas received a 5% increase on a salary of $240 per week. Recently her salary was reduced 5%. How does her present salary compare with her original salary before the increase? (6–15)

57. Find the square root of each of the following numbers. If there is a remainder, find answer correct to nearest hundredth: (7–2)

a. 43,681   **b.** 473,344   **c.** 92,679,129   **d.** 5.9   **e.** 85

CHAPTER 8
Units of Measure and Measurement

Many years ago there were no standard units of measure. Early humans used their fingers, feet, and arms to measure length or distance. The width across the open hand at the base of the fingers, called the *palm*, the breadth of a finger, called a *digit*, the greatest stretch of the open hand, called the *span*, and the length of the forearm from the elbow to the end of the middle finger, called the *cubit*, were some of the units used. However, since these measurements varied depending upon the size of the person, they were unsatisfactory.

Today we use metric and customary units of measure which are standard. See pages 490–491 for the tables of measure. Probably in the near future we shall be using in the United States a modernized metric system, the International System of Units, generally known as SI. It should be noted that sometimes the metric unit *meter* is spelled as *metre* and *liter* as *litre*.

UNITS OF MEASURE

CHANGING TO A SMALLER UNIT OF MEASURE

To change a given number of units of one denomination to units of smaller denomination:

We find the number of units of the smaller denomination that is equivalent to one unit of the larger denomination. This number is sometimes called the *conversion factor*. Then we multiply the given number of units of the larger denomination by this conversion factor.

Since each conversion factor in the metric system is some power of ten, short methods of computation may be used. See section 5–10.

On the opposite page are several examples of changing to a smaller unit of measure and references to sections where you will find additional practice exercises.

228

CHAPTER 8

8–1 Metric—Length

14 centimeters to millimeters:

$10 \times 14 = 140$

Answer, 140 millimeters

8–2 Metric—Weight

9 kilograms to grams:

$1,000 \times 9 = 9,000$

Answer, 9,000 grams

8–3 Metric—Capacity

6 liters to centiliters:

$100 \times 6 = 600$

Answer, 600 centiliters

8–4 Metric—Area

5 km² to m²:

$1,000,000 \times 5 = 5,000,000$

Answer, 5,000,000 m²

8–5 Metric—Volume

8 dm³ to cm³:

$1,000 \times 8 = 8,000$

Answer, 8,000 cm³

8–6 Customary—Length

8 feet to inches:

$12 \times 8 = 96$

Answer, 96 inches

8–7 Customary—Weight

7 pounds to ounces:

$16 \times 7 = 112$

Answer, 112 ounces

8–8 Customary—Liquid

18 gallons to quarts:

$4 \times 18 = 72$

Answer, 72 quarts

8–9 Customary—Dry

5 bushels to pecks:

$4 \times 5 = 20$

Answer, 20 pecks

8–10 Customary—Area

15 sq. yd. to sq. ft.:

$9 \times 15 = 135$

Answer, 135 sq. ft.

8–11 Customary—Volume

6 cu. ft. to cu. in.:

$1,728 \times 6 = 10,368$

Answer, 10,368 cu. in.

8–13 Time

14 hours to minutes:

$60 \times 14 = 840$

Answer, 840 minutes

8–14 Angles and Arcs

25 degrees to minutes:

$60 \times 25 = 1,500$

Answer, 1,500 minutes

CHANGING TO A LARGER
UNIT OF MEASURE

To change a given number of units of one denomination to units of a larger denomination:

We find the number of units of the smaller denomination that is equivalent to one of the larger denomination. Then we divide the given number of units of the smaller denomination by this conversion factor.

Since each conversion factor in the metric system is some power of ten, short methods of computation may be used. See section 5–12.

Below are several examples of changing to a larger unit of measure and references to sections where you will find additional practice exercises.

8–1 Metric—Length	8–2 Metric—Weight
3,000 meters to kilometers:	67 milligrams to centigrams:
$3,000 \div 1,000 = 3$	$67 \div 10 = 6.7$
Answer, 3 kilometers	*Answer,* 6.7 centigrams
8–3 Metric—Capacity	**8–4 Metric—Area**
945 centiliters to liters:	480 mm² to cm²:
$945 \div 100 = 9.45$	$480 \div 100 = 4.8$
Answer, 9.45 liters	*Answer,* 4.8 cm²

8–5 Metric—Volume

250,000 dm³ to m³:

$250,000 \div 1,000 = 250$

Answer, 250 m³

8–6 Customary—Length	8–7 Customary—Weight
15 feet to yards:	12,000 lb. to short tons:
$15 \div 3 = 5$	$12,000 \div 2,000 = 6$
Answer, 5 yards	*Answer,* 6 short tons

8–8 Customary—Liquid

14 pints to quarts:

$14 \div 2 = 7$

Answer, 7 quarts

8–9 Customary—Dry

36 pecks to bushels:

$36 \div 4 = 9$

Answer, 9 bushels

8–10 Customary—Area

576 sq. in. to sq. ft.:

$576 \div 144 = 4$

Answer, 4 sq. ft.

8–11 Customary—Volume

216 cu. ft. to cu. yd.:

$216 \div 27 = 8$

Answer, 8 cu. yd.

8–13 Time

60 months to years:

$60 \div 12 = 5$

Answer, 5 years

8–14 Angles and Arcs

240 minutes to degrees:

$240 \div 60 = 4$

Answer, 4 degrees

METRIC SYSTEM

Our monetary system is a decimal system in which the *dollar* is the basic unit. In the metric system, the *meter* (m) is the basic unit of length, the *gram* (g) is the basic unit of weight or mass, and the *liter* (L) is the basic unit of capacity (dry and liquid measures). Other metric units of length, weight, and capacity are named by adding the following prefixes to the basic unit of measure:

Prefix	Symbol		Value
kilo-	k	meaning	thousand (1,000)
hecto-	h	meaning	hundred (100)
deka-	da	meaning	ten (10)
deci-	d	meaning	one-tenth (.1 or $\frac{1}{10}$)
centi-	c	meaning	one-hundredth (.01 or $\frac{1}{100}$)
milli-	m	meaning	one-thousandth (.001 or $\frac{1}{1000}$)

Units of Measure and Measurement

The chart below shows the relationship among units. Observe the similarity of the metric system of measures to our decimal numeration system and to our monetary system.

It should be noted that just as 3 dollars 8 dimes 5 cents may be written as a single numeral, 3.85 *dollars* or $3.85; so 3 meters 8 decimeters 5 centimeters may also be written as a single numeral, 3.85 *meters*.

Abbreviations or symbols are written without the period after the last letter. The same symbol is used for both one or more quantities. Thus, *cm* is the symbol for *centimeter* or *centimeters*.

UNITS OF MEASURE

	1,000	100	10	1	.1	.01	.001
Decimal Place Value	thousands	hundreds	tens	ones	tenths	hundredths	thousandths
United States Money	$1,000 bill	$100 bill	$10 bill	dollar	dime	cent	mill
Metric Length	kilometer km	hectometer hm	dekameter dam	meter m	decimeter dm	centimeter cm	millimeter mm
Metric Weight	kilogram kg	hectogram hg	dekagram dag	gram g	decigram dg	centigram cg	milligram mg
Metric Capacity	kiloliter kL	hectoliter hL	dekaliter daL	liter L	deciliter dL	centiliter cL	milliliter mL

The above chart reveals that in the metric system ten (10) of any unit of measure is equivalent to one (1) unit of the next larger size.

The prefix "micro" means one-millionth, and the prefix "mega" means one million. There is a *micrometer* (one-millionth of a meter), a *microgram* (one-millionth of a gram), and a *microliter* (one-millionth of a liter). A *megameter* is one million (1,000,000) meters, a *megagram* is one million grams, and a *megaliter* is one million liters.

8–1 MEASURE OF LENGTH—METRIC

Let us examine the following section of a metric ruler:

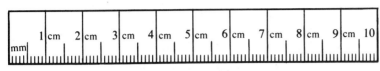

ONE DECIMETER

Each of the smallest subdivisions shown here indicates a measure of 1 *millimeter* (mm). Observe that ten (10) of these millimeter subdivisions form the next larger subdivision, called a *centimeter* (cm), and that ten (10) of the centimeter subdivisions form the next larger subdivision, called a *decimeter* (dm). The meter stick measuring one meter (m), the basic metric unit measuring length, has markings that show 10 decimeter divisions, 100 centimeter divisions, and 1,000 millimeter divisions.

To change a given number of units of one metric denomination to units of another metric denomination, we follow the procedures explained on pages 228–230. For short methods of computation, see sections 5–10 and 5–12.

EXERCISES

1. What metric unit of length does each of these symbols represent?

   a. dm   **b.** dam   **c.** km   **d.** cm   **e.** mm   **f.** m   **g.** hm

2. Use this section of the metric ruler to answer the following questions:

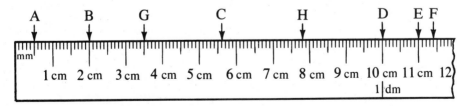

   a. What measurement is indicated by the point labeled:

   B?   *A?*   *D?*   *G?*   *E?*   *C?*   *F?*   *H?*

b. How far from point D is point E? From point G is point A? From point B is point H? From point F is point A? From point C is point H?

c. How many centimeters is it from point B to point E? From point D to point B? From point A to point G?

d. How many millimeters is it from point C to point D? From point G to point F? From point A to point H?

e. How many millimeters are in the length from 0 to each of the following markings:

4 cm?   5 cm 8 mm?

7 cm 3 mm?   1 dm 1 cm 4 mm?

f. In each of the following find the sum of the measurements by locating the mark for the first measurement on the ruler and adding on to this the second measurement. Simplify each sum as indicated:

8 mm + 9 mm = __ mm = __ cm __ mm

42 mm + 23 mm = __ mm = __ cm __ mm

3 cm 4 mm + 2 cm 5 mm = __ cm __ mm

7 cm 8 mm + 1 cm 6 mm = __ cm __ mm = __ cm __ mm

4 cm 6 mm + 2 cm 4 mm = __ cm __ mm = __ cm

1 dm 3 mm + 1 cm 5 mm = __ dm __ cm __ mm

3 cm 9 mm + 6 cm 1 mm = __ cm __ mm = __ cm = __ dm

g. In each of the following locate the marking for the first measurement on the ruler and take away from this the second measurement to find your answer:

16 mm − 9 mm = __ mm

5 cm 6 mm − 2 cm 4 mm = __ cm __ mm

7 cm − 6 mm = __ cm __ mm

2 cm 5 mm − 8 mm = __ cm __ mm

6 cm 3 mm − 5 cm 9 mm = __ cm __ mm

4 cm − 1 cm 7 mm = __ cm __ mm

1 dm − 3 cm 5 mm = __ cm __ mm

h. Find the 106 mm mark on the metric ruler. Subtract from it a measurement of 2.7 cm. What measurement does the mark you reach indicate?

3. Complete each of the following:

a. __ mm = 1 cm   e. __ dam = 1 hm   i. __ m = 1 dm
b. __ cm = 1 dm   f. __ hm = 1 km   j. __ dam = 1 m
c. __ dm = 1 m   g. __ cm = 1 mm   k. __ hm = 1 dam
d. __ m = 1 dam   h. __ dm = 1 cm   l. __ km = 1 hm

4. Complete each of the following:

a. __ mm = 1 m
b. __ cm = 1 m
c. __ dm = 1 m
d. __ mm = 1 cm
e. __ mm = 1 dm
f. __ m = 1 km
g. __ km = 1 m

h. __ m = 1 cm
i. __ m = 1 mm
j. __ m = 1 dm
k. 1 m = __ dm = __ cm = __ mm
l. 1 km = __ hm = __ dam = __ m
m. 1 km = __ m = __ dm = __ cm = __ mm
n. 1 mm = __ m = __ km

5. Express each of the following in meters:

a. 9 km 6 hm 4 dam 8 m = _____ m
b. 6 m 5 dm 1 cm 9 mm = _____ m
c. 5 m 3 cm 2 mm = _____ m
d. 6 km 4 m 2 cm 7 mm = _____ m
e. 2 km 1 hm 7 dam 5 m 2 dm 8 cm 3 mm = _____ m

6. Change each of the following to millimeters:

53 cm;   9.5 m;   2 km;   7.4 cm;   3.7 m

7. Change each of the following to centimeters:

1.8 dm;   46 m;   308 mm;   5 km;   2.9 m

8. Change each of the following to decimeters:

638 m;   590 cm;   4,829 mm;   1.3 km;   18.2 m

9. Change each of the following to meters:

75 dam;   298 mm;   8.6 hm;   40.5 dm;   5,928 cm
0.62 km;   19.1 dam;   11,520 mm;   3.475 km;   859 cm

10. Change each of the following to dekameters:

89 m;   43 hm;   6.4 km;   27.8 m;   2,589 cm

11. Change each of the following to hectometers:

40 km;   500 dam;   15.9 m;   3.2 km;   658.45 m

12. Change each of the following to kilometers:

61 hm;   3,582 m;   628,000 cm;   7,150,000 mm;   489.6 dam

13. Find the missing equivalent measurement:

	km	hm	dam	m	dm	cm	mm
a.	?	?	?	500	?	?	?
b.	8	?	?	?	?	?	?
c.	?	?	?	?	?	4,000	?
d.	?	?	?	?	?	?	3,800,000

14. Complete each of the following:

a. 8 cm 3 mm = __ mm   **d.** 7 cm 1 mm = __ mm

b. 9 km 450 m = __ m   **e.** 6 m 7 mm = __ mm

c. 3 m 9 cm = __ cm   **f.** 5 m 18 cm = __ cm

15. Complete each of the following:

a. 2 m 9 dm 4 cm = __ cm   **c.** 2 km 5 m 6 cm = __ cm

b. 5 m 6 cm 3 mm = __ mm   **d.** 3 m 7 cm 8 mm = __ mm

16. Complete each of the following:

a. 2 cm 9 mm = __ cm   **d.** 6 km 195 m = __ km

b. 7 km 8 m = __ km   **e.** 8 cm 2 mm = __ cm

c. 4 m 7 cm = __ m   **f.** 3 m 48 mm = __ m

17. Complete each of the following:

a. 6 m 5 cm 2 mm = __ m   **c.** 4 m 9 cm 1 mm = __ m

b. 8 km 4 m 9 cm = __ km   **d.** 2 km 18 m 25 cm = __ km

18. Complete each of the following:

a. 2 m 9 cm 4 mm = __ cm   **c.** 75 m 8 cm = __ km

b. 5 km 2 m 1 cm = __ m   **d.** 3 cm 9 mm = __ m

19. Sound travels in water at a speed of 1,450 meters per second. How many kilometers does it travel in 10 seconds?

20. If the acceleration of gravity is 9.8 meters per second per second, what is it in terms of centimeters per second per second?

21. Scott has two pieces of wood, one piece measuring 2 m 8 cm and the other three times as long. What is the length of the larger piece of wood? What is the total length of the two pieces of wood? What is the difference between the two pieces of wood? If the larger piece of wood is cut into 8 pieces of equal length, how long is each piece of wood?

22. Which measurement is greater:
    a. 6 km or 5,000 m?
    b. 8,000 mm or 8 m?
    c. 9 m or 2,000 cm?
    d. 500 mm or 4 m?
    e. 6.1 cm or 74 mm?
    f. 2.2 m or 220 mm?

23. Which measurement is smaller:
    a. 80 cm or 6 m?
    b. 3 km or 40,000 mm?
    c. 9 m or 6 km?
    d. 58 mm or 4.4 cm?
    e. 6.45 m or 645 mm?
    f. 8.5 km or 775 m?

24. Arrange the following measurements in order of size (longest first):

    2,800 m;   975,000 mm;   5.8 km;   629,600 cm

25. Arrange the following measurements in order of size (shortest first):

    345 m;   3.45 km;   3,450,000 cm;   34.5 mm

8–2 MEASURE OF MASS OR WEIGHT—METRIC

Technically, the kilogram is a unit used to measure the *mass* of an object. However, in everyday use the word "weight" almost always means "mass." Therefore, for our purposes we will continue to speak of the kilogram as a unit of *weight*.

Since the weight of one (1) gram is so small, the *kilogram* is generally considered as the practical basic unit of weight. Note also that the weight of 1,000 kilograms is equivalent to one (1) metric ton (t).

To change a given number of units of one metric denomination to units of another denomination, we follow the procedures explained on pages 228–230. For short methods of computation, see sections 5–10 and 5–12.

EXERCISES

1. What metric unit of weight does each of these symbols represent?

    a. mg   b. kg   c. cg   d. g   e. dg   f. dag   g. hg

2. Complete each of the following:

a. __ mg = 1 cg   **e.** __ dag = 1 hg   **i.** __ g = 1 dg

b. __ cg = 1 dg   **f.** __ hg = 1 kg   **j.** __ dag = 1 g

c. __ dg = 1 g   **g.** __ cg = 1 mg   **k.** __ hg = 1 dag

d. __ g = 1 dag   **h.** __ dg = 1 cg   **l.** __ kg = 1 hg

3. Complete each of the following:

a. __ mg = 1 g   **g.** 1 kg = __ g = __ mg   **m.** __ mg = 1 kg

b. __ cg = 1 g   **h.** 1 mg = __ g = __ kg   **n.** __ kg = 1 hg

c. __ g = 1 cg   **i.** __ hg = 1 kg   **o.** __ kg = 1 dag

d. __ g = 1 mg   **j.** __ dag = 1 kg   **p.** __ kg = 1 dg

e. __ g = 1 kg   **k.** __ dg = 1 kg   **q.** __ kg = 1 cg

f. __ kg = 1 g   **l.** __ cg = 1 kg   **r.** __ kg = 1 mg

4. Change each of the following to milligrams:

6 cg;   25 g;   0.375 g;   4.19 kg;   5.6 cg

5. Change each of the following to centigrams:

8.25 dg;   43 g;   23 kg;   5 mg;   9.6 g

6. Change each of the following to decigrams:

17 g;   82 cg;   3,400 mg;   7.9 kg;   4.25 g

7. Change each of the following to grams:

450 mg;   3 kg;   67.5 cg;   920 dg;   80 dag

8. Change each of the following to dekagrams:

2,000 g;   41 kg;   3,500 mg;   7.83 hg;   54.5 cg

9. Change each of the following to hectograms:

30 kg;   5,000 g;   498 dag;   2.7 kg;   325.9 g

10. Change each of the following to kilograms:

75 hg;   2,972 g;   6,100,000 mg;   928,000 cg;   854.7 dag

11. Change each of the following to metric tons:

4,000 kg;   650 kg;   5,100,000 g;   34,000 hg;   92,400 kg

12. Change each of the following to grams:

    16.3 kg;   5,800 mg

13. Change each of the following to kilograms:

    9,720 g;   245,000 mg

14. Complete each of the following:

    a. 8 cg 9 mg = __ mg   **c.** 2 g 17 cg = __ cg   **e.** 7 kg 160 g = __ g
    b. 5 kg 750 g = __ g   **d.** 6 g 25 mg = __ mg   **f.** 4 cg 8 mg = __ mg

15. Complete each of the following:

    a. 4 g 5 dg 3 cg = __ cg   **c.** 3 kg 8 g 9 cg = __ cg
    b. 9 g 5 cg 3 mg = __ mg   **d.** 1 kg 54 g 2 mg = __ mg

16. Complete each of the following:

    a. 6 cg 8 mg = __ cg   **c.** 9 g 6 mg = __ g   **e.** 6 kg 5 g = __ kg
    b. 4 g 3 cg = __ g   **d.** 14 kg 250 g = __ kg **f.** 11 g 92 mg = __ g

17. Complete each of the following:

    a. 3 g 8 cg 5 mg = __ g   **c.** 5 kg 1 g 7 mg = __ kg
    b. 2 kg 9 g 3 cg = __ kg   **d.** 6 g 4 cg 2 mg = __ g

18. Complete each of the following:

    a. 4 g 1 cg 8 mg = __ cg   **c.** 3 cg 5 mg = __ g
    b. 6 kg 5 g 2 cg = __ g   **d.** 250 g 17 cg = __ kg

19. How many 25 mg tablets will be equivalent to a dose of 1 gram?

20. How many kg will 325 coins weigh if each coin weighs 8 grams?

21. Which weight is heavier:

    a. 5 kg or 5,000 g?   **c.** 25 g or 190 mg?   **e.** 18 mg or 3.1 g?
    b. 47 mg or 6.3 cg?   **d.** 9,000 cg or 6 kg?   **f.** 400 g or 2.5 kg?

22. Which weight is lighter:

    a. 40 cg or 1.5 g?   **c.** 35 mg or 3.5 cg?   **e.** 4.8 g or 5,100 mg?
    b. 8,400 g or 9 kg?   **d.** 6,100 g or 7.3 kg?   **f.** 6.53 kg or 7,250 g?

23. Arrange in order of weight (lightest first):

    4.7 kg;   53,000 cg;   6,100 g;   750,000 mg

24. Arrange in order of weight (heaviest first):

    224 g;   6.25 kg;   4,378,000 mg;   248.5 cg

8–3 MEASURE OF CAPACITY—METRIC

The units that measure capacity also measure volume. See section 8–5 on page 244 where units of cubic measure are studied.

To change a given number of units of one metric denomination to units of another denomination, we follow the procedures explained on pages 228–230. For short methods of computation, see sections 5–10 and 5–12.

EXERCISES

1. What metric unit of capacity does each of these symbols represent?

   a. cL   **b.** kL   **c.** L   **d.** mL   **e.** daL   **f.** hL   **g.** dL

2. Complete each of the following:

   a. __ mL = 1 cL   **e.** __ daL = 1 hL   **i.** __ L = 1 dL
   b. __ cL = 1 dL   **f.** __ hL = 1 kL   **j.** __ daL = 1 L
   c. __ dL = 1 L   **g.** __ cL = 1 mL   **k.** __ hL = 1 daL
   d. __ L = 1 daL   **h.** __ dL = 1 cL   **l.** __ kL = 1 hL

3. Complete each of the following:

   a. __ mL = 1 L   **e.** __ L = 1 cL
   b. __ cL = 1 L   **f.** __ L = 1 mL
   c. __ L = 1 kL   **g.** kL = __ L = __ mL
   d. __ kL = 1 L   **h.** 1 mL = __ L = __ kL

4. Change each of the following to milliliters:

   5 cL;   3.2 L;   47 dL;   0.125 L;   41.7 cL

5. Change each of the following to centiliters:

   67 L;   7 dL;   40 mL;   9.2 L;   50.6 mL

6. Change each of the following to deciliters:

   21 L;   85 cL;   1.75 L;   340 mL;   584 cL

7. Change each of the following to liters:

   8 dL;   30 hL;   12.75 kL;   600 cL;   9,278 mL

8. Change each of the following to dekaliters:

17 hL;   139 L;   19.7 L;   2.5 hL;   468 dL

9. Change each of the following to hectoliters:

9.4 kL;   7.1 daL;   4,305 L;   51.98 kL;   945.7 L

10. Change each of the following to kiloliters:

7,853 L;   26 hL;   685 L;   49.6 hL;   300 daL

11. Find the missing equivalent capacities:

	L	dL	cL	mL
a.	6	?	?	?
b.	?	428	?	?
c.	?	?	?	500
d.	9.1	?	?	?
e.	?	?	327.4	?

12. Complete each of the following:

    a. 2 cL 9 mL = __ mL   **d.** 3 kL 400 L = __ L

    b. 7 L 4 cL = __ cL   **e.** 9 L 56 mL = __ mL

    c. 8 L 5 mL = __ mL   **f.** 12 L 35 cL = __ cL

13. Complete each of the following:

    a. 1 L 4 cL 8 mL = __ mL   **b.** 5 L 93 cL 3 mL = __ mL

14. Complete each of the following:

    a. 4 cL 9 mL = __ cL   **d.** 2 L 7 mL = __ L

    b. 6 L 6 cL = __ L   **e.** 8 L 25 cL = __ L

    c. 2 kL 75 L = __ kL   **f.** 9 cL 4 mL = __ cL

15. Complete each of the following:

    a. 7 L 5 cL 8 mL = __ L   **b.** 4 L 9 cL 3 mL = __ L

16. Complete each of the following:

    a. 3 L 6 cL 7 mL = __ cL   **b.** 6 L 8 cL 5 mL = __ cL

17. Marilyn mixed 79 cL of warm water with 68 cL of cold water. How many liters of water did she mix?

18. If a tank holds 1.5 kiloliters of water, how long will it take to fill it if water flows in at the rate of 25 liters per minute?

19. Which capacity is smaller:

a. 30 cL or 56 mL? **c.** 84.3 mL or 1 L? **e.** 25 dL or 25 daL?

b. 4.9 L or 1,000 cL? **d.** 4.7 cL or 5 mL? **f.** 5.6 L or 8,300 mL?

20. Arrange the following capacities in order of size (largest capacity first):

54.7 cL; 546 mL; 0.549 L; 5.48 dL

21. Arrange the following capacities in order of size (smallest capacity first):

27 L; 4,325 mL; 38.6 dL; 429 cL

8–4 MEASURE OF AREA—METRIC

We have found in linear measure that ten (10) of any metric unit is equivalent to one (1) of the next higher metric unit. However, in the square measure one hundred (100) of any metric unit is equivalent to one (1) of the next higher unit. As we see in the following table, in the metric measure of area the exponent ^{2} is used to represent the word "square."

100 square millimeters (mm^2) = 1 square centimeter (cm^2)

100 square centimeters (cm^2) = 1 square decimeter (dm^2)

100 square decimeters (dm^2) = 1 square meter (m^2)

100 square meters (m^2) = 1 square dekameter (dam^2)

100 square dekameters (dam^2) = 1 square hectometer (hm^2)

100 square hectometers (hm^2) = 1 square kilometer (km^2)

1 cm

Area = 1 cm^2

Special names are sometimes used. *Centare* may be used instead of square meter, *are* instead of square dekameter, and *hectare* instead of square hectometer. The hectare is widely used. Thus,

100 centares = 1 are (a)

100 ares = 1 hectare (ha)

100 hectares = 1 square kilometer

To change from one metric unit of square measure to another metric unit of square measure, we follow the procedures explained on pages 228–230.

1. What unit of metric square measure does each of these symbols represent?

   a. cm^2 **b.** m^2 **c.** km^2 **d.** mm^2 **e.** ha   **f.** dm^2 **g.** dam^2

2. **a.** How many square centimeters are in 1 square meter?
   b. How many square millimeters are in 1 square meter?
   c. How many square meters are in 1 square kilometer?
   d. How many square meters are in 1 hectare?
   e. How many hectares are in 1 square kilometer?

3. Change each of the following to square millimeters:

   7 cm^2; 1.09 m^2; 1.5 dm^2; 23.4 cm^2; 0.54 m^2

4. Change each of the following to square centimeters:

   43 dm^2; 6.5 m^2; 300 mm^2; 0.89 m^2; $4,500 \text{ mm}^2$

5. Change each of the following to square decimeters:

   924 cm^2; 20 m^2; $500,000 \text{ mm}^2$; 6.2 m^2; 430.6 cm^2

6. Change each of the following to square meters (or centares):

   25 km^2; 16 dm^2; $50,000 \text{ cm}^2$; $624,000 \text{ mm}^2$; 0.318 km^2

7. Change each of the following to square dekameters (or ares):

   $2,000 \text{ m}^2$;   28 hectares; 4.97 m^2;   8.7 hectares; $10,500 \text{ m}^2$

8. Change each of the following to hectares (or square hectometers):

   $45,000 \text{ m}^2$; 89.6 dam^2; 18 km^2; 275.6 m^2; 3.4 km^2

9. Change each of the following to square kilometers:

   300 hectares; $6,000 \text{ m}^2$;   83.3 hectares; $2,960,000 \text{ m}^2$; $527,140 \text{ m}^2$

10. A farm contains 80 hectares of land. How many square meters does it measure? What part of a square kilometer is it?

8–5 MEASURE OF VOLUME—METRIC

The *volume,* also called capacity, is generally the number of units of cubic measure contained in a given space. However, the units of capacity (see section 8–3 on page 240) also are used to measure volume. Refer to the relationship given below between the cubic decimeter and the liter.

In linear measure ten (10) of any metric unit is equivalent to one (1) of the next higher metric unit. In the square measure one hundred (100) of any metric unit is equivalent to one (1) of the next higher unit. However,

Volume = 1 cm³

in the cubic measure one thousand (1,000) of any metric unit is equivalent to one (1) of the next higher unit. As shown below, in the metric measure of volume the exponent ³ is used to represent the word "cubic."

1,000 cubic millimeters (mm³) = 1 cubic centimeter (cm³)
1,000 cubic centimeters (cm³) = 1 cubic decimeter (dm³)
1,000 cubic decimeters (dm³) = 1 cubic meter (m³)

To change from one metric unit of cubic measure to another unit of cubic measure, we follow the procedures explained on pages 228–230.

Also note the following relationships:

The volume of one cubic decimeter has the same capacity as one (1) liter. Since 1 cubic decimeter is equivalent to 1,000 cubic centimeters (cm³) and 1 liter is equivalent to 1,000 milliliters (mL), then the volume of 1 cubic centimeter (cm³) has the same capacity as 1 milliliter (mL).

Also a gram is the weight of one (1) cubic centimeter (or 1 milliliter) of water at a temperature of 4 degrees Celsius, and a kilogram is the weight of 1,000 cubic centimeters (or 1 liter) of water at a temperature of 4 degrees Celsius.

MISCELLANEOUS EQUIVALENTS

1 liter = 1 cubic decimeter (dm³) = 1,000 cubic centimeters (cm³)
1 milliliter (mL) = 1 cubic centimeter (cm³)
1 liter of water weighs 1 kilogram (kg)
1 milliliter (mL) or cubic centimeter (cm³) of water weighs 1 gram (g)

1. What unit of metric cubic measure does each of the following symbols represent?

   a. m^3 **b.** cm^3 **c.** mm^3 **d.** km^3 **e.** dam^3 **f.** hm^3 **g.** dm^3

2. **a.** How many cubic millimeters are in 1 cubic decimeter?
   b. How many cubic millimeters are in 1 cubic meter?
   c. How many cubic centimeters are in 1 cubic meter?

3. Change each of the following to cubic millimeters:

   $6 \ cm^3$; $12 \ m^3$; $5.5 \ cm^3$; $23.4 \ dm^3$; $48.5 \ m^3$

4. Change each of the following to cubic centimeters:

   $24 \ m^3$; $3.59 \ dm^3$; $4,631 \ mm^3$; $9.6 \ m^3$; $850 \ mm^3$

5. Change each of the following to cubic decimeters:

   $49 \ m^3$; $4,780 \ cm^3$; $14.2 \ m^3$; $52,750 \ mm^3$; $94.8 \ cm^3$

6. Change each of the following to cubic meters:

   $19,000 \ dm^3$; $8,300,000 \ mm^3$; $26,500 \ cm^3$; $625 \ dm^3$; $500,000 \ cm^3$

7. **a.** 18 milliliters of liquid will occupy a space of how many cubic centimeters?
   b. 5 liters of liquid will occupy a space of how many cubic centimeters?
   c. A space of 340 cubic centimeters will hold how many milliliters of liquid?
   d. A space of 15.7 cubic decimeters will hold how many liters of liquid?
   e. A space of 6,800 cubic centimeters will hold how many liters of liquid?
   f. 2 liters of water weigh approximately how many kilograms?
   g. 85 milliliters of water weigh how many grams?
   h. 73 centiliters of water weigh how many grams?
   i. 4.5 liters of water weigh how many kilograms?
   j. 0.327 liter of water weighs how many grams?
   k. How many liters of water are in a container if the water weighs 9 kilograms?
   l. How many milliliters of water weigh 87 grams?

Units of Measure and Measurement

m. How many liters of water are in a container if the water weighs 325 grams?

n. How many cubic decimeters are occupied by 32 kilograms of water?

o. Water weighing 17 grams occupies a space of how many cubic centimeters?

p. Water weighing 4.7 kilograms fills a space of how many cubic centimeters?

8. How much space is occupied by each of the following capacities?

    a. In cubic centimeters (cm³):
      9 mL;   31.4 mL;   25 cL;   6 dL;   0.83 L

    b. In cubic decimeters (dm³):
      4 L;   97 dL;   367 cL;   19.3 L;   7.75 L

9. Find the capacity that will fill each of the following volumes:

    a. In milliliters (mL):
      11 cm³;   2.6 cm³;   700 mm³;   8 dm³;   0.05 m³

    b. In centiliters (cL):
      5 cm³;   2.58 m³;   6.3 dm³;   9.46 cm³;   8,400 mm³

    c. In liters (L):
      6 dm³;   25.9 dm³;   3.8 m³;   4,000 cm³;   87,000 mm³

10. Find the weight of each of the following volumes or capacities of water:

    a. In kilograms (kg):
      4 dm³;   87 L;   156 cm³;   6.92 L;   5,200 cm³

    b. In grams (g):
      21 cm³;   .367 L;   9.7 mL;   3.25 cL;   6,300 mm³

11. Find the volume or capacity occupied by each of the following weights of water:

    a. In cubic centimeters (cm³):
      7 kg;   40 g;   0.3 kg;   850 mg;   4.92 g

    b. In liters (L):
      16 kg;   5,100 g;   475 g;   0.006 kg;   7,260 mg

    c. In milliliters (mL):
      5 g;   157.3 g;   2.6 kg;   9,140 mg;   8,500 cg

    d. In centiliters (cL):
      31 g;   8.4 kg;   425 g;   18,300 cg;   7,000 mg

12. A tank holds 25 liters of gasoline. How many cubic decimeters of space are in the tank? How many cubic centimeters?
13. How many liters of water will fill an aquarium if it occupies a space of 4,800 cubic centimeters? What is the weight of the water when the aquarium is full?
14. It takes 200,000 liters of water to fill a swimming pool. How many cubic decimeters does the water occupy when the swimming pool is full? How many kilograms does the water weigh when the swimming pool is three-fourths full?
15. A water tank has a volume of 4.37 cubic meters. How many liters of water can the tank hold? What is the weight of the water when the tank is full?

CUSTOMARY SYSTEM

Since the complete changeover to the metric system is a gradual one, we will find the customary units of measure still being used. Consequently the following sections deal with the customary units of measure for possible use in our everyday affairs.

We find that the conversion factors used in the customary system consist of many different numbers such as 12; 3; 36; 5,280; 1,760; 16; 2,000; etc. When we change from a small customary unit of measure to a larger unit, we sometimes get complicated answers. For example:

49 inches changed to yards is $1\frac{13}{36}$ yards.

39 ounces changed to pounds is $2\frac{7}{16}$ pounds.

However, we have seen that the conversion factors used in the metric system are all some power of ten. When we change from any unit of measure to another unit in the metric system, the computation is quick and easy because we work with the decimal system. For example:

46.2 millimeters = 4.62 centimeters

825 centimeters = 8.25 meters

9,573 milligrams = 9.573 grams

In the following sections 8–6 to 8–11 inclusive, to change a given number of units of one customary denomination to units of another denomination, we follow the procedures that are explained on pages 228–231. See pages 490–491 for tables of measure.

FUNDAMENTAL OPERATIONS WITH DENOMINATE NUMBERS

Any numbers which are expressed in terms of units of measure are called *denominate numbers*.

Addition

To add denominate numbers, we arrange like units in columns, then add each column. Where the sum of any column is greater than the number of units that make the next larger unit, it is simplified as illustrated in the model.

> Add:
>
> 5 ft. 11 in.
> 3 ft. 7 in.
> 8 ft. 18 in. = 9 ft. 6 in.
>
> *Answer,* 9 ft. 6 in.

Subtraction

To subtract denominate numbers, we arrange like units under each other, then subtract, starting from the right. When the number of units in the subtrahend is greater than the number of corresponding units in the minuend, we take one of the next larger units in the minuend and change it to an equivalent number of smaller units to permit subtraction as shown in the model.

> Subtract:
>
> 6 hr. 20 min. = 5 hr. 80 min.
> 1 hr. 45 min. = 1 hr. 45 min.
>   4 hr. 35 min.
>
> *Answer,* 4 hr. 35 min.

Multiplication

To multiply denominate numbers, we multiply each unit by the multiplier. Where the product of any column is greater than the number of units that make the next larger unit, it is simplified as shown in the model.

> Multiply:
>
> 2 yd. 10 in.
>   4
> 8 yd. 40 in. = 9 yd. 4 in.
>
> *Answer,* 9 yd. 4 in.

Division

To divide denominate numbers, we divide each unit by the divisor. If the unit is not exactly divisible, we change the remainder to the next smaller unit and combine with the given number of the smaller unit to form the next partial dividend.

> Divide:
>
> $$\begin{array}{r} 2 \text{ lb. } 7 \text{ oz.} \\ 6\overline{)14 \text{ lb. } 10 \text{ oz.}} \\ 12 \text{ lb.} \hphantom{abc} \\ \overline{2 \text{ lb. } 10 \text{ oz.}} = 42 \text{ oz.} \\ 42 \text{ oz.} \end{array}$$
>
> *Answer,* 2 lb. 7 oz.

8–6 MEASURE OF LENGTH—CUSTOMARY

1. Find the number of inches in:

    a. 2 ft.,   19 ft., $6\frac{1}{2}$ ft., $\frac{3}{4}$ ft.

    b. 4 yd.,   27 yd., $9\frac{3}{4}$ yd., $1\frac{5}{8}$ yd.

    c. 1 ft. 6 in.,   5 ft. 11 in.,   1 yd. 9 in.,   6 yd. 23 in.

2. Find the number of feet in:

    a. 8 yd.,   21 yd., $\frac{2}{3}$ yd., $5\frac{1}{2}$ yd.

    b. 3 mi.,   15 mi., $\frac{5}{8}$ mi., $10\frac{1}{4}$ mi.

    c. 6 rd.,   34 rd., $\frac{1}{2}$ rd., $4\frac{3}{4}$ rd.

    d. 10 yd. 2 ft.,   45 yd. 1 ft.,   2 mi. 700 ft.,   7 rd. 5 ft.

    e. 48 in.,   144 in.,   900 in.,   468 in.

3. Find the number of yards in:

    a. 2 mi.,   28 mi., $\frac{1}{2}$ mi., $3\frac{7}{8}$ mi.

    b. 4 rd.,   9 rd., $\frac{3}{4}$ rd., $8\frac{1}{2}$ rd.

    c. 1 mi. 660 yd.,   12 mi. 1,000 yd.,   7 rd. 4 yd.,   10 rd. 2 yd.

    d. 108 in.,   504 in.,   720 in.,   648 in.

    e. 9 ft.,   42 ft.,   75 ft.,   96 ft.

4. Find the number of rods in:

    a. 5 mi.,   12 mi., $7\frac{3}{4}$ mi., $9\frac{1}{8}$ mi.

    b. 33 ft., $49\frac{1}{2}$ ft.,   22 yd., $16\frac{1}{2}$ yd.

5. Find the number of miles in:

    a. 10,560 ft.,   47,520 ft.,   26,400 ft.,   79,200 ft.

    b. 7,040 yd.,   17,600 yd.,   21,120 yd.,   44,000 yd.

6. a. What part of a foot is:

    6 in.,   8 in.,   9 in.,   5 in.,   10 in.,   3 in.,   1 in.?

    b. What part of a yard is:

    27 in.,   24 in.,   30 in.,   11 in.,   2 ft.,   1 ft., $1\frac{1}{2}$ ft.?

    c. What part of a mile is:

    880 yd.,   1,320 ft.,   1,540 yd.,   80 rd.,   110 yd.,   3,520 ft.?

7. Add and simplify:

		3 mi. 600 yd.	6 yd. 1 ft. 8 in.
1 ft. 5 in.	2 yd. 18 in.	5 mi. 900 yd.	3 yd. 2 ft. 10 in.
1 ft. 2 in.	3 yd. 26 in.	1 mi. 440 yd.	1 yd. 1 ft. 9 in.

8. Subtract:

8 yd. 9 in.	4 ft.	5 mi. 2,000 ft.	7 yd. 1 ft. 2 in.
5 yd. 3 in.	2 ft. 7 in.	5,000 ft.	3 yd. 2 ft. 6 in.

9. Multiply and simplify:

1 ft. 3 in.	2 mi. 440 yd.	10 yd. 9 in.	4 yd. 2 ft. 8 in.
3	6	4	5

10. Divide:

4)12 mi. 220 yd.   3)7 ft. 9 in.   8)25 yd. 20 in.   5)8 yd. 2 ft. 3 in.

8–7 MEASURE OF WEIGHT—CUSTOMARY

EXERCISES

1. Find the number of ounces in:

a. 7 lb.,   18 lb., $4\frac{1}{2}$ lb., $3\frac{3}{4}$ lb.

b. 1 lb. 9 oz.,   2 lb. 14 oz.,   5 lb. 3 oz.,   9 lb. 10 oz.

2. Find the number of pounds in:

a. 3 s.t.,   25 s.t., $8\frac{1}{2}$ s.t., $12\frac{2}{5}$ s.t.

b. 5 l.t.,   49 l.t., $2\frac{3}{4}$ l.t., $6\frac{1}{2}$ l.t.

c. 4 s.t. 500 lb.,   7 l.t. 300 lb.,   10 s.t. 900 lb.,   8 l.t. 1,500 lb.

d. 80 oz.,   128 oz.,   400 oz.,   272 oz.

3. Find the number of short tons in: 8,000 lb.,   20,000 lb.,   5,000 lb.

4. Find the number of long tons in: 4,480 lb.,   20,160 lb.,   7,840 lb.

5. a. What part of a pound is:

8 oz.,   12 oz.,   10 oz.,   3 oz.?

b. What part of a short ton is:

500 lb.,   1,000 lb.,   200 lb.,   1,200 lb.?

c. What part of a long ton is:

1,120 lb.,   280 lb.,   1,680 lb.,   1,960 lb.?

6. Add and simplify:

		7 lb. 9 oz.	1 l.t. 800 lb.
6 lb. 4 oz.	4 s.t. 1,500 lb.	8 lb. 11 oz.	5 l.t. 1,600 lb.
3 lb. 8 oz.	2 s.t. 1,000 lb.	3 lb. 12 oz.	2 l.t. 750 lb.

7. Subtract:

5 lb. 11 oz.	8 lb. 4 oz.	3 s.t. 500 lb.	6 lb.
2 lb. 5 oz.	7 lb. 15 oz.	1 s.t. 1,600 lb.	4 lb. 8 oz.

8. Multiply and simplify:

4 lb. 3 oz.	6 s.t. 200 lb.	2 lb. 9 oz.	5 lb. 12 oz.
5	10	6	8

9. Divide:

3)15 lb. 6 oz.   9)27 l.t. 1,800 lb.   7)9 lb. 10 oz.   12)5 lb. 4 oz.

8–8 LIQUID MEASURE—CUSTOMARY

EXERCISES

1. Find the number of ounces in:
  a. 5 pt., 16 pt., $3\frac{1}{2}$ pt., $1\frac{3}{4}$ pt.
  b. 3 qt., 20 qt., $5\frac{1}{4}$ qt., $\frac{1}{2}$ qt.
  c. 2 gal., 5 gal., $\frac{1}{2}$ gal., $1\frac{1}{4}$ gal.
  d. 1 pt. 9 oz., 7 qt. 14 oz., 1 gal. 5 oz.

2. Find the number of pints in:
  a. 6 qt., 40 qt., $8\frac{1}{2}$ qt., $19\frac{1}{4}$ qt.
  b. 2 gal., 9 gal., $5\frac{1}{2}$ gal., $6\frac{3}{4}$ gal.
  c. 3 qt. 1 pt., 8 qt. 1 pt., 10 qt. 1 pt.
  d. 32 oz., 224 oz., 480 oz., 800 oz.

3. Find the number of quarts in:
  a. 2 gal., 15 gal., $9\frac{1}{2}$ gal., $7\frac{3}{4}$ gal.
  b. 5 gal. 3 qt., 1 gal. 2 qt., 8 gal. 1 qt.
  c. 4 pt., 34 pt., 9 pt., 25 pt.
  d. 64 oz., 180 oz., 320 oz., 288 oz.

4. Find the number of gallons in:

a. 12 qt.,	56 qt.,	10 qt.,	19 qt.
b. 16 pt.,	40 pt.,	27 pt.,	82 pt.
c. 128 oz.,	384 oz.,	96 oz.,	192 oz.

5. a. What part of a pint is:

  8 oz.,   4 oz.,   14 oz.,   5 oz.,   3 oz.,   12 oz.?

b. What part of a quart is:

1 pt.,   24 oz.,   16 oz., $\frac{1}{2}$ pt., $1\frac{1}{2}$ pt.,   8 oz.?

c. What part of a gallon is:

3 qt.,   2 qt.,   1 pt.,   64 oz., $2\frac{1}{2}$ qt.,   3 pt.?

6. Add and simplify:

		6 gal. 3 qt.	3 pt. 12 oz.
2 gal. 1 qt.	1 qt. 14 oz.	4 gal. 2 qt.	5 pt. 7 oz.
4 gal. 2 qt.	1 qt. 9 oz.	3 gal. 3 qt.	1 pt. 9 oz.

7. Subtract:

3 qt. 1 pt.	1 pt. 12 oz.	7 gal.	3 qt. 1 pt. 5 oz.
2 qt. 1 pt.	15 oz.	4 gal. 3 qt.	1 qt. 1 pt. 12 oz.

8. Multiply and simplify:

5 gal. 1 qt.	3 qt. 7 oz.	1 pt. 9 oz.	4 gal. 3 qt.
3	8	6	9

9. Divide:

$3\overline{)12 \text{ gal. } 3 \text{ qt.}}$ $5\overline{)5 \text{ pt. } 15 \text{ oz.}}$ $7\overline{)9 \text{ qt. } 6 \text{ oz.}}$ $10\overline{)32 \text{ gal. } 2 \text{ qt.}}$

10. How many ounces of water must be added to:

a. A 6 oz. can of frozen grape concentrate to make $1\frac{1}{2}$ pints of grape juice?

b. A 6 oz. can of frozen lemon concentrate to make 1 quart of lemonade?

c. A 27 oz. can of frozen orange concentrate to make one gallon of juice?

8–9 DRY MEASURE—CUSTOMARY

EXERCISES

1. Find the number of pints in: 6 qt.,   25 qt., $9\frac{1}{2}$ qt.,   4 qt. 1 pt.

2. Find the number of quarts in:

a. 5 pk.,   18 pk., $8\frac{3}{4}$ pt.,   7 pk. 5 qt.

b. 48 pt.,   70 pt.,   1 pt.,   25 pt.

3. Find the number of pecks in:

    a. 7 bu.,   24 bu., $2\frac{1}{2}$ bu., $9\frac{3}{4}$ bu.

    b. 3 bu. 3 pk.,   29 bu. 1 pk.,   16 qt.,   28 qt.

4. Find the number of bushels in: 20 pk.,   48 pk.,   35 pk.,   64 qt.
5. **a.** What part of a bushel is: 2 pk.,   3 pk.,   1 pk.,   4 qt.?
    b. What part of a peck is: 4 qt.,   6 qt.,   3 qt.,   1 pt.?

6. Add and simplify:

		5 bu. 3 pk.	3 pk. 4 qt.
3 bu. 2 pk.	2 pk. 3 qt.	1 bu. 2 pk.	7 pk. 2 qt.
6 bu. 1 pk.	5 pk. 4 qt.	3 bu. 3 pk.	2 pk. 3 qt.

7. Subtract:

		2 pk. 5 qt.	10 bu. 2 pk.
9 pk. 7 qt.	8 bu.	7 qt.	5 bu. 3 pk.
2 pk. 3 qt.	3 bu. 2 pk.		

8. Multiply and simplify:

1 pk. 3 qt.	8 bu. 3 pk.
2	7

9. Divide:

2)14 pk. 6 qt.   5)18 bu. 3 pk.

8–10   MEASURE OF AREA—CUSTOMARY

EXERCISES

Change:

1. To square inches: 17 sq. ft.,   4 sq. yd.,   20 sq. ft.,   5 sq. yd.
2. To square feet: 1,296 sq. in.,   15 sq. yd.,   42 sq. rd.,   4 acres.
3. To square yards: 63 sq. ft.,   10,368 sq. in.,   8 acres,   5 sq. mi.
4. To square rods: 50 acres,   968 sq. yd.,   1,089 sq. yd.,   13 acres.
5. To acres: 5,600 sq. rd.,   11 sq. mi.,   87,120 sq. yd.,   2,400 sq. rd.
6. To square miles: 10,880 acres,   18,585,600 sq. yd.,   14,720 acres
7. What part of a square foot is: 108 sq. in.?   16 sq. in.?   60 sq. in.?
8. What part of a square yard is: 6 sq. ft.?   5 sq. ft.?   432 sq. in.?
9. What part of a square mile is: 480 acres?   1,936 sq. yd.?   21,780 sq. ft.?

EXERCISES

Change:

1. To cubic inches: 15 cu. ft.,   7 cu. yd.,   40 cu. ft.
2. To cubic inches: 23 cu. yd., $6\frac{1}{2}$ cu. ft.,   35 cu. yd.
3. To cubic feet: 30 cu. yd.,   16 cu. yd.,   6,912 cu. in.
4. To cubic feet: 15,552 cu. in.,   34,560 cu. in.,   189 cu. yd.
5. To cubic yards: 108 cu. ft.,   186,624 cu. in.,   513 cu. ft.
6. To cubic yards: 419,904 cu. in.,   1,350 cu. ft.,   933,120 cu. in.
7. What part of a cubic foot is: 864 cu. in.?   108 cu. in.?   1,296 cu. in.?
8. What part of a cubic yard is: 18 cu. ft? $13\frac{1}{2}$ cu. ft.?   6 cu. ft.?
9. What part of a cubic foot is: 648 cu. in.?   432 cu. in.?   972 cu. in.?
10. What part of a cubic yard is: 9 cu. ft.? $22\frac{1}{2}$ cu. ft.?   3 cu. ft.?

8-12 VOLUME, CAPACITY, AND WEIGHT RELATIONSHIPS—CUSTOMARY

See page 490 for table of equivalents.

EXERCISES

1. Find the capacity in gallons equal to a volume of 1,848 cu. in.
2. Find the volume in cubic inches equal to a capacity of 15 gallons.
3. Find the capacity in gallons equal to a volume of 60 cu. ft.
4. Find the volume in cubic feet equal to a capacity of 135 gallons.
5. What is the weight in pounds of 42 cu. ft. of sea water?
6. What volume in cubic feet do 5,120 lb. of sea water occupy?
7. What is the weight in pounds of 110 cu. ft. of fresh water?
8. What volume in cubic feet do 4,500 lb. of fresh water occupy?
9. Find the capacity in bushels equal to a volume of 20 cu. ft.
10. Find the volume in cubic feet equal to a capacity of 84 bushels.

11. Find the equivalent:

    a. Capacity in gallons: 3,234 cu. in.,   46 cu. ft.,   100 cu. ft.

    b. Capacity in bushels: 50 cu. ft.,   365 cu. ft.,   34 cu. yd.

    c. Volume in cubic feet: 75 gal.,   1,200 gal.,   236 bu.

    d. Volume in cubic inches: 8 gal.,   14 gal., $10\frac{1}{2}$ gal.

    e. Volume in cubic feet: 3,200 lb. of sea water,   7,500 lb. of fresh water.

    f. Weight in pounds: 90 cu. ft. of fresh water,   135 cu. ft. of sea water.

8–13 MEASURE OF TIME

See pages 229–231 for directions to change units of time and page 248 for directions to compute with these units. The table of measure is found on page 491.

EXERCISES

---

1. Find the number of seconds in:

    a. 18 min.,   30 min., $7\frac{1}{3}$ min., $2\frac{3}{4}$ min.

    b. 3 hr.,   12 hr., $4\frac{1}{2}$ hr., $\frac{2}{3}$ hr.

    c. 3 min. 15 sec.,   12 min. 48 sec.,   45 min. 30 sec.,   1 hr. 18 min. 29 sec.

2. Find the number of minutes in:

    a. 4 hr.,   17 hr., $2\frac{1}{2}$ hr., $10\frac{5}{6}$ hr.

    b. 7 hr. 45 min.,   9 hr. 23 min.,   14 hr. 56 min.,   21 hr. 4 min.

    c. 240 sec.,   3,600 sec.,   90 sec.,   500 sec.

3. Find the number of hours in:

    a. 2 da.,   7 da., $4\frac{5}{8}$ da., $3\frac{2}{3}$ da.

    b. 1 da. 9 hr.,   3 da. 14 hr.,   2 da. 23 hr.,   10 da. 5 hr.

    c. 180 min.,   1,440 min.,   270 min.,   7,200 sec.

4. Find the number of days in:

    a. 5 wk.,   13 wk.,   52 wk., $3\frac{4}{7}$ wk.

    *b. 3 yr.,   2 yr., $1\frac{3}{4}$ yr., $2\frac{1}{4}$ yr.

    c. 1 wk. 3 da.,   7 wk. 5 da.,   1 yr. 100 da.,   2 yr. 263 da.

    d. 72 hr.,   216 hr.,   36 hr.,   100 hr.

---

* Where 4 or more years are involved, use 366 days for every fourth year.

Units of Measure and Measurement

5. Find the number of months in:

   a. 3 yr.,   8 yr., $\frac{3}{4}$ yr., $4\frac{2}{3}$ yr.

   b. 2 yr. 8 mo.,   5 yr. 11 mo.,   7 yr. 7 mo.,   11 yr. 4 mo.

6. Find the number of weeks in:

   2 yr., $1\frac{3}{4}$ yr.,   1 yr. 40 wk.,   2 yr. 29 wk.

7. Find the number of years in:

   a. 48 mo.,   120 mo.,   30 mo.,   64 mo.

   b. 104 wk.,   156 wk.,   78 wk.,   169 wk.

   c. 730 da.,   511 da.,   1,168 da.,   1,461 da.

8. a. What part of a minute is: 15 sec.,   40 sec.,   24 sec.,   35 sec.?

   b. What part of an hour is: 45 min.,   30 min.,   5 min.,   48 sec.?

   c. What part of a day is: 6 hr.,   15 hr.,   12 hr.,   20 hr.?

   d. What part of a week is: 3 da.,   1 da.,   5 da., $3\frac{1}{2}$ da.?

   e. What part of a year is: 8 mo.,   26 wk.,   292 da.,   3 mo.?

9. Add and simplify:

                                          6 yr. 8 mo.   5 hr. 25 min. 32 sec.

    48 hr. 28 min.   5 wk. 4 da.   9 yr. 1 mo.   3 hr. 17 min. 51 sec.

     8 hr. 39 min.   4 wk. 6 da.   2 yr. 5 mo.   7 hr. 38 min. 47 sec.
    ——————————   ——————————   ——————————   ——————————————

10. Subtract:

    6 da. 18 hr.   15 yr. 6 mo.   10 min.   8 hr. 19 min. 15 sec.

    4 da.   5 hr.   8 mo.   4 min. 36 sec.   2 hr. 30 min. 42 sec.
    ————————   ————————   ————————————   ——————————————

11. Multiply and simplify:

    7 yr. 2 mo.   4 da. 3 hr.   3 hr. 12 min.   1 hr. 38 min. 6 sec.

        4   9   10   15
    ————————   ———————   ———————   ————————————

12. Divide:

    3)15 yr. 9 mo.   4)18 hr. 32 min.   7)9 da. 15 hr.   15)7 hr. 41 min. 30 sec.

13. Which is greater: **14.** Which is less:

   a. A half-hour or 40 minutes?   **a.** A quarter-minute or 20 seconds?

   b. 7 months or two-thirds of a year?   **b.** 11 hours or a half-day?

15. Find the length of time:

   a. From 1 A.M. to 5 P.M. the same day.

   b. From 12:45 P.M. to 9:30 A.M. the following day.

8–14 MEASURE OF ANGLES AND ARCS

See pages 229–231 for directions to change units measuring angles and arcs and page 248 for directions to compute with these units. The table of measure is found on page 491.

EXERCISES

Change:

1. To minutes: 36°,   18° 25′,   2,580″,   54°

2. To seconds: 51′,   3°,   24′30″,   1° 24′45″

3. To degrees: 840′,   21,660′,   3,600″,   21,660″

4. Add and simplify:

48° 25′	127° 7′ 29″	11° 16′ 30″	82° 29′ 15″
29° 31′	38° 15′ 52″	54° 35′ 25″	36° 50′ 28″
		98° 3′ 18″	60° 40′ 17″

5. Subtract:

160° 25′	90°	81° 34′ 40″	180°
96° 17′	36° 15′	40° 50′ 37″	96° 29′ 46″

6. Multiply and simplify:

26° 14′	7° 38′	47° 12′ 53″	6° 28′ 30″
4	15	3	15

7. Divide:

$5\overline{)40° 35′}$ $15\overline{)10° 30′}$ $6\overline{)49° 12′}$ $15\overline{)18° 31′ 45″}$

8. Find the sum of measures of two angles when one angle measures 38° and the other measures 153°.

9. An angle measuring 102° is to be divided into 3 equal angles. What is the measure of each equal angle?

10. One angle measures 60°. A second angle measures 49°32′. How much greater is the measure of the first angle?

11. Angle A is 6 times the size of angle B. Angle B measures 17°20′. What is the measure of angle A?

12. A circle, measuring 360° of arc, is divided into 8 equal arcs. What is the measure of each equal arc?

8-15 RATES OF SPEED

We change the given units to the required units (in the metric model: kilometer to 1,000 meters and hour to 3,600 seconds; in the customary model: mile to 5,280 ft. and hour to 3,600 sec.), then we perform the necessary arithmetical operations. A *knot* is one (1) nautical mile per hour. A nautical mile is approximately equivalent to 6,080 ft. or 1.15 statute miles or 1.85 km. A kilometer is approximately equal to 0.54 nautical mile. See table of measure on page 490.

Note that in the metric system rates of speed are abbreviated in the following ways: meters per second (m/s); kilometers per hour (km/h); centimeters per second (cm/s); millimeters per minute (mm/min); and so on.

METRIC	CUSTOMARY
Change 72 km/h to m/s:	Change 30 m.p.h. to ft. per sec.:
$72 \text{ km/h} = \dfrac{72 \text{ km}}{1 \text{ h}}$	$30 \text{ m.p.h.} = \dfrac{30 \text{ mi.}}{1 \text{ hr.}}$
$\dfrac{72 \times 1,000}{3,600} = 20 \text{ m/s}$	$\dfrac{30 \times 5,280}{3,600} = 44 \text{ ft. per sec.}$
Answer, 20 m/s	*Answer,* 44 ft. per sec.

EXERCISES

Change, finding answers to the nearest hundredth wherever necessary:

1. To meters per second:	300 cm/s;	50 km/h;	160 mm/min
2. To meters per minute:	85 mm/s;	240 cm/min;	80 km/h
3. To centimeters per second:	60 km/h;	75 m/min;	630 mm/s
4. To kilometers per hour:	90 m/s;	480 cm/s;	225 knots
5. To knots:	80 km/h;	900 m/s;	350 km/h

6. To feet per second: 300 stat. m.p.h.;   225 stat. m.p.h.;   24 knots

7. To statute miles per hour: 506 ft. per sec.;   140 knots: 858 ft. per min.

8. To nautical miles per hour: 175 knots;   100 stat. m.p.h.;   440 ft. per sec.

9. To knots: 34.8 naut. m.p.h.;   56 stat. m.p.h.;   154 ft. per sec.

10. To feet per minute: 540 ft. per sec.;   165 stat. m.p.h.;   210 knots

8–16   TEMPERATURE

The three thermometer scales that are used to measure temperature are the *Celsius*, the *Fahrenheit*, and the *Kelvin*. The Celsius scale (formerly called centigrade) is based on 100 divisions, each called a *degree*. On the Celsius scale the freezing point of water is indicated as 0° and the boiling point as 100°. On the Fahrenheit scale the freezing point and the boiling point of water are indicated as 32° and 212° respectively for a 180° interval. It now appears that the Celsius scale will soon replace the Fahrenheit scale in the United States.

The Kelvin temperature scale, used in SI measurement, is related to the Celsius scale. One degree Celsius is exactly equal to one *kelvin* (the name used to mean degree Kelvin). The reading of a specific temperature on the Kelvin scale is approximately 273 kelvins more than its reading on the Celsius scale.

To change a Celsius temperature reading to a kelvin reading, we add 273° to the Celsius reading or use the formula:

$$K = C + 273.$$

To change a kelvin temperature reading to a Celsius reading, we subtract 273° from the kelvin reading or use the formula:

$$C = K - 273.$$

To change a Celsius temperature reading to a Fahrenheit reading, we add 32° to nine-fifths of the Celsius temperature reading or use the formula:

$$F = \tfrac{9}{5}C + 32.$$

To change a Fahrenheit temperature reading to a Celsius reading, we subtract 32° from the Fahrenheit temperature reading and take five-ninths of this answer or use the formula:

$$C = \tfrac{5}{9}(F - 32).$$

Units of Measure and Measurement   **259**

1. Change each of the following Celsius temperature readings to a corresponding kelvin reading:

   a. 40°C **c.** 0°C **e.** 200°C
   b. 98°C **d.** 9°C

2. Change each of the following kelvin temperature readings to a corresponding Celsius reading:

   a. 275 K **c.** 400 K **e.** 381 K
   b. 358 K **d.** 323 K

3. Change each of the following Fahrenheit readings to a corresponding Celsius temperature reading:

   a. 77°F **c.** 185°F **e.** 100°F
   b. 212°F **d.** 32°F

4. Change each of the following Celsius temperature readings to a corresponding Fahrenheit temperature reading:

   a. 40°C **c.** 7°C **e.** 0°C
   b. 100°C **d.** 65°C

5. The classroom thermostat is set at 68°F. What would it be on the Celsius temperature scale? What is it in kelvins?

6. Copper has a melting point of 1,083°C and a boiling point of 2,336°C, silver has a melting point of 960.8°C and a boiling point of 2,600°C. Express each of these as a Fahrenheit temperature reading. Also express in kelvins.

7. The average temperatures in some of the larger cities of Europe during the month of April are as follows: Paris, 10°C; London, 9°C; Rome, 14°C; Madrid, 12°C; Lisbon, 15°C; Helsinki, 3°C; and Athens, 16°C. Express each of these Celsius temperature readings as a Fahrenheit temperature reading to the nearest degree. Also express in kelvins.

8. If the temperature of standard air at sea level is 59°F, what is the corresponding temperature reading on the Celsius scale? What is it in kelvins?

8–17 TWENTY-FOUR HOUR CLOCK

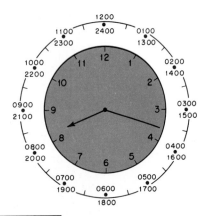

To tell time on a 24-hour clock, a 4-digit numeral is used, the first two digits indicating the hour and the last two the minutes. 1 P.M. is thought of as the 13th hour, 2 P.M. the 14th hour, etc. Thus 1200 is added to the given digits when expressing time from 1 P.M. to 12 midnight. The numeral 12 representing the hour is replaced by two zeros when expressing the time from midnight to 1 A.M.

8:43 A.M. = 0843	5:09 P.M. = 1709

12:37 A.M. = 0037	12:28 P.M. = 1228

EXERCISES

1. Using the 24-hour system express each of the following:

   a. 11:42 A.M.
   b. 2:59 A.M.
   c. 6:00 A.M.
   d. 9:00 P.M.

   e. 3:24 P.M.
   f. 10:05 P.M.
   g. 12:14 A.M.
   h. 12:40 P.M.

   i. 10:30 A.M.
   j. 4:15 P.M.
   k. 12:23 P.M.
   l. 5:50 A.M.

2. Express each of the following in A.M. or P.M. time:

   a. 0125
   b. 1106
   c. 0400
   d. 1800

   e. 2130
   f. 0028
   g. 2336
   h. 1217

   i. 0754
   j. 1000
   k. 0002
   l. 1745

3. Find the difference in times between:

   a. 0043 and 0800   b. 0935 and 1710   c. 1122 and 2309

4. An aircraft carrier left port at 0517 and arrived at its destination at 2005. How long did it take the aircraft carrier to reach its destination?

5. An airplane took off from Miami at 0945 and arrived in Boston at 1320. A second airplane traveled the same route, taking off at 2155 and landing at 0043 the next day. Which airplane made the faster time and how much faster?

8–18 TIME ZONES

There are four standard *time belts* in the United States, excluding Alaska and Hawaii: Eastern (EST), Central (CST), Mountain (MST), and Pacific (PST). Central time is one hour earlier than Eastern time, Mountain time is one hour earlier than Central time, and Pacific time is one hour earlier than Mountain time. The meridians at 75°, 90°, 105°, and 120° west longitude are used to determine the time in these zones.

Alaska has four time zones determined by the meridians at 120°, 135°, 150°, and 165° west longitude. Hawaii uses the time zone of the meridian at 150° west longitude. Parts of Canada east of Maine are in another time zone, the Atlantic Standard Time Zone, which is one hour later than Eastern Standard Time.

EXERCISES

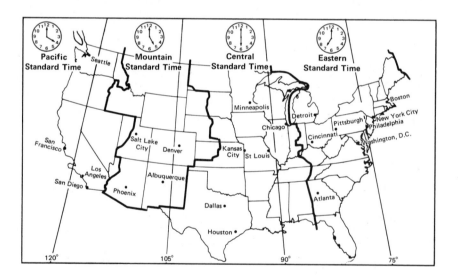

1. In what time zone is your city located?

2. If it is 1 P.M. in the Mountain Time Zone, what time is it in:

   a. Central Zone?
   b. Pacific Zone?
   c. Eastern Zone?

3. If it is 8 A.M. in Chicago, what time is it in:

    a. San Francisco?   **d.** Washington?   **g.** Atlanta?
    b. Minneapolis?   **e.** Denver?   **h.** Los Angeles?
    c. Cincinnati?   **f.** Boston?   **i.** Your city?

4. If a nationwide program is telecast at 5 P.M. from New York City, what time is it seen in:

    a. Pittsburgh?   **c.** St. Louis?   **e.** Detroit?
    b. Los Angeles?   **d.** Salt Lake City?   **f.** Your city?

5. How long did it take an airplane to fly from San Francisco to Philadelphia if it left San Francisco at 10:15 A.M. (PST) and arrived in Philadelphia at 6:27 P.M. (EST)?

6. If, exactly at midnight, you place a telephone call in Pittsburgh for Denver, what time is it in Denver?

MEASUREMENT

8–19 PRECISION AND ACCURACY IN MEASUREMENT

Measurement is never exact, it is approximate. The same length measured on each of the following scales shows a measurement of:

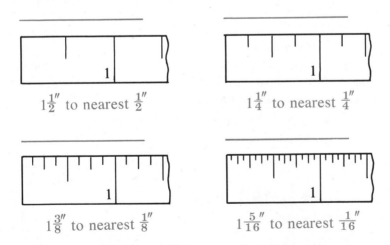

$1\frac{1}{2}''$ to nearest $\frac{1}{2}''$

$1\frac{1}{4}''$ to nearest $\frac{1}{4}''$

$1\frac{3}{8}''$ to nearest $\frac{1}{8}''$

$1\frac{5}{16}''$ to nearest $\frac{1}{16}''$

Observe that $1\frac{1}{2}''$ is precise to the nearest $\frac{1}{2}''$; $1\frac{1}{4}''$ is precise to the nearest $\frac{1}{4}''$; $1\frac{3}{8}''$ is precise to the nearest $\frac{1}{8}''$; $1\frac{5}{16}''$ is precise to the nearest $\frac{1}{16}''$. The smaller the unit, the more precise is the measurement. The measurement $1\frac{5}{16}''$ is the most precise of the above measurements.

Precision is the closeness to the true measurement. It is determined by the smallest unit of measure used to make the measurement.

The precision of a measurement named by a numeral for a whole number ending in zeros is indicated by an underlined zero as shown below. (Also see page 266.)

25,00<u>0</u> kilometers is precise to the nearest kilometer.

25,0<u>0</u>0 kilometers is precise to the nearest 10 kilometers.

25,<u>0</u>00 miles is precise to the nearest 100 miles.

25,000 miles is precise to the nearest 1,000 miles.

25,000.0 miles is precise to the nearest tenth of a mile.

In measuring the above length $1\frac{5}{16}''$, the unit used was $\frac{1}{16}$ of an inch. The real length is between $1\frac{9}{32}''$ and $1\frac{11}{32}''$. The greatest possible error between the measurement $1\frac{5}{16}''$ and the true measurement can only be $\frac{1}{32}''$ since the *greatest possible error* is one-half of the unit used to measure.

The *relative error* is the ratio of the greatest possible error to the measurement. The *accuracy* of the measurement is determined by the relative error. The smaller the relative error, the more accurate is the measurement.

The measurement $1\frac{5}{16}''$ has the greatest possible error of $\frac{1}{32}''$.

The ratio of $\frac{1}{32}''$ to $1\frac{5}{16}''$ is $\frac{1}{42}$. The relative error is $\frac{1}{42}$.

$\frac{1}{32}$ to $1\frac{5}{16}$

$\frac{1}{32} \div 1\frac{5}{16}$

$\frac{1}{32} \times \frac{16}{21} = \frac{1}{42}$

Sometimes to make quick comparisons the relative error is expressed as a percent. To do this we multiply the relative error by 100 (or see table on page 187).

The allowance for error in measurement is called *tolerance*. A required measurement of 8.2 inches with a tolerance of .05 inch allowed in both directions would be indicated as 8.2″ ± .05″ and would represent any measurement from 8.15 inches to 8.25 inches inclusive.

EXERCISES

1. To what unit of measure are these measurements precise?

a. $1\frac{7}{8}$ in. **d.** $2\frac{1}{2}$ pt. **g.** .05 mm **j.** .070 cm **m.** 6 kg 3 g

b. $5\frac{22}{32}$ in. **e.** $6\frac{2}{3}$ hr. **h.** .324 cm **k.** 8.6 kg **n.** 9 hr. 17 min.

c. $8\frac{3}{4}$ lb. **f.** $1\frac{5}{6}$ yd. **i.** 12.8 km **l.** 4.89 m **o.** 2 ft. $4\frac{1}{2}$ in.

2. Find the unit of measure or precision of each of the following measurements:

a. 237 km **c.** 18 g **e.** 930 sec. **g.** 2,583 cL

b. 15,000 ft. **d.** 40,000 tons **f.** 270,000 persons **h.** 5,600,000,000 mi.

3. Which measurement in each of the following is more precise?

a. 0.065 m or 0.0126 m? **c.** 8.0 cm or 4.05 cm? **e.** $6\frac{5}{8}$ lb. or 3 lb. 5 oz.?

b. $9\frac{3}{4}$ in. or $7\frac{1}{8}$ in.? **d.** $4\frac{3}{16}$ mi. or $8\frac{1}{2}$ in.? **f.** $2\frac{1}{4}$ ft. or 2 ft. 3 in.?

4. Find the greatest possible error in each of these measurements:

a. $3\frac{1}{2}$ in. **f.** $1\frac{3}{5}$ hr. **k.** 942 m **p.** 1 ft. 8 in.

b. $4\frac{3}{4}$ in. **g.** 2.5 L **l.** 680 yd. **q.** $4\frac{10}{16}$ in.

c. $1\frac{7}{8}$ in. **h.** 1.06 cm **m.** 4,000 ft. **r.** 1 hr. 40 min.

d. $2\frac{9}{32}$ in. **i.** 0.098 mm **n.** 120,000 km **s.** 2.0014 mm

e. $6\frac{11}{16}$ lb. **j.** 34 kg **o.** 3,000,000 mi. **t.** $5\frac{28}{64}$ in.

5. Find the relative error in each of the measurements given in Exercise 4.

6. Find the relative error as a percent for each of the following measurements:

a. 0.8 lb. **b.** 40 km **c.** $6\frac{1}{4}$ in. **d.** $2\frac{2}{3}$ hr. **e.** 25 m

7. Which measurement in each of the following is more accurate?

 a. $2\frac{7}{8}$ in. or $3\frac{5}{16}$ in.?   **c.** 5.4 mm or 0.54 mm?   **e.** 30,0̲0̲0 mi. or $1\frac{1}{4}$ in.?

 b. 18.5 cm or 1.92 cm?   **d.** 69 ft. or 6.9 in.?   **f.** 0.02 m or 230 m?

8. Which is more precise: 0.9 mm or 0.03 mm? Which is more accurate?

9. Arrange the following measurements in order of precision, least precise first, and also in order of accuracy, least accurate first:

 a. 0.04 mm,   0.040 mm,   4.0 mm,   40 mm,   4 mm,   0.004 mm

 b. 8.45 mi.,   6.9 in.,   5.207 ft.,   290 yd.

10. What range of measurements does each of the following represent?

 a. $4.6'' \pm .05''$ **d.** 6.09 mm $\pm$ .025 mm   **g.** $9\frac{3''}{4} \pm \frac{19''}{64}$

 b. $5\frac{1''}{2} \pm \frac{1''}{4}$ **e.** $3\frac{7''}{8} \pm \frac{3''}{16}$ **h.** $1'' \pm .001''$

 c. 17.5 cm $\pm$ .07 cm   **f.** $2.934'' \pm .0001''$ **i.** 4.9 mm $\pm$ .15 mm

8–20 SIGNIFICANT DIGITS

Digits are *significant* in an approximate number when they indicate the precision which is determined by the value of the place of the last significant digit on the right.

> In 46.25, the significant digit 5 indicates precision to the nearest hundredth.
> In 94,0̲0̲, the underlined 0 indicates precision to the nearest ten.

The digits described below in items (1) to (4) inclusive are significant, those described in items (5) and (6) are not significant except as noted in (5).

(1) All non-zero digits are significant.

(2) Zeros located between non-zero digits are significant.

(3) When a decimal or mixed decimal ends in zeros, these zeros are significant.

---

(1) 825 has 3 significant digits.

(2) 2,007 has 4 significant digits.

(3) 43.270 has 5 significant digits.

---

(4) When numbers are expressed in scientific notation, all the digits in the first factor are significant.

(5) When a number ends in zeros, these zeros are not significant unless they are specified as being significant or indicated as significant by a line drawn under them.

(6) In a decimal fraction (when the number is between 0 and 1) the zeros immediately following the decimal point are not significant.

(4) In 8.59×10^6, digits 8, 5, and 9 are significant.

(5) 35,000 has 2 significant digits (3,5)

35,0̲00 has 3 significant digits (3,5,0)

35,00̲0 has 5 significant digits (3,5,0,0,0)

2,070 has 3 significant digits (2,0,7)

(6) .00572 has 3 significant digits (5,7,2) but

5.0072 has 5 significant digits (5,0,0,7,2)

.0050 has 2 significant digits (5,0)

EXERCISES

Determine the number of significant digits in each of the following:

1. 47
2. 9.386
3. 590
4. 6,080,000
5. 940,500,000
6. 5
7. .1468
8. .002
9. .0163
10. .30
11. .00060
12. .010020
13. 84.09
14. 6.00325

15. 96,0̲00
16. 420,0̲00
17. 9.8×10^8
18. 3.05×10^{12}
19. 5,006
20. 5,600
21. .0465
22. 4.0650
23. 250,00̲0
24. 6.7×10^4
25. 65,273
26. 82.040
27. .0009
28. 3,910

29. 50,0̲00
30. .00000013
31. 4.000208
32. 1.93×10^7
33. 24.0
34. 3.1416
35. 5.987×10^9
36. 42̲0,000
37. 37.004
38. .000025
39. 9,248,017
40. 32.680
41. .002005
42. 6.0080

8–21 APPROXIMATE NUMBERS

Numbers may be exact or approximate. Numbers used to count are exact; numbers used to measure are approximate. Estimated numbers are approximate numbers. An approximate number is a number that is almost equal to the true number.

Since measurement is approximate, we may be required to compute with approximate numbers arising through measurement. A measurement of 6.4 inches could mean any measurement from 6.35 inches to 6.45 inches. When written as 6.4″ ± .05″, it shows the measurement plus and minus the greatest possible error. The result of a computation with approximate numbers cannot be more accurate than the least accurate approximate number involved in the computation.

There are several methods of computing with approximate numbers. Observe the alternative methods on the next page.

Addition

To add approximate numbers, we add as we usually do, then round the sum using the unit of the least precise addend.

Subtraction

To subtract approximate numbers, we subtract as we usually do, then round the difference using the unit of the less precise of the given numbers.

Multiplication

To multiply approximate numbers, we multiply as we usually do, then round the product so that it contains the same number of significant digits as the factor having the smaller number of significant digits.

Add:

$$\begin{array}{r} 1.82 \\ 4.363 \\ +3.1 \\ \hline 9.283 = 9.3 \end{array}$$

Subtract:

$$\begin{array}{r} 9.621 \\ -4.21 \\ \hline 5.411 = 5.41 \end{array}$$

Multiply:

$$\begin{array}{r} 2.53 \\ 1.7 \\ \hline 1\ 771 \\ 2\ 53 \\ \hline 4.301 = 4.3 \end{array}$$

Division

To divide approximate numbers, we divide as we usually do, then round the quotient so that it contains the same number of significant digits as there are in either the dividend or divisor, whichever is less.

Divide:

$$
\begin{array}{r}
1.77 = 1.8 \\
2.5_\wedge\overline{)4.4_\wedge25} \\
25 \\
\overline{192} \\
175 \\
\overline{175} \\
175 \\
\cdots
\end{array}
$$

Alternate Methods

To add or subtract we first round the given approximate numbers to the least precise number, then perform the required operation.

To multiply when one of two factors contains more significant digits than the other, we round the factor which has more significant digits so that it contains only one more significant digit than the other. Then we multiply and round the product so that it contains the same number of significant digits as the factor having the smaller number of significant digits.

EXERCISES

Compute the following approximate numbers as indicated:

1. Add:

   a. $4.6 + 2.52$
   b. $9.385 + 3.4 + 8.19$
   c. $.0038 + .005 + .01$
   d. $16 + .93 + 6.4$
   e. $185.2 + 4.0094 + 17.83$

2. Subtract:

   a. $68.953 - 7.82$
   b. $19.526 - 8.6$
   c. $75 - 2.3$
   d. $84.6 - .0087$
   e. $6.2509 - 1.39256$

3. Multiply:

   a. $65 \times .807$
   b. 4.3×9.6
   c. 12.84×8.3015
   d. $.0092 \times 1.04$
   e. $4.751 \times .0283$

4. Divide:

   a. $24\overline{)9.35}$
   b. $1.9\overline{)842.03}$
   c. $7\overline{).015}$
   d. $.023\overline{)10.2471}$
   e. $3.86\overline{)958.3059}$

To estimate a sum, a difference, a product, or a quotient, first round the given fractions to nearest whole numbers and the given whole numbers to convenient place values and then perform the operation or operations.

For each of the following select your nearest estimate:

1. 42 times 71 is approximately: 280;   3,000;   28,000;   2,500

2. $4\frac{7}{8}$ times $3\frac{1}{2}$ is approximately: 7;   12;   17;   25

3. 5% of 3,956 is approximately: 18,000;   200;   1,900;   15

4. 890 divided by 15 is approximately: 450;   1,000;   30;   60

5. .061 divided by .2 is approximately: 35;   .3;   305;   .035

6. 8 divided by $\frac{3}{4}$ is approximately: 6;   11;   24;   35

7. 20% of 324 is approximately: 628;   65;   6;   .06

8. 4,483 divided by 50 is approximately: 890;   2,000;   30;   90

9. 798 times 699 is approximately: 42,000;   1,500;   560,000;   9,000

10. .03 times 9.8 is approximately: .3;   270;   .01;   29

11. 90% of 437 is approximately: 500;   400;   43;   5

12. 78,926 divided by 198 is approximately: 700;   150;   400;   1,200

13. 47 divided by .6 is approximately: 8;   800;   .8;   80

14. 2.9 times .11 is approximately: 30;   290;   .3;   2.99

15. $19\frac{1}{2}$ divided by $2\frac{1}{2}$ is approximately: 38;   8;   40;   17

16. $66\frac{2}{3}$% of 4,152 is approximately: 4,000;   50;   2,800; $\frac{2}{3}$

17. $10\frac{1}{4}$ times $5\frac{1}{8}$ is approximately: 600; $\frac{1}{32}$;   50;   2

18. 117 times 76 is approximately: 190;   9,000;   10,000;   2,000

19. $\frac{7}{8}$ divided by 3 is approximately: 3; $\frac{1}{3}$; $\frac{3}{4}$;   1

20. $12\frac{1}{2}$% of 325 is approximately: 360;   40;   20;   1,000

21. $3\frac{1}{7}$ times 16 is approximately: 5;   13;   28;   50

22. 66 divided by $1\frac{7}{8}$ is approximately: 30;   60;   120;   15

23. .7 divided by .04 is approximately: .28;   18;   2;   1.7

24. 3% of $14.85 is approximately: $45; $4.48; $.45; $14.85

25. $6\frac{1}{3}$ times $9\frac{5}{6}$ is approximately: 60;   54;   27;   18

26. 156,918 divided by 406 is approximately: 700;   60;   2,500;   400

27. .26 times 728 is approximately: 500;   200;   14;   1.6

28. $\frac{3}{4}$ of 587 is approximately: 500;   120;   450;   60

29. 60% of 2,150 is approximately: 120;   1,300;   1,500;   13

30. $4\frac{5}{8}$ times $2\frac{7}{8}$ is approximately: 8;   11;   13;   16

31. 825,000 divided by 195 is approximately: 5,000;   450;   4,000;   30

32. 2% of $8.91 is approximately: $.18; $1.60; $17.82; $.02

33. 102 divided by .4 is approximately: 2,500;   25;   2.5;   250

34. 913 times 69 is approximately: 5,400;   63,000;   500;   100,000

35. $\frac{4}{5}$ of 247 is approximately: 50;   100;   200;   500

CHAPTER REVIEW

1. Change: **a.** 96 m to mm   **b.** 530 m to km   (8–1)

2. Which measurement is greater: 6.7 cm or 49 mm?   (8–1)

3. Change: **a.** 380 g to kg   **b.** 4.5 cg to mg   (8–2)

4. Arrange according to weight (lightest first):   (8–2)

     7,800 g   4.6 kg   810,000 mg   54,000 cg

5. How many: **a.** cL are in 12 L?   **b.** dL are in 1,500 mL?   (8–3)

6. How many: hectares are in 25 km²?   cm² are in 600 m²?   (8–4)

7. Change: **a.** 5.9 m³ to cm³   **b.** 4,750 cm³ to dm³   (8–5)

8. 1.25 liters of water occupies a space of __ cm³ and weighs __ kg.   (8–5)

9. How many feet are in $5\frac{1}{4}$ miles?   (8–6)

10. How many ounces are in 8 pounds?   (8–7)

11. How many quarts are in 7 gallons?   (8–8)

12. What part of a peck is 6 quarts?   (8–9)

13. Change 1,152 sq. in. to sq. ft. (8–11)

14. Change 14 cu. ft. to cu. in. (8–10)

15. From 8 hr. 30 min. subtract 3 hr. 17 min. 35 sec. (8–13)

16. Multiply 40°15′ by 7. Simplify your answer. (8–14)

17. Change 144 km/h to m/s. (8–15)

18. Is a temperature of 84°F warmer than a temperature of 30°C? (8–16)

19. Express as A.M. or P.M. time: **a.** 1830 **b.** 0015 (8–17)

20. If it is 10 P.M. in Los Angeles, what time is it in New York City? (8–18)

21. Find the greatest possible error and the relative error in each of the following measurements: (8–19)

    a. $2\frac{1}{2}$ in.   **b.** $9\frac{3}{8}$ lb.   **c.** 6.25 g   **d.** 150,000 km   **e.** 500 m

22. Which is more precise, 0.02 in. or 0.020 in.? Which is more accurate? (8–19)

23. Arrange the following measurements in order of precision, most precise first; and also in order of accuracy, most accurate first: (8–19)

    50 yd.,   2.93 ft.,   8.5 in.,   760,000 mi.

24. How many significant digits are in each of the following? (8–20)

    a. .00010   **b.** 9,040   **c.** 2.6×10^8 **d.** 8.0297   **e.** 400,000

25. Compute the following approximate numbers as indicated: (8–21)

    a. 1.674 + 2.53 + 4.6   **c.** 6.91 × .452

    b. 78.562 − 9.42   **d.** $8.9\overline{)\,.9534}$

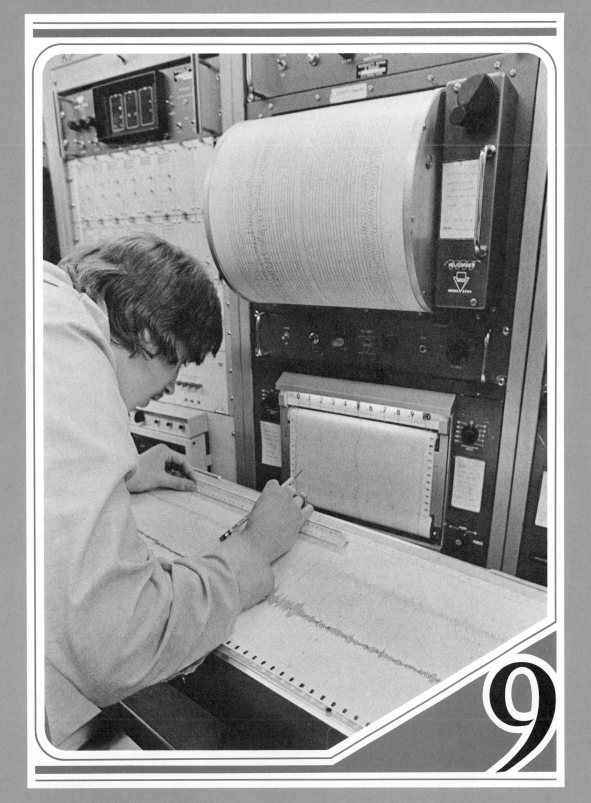

CHAPTER 9
Graphs and Statistics

9–1 BAR GRAPHS

The *bar graph* is used to compare the size of quantities in statistics.

To construct a bar graph, we draw a horizontal guide line on the bottom of the squared paper and a vertical guide line on the left. We select a convenient scale for the numbers that are being compared, first rounding large numbers. For a vertical bar graph, we place and label the number scale along the vertical guide line; for a horizontal bar graph, we use the horizontal guide line.

We print the items being compared in alternate squares along the second guide line, labeling these items. We mark off for each item the height corresponding to the given number and draw lines to complete bars. All bars should have the same width. We select and print an appropriate title describing the graph.

EXERCISES

1. Use the graph on the right to answer the following questions regarding the heights of some famous dams in the United States.

   a. How many feet does the side of a small square represent in the vertical scale of the bar graph? $\frac{1}{2}$ of the side of a square?
   b. Which dam is the highest?
   c. Find the height of each dam:

Davis	Shasta
Grand Coulee	Fort Peck
Fort Randall	Dix River
Arrowrock	Mud Mt.
Hoover	

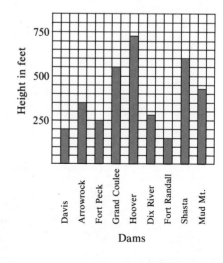

d. How much higher is the Grand Coulee than the Mud Mountain Dam?

e. How many times as high as the Davis Dam is the Shasta?

2. Draw a vertical bar graph showing the sales of tickets for the school show by classes. Freshmen, 360 tickets; sophomores, 300 tickets; juniors, 270 tickets; and seniors, 410 tickets.

3. Draw a vertical bar graph picturing the number of accidental deaths by causes during a recent year. Motor vehicle, 56,000; falls, 16,900; burns, 6,400; drowning, 8,700; railroad, 2,300; firearms, 2,700; and poisons and gases, 4,200.

4. Draw a horizontal bar graph representing the stopping distances of good brakes on good pavement.

Speed in m.p.h.	20	30	40	50	60	70
Stopping distance	43 ft.	79 ft.	126 ft.	183 ft.	251 ft.	328 ft.

5. Draw a vertical bar graph showing the areas of the Great Lakes: Superior, 88,389 km²; Erie, 27,611 km²; Michigan, 62,222 km²; Ontario, 20,944 km²; Huron, 63,917 km².

9–2 LINE GRAPHS

The *line graph* is used to show changes and the relationship between quantities.

To construct a line graph, we draw a horizontal guide line on the bottom of the squared paper and a vertical guide line on the left. We select a convenient scale for the related numbers, first rounding large numbers. We place and label this scale along one of the guide lines.

We print and label items below the other guide line, using a separate line for each item. On each of these lines we mark with a dot the location of the value corresponding to the given number. We then draw straight lines to connect successive dots. We select and print an appropriate title describing the graph.

EXERCISES

1. Use the graph on page 276 to answer the following questions regarding the monthly normal precipitation in Cincinnati (solid line) and Phoenix (dotted line).

a. During what month does the most rain fall in Phoenix? How many inches?

b. During what month does the least amount of rain fall in Cincinnati? How many inches?

c. How many inches less rain falls in Phoenix than in Cincinnati during the month of September?

d. How many times as much rain falls in Cincinnati as in Phoenix during the month of December?

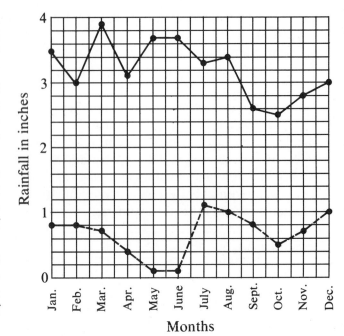

2. Draw a line graph showing that in ten successive progress tests in arithmetic, each containing 30 examples, John solved 14, 17, 19, 20, 25, 24, 28, 27, 29, and 26 examples correctly.

3. Use a solid line to show changes in the retail price of a dozen eggs and a dotted line for the changes in the price of a pound of sliced bacon.

Food	1971	1972	1973	1974	1975	1976	1977	1978	1979	1980
Eggs	52.9¢	52.4¢	78.1¢	78.3¢	77.0¢	84.1¢	82.3¢	81.5¢	84.0¢	84.4¢
Bacon	80.0¢	96.2¢	132.5¢	132.0¢	175.6¢	171.1¢	156.2¢	173.2¢	154.6¢	146.5¢

4. Use a solid line to represent monthly normal temperatures in San Francisco and a dotted line for the temperatures in Baltimore.

CITY	Jan.	Feb.	Mar.	Apr.	May	June	July	Aug.	Sept.	Oct.	Nov.	Dec.
San Francisco	50	52	54	55	57	58	58	59	61	60	56	51
Baltimore	35	36	43	54	67	73	78	76	69	58	47	37

5. Use a solid line to represent the receipts and a dotted line for the expenditures of the United States government, expressed in billions of dollars.

	1972	1973	1974	1975	1976	1977	1978	1979	1980
Receipts	215.3	232.2	264.8	280.9	300.0	356.8	401.9	465.9	517.9
Expenditures	238.3	246.6	268.3	325.1	365.6	401.8	450.7	493.2	578.8

9–3 CIRCLE GRAPHS

The *circle graph* is used to show the relation of the parts to the whole and to each other.

To construct a circle graph, we make a table showing: (a) given facts; (b) fractional part or percent each quantity is of the whole; (c) the number of degrees representing each fractional part or percent, obtained by multiplying 360° by the fraction or percent.

We draw a convenient circle and with a protractor construct successive central angles, using the number of degrees representing each part. We label each sector and select and print an appropriate title describing the graph.

EXERCISES

1. Use the graph on the right to answer the following questions regarding the distribution of marks in a social studies test.

    a. What fractional part of the class received A? B? E? D? C?

    b. How many degrees of the circle represent the number of pupils receiving B? C? A? E?

    c. What is the ratio of the C's to the A's? Of the E's to the B's?

    d. If there are 36 pupils in the class, how many received A? E? C? B? D?

MARKS IN A
SOCIAL STUDIES TEST

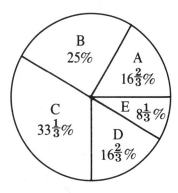

Draw circle graphs showing the following data:

2. A family budget: food, 30%; clothing, 15%; shelter, 25%; operating expenses, 10%; savings, 5%; automobile, 8%; other expenses, 7%.
3. In an eighth grade class, 12 pupils plan to stay home during the summer, 10 are going to the seashore, 4 are going on motor trips, 8 are going camping, and 6 are going to the mountains.
4. The Amerigo Vespucci High School has the following enrollment: 240 freshmen, 216 sophomores, 184 juniors, and 160 seniors.
5. The operating expenses of Thomas and Company during the month of June were as follows: General expense, $600; rent, $800; salaries, $3,840; insurance, $72; depreciation on furniture and equipment, $400; delivery expense, $288.
6. The sources of United States taxes for a recent year were: individual income taxes, $240,700,000,000; corporation income taxes, $65,500,000,000; social insurance taxes and contributions, $160,500,000,000; estate and gift taxes, $6,100,000,000; excise taxes, $25,400,000,000; and custom duties, $7,000,000,000.

9–4 AVERAGES

An *average* is a measure of central tendency of data. Three commonly used averages are the arithmetic mean (or simply mean), the median, and the mode.

The *arithmetic mean* of a list of numbers is determined by dividing the sum of numbers by the number in the list. High numbers and low numbers are balanced off to make all numbers the same size. An extremely high number or an extremely low number distorts the picture of central tendency if the arithmetic mean is used.

Find the arithmetic mean of the following set of scores: 80, 96, 85, and 91:

$$\frac{80 + 96 + 85 + 91}{4} = \frac{352}{4} = 88$$

Answer, 88

The *median* of a list of numbers is the middle number when the numbers are arranged in order of size. To find this number we may count from either end, smallest to largest or vice-versa. If the number of members is even, the median is determined by dividing the sum of the two middle numbers by 2. Since the median is a positional average, an extremely high or low number does not affect it.

The *mode* of a list of numbers is the number that occurs most frequently in the set. There may be more than one mode.

The *range* is the difference between the highest and lowest numbers in the list of numbers.

The members of a class of 25 pupils made the following scores in a test:

8, 6, 10, 9, 9, 8, 7, 10, 9, 7, 9, 8, 6, 10, 6, 9, 7, 8, 9, 8, 7, 9, 6, 7, and 8.

We make a tally of data:

Score	Number
10				
9								
8							
7						
6					

We arrange data in a frequency table:

Score	Number
10	3
9	7
8	6
7	5
6	4
Total	25

Arithmetic Mean:

$10 \times 3 = 30$
$9 \times 7 = 63$
$8 \times 6 = 48$
$7 \times 5 = 35$
$6 \times 4 = 24$

sum = 200

$\frac{200}{25} = 8$

Arithmetic mean = 8

Median or Middle Score is the 13th score from top or bottom = 8

Mode or most frequent score = 9

Range 10 − 6 = 4

The Greek letter Σ, capital sigma, is the symbol that is generally used to indicate in a concise way the sum of a list of numbers.

Graphs and Statistics

1. Find the mean for each of the following lists of scores:
   a. 72, 75, 72, 78, 73, 70, 76, 79, 71
   b. 3, 8, 6, 2, 9, 5, 8, 9, 10, 7, 4, 0, 5, 6, 8, 7, 6, 8, 9, 5, 3, 4

2. Find the median for each of the following lists of scores:
   a. 12, 17, 20, 13, 18, 15, 14, 17, 11   b. 5.8, 4.9, 7.4, 6.5, 5.6, 6.3, 8.1, 6.8

3. Find the mode and range for each of the following lists of scores:
   a. 23, 28, 32, 20, 29, 31, 26, 28, 25, 27, 32, 30, 23, 28, 34
   b. 85, 93, 97, 86, 90, 95, 89, 91, 98, 94, 82, 97, 89, 90, 96, 92

4. Find the mean, median, mode, and range for each of the following:
   a. 44, 50, 43, 48, 46, 40, 48, 44, 42, 48, 45, 49, 43, 48, 41, 44, 42
   b. 80, 65, 75, 90, 100, 75, 85, 100, 95, 60, 90, 80, 95, 90, 65, 75, 90, 85, 95, 80, 75

5. Tally and arrange each of the following lists of scores in a frequency table, then find the mean, median, mode, and range:
   a. 63, 67, 60, 59, 72, 65, 69, 64, 67, 71, 66, 70, 62, 69, 63, 67, 62, 60, 67, 69, 72, 66, 67, 66, 65, 66, 68
   b. 8, 5, 2, 9, 4, 3, 7, 8, 9, 8, 10, 7, 5, 6, 8, 10, 9, 6, 7, 8, 2, 1, 8, 4, 3, 5, 6, 9, 9, 10

CHAPTER REVIEW

1. Draw a vertical bar graph showing the number of coins manufactured during 1974 by the U.S. Mints: 191,231,000 half-dollars; 584,669,000 quarters; 1,041,331,000 dimes; 8,879,277,751 nickels; and 9,758,402,751 pennies.   (9–1)

2. Draw a line graph showing the United States gross national product (GNP) in billions of dollars for the ten years shown: (9–2)

	1971	1972	1973	1974	1975	1976	1977	1978	1979	1980
GNP	1,063.4	1,171.1	1,306.3	1,406.9	1,528.8	1,706.5	1,887.2	2,127.6	2,368.8	2,626.1

3. Draw a circle graph showing how a certain city planned to spend its income: schools, 35%; public safety, 15%; health and welfare, 10%; interest on debt, 20%; public works, 15%; other, 5%.   (9–3)

4. Find the mean, median, mode, and range for the following scores: 95, 70, 65, 80, 90, 85, 75, 85, 65, 85, 70, 90, 85.   (9–4)

CHAPTER 10
Introduction to Algebra

EXTENSION OF THE NUMBER SYSTEM

When we add any two whole numbers, we find that the sum is always a whole number. Thus, the whole numbers are said to be *closed* under the operation of addition.

However, when we subtract one whole number from another whole number, the difference is not always a whole number.

For example:

In each of the following subtractions the difference is a whole number.

5	5	5	5	5
−1	−2	−3	−4	−5
4	3	2	1	0

But in each of the following subtractions the difference cannot be a whole number.

5	5	5	5	5
−6	−7	−8	−9	−10
?	?	?	?	?

Thus we see that the whole numbers are not closed under the operation of subtraction. In order to be able to subtract in problems like those above, let us now enlarge our number system.

10–1 INTEGERS

Positive and Negative Numbers

In section 1–5 we found that the numerals naming whole numbers may be arranged in a definite order on the number line so that they correspond one-to-one with points on the number line to the right of the point labeled 0.

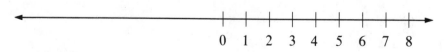

Now let us extend the number line to the left of the point marked 0. Using the interval between 0 and 1 as the unit of measure, we locate equally spaced points to the left of 0. The first new point is labeled ⁻1, read "negative one"; the second point ⁻2, read "negative two"; the third point ⁻3, etc.

The numbers corresponding to the points to the left of 0 are *negative numbers* and their numerals are identified by the raised dash (⁻) symbols that precede the digits. The numbers corresponding to the points to the right of 0 are *positive numbers* and their numerals may either contain no sign or for emphasis are identified by the raised plus (⁺) symbols that precede the digits, in which case the number line would look like this:

Positive and negative numbers are sometimes called *signed numbers* or *directed numbers*. The numeral ⁻8 names the number *negative eight*. The numeral ⁺7 or simply 7 names the number *positive seven*. 0 is neither positive nor negative. All numbers greater than 0 are positive numbers.

Opposites

Examination of the number line below will show that the points that correspond to ⁺6 and ⁻6 fall on opposite sides of the point marked 0 but are the same distance from 0.

A pair of numbers, one positive and the other negative, such as ⁺6 and ⁻6, which have the same absolute value (see section 10–3) are called *opposites*. ⁻6 is the opposite of ⁺6 and ⁺6 is the opposite of ⁻6. Each is the opposite of the other. The opposite of zero is zero.

Introduction to Algebra

Integers

The group of numbers which consists of all the whole numbers and their opposites is called the *integers*. Both . . . , ⁻2, ⁻1, 0, 1, 2, . . . and . . . , ⁻2, ⁻1, 0, ⁺1, ⁺1, . . . describe the *integers*. Observe that the three dots are used at both ends since the integers continue in both directions without ending. Thus, 1, 2, 3, . . . describes the *positive integers* (or the natural numbers); 0, 1, 2, 3, . . . describes the *non-negative integers* (or the whole numbers); . . . , ⁻3, ⁻2, ⁻1 describes the *negative integers;* and . . . , ⁻3, ⁻2, ⁻1, 0 describes the *non-positive integers.*

The *even integers* consist of the integers that are divisible by two (2). The even integers are described by . . . , ⁻4, ⁻2, 0, 2, 4, ... The *odd integers* consist of all the integers that are not divisible by two (2). The odd integers are described by . . . , ⁻3, ⁻1, 1, 3, ...

EXERCISES

1. Read or write in words, each of the following:

a. ⁻10	**d.** ⁺11	**g.** ⁺72
b. ⁺8	**e.** ⁻27	**h.** ⁻125
c. ⁻4	**f.** ⁺51	**i.** ⁻39

2. Write symbolically:

a. Positive four	**e.** Positive fifteen
b. Negative two	**f.** Negative twenty
c. Negative twelve	**g.** Negative nineteen
d. Positive one	**h.** Positive sixty-six

3. What number is the opposite of each of the following?

a. ⁺3	**d.** 0	**g.** ⁻64
b. ⁻9	**e.** ⁻18	**h.** ⁻100
c. ⁺12	**f.** ⁺37	**i.** ⁺43

4. a. Does ⁻7 name a whole number? An integer?
b. Does 16 name a whole number? An integer?

5. List all the numbers described by each of the following:

a. ⁻10, ⁻9, ⁻8, . . . , 4
b. ⁻8, ⁻6, ⁻4, . . . , 6
c. ⁻11, ⁻9, ⁻7, . . . , 11

10–2 RATIONAL NUMBERS; REAL NUMBERS

In section 4–7 we found that numerals naming the fractional numbers of arithmetic may be arranged in a definite order on the number line to the right of the point labeled 0. There is a point on the number line corresponding to each fractional number.

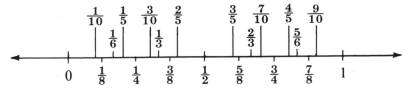

Examination of the number line below will show that there are fractional subdivisions to the left of zero matching those to the right of zero with each point of division corresponding to a fractional number. Since there are an infinite number of positive and negative fractional numbers, only a few are indicated. However, there is a point on the number line corresponding to each positive and negative fractional number.

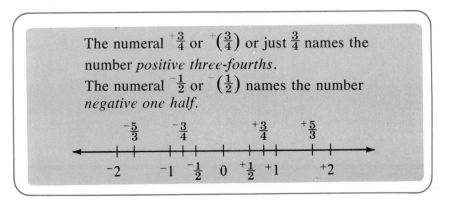

The numeral $^+\frac{3}{4}$ or $^+\left(\frac{3}{4}\right)$ or just $\frac{3}{4}$ names the number *positive three-fourths*.
The numeral $^-\frac{1}{2}$ or $^-\left(\frac{1}{2}\right)$ names the number *negative one half*.

Observe in numerals like $^-\frac{1}{2}$ or $^+\frac{3}{4}$ where parentheses are not used the $-$ or $+$ symbol belongs to the entire fraction although it may appear that the symbol belongs to the numerator alone.

Each positive fractional number has an opposite negative fractional number and each negative fractional number has an opposite positive fractional number.

$^-\frac{4}{5}$ is the opposite of $^+\frac{4}{5}$.
$^+1\frac{5}{8}$ is the opposite of $^-1\frac{5}{8}$.

Introduction to Algebra

All the fractional numbers and their opposites are called the *rational numbers*. This includes the integers since each integer may be named in fraction form. For example $^-5 = \frac{^-5}{1}$, $^+3 = \frac{^+3}{1}$, and $0 = \frac{0}{1} = \frac{0}{2} = \frac{0}{3}$, etc. A rational number may be described as a number named by a numeral that expresses a quotient of two integers with division by zero excluded.

An *irrational number* is a number that is both a non-terminating and non-repeating decimal. See pages 162 and 216. An irrational number cannot be named by a quotient of two integers with division by zero excluded. All the positive and negative irrational numbers are called the *irrational numbers*.

All the rational numbers and all the irrational numbers are *real numbers*. They include all the integers, all the positive and negative fractional numbers, and all the positive and negative irrational numbers. There are an infinite number of real numbers.

EXERCISES

1. Read, or write in words, each of the following:

   a. $\frac{^-7}{8}$ b. $\frac{^+6}{5}$ c. $^-2\frac{3}{4}$ d. $^+.85$ e. $^-7.4$ f. $^+\frac{1}{16}$ g. $\frac{^-17}{4}$ h. $^-.001$

2. Write symbolically:

   a. Negative one fourth
   b. Positive three tenths
   c. Positive seven hundredths
   d. Negative two and five tenths
   e. Negative seven and fifty-two hundredths
   f. Positive one hundred forty-six thousandths

3. What number is the opposite of each of the following?

   a. $^+\frac{3}{16}$ b. $\frac{^-7}{2}$ c. $^+.03$ d. $^-1.98$ e. $^-4\frac{5}{9}$ f. $^+.006$ g. $^+3\frac{8}{11}$ h. $^-47.2$

4. a. Is $\frac{^-9}{10}$ a whole number? An integer? A rational number? A real number?

   b. Is $^+6\frac{1}{8}$ a whole number? An integer? A rational number? A real number?

   c. Is $^+.25$ a whole number? An integer? A rational number? A real number?

   d. Is $^-7.6$ a whole number? An integer? A rational number? A real number?

   e. Is $^-5$ a whole number? An integer? A rational number? A real number?

   f. Is $^-\sqrt{23}$ a whole number? An integer? A rational number? A real number?

5. Which of the following numerals name integers? Which name rational numbers? Which name irrational numbers? Which name real numbers?

   a. $^-14$; $^+.07$; $\frac{^-3}{10}$; $^-\sqrt{41}$; $\frac{12}{3}$; $^-8\frac{1}{7}$ c. $^-.125$; $\frac{^-1}{16}$; $^+\sqrt{25}$; $\frac{^-56}{8}$; $^-84$; $^+9\frac{3}{4}$
   b. $^+\frac{8}{15}$; $^-200$; $^-1\frac{4}{5}$; $^-2.01$; $^+\sqrt{17}$; $\frac{^-27}{9}$ d. $^+29$; $^-\sqrt{3}$; $\frac{^-11}{32}$; $^-.67$; $^-1\frac{5}{12}$; $^+\frac{19}{6}$

10-3 ABSOLUTE VALUE

The *absolute value* of any number is the value of the corresponding arithmetic number which has no sign. The absolute value of ⁻3 is 3 and the absolute value of ⁺3 is 3. The absolute value of 0 is 0.

A pair of vertical bars | | is the symbol used to designate absolute value.

| ⁻6| is read "the absolute value of negative 6."

EXERCISES

1. Read, or write in words, each of the following:

 a. $|17|$ **b.** $|^-1|$ **c.** $|^+26|$ **d.** $\left|^-\frac{6}{11}\right|$ **e.** $|^-.08|$ **f.** $\left|^+4\frac{3}{8}\right|$

2. Write symbolically, using the absolute value symbol:

 a. The absolute value of negative eleven

 b. The absolute value of positive six sevenths

 c. The absolute value of negative nine and three tenths

 d. The absolute value of positive seven thousandths

3. Find the absolute value of each of the following:

 a. $|^-4|$ **d.** $|0|$ **g.** $\left|^-1\frac{3}{4}\right|$ **j.** $|^-.53|$

 b. $|^+8|$ **e.** $|^+.6|$ **h.** $|^+16|$ **k.** $\left|^+\frac{12}{5}\right|$

 c. $|^-9|$ **f.** $\left|^-\frac{5}{8}\right|$ **i.** $|^-12|$ **l.** $|^-100|$

In each of the following first find the absolute value of each number as required, then apply the necessary operation to obtain the answer:

4. a. $|^-6| + |^-5|$ **b.** $\left|^+\frac{1}{2}\right| + \left|^-\frac{1}{2}\right|$ **c.** $\left|^-1\frac{3}{4}\right| + \left|^+2\frac{1}{3}\right|$ **d.** $|^-.82| + |^-1.6|$

5. a. $|^-15| - |^+6|$ **b.** $\left|^+\frac{7}{8}\right| - \left|^-\frac{2}{3}\right|$ **c.** $\left|^-5\frac{1}{5}\right| - \left|^-4\frac{3}{8}\right|$ **d.** $|^+1.9| - |^-.05|$

6. a. $|^+7| \times |^-8|$ **b.** $\left|^-\frac{3}{4}\right| \times \left|^-\frac{9}{10}\right|$ **c.** $\left|^+2\frac{5}{6}\right| \times |^-12|$ **d.** $|^-4.16| \times |^+.04|$

7. a. $|^-56| \div |^+14|$ **b.** $\left|^+\frac{5}{6}\right| \div \left|^-\frac{3}{5}\right|$ **c.** $\left|^-1\frac{2}{3}\right| \div \left|^-2\frac{11}{12}\right|$ **d.** $|^+7.5| \div |^-.03|$

10–4 THE REAL NUMBER LINE; GRAPH OF A GROUP OF NUMBERS

The *real number line* is the complete collection of points which corresponds to all the real numbers. The real number line is endless in both directions and only a part of it is shown at any one time. There are an infinite number of points on the real number line. However, there is one and only one point that corresponds to each real number and one and only one real number that corresponds to each point on the real number line.

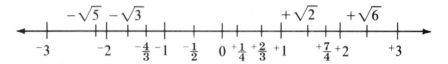

Usually the real number line is labeled only with the numerals naming the integers.

Each point on the number line is called the *graph* of the number to which it corresponds and each number is called the *coordinate* of the related point on the line. Capital letters are generally used to identify particular points.

Thus, the graph of a number is a point on the number line whose coordinate is the number.

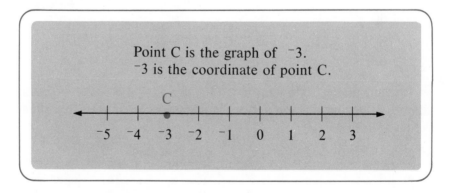

Point C is the graph of $^-3$.
$^-3$ is the coordinate of point C.

The *graph of a group of numbers* is made up of the points on the number line whose coordinates are the numbers.

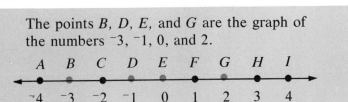

The points *B*, *D*, *E*, and *G* are the graph of the numbers ⁻3, ⁻1, 0, and 2.

To draw the graph of a group of numbers, we first draw an appropriate number line and locate the point or points whose coordinate or coordinates are listed in the given numbers. We use heavy solid or colored dots to indicate these points.

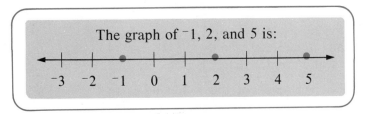

The graph of ⁻1, 2, and 5 is:

Sometimes a restricted number line is required. To construct this kind of number line, we draw a straight line and, using a convenient unit of measure, we locate the required points of division. These points of division are then properly labeled.

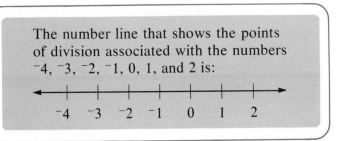

The number line that shows the points of division associated with the numbers ⁻4, ⁻3, ⁻2, ⁻1, 0, 1, and 2 is:

EXERCISES

L M N P Q R S T U V A B C D E F G H I J K

⁻10 ⁻9 ⁻8 ⁻7 ⁻6 ⁻5 ⁻4 ⁻3 ⁻2 ⁻1 0 ⁺1 ⁺2 ⁺3 ⁺4 ⁺5 ⁺6 ⁺7 ⁺8 ⁺9 ⁺10

1. a. What number corresponds to point *K*? *E*? *P*? *D*? *V*? *L*? *J*? *T*? *S*? *A*?

Introduction to Algebra

b. What letter labels the point corresponding to each of the following numbers?

⁻5   ⁺6   ⁻2   ⁺2   ⁺8   0   ⁻9   ⁺7   ⁺1   ⁻6

2. Draw the graph of each of the following groups of numbers on a number line:

a. ⁻5

b. ⁻7, ⁺3

c. ⁻8, ⁻4, 0, ⁺2

d. ⁻3, ⁻1, 3, 5, 7

e. ⁻5, ⁻4, ⁻1, 0, 1, 4

f. ⁻2, ⁺6, ⁻3

g. ⁺3, ⁻5, ⁺2, ⁻8, ⁺9, ⁺4, ⁻1

h. ⁻9, 0, 1, ⁻6, ⁻2, 8, ⁻4, 7

i. ⁻6, ⁻5, ⁻4, . . . , 3

j. ⁻10, ⁻8, ⁻6, . . . , 4

3. Draw the graph of each of the following on a number line:

a. all integers less than ⁺1 and greater than ⁻1

b. all integers greater than ⁻3 and less than 0

c. all integers less than ⁺4 and greater than ⁻4

4. Write the coordinates of which each of the following is the graph:

a.

b.

c.
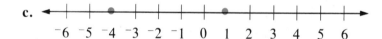

d.

e.

f.
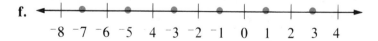

g.
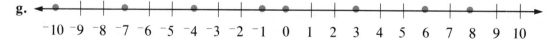

10–5 COMPARING INTEGERS

The number line may be drawn horizontally or vertically.

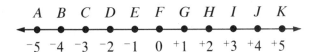

A   B   C   D   E   F   G   H   I   J   K

⁻5 ⁻4 ⁻3 ⁻2 ⁻1   0 ⁺1 ⁺2 ⁺3 ⁺4 ⁺5

On the horizontal number line, of two numbers the number corresponding to the point on the line *farther to the right* is the greater number.

On the vertical number line, the numbers *above* zero are positive and those *below* zero are negative. Any number corresponding to a point is greater than any number corresponding to a point located below it.

1. On the horizontal number line, which point corresponds to the greater number:

   a. Point J or point B?
   b. Point C or point H?
   c. Point E or point D?
   d. Point F or point A?

2. On the vertical number line, which point corresponds to the greater number:

   a. Point P or point T?
   b. Point W or point N?
   c. Point R or point M?
   d. Point V or point S?

3. On the horizontal number line is the point corresponding to ⁻1 to the left or to the right of the point corresponding to ⁻5? Which number is greater, ⁻1 or ⁻5?

4. On the vertical number line is the point corresponding to ⁻4 above or below the point corresponding to ⁻2? Which number is greater, ⁻2 or ⁻4?

5. Which of the following sentences are true?

   a. $^{+}6 > {^{+}}9$
   b. $^{-}6 > {^{-}}9$
   c. $^{+}2 < 0$
   d. $^{+}3 < {^{-}}8$
   e. $0 > {^{-}}7$
   f. $^{-}5 > {^{-}}5$
   g. $^{-}1 < {^{+}}1$
   h. $^{-}2 \not> {^{-}}4$
   i. $^{-}7 \not< {^{-}}7$
   j. $^{+}8 < {^{-}}10$
   k. $^{-}4 \not> {^{-}}1$
   l. $^{-}3 \not< 0$
   m. $7 > {^{-}}50$
   n. $^{-}12 \not< {^{-}}6$
   o. $^{+}20 \not> {^{-}}45$

6. Rewrite each of the following and insert between the two numerals the symbol =, <, or > which will make the sentence true:

a. $^-6$? $^-2$ d. $^-8$? $^-8$ g. $^-4$? $^-6$

b. $^+9$? $^+7$ e. $^+17$? $^-20$ h. 0 ? $^-9$

c. $^-5$? $^+3$ f. $^-10$? 0 i. $^-16$? $^+1$

7. Name the following numbers in order of size (smallest first):

a. $^-2$, $^+9$, $^-10$, $^+14$, $^-6$, $^+5$, 0, $^+10$, $^-3$, $^-1$

b. $^+7$, $^-4$, $^-8$, 0, $^+5$, $^-12$, $^+1$, $^-2$, $^-7$, $^+3$

8. Name the following numbers in order of size (greatest first):

a. $^-8$, $^+5$, $^-3$, $^+9$, 0, $^-4$, $^+4$, $^-11$, $^+15$, $^-6$

b. $^+6$, $^-7$, $^+2$, $^-1$, $^+12$, $^-5$, $^+3$, 0, $^-2$, $^-13$

9. Which is greater:

a. The absolute value of $^-7$ or the absolute value of $^+2$?

b. The absolute value of $^+10$ or the absolute value of $^-10$?

10. Which has the greater opposite number?

a. $^+9$ or $^+5$ b. $^-4$ or $^-7$ c. $^-6$ or $^+8$ d. $^+3$ or $^-5$

10–6 OPPOSITE MEANINGS

Positive and negative numbers are used in science, statistics, weather reports, stock reports, sports, and many other fields to express opposite meanings or directions. For example:

If $^+3\%$ indicates an *increase* of 3% in the cost of living, $^-4\%$ would indicate a 4% *decrease* in the cost of living.

EXERCISES

1. If $^+1\frac{1}{2}$ points represents a $1\frac{1}{2}$-point gain in a stock, what does $^-2$ points represent?

2. If $^-15°$ indicates a temperature of 15° below zero, how can a temperature of 23° above zero be indicated?

3. If 50° west longitude is represented by $^-50°$, what does $^+65°$ represent?

4. If $^+58,000$ people represents an increase of 58,000 in population, how can a decrease of 17,000 in population be represented?

5. If $^-10$ amperes means a discharge of 10 amperes of electricity, what does $^+8$ amperes mean?

6. If $^+40$ km/h indicates a tail wind of 40 km/h, how can a head wind of 48 km/h be indicated?

7. If $^+1,500$ feet represents 1,500 feet above sea level, what does $^-700$ feet represent?

8. If an excess of 43.7 mm of rainfall is indicated by $^+43.7$ mm, how can a deficiency of 59.5 mm be indicated?

9. If 9 degrees below normal is represented by $^-9°$, how can 17 degrees above normal be represented?

10. If 36° north latitude is indicated by $^+36°$, how can 51° south latitude be indicated?

10–7 OPPOSITE DIRECTIONS; VECTORS

Positive and negative numbers, used as directed numbers, indicate movements in opposite directions. A movement to the right of a particular point is generally considered as moving in a positive direction from the point and a movement to the left of a point as moving in a negative direction from the point.

The sign in the numeral naming a directed number indicates the direction, and the absolute value of the directed number represents the magnitude (distance in units) of the movement.

> For example,
> $^+7$ means moving 7 units to the right.
> $^-4$ means moving 4 units to the left.

An arrow that represents a directed line segment is called a *vector*. It is used to picture the size and the direction of the movement that is indicated by a signed number. The absolute value of the signed number indicates the length of the arrow and the sign indicates the direction.

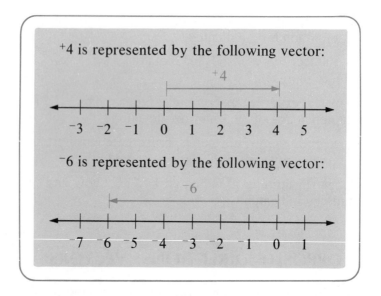

+4 is represented by the following vector:

⁻6 is represented by the following vector:

To determine the numeral that describes the movement from one point to another point on the number line, we draw the vector between the points with the arrowhead pointing in the direction of the movement. We use the number of units of length in the vector as the absolute value of the numeral. We select the sign according to the direction of the vector. If it points to the right, the sign is positive (⁺), if it points to the left, the sign is negative (⁻).

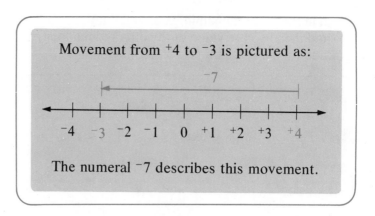

Movement from ⁺4 to ⁻3 is pictured as:

The numeral ⁻7 describes this movement.

1. A movement of how many units of distance and in what direction is represented by each of the following numbers?

   a. $^-8$ **b.** $^+10$ **c.** $^-1$ **d.** $^+3$ **e.** 18   **f.** $^-2\frac{1}{4}$ **g.** $^-3.75$ **h.** $^+\frac{5}{6}$

2. Represent each of the following movements by a numeral naming a signed number:

   a. Moving 5 units to the left
   b. Moving 9 units to the right
   c. Moving $10\frac{3}{4}$ units to the right
   d. Moving 8.5 units to the left

3. Write the numeral that is represented by each of the following vectors?

   a.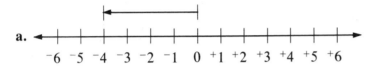

   b.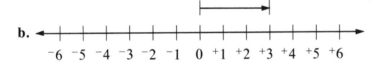

   c.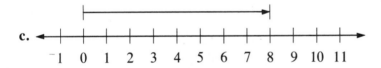

   d.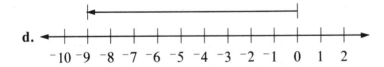

4. Using the number line as a scale, draw a vector representing:

   a. $^-3$ **b.** $^+6$ **c.** $^-7$ **d.** 5   **e.** $^+1\frac{1}{2}$ **f.** $^-4.6$ **g.** $^-10$ **h.** $^+3\frac{3}{4}$

5. Write the numeral that is represented by each of the following vectors:

   a.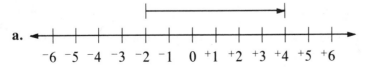

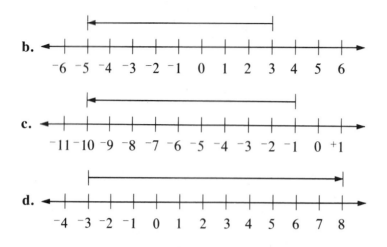

b.

c.

d.

6. Use the number line as a scale to draw a vector that illustrates each of the following movements. Write the numeral that is represented by each of these vectors.

a. From 0 to $^+8$
b. From 0 to $^-6$
c. From $^-5$ to 0
d. From $^+4$ to 0
e. From $^+5$ to $^+9$
f. From $^+11$ to $^+1$

g. From $^-2$ to $^-7$
h. From $^-5$ to $^-1$
i. From $^+3$ to $^-3$
j. From $^-8$ to $^+11$
k. From $^+10$ to $^-9$
l. From $^+5$ to $^+15$

m. From $^-4$ to $^-8$
n. From $^-8$ to $^-4$
o. From $^+1$ to $^-3$
p. From $^-12$ to $^+12$
q. From $^+8$ to $^-2$
r. From $^+9$ to $^+2$

10–8 ADDITIVE INVERSE OF A NUMBER; MORE ABOUT OPPOSITES

Sometimes the *opposite of a number* is called the *additive inverse of the number.*

When the sum of two numbers is zero, each addend is said to be the *additive inverse* of the other addend. We shall see in sections 10–9 and 10–10 that the sum of a number and its opposite is zero.

$^-5$ is the opposite of or the additive inverse of $^+5$ (or 5).

$^+5$ (or 5) is the opposite of or the additive inverse of $^-5$.

A centered dash symbol is used in algebra to indicate the opposite of a number.

The expression $-(5)$ and sometimes -5 are read as:
"The opposite of five."

The sentence $-(^-5) = {}^+5$ is read as:
"The opposite of negative five is positive five."

The sentence $-5 = {}^-5$ is read as:
"The opposite of five is negative five."

EXERCISES

1. What number is the additive inverse of each of the following numbers?

   a. $^-4$ **b.** 0   **c.** $^+58$ **d.** $^-\frac{7}{16}$ **e.** $^+1.04$ **f.** $^+\frac{2}{3}$ **g.** $^-6\frac{5}{8}$ **h.** $^-\frac{9}{4}$

2. What number is the opposite of each of the following numbers?

   a. $^+11$ **b.** $^-7$ **c.** $^-\frac{5}{8}$ **d.** $^-.27$ **e.** $^+\frac{13}{5}$ **f.** 0   **g.** $^-2\frac{3}{4}$ **h.** $^+25$

3. Read, or write in words, each of the following:

   a. -10 **c.** $-\left(^-\frac{3}{8}\right)$ **e.** $-(^-3) = {}^+3$ **g.** $-20 = {}^-20$

   b. $-(^+7)$ **d.** $-(-6)$ **f.** $-(^+12) = {}^-12$ **h.** $-(-8.2) = 8.2$

4. Write symbolically, using the "opposite symbol":

   a. The opposite of forty-seven
   b. The opposite of positive nine
   c. The opposite of negative one
   d. The opposite of positive sixteen
   e. The opposite of negative sixteen
   f. The opposite of twelve is negative twelve
   g. The opposite of negative two is positive two
   h. The opposite of positive eighty-four is negative eighty-four
   i. The opposite of negative forty is positive forty
   j. The opposite of the opposite of fifty-three is fifty-three

5. Find the:

   a. Opposite of the opposite of: $^+1$; $^-9$; $^+\frac{5}{12}$; $^-.7$; $^-5\frac{3}{8}$

   b. What is always true about the opposite of the opposite of a number?

Introduction to Algebra

10–9 ADDITION ON THE NUMBER LINE

If we move 5 units to the right from the point marked 0, we reach the point whose coordinate is ⁺5. If we then move 3 units to the right of this point, we reach the point whose coordinate is ⁺8. The sum of these two movements is the same as a single movement of 8 units to the right.

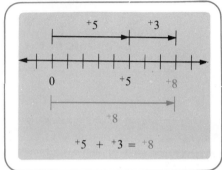

Observe in the illustration that a vector is drawn to represent the sum and each addend. To avoid confusion, we draw the vectors representing the addends above the number line and the vector representing the sum below the number line. The vector representing the first addend begins at the point 0 and the second vector representing the second addend is drawn from the point reached by the first vector. The resultant vector that represents the sum is drawn from the point 0 to the point reached by the vector representing the second addend.

If we move 5 units to the left from the point marked 0, we reach the point whose coordinate is ⁻5. If we then move 3 units to the left of this point, we reach the point whose coordinate is ⁻8. The sum of these two movements is the same as a single movement of 8 units to the left. Observe how vectors are used to illustrate this.

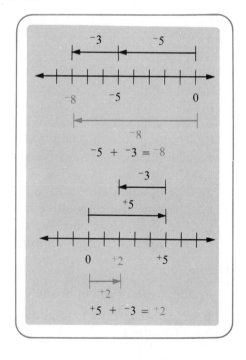

If we first move 5 units to the right from the point marked 0 and then from the point reached we move 3 units to the left, we reach the point whose coordinate is ⁺2. The sum of these two movements is the same as a single movement of 2 units to the right.

If we first move 5 units to the right from the point marked 0 and then from the point reached we move 8 units to the left, we reach the point whose coordinate is $^-3$. The sum of these two movements is the same as a single movement of 3 units to the left.

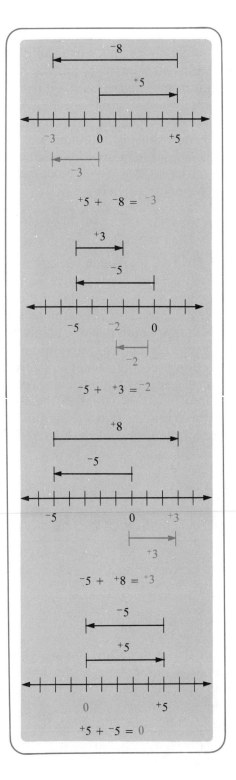

$^+5 + {}^-8 = {}^-3$

If we first move 5 units to the left from the point marked 0 and then from the point reached we move 3 units to the right, we reach the point whose coordinate is $^-2$. The sum of these two movements is the same as a single movement of 2 units to the left.

$^-5 + {}^+3 = {}^-2$

If we first move 5 units to the left from the point marked 0 and then from the point reached we move 8 units to the right, we reach the point whose coordinate is $^+3$. The sum of these two movements is the same as a single movement of 3 units to the right.

$^-5 + {}^+8 = {}^+3$

If we first move 5 units to the right from the point marked 0 and then from the point reached we move 5 units to the left, we reach the point whose coordinate is 0. The first movement is offset by an equal opposite movement. The sum of these two movements is a movement of zero units.

$^+5 + {}^-5 = 0$

We may add rational numbers on the number line. For example:

If we first move $2\frac{1}{2}$ units to the right from the point marked 0 and then from the point reached we move $6\frac{1}{2}$ units to the left, we reach a point whose coordinate is ⁻4. The sum of these two movements is the same as a single movement of 4 units to the left.

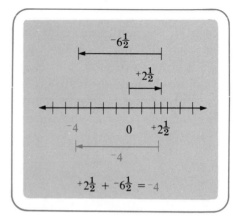

$$+2\tfrac{1}{2} + {}^-6\tfrac{1}{2} = {}^-4$$

Observe that when vectors are used, the sum of two positive numbers or the sum of two negative numbers is represented by a vector whose length is equal to the sum of the lengths of the vectors representing the two addends. This resultant vector has a positive direction when the two addends are both positive numbers and a negative direction when the two addends are both negative numbers.

However, the sum of a positive number and a negative number or the sum of a negative number and a positive number is represented by a vector whose length is equal to the difference in the lengths of the vectors representing the two addends and its direction is determined by the direction of the longer of the two vectors representing the two addends.

EXERCISES

In each of the following add as indicated, using the number line to find the sum:

1. a. ⁺2 + ⁺3   **c.** ⁺4 + ⁺4   **e.** ⁺9 + ⁺2   **g.** ⁺3 + ⁺6
  b. ⁺6 + ⁺1   **d.** ⁺7 + ⁺3   **f.** ⁺5 + ⁺5   **h.** ⁺8 + ⁺4

In each of the above problems do you see that the absolute value of the sum is the sum of the absolute values of the two addends and that the sum of two positive integers is a positive integer?

2. a. ⁻5 + ⁻2   **c.** ⁻1 + ⁻9   **e.** ⁻6 + ⁻5   **g.** ⁻2 + ⁻2
  b. ⁻3 + ⁻4   **d.** ⁻2 + ⁻8   **f.** ⁻4 + ⁻1   **h.** ⁻7 + ⁻6

In each of the above problems do you see that the absolute value of the sum is the sum of the absolute values of the two addends and that the sum of two negative integers is a negative integer?

3. a. $^+6 + {}^-1$ **c.** $^+4 + {}^-7$ **e.** $^+5 + {}^-2$ **g.** $^+10 + {}^-7$

   b. $^+8 + {}^-3$ **d.** $^+2 + {}^-9$ **f.** $^+1 + {}^-6$ **h.** $^+3 + {}^-11$

In each of the above problems do you see that the absolute value of the sum is the difference in the absolute values of the two addends and that the sign in the sum, when we add a positive number and a negative number, corresponds to the sign of the addend having the greater absolute value?

4. a. $^-7 + {}^+2$ **c.** $^-1 + {}^+3$ **e.** $^-8 + {}^+11$ **g.** $^-10 + {}^+7$

   b. $^-5 + {}^+9$ **d.** $^-4 + {}^+8$ **f.** $^-2 + {}^+1$ **h.** $^-6 + {}^+12$

In each of the above problems do you see that the absolute value of the sum is the difference in the absolute values of the two addends and that the sign in the sum, when we add a negative number and a positive number, corresponds to the sign of the addend having the greater absolute value?

5. a. $^+3 + {}^-3$ **c.** $^-2 + {}^+2$ **e.** $^+10 + {}^-10$ **g.** $^-11 + {}^+11$

   b. $^+6 + {}^-6$ **d.** $^-7 + {}^+7$ **f.** $^-8 + {}^+8$ **h.** $^+9 + {}^-9$

In each of the above problems do you see that the sum of an integer and its opposite is zero?

6. a. $0 + {}^-4$ **c.** $0 + {}^+6$ **e.** $^+8 + 0$ **g.** $^-10 + 0$

   b. $^+3 + 0$ **d.** $^-2 + 0$ **f.** $0 + {}^+9$ **h.** $0 + {}^-7$

In each of the above problems do you see that the sum of any non-zero integer and zero is the non-zero integer?

7. a. $^+\frac{1}{2} + {}^+1\frac{1}{2}$ **c.** $^+5\frac{1}{2} + {}^-6$ **e.** $^-2\frac{7}{8} + 0$ **g.** $^-3\frac{1}{3} + {}^-\frac{5}{6}$

   b. $^-2\frac{3}{4} + {}^-2\frac{3}{4}$ **d.** $^-3\frac{2}{3} + {}^+4\frac{1}{3}$ **f.** $^+4\frac{1}{4} + {}^-4\frac{1}{4}$ **h.** $^-5 + {}^+7\frac{1}{2}$

In the above problems do you see that the same procedures are used to add rational numbers that are used to add integers?

8. a. $^+3 + {}^+4$ **e.** $^+8 + {}^-10$ **i.** $^-12 + {}^+9$ **m.** $^+1 + {}^-1$

   b. $^+7 + {}^-2$ **f.** $0 + {}^-7$ **j.** $^+1 + {}^+8$ **n.** $^-6 + {}^-6$

   c. $^-4 + {}^+4$ **g.** $^-6 + {}^-5$ **k.** $^+1\frac{3}{8} + {}^-\frac{3}{4}$ **o.** $^-2 + {}^+10$

   d. $^-1 + {}^-6$ **h.** $^-4 + {}^+2$ **l.** $^-2\frac{1}{4} + {}^-3\frac{1}{2}$ **p.** $^+5 + {}^-13$

10–10 ADDITION OF INTEGERS; PROPERTIES

Our observations in adding on the number line lead us to conclude that:

To add two positive integers, we find the sum of their absolute values and prefix the numeral with a positive sign. Observe that addition may be indicated horizontally or vertically.

In $^+5 + {}^+3 = {}^+8$, the absolute value of the sum (8) is the sum of the absolute values of the addends (5 + 3) and the sign is the common sign, $^+$ in this case.

To add two negative integers, we find the sum of their absolute values and prefix the numeral with a negative sign.

In $^-5 + {}^-3 = {}^-8$, the absolute value of the sum (8) is the sum of the absolute values of the addends (5 + 3) and the sign is the common sign, $^-$ in this case.

To add a positive integer and a negative integer or *a negative integer and a positive integer,* we subtract the smaller absolute value from the greater absolute value of the two addends and prefix the difference with the sign of the number having the greater absolute value.

In $^+5 + {}^-3 = {}^+2$, the absolute value of the sum (2) is equal to the difference in the absolute values of the addends (5 − 3) and the sign of the sum ($^+$) is the same as the sign of the addend with the greater absolute value (the sign of $^+5$).

Horizontally:

$$^+5 + {}^+3 = {}^+(5 + 3) = {}^+8$$

Vertically:

$$\begin{array}{r} ^+5 \\ {}^+3 \\ \hline {}^+8 \end{array}$$

Answer, $^+8$

Horizontally:

$$^-5 + {}^-3 = {}^-(5 + 3) = {}^-8$$

Vertically:

$$\begin{array}{r} ^-5 \\ {}^-3 \\ \hline {}^-8 \end{array}$$

Answer, $^-8$

Horizontally:

$$^+5 + {}^-3 = {}^+(5 - 3) = {}^+2$$

Vertically:

$$\begin{array}{r} ^+5 \\ {}^-3 \\ \hline {}^+2 \end{array}$$

Answer, $^+2$

In $^+5 + ^-8 = ^-3$, the absolute value of the sum (3) is equal to the difference in the absolute values of the addends (8 − 5) and the sign of the sum (⁻) is the same as the sign of the addend with the greater absolute value (the sign of $^-8$).

In $^-5 + ^+3 = ^-2$, the absolute value of the sum (2) is equal to the difference in the absolute values of the addends (5 − 3) and the sign of the sum (⁻) is the same as the sign of the addend with the greater absolute value (the sign of $^-5$).

In $^-5 + ^+8 = ^+3$, the absolute value of the sum (3) is equal to the difference in the absolute values of the addends (8 − 5) and the sign of the sum (⁺) is the same as the sign of the addend with the greater absolute value (the sign of $^+8$).

The sum of any integer and its opposite is zero.

The sum of any non-zero integer and zero is the non-zero integer.

The numeral naming a positive integer does not require the positive (⁺) sign.

To add three or more integers, we either add successively as shown in the model or we add first the positive numbers, then the negative numbers, and finally the two answers.

Horizontally: Vertically:

$^+5 + ^-8 = ^-(8 − 5) = ^-3$ $^+5$
                                       $^-8$
                                       ————
                                       $^-3$

Answer, $^-3$

Horizontally: Vertically:

$^-5 + ^+3 = ^-(5 − 3) = ^-2$ $^-5$
                                       $^+3$
                                       ————
                                       $^-2$

Answer, $^-2$

Horizontally: Vertically:

$^-5 + ^+8 = ^+(8 − 5) = ^+3$ $^-5$
                                       $^+8$
                                       ————
                                       $^+3$

Answer, $^+3$

$^+5 + ^-5 = 0$ *Answer,* 0
$^-8 + ^+8 = 0$ *Answer,* 0

$^-7 + 0 = ^-7$ *Answer,* $^-7$
$0 + ^+1 = ^+1$ *Answer,* $^+1$

$6 + ^-11 = ^-5$ *Answer,* $^-5$
$^-4 + 7 = 3$ *Answer,* 3

$^+6 + ^-9 + ^+2$
$= ^-3 + ^+2$
$= ^-1$ *Answer,* $^-1$

Introduction to Algebra   **303**

Add as indicated:

1. **a.** $^+5 + {}^+7$ **b.** $^+36 + {}^+8$ **c.** $^+19 + {}^+43$ **d.** $^+127 + {}^+99$

2. **a.** $^-6 + {}^-11$ **b.** $^-18 + {}^-49$ **c.** $^-56 + {}^-25$ **d.** $^-34 + {}^-67$

3. **a.** $^+8 + {}^-2$ **b.** $^+21 + {}^-14$ **c.** $^+33 + {}^-27$ **d.** $^+61 + {}^-42$

4. **a.** $^+3 + {}^-9$ **b.** $^+6 + {}^-20$ **c.** $^+46 + {}^-62$ **d.** $^+59 + {}^-85$

5. **a.** $^-7 + {}^+1$ **b.** $^-45 + {}^+12$ **c.** $^-51 + {}^+35$ **d.** $^-101 + {}^+74$

6. **a.** $^-2 + {}^+10$ **b.** $^-17 + {}^+40$ **c.** $^-29 + {}^+74$ **d.** $^-87 + {}^+120$

7. **a.** $^+4 + 0$ **b.** $0 + {}^-13$ **c.** $0 + {}^+21$ **d.** $^-52 + 0$

8. **a.** $^+15 + {}^-15$ **b.** $^-47 + {}^+47$ **c.** $^+92 + {}^-92$ **d.** $^-66 + {}^+66$

9. **a.** $8 + {}^-14$ **b.** $^-31 + 16$ **c.** $17 + {}^-25$ **d.** $^-42 + 80$

10. **a.** $^+3 + {}^+2 + {}^+6$ **d.** $^+20 + {}^-18 + {}^-5$ **g.** $^-3 + {}^+4 + {}^-7 + {}^+2$

     b. $^-8 + {}^+9 + {}^-1$ **e.** $^+19 + {}^+8 + {}^-24$ **h.** $^-11 + {}^+16 + {}^-3 + {}^-5$

     c. $^-11 + {}^-6 + {}^-28$ **f.** $^-25 + {}^-47 + {}^+56$ **i.** $^+17 + {}^-23 + {}^-35 + {}^+46$

11. **a.** $^-16 + {}^-5$ **e.** $^-64 + {}^+73$ **i.** $^-26 + {}^+75 + {}^-48$

     b. $^-8 + {}^+13$ **f.** $^+32 + {}^-32$ **j.** $^+15 + {}^-6 + {}^-37$

     c. $^+21 + {}^-9$ **g.** $^-99 + {}^-89$ **k.** $^+83 + {}^-19 + {}^-67 + {}^+8$

     d. $^+56 + {}^+75$ **h.** $0 + {}^-24$ **l.** $^-55 + {}^+28 + {}^-36 + {}^+57$

12. **a.** $(^+6 + {}^+5) + {}^-3$ **c.** $(^-11 + {}^+16) + {}^-6$ **e.** $^-20 + ({}^+37 + {}^-15)$

     b. $^+8 + ({}^-9 + {}^-7)$ **d.** $^-12 + ({}^-7 + {}^-25)$ **f.** $(^+26 + {}^-40) + {}^+34$

13. Add:

a.

$^+3$	$^-7$	$^-16$	$^+34$	$^-42$	$^+31$	$^-20$	$^+11$
$^+9$	$^-17$	$^+8$	$^-19$	$^+42$	0	$^-20$	$^-52$

b.

$^+28$	$^-81$	$^-67$	$^+95$	0	$^+44$	$^-39$	$^-19$
$^-67$	$^+25$	$^-67$	$^+107$	$^-75$	$^-5$	$^+46$	$^-1$

c.

$^-35$	$^-28$	$^+43$	$^-55$	$^+29$	$^+82$	0	$^-101$
$^-49$	$^+8$	$^-71$	$^+63$	$^-29$	$^+19$	$^-56$	$^+63$

d.

$^+3$	$^-12$	$^-27$	$^+6$	$^-27$	$^-6$	$^+103$	$^-38$
$^-9$	$^+8$	$^+53$	$^-8$	$^-9$	$^+34$	$^-96$	$^-53$
$^+5$	$^-2$	$^-19$	$^+1$	$^-15$	$^-57$	$^-42$	$^-67$
			$^-2$	$^+60$	$^+31$	$^+29$	$^-95$

14. Find the missing numbers:

a. $^+3 + {}^-9 = ?$ **d.** $^-5 + {}^-16 = \square$ **g.** $^-26 + {}^+19 = n$

b. $^-13 + {}^+8 = \square$ **e.** $^-17 + {}^+17 = n$ **h.** $^-38 + {}^-56 = n$

c. $^+21 + {}^-31 = n$ **f.** $^+34 + {}^+43 = ?$ **i.** $^+45 + {}^-27 = n$

15. Find the missing numbers:

a. $? + {}^+6 = {}^+8$ **d.** $\square + {}^-19 = {}^-3$ **g.** $n + {}^+5 = {}^-18$

b. $\square + {}^-4 = {}^-11$ **e.** $? + {}^+21 = {}^+6$ **h.** $n + {}^-43 = 0$

c. $n + {}^-2 = {}^-2$ **f.** $n + {}^-32 = {}^+8$ **i.** $n + {}^-59 = {}^-22$

16. Find the missing numbers:

a. $^+7 + ? = {}^+12$ **d.** $^-13 + \square = {}^-4$ **g.** $^+36 + n = {}^+7$

b. $^-2 + \square = {}^-9$ **e.** $^+25 + n = 0$ **h.** $^-53 + n = {}^-53$

c. $^+6 + n = {}^-1$ **f.** $^-18 + ? = {}^-2$ **i.** $^-41 + n = {}^+14$

Properties

In the following exercises we determine the properties that hold for the integers under the operation of addition.

1. Commutative Property

a. What do we mean when we say that the commutative property holds for the addition of a certain group of numbers?

b. In each of the following find the two sums by adding on the number line using vectors. Compare the two sums by comparing their vectors.

   (1) $^+2 + {}^+5;\ {}^+5 + {}^+2.$ Does $^+2 + {}^+5 = {}^+5 + {}^+2$?

   (2) $^-6 + {}^+4;\ {}^+4 + {}^-6.$ Does $^-6 + {}^+4 = {}^+4 + {}^-6$?

c. In each of the following add as indicated, then compare the sums:

   (1) $^+7 + {}^+8;\ {}^+8 + {}^+7.$ Does $^+7 + {}^+8 = {}^+8 + {}^+7$?

   (2) $^-3 + {}^-1;\ {}^-1 + {}^-3.$ Does $^-3 + {}^-1 = {}^-1 + {}^-3$?

   (3) $^+9 + {}^-4;\ {}^-4 + {}^+9.$ Does $^+9 + {}^-4 = {}^-4 + {}^+9$?

   (4) $^-6 + {}^+5;\ {}^+5 + {}^-6.$ Does $^-6 + {}^+5 = {}^+5 + {}^-6$?

d. Can you find two integers for which the commutative property of addition does not hold?

e. Can we say that the commutative property holds for the addition of integers?

Introduction to Algebra

2. Associative Property

a. What do we mean when we say that the associative property holds for the addition of a certain group of numbers?

b. In each of the following find the two sums by adding on the number line using vectors. Compare the two sums by comparing their vectors.

(1) $(^-6 + {}^+7) + {}^+3$; $^-6 + ({}^+7 + {}^+3)$.
   Does $(^-6 + {}^+7) + {}^+3 = {}^-6 + ({}^+7 + {}^+3)$?
(2) $(^+8 + {}^-4) + {}^-5$; $^+8 + ({}^-4 + {}^-5)$.
   Does $(^+8 + {}^-4) + {}^-5 = {}^+8 + ({}^-4 + {}^-5)$?

c. In each of the following add as indicated, then compare the sums:

(1) $(^-3 + {}^-8) + {}^+14$; $^-3 + ({}^-8 + {}^+14)$.
   Does $(^-3 + {}^-8) + {}^+14 = {}^-3 + ({}^-8 + {}^+14)$?
(2) $(^+2 + {}^-10) + {}^-1$; $^+2 + ({}^-10 + {}^-1)$.
   Does $(^+2 + {}^-10) + {}^-1 = {}^+2 + ({}^-10 + {}^-1)$?

d. Can you find three integers for which the associative property of addition does not hold?

e. Can we say that the associative property holds for the addition of integers?

3. Closure

a. What do we mean when we say that a certain group of numbers is closed under the operation of addition?

b. Is the sum of each of the following an integer?

(1) $^+4 + {}^-7$ (4) $^-5 + {}^+3$ (7) $^+9 + 0$
(2) $^-2 + {}^-2$ (5) $0 + {}^-10$ (8) $^-15 + {}^+7$
(3) $^+8 + {}^+12$ (6) $^-11 + {}^+11$ (9) $^+20 + {}^-20$

c. Can you find two integers for which the sum is not an integer?

d. Is the sum of two integers always an integer?

e. Can we say that the integers are closed under the operation of addition?

4. Additive Identity

a. What do we mean when we say that a certain group of numbers has an additive identity?

b. What is the sum of each of the following?

(1) $^-7 + 0$ (3) $^+8 + 0$ (5) $0 + {^+16}$ (7) $^+11 + 0$
(2) $0 + {^+3}$ (4) $0 + {^-1}$ (6) $^-14 + 0$ (8) $0 + {^-2}$

c. In each case in problem **4b** is the sum of the integer and zero the integer itself?

d. Can you find any integer which when added to zero does not have the given integer as the sum?

e. Do the integers have an additive identity? If so, what is it?

5. Additive Inverse

a. What do we mean by an additive inverse of an integer?

b. What is the sum of each of the following?

(1) $^-2 + {^+2}$ (4) $^-5 + {^+5}$ (7) $^+82 + {^-82}$
(2) $^+7 + {^-7}$ (5) $0 + 0$ (8) $^-100 + {^+100}$
(3) $^+13 + {^-13}$ (6) $^+27 + {^-27}$

c. Are we adding in each case in problem **5b** an integer and its additive inverse? What is the sum in each case?

d. Can you find any integer which when added to its additive inverse does not have zero as the sum?

e. Does each integer have an additive inverse?

10–11   ADDITION OF RATIONAL NUMBERS; PROPERTIES

Examination of addition on the number line reveals that to add positive and negative fractional numbers, we follow the same procedures as we do when we add integers. See sections 10–9 and 10–10. Since in the addition of rational numbers we sometimes add the absolute values and at other times subtract the absolute values, we should review at this time both the addition and the subtraction of the fractional numbers of arithmetic. See sections 4–11 and 4–12. Although the model problems below only illustrate common fractions, rational numbers may also be named by decimal fraction numerals. Thus sections 5–7 and 5–8 should also be reviewed at this time.

To add two positive rational numbers, we find the sum of their absolute values and prefix the numeral with a positive sign.

To add two negative rational numbers, we find the sum of their absolute values and prefix the numeral with a negative sign.

Add: $\dfrac{^-4}{9} + \dfrac{^-2}{9} = ?$

$$\frac{^-4}{9} + \frac{^-2}{9} = {}^-\left(\left|\frac{^-4}{9}\right| + \left|\frac{^-2}{9}\right|\right) = {}^-\left(\frac{4}{9} + \frac{2}{9}\right) = {}^-\left(\frac{4+2}{9}\right) = \frac{^-6}{9} = \frac{^-2}{3}$$

or, Vertically:

$$\frac{^-4}{9}$$
$$\frac{^-2}{9}$$
$$\frac{^-6}{9} = \frac{^-2}{3}$$

Horizontally:

$$\frac{^-4}{9} + \frac{^-2}{9} = \frac{^-4 + {}^-2}{9} = \frac{^-6}{9} = \frac{^-2}{3}$$

Answer, $\dfrac{^-2}{3}$

To add a positive rational number and a negative rational num-*ber* or *a negative rational number and a positive rational number,* subtract the smaller absolute value from the greater absolute value of the two addends and prefix the difference with the sign of the number having the greater absolute value.

Add: $\dfrac{^+3}{4} + \dfrac{^-2}{3} = ?$

$$\frac{^+3}{4} + \frac{^-2}{3} = {}^+\left(\left|\frac{^+3}{4}\right| - \left|\frac{^-2}{3}\right|\right) = {}^+\left(\frac{3}{4} - \frac{2}{3}\right) = {}^+\left(\frac{3}{4} \times \frac{3}{3} - \frac{2}{3} \times \frac{4}{4}\right)$$
$$= {}^-\left(\frac{9}{12} - \frac{8}{12}\right) = \frac{^+1}{12}$$

or, Vertically:

Add: $\dfrac{^+3}{4} = \dfrac{^+3}{4} \times \dfrac{3}{3} = \dfrac{^+9}{12}$

$\phantom{\text{Add: }}\dfrac{^-2}{3} = \dfrac{^-2}{3} \times \dfrac{4}{4} = \dfrac{^-8}{12}$

$\phantom{\text{Add: }\dfrac{^-2}{3} = \dfrac{^-2}{3} \times \dfrac{4}{4} = }\dfrac{^+1}{12}$

Horizontally:

$$\frac{^+3}{4} + \frac{^-2}{3} = \frac{^+3 \times 3}{4 \times 3} + \frac{^-2 \times 4}{3 \times 4} = \frac{^+9}{12} + \frac{^-8}{12} = \frac{^+9 + {}^-8}{12} = \frac{^+1}{12}$$

Answer, $\dfrac{^+1}{12}$

Observe in the model problem below that sometimes it is necessary to interchange the absolute values to make this subtraction possible.

Add: $\dfrac{^+1}{2} + \dfrac{^-7}{8} = ?$

$$\dfrac{^+1}{2} + \dfrac{^-7}{8} = {}^-\left(\left|\dfrac{^-7}{8}\right| - \left|\dfrac{^+1}{2}\right|\right)^* =$$

$$^-\left(\dfrac{7}{8} - \dfrac{1}{2}\right) = {}^-\left(\dfrac{7}{8} - \dfrac{1}{2} \times \dfrac{4}{4}\right) = {}^-\left(\dfrac{7}{8} - \dfrac{4}{8}\right) = \dfrac{^-3}{8}$$

* (Since the smaller absolute value happens to be in the first addend in this problem, we interchange absolute values in order to subtract.)

or,

Vertically:

$$\text{Add: } \dfrac{^+1}{2} = \dfrac{^+4}{8}$$
$$\dfrac{^-7}{8} = \dfrac{^-7}{8}$$
$$\overline{\dfrac{^-3}{8}}$$

Horizontally:

$$\dfrac{^+1}{2} + \dfrac{^-7}{8} = \dfrac{^+4}{8} + \dfrac{^-7}{8} = \dfrac{^+4 + {}^-7}{8} = \dfrac{^-3}{8}$$

Answer, $\dfrac{^-3}{8}$

The sum of any rational number and its opposite is zero.

The sum of any non-zero rational number and zero is the non-zero rational number.

The numeral naming a positive rational number does not require the positive ($^+$) sign.

To add three or more rational numbers, we either add successively or first add the positive numbers, then the negative numbers, and finally the two answers.

$$^+1\tfrac{1}{2} + {}^-3\tfrac{1}{4} + {}^+2\tfrac{5}{6} = {}^+1\tfrac{6}{12} + {}^-3\tfrac{3}{12} + {}^+2\tfrac{10}{12}$$
$$= {}^+1\tfrac{6}{12} + {}^+2\tfrac{10}{12} + {}^-3\tfrac{3}{12}$$
$$= {}^+3\tfrac{16}{12} + {}^-3\tfrac{3}{12}$$
$$= {}^+\tfrac{13}{12} = {}^+1\tfrac{1}{12}$$

Answer, $^+1\tfrac{1}{12}$

Introduction to Algebra

Add as indicated:

1. **a.** $^+\frac{1}{8} + \,^+\frac{3}{8}$ **b.** $^+\frac{2}{3} + \,^+\frac{7}{12}$ **c.** $^+1\frac{1}{4} + \,^+3\frac{5}{6}$ **d.** $^+7\frac{9}{16} + \,^+4\frac{3}{10}$

2. **a.** $^+.7 + \,^+.9$ **b.** $^+3.6 + \,^+.15$ **c.** $^+.019 + \,^+.03$ **d.** $^+20.69 + \,^+5.386$

3. **a.** $^-\frac{5}{6} + \,^-\frac{1}{6}$ **b.** $^-\frac{4}{5} + \,^-\frac{1}{2}$ **c.** $^-2\frac{7}{8} + \,^-1\frac{5}{8}$ **d.** $^-6\frac{11}{12} + \,^-8\frac{5}{16}$

4. **a.** $^-.84 + \,^-.5$ **b.** $^-.07 + \,^-.17$ **c.** $^-16 + \,^-2.8$ **d.** $^-9.62 + \,^-84.9$

5. **a.** $^+\frac{3}{4} + \,^-\frac{1}{8}$ **b.** $^+2\frac{1}{3} + \,^-3\frac{1}{4}$ **c.** $^+6\frac{3}{8} + \,^-\frac{11}{16}$ **d.** $^+7\frac{1}{2} + \,^-9\frac{7}{12}$

6. **a.** $^+1.4 + \,^-2.5$ **b.** $^+.9 + \,^-1.1$ **c.** $^+.359 + \,^-.29$ **d.** $^+27.6 + \,^-2.76$

7. **a.** $^-\frac{2}{5} + \,^+\frac{7}{100}$ **b.** $^-8\frac{1}{6} + \,^+1\frac{2}{3}$ **c.** $^-3\frac{1}{2} + \,^+7\frac{1}{16}$ **d.** $^-1\frac{3}{10} + \,^+1\frac{7}{16}$

8. **a.** $^-9.6 + \,^+6.9$ **b.** $^-.71 + \,^+.8$ **c.** $^-.004 + \,^+.0037$ **d.** $^-1.16 + \,^+11.3$

9. **a.** $^+1\frac{1}{2} + \,^-1\frac{1}{2}$ **b.** $^-\frac{11}{12} + \,^+\frac{11}{12}$ **c.** $^+7\frac{2}{3} + \,^-7\frac{2}{3}$ **d.** $^-5\frac{13}{16} + \,^+5\frac{13}{16}$

10. **a.** $^-3.9 + \,^+3.9$ **b.** $^+.7 + \,^-.7$ **c.** $^-.046 + \,^+.046$ **d.** $^+9.183 + \,^-9.183$

11. **a.** $^-5\frac{7}{9} + 0$ **b.** $0 + \,^+8\frac{2}{3}$ **c.** $^-1.6 + 0$ **d.** $0 + \,^+.055$

12. **a.** $^-9\frac{1}{4} + 5\frac{3}{16}$ **b.** $7\frac{1}{2} + \,^-1\frac{3}{8}$ **c.** $^-.63 + 1.4$ **d.** $5.81 + \,^-3.142$

13. **a.** $^+\frac{3}{5} + \,^-\frac{1}{2} + \,^-\frac{7}{10}$ **c.** $^-5\frac{1}{4} + \,^-4\frac{2}{3} + \,^-2\frac{5}{8}$ **e.** $^-6.29 + \,^-.518 + \,^+73.4$

    b. $^+2\frac{2}{3} + \,^-9\frac{5}{6} + \,^+6\frac{1}{2}$ **d.** $^-1\frac{1}{6} + \,^+2\frac{7}{8} + \,^-\frac{3}{4}$ **f.** $^+.193 + \,^-.3621 + \,^+.27$

14. **a.** $\left(^-\frac{2}{3} + \,^-\frac{11}{12}\right) + \,^-\frac{5}{6}$ **d.** $\left(^-\frac{4}{5} + \,^-1\frac{5}{6}\right) + \,^+3$ **g.** $(^-.7 + \,^+.82) + \,^-.1$

    b. $\left(^+3\frac{1}{2} + \,^+7\frac{3}{4}\right) + \,^+4\frac{1}{3}$ **e.** $^+6\frac{1}{4} + \left(^-4\frac{7}{12} + \,^+2\frac{3}{16}\right)$ **h.** $^-2.5 + (^-.96 + \,^-1.4)$

    c. $^-1\frac{5}{8} + \left(^+2\frac{1}{4} + \,^+\frac{9}{16}\right)$ **f.** $^-4\frac{1}{6} + \left(^+5\frac{1}{2} + \,^-10\frac{7}{8}\right)$ **i.** $(^+8.17 + \,^-91.3) + \,^+.796$

15. Add:

$^-\frac{11}{16}$	$^+\frac{5}{6}$	$^-\frac{4}{5}$	$^+1\frac{1}{2}$	$^+7\frac{5}{12}$	$^-6\frac{9}{10}$	$^-4\frac{9}{16}$
$^-\frac{9}{16}$	$^-\frac{17}{18}$	$^+\frac{3}{4}$	$^-\frac{5}{8}$	$^+3\frac{1}{4}$	$^+8\frac{5}{6}$	$^-9\frac{7}{12}$

16. Add:

$^-\frac{7}{8}$	$^+\frac{2}{3}$	$^-\frac{1}{4}$	$^+4\frac{3}{4}$	$^-3\frac{2}{3}$	$^+9\frac{3}{8}$	$^-5\frac{13}{16}$
$^-\frac{5}{16}$	$^-\frac{1}{2}$	$^-\frac{11}{12}$	$^+2\frac{1}{2}$	$^-1\frac{3}{5}$	$^-3\frac{7}{12}$	$^+4\frac{11}{12}$
$^+\frac{3}{4}$	$^+\frac{3}{8}$	$^-\frac{9}{16}$	$6\frac{7}{8}$	$^+5\frac{1}{2}$	$^-7\frac{5}{6}$	$^-2\frac{5}{8}$

17. Add:

$^-8.7$	$^+.126$	$^-5.98$	$^-17.5$	$^-7.48$	$^-.045$	$^-6.5$
$^+4.9$	$^-.318$	$^-3.02$	$^+28.2$	$^+3.91$	$^-.039$	$^+7.12$
			$^-10.4$	$^+4.86$	$^+.024$	$^-1.839$

18. Find the missing numbers:

a. $^+\frac{7}{8} + ^-\frac{1}{8} = ?$ c. $^-2\frac{3}{4} + ^-1\frac{5}{16} = \square$ e. $^-1\frac{7}{10} + ^+2\frac{5}{8} = n$

b. $^-\frac{4}{5} + ^+\frac{2}{3} = n$ d. $^+5\frac{5}{6} + ^+3\frac{7}{12} = n$ f. $^+7\frac{1}{3} + ^-5\frac{3}{4} = n$

19. Find the missing numbers:

a. $^-.9 + ^-.3 = \square$ c. $^-3.4 + ^+2 = ?$ e. $^+5.4 + ^-.54 = n$

b. $^+.14 + ^-2.5 = n$ d. $^+6.7 + ^-6.7 = n$ f. $^-.825 + ^+.91 = n$

20. Find the missing numbers:

a. $? + ^+\frac{2}{3} = ^+1\frac{1}{6}$ c. $\square + ^-2\frac{5}{6} = ^-8\frac{1}{3}$ e. $n + ^+1\frac{3}{4} = ^+\frac{11}{12}$

b. $n + ^-\frac{7}{8} = ^-\frac{11}{16}$ d. $n + ^-7\frac{4}{9} = 0$ f. $n + ^-9\frac{4}{5} = ^-4\frac{2}{3}$

21. Find the missing numbers:

a. $? + ^+.6 = ^+1.3$ c. $n + ^+9.6 = ^+1.82$ e. $n + ^-.469 = ^-.469$

b. $n + ^-2.7 = ^-5.2$ d. $\square + ^-10 = ^-16.7$ f. $n + ^+7.25 = ^-2.986$

22. Find the missing numbers:

a. $^-\frac{1}{2} + \square = ^-\frac{1}{4}$ c. $^+2\frac{2}{3} + ? = ^+7\frac{5}{6}$ e. $^-3\frac{3}{8} + n = ^-9\frac{3}{4}$

b. $^+1\frac{1}{8} + n = ^-1\frac{1}{2}$ d. $^-4\frac{11}{16} + ? = ^+4\frac{11}{16}$ f. $^-7\frac{2}{5} + n = ^+5$

23. Find the missing numbers:

a. $^+.8 + ? = ^+1.4$ c. $^-3.6 + \square = 0$ e. $^-4.8 + n = ^+3.1$

b. $^-1.7 + n = ^-2$ d. $^+.5 + n = ^+.27$ f. $^+.699 + n = ^-.0001$

Properties

In the following exercises we determine the properties that hold for the rational numbers under the operation of addition.

1. Commutative Property

   a. What do we mean when we say that the commutative property holds for the addition of a certain group of rational numbers?

   b. In each of the following find the two sums by adding on the number line, using vectors. Compare the two sums by comparing their vectors.

     (1) $^+\frac{1}{2} + ^-\frac{3}{4}$; $^-\frac{3}{4} + ^+\frac{1}{2}$. Does $^+\frac{1}{2} + ^-\frac{3}{4} = ^-\frac{3}{4} + ^+\frac{1}{2}$?

     (2) $^-2\frac{1}{2} + ^-1\frac{1}{4}$; $^-1\frac{1}{4} + ^-2\frac{1}{2}$. Does $^-2\frac{1}{2} + ^-1\frac{1}{4} = ^-1\frac{1}{4} + ^-2\frac{1}{2}$?

c. In each of the following add as indicated, then compare the sums:

(1) $\frac{-2}{3} + \frac{+5}{6}$; $\frac{+5}{6} + \frac{-2}{3}$. Does $\frac{-2}{3} + \frac{+5}{6} = \frac{+5}{6} + \frac{-2}{3}$?

(2) $+3\frac{7}{8} + +2\frac{3}{8}$; $+2\frac{3}{8} + +3\frac{7}{8}$.

Does $+3\frac{7}{8} + +2\frac{3}{8} = +2\frac{3}{8} + +3\frac{7}{8}$?

(3) $+4\frac{3}{4} + -5\frac{11}{16}$; $-5\frac{11}{16} + +4\frac{3}{4}$.

Does $+4\frac{3}{4} + -5\frac{11}{16} = -5\frac{11}{16} + +4\frac{3}{4}$?

(4) $-1.48 + -.357$; $-.357 + -1.48$.

Does $-1.48 + -.357 = -.357 + -1.48$?

d. Can you find two rational numbers for which the commutative property of addition does not hold?

e. Can we say that the commutative property holds for the addition of rational numbers?

2. Associative Property

a. What do we mean when we say that the associative property holds for the addition of a certain group of numbers?

b. In each of the following find the two sums by adding on the number line, using vectors. Compare the two sums by comparing their vectors.

(1) $\left(\frac{-3}{4} + \frac{-3}{4}\right) + \frac{-1}{2}$; $\frac{-3}{4} + \left(\frac{-3}{4} + \frac{-1}{2}\right)$.

Does $\left(\frac{-3}{4} + \frac{-3}{4}\right) + \frac{-1}{2} = \frac{-3}{4} + \left(\frac{-3}{4} + \frac{-1}{2}\right)$?

(2) $\left(+1\frac{2}{3} + -3\frac{1}{3}\right) + \frac{+2}{3}$; $+1\frac{2}{3} + \left(-3\frac{1}{3} + \frac{+2}{3}\right)$.

Does $\left(+1\frac{2}{3} + -3\frac{1}{3}\right) + \frac{+2}{3} = +1\frac{2}{3} + \left(-3\frac{1}{3} + \frac{+2}{3}\right)$?

c. In each of the following add as indicated, then compare the sums:

(1) $\left(-2\frac{5}{8} + +1\frac{3}{4}\right) + -5\frac{1}{2}$; $-2\frac{5}{8} + \left(+1\frac{3}{4} + -5\frac{1}{2}\right)$.

Does $\left(-2\frac{5}{8} + +1\frac{3}{4}\right) + -5\frac{1}{2} = -2\frac{5}{8} + \left(+1\frac{3}{4} + -5\frac{1}{2}\right)$?

(2) $(-5.2 + +4.25) + +.84$; $-5.2 + (+4.25 + +.84)$.

Does $(-5.2 + +4.25) + +.84 = -5.2 + (+4.25 + +.84)$?

d. Can you find three rational numbers for which the associative property of addition does not hold?

e. Can we say that the associative property holds for the addition of rational numbers?

3. Closure

   a. What do we mean when we say that a certain group of numbers is closed under the operation of addition?

   b. Is the sum of each of the following a rational number?

   (1) $^+\frac{3}{5} + {}^+\frac{4}{5}$ (4) $^-5\frac{1}{6} + 0$ (7) $^-.276 + {}^-3.84$

   (2) $^-\frac{7}{8} + {}^+\frac{3}{4}$ (5) $^-4\frac{3}{8} + {}^+1\frac{11}{12}$ (8) $^+.04 + {}^-.004$

   (3) $^-\frac{2}{3} + {}^-\frac{7}{16}$ (6) $^+2\frac{2}{5} + {}^-7\frac{1}{4}$ (9) $^-6.08 + {}^+2.5$

   c. Can you find two rational numbers for which the sum is not a rational number?

   d. Is the sum of two rational numbers always a rational number?

   e. Can we say that the rational numbers are closed under the operation of addition?

4. Additive Identity

   a. What do we mean when we say that a certain group of numbers has an additive identity?

   b. What is the sum of each of the following?

   (1) $^+\frac{7}{8} + 0$ (3) $0 + {}^+3.9$ (5) $^-\frac{11}{4} + 0$ (7) $0 + {}^-.6$

   (2) $0 + {}^-1\frac{1}{3}$ (4) $^-.01 + 0$ (6) $0 + {}^+3.72$ (8) $^-9\frac{11}{16} + 0$

   c. In each case in problem **4b,** is the sum of the rational number and zero the rational number itself?

   d. Can you find any rational number which when added to zero does not have the given rational number as the sum?

   e. Do the rational numbers have an additive identity? If so, what is it?

5. Additive Inverse

   a. What do we mean by an additive inverse of a rational number?

   b. What is the sum of each of the following?

   (1) $^-\frac{7}{12} + {}^+\frac{7}{12}$ (4) $^-6.33 + {}^+6.33$ (7) $^+10\frac{3}{4} + {}^-10\frac{3}{4}$

   (2) $^+2\frac{1}{2} + {}^-2\frac{1}{2}$ (5) $^-\frac{15}{8} + {}^+\frac{15}{8}$ (8) $^-9.6 + {}^+9.6$

   (3) $^+.9 + {}^-.9$ (6) $^+.002 + {}^-.002$

   c. Are we adding in each case in problem **5b** a rational number and its additive inverse? What is the sum in each case?

   d. Can you find a rational number which when added to its additive inverse does not have zero as the sum?

   e. Does each rational number have an additive inverse?

Introduction to Algebra

10–12 SUBTRACTION ON THE NUMBER LINE

Since subtraction is the inverse operation of addition, to subtract we find the addend which when added to the given addend (subtrahend) will equal the given sum (minuend).

$$^+5 - {}^-3 = ?$$

is thought of as

$$^-3 + ? = {}^+5$$

Using this idea of inverse operation, to subtract on the number line we locate the points reached by the movements represented by the given sum and by the given addend, moving in both cases from the point marked 0.

We draw (1) a vector below the number line to represent the movement indicated by the given sum and (2) a vector above the number line to represent the movement indicated by the given addend.

To find the missing addend, we draw (3) a vector *from* the point reached by the vector representing the given addend *to* the point reached by the vector representing the sum. The length of this vector is the absolute value and the direction of the vector indicates the sign of the missing addend.

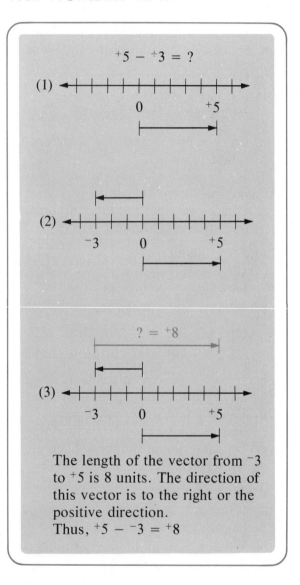

The length of the vector from $^-3$ to $^+5$ is 8 units. The direction of this vector is to the right or the positive direction.
Thus, $^+5 - {}^-3 = {}^+8$

EXERCISES

In each of the following subtract as indicated on the number line, using vectors to find the difference:

1. a. $^+6 - {}^+3$ **b.** $^+4 - {}^+2$ **c.** $^+9 - {}^+5$ **d.** $^+8 - {}^+6$

2. a. $^+4 - ^+7$ **b.** $^+2 - ^+8$ **c.** $^+3 - ^+6$ **d.** $^+1 - ^+9$
3. a. $^-8 - ^-5$ **b.** $^-6 - ^-1$ **c.** $^-7 - ^-3$ **d.** $^-10 - ^-2$
4. a. $^-1 - ^-7$ **b.** $^-5 - ^-9$ **c.** $^-2 - ^-11$ **d.** $^-4 - ^-6$
5. a. $^+5 - ^-4$ **b.** $^+7 - ^-8$ **c.** $^+9 - ^-6$ **d.** $^+8 - ^-10$
6. a. $^-7 - ^+2$ **b.** $^-1 - ^+12$ **c.** $^-4 - ^+4$ **d.** $^-9 - ^+12$
7. a. $^-6 - ^-6$ **b.** $^+3 - ^-3$ **c.** $^-8 - ^-8$ **d.** $^+4 - ^+4$
8. a. $0 - ^-4$ **b.** $0 - ^+7$ **c.** $^-3 - 0$ **d.** $^+8 - 0$
9. a. $^-2\frac{1}{2} - ^+3\frac{1}{2}$ **b.** $^-4 - ^-5\frac{3}{4}$ **c.** $^+3\frac{1}{3} - ^-2\frac{2}{3}$ **d.** $^-6\frac{1}{4} - ^-6\frac{1}{4}$

10–13 SUBTRACTION OF INTEGERS; PROPERTIES

In the addition of integers we learned that $^+5 + ^+3 = ^+8$. In subtracting integers on the number line we found that $^+5 - ^-3 = ^+8$.

A comparison of $^+5 - ^-3 = ^+8$
and $^+5 + ^+3 = ^+8$

shows that subtracting $^-3$ from $^+5$ gives the same answer ($^+8$) as adding $^+3$ to $^+5$. Since $^+3$ is the opposite of $^-3$, we may say in this case that *subtracting a number* gives the same answer as *adding its opposite*. Let us determine whether this is true in other cases.

a. $^+2 - ^+6 = ?$ means "What number added to $^+6$ equals $^+2$?" The answer is $^-4$. Thus, $^+2 - ^+6 = ^-4$.

b. $^-7 - ^+3 = ?$ means "What number added to $^+3$ equals $^-7$?" The answer is $^-10$. Thus, $^-7 - ^+3 = ^-10$.

c. $^-4 - ^-9 = ?$ means "What number added to $^-9$ equals $^-4$?" The answer is $^+5$. Thus, $^-4 - ^-9 = ^+5$.

d. $0 - ^-6 = ?$ means "What number added to $^-6$ equals 0?" The answer is $^+6$. Thus, $0 - ^-6 = ^+6$.

When we compare:

a. $^+2 - ^+6 = ^-4$	**c.** $^-4 - ^-9 = ^+5$
$^+2 + ^-6 = ^-4$	$^-4 + ^+9 = ^+5$
b. $^-7 - ^+3 = ^-10$	**d.** $0 - ^-6 = ^+6$
$^-7 + ^-3 = ^-10$	$0 + ^+6 = ^+6$

we conclude that both subtracting a number and adding the

opposite of the number which is to be subtracted give the same answer.

Thus, *to subtract any integer from another integer,* we add to the minuend the opposite (or additive inverse) of the integer which is to be subtracted. The problem first could be rewritten, arranged horizontally or vertically. For example:

Subtract: $^-6 - ^+4 = ?$

Horizontally:

$^-6 - ^+4 = ^-6 + ^-4 = ^-10$

Answer, $^-10$

Vertically:

Subtract:		Add:
$^-6$		$^-6$
$^+4$	$\longrightarrow$	$^-4$
		$^-10$

Subtract: $^-1 - ^-3 = ?$

Horizontally:

$^-1 - ^-3 = ^-1 + ^+3 = ^+2$

Answer, $^+2$

Vertically:

Subtract:		Add:
$^-1$		$^-1$
$^-3$	$\longrightarrow$	$^+3$
		$^+2$

Subtract: $0 - ^+2 = ?$

Horizontally:

$0 - ^+2 = 0 + ^-2 = ^-2$

Answer, $^-2$

Vertically:

0		0
$^+2$	$\longrightarrow$	$^-2$
		$^-2$

The numeral naming a positive number does not require the positive ($^+$) sign.

$8 - 11 = 8 + ^-11 = ^-3$

Answer, $^-3$

Subtract as indicated:

1. **a.** $^+7 - {}^+2$ **b.** $^+11 - {}^+5$ **c.** $^+33 - {}^+19$ **d.** $^+57 - {}^+27$
2. **a.** $^+1 - {}^+8$ **b.** $^+9 - {}^+32$ **c.** $^+16 - {}^+54$ **d.** $^+49 - {}^+90$
3. **a.** $^-10 - {}^-5$ **b.** $^-61 - {}^-28$ **c.** $^-73 - {}^-36$ **d.** $^-110 - {}^-42$
4. **a.** $^-2 - {}^-9$ **b.** $^-12 - {}^-40$ **c.** $^-27 - {}^-65$ **d.** $^-76 - {}^-103$
5. **a.** $^+14 - {}^-6$ **b.** $^+27 - {}^-39$ **c.** $^+60 - {}^-43$ **d.** $^+51 - {}^-51$
6. **a.** $^-24 - {}^+18$ **b.** $^-48 - {}^+65$ **c.** $^-94 - {}^+38$ **d.** $^-169 - {}^+250$
7. **a.** $^+9 - 0$ **b.** $^-17 - 0$ **c.** $^-56 - 0$ **d.** $^+31 - 0$
8. **a.** $0 - {}^-6$ **b.** $0 - {}^+24$ **c.** $0 - {}^-61$ **d.** $0 - {}^+108$
9. **a.** $^-12 - {}^-12$ **b.** $^+92 - {}^+92$ **c.** $^-75 - {}^-75$ **d.** $^-29 - {}^-29$
10. **a.** $6 - 11$ **b.** $2 - 28$ **c.** $19 - 54$ **d.** $67 - 100$
11. **a.** $(^-9 - {}^+6) - {}^+10$ **c.** $^-24 - (^+11 - {}^+16)$ **e.** $(^+10 - {}^-5) - {}^+15$
    b. $(^+8 - {}^+14) - {}^-7$ **d.** $^+18 - (^-5 - {}^-21)$ **f.** $^-1 - (^-45 - {}^+45)$

12. Subtract in each of the following:

a.
$^+17$	$^-97$	$^-40$	$^+9$	$^-18$	0	$^-85$	29
$^+28$	$^+39$	$^-15$	$^-56$	$^-72$	$^-34$	$^+114$	52

b.
$^+65$	$^-91$	$^-54$	$^+18$	$^-87$	8	$^-99$	$^-45$
$^-35$	$^-76$	$^+6$	$^+30$	$^+87$	43	0	$^-78$

c.
$^-42$	$^-26$	$^+62$	0	93	$^+7$	$^-59$	$^-32$
$^-81$	$^+19$	$^+75$	$^+10$	200	$^-38$	$^-59$	$^+32$

13. Find the missing numbers:

   a. $^+6 - {}^+11 = ?$ **d.** $0 - {}^-63 = \square$ **g.** $^-24 - {}^-57 = n$
   b. $^-19 - {}^-12 = \square$ **e.** $^+18 - {}^-18 = ?$ **h.** $^+100 - {}^-78 = n$
   c. $^-31 - {}^+45 = n$ **f.** $^-50 - {}^-50 = n$ **i.** $^+45 - {}^+82 = n$

14. Find the missing numbers:

   a. $? - {}^+3 = {}^+9$ **d.** $\square - {}^+6 = {}^-13$ **g.** $n - {}^-12 = 10$
   b. $\square - {}^-14 = {}^-20$ **e.** $? - {}^-15 = 0$ **h.** $n - 0 = {}^-36$
   c. $n - {}^-1 = {}^+8$ **f.** $n - 9 = {}^-5$ **i.** $n - {}^+23 = {}^-18$

15. Find the missing numbers:

   a. $^-7 - \square = {}^-15$ **d.** $^-24 - ? = 0$ **g.** $^+100 - n = {}^+275$
   b. $^+11 - ? = {}^-2$ **e.** $0 - n = {}^-19$ **h.** $^-49 - n = {}^-50$
   c. $^-4 - n = {}^+12$ **f.** $^-35 - \square = {}^+25$ **i.** $^+63 - n = {}^-36$

Properties

In the following exercises we determine the properties that hold for the integers under the operation of subtraction.

1. Commutative Property

    a. If the commutative property holds for the subtraction of integers, what would have to be true?

    b. In each of the following subtract as indicated, then compare answers:

    (1) $^+9 - {}^+5$; $^+5 - {}^+9$. Does $^+9 - {}^+5 = {}^+5 - {}^+9$?
    (2) $^-16 - {}^-21$; $^-21 - {}^-16$. Does $^-16 - {}^-21 = {}^-21 - {}^-16$?
    (3) $^+7 - {}^-9$; $^-9 - {}^+7$. Does $^+7 - {}^-9 = {}^-9 - {}^+7$?
    (4) $^-6 - {}^+3$; $^+3 - {}^-6$. Does $^-6 - {}^+3 = {}^+3 - {}^-6$?

    c. Does the commutative property hold for the subtraction of integers?

2. Associative Property

    a. If the associative property holds for the subtraction of integers, what would have to be true?

    b. If each of the following subtract as indicated, then compare answers:

    (1) $(^-10 - {}^+8) - {}^-6$; $^-10 - (^+8 - {}^-6)$.
        Does $(^-10 - {}^+8) - {}^-6 = {}^-10 - (^+8 - {}^-6)$?
    (2) $(^-3 - {}^-9) - {}^+2$; $^-3 - (^-9 - {}^+2)$.
        Does $(^-3 - {}^-9) - {}^+2 = {}^-3 - (^-9 - {}^+2)$?

    c. Does the associative property hold for the subtraction of integers?

3. Closure

    a. What do we mean when we say that a certain group of numbers is closed under the operation of subtraction?

    b. When you subtract in each of the following, is the difference in each case an integer?

(1) $^-8 - {}^-1$	(4) $^+12 - {}^-12$	(7) $4 - 9$
(2) $^+7 - {}^+10$	(5) $0 - {}^+5$	(8) $^+3 - {}^-11$
(3) $^-1 - {}^+6$	(6) $^-2 - 0$	(9) $^-6 - {}^-6$

    c. Can you find two integers for which the difference is not an integer?

    d. Is the difference of two integers always an integer?

    e. Can we say that the integers are closed under the operation of subtraction?

10–14 SUBTRACTION OF RATIONAL NUMBERS; PROPERTIES

Examination of subtraction on the number line in section 10–12 and the development in section 10–13, that subtracting a number and adding the opposite of the number which is to be subtracted both give the same answer, lead us to conclude that:

To subtract any rational number from another rational number, we add to the minuend the opposite (or additive inverse) of the rational number which is to be subtracted. The problem first could be rewritten, arranged horizontally or vertically. For example:

Subtract: $\frac{^+1}{5} - \frac{^+2}{5} = ?$

Horizontally:

$$\frac{^+1}{5} - \frac{^+2}{5} = \frac{^+1}{5} + \frac{^-2}{5} = \frac{^+1 + {}^-2}{5} = \frac{^-1}{5}$$

Answer, $\frac{^-1}{5}$

Vertically:

Subtract: Add:

$$\begin{array}{cc} \dfrac{^+1}{5} & \dfrac{^+1}{5} \\[2mm] \dfrac{^+2}{5} & \longrightarrow \ \dfrac{^-2}{5} \\[2mm] \hline & \dfrac{^-1}{5} \end{array}$$

Subtract: $^-3\frac{1}{2} - {}^+2\frac{3}{8} = ?$

Horizontally:

$$^-3\frac{1}{2} - {}^+2\frac{3}{8} = {}^-3\frac{1}{2} + {}^-2\frac{3}{8} =$$
$$^-3\frac{4}{8} + {}^-2\frac{3}{8} = {}^-5\frac{7}{8}$$

Answer, $^-5\frac{7}{8}$

Vertically:

Subtract: Add:

$$\begin{array}{ccc} ^-3\frac{1}{2} & ^-3\frac{1}{2} = & ^-3\frac{4}{8} \\[2mm] ^+2\frac{3}{8} \longrightarrow & ^-2\frac{3}{8} = & ^-2\frac{3}{8} \\[2mm] \hline & & ^-5\frac{7}{8} \end{array}$$

Subtract: $0 - {}^-6.8 = ?$

Horizontally:
$$0 - {}^-6.8 = 0 + {}^+6.8 = {}^+6.8$$

Answer, $^+6.8$

Vertically:

Subtract: Add:

$$\begin{array}{cc} 0 & 0 \\ ^-6.8 & \longrightarrow \ ^+6.8 \\ \hline & ^+6.8 \end{array}$$

It may be necessary to review at this time both the addition and the subtraction of the rational numbers of arithmetic (common fractions, mixed numbers, and decimal fractions). See sections 4–11, 4–12, 5–7, and 5–8.

EXERCISES

Subtract as indicated:

1. **a.** $^+\frac{2}{3} - ^+\frac{1}{3}$ **b.** $^+\frac{5}{6} - ^+\frac{7}{12}$ **c.** $^+4\frac{7}{8} - ^+1\frac{3}{8}$ **d.** $^+6\frac{1}{3} - ^+3\frac{3}{4}$

2. **a.** $^+\frac{1}{9} - ^+\frac{5}{9}$ **b.** $^+\frac{9}{16} - ^+\frac{3}{4}$ **c.** $^+1\frac{1}{2} - ^+3\frac{4}{5}$ **d.** $^+\frac{11}{12} - ^+1\frac{2}{3}$

3. **a.** $^+.63 - ^+.59$ **b.** $^+.8 - ^+.08$ **c.** $^+1.6 - ^+.19$ **d.** $^+.832 - ^+.83$

4. **a.** $^+.85 - ^+1.2$ **b.** $^+.62 - ^+.7$ **c.** $^+.43 - ^+4.3$ **d.** $^+.1689 - ^+.169$

5. **a.** $^-\frac{5}{7} - ^-\frac{3}{7}$ **b.** $^-\frac{5}{8} - ^-\frac{1}{6}$ **c.** $^-2\frac{2}{3} - ^-2\frac{1}{4}$ **d.** $^-7\frac{1}{2}$ $^-5\frac{11}{12}$

6. **a.** $^-\frac{1}{10} - ^-\frac{7}{10}$ **b.** $^-\frac{3}{4} - ^-\frac{4}{5}$ **c.** $^-1\frac{1}{6} - ^-5\frac{3}{8}$ **d.** $^-4\frac{2}{3} - ^-6\frac{11}{16}$

7. **a.** $^-8.6 - ^-1.4$ **b.** $^-9 - ^-.83$ **c.** $^-.106 - ^-.0081$ **d.** $^-25.6 - ^-.907$

8. **a.** $^-.05 - ^-.2$ **b.** $^-4.8 - ^-11.4$ **c.** $^-6.96 - ^-27.1$ **d.** $^-.0004 - ^-.1$

9. **a.** $^+\frac{13}{16} - ^-\frac{3}{16}$ **b.** $^+\frac{5}{6} - ^-\frac{1}{8}$ **c.** $^+3\frac{1}{2} - ^-1\frac{2}{3}$ **d.** $^+1\frac{11}{12} - ^-4\frac{3}{4}$

10. **a.** $^+.25 - ^-.2$ **b.** $^+8.9 - ^-.105$ **c.** $^+4 - ^-.04$ **d.** $^+.517 - ^-.25$

11. **a.** $^-\frac{4}{5} - ^+\frac{2}{3}$ **b.** $^-\frac{9}{16} - ^+\frac{7}{12}$ **c.** $^-8\frac{1}{6} - ^+7\frac{5}{8}$ **d.** $^-10\frac{1}{2} - ^+6\frac{29}{32}$

12. **a.** $^-.79 - ^+.157$ **b.** $^-9.584 - ^+1.269$ **c.** $^-9.47 - ^+.9$ **d.** $^-2.7 - ^+5$

13. **a.** $^-\frac{11}{12} - 0$ **b.** $^+4\frac{2}{3} - 0$ **c.** $^+2.8 - 0$ **d.** $^-.039 - 0$

14. **a.** $0 - ^-\frac{19}{25}$ **b.** $0 - ^+8\frac{15}{16}$ **c.** $0 - ^+.735$ **d.** $0 - ^-5.26$

15. **a.** $^-\frac{9}{11} - ^-\frac{9}{11}$ **b.** $^+5\frac{3}{4} - ^+5\frac{3}{4}$ **c.** $^-.6 - ^-.6$ **d.** $^+7.834 - ^+7.834$

16. **a.** $\frac{3}{8} - \frac{7}{8}$ **b.** $2\frac{13}{16} - 9$ **c.** $.56 - 1.3$ **d.** $.092 - .25$

17. **a.** $\left(^-\frac{1}{4} - ^-\frac{2}{3}\right) - ^-\frac{1}{6}$ **c.** $^-1\frac{1}{3} - \left(^-2\frac{2}{5} - ^+4\frac{3}{4}\right)$ **e.** $(^+.07 - ^-.4) - ^-.203$

    b. $^+6\frac{1}{2} - \left(^-3\frac{5}{8} - ^-4\frac{11}{16}\right)$ **d.** $(^-3.5 - ^+8.2) - ^+5.4$ **f.** $^+.632 - (^+.92 - ^+.2)$

18. Subtract in each of the following:

a.
$$^+\frac{5}{8} \quad ^-\frac{1}{2} \quad ^+\frac{3}{8} \quad ^-4\frac{3}{4} \quad ^-5 \quad ^+6\frac{5}{6} \quad 2\frac{3}{10}$$
$$^+\frac{1}{8} \quad ^-\frac{5}{6} \quad ^-\frac{1}{5} \quad ^+\frac{15}{16} \quad ^-1\frac{11}{12} \quad ^-3\frac{1}{4} \quad 8\frac{2}{3}$$

b.
$$6\frac{1}{3} \quad ^+5\frac{1}{3} \quad ^-1\frac{9}{16} \quad ^-6\frac{1}{2} \quad 3\frac{7}{8} \quad ^+6\frac{7}{12} \quad ^-10\frac{7}{32}$$
$$9\frac{2}{3} \quad ^-3\frac{2}{5} \quad ^-2\frac{5}{8} \quad ^+4\frac{5}{6} \quad 7\frac{11}{12} \quad ^-5\frac{13}{16} \quad ^-2\frac{3}{4}$$

c.
$$^-.8 \quad ^+1.6 \quad .035 \quad ^-7.495 \quad ^-10.27 \quad 2.87 \quad ^-.67$$
$$^-.9 \quad ^-.7 \quad .04 \quad ^+1.53 \quad ^-.8 \quad 5 \quad ^-.8924$$

19. Find the missing numbers:

a. $^+\frac{4}{5} - {}^+\frac{1}{5} = ?$

b. $^-\frac{11}{16} - {}^-\frac{13}{20} = n$

c. $^+1\frac{1}{2} - {}^+\frac{5}{6} = \square$

d. $^+2\frac{7}{8} - {}^-1 = n$

e. $^-6\frac{1}{3} - {}^-7\frac{5}{12} = n$

f. $^+4\frac{5}{8} - 9\frac{3}{16} = n$

20. Find the missing numbers:

a. $^+.6 - {}^-.1 = \square$

b. $^-8.7 - {}^-4.9 = n$

c. $^-8 - {}^+.07 = ?$

d. $.35 - .91 = n$

e. $^+5.07 - {}^-.829 = n$

f. $^-.8 - {}^-3.58 = n$

21. Find the missing numbers:

a. $? - {}^-\frac{5}{16} = {}^+\frac{13}{16}$

b. $n - {}^+\frac{5}{6} = {}^-\frac{1}{3}$

c. $\square - {}^-2\frac{1}{4} = {}^-6\frac{1}{2}$

d. $n - 5\frac{7}{12} = 3\frac{5}{6}$

e. $n - {}^-7\frac{5}{8} = 10$

f. $n - 1\frac{3}{4} = \frac{11}{16}$

22. Find the missing numbers:

a. $? - {}^-.4 = {}^+.7$

b. $n - {}^+1.6 = {}^-8$

c. $n - {}^-.59 = {}^-1.2$

d. $\square - {}^+6.3 = {}^-3.27$

e. $n - {}^-.225 = {}^-.001$

f. $n - 30.8 = 6.54$

23. Find the missing numbers:

a. $^+\frac{1}{12} - \square = {}^+\frac{7}{12}$

b. $^-\frac{9}{10} - n = {}^+\frac{2}{5}$

c. $^-8\frac{1}{2} - ? = {}^-4\frac{3}{8}$

d. $11 - n = {}^-\frac{5}{6}$

e. $^-3\frac{11}{16} - n = {}^-4\frac{2}{3}$

f. $^-9\frac{5}{12} - n = 5\frac{3}{4}$

24. Find the missing numbers:

a. $^-.7 - ? = 0$

b. $^+4.2 - n = {}^-3.1$

c. $.925 - \square = 7.6$

d. $^-.489 - n = {}^-5$

e. $^-16.2 - n = 6.8$

f. $.375 - n = .2635$

Properties

In the following exercises we determine the properties that hold for the rational numbers under the operation of subtraction.

1. Commutative Property

a. If the commutative property holds for the subtraction of rational numbers, what would have to be true?

b. In each of the following subtract as indicated, then compare answers:

(1) $^-\frac{2}{3} - {}^+\frac{1}{6}$; $^+\frac{1}{6} - {}^-\frac{2}{3}$. Does $^-\frac{2}{3} - {}^+\frac{1}{6} = {}^+\frac{1}{6} - {}^-\frac{2}{3}$?

(2) $^-1\frac{3}{8} - {}^-2\frac{1}{4}$; $^-2\frac{1}{4} - {}^-1\frac{3}{8}$. Does $^-1\frac{3}{8} - {}^-2\frac{1}{4} = {}^-2\frac{1}{4} - {}^-1\frac{3}{8}$?

(3) $^+6 - {}^+\frac{13}{16}$; $^+\frac{13}{16} - {}^+6$. Does $^+6 - {}^+\frac{13}{16} = {}^+\frac{13}{16} - {}^+6$?

(4) $^+8.7 - {}^-9.3$; $^-9.3 - {}^+8.7$. Does $^+8.7 - {}^-9.3 = {}^-9.3 - {}^+8.7$?

c. Does the commutative property hold for the subtraction of rational numbers?

Introduction to Algebra

2. Associative Property

   a. If the associative property holds for the subtraction of rational numbers, what would have to be true?

   b. In each of the following subtract as indicated, then compare answers:

   (1) $\left(^{+}\frac{4}{5} - ^{-}\frac{7}{10}\right) - ^{-}\frac{1}{2}$; $^{+}\frac{4}{5} - \left(^{-}\frac{7}{10} - ^{-}\frac{1}{2}\right)$.

   Does $\left(^{+}\frac{4}{5} - ^{-}\frac{7}{10}\right) - ^{-}\frac{1}{2} = ^{+}\frac{4}{5} - \left(^{-}\frac{7}{10} - ^{-}\frac{1}{2}\right)$?

   (2) $\left(^{-}2\frac{3}{4} - ^{-}1\frac{5}{8}\right) - ^{+}\frac{11}{12}$; $^{-}2\frac{3}{4} - \left(^{-}1\frac{5}{8} - ^{+}\frac{11}{12}\right)$.

   Does $\left(^{-}2\frac{3}{4} - ^{-}1\frac{5}{8}\right) - ^{+}\frac{11}{12} = ^{-}2\frac{3}{4} - \left(^{-}1\frac{5}{8} - ^{+}\frac{11}{12}\right)$?

   c. Does the associative property hold for the subtraction of rational numbers?

3. Closure

   a. What do we mean when we say that a certain group of numbers is closed under the operation of subtraction?

   b. When you subtract in each of the following, is the difference in each case a rational number?

   (1) $^{+}\frac{3}{4} - ^{-}\frac{5}{6}$ (4) $^{-}5\frac{3}{8} - 0$ (7) $^{+}1\frac{2}{5} - ^{+}3\frac{2}{3}$

   (2) $^{-}\frac{7}{12} - ^{+}1\frac{1}{4}$ (5) $^{-}.07 - ^{-}.003$ (8) $0 - ^{-}4\frac{3}{7}$

   (3) $^{-}3\frac{1}{2} - ^{-}5\frac{1}{3}$ (6) $^{+}8\frac{7}{16} - ^{-}8\frac{7}{16}$ (9) $^{-}3.8 - ^{+}.17$

   c. Can you find two rational numbers for which the difference is not a rational number?

   d. Can we say that the rational numbers are closed under the operation of subtraction?

10–15 MULTIPLICATION OF INTEGERS; PROPERTIES

To develop the procedure of determining the product of two positive integers (like $^{+}4 \times ^{+}5$), or of two negative integers (like $^{-}4 \times ^{-}5$), or of a positive integer and a negative integer (like $^{+}4 \times ^{-}5$), or of a negative integer and a positive integer (like $^{-}4 \times ^{+}5$), let us analyze the following:

Representing a bank deposit of $5 by $^{+}5$, a withdrawal of $5 by $^{-}5$, 4 weeks from now by $^{+}4$, and 4 weeks ago by $^{-}4$, let us find the answers to the following situations using signed numbers.

a. If we deposit in our bank account $5 each week for 4 weeks, how will our bank account 4 weeks from now compare with our present bank account?

There will be $20 more in the account 4 weeks from now. $^{+}4 \times {}^{+}5 = {}^{+}20$

b. If we deposited in our bank account $5 each week for the past 4 weeks, how did our bank account 4 weeks ago compare with our present bank account?

There was $20 less in the account 4 weeks ago. $^{-}4 \times {}^{+}5 = {}^{-}20$

c. If we withdraw from our bank account $5 each week for the next 4 weeks, how will our bank account 4 weeks from now compare with our present bank account?

There will be $20 less in the account 4 weeks from now. $^{+}4 \times {}^{-}5 = {}^{-}20$

d. If we withdrew from our bank account $5 each week for the past 4 weeks, how did our bank account 4 weeks ago compare with our present bank account?

There was $20 more in the account 4 weeks ago. $^{-}4 \times {}^{-}5 = {}^{+}20$

From the above it appears that the product of two positive integers is a positive integer, the product of two negative integers is a positive integer, and the product of a positive integer and a negative integer or a negative integer and a positive integer is a negative integer. Let us check this further.

Multiplication may be thought of as repeated addition. *Four times three,* expressed as 4×3, is the sum of four 3's: $(3 + 3 + 3 + 3)$ or 12. The expression four times three may be written as 4×3, $4 \cdot 3$, $(4) \times (3)$, $4(3)$, $(4)3$, or $(4)(3)$. Observe that the $\times$ symbol may be replaced by a raised dot or the factors may be written next to each other within parentheses without any multiplication symbol.

Since a numeral without a sign represents a positive number, 4 × 3 may be expressed as ⁺4 × ⁺3 or (⁺4)(⁺3).

Thus, 4 × 3 or ⁺4 × ⁺3 = ⁺3 + ⁺3 + ⁺3 + ⁺3 = ⁺12.

That is: ⁺4 × ⁺3 = ⁺12

This is illustrated on the number line as:

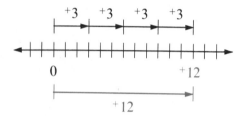

Thus, the product of two positive integers is a positive integer whose absolute value is the product of the absolute values of the two given factors.

The product of zero and any integer is zero.

$$^-3 \times 0 = 0 \qquad ^+8 \times 0 = 0$$
$$0 \times {}^+7 = 0 \qquad 0 \times {}^-2 = 0$$

The indicated product ⁺4 × ⁻3 means four ⁻3's, or the sum of ⁻3 + ⁻3 + ⁻3 + ⁻3, which is ⁻12.

That is: ⁺4 × ⁻3 = ⁻12

This is illustrated on the number line as:

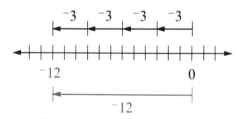

Let us examine the sequence at the right:

Observe that each time the second factor decreases by 1, the product decreases by 4.

Thus, the product ⁺4 × ⁻1 should be 4 less than 0, the product of ⁺4 × 0. This is ⁻4.

The product of ⁺4 × ⁻2 should be 4 less than ⁻4, the product of ⁺4 × ⁻1. This is ⁻8.

$$^+4 \times {}^+3 = {}^+12$$
$$^+4 \times {}^+2 = {}^+8$$
$$^+4 \times {}^+1 = {}^+4$$
$$^+4 \times 0 = 0$$
$$^+4 \times {}^-1 = {}^-4$$
$$^+4 \times {}^-2 = {}^-8$$
$$^+4 \times {}^-3 = {}^-12$$

The product of ⁺4 × ⁻3 should be 4 less than ⁻8, the product of ⁺4 × ⁻2. This is ⁻12.

Thus, ⁺4 × ⁻3 = ⁻12.

This also illustrates that ⁺4 × ⁻3 = ⁻12.

Thus, the product of a positive integer and a negative integer is a negative integer whose absolute value is the product of the absolute values of the two given factors.

Let us examine the sequence at the right:

Observe that each time the first factor decreases by 1, the product decreases by 3.

• Thus, the product of ⁻1 × ⁺3 should be 3 less than 0, the product of 0 × ⁺3. This is ⁻3.

The product of ⁻2 × ⁺3 should be 3 less than ⁻3, the product of ⁻1 × ⁺3. This is ⁻6.

The product of ⁻3 × ⁺3 should be 3 less than ⁻6, the product of ⁻2 × ⁺3. This is ⁻9.

$$
\begin{array}{rcl}
^{+}4 \times {}^{+}3 &=& {}^{+}12 \\
^{+}3 \times {}^{+}3 &=& {}^{+}9 \\
^{+}2 \times {}^{+}3 &=& {}^{+}6 \\
^{+}1 \times {}^{+}3 &=& {}^{+}3 \\
0 \times {}^{+}3 &=& 0 \\
^{-}1 \times {}^{+}3 &=& {}^{-}3 \\
^{-}2 \times {}^{+}3 &=& {}^{-}6 \\
^{-}3 \times {}^{+}3 &=& {}^{-}9 \\
^{-}4 \times {}^{+}3 &=& {}^{-}12 \\
\end{array}
$$

The product of ⁻4 × ⁺3 should be 3 less than ⁻9, the product of ⁻3 × ⁺3. This is ⁻12.

Thus, ⁻4 × ⁺3 = ⁻12.

This illustrates that ⁻4 × ⁺3 = ⁻12.

Thus, the product of a negative integer and a positive integer is a negative integer whose absolute value is the product of the absolute values of the two given factors.

Let us examine the sequence at the right:

Observe that each time the second factor decreases by 1, the product increases by 4.

Thus, the product of ⁻4 × ⁻1 should be 4 more than 0, the product ⁻4 × 0. This is ⁺4.

The product of ⁻4 × ⁻2 should be 4 more than ⁺4, the product of ⁻4 × ⁻1. This is ⁺8.

$$
\begin{array}{rcl}
^{-}4 \times {}^{+}3 &=& {}^{-}12 \\
^{-}4 \times {}^{+}2 &=& {}^{-}8 \\
^{-}4 \times {}^{+}1 &=& {}^{-}4 \\
^{-}4 \times 0 &=& 0 \\
^{-}4 \times {}^{-}1 &=& {}^{+}4 \\
^{-}4 \times {}^{-}2 &=& {}^{+}8 \\
^{-}4 \times {}^{-}3 &=& {}^{+}12 \\
\end{array}
$$

The product ⁻4 × ⁻3 should be 4 more than ⁺8, the product of ⁻4 × ⁻2. This is ⁺12.

Thus, ⁻4 × ⁻3 = ⁺12.

This illustrates that ⁻4 × ⁻3 = ⁺12.

Introduction to Algebra

Thus, the product of two negative integers is a positive integer whose absolute value is the product of the absolute values of the two given factors.

Summarizing, *to multiply two positive integers* or *two negative integers,* we find the product of their absolute values and prefix the numeral for this product with a positive sign.

Multiply: $^+7 \times {}^+6 = ?$ Multiply: $^-4 \times {}^-9 = ?$

$^+7 \times {}^+6 = {}^+(7 \times 6) = {}^+42$ $^-4 \times {}^-9 = {}^+(4 \times 9) = {}^+36$

$$
\begin{array}{r} ^+7 \\ \text{or} \quad \underline{^+6} \\ ^+42 \end{array}
\qquad\qquad
\begin{array}{r} ^-4 \\ \text{or} \quad \underline{^-9} \\ ^+36 \end{array}
$$

Answer, $^+42$ Answer, $^+36$

To multiply a positive integer by a negative integer or *a negative integer by a positive integer,* we find the product of their absolute values and prefix the numeral for this product with a negative sign.

Multiply: $^+8 \times {}^-3 = ?$ Multiply: $^-5 \times {}^+7 = ?$

$^+8 \times {}^-3 = {}^-(8 \times 3) = {}^-24$ $^-5 \times {}^+7 = {}^-(5 \times 7) = {}^-35$

$$
\begin{array}{r} ^+8 \\ \text{or} \quad \underline{^-3} \\ ^-24 \end{array}
\qquad\qquad
\begin{array}{r} ^-5 \\ \text{or} \quad \underline{^+7} \\ ^-35 \end{array}
$$

Answer, $^-24$ Answer, $^-35$

The numeral naming a positive integer does not require the positive ($^+$) sign.

$^-8 \times 7 = {}^-56$ Answer, $^-56$

The product of zero and any integer is zero.

$0 \times {}^-4 = 0$ Answer, 0

$^+6 \times 0 = 0$ Answer, 0

To multiply three or more factors, we multiply successively. Observe that an odd number of negative factors produces a negative number as the product, while an even number of negative factors produces a positive number as the product, provided zero is not a factor. In each case the absolute value of the product is equal to the product of the absolute values of the given factors.

Multiply:

$$(^-2)(^+4)(^-1)(^-6) = {^-48}$$

Answer, $^-48$

Multiply:

$$(^-1)(^-3)(^-2)(^-4) = {^+24}$$

Answer, $^+24$

EXERCISES

Multiply as indicated:

1. a. $^+9 \times {^+7}$	**b.** $^+5 \times {^+11}$	**c.** $^+3 \times {^+25}$	**d.** $^+42 \times {^+58}$
2. a. $^-8 \times {^-6}$	**b.** $^-2 \times {^-16}$	**c.** $^-30 \times {^-14}$	**d.** $^-1 \times {^-125}$
3. a. $^+4 \times {^-9}$	**b.** $^+15 \times {^-6}$	**c.** $^+27 \times {^-100}$	**d.** $^+64 \times {^-75}$
4. a. $^-7 \times {^+8}$	**b.** $^-4 \times {^+17}$	**c.** $^-10 \times {^+36}$	**d.** $^-53 \times {^+29}$
5. a. $^-6 \times 6$	**b.** $^-12 \times 5$	**c.** $8 \times {^-47}$	**d.** $34 \times {^-18}$
6. a. $0 \times {^-19}$	**b.** $^+28 \times 0$	**c.** $^-16 \times 0$	**d.** $0 \times {^+41}$

7. a. $(^-1)(^-2)$	**f.** $(^-4)(^-5)$	**k.** $(^-13)(^-13)$	**p.** $^-7(^-4)$
b. $(^-9)(^+5)$	**g.** $(0)(^-1)$	**l.** $(^-45)(20)$	**q.** $^-9(10)$
c. $(^+11)(^-4)$	**h.** $(^-14)(3)$	**m.** $(106)(^-51)$	**r.** $8(^-5)$
d. $(^-3)(^-10)$	**i.** $(^-6)(^-12)$	**n.** $(^-59)(^-200)$	**s.** $12(^-6)$
e. $(^+8)(^+8)$	**j.** $(8)(^-7)$	**o.** $(^-325)(^-198)$	**t.** $^-16(^-12)$

8. Multiply in each of the following:

$^-4$	$^+8$	$^-9$	$^+6$	$^-14$	$^+11$	$^-1$	$^-25$
$^-3$	$^-5$	$^+9$	$^+7$	$^-6$	$^-8$	$^-4$	$^+2$

$^+7$	$^-19$	0	$^-45$	18	$^-67$	$^-29$	$^-100$
$^-12$	$^-9$	$^-23$	$^+1$	$^-6$	34	$^-48$	$^-100$

9. a. $(^-4 \times {^-6}) \times {^+2}$	**c.** $^+7 \times (^-2 \times {^+5})$	**e.** $(^-4 \times {^-4}) \times {^-4}$
b. $(^+8 \times {^-3}) \times {^-1}$	**d.** $^-3 \times (^-9 \times {^-2})$	**f.** $^+8 \times (^-5 \times {^-3})$

10. a. $^+5 \times {^-8} \times {^+3}$	**c.** $^-10 \times {^-10} \times {^-10}$	**e.** $^-3 \times {^+6} \times {^-1} \times {^-2}$
b. $^+7 \times {^-4} \times {^-5}$	**d.** $^-15 \times {^+4} \times {^-1}$	**f.** $^-2 \times {^-2} \times {^-2} \times {^-2}$

11. a. $(^-2)(3)(^-1)$	**c.** $(5)(2)(^-3)(4)$	**e.** $(4)(^-3)(2)(^-1)(5)$
b. $(^-1)(^-1)(^-1)$	**d.** $(^-3)(6)(^-4)(^-2)$	**f.** $(^-2)(^-3)(^-1)(^-3)(^-4)$

12. Find the missing numbers:

a. $^-9 \times {}^-6 = ?$ **d.** $6 \times {}^-10 = \square$ **g.** $20 \times {}^-1 = n$
b. $7 \times {}^-3 = \square$ **e.** $^-15 \times {}^-7 = ?$ **h.** $^-36 \times 8 = n$
c. $^-8 \times 4 = n$ **f.** $^-12 \times 9 = n$ **i.** $^-3 \times {}^-32 = n$

13. Find the missing numbers:

a. $3 \times ? = {}^-12$ **d.** $^-1 \times \square = 16$ **g.** $^-20 \times n = {}^-100$
b. $5 \times n = {}^-30$ **e.** $9 \times ? = {}^-63$ **h.** $7 \times n = 42$
c. $^-12 \times \square = {}^-72$ **f.** $^-8 \times n = 0$ **i.** $^-2 \times n = 34$

14. Find the missing numbers:

a. $? \times 4 = {}^-20$ **d.** $\square \times {}^-8 = 64$ **g.** $n \times {}^-7 = 56$
b. $\square \times {}^-3 = 30$ **e.** $n \times {}^-5 = {}^-45$ **h.** $n \times 2 = {}^-66$
c. $n \times {}^-6 = {}^-48$ **f.** $? \times 12 = 72$ **i.** $n \times {}^-25 = {}^-200$

Properties

In the following exercises we determine the properties that hold for the integers under the operation of multiplication.

1. Commutative Property

 a. What do we mean when we say that the commutative property holds for the multiplication of a certain group of numbers?

 b. In each of the following multiply as indicated, then compare the products:

  (1) $^+7 \times {}^+5$; $^+5 \times {}^+7$. Does $^+7 \times {}^+5 = {}^+5 \times {}^+7$?
  (2) $^-6 \times {}^-8$; $^-8 \times {}^-6$. Does $^-6 \times {}^-8 = {}^-8 \times {}^-6$?
  (3) $^+12 \times {}^-3$; $^-3 \times {}^+12$. Does $^+12 \times {}^-3 = {}^-3 \times {}^+12$?
  (4) $^-9 \times {}^+9$; $^+9 \times {}^-9$. Does $^-9 \times {}^+9 = {}^+9 \times {}^-9$?

 c. Can you find two integers for which the commutative property of multiplication does not hold?

 d. Can we say that the commutative property holds for the multiplication of integers?

2. Associative Property

 a. What do we mean when we say that the associative property holds for the multiplication of a certain group of numbers?

 b. In each of the following multiply as indicated, then compare the products:

  (1) $(^+8 \times {}^-2) \times {}^-3$; $^+8 \times (^-2 \times {}^-3)$.
   Does $(^+8 \times {}^-2) \times {}^-3 = {}^+8 \times {}^-2 \times {}^-3$?

(2) $(^-5 \times {}^-9) \times {}^+7$; $^-5 \times (^-9 \times {}^+7)$.
     Does $(^-5 \times {}^-9) \times {}^+7 = {}^-5 \times (^-9 \times {}^+7)$?

  c. Can you find three integers for which the associative property of multiplication does not hold?

  d. Can we say that the associative property holds for the multiplication of integers?

3. Distributive Property

  a. What do we mean when we say that the distributive property of multiplication over addition holds for the integers?

  b. In each of the following perform the indicated operations, then compare answers:

    (1) $^+6 \times (^-7 + {}^+5)$; $(^+6 \times {}^-7) + (^+6 \times {}^+5)$.
       Does $^+6 \times (^-7 + {}^+5) = (^+6 \times {}^-7) + (^+6 \times {}^+5)$?
    (2) $^-3 \times (^+8 + {}^-9)$; $(^-3 \times {}^+8) + (^-3 \times {}^-9)$.
       Does $^-3 \times (^+8 + {}^-9) = (^-3 \times {}^+8) + (^-3 \times {}^-9)$?

  c. Can you find any integers for which multiplication is not distributed over addition?

  d. Can we say that the distributive property of multiplication over addition holds for the integers?

4. Closure

  a. What do we mean when we say that a certain group of numbers is closed under the operation of multiplication?

  b. Is the product of each of the following an integer?

(1) $^-4 \times {}^+2$	(4) $^+6 \times {}^+12$	(7) $0 \times {}^+3$
(2) $^+10 \times {}^-9$	(5) $^-7 \times 0$	(8) $^-11 \times {}^-11$
(3) $^-8 \times {}^-8$	(6) $^-1 \times {}^-15$	(9) $^-24 \times {}^+1$

  c. Can you find two integers for which the product is not an integer?

  d. Is the product of two integers always an integer?

  e. Can we say that the integers are closed under the operation of multiplication?

5. Multiplicative Identity

  a. What do we mean when we say that a certain group of numbers has a multiplicative identity?

  b. What is the product of each of the following?

(1) $^-9 \times 1$	(3) $^+13 \times 1$	(5) $^-1 \times 1$	(7) $1 \times {}^+35$
(2) $1 \times {}^+7$	(4) $1 \times {}^-20$	(6) 1×0	(8) $^-100 \times 1$

c. In each case in problem **5b** is the product of the integer and one (1) the integer itself?

d. Can you find any integer which when multiplied by one (1) does not have the given integer as the product?

e. Do the integers have a multiplicative identity? If so, what is it?

10–16 MULTIPLICATION OF RATIONAL NUMBERS; PROPERTIES

We follow the same procedures to multiply rational numbers as we do to multiply integers. See section 10–15. To review the multiplication of the rational numbers of arithmetic (common fractions, mixed numbers, and decimal fractions) see sections 4–13 and 5–9.

To multiply two positive rational numbers or *two negative rational numbers,* we find the product of their absolute values and prefix the numeral for this product with a positive sign.

Multiply: $^+\frac{1}{3} \times \ ^+\frac{5}{8} = ?$

$^+\frac{1}{3} \times \ ^+\frac{5}{8} = \ ^+\left(\frac{1}{3} \times \frac{5}{8}\right) = \ ^+\frac{5}{24}$ $\qquad$ *Answer,* $^+\frac{5}{24}$

Multiply: $^-\frac{3}{4} \times \ ^-1\frac{1}{2} = ?$

$^-\frac{3}{4} \times \ ^-1\frac{1}{2} = \ ^+\left(\frac{3}{4} \times 1\frac{1}{2}\right) = \ ^+\left(\frac{3}{4} \times \frac{3}{2}\right) = \ ^+\frac{9}{8} = \ ^+1\frac{1}{8}$

$\qquad\qquad\qquad\qquad\qquad\qquad\qquad\qquad$ *Answer,* $^+1\frac{1}{8}$

To multiply a positive rational number by a negative rational number or *a negative rational number by a positive rational number,* we find the product of their absolute values and prefix the numeral for this product with a negative sign. The numeral naming a positive rational number does not require the positive ($^+$) sign.

Multiply: $^+2\frac{2}{3} \times \ ^-1\frac{1}{5} = ?$

$^+2\frac{2}{3} \times \ ^-1\frac{1}{5} = \ ^-\left(2\frac{2}{3} \times 1\frac{1}{5}\right) = \ ^-\left(\frac{8}{3} \times \frac{6}{5}\right) = \ ^-\frac{48}{15} = \ ^-3\frac{1}{5}$

$\qquad\qquad\qquad\qquad\qquad\qquad\qquad\qquad$ *Answer,* $^-3\frac{1}{5}$

Multiply: $^-1.2 \times \ ^+.7 = ?$

$^-1.2 \times \ ^+.7 = \ ^-(1.2 \times .7) = \ ^-.84$ $\qquad\qquad$ *Answer,* $^-.84$

The product of zero and any rational number is zero.

$$0 \times {}^-2\tfrac{7}{8} = 0 \qquad Answer,\ 0$$
$$ {}^+3.095 \times 0 = 0 \qquad Answer,\ 0$$

To multiply three or more factors, we multiply successively. The absolute value of the product is equal to the product of the absolute values of the given factors. An odd number of negative factors produces a negative number as the product, while an even number of negative factors produces a positive number as the product, provided zero is not a factor.

$$({}^-.6)({}^-9)({}^-.02) = {}^-.108 \qquad Answer,\ .108$$
$$\left({}^{-}\tfrac{2}{3}\right)\left({}^{+}\tfrac{1}{2}\right)\left({}^{-}\tfrac{3}{4}\right) = {}^{+}\tfrac{1}{4} \qquad Answer,\ {}^{+}\tfrac{1}{4}$$

EXERCISES

Multiply as indicated:

1. a. ${}^{+}\tfrac{1}{2} \times {}^{+}\tfrac{3}{8}$ b. ${}^{+}\tfrac{3}{4} \times {}^{+}16$ c. ${}^{+}\tfrac{5}{6} \times {}^{+}2\tfrac{1}{10}$ d. ${}^{+}4\tfrac{1}{2} \times {}^{+}1\tfrac{5}{12}$

2. a. ${}^{+}.9 \times {}^{+}.4$ b. ${}^{+}67 \times {}^{+}.03$ c. ${}^{+}1.4 \times {}^{+}2.5$ d. ${}^{+}.375 \times {}^{+}.48$

3. a. ${}^{-}\tfrac{5}{8} \times {}^{+}\tfrac{16}{25}$ b. ${}^{-}5 \times {}^{-}\tfrac{7}{10}$ c. ${}^{-}\tfrac{9}{16} \times {}^{-}1\tfrac{1}{6}$ d. ${}^{-}3\tfrac{3}{4} \times {}^{-}2\tfrac{2}{3}$

4. a. ${}^{-}.02 \times {}^{-}.3$ b. ${}^{-}.4 \times {}^{-}50$ c. ${}^{-}.68 \times {}^{-}8.1$ d. ${}^{-}.001 \times {}^{-}.001$

5. a. ${}^{+}\tfrac{2}{3} \times {}^{-}\tfrac{1}{2}$ b. ${}^{+}24 \times {}^{-}3\tfrac{1}{8}$ c. ${}^{+}6\tfrac{2}{3} \times {}^{-}\tfrac{11}{12}$ d. ${}^{+}3\tfrac{1}{7} \times {}^{-}5\tfrac{5}{6}$

6. a. ${}^{+}.125 \times {}^{-}.8$ b. ${}^{+}100 \times {}^{-}.002$ c. ${}^{+}.01 \times {}^{-}.005$ d. ${}^{+}6.2 \times {}^{-}83.6$

7. a. ${}^{-}\tfrac{9}{10} \times {}^{+}\tfrac{15}{16}$ b. ${}^{-}5\tfrac{1}{4} \times {}^{+}2$ c. ${}^{-}2\tfrac{3}{16} \times {}^{+}\tfrac{4}{7}$ d. ${}^{-}5\tfrac{1}{3} \times {}^{+}2\tfrac{1}{4}$

8. a. ${}^{-}.009 \times {}^{+}.003$ b. ${}^{-}24 \times {}^{+}8.5$ c. ${}^{-}3.27 \times {}^{+}.42$ d. ${}^{-}1.05 \times {}^{+}.0015$

9. a. $8 \times {}^{-}\tfrac{11}{16}$ b. $1\tfrac{2}{3} \times {}^{-}30$ c. ${}^{-}.7 \times 5.6$ d. $.04 \times {}^{-}.928$

10. a. $0 \times {}^{-}\tfrac{7}{8}$ b. ${}^{+}6\tfrac{3}{5} \times 0$ c. ${}^{-}.63 \times 0$ d. $0 \times {}^{-}8.25$

11. a. $\left(\tfrac{-1}{2}\right)\left(\tfrac{-1}{2}\right)$ f. $\left(\tfrac{-1}{2}\right)\left(-2\tfrac{1}{3}\right)$ k. $({}^-.3)({}^-.3)$ p. $\tfrac{1}{2}\left(-4\tfrac{1}{4}\right)$

    b. $\left(\tfrac{-2}{3}\right)\left(\tfrac{3}{4}\right)$ g. $(36)\left(-3\tfrac{5}{6}\right)$ l. $(.8)({}^-.14)$ q. $\tfrac{-3}{8}(70)$

    c. $\left(\tfrac{1}{4}\right)\left(\tfrac{-7}{8}\right)$ h. $\left(\tfrac{7}{10}\right)\left(-6\tfrac{1}{4}\right)$ m. $({}^-4.2)(.57)$ r. $\tfrac{-2}{3}\left(-7\tfrac{2}{5}\right)$

    d. $(24)\left(\tfrac{-15}{16}\right)$ i. $\left(-1\tfrac{9}{16}\right)\left(-4\tfrac{2}{3}\right)$ n. $({}^-.009)({}^-.06)$ s. ${}^-.9(8.35)$

    e. $\left(\tfrac{-11}{12}\right)({}^-60)$ j. $\left(-3\tfrac{1}{8}\right)\left(1\tfrac{3}{5}\right)$ o. $(2.5)({}^-.309)$ t. $3.4({}^-.001)$

12. Multiply in each of the following:

$^-.02$	$^-57$	0.3	$^-.006$	$^-200$	$^-1.1$	$^-.3197$
$^-.2$	$.09$	$^-.47$	$^-.001$	$.005$	$^-.11$	2.5

13. a. $\left(\frac{+5}{6} \times \frac{-1}{4}\right) \times \frac{+2}{5}$ **c.** $\left(^-1\frac{1}{8} \times ^-3\frac{1}{3}\right) \times ^-2\frac{1}{2}$ **e.** $(^-.8 \times ^+.12) \times ^-.05$

    b. $\frac{+3}{10} \times \left(\frac{-5}{8} \times \frac{+2}{3}\right)$ **d.** $^-2\frac{4}{7} \times \left(^+7\frac{5}{16} \times ^-2\frac{2}{3}\right)$ **f.** $^-3.6 \times (^-.25 \times ^-7.4)$

14. a. $\frac{-1}{3} \times \frac{1}{2} \times \frac{-1}{4}$ **c.** $^-4\frac{1}{5} \times \frac{-5}{8} \times 3\frac{1}{7}$ **e.** $.08 \times ^-4.3 \times .5$

    b. $\frac{-5}{6} \times \frac{-3}{8} \times \frac{-4}{5}$ **d.** $^-6\frac{2}{3} \times ^-2\frac{1}{2} \times ^-1\frac{4}{5}$ **f.** $^-1.25 \times ^-.004 \times ^-.039$

15. a. $\left(\frac{3}{10}\right)\left(\frac{-1}{2}\right)\left(\frac{5}{6}\right)$ **c.** $\left(^-1\frac{3}{5}\right)(10)\left(\frac{-15}{16}\right)$ **e.** $(^-.5)(^-.1)(^-.2)$

    b. $\left(\frac{-3}{8}\right)\left(\frac{-3}{4}\right)\left(\frac{-2}{3}\right)$ **d.** $\left(^-2\frac{1}{4}\right)\left(\frac{-5}{6}\right)\left(3\frac{1}{3}\right)(^-36)$ **f.** $(^-1.4)(^-.32)(^-.25)(^-.008)$

16. Find the missing numbers:

    a. $\frac{-3}{4} \times \frac{-3}{4} = ?$ **c.** $\frac{-7}{12} \times ^-90 = \square$ **e.** $^-4\frac{7}{8} \times ^-2\frac{1}{2} = n$

    b. $\frac{5}{8} \times \frac{-2}{3} = n$ **d.** $^-3\frac{1}{8} \times 1\frac{3}{5} = n$ **f.** $20 \times ^-8\frac{1}{6} = n$

17. Find the missing numbers:

    a. $.1 \times ^+.02 = \square$ **c.** $^-.15 \times 40 = ?$ **e.** $^-.0062 \times ^-.05 = n$

    b. $^-.006 \times ^-.006 = n$ **d.** $3.75 \times ^-.132 = n$ **f.** $^-.0015 \times 2.8 = n$

Properties

In the following exercises we determine the properties that hold for the rational numbers under the operation of multiplication.

1. Commutative Property

    a. What do we mean when we say that the commutative property holds for the multiplication of a certain group of numbers?

    b. In each of the following multiply as indicated, then compare the products:

        (1) $\frac{-3}{8} \times \frac{-4}{5}$; $\frac{-4}{5} \times \frac{-3}{8}$. Does $\frac{-3}{8} \times \frac{-4}{5} = \frac{-4}{5} \times \frac{-3}{8}$?

        (2) $^-2\frac{1}{2} \times ^+16$; $^+16 \times ^-2\frac{1}{2}$. Does $^-2\frac{1}{2} \times ^+16 = ^+16 \times ^-2\frac{1}{2}$?

        (3) $^+3\frac{5}{8} \times ^+1\frac{1}{3}$; $^+1\frac{1}{3} \times ^+3\frac{5}{8}$. Does $^+3\frac{5}{8} \times ^+1\frac{1}{3} = ^+1\frac{1}{3} \times ^+3\frac{5}{8}$?

        (4) $^+8.7 \times ^-.04$; $^-.04 \times ^+8.7$.

           Does $^+8.7 \times ^-.04 = ^-.04 \times ^+8.7$?

    c. Can you find two rational numbers for which the commutative property of multiplication does not hold?

    d. Can we say that the commutative property holds for the multiplication of rational numbers?

2. Associative Property

    a. What do we mean when we say that the associative property holds for the multiplication of a certain group of numbers?

    b. In each of the following multiply as indicated, then compare the products:

        (1) $\left(\frac{-3}{5} \times \frac{-2}{3}\right) \times \frac{+5}{6}$; $\frac{-3}{5} \times \left(\frac{-2}{3} \times \frac{+5}{6}\right)$.

            Does $\left(\frac{-3}{5} \times \frac{-2}{3}\right) \times \frac{+5}{6} = \frac{+3}{5} \times \left(\frac{-2}{3} \times \frac{+5}{6}\right)$?

        (2) $\left(^{+}2\frac{1}{4} \times ^{+}1\frac{3}{5}\right) \times ^{-}4\frac{1}{2}$; $^{+}2\frac{1}{4} \times \left(^{+}1\frac{3}{5} \times ^{-}4\frac{1}{2}\right)$.

            Does $\left(^{+}2\frac{1}{4} \times ^{+}1\frac{3}{5}\right) \times ^{-}4\frac{1}{2} = ^{+}2\frac{1}{4} \times \left(^{+}1\frac{3}{5} \times ^{-}4\frac{1}{2}\right)$?

    c. Can you find three rational numbers for which the associative property of multiplication does not hold?

    d. Can we say that the associative property holds for the multiplication of rational numbers?

3. Distributive Property

    a. What do we mean when we say that the distributive property of multiplication over addition holds for the rational numbers?

    b. In each of the following perform the indicated operations, then compare answers:

        (1) $\frac{-1}{2} \times \left(\frac{+7}{8} + \frac{-1}{4}\right)$; $\left(\frac{-1}{2} \times \frac{+7}{8}\right) + \left(\frac{-1}{2} \times \frac{-1}{4}\right)$.

            Does $\frac{-1}{2} \times \left(\frac{+7}{8} + \frac{-1}{4}\right) =$

            $\left(\frac{-1}{2} \times \frac{+7}{8}\right) + \left(\frac{-1}{2} \times \frac{-1}{4}\right)$?

        (2) $^{+}3\frac{1}{3} \times \left(^{-}1\frac{1}{2} + ^{+}1\frac{1}{5}\right)$; $\left(^{+}3\frac{1}{3} \times ^{-}1\frac{1}{2}\right) + \left(^{+}3\frac{1}{3} \times ^{+}1\frac{1}{5}\right)$.

            Does $^{+}3\frac{1}{3} \times \left(^{-}1\frac{1}{2} + ^{+}1\frac{1}{5}\right) =$

            $\left(^{+}3\frac{1}{3} \times ^{-}1\frac{1}{2}\right) + \left(^{+}3\frac{1}{3} \times ^{+}1\frac{1}{5}\right)$?

    c. Can you find any rational numbers for which multiplication is not distributed over addition?

    d. Can we say that the distributive property of multiplication over addition holds for the rational numbers?

4. Closure

    a. What do we mean when we say that a certain group of numbers is closed under the operation of multiplication?

    b. Is the product of each of the following a rational number?

        (1) $^{+}\frac{7}{8} \times ^{+}\frac{3}{4}$ (4) $^{-}\frac{5}{12} \times ^{-}48$ (7) $^{+}0.6 \times ^{-}5.8$

        (2) $^{+}1\frac{1}{2} \times ^{-}\frac{5}{6}$ (5) $^{-}1 \times ^{+}7\frac{1}{3}$ (8) $^{-}1.75 \times ^{-}3.04$

        (3) $^{-}4\frac{2}{3} \times ^{+}3\frac{1}{7}$ (6) $0 \times ^{-}5\frac{11}{16}$ (9) $^{-}7.3 \times ^{+}.001$

c. Can you find two rational numbers for which the product is not a rational number?

d. Is the product of two rational numbers always a rational number?

e. Can we say that the rational numbers are closed under the operation of multiplication?

5. Multiplicative Identity

    a. What do we mean when we say that a certain group of numbers has a multiplicative identity?

    b. What is the product of each of the following?

        (1) $1 \times {}^+\frac{5}{6}$ (3) $1 \times {}^-2\frac{1}{8}$ (5) ${}^-7\frac{3}{4} \times 1$ (7) $1 \times {}^-3.69$

        (2) ${}^-\frac{11}{12} \times 1$ (4) ${}^+6\frac{2}{5} \times 1$ (6) $1 \times {}^+5\frac{2}{3}$ (8) ${}^+10.5 \times 1$

    c. In each case in problem **5b**, is the product of the rational number and one (1) the rational number itself?

    d. Can you find any rational number which when multiplied by one (1) does not have the given rational number as the product?

    e. Do the rational numbers have a multiplicative identity? If so, what is it?

6. Multiplicative Inverse

    a. What do we mean by a multiplicative inverse of a rational number?

    b. What is the multiplicative inverse of:

        ${}^-9$? ${}^+\frac{1}{10}$? ${}^-\frac{5}{8}$? ${}^+\frac{11}{3}$? ${}^-1\frac{3}{4}$?

    c. Is each of the following given indicated products a product of a rational number and its multiplicative inverse? Multiply each of the following:

        (1) ${}^+\frac{2}{3} \times {}^+\frac{3}{2}$ (4) ${}^+\frac{5}{4} \times {}^+\frac{4}{5}$ (7) ${}^+12 \times {}^+\frac{1}{12}$

        (2) ${}^-\frac{1}{6} \times {}^-6$ (5) ${}^+1\frac{1}{6} \times {}^+\frac{6}{7}$ (8) ${}^-\frac{3}{8} \times {}^-2\frac{2}{3}$

        (3) ${}^-\frac{5}{16} \times {}^-\frac{16}{5}$ (6) ${}^-2\frac{1}{4} \times {}^-\frac{4}{9}$

    d. In each case is the product of the two non-zero rational numbers one (1)?

    e. Can you find any non-zero rational number that does not have a multiplicative inverse?

    f. Does each non-zero rational number have a multiplicative inverse?

10–17 DIVISION OF INTEGERS; PROPERTIES

Since division is the inverse operation of multiplication, to divide we find the factor (quotient) which multiplied by the given factor (divisor) will equal the given product (dividend).

> To divide $^+20$ by $^+5$ means to find the number which multiplied by $^+5$ will equal $^+20$.
> That is: $^+20 \div {}^+5 = ?$ becomes $^+5 \times ? = {}^+20$.
>   Since $^+5 \times {}^+4 = {}^+20$,
>   then $^+20 \div {}^+5 = {}^+4$.
>
> $^+20 \div {}^+5 = {}^+4$ is also written as $\dfrac{^+20}{^+5} = 4$

Thus, the quotient of a positive integer divided by a positive integer is a positive number whose absolute value is the quotient of the absolute values of the two given integers.

> To divide $^-20$ by $^-5$ means to find the number which multiplied by $^-5$ will equal $^-20$.
> That is: $^-20 \div {}^-5 = ?$ becomes $^-5 \times ? = {}^-20$.
>   Since $^-5 \times {}^+4 = {}^-20$,
>   then $^-20 \div {}^-5 = {}^+4$.
>
> $^-20 \div {}^-5 = {}^+4$ is also written as $\dfrac{^-20}{^-5} = {}^+4$

Thus, the quotient of a negative integer divided by a negative integer is a positive number whose absolute value is the quotient of the absolute values of the two given integers.

> To divide $^-20$ by $^+5$ means to find the number which multiplied by $^+5$ will equal $^-20$.
> That is: $^-20 \div {}^+5 = ?$ becomes $^+5 \times ? = {}^-20$.
>   Since $^+5 \times {}^-4 = {}^-20$,
>   then $^-20 \div {}^+5 = {}^-4$.
>
> $^-20 \div {}^+5 = {}^-4$ is also written as $\dfrac{^-20}{^+5} = {}^-4$

Thus, the quotient of a negative integer divided by a positive integer is a negative number whose absolute value is the quotient of the absolute values of the two given integers.

To divide $^+20$ by $^-5$ means to find the number which multiplied by $^-5$ will equal $^+20$.

That is $^+20 \div {}^-5 = ?$ becomes $^-5 \times ? = {}^+20$.

Since $^-5 \times {}^-4 = {}^+20$,

then $^+20 \div {}^-5 = {}^-4$.

$^+20 \div {}^-5 = {}^-4$ is also written as $\dfrac{20}{-5} = {}^-4$

Thus, the quotient of a positive integer divided by a negative integer is a negative number whose absolute value is the quotient of the absolute values of the two given integers.

Summarizing, *to divide a positive integer by a positive integer or a negative integer by a negative integer,* we divide their absolute values and prefix the numeral for this quotient with a positive sign.

Divide: $^+36 \div {}^+3 = ?$ Divide: $^-45 \div {}^-5 = ?$

$^+36 \div {}^+3 = {}^+(36 \div 3) = {}^+12$ $^-45 \div {}^-5 = {}^+(45 \div 5) = {}^+9$

or $\dfrac{^+36}{^+3} = {}^+12$ or $\dfrac{^-45}{^-5} = {}^+9$

Answer, $^+12$ *Answer,* $^+9$

To divide a positive integer by a negative integer or *a negative integer by a positive integer,* we divide their absolute values and prefix the numeral for this quotient with a negative sign.

Divide: $^-30 \div {}^+6 = ?$ Divide: $^+24 \div {}^-3 = ?$

$^-30 \div {}^+6 = {}^-(30 \div 6) = {}^-5$ $^+24 \div {}^-3 = {}^-(24 \div 3) = {}^-8$

or $\dfrac{^-30}{^+6} = {}^-5$ or $\dfrac{^+24}{^-3} = {}^-8$

Answer, $^-5$ *Answer,* $^-8$

Any non-zero integer divided by itself is one.

Divide: $^-2 \div ^-2 = ?$

$^-2 \div ^-2 = {}^+(2 \div 2) = {}^+1$ or $\dfrac{^-2}{^-2} = {}^+1$

Answer, $^+1$

Zero divided either by a positive integer or by a negative integer is zero. We cannot divide a positive integer or a negative integer by zero.

$0 \div {}^+8 = 0$ $\qquad\qquad \dfrac{0}{^-3} = 0$

Answer, 0 $\qquad\qquad$ *Answer,* 0

The numeral naming a positive number does not require the positive ($^+$) sign.

$^-16 \div 8 = {}^-2$ $\qquad$ or $\qquad \dfrac{^-16}{8} = {}^-2$

Answer, $^-2$

Sometimes when an integer is divided by a non-zero integer, the quotient is not an integer but a rational number.

Divide: $9 \div {}^-2 = ?$

$9 \div {}^-2 = {}^-(9 \div 2) = \dfrac{^-9}{2} = {}^-4\frac{1}{2}$

Answer, $^-4\frac{1}{2}$

Divide: $^-8 \div {}^-12 = ?$

$^-8 \div {}^-12 = {}^+(8 \div 12) = \dfrac{^+8}{12} = \dfrac{^+2}{3}$

Answer, $^+\frac{2}{3}$

Introduction to Algebra

Divide as indicated:

1. **a.** $^{+}16 \div {}^{+}2$ **b.** $^{+}55 \div {}^{+}5$ **c.** $^{+}36 \div {}^{+}4$ **d.** $^{+}100 \div {}^{+}20$
2. **a.** $^{-}32 \div {}^{-}8$ **b.** $^{-}90 \div {}^{-}10$ **c.** $^{-}27 \div {}^{-}9$ **d.** $^{-}84 \div {}^{-}6$
3. **a.** $^{-}42 \div {}^{+}7$ **b.** $^{-}56 \div {}^{+}4$ **c.** $^{-}144 \div {}^{+}12$ **d.** $^{-}72 \div {}^{+}18$
4. **a.** $^{+}35 \div {}^{-}5$ **b.** $^{+}64 \div {}^{-}8$ **c.** $^{+}19 \div {}^{-}1$ **d.** $^{+}150 \div {}^{-}25$
5. **a.** $0 \div {}^{-}3$ **b.** $0 \div {}^{+}11$ **c.** $0 \div {}^{-}24$ **d.** $0 \div {}^{+}60$
6. **a.** $^{-}80 \div 10$ **b.** $28 \div {}^{-}7$ **c.** $^{-}65 \div 13$ **d.** $132 \div {}^{-}12$
7. **a.** $^{-}9 \div {}^{-}9$ **b.** $^{-}15 \div 15$ **c.** $21 \div {}^{-}21$ **d.** $^{-}100 \div {}^{-}100$
8. **a.** $7 \div {}^{-}3$ **b.** $^{-}14 \div {}^{-}5$ **c.** $^{-}21 \div 9$ **d.** $^{-}40 \div {}^{-}6$
9. **a.** $^{-}2 \div {}^{-}5$ **b.** $^{-}4 \div 24$ **c.** $6 \div {}^{-}15$ **d.** $^{-}56 \div 63$

10. Divide in each of the following:

   a. $\dfrac{^{-}15}{^{-}3}$ $\dfrac{^{+}21}{^{-}7}$ $\dfrac{^{-}56}{^{+}8}$ $\dfrac{^{-}60}{^{-}12}$ $\dfrac{^{+}75}{^{-}5}$ $\dfrac{^{+}110}{^{+}10}$ $\dfrac{^{-}96}{^{+}24}$ $\dfrac{^{-}350}{^{-}50}$

   b. $\dfrac{^{-}16}{^{+}2}$ $\dfrac{^{+}81}{^{-}9}$ $\dfrac{^{-}47}{^{-}1}$ $\dfrac{^{-}78}{^{+}6}$ $\dfrac{^{+}92}{^{+}4}$ $\dfrac{^{-}80}{^{-}16}$ $\dfrac{^{+}108}{^{-}12}$ $\dfrac{^{-}68}{^{+}68}$

   c. $\dfrac{40}{^{-}5}$ $\dfrac{^{-}104}{8}$ $\dfrac{^{-}48}{^{-}3}$ $\dfrac{^{-}370}{10}$ $\dfrac{126}{^{-}18}$ $\dfrac{17}{^{-}17}$ $\dfrac{^{-}99}{^{-}11}$ $\dfrac{775}{^{-}25}$

   d. $\dfrac{^{-}48}{4}$ $\dfrac{^{-}33}{1}$ $\dfrac{98}{^{-}7}$ $\dfrac{^{-}180}{9}$ $\dfrac{56}{^{-}2}$ $\dfrac{^{-}91}{^{-}13}$ $\dfrac{165}{^{-}15}$ $\dfrac{^{-}520}{^{-}40}$

11. **a.** $(^{-}12 \div {}^{+}3) \div {}^{-}2$ **c.** $(^{-}36 \div {}^{-}12) \div {}^{-}3$ **e.** $^{-}100 \div ({}^{-}10 \div {}^{-}5)$
    b. $^{+}60 \div ({}^{+}6 \div {}^{-}2)$ **d.** $^{-}80 \div ({}^{-}20 \div {}^{+}4)$ **f.** $(^{-}64 \div {}^{+}8) \div {}^{+}4$

12. Find the missing numbers:

   a. $^{-}18 \div 6 = ?$ **d.** $^{-}40 \div {}^{-}5 = \square$ **g.** $96 \div {}^{-}8 = n$
   b. $36 \div {}^{-}4 = \square$ **e.** $^{-}72 \div 9 = ?$ **h.** $^{-}85 \div {}^{-}17 = n$
   c. $\dfrac{7}{^{-}1} = n$ **f.** $\dfrac{^{-}56}{^{-}7} = n$ **i.** $\dfrac{^{-}180}{12} = n$

13. Find the missing numbers:

   a. $? \div 2 = {}^{-}8$ **d.** $\square \div {}^{-}6 = {}^{-}11$ **g.** $n \div {}^{-}13 = 0$
   b. $\square \div {}^{-}1 = 19$ **e.** $? \div 3 = {}^{-}1$ **h.** $n \div {}^{-}9 = {}^{-}108$
   c. $\dfrac{n}{^{-}7} = 4$ **f.** $\dfrac{n}{8} = {}^{-}9$ **i.** $\dfrac{n}{^{-}2} = 29$

14. Find the missing numbers:

   a. $20 \div ? = {}^{-}10$ **d.** $^{-}76 \div n = {}^{-}19$ **g.** $^{-}5 \div n = 5$
   b. $^{-}16 \div \square = 4$ **e.** $^{-}100 \div ? = 10$ **h.** $42 \div n = {}^{-}6$
   c. $\dfrac{^{-}15}{n} = 1$ **f.** $\dfrac{35}{n} = {}^{-}7$ **i.** $\dfrac{^{-}50}{n} = {}^{-}2$

Properties

In the following exercises we determine the properties that hold for the integers under the operation of division.

1. Commutative Property

a. If the commutative property holds for the division of integers, what would have to be true?

b. In each of the following divide as indicated, then compare quotients:

(1) $^+18 \div {}^+3$; $^+3 \div {}^+18$. Does $^+18 \div {}^+3 = {}^+3 \div {}^+18$?
(2) $^-21 \div {}^-7$; $^-7 \div {}^-21$. Does $^-21 \div {}^-7 = {}^-7 \div {}^-21$?
(3) $^+56 \div {}^-8$; $^-8 \div {}^+56$. Does $^+56 \div {}^-8 = {}^-8 \div {}^+56$?
(4) $^-63 \div {}^+9$; $^+9 \div {}^-63$. Does $^-63 \div {}^+9 = {}^+9 \div {}^-63$?

c. Does the commutative property hold for the division of integers?

2. Associative Property

a. If the associative property holds for the division of integers, what would have to be true?

b. In each of the following divide as indicated, then compare quotients:

(1) $(^+24 \div {}^-8) \div {}^-2$; $^+24 \div (^-8 \div {}^-2)$.
    Does $(^+24 \div {}^-8) \div {}^-2 = {}^+24 \div (^-8 \div {}^-2)$?
(2) $(^-90 \div {}^-6) \div {}^+3$; $^-90 \div (^-6 \div {}^+3)$.
    Does $(^-90 \div {}^-6) \div {}^+3 = {}^-90 \div (^-6 \div {}^+3)$?

c. Does the associative property hold for the division of integers?

3. Distributive Property

a. If the distributive property of division over addition holds for the integers, what would have to be true?

b. In each of the following perform the indicated operations, then compare answers:

(1) $^+48 \div (^+12 + {}^-4)$; $(^+48 \div {}^+12) + (^+48 \div {}^-4)$.
    Does $^+48 \div (^+12 + {}^-4) = (^+48 \div {}^+12) + (^+48 \div {}^-4)$?
(2) $(^-30 + {}^-25) \div {}^-5$; $(^-30 \div {}^-5) + (^-25 \div {}^-5)$.
    Does $(^-30 + {}^-25) \div {}^-5 = (^-30 \div {}^-5) + (^-25 \div {}^-5)$?

c. Is division distributed over addition in problem **3b** (1)? In problem **3b** (2)? When is division distributed over addition in the integers?

4. Closure

    a. What do we mean when we say that a certain group of numbers is closed under the operation of division?

    b. When you divide in each of the following, is the quotient in each case an integer?

(1) $^-20 \div ^-4$	(4) $^-1 \div ^+6$	(7) $^+9 \div ^-10$
(2) $^+6 \div ^+9$	(5) $^+17 \div ^-25$	(8) $^-36 \div ^-1$
(3) $0 \div ^-5$	(6) $^-72 \div ^+18$	(9) $^-21 \div ^+14$

    c. Can you find two integers for which the quotient is not an integer provided that division by zero is excluded?

    d. Can we say that the integers are closed under the operation of division provided that division by zero is excluded?

10–18   DIVISION OF RATIONAL NUMBERS; PROPERTIES

We follow the same procedures to divide rational numbers as we do when we divide integers. See section 10–17. However, it may be necessary to review at this time the division of the rational numbers of arithmetic (common fractions, mixed numbers, and decimal fractions). See sections 4–15 and 5–11.

To divide a positive rational number by a positive rational number or *a negative rational number by a negative rational number,* we divide their absolute values and prefix the numeral for this quotient with a positive sign.

> Divide: $\dfrac{^-2}{3} \div \dfrac{^-4}{5} = ?$
>
> $\dfrac{^-2}{3} \div \dfrac{^-4}{5} = {}^+\left(\dfrac{2}{3} \div \dfrac{4}{5}\right) = {}^+\left(\dfrac{2}{3} \times \dfrac{5}{4}\right) = \dfrac{^+5}{6}$
>
> *Answer,* $\dfrac{^+5}{6}$

To divide a positive rational number by a negative rational number or *a negative rational number by a positive rational number,* we divide their absolute values and prefix the numeral for this quotient with a negative sign.

Divide: $^-1\frac{7}{8} \div \,^+1\frac{1}{2} = ?$

$^-1\frac{7}{8} \div \,^+1\frac{1}{2} = \,^-\left(1\frac{7}{8} \div 1\frac{1}{2}\right)$

$\qquad\qquad = \,^-\left(\frac{15}{8} \times \frac{2}{3}\right) = \,^-\frac{5}{4} = \,^-1\frac{1}{4}$

Answer, $^-1\frac{1}{4}$

Any non-zero rational number divided by itself is one (1).

Divide: $^-.7 \div \,^-.7 = ?$

$^-.7 \div \,^-.7 = \,^+(.7 \div .7) = \,^+1$ or $\frac{^-.7}{^-.7} = \,^+1$

Answer, $^+1$

Zero divided either by a positive rational number or by a negative rational number is zero. We cannot divide a positive rational number or a negative rational number by zero.

$0 \div \,^-2\frac{1}{2} = 0$ $\qquad\qquad$ *Answer,* 0

$0 \div \,^-8.5 = 0$ $\qquad\qquad$ *Answer,* 0

The numeral naming a positive rational number does not require the positive ($^+$) sign.

EXERCISES

Divide as indicated:

1. a. $^+\frac{13}{16} \div \,^+\frac{7}{8}$ $\quad$ **b.** $^+12 \div \,^+\frac{3}{5}$ $\quad$ **c.** $^+4\frac{1}{2} \div \,^+27$ $\quad$ **d.** $^+9\frac{1}{3} \div \,^+1\frac{1}{6}$

2. a. $^+.8 \div \,^+.4$ $\quad$ **b.** $^+15 \div \,^+.5$ $\quad$ **c.** $^+5.6 \div \,^+.14$ $\quad$ **d.** $^+.005 \div \,^+.0002$

3. a. $^-\frac{3}{4} \div \,^-\frac{3}{8}$ $\quad$ **b.** $^-\frac{5}{6} \div \,^-2$ $\quad$ **c.** $^-1\frac{1}{8} \div \,^-\frac{3}{32}$ $\quad$ **d.** $^-7\frac{1}{2} \div \,^-1\frac{1}{4}$

4. a. $^-7.6 \div \,^-.4$ $\quad$ **b.** $^-6.9 \div \,^-3$ $\quad$ **c.** $^-.004 \div \,^-.02$ $\quad$ **d.** $^-27 \div \,^-.09$

5. a. $\dfrac{-9}{10} \div \dfrac{+1}{3}$ **b.** $-7 \div \dfrac{+1}{6}$ **c.** $\dfrac{-9}{16} \div +1\dfrac{3}{5}$ **d.** $-2\dfrac{1}{16} \div +1\dfrac{3}{8}$

6. a. $-.72 \div +.08$ **b.** $-.0028 \div +.7$ **c.** $-14 \div +5.6$ **d.** $-.168 \div +24$

7. a. $+\dfrac{5}{8} \div -\dfrac{5}{6}$ **b.** $+\dfrac{11}{12} \div -2$ **c.** $+10\dfrac{5}{8} \div -5$ **d.** $+1\dfrac{11}{16} \div -2\dfrac{1}{4}$

8. a. $+8.4 \div -1.2$ **b.** $+2 \div -.8$ **c.** $+7.686 \div -.06$ **d.** $+.0016 \div -.4$

9. a. $0 \div -\dfrac{11}{16}$ **b.** $0 \div -3\dfrac{2}{3}$ **c.** $0 \div -.7$ **d.** $0 \div -4.9$

10. a. $-\dfrac{2}{3} \div \dfrac{5}{6}$ **b.** $3\dfrac{3}{4} \div -4\dfrac{2}{5}$ **c.** $-2.4 \div .03$ **d.** $90 \div -1.5$

11. a. $-\dfrac{3}{4} \div -\dfrac{3}{4}$ **b.** $-7\dfrac{5}{12} \div 7\dfrac{5}{12}$ **c.** $.68 \div -.68$ **d.** $-3.517 \div -3.517$

12. Divide in each of the following:

a. $\dfrac{\frac{-3}{4}}{\frac{7}{8}}$ $\dfrac{-10}{\frac{-15}{16}}$ $\dfrac{\frac{2}{3}}{-12}$ $\dfrac{\frac{-15}{16}}{-1\frac{1}{8}}$ $\dfrac{3\frac{3}{8}}{-4\frac{1}{2}}$ $\dfrac{\frac{-7}{12}}{2\frac{1}{3}}$ $\dfrac{-5\frac{1}{4}}{-3\frac{2}{3}}$

b. $\dfrac{-62.5}{.5}$ $\dfrac{1.08}{-9}$ $\dfrac{-6}{-1.2}$ $\dfrac{-.1}{.4}$ $\dfrac{-.02}{-.004}$ $\dfrac{9.07}{-9.07}$ $\dfrac{-.003}{-.15}$

13. a. $\left(\dfrac{-7}{8} \div \dfrac{-9}{16}\right) \div \dfrac{+2}{3}$ **c.** $\left(-2\dfrac{1}{3} \div +5\dfrac{1}{2}\right) \div +1\dfrac{3}{4}$ **e.** $(+1.2 \div -.2) \div -.3$

b. $\dfrac{-3}{4} \div \left(\dfrac{-4}{5} \div \dfrac{-9}{10}\right)$ **d.** $-4\dfrac{1}{6} \div \left(+20 \div -3\dfrac{3}{4}\right)$ **f.** $-14.4 \div (-7.2 \div -.04)$

14. Find the missing numbers:

a. $\dfrac{-11}{16} \div \dfrac{-5}{8} = ?$ **d.** $\dfrac{-7}{8} \div \dfrac{-7}{8} = \square$ **g.** $2\dfrac{5}{12} \div -2 = n$

b. $\dfrac{7}{12} \div \dfrac{-9}{10} = \square$ **e.** $-1\dfrac{9}{16} \div \dfrac{5}{6} = ?$ **h.** $-3\dfrac{3}{8} \div -4\dfrac{1}{2} = n$

c. $\dfrac{-\frac{1}{2}}{\frac{3}{4}} = n$ **f.** $\dfrac{5}{-3\frac{1}{8}} = n$ **i.** $\dfrac{-1\frac{1}{6}}{-9\frac{1}{3}} = n$

15. Find the missing numbers:

a. $-.8 \div -.2 = \square$ **d.** $.3 \div -.12 = ?$ **g.** $64.8 \div -.27 = n$

b. $-3.24 \div 6 = ?$ **e.** $-.504 \div -6.3 = \square$ **h.** $-.006 \div .006 = n$

c. $\dfrac{7.6}{-.4} = n$ **f.** $\dfrac{-10}{.25} = n$ **i.** $\dfrac{-.3}{-.01} = n$

Properties

In the following exercises we determine the properties that hold for the rational numbers under the operation of division.

1. Commutative Property

a. If the commutative property holds for the division of rational numbers, what would have to be true?

b. In each of the following divide as indicated, then compare quotients:

(1) $^{+}\frac{3}{4} \div {}^{-}\frac{1}{4}; \ {}^{-}\frac{1}{4} \div {}^{+}\frac{3}{4}$. Does $^{+}\frac{3}{4} \div {}^{-}\frac{1}{4} = {}^{-}\frac{1}{4} \div {}^{+}\frac{3}{4}$?

(2) $^{-}1\frac{1}{2} \div {}^{-}\frac{3}{8}; \ {}^{-}\frac{3}{8} \div {}^{-}1\frac{1}{2}$. Does $^{-}1\frac{1}{2} \div {}^{-}\frac{3}{8} = {}^{-}\frac{3}{8} \div {}^{-}1\frac{1}{2}$?

(3) $^{-}6\frac{1}{4} \div {}^{+}3\frac{1}{3}; \ {}^{+}3\frac{1}{3} \div {}^{-}6\frac{1}{4}$. Does $^{-}6\frac{1}{4} \div {}^{+}3\frac{1}{3} = {}^{+}3\frac{1}{3} \div {}^{-}6\frac{1}{4}$?

(4) $^{+}.8 \div {}^{+}.02; \ {}^{+}.02 \div {}^{+}.8$. Does $^{+}.8 \div {}^{+}.02 = {}^{+}.02 \div {}^{+}.8$?

c. Does the commutative property hold for the division of rational numbers?

2. **Associative Property**

a. If the associative property holds for the division of rational numbers, what would have to be true?

b. In each of the following divide as indicated, then compare quotients:

(1) $\left(\frac{-5}{6} \div {}^{+}\frac{1}{2}\right) \div \frac{-2}{3}; \ \frac{-5}{6} \div \left(\frac{+1}{2} \div \frac{-2}{3}\right)$.
   Does $\left(\frac{-5}{6} \div {}^{+}\frac{1}{2}\right) \div \frac{-2}{3} = \frac{-5}{6} \div \left(\frac{+1}{2} \div \frac{-2}{3}\right)$?

(2) $\left(^{+}3\frac{1}{8} \div {}^{-}1\frac{1}{4}\right) \div {}^{-}2\frac{1}{2}; \ {}^{+}3\frac{1}{8} \div \left(^{-}1\frac{1}{4} \div {}^{-}2\frac{1}{2}\right)$.
   Does $\left(^{+}3\frac{1}{8} \div {}^{-}1\frac{1}{4}\right) \div {}^{-}2\frac{1}{2} = {}^{+}3\frac{1}{8} \div \left(^{-}1\frac{1}{4} \div {}^{-}2\frac{1}{2}\right)$?

c. Does the associative property hold for the division of rational numbers?

3. **Distributive Property**

a. If the distributive property of division over addition holds for the rational numbers, what would have to be true?

b. In each of the following perform the indicated operations, then compare answers:

(1) $\frac{-3}{4} \div \left(^{+}\frac{9}{16} + {}^{-}\frac{3}{8}\right); \ \left(\frac{-3}{4} \div {}^{+}\frac{9}{16}\right) + \left(\frac{-3}{4} \div {}^{-}\frac{3}{8}\right)$.
   Does $\frac{-3}{4} \div \left(^{+}\frac{9}{16} + {}^{-}\frac{3}{8}\right) = \left(\frac{-3}{4} \div {}^{+}\frac{9}{16}\right) + \left(\frac{-3}{4} \div {}^{-}\frac{3}{8}\right)$?

(2) $\left(^{+}4\frac{1}{2} + {}^{-}6\frac{2}{3}\right) \div {}^{-}1\frac{1}{4}; \ \left(^{+}4\frac{1}{2} \div {}^{-}1\frac{1}{4}\right) + \left(^{-}6\frac{2}{3} \div {}^{-}1\frac{1}{4}\right)$.
   Does $\left(^{+}4\frac{1}{2} + {}^{-}6\frac{2}{3}\right) \div {}^{-}1\frac{1}{4} = \left(^{+}4\frac{1}{2} \div {}^{-}1\frac{1}{4}\right) + \left(^{-}6\frac{2}{3} \div {}^{-}1\frac{1}{4}\right)$?

c. Is division distributed over addition in problem **3b** (1)? In problem **3b** (2)? When is division distributed over addition in the rational numbers?

4. **Closure**

a. What do we mean when we say that a certain group of numbers is closed under the operation of division?

b. When you divide in each of the following, is the quotient in each case a rational number?

(1) $\dfrac{-5}{8} \div \dfrac{-1}{8}$ (4) $^-2\tfrac{3}{5} \div {}^+4\tfrac{1}{2}$ (7) $^+1.28 \div {}^-.04$

(2) $\dfrac{+2}{3} \div \dfrac{-4}{5}$ (5) $^+\tfrac{13}{16} \div {}^-1\tfrac{7}{8}$ (8) $^+.06 \div {}^+.15$

(3) $0 \div \dfrac{-9}{16}$ (6) $^-3\tfrac{5}{12} \div {}^-4$ (9) $^-10 \div {}^-.1$

c. Can you find two rational numbers for which the quotient is not a rational number provided that division by zero is excluded?

d. Can we say that the rational numbers are closed under the operation of division provided that division by zero is excluded?

10–19 COMPUTATION—USING NUMERALS WITH CENTERED SIGNS

The number that is the *opposite of six,* named by the numeral −6, and the number *negative six,* named by the numeral ⁻6 are one and the same number. Since there is no need to have two symbols that differ so slightly to name the same number, to simplify matters we shall discard the use of the raised sign and henceforth use only numerals with centered signs to name numbers. The numeral −6 represents both the *opposite of six* and the number *negative six.* The numeral +6 or 6 names the number *positive six.*

While both sign locations are correct in naming signed numbers, the numerals having the signs centered are more generally used.

To compute with signed numbers named by numerals with centered signs, we follow the same procedures as with numbers named by numerals having raised signs.

Also, *to simplify an algebraic expression* such as 8 − 10 + 7 − 2, we may take it to mean (+8) + (−10) + (+7) + (−2) where the given signs tell you which numbers are positive and which are negative but the operation is considered to be addition.

$$8 - 10 + 7 - 2 = (+8) + (-10) + (+7) + (-2) = +3$$

1. Add:

a.

$+9$	-7	$+6$	$+1$	-8	-10	-4	$+2$	-15	-5
$+4$	-8	-3	-5	$+2$	$+16$	-7	-12	$+14$	$+21$

b.

$+7$	-9	-8	0	-3	$+\frac{2}{5}$	$+\frac{7}{8}$	$-\frac{3}{4}$	$-.5$	-3.94
-7	$+9$	$+8$	$+11$	0	$+\frac{1}{5}$	$-\frac{3}{8}$	$-\frac{2}{3}$	$+1.8$	-1.06

2. Add as indicated:

a. $(+3) + (-9)$

b. $(-2) + (+8) + (-5)$

c. $[(-6) + (-10)] + (-4)$

d. $(+1) + [(+7) + (-9)]$

e. $(-11) + (+4) + (+9) + (-1)$

f. $[(15) + (-8)] + [(+2) + (-9)]$

3. Simplify:

a. $8 + 4$

b. $6 - 7$

c. $-5 + 6$

d. $-4 - 10$

e. $9 - 15$

f. $-2 - 4$

g. $7 - 2 - 3$

h. $12 + 7 - 9$

i. $16 - 8 + 2$

j. $5 - 8 + 1$

k. $6 - 9 - 3$

l. $-2 + 5 - 2$

m. $11 - 4 + 8 - 10$

n. $-3 + 5 + 2 - 5$

o. $1 - 8 + 2 - 4 + 3$

p. $5 + 2 - 9 + 6 - 4$

4. Subtract:

a.

$+21$	$+8$	11	2	-5	-1	$+9$	-3	-8	$+12$
$+18$	$+9$	3	10	-2	-11	-4	$+15$	$+1$	-12

b.

$+7$	-2	0	7	0	$+\frac{3}{4}$	$-.18$	$-1\frac{1}{2}$	$+1.05$	$-4\frac{1}{2}$
$+7$	-2	$+6$	0	-1	$-\frac{1}{4}$	$-.25$	$+\frac{2}{3}$	$+2.75$	$+2\frac{1}{2}$

5. Subtract as indicated:

a. $(-9) - (+7)$

b. $(-8) - (-3)$

c. $(0) - (8)$

d. $(+6) - (-5)$

e. $(6 - 5) - (2 - 9)$

f. $(8 - 11) - (4 - 5)$

g. $[(-9) + (-3)] - (-15)$

h. $(+6) - [(-8) - (+4)]$

i. $[(-11) - (+6)] - (-2)$

6. a. From -8 subtract 4.

b. Subtract 7 from 0.

c. Take 11 from 9.

d. From -1 take -1.

e. Subtract 12 from 5.

f. From 8 take -6.

7. Multiply:

a.

6	$+9$	-7	-6	-8	-4	$+7$	$+16$	-1	$+12$
7	$+8$	-7	-9	6	$+4$	-8	-3	-1	-12

b.

0	−8	0	+5	0	+.3	+.04	$-1\frac{1}{2}$	$-3\frac{3}{4}$	−1.5
9	0	−4	0	+6	−.2	+.78	−6	$+4\frac{1}{3}$	−.07

8. Multiply as indicated:

a. $(-9) \times (-8)$ **e.** $(+6)(-.8)$ **i.** $(-9) \times [(-2)(-5)]$

b. $(+6) \cdot (-7)$ **f.** $(-\frac{2}{3})(-9)$ **j.** $-6(2 - 9) - (2 - 3)$

c. $(-2)(+2)$ **g.** $(-11)(0)(-2)$ **k.** $(-3)(-4)(+1)(-4)$

d. $-5(4 - 10)$ **h.** $[(+16)(-1)] \times (-4)$ **l.** $(-5)(-2)(-1)(-3)$

9. Find the value of each of the following:

a. $(-2)^2$ **d.** $(+3)^4$ **g.** $(-1)^6$

b. $(+5)^2$ **e.** $(-1)^5$ **h.** $(+4)^4$

c. $(-6)^3$ **f.** $(-5)^4$ **i.** $(-7)^3$

10. Divide as indicated:

a. $\dfrac{+18}{+3}$ $\dfrac{-30}{-5}$ $\dfrac{+21}{-7}$ $\dfrac{-56}{+8}$ $\dfrac{-72}{-18}$ $\dfrac{+54}{-9}$ $\dfrac{-80}{+20}$ $\dfrac{+35}{+7}$ $\dfrac{-90}{+18}$ $\dfrac{-60}{-4}$

b. $\dfrac{-6}{-6}$ $\dfrac{+18}{-18}$ $\dfrac{-29}{+29}$ $\dfrac{-8}{-1}$ $\dfrac{-25}{+1}$ $\dfrac{+7}{-1}$ $\dfrac{0}{+5}$ $\dfrac{0}{-6}$ $\dfrac{0}{+8}$ $\dfrac{0}{-3}$

11. Divide as indicated:

a. $(-24) \div (+6)$ **c.** $(-12) \div (-\frac{2}{3})$ **e.** $(-25) \div (-25)$

b. $(+40) \div (-8)$ **d.** $(+.36) \div (-.9)$ **f.** $(+4\frac{1}{6}) \div (-4\frac{1}{6})$

12. Simplify by performing the indicated operations:

a. $\dfrac{6 - 16}{2}$ **c.** $\dfrac{9(-2) + 3(-6)}{6(-1 - 1)}$ **e.** $\dfrac{(-5)^2 - (-3)^2}{(-2)^2}$

b. $\dfrac{10 - 2(3)}{-4}$ **d.** $\dfrac{8(1 - 4) - 6(9 - 1)}{-5(14 - 2)}$ **f.** $\dfrac{-3(-1 - 3)}{5(-4) - 2(2 - 9)}$

13. a. Does $(-5) + (-4) = |-5| + |-4|$?

b. Does $(+6) + (-9) = |+6| + |-9|$?

c. Does $|-2| + |-7| = |(-2) + (-7)|$?

d. Does $|+8| + |-3| = |(+8) + (-3)|$?

e. Does $(-6)(-2) = |-6| \times |-2|$?

f. Does $(-3)(+7) = |-3| \times |+7|$?

346

LANGUAGE OF ALGEBRA

10–20 SYMBOLS—REVIEW

In algebra we continue to use the operational symbols of arithmetic.

The signs of operation may assume any one of several meanings, as follows:

The *addition* symbol or plus symbol $+$ means sum, add, more than, increased by, exceeded by.

The *subtraction* symbol or minus symbol $-$ means difference, subtract, take away, less, less than, decreased by, diminished by.

The *multiplication* symbol $\times$ or the raised dot $(\cdot)$ means product, multiply, times.

The *division* symbol $\div$ or $\overline{)}$ means quotient, divide. The fraction bar, as in $\frac{a}{b}$, is generally used in algebra to indicate division. The word "over" is sometimes used to express the relationship of the numerator to the denominator.

Other symbols used in both algebra and arithmetic include exponents, the square root symbol, parentheses, the verbs of mathematical sentences such as $=$, $\neq$, $>$, $\not>$, $<$, $\not<$, $\geq$, $\not\geq$, $\leq$, and $\not\leq$.

An *exponent* is the small numeral written to the upper right (superscript) of the base. When it names a natural number, it tells how many times the factor is being used in multiplication. 8^2 represents 8×8 and is read "the square of eight" and 8^3 represents $8 \times 8 \times 8$ and is read "the cube of eight." The factor that is being repeated is called the *base*. The number 8^4 uses 8 as the base and 4 as the exponent. Numbers such as 8^2, 8^3, 8^4, 8^5, etc. are called *powers* of 8.

The *square root* symbol $\sqrt{}$ written over the numeral indicates the square root of the corresponding number. The *square root* of a number is that number which when multiplied by itself produces the given number.

Parentheses ( ) are generally used to group together two or more numerals so that they are treated as a single quantity. Sometimes parentheses are used to set off a numeral from another so that the meaning will not be misunderstood.

A numeral is sometimes called a *constant* because it names a definite number.

A *variable* is a letter (small letter, capital letter, letter with a subscript such as b_1, read "*b* sub one," or letter with prime marks such as S', read "*S* prime") or a frame (such as □, □, ○, and △) or a blank which holds a place open for a number. Sometimes the first letter of a key word is used as the variable. A variable may represent any number, but under certain conditions it represents a specific number or numbers.

EXERCISES

1. Read, or write in words, each of the following:

   a. 24×75 **d.** 21^2 **g.** 19^3 **j.** $(^-46)(^-9)$ **m.** $|^-12|$

   b. $^-3 + {}^+7$ **e.** $\sqrt{39}$ **h.** $68 \cdot 27$ **k.** 11^7 **n.** $15 - (23 - 4)$

   c. $\frac{54}{9}$ **f.** $10 - 25$ **i.** $\sqrt{53}$ **l.** $8(12 + 6)$ **o.** $7 \times (6 \times 9)$

2. What symbol represents the variable in each of the following?

   a. $? + 5 = 11$ **c.** $n + 1 = 9$ **e.** $\triangle - 16 = 16$ **g.** $^-6 + {}^-9 = R'$

   b. $12 - \square = 3$ **d.** $3x = 18$ **f.** $\frac{y}{8} = 7$ **h.** $30 = b + 8$

10–21 MATHEMATICAL PHRASES OR MATHEMATICAL EXPRESSIONS

A *numerical expression* or *numerical phrase* consists of a single numeral with or without operational symbols like 15 or 2^5 or two or more numerals with operational symbols like $8 + 9$; $63 - 27$; 8×36; $54 \div 9$; $6 \times (5 + 7)$; etc.

An *algebraic expression* or *algebraic phrase* may be a numerical expression as described above or an expression containing one or more variables joined by operational symbols like a; $c - 3d$; $5x^2 - 3x + 7$; etc.

Both numerical expressions and algebraic expressions are *mathematical expressions*.

In an algebraic expression no multiplication symbol is necessary when the factors are two letters (variables) or a numeral and a letter. In the latter case the numeral always precedes the letter or the variable. This numeral is usually called the *numerical coefficient* of the variable. a times b may be expressed as $a \times b$, $a \cdot b$, ab (preferred), $(a)(b)$, $a(b)$, or $(a)b$. In $4a^3$, the 4 is the numerical coefficient of a^3.

To write algebraic expressions, we write numerals, variables, and operational symbols as required in the proper order.

The sum of eight and six.   *Answer,* $8 + 6$

The product of n and three. *Answer,* $3n$

The square of the edge (e). *Answer,* e^2

The difference between the length (l) and the width (w).
    Answer, $l - w$

The area (A) divided by pi (π). *Answer,* $\dfrac{A}{\pi}$

The square root of the distance (d). *Answer,* $\sqrt{d}$

Twelve times the sum of n and seven.
    Answer, $12(n + 7)$

EXERCISES

1. Write each of the following as an algebraic expression:

    a. Twenty added to fifteen.
    b. The quotient of ten divided by five.
    c. The difference between eight and four.
    d. x times y.
    e. The square root of twelve.
    f. From s subtract d.
    g. The product of n and eight.
    h. The square of T.
    i. The sum of b and r.
    j. The quotient of E divided by R.
    k. Six times some number n.
    l. Some number x increased by eleven.
    m. Some number b decreased by fourteen.
    n. Some number y divided by ten.
    o. Nine times the sum of x and four.
    p. The square root of the product of v and t.

2. Write each of the following as an algebraic expression:

    a. The discount (d) divided by the list price (l).
    b. One half the product of the altitude (a) and the base (b).
    c. 90° decreased by angle A.
    d. The sum of twice the length (l) and twice the width (w).
    e. The square root of the difference between the square of the hypotenuse (h) and the square of the altitude (a).
    f. Twice pi (π) times the radius (r) times the sum of the height (h) and the radius.

3. Read, or write in words, each of the following:

a. $10\,m$ **d.** s^2 **g.** $15 - d$ **j.** $c + g$ **m.** abc

b. $n + 6$ **e.** $y - 3$ **h.** e^3 **k.** $16\,t^2$ **n.** $10\,b^5$

c. $\dfrac{x}{9}$ **f.** $\sqrt{A}$ **i.** lw **l.** $\dfrac{d}{r}$ **o.** $h(b_1 + b_2)$

10–22 MATHEMATICAL SENTENCES—OPEN SENTENCES; EQUATIONS; INEQUALITIES

Sentences such as:

"Some number n increased by eight is equal to twelve"
expressed in symbols as $n + 8 = 12$

or "Nine times each number b is greater than fifty"
expressed in symbols as $9\,b > 50$

or "Each number x decreased by six is less than fourteen"
expressed in symbols as $x - 6 < 14$

are *mathematical sentences*. A mathematical sentence that contains a variable is called an *open sentence*. $n + 8 = 12, 9\,b > 50$, and $x - 6 < 14$ are open sentences. A verbal (word) sentence may be expressed as an equivalent algebraic sentence and vice-versa.

An open sentence that has the equality sign $=$ as its verb is called an *equation*. If the sentence uses $\neq, >, <, \not>, \not<, \geq, \leq,$ $\not\geq,$ or $\not\leq$ as its verb, it is called an *inequation* or *inequality*.

The sentence $n + 8 = 12$ is an equation; the sentences $9\,b > 50$ and $x - 6 < 14$ are inequalities.

Symbolic verbs used in mathematical sentences include:

$=$ meaning "is equal to."
$\neq$ meaning "is not equal to."
$<$ meaning "is less than."
$\not<$ meaning "is not less than."
$>$ meaning "is greater than."
$\not>$ meaning "is not greater than."
$\leq$ or $\leqq$ meaning "is less than or equal to."
$\not\leq$ or $\not\leqq$ meaning "is not less than or not equal to."
$\geq$ or $\geqq$ meaning "is greater than or equal to."
$\not\geq$ or $\not\geqq$ meaning "is not greater than or not equal to."

Observe that the symbol $\not<$ is equivalent to symbol $\geq$; symbol $\not>$ is equivalent to symbol $\leq$; symbol $\not\leq$ is equivalent to symbol $>$; and symbol $\not\geq$ is equivalent to symbol $<$.

An open sentence is not a statement. We cannot tell whether it is true or false. It is only after we substitute a number for the variable that the open sentence becomes a statement. Then we can determine whether the sentence is true or false.

The sentence "$9\,x \leq 63$" is the shortened form of "$9\,x < 63$ or $9\,x = 63$" and is read "Nine times each number x is less than or equal to sixty-three."

The sentence "$1 < y < 6$" is the shortened form of "$1 < y$ and $y < 6$" and is read "One is less than each number y which is less than six" or "Each number y is greater than one and less than six."

The sentence "$10 \geq a \geq 2$" is read "Ten is greater than or equal to each number a which is greater than or equal to two" or "Each number a is less than or equal to ten and greater than or equal to two."

EXERCISES

1. Read, or write in words, each of the following:

   a. $6\,x = 42$ **g.** $2\,b + 1 \nless 5$ **m.** $10\,x - 5 = 0$
   b. $h < 0$ **h.** $9\,n - 3\,n = 57$ **n.** $7\,r \nleq 35$
   c. $12\,n > 96$ **i.** $15\,y \leq 90$ **o.** $^-4 < a < 6$
   d. $c + 0 \neq 28$ **j.** $r + 25 \geq 32$ **p.** $15 > 3\,d > 0$
   e. $t - 5 \ngtr 17$ **k.** $5\,a + 6 < 51$ **q.** $1 \leq n \leq 14$
   f. $\dfrac{m}{8} = 4$ **l.** $8\,w - 11 > 99$ **r.** $^-3 \geq x \geq ^-9$

2. Write each of the following as an open sentence symbolically:

   a. Some number x increased by four is equal to thirty.
   b. Five times some number n decreased by seven is equal to sixty-three.
   c. Each number d is less than forty-five.
   d. Nine times each number h is greater than eighteen.
   e. Twelve times each number a plus eleven is not equal to fifty.
   f. Each number b decreased by five is not less than twenty.
   g. Each number n divided by ten is not greater than seven.
   h. Four times each number g increased by one is greater than or equal to six.
   i. Two times each number c decreased by five is less than or equal to three.
   j. Each number t is greater than negative six and less than positive two.

Introduction to Algebra   **351**

10-23 FORMULAS

A special kind of equation, called a *formula*, is a mathematical rule expressing the relationship of two or more quantities by means of numerals, variables, and operating symbols. The formula contains algebraic expressions.

To express mathematical and scientific principles as formulas, we write numerals, operating symbols, and letters (variables) representing the given quantities in the required order to show the relationship between quantities. A quantity may be represented by the first letter of a key word.

Write as a formula:

The selling price (s) is equal to the cost (c) increased by the margin (m).

Answer, $s = c + m$

Write as a formula:

The pitch of a roof (p) is equal to the rise (r) divided by the span (s).

Answer, $p = \dfrac{r}{s}$

To translate a formula to a word statement, we write a word rule stating the relationship expressed by the formula.

Translate:

$c = \pi d$ where c = circumference of circle,
π = pi or 3.14,
and d = diameter of circle.

Answer, The circumference of a circle equals pi times the diameter of the circle.

---

1. Express each of the following as a formula:

   a. The perimeter of a square (p) is equal to four times the length of the side (s).

   b. The net price (n) is equal to the list price (l) less the discount (d).

   c. The radius of a circle (r) is equal to the diameter (d) divided by two.

   d. The Kelvin temperature reading (K) is equal to the Celsius temperature reading (C) increased by 273°.

   e. The area of a circle (A) is equal to pi (π) times the square of the radius (r).

   f. The perimeter of an isosceles triangle (p) is equal to the base (b) added to twice the length of one of the equal sides (e).

   g. The interest (i) is equal to the principal (p) times the rate of interest per year (r) times the time in years (t).

   h. The rate of commission (r) is equal to the commission (c) divided by the sales (s).

   i. The perimeter of a rectangle (p) is equal to twice the sum of the length (l) and the width (w).

   j. The altitude of a right triangle (a) is equal to the square root of the difference between the square of the hypotenuse (h) and the square of the base (b).

2. Express each of the following formulas as a word statement:

   a. $A = lw$ where A = area of a rectangle, l = length, and w = width.

   b. $r = \dfrac{d}{t}$ where r = average rate of speed, d = distance traveled, and t = time of travel.

   c. $i = A - p$ where i = interest, A = total amount, and p = principal.

   d. $d = \frac{1}{2} gt^2$ where d = distance a freely falling body drops, g = acceleration due to gravity, and t = time of falling.

   e. $F = \frac{9}{5} C + 32°$ where F = Fahrenheit temperature reading and C = Celsius temperature reading.

Introduction to Algebra

10–24 INTRODUCTION TO THE SOLUTION OF EQUATIONS IN ONE VARIABLE

To solve an equation in one variable means to find the number represented by the variable which, when substituted for the variable, will make the sentence true.

Any number that makes the sentence true is said to *satisfy* the equation and to be the *root* or the *solution* of the open sentence.

> The equation $n + 2 = 8$ indicates that some number n plus two equals eight. When 6 is substituted for the variable n, the resulting sentence $6 + 2 = 8$ is a true sentence. Thus 6 is said to be the root of the equation $n + 2 = 8$.

Checking an equation is testing whether some number is a solution to this equation by substituting the number for the variable in the equation. If the resulting sentence is true, the number is a solution; if not, the number is not a solution.

> 6 is a solution to $n + 2 = 8$ because $6 + 2 = 8$.
> 5 is not a solution because $5 + 2 \neq 8$.

The expressions at the left and at the right of the equality sign in an equation are called *members* or *sides* of the equation.

> In the equation $n + 2 = 8$, the expression $n + 2$ is the left member and the expression 8 is the right member.

Equations which have exactly the same solutions are called *equivalent equations*. The equation $n + 2 = 8$ and $n = 6$ are equivalent equations because they both have the same solution, 6. An equation is considered to be in its *simplest form* when one member contains only the variable itself and the other member is a constant term. The equation $n = 6$ is an equation in the simplest form.

EXERCISES

1. Which of the following numbers will make the sentence $n + 5 = 10$ true?

   a. $n = 15$ **b.** $n = 2$ **c.** $n = {}^-10$ **d.** $n = \frac{1}{2}$ **e.** $n = 5$

2. Which of the following numbers will make the sentence $x - 3 = 11$ true?

   a. $x = 8$ **b.** $x = 0$ **c.** $x = {}^-8$ **d.** $x = 14$ **e.** $x = 12$

3. Which of the following numbers will make the sentence $8\,y = 32$ true?

   a. $y = 24$ **b.** $y = \frac{1}{4}$ **c.** $y = 40$ **d.** $y = 4$ **e.** $y = 0$

4. Which of the following numbers will make the sentence $\frac{r}{4} = 12$ true?

   a. $r = 3$ **b.** $r = 12$ **c.** $r = \frac{1}{3}$ **d.** $r = 36$ **e.** $r = 48$

5. Which of the following numbers is the root of the equation $w + 8 = 8$?

   a. $w = 1$ **b.** $w = 16$ **c.** $w = 0$ **d.** $w = {}^-1$ **e.** $w = 2$

6. Which of the following numbers is the root of the equation $9\,n = 54$?

   a. $n = 45$ **b.** $n = 63$ **c.** $n = 7$ **d.** $n = 6$ **e.** $n = \frac{1}{6}$

7. Which of the following numbers is the root of the equation $s - 7 = 3$?

   a. $s = 4$ **b.** $s = {}^-4$ **c.** $s = 10$ **d.** $s = {}^-21$ **e.** $s = 21$

8. Which of the following numbers is the root of the equation $\frac{x}{6} = 5$?

   a. $x = 6$ **b.** $x = 5$ **c.** $x = 11$ **d.** $x = 1$ **e.** $x = 30$

9. Which of the following is a solution to the equation $6\,z = 72$?

   a. 66   **b.** 15   **c.** 9   **d.** 12   **e.** 78

Introduction to Algebra

10. Which of the following is a solution to the equation $m + 9 = 27$?

   a. 36   **b.** 3   **c.** 18   **d.** 47   **e.** $^-36$

11. Which of the following is a solution to the equation $\frac{t}{12} = 16$?

   a. 4   **b.** $\frac{3}{4}$ **c.** 28   **d.** 192   **e.** 144

12. Which of the following is a solution to the equation $x - 6 = 6$?

   a. 0   **b.** $^-12$ **c.** 12   **d.** 1   **e.** 36

13. a. Write the left member of the equation $9\,n + 2 = 27$.
    b. Write the right member of the equation $3\,x - 5 = 85$.

14. Which of the following equations have 3 as a root? Which are equivalent equations?

   a. $x - 1 = 2$ **b.** $7\,x = 21$ **c.** $x + 14 = 11$ **d.** $x = 3$ **e.** $\frac{x}{3} = 1$

15. Which of the following equations have 4 as a root? Which are equivalent equations? Which equation of the equivalent equations is in the simplest form?

   a. $y - 5 = 9$ **b.** $14\,y = 56$ **c.** $y + 16 = 20$ **d.** $y = 4$ **e.** $\frac{y}{2} = 2$

10–25 INVERSE OPERATIONS; PROPERTIES OF EQUALITY

In section 2–2 we studied that *inverse operations undo each other.* That is: subtraction undoes addition, addition undoes subtraction, division undoes multiplication, and multiplication undoes division.

We found that:

(1) When we first add a number to the given number n and then subtract this number from the sum, we return to the given number n.

That is: $(n + 1) - 1 = n$; $(n + 2) - 2 = n$; $(n + 3) - 3 = n$.

(2) When we first subtract a number from the given number n and then add this number to the answer, we return to the given number n.

That is: $(n - 1) + 1 = n$; $(n - 2) + 2 = n$; $(n - 3) + 3 = n$.

(3) When we first multiply the given number n by a number and then we divide the product by this number, we return to the given number n.

That is: $(n \times 2) \div 2 = n$ or $\dfrac{2n}{2} = n$;

$(n \times 3) \div 3 = n$ or $\dfrac{3n}{3} = n$;

$(n \times 4) \div 4 = n$ or $\dfrac{4n}{4} = n$; etc.

(4) When we first divide the given number n by a number and then we multiply the quotient by this number, we return to the given number n.

That is: $(n \div 2) \times 2 = n$ or $\dfrac{n}{2} \times 2 = n$;

$(n \div 3) \times 3 = n$ or $\dfrac{n}{3} \times 3 = n$;

$(n \div 4) \times 4 = n$ or $\dfrac{n}{4} \times 4 = n$; etc.

The *properties of equality* which state that the results are equal when equals are increased or decreased or multiplied or divided by equals, with division by zero excluded, are called *axioms*.

These axioms allow us in each of the following cases to obtain an equation in the simplest form.

a. When we subtract the same number from both sides of a given equation.

For example: Given: $n + 5 = 30$

Subtracting 5 from each side: $(n + 5) - 5 = 30 - 5$

we get: $n = 25$

b. When we add the same number to both sides of a given equation.

For example: Given: $n - 5 = 30$

Adding 5 to each side: $(n - 5) + 5 = 30 + 5$

we get: $n = 35$

c. When we divide both sides of given equation by the same non-zero number.

For example: Given: $5\,n = 30$

Dividing each side by 5: $\dfrac{5\,n}{5} = \dfrac{30}{5}$

we get: $n = 6$

Introduction to Algebra

d. When we multiply both sides of a given equation by the same non-zero number.

For example: Given: $\frac{n}{5} = 30$

Multiplying each side by 5: $5 \cdot \frac{n}{5} = 5 \cdot 30$

we get: $n = 150$

EXERCISES

In each of the following, find the missing number and, where required, the missing operation:

1. a. $(12 + 9) - \square = 12$ **b.** $(15 + 21) \,?\, \square = 15$ **c.** $(x + 6) \,?\, \square = x$

2. a. $(17 - 5) + \,?\, = 17$ **b.** $(30 - 14) \,?\, \square = 30$ **c.** $(y - 10) \,?\, \square = y$

3. a. $(9 \times 8) \div \square = 9$ **b.** $(52 \times 23) \,?\, \square = 52$ **c.** $(b \times 7) \,?\, \square = b$

4. a. $(4 \times 3) \div \square = 3$ **b.** $(27 \times 36) \,?\, \square = 36$ **c.** $(8\,d) \,?\, \square = d$

5. a. $(42 \div 6) \times \square = 42$ **b.** $(8 \div 3) \,?\, \square = 8$ **c.** $(m \div 4) \,?\, \square = m$

6. a. $\frac{11}{16} \times \,?\, = 11$ **b.** $\frac{19}{7} \,?\, \square = 19$ **c.** $\frac{x}{5} \,?\, \square = x$

7. a. $(t - 11) \,?\, \square = t$ **c.** $(n + 34) \,?\, \square = n$ **e.** $(25\,w) \,?\, \square = w$

b. $(18\,r) \,?\, \square = r$ **d.** $(h - 40) \,?\, \square = h$ **f.** $\frac{z}{27} \,?\, \square = z$

8. In each of the following, what number do you subtract from both sides of the given equation to get an equivalent equation in simplest form? Also write this equivalent equation.

a. $x + 9 = 23$ **b.** $n + 1 = 17$ **c.** $b + 14 = 25$ **d.** $y + 50 = 83$

9. In each of the following, what number do you add to both sides of the given equation to get an equivalent equation in simplest form? Also write this equivalent equation.

a. $r - 2 = 7$ **b.** $w - 18 = 5$ **c.** $t - 21 = 21$ **d.** $p - 12 = 0$

10. In each of the following, by what number do you divide both sides of the given equation to get an equivalent equation in simplest form? Also write this equivalent equation.

a. $8\,n = 48$ **b.** $25\,a = 100$ **c.** $9\,m = 15$ **d.** $10\,y = 7$

11. In each of the following, by what number do you multiply both sides of the given equation to get an equivalent equation in simplest form? Also write this equivalent equation.

   a. $\frac{x}{4} = 16$ **b.** $\frac{t}{9} = 3$ **c.** $\frac{d}{12} = 11$ **d.** $\frac{b}{19} = 21$

12. What operation with what number do you use on both sides of each of the following equations to get an equivalent equation in simplest form? Also write this equivalent equation.

a. $7w = 21$	**f.** $t - 13 = 7$	**k.** $x + 57 = 110$	**p.** $20c = 11$
b. $y - 6 = 30$	**g.** $10b = 35$	**l.** $16r = 12$	**q.** $p + 96 = 300$
c. $n + 18 = 62$	**h.** $\frac{s}{8} = 1$	**m.** $g - 105 = 27$	**r.** $\frac{n}{6} = 14$
d. $6x = 72$	**i.** $w + 59 = 59$	**n.** $60 = b + 7$	**s.** $85 = n - 21$
e. $\frac{a}{9} = 5$	**j.** $28y = 21$	**o.** $10 = \frac{x}{5}$	**t.** $3 = 9c$

10–26 SOLVING EQUATIONS IN ONE VARIABLE

To solve an equation in one variable, we transform the given equation to the simplest equivalent equation which has only the variable itself as one member and a constant naming a number as the other member. To make this transformation we use the properties of equality (axioms) with inverse operations or with the additive inverse or multiplicative inverse as required.

An equation may be compared to balanced scales. To keep the equation in balance, any change on one side of the equality sign must be balanced by an equal change on the other side of the equality sign.

Observe in the models on the next several pages the following four basic types of equations:

$$\textbf{Type I} \quad n + 2 = 8$$

$$\textbf{Type II} \quad n - 2 = 8$$

$$\textbf{Type III} \quad 2n = 8$$

$$\textbf{Type IV} \quad \frac{n}{2} = 8$$

These equations are solved both by inverse operations and by the additive inverse or the multiplicative inverse. When the inverse operation method is used, the operation indicated in the given equation by the variable and its connected constant is undone by performing the inverse operation on both sides of the equation.

To check whether the number found is a solution, we substitute this number for the variable in the given equation. If the resulting sentence is true, then the number is a solution. A check mark is sometimes used to indicate that the resulting sentence is true. In this section the solutions will be only one number.

Basic Type I

Solve and check: $n + 2 = 8$

Solution by inverse operation:
The indicated operation of $n + 2$ is addition. To find the root we subtract 2 from each member.

$$n + 2 = 8$$
$$n + 2 - 2 = 8 - 2$$
$$n = 6$$

The root is 6.
Answer, 6

Solution by additive inverse:
The additive inverse of $^+2$ is $^-2$. We add the additive inverse to both members, using the addition axiom.

$$n + 2 = 8$$
$$n + 2 + (^-2) = 8 + (^-2)$$
$$n = 6$$

Answer, 6

Check:
$$n + 2 = 8$$
$$6 + 2 = 8$$
$$8 = 8 \checkmark$$

Observe that the equation $n + 2 = 8$ may also appear as $2 + n = 8$ or $8 = n + 2$ or $8 = 2 + n$. These are forms of the same equation. In each case the constant 2 must be eliminated in order to get an equivalent equation in the simplest form. This is $n = 6$ when solving $n + 2 = 8$ or $2 + n = 8$, and $6 = n$ when solving $8 = n + 2$ or $8 = 2 + n$. The equation $6 = n$ may be rewritten as $n = 6$.

Solve and check:

1. $n + 5 = 25$
2. $y + 12 = 53$
3. $r + 29 = 71$
4. $p + 87 = 110$
5. $9 + a = 15$
6. $18 + x = 33$
7. $64 + d = 72$
8. $78 + t = 100$

9. $17 = x + 6$
10. $34 = m + 25$
11. $75 = c + 58$
12. $91 = g + 43$
13. $9 = 2 + z$
14. $23 = 18 + b$
15. $80 = 53 + n$
16. $56 = 26 + y$

17. $b + 27 = 27$
18. $s + .3 = 1.6$
19. $\frac{1}{2} + n = 2\frac{1}{4}$
20. $c + \$.15 = \$.70$
21. $8 = t + \frac{2}{3}$
22. $5 = 2.7 + x$
23. $94 = n + 94$
24. $\$1.25 = \$.50 + m$

25. $3\frac{3}{4} + a = 12$
26. $.6 = r + .08$
27. $\$20 = \$4.75 + d$
28. $d + \frac{5}{8} = 1\frac{3}{16}$
29. $5.9 = y + 4$
30. $n + 1\frac{4}{5} = 7\frac{1}{2}$
31. $c + \$9 = \$11.75$
32. $4\frac{3}{8} = 4\frac{3}{8} + x$

Basic Type II

Solve and check: $n - 2 = 8$

Solution by inverse operation:
The indicated operation of $n - 2$ is subtraction. To find the root we add 2 to both members.

$$n - 2 = 8$$
$$n - 2 + 2 = 8 + 2$$
$$n = 10$$

The root is 10.
Answer, 10

Solution by additive inverse:
The additive inverse of $^-2$ is $^+2$. We add the additive inverse to both members, using the addition axiom.

$$n - 2 = 8$$
$$n + (^-2) = 8$$
$$n + (^-2) + (^+2) = 8 + (^+2)$$
$$n = 10$$

Answer, 10

Check:
$$n - 2 = 8$$
$$10 - 2 = 8$$
$$8 = 8\surd$$

Introduction to Algebra

Observe that the equation $n - 2 = 8$ may also appear as $8 = n - 2$ but not as $2 - n = 8$ or $8 = 2 - n$. When solving $n - 2 = 8$ or $8 = n - 2$, the constant 2 must be eliminated in each case in order to get an equivalent equation in the simplest form. This is $n = 10$ when solving $n - 2 = 8$, or $10 = n$ when solving $8 = n - 2$. The equation $10 = n$ may be rewritten as $n = 10$.

EXERCISES

Solve and check:

1. $b - 4 = 7$
2. $n - 9 = 3$
3. $x - 15 = 42$
4. $h - 50 = 28$
5. $11 = a - 9$
6. $8 = m - 17$
7. $75 = c - 36$
8. $97 = g - 40$
9. $x - 9 = 9$
10. $24 = r - 24$
11. $d - 12 = 0$

12. $0 = y - 27$
13. $b - \frac{1}{4} = \frac{1}{2}$
14. $5 = t - 3\frac{5}{8}$
15. $x - 2\frac{3}{4} = 7\frac{2}{3}$
16. $8\frac{1}{2} = s - 6$
17. $m - .7 = 3.1$
18. $v - 4.2 = 29$
19. $9.6 = p - 7$
20. $.005 = k - .05$
21. $x - \$.09 = \$.16$
22. $\$32 = y - \$5.80$

23. $z - \$1.39 = \$8.46$
24. $\$10 = n - \$.75$
25. $0 = a - 200$
26. $f - 1\frac{1}{2} = 1\frac{1}{2}$
27. $y - 64 = 25$
28. $64 = c - 25$
29. $d - .6 = .2$
30. $80 = w - 90$
31. $1\frac{5}{6} = b - 4\frac{2}{3}$
32. $m - \$8 = \$2.25$
33. $\$.98 = r - \$.98$

Basic Type III

Solve and check: $2n = 8$
Solution by inverse operation:
The indicated operation of $2n$ is multiplication. To find the root we divide both members by 2.

$$2n = 8$$
$$\frac{2n}{2} = \frac{8}{2}$$
$$n = 4$$

The root is 4.
Answer; 4

Solution by multiplicative inverse: | $2\,n = 8$
The multiplicative inverse of 2 is $\frac{1}{2}$. | $\frac{1}{2} \cdot 2\,n = \frac{1}{2} \cdot 8$
We multiply both members by $\frac{1}{2}$, | $n = 4$
using the multiplication axiom. |

Answer, 4

Check:
$$2\,n = 8$$
$$2 \cdot 4 = 8$$
$$8 = 8\,\checkmark$$

Observe that the equation $2\,n = 8$ may also appear as $8 = 2\,n$. When solving $2\,n = 8$ or $8 = 2\,n$, the numerical coefficient 2 must be eliminated in each case in order to get an equivalent equation in simplest form. This is $n = 4$ when solving $2\,n = 8$, or $4 = n$ when solving $8 = 2\,n$. The equation $4 = n$ may be rewritten as $n = 4$.

EXERCISES

Solve and check:

1. $5\,x = 20$
2. $12\,b = 36$
3. $8\,c = 56$
4. $9\,n = 9$
5. $16\,y = 0$
6. $100 = 10\,s$
7. $72 = 8\,m$
8. $56 = 14\,b$
9. $15 = 15\,z$
10. $132 = 11\,d$
11. $7\,x = 91$
12. $20\,n = 100$
13. $96 = 4\,a$
14. $150 = 25\,w$

15. $5\,c = 18$
16. $7\,a = 23$
17. $15\,r = 37$
18. $43 = 6\,y$
19. $6\,m = 9$
20. $16\,y = 24$
21. $40 = 12\,t$
22. $67 = 21\,g$
23. $7\,c = 5$
24. $15\,c = 1$
25. $9\,d = 15$
26. $21 = 18\,n$
27. $11\,x = 32$
28. $10\,r = 7$

29. $24\,n = 11$
30. $37 = 50\,a$
31. $10\,b = 4$
32. $39\,x = 26$
33. $16 = 24\,y$
34. $6\,x = .36$
35. $.4\,y = 24$
36. $3\,x = \$.48$
37. $.05\,c = 10$
38. $1.04\,a = 5.2$
39. $8\,y = 12$
40. $8 = 12\,y$
41. $.06\,n = 18$
42. $1.02\,c = 51$

43. $\frac{1}{2}\,n = 15$
44. $\frac{1}{5}\,y = 20$
45. $\frac{2}{3}\,n = 42$
46. $\frac{7}{8}\,c = 56$
47. $72 = \frac{3}{4}\,s$
48. $0 = 18\,r$
49. $21\,c = 21$
50. $18\,x = 144$
51. $45 = .3\,y$
52. $\frac{5}{16}\,n = 40$
53. $15\,a = 9$
54. $24\,x = 42$
55. $100 = .04\,n$
56. $\frac{3}{8}\,y = 48$

Introduction to Algebra

363

Basic Type IV

Solve and check: $\dfrac{n}{2} = 8$

Solution by inverse operation:

The indicated operation of $\dfrac{n}{2}$ is division. To find the root we multiply both members by 2.

$$\dfrac{n}{2} = 8$$

$$2 \cdot \dfrac{n}{2} = 2 \cdot 8$$

$$n = 16$$

The root is 16.
Answer, 16

Solution by multiplicative inverse:

Since $\dfrac{n}{2} = \dfrac{1}{2}n$, we use the multiplicative inverse of $\dfrac{1}{2}$, which is 2. We multiply both members by 2, using the multiplication axiom.

$$\dfrac{n}{2} = 8$$

$$2 \cdot \dfrac{1}{2}n = 2 \cdot 8$$

$$n = 16$$

Answer, 16

Check:

$$\dfrac{n}{2} = 8$$

$$\dfrac{16}{2} = 8$$

$$8 = 8\;\checkmark$$

Observe that the equation $\dfrac{n}{2} = 8$ may also appear as $8 = \dfrac{n}{2}$. When solving $\dfrac{n}{2} = 8$ or $8 = \dfrac{n}{2}$, the denominator 2 must be eliminated in each case in order to get an equivalent equation in simplest form. This is $n = 16$ when solving $\dfrac{n}{2} = 8$, or $16 = n$ when solving $8 = \dfrac{n}{2}$. The equation $16 = n$ may be rewritten as $n = 16$.

Solve and check:

1. $\frac{n}{5} = 3$ **6.** $40 = \frac{s}{5}$ **11.** $\frac{1}{2} b = 15$ **16.** $\frac{v}{9} = 6$

2. $\frac{x}{2} = 10$ **7.** $18 = \frac{y}{32}$ **12.** $\frac{1}{3} a = 24$ **15.** $63 = \frac{t}{7}$

3. $\frac{c}{9} = 0$ **8.** $1.4 = \frac{d}{9}$ **13.** $25 = \frac{1}{6} c$ **17.** $\frac{1}{4} x = \$1.20$

4. $\frac{m}{12} = 1$ **9.** $80 = \frac{b}{102}$ **14.** $70 = \frac{1}{10} n$ **19.** $\frac{r}{36} = 18$

5. $\frac{r}{6} = 6$ **10.** $21 = \frac{w}{14}$ **15.** $\frac{1}{100} y = 3.5$ **20.** $\frac{x}{4} = 5$

The solution of more difficult equations may involve the use of more than one axiom. When a member of a given equation consists of two or more terms containing the variable, we first combine these terms.

Solve and check: $7n + 6 = 41$

$$7n + 6 = 41$$
$$7n + 6 - 6 = 41 - 6$$
$$7n = 35$$
$$\frac{7n}{7} = \frac{35}{7}$$
$$n = 5$$

Check:
$$7n + 6 = 41$$
$$(7 \cdot 5) + 6 = 41$$
$$35 + 6 = 41$$
$$41 = 41 \checkmark$$

Answer, 5

Solve and check: $3x + 2x = 20$

$$3x + 2x = 20$$
$$5x = 20$$
$$\frac{5x}{5} = \frac{20}{5}$$
$$x = 4$$

Check:
$$3x + 2x = 20$$
$$(3 \cdot 4) + (2 \cdot 4) = 20$$
$$12 + 8 = 20$$
$$20 = 20 \checkmark$$

Answer, 4

Introduction to Algebra

Solve and check:

1. $6\,a + 5 = 47$
2. $3 + 7\,c = 66$
3. $58 = 11\,y + 25$
4. $103 = 19 + 12\,x$
5. $8\,z - 7 = 89$
6. $127 = 15\,n - 8$
7. $13\,m - 65 = 0$
8. $24\,y - 31 = 89$
9. $x + x = 36$
10. $5\,b + 7\,b = 132$
11. $16\,y - 9\,y = 56$

12. $14\,s - 5\,s = 108$
13. $90 = 7\,d - d$
14. $c + .04\,c = 208$
15. $a - .06\,a = 329$
16. $p + .15\,p = 483$
17. $\frac{2}{3}\,b = 14$
18. $\frac{3}{8}\,n = 48$
19. $\frac{5}{6}\,x = \$9.40$
20. $n + \frac{1}{2}\,n = 7\frac{1}{2}$
21. $\frac{3}{4}\,a - 5 = 10$
22. $l - .45\,l = 11$

23. $3\,c + 25 = 53$
24. $4\,d - 1 = 2$
25. $7\,a - 5 = 12$
26. $7\,a - 5\,a = 12$
27. $11\,b + 3\,b = 70$
28. $0 = 35\,x - 28$
29. $a + .02\,a = 51$
30. $16\,y + 10\,y = 194$
31. $9\,c = 16 + 29$
32. $n - .05\,n = 285$
33. $p - .1\,p = \$302.50$

10–27 SOLVING EQUATIONS WHEN THE REPLACEMENTS FOR THE VARIABLE ARE RESTRICTED

The solution of an equation depends not only on the equation but also on how restricted the replacements for the variable are. The same equation with different replacements for the variable may have different solutions.

For the equation $3x = 12$

When the replacements are all the whole numbers, the solution is 4.

When the replacements are all the even numbers, the solution is 4.

When the replacements are all the prime numbers, there is no solution.

For the equation $4y = 3$

When the replacements are all the real numbers, the solution is $\frac{3}{4}$.

When the replacements are all the whole numbers, there is no solution.

In the latter case, since the solution is a fraction and only whole numbers may be used as the replacements for the variable, there is no solution.

When the replacements for the variables are not given in this book, use all the real numbers as the replacements.

EXERCISES

1. In each of the following, substitute for the variable each number of the given replacement group to determine which is the root of the open sentence:

Open Sentence	Replacements	Open Sentence	Replacements
a. $n + 6 = 8$	0, 1, and 2	**f.** $10\,t - 3\,t = 7$	0, 1, 2, 3, 4, and 5
b. $x - 3 = 4$	3, 7, and 9	**g.** $8\,c - 15 = 49$	2, 4, 6, 8, and 10
c. $12\,y = 36$	1, 3, and 5	**h.** $15\,x + 11 = 86$	1, 3, 5, 7, and 9
d. $4\,m + 5 = 5$	0, 1, 2, and 3	**i.** $9\,n + 4\,n = 104$	2, 5, 6, 8, and 12
e. $\frac{a}{3} = 1$	0, 1, 2, 3, and 4	**j.** $7\,b - 13 = 120$	8, 11, 13, 17, 19, and 21

Find the solution of each of the following:

2. When the replacements for the variable are all the natural numbers:

   a. $7\,x = 56$ **b.** $n + 18 = 18$ **c.** $y - 3 = 11$ **d.** $\frac{b}{6} = 10$

3. When the replacements for the variables are all the whole numbers:

   a. $c + 2 = 7$ **b.** $\frac{x}{12} = 4$ **c.** $9\,n = 25$ **d.** $4\,h - 19 = 13$

4. When the replacements for the variable are all the real numbers:

   a. $m - 35 = 28$ **b.** $16\,a = 14$ **c.** $18\,d + 17 = 53$ **d.** $y + y = 26$

Introduction to Algebra   **367**

5. When the replacements for the variable are 0, 2, 4, 6, . . . :

    a. $\dfrac{n}{7} = 9$ **b.** $25\,b = 500$ **c.** $3\,x - 11 = 72$ **d.** $8\,n + 15 = 95$

6. When the replacements for the variable are all the prime numbers:

    a. $8\,n = 24$ **b.** $x - 5 = 4$ **c.** $4\,t + 8 = 60$ **d.** $\dfrac{r}{2} = 1$

7. When the replacements for the variable are all the multiples of 5:

    a. $y + 9 = 54$ **b.** $3 \cdot m - 12 = 75$ **c.** $6\,x + x = 140$ **d.** $\dfrac{a}{10} = 6$

8. When the replacements for the variable are all the integers:

    a. $16\,c = 96$ **b.** $10\,d - 6\,d = 72$ **c.** $11\,n + 4 = 4$ **d.** $9\,x - 7 = 7$

10–28 SOLVING EQUATIONS WITH ABSOLUTE VALUES

Since $|{}^{+}2| = 2$ and $|{}^{-}2| = 2$, replacement of the variable in the equation $|x| = 2$ by either $^{+}2$ or $^{-}2$ will make the sentence true. Therefore, the roots of $|x| = 2$ and $^{+}2$ and $^{-}2$ or its solutions are $^{+}2$ and $^{-}2$. Observe that there are two solutions.

> We use the equality axioms to solve equations of the basic types:
>
> $$|x| + 7 = 12$$
> $$|x| + 7 - 7 = 12 - 7$$
> $$|x| = 5$$
> $$x = {}^{+}5 \text{ or } {}^{-}5$$
>
> *Answers,* $^{+}5$ and $^{-}5$

EXERCISES

Find the solutions of each of the following equations:

1. $|n| = 3$ **4.** $5 \times |y| = 40$ **7.** $|z| - 54 = 0$ **9.** $12 \times |g| = 96$

2. $|b| = 18$ **5.** $|a| - 6 = 2$

3. $|x| + 4 = 11$ **6.** $|w| + 19 = 25$ **8.** $\dfrac{|m|}{9} = 4$ **10.** $\dfrac{|r|}{2} = 10$

10-29 GRAPHING AN EQUATION IN ONE VARIABLE ON THE NUMBER LINE

Since the graph of an equation is the graph of its solutions, the graph of an equation in one variable on the number line is all points on the number line whose coordinates are the solutions to the equation.

The solutions to the equations studied thus far consisted mostly of one number, although some consisted of two numbers. Where the solution is one number, the graph will consist of one point; where there are two solutions, the graph will consist of two points. Observe in illustration (5) that the solution of the given equation is an infinite collection of numbers which is shown as the entire number line. (See page 370.)

To draw the graph of an equation in one variable on the number line, we first solve the given equation to find its solutions. We then locate the point or points whose coordinate or coordinates are numbers forming all the solutions to the given equation. We indicate these points by solid or colored dots. Also see section 10-4.

---

(1) The solution of the equation $n + 2 = 8$ is 6. The graph of $n + 2 = 8$ is the point whose coordinate is 6.

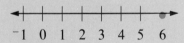

(2) The solution of the equation $7n + 6 = 41$ is 5. The graph of $7n + 6 = 41$ is the point whose coordinate is 5.

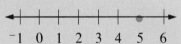

(3) There is no solution to the equation $x = x + 3$ since there is no number that is greater than or less than itself. We have no points to draw the graph.

(4) The solutions of $|x| = 2$ are ⁻2 and ⁺2. The graph of $|x| = 2$ is the points whose coordinates are ⁻2 and ⁺2.

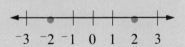

Introduction to Algebra

(5) The solution of $3x + 12 = 3(x + 4)$ is an infinite collection of numbers since the equation (identity) is satisfied by every real number. The graph of $3x + 12 = 3(x + 4)$ is the entire number line indicated by a solid or colored line with an arrowhead in each direction to show that it is endless.

$$\begin{array}{ccccccccc} & & & & & & & & \\ -4 & -3 & -2 & -1 & 0 & 1 & 2 & 3 & 4 \end{array}$$

(6) The graph 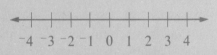 is a picture of

$$\begin{array}{cccccccc} -2 & -1 & 0 & 1 & 2 & 3 & 4 \end{array}$$

the equation $x = 3$ or any equivalent equation such as $4x = 12$, $x + 2 = 5$, $x - 1 = 2$, etc.

EXERCISES

For each of the following equations first draw an appropriate number line, then graph its solution. The replacements for the variables are all the real numbers.

1. $x = 4$
2. $y = 2$
3. $4n = 20$
4. $x + 9 = 15$
5. $b - 2 = 2$
6. $w + 3 = 3$
7. $9x = 72$
8. $\frac{n}{2} = 5$

9. $v - 3 = 4$
10. $8t = 8$
11. $n + 37 = 37$
12. $\frac{b}{4} = 2$
13. $7 = x - 1$
14. $84 = 12a$
15. $23 = 14 + y$
16. $10c = 5$

17. $6n + 15 = 69$
18. $10a + 7 = 7$
19. $17x - 5x = 24$
20. $11y - 5 = 6$
21. $3x + 19 = 43$
22. $6n - n = 20$
23. $11 = 2w + 8$
24. $29 = 4m - 5$

25. $n = n + 4$
26. $2x + 18 = 2(x + 9)$
27. $x = x - 1$
28. $\frac{m}{7} = 1$
29. $n + 9 = n$
30. $|x| = 4$
31. $x + 6 = 6 + x$
32. $|n| = 7$

10–30 SOLVING AND GRAPHING INEQUALITIES WHEN THE REPLACEMENTS FOR THE VARIABLE ARE RESTRICTED

This section is a brief introduction to the solution and graphing of inequalities when the replacements for the variable are limited to just a few numbers.

The *solutions of an inequality* are all the numbers each of which, when substituted for the variable, will make the inequality a true sentence.

The solutions of $x < 3$ when the replacements for the variable are limited to 0, 1, 2, 3, 4, and 5 are 0, 1, and 2 because 0, 1, and 2, as we see by the following, are the only given replacements that will make the sentence $x < 3$ true.

To find the solutions of $x < 3$ when the replacements for the variable are 0, 1, 2, 3, 4, and 5, we substitute each of the replacements for the variable x in the sentence $x < 3$:

$x < 3$	$x < 3$	$x < 3$	$x < 3$	$x < 3$	$x < 3$
$0 < 3$	$1 < 3$	$2 < 3$	$3 < 3$	$4 < 3$	$5 < 3$
true	true	true	false	false	false

Answer, Solutions are 0, 1, and 2

The graph of an inequality is the graph of its solutions. To draw the graph of an inequality on a number line, we first find the solutions of the inequality. We then locate the point or points whose coordinate or coordinates are numbers forming the solutions to the given inequality. We indicate these points by solid or colored dots. Also see section 10–4.

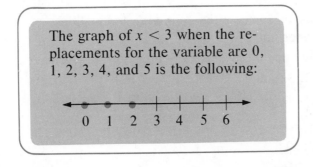

The graph of $x < 3$ when the replacements for the variable are 0, 1, 2, 3, 4, and 5 is the following:

Introduction to Algebra

1. Substitute for the variable each number given in the replacement group to determine which values make each sentence true:

Sentence	Replacements
a. $x < 4$	1, 2, 3, 4, 5, 6, and 7
b. $y > 5$	2, 3, 5, 10, 13, 20, and 34
c. $z < 2$	$^-3$, $^-2$, $^-1$, 0, 1, 2, and 3
d. $w > {}^-2$	$^-4$, $^-3$, $^-1$, 1, 2, and 4
e. $x < {}^-3$	$^-6$, $^-5$, $^-4$, . . . , 6
f. $n > 3$	0, 1, 2, . . . , 10
g. $b < 1$	all the whole numbers
h. $a > 4$	all the whole numbers less than 5
i. $x + 1 < 12$	1, 3, 5, . . . , 19
j. $y - 2 > 11$	2, 4, 6, . . . , 24
k. $n + 9 > 14$	$^-4$, $^-3$, $^-2$, . . . , 7
l. $y - 4 < 11$	3, 6, 9, . . . , 30
m. $3\,x < 15$	0, 1, 4, 6, 9, and 11
n. $5\,b > 30$	1, 2, 3, 6, 10, 15, and 18
o. $2\,x < 10$	all the integers greater than $^-3$ and less than 7
p. $7\,z > 63$	all the odd whole numbers less than 11
q. $2\,x + 3 < 5$	$^-1$, 0, and 1
r. $4\,y - 1 < 29$	0, 2, 4, . . . , 12
s. $3\,n + 5 > 23$	1, 3, 4, 7, 8, 12, and 16
t. $9\,b - 8 > 19$	$^-10$, $^-9$, $^-8$, . . . , 10

2. Find the solutions of $3\,x + 1 < 10$ when the replacements are:

   a. all the natural numbers   **b.** all the whole numbers   **c.** $^-4$, $^-3$, $^-2$, . . . , 4

3. When the replacements are $^-5$, $^-4$, $^-3$, . . . , 5, find the solutions of each of the following inequalities:

   a. $x < 0$ **c.** $4\,n < 12$ **e.** $x - 2 > 0$ **g.** $2\,x - 5 > 5$

   b. $y > 1$ **d.** $9\,b > 36$ **f.** $y + 4 < 4$ **h.** $\frac{n}{2} < 1$

4. First find the solutions of each of the following inequalities. Then draw on the number line the graph of its solutions.

Sentence	Replacements	Sentence	Replacements
a. $n > 2$	0, 1, 2, 3, and 4	**f.** $n - 5 > 1$	0, 1, 2, . . . , 12
b. $x < 5$	1, 2, 3, . . . , 10	**g.** $r - 8 < 1$	1, 2, 3, . . . , 15
c. $6\,b > 24$	0, 1, 2, . . . , 8	**h.** $d + 4 > 7$	$^-5$, $^-4$, $^-3$, . . . , 5
d. $7\,m < 7$	$^-2$, $^-1$, 0, 1, and 2	**i.** $2\,x + 1 > 6$	0, 1, 2, . . . , 10
e. $x + 3 < 5$	$^-3$, $^-2$, $^-1$, . . . , 3	**j.** $3\,t - 4 < 11$	$^-2$, $^-1$, 0, . . . , 9

5. Draw a graph of each of the following inequalities on the number line:

	Sentence	Replacements		Sentence	Replacements
a.	$x < 4$	1, 2, 3, 4, 5, and 6	**f.**	$b + 3 < 3$	$^-4, ^-3, ^-2, \ldots, 4$
b.	$n > 0$	$0, 1, 2, \ldots, 8$	**g.**	$w - 4 > 1$	$1, 2, 3, \ldots, 9$
c.	$11\,a < 11$	$^-3, ^-2, ^-1, \ldots, 3$	**h.**	$2n + 7 < 15$	$^-6, ^-5, ^-4, \ldots, 6$
d.	$8\,t > 64$	$1, 2, 3, \ldots, 10$	**i.**	$6\,y - 5 > 25$	$0, 1, 2, \ldots, 15$
e.	$m - 2 < 5$	$0, 1, 2, \ldots, 12$	**j.**	$\frac{n}{4} < 2$	$^-2, ^-1, 0, \ldots, 12$

10–31 RATIO

We may compare two numbers by subtraction or by division. When we compare 20 with 5, we find by subtraction that 20 is fifteen more than 5 and by division that 20 is four times as large as 5. When we compare 5 with 20, we find by subtraction that 5 is fifteen less than 20 and by division that 5 is one-fourth as large as 20.

The answer we obtain when we compare two quantities by division is called the *ratio* of the two quantities.

When 20 is compared to 5, 20 is divided by 5 as $\frac{20}{5}$ which equals $\frac{4}{1}$. The ratio is $\frac{4}{1}$ or 4 to 1.

When 5 is compared to 20, 5 is divided by 20 as $\frac{5}{20}$ which equals $\frac{1}{4}$. The ratio is $\frac{1}{4}$ or 1 to 4.

A ratio has two terms, the number that is being compared (found in the numerator) and the number to which the first number is being compared (found in the denominator). The ratio in fraction form is usually expressed in lowest terms.

The ratio of 5 miles to 6 miles is $\frac{5}{6}$. The fraction $\frac{5}{6}$ is an indicated division meaning $5 \div 6$. Usually the ratio is expressed as a common fraction but it may also be expressed as a decimal fraction or a percent.

The ratio $\frac{5}{6}$ is sometimes written as $5:6$. The colon may be used instead of the fraction bar. The ratio in either form is read "5 to 6" "(five to six)."

If the quantities compared are denominate numbers, they must first be expressed in the same units. The ratio is an abstract number; it contains no unit of measurement.

A ratio may be used to express a *rate*. The average rate of speed of an automobile when it travels 150 miles in 3 hours may be expressed by the ratio which is $\frac{150}{3}$ or 50 miles per hour. If pears sell at the rate of 3 for 89¢, the ratio expressing this rate is $\frac{3}{89}$ and is read "3 for 89."

When a ratio is used to express a rate, the two quantities have different names like miles and hours, pears and cents, etc.

Ratios such as $\frac{2}{6}$, $\frac{3}{9}$, $\frac{4}{12}$, $\frac{5}{15}$, although written with different number pairs, express the same comparison or rate. These ratios are called *equivalent ratios*. In simplest form they are the same, the ratio $\frac{1}{3}$.

EXERCISES

1. Find the ratio of:

   a. 3 to 18
   b. 6 to 14
   c. 2 to 3
   d. 25 to 75
   e. 49 to 56

   f. 12 to 4
   g. 9 to 5
   h. 16 to 2
   i. 36 to 8
   j. 63 to 54

   k. 24 to 6
   l. 3 to 15
   m. 18 to 20
   n. 40 to 16
   o. 72 to 108

2. Find the ratio of:

   a. 8 mm to 10 mm
   b. 9 cm to 1 m
   c. 1 yd. to 27 in.
   d. 2 lb. to 12 oz.
   e. 3 kg to 2 g

   f. 1 pt. to 1 gal.
   g. A nickel to a quarter
   h. A dollar to a dime
   i. 9 things to 1 dozen
   j. 1 dozen to 10 things

   k. 45 min. to 3 hr.
   l. 2 min. to 20 sec.
   m. 15 mo. to 4 yr.
   n. 125 mm to 3 m
   o. 50 min. to 2 hr. 30 min.

3. Express each of the following rates as a ratio:

   a. 6 boxes for 25¢
   b. 900 meters per second
   c. 1,250 liters in 10 minutes
   d. 90¢ for 4 quarts
   e. 750 miles in 3 hours

   f. 5,400 revolutions in 9 minutes
   g. 128 kilometers on 8 liters
   h. $41 for 5 ties
   i. 12 tablets for 75¢
   j. $115 for 20 square meters

4. The class marks in mathematics for the semester were distributed as follows: 4 A's, 10 B's, 12 C's, 8 D's, and 2 E's. What is the ratio of the number of pupils receiving C to those receiving A? B's to E's? A's to D's? D's to B's?

5. There are 320 boys and 280 girls enrolled in a school. What is the ratio of: boys to girls? girls to boys? boys to entire enrollment? girls to entire enrollment? If there are 24 teachers, what is the ratio of pupils to teachers?

10–32 PROPORTIONS

A *proportion* is a mathematical sentence which states that two ratios are equivalent.

Using the equivalent ratios $\frac{4}{8}$ and $\frac{12}{24}$ we may write the proportion $\frac{4}{8} = \frac{12}{24}$. This proportion may also be expressed as $4:8 = 12:24$. The proportion in both forms is read "4 is to 8 as 12 is to 24."

There are four terms in a proportion as shown:

$$\begin{array}{c} \text{first} \to 4 \\ \text{second} \to 8 \end{array} = \begin{array}{c} 12 \leftarrow \text{third} \\ 24 \leftarrow \text{fourth} \end{array} \qquad \begin{array}{cccc} \text{1st} & \text{2nd} & \text{3rd} & \text{4th} \\ \downarrow & \downarrow & \downarrow & \downarrow \\ 4 & : 8 & = 12 & : 24 \end{array}$$

In the proportion $4:8 = 12:24$, the first term (4) and the fourth term (24) are called the *extremes* and the second term (8) and the third (12) are called the *means*. Observe that the product of the extremes (4×24) is equal to the product of the means (8×12). In the form $\frac{4}{8} = \frac{12}{24}$ observe that the cross products are equal ($4 \times 24 = 8 \times 12$). These products are equal *only* when the ratios are equivalent. We can check whether two ratios are equivalent by either expressing each ratio in lowest terms or by determining whether the cross products are equal.

If any three of the four terms of the proportion are known quantities, the fourth may be determined. We use the idea that the product of the extremes is equal to the product of the means to transform the given proportion to a simpler equation.

Thus we find the cross products by multiplying the numerator of the first fraction by the denominator of the second fraction and the numerator of the second fraction by the denominator of the first fraction. We write one product equal to the other, then we solve the resulting equation.

Solve and check: $\dfrac{n}{54} = \dfrac{5}{6}$

Solution:

$$\frac{n}{54} = \frac{5}{6}$$
$$6 \times n = 5 \times 54$$
$$6n = 270$$
$$\frac{6n}{6} = \frac{270}{6}$$
$$n = 45 \qquad \textit{Answer, } 45$$

Check:

$$\frac{45}{54} = \frac{5}{6}$$
$$\frac{5}{6} = \frac{5}{6} \checkmark$$

Introduction to Algebra

1. Write each of the following as a proportion:

    a. 10 compared to 12 is the same as 5 compared to 6.

    b. 36 compared to 9 is the same as 28 compared to 7.

    c. A number n compared to 15 is the same as 2 compared to 3.

    d. 90 compared to 100 is the same as some number n compared to 25.

2. Solve and check:

    a. $\dfrac{n}{20} = \dfrac{3}{5}$ **e.** $\dfrac{7}{8} = \dfrac{d}{16}$ **i.** $\dfrac{96}{c} = \dfrac{12}{25}$ **m.** $\dfrac{5}{16} = \dfrac{35}{b}$ **q.** $\dfrac{x}{9} = \dfrac{5}{8}$

    b. $\dfrac{x}{45} = \dfrac{7}{9}$ **f.** $\dfrac{4}{5} = \dfrac{n}{65}$ **j.** $\dfrac{72}{g} = \dfrac{9}{5}$ **n.** $\dfrac{2}{7} = \dfrac{26}{n}$ **r.** $\dfrac{19}{21} = \dfrac{a}{21}$

    c. $\dfrac{a}{12} = \dfrac{25}{36}$ **g.** $\dfrac{7}{6} = \dfrac{y}{9}$ **k.** $\dfrac{27}{x} = \dfrac{18}{56}$ **o.** $\dfrac{108}{18} = \dfrac{18}{r}$ **s.** $\dfrac{3}{d} = \dfrac{7}{2}$

    d. $\dfrac{b}{8} = \dfrac{28}{32}$ **h.** $\dfrac{11}{16} = \dfrac{m}{100}$ **i.** $\dfrac{8}{n} = \dfrac{120}{75}$ **p.** $\dfrac{32}{7} = \dfrac{5}{x}$ **t.** $\dfrac{n}{4} = \dfrac{25}{10}$

    Using proportions, solve each of the following:

3. a. What number compared to 56 is the same as 9 compared to 14?

    b. 12 compared to 75 is the same as what number compared to 100?

    c. 27 compared to what number is the same as 105 compared to 35?

    d. 96 compared to 180 is the same as 16 compared to what number?

4. At the rate of 4 for 15¢, how many can you buy for 90¢?

5. At the rate of 5 items for $8, how much will 7 items cost?

6. A motorist traveled 172 kilometers on the turnpike in 2 hours. How long will it take him at that rate to travel 301 kilometers?

7. How many square meters of lawn will 10 kg of grass seed cover if 2 kg of seed are required for 130 square meters?

8. If it takes 24 yards of material to make 4 pairs of window drapes, how many yards of material are required to make 9 pairs of drapes?

9. Find the value of c if $c' = 44$, $d = 70$, and $d' = 14$, using the formula, $\dfrac{c}{c'} = \dfrac{d}{d'}$

10. Find the value of R_3 if $R_1 = 150$, $R_2 = 96$, and $R_4 = 144$, using the formula, $\dfrac{R_1}{R_2} = \dfrac{R_3}{R_4}$

CHAPTER REVIEW

1. Which of the following numerals name integers? Which name (10–1)
   rational numbers? Which name irrational numbers? Which (10–2)
   name real numbers?

   $^+.67$ $-\frac{9}{10}$ $^+\sqrt{73}$ $^-99$ $^+6\frac{3}{8}$ $-\frac{36}{12}$

2. Find the absolute value of: **a.** $|^-16|$ **b.** $|^+10|$ (10–3)
3. Draw the graph of $^-4$, $^-2$, 0, $^+1$, $^+3$ on a number line.   (10–4)
4. Which of the following are true?   (10–5)

   a. $^+2 < {}^+8$ **c.** $^+3 \not< {}^-4$ **e.** $^+1 < {}^-3$
   b. $0 > {}^-1$ **d.** $^-5 \not> {}^-2$

5. If $^+300$ feet represents 300 feet above sea level, how can 50
   feet below sea level be represented?   (10–6)
6. Use the number line as a scale to draw a vector that illustrates
   each of the following movements. Write the numeral that is
   represented by each of these vectors.   (10–7)

   a. From $^-3$ to $^+6$ **b.** From $^+1$ to $^-5$

7. **a.** What is the opposite of $^+9$?   (10–1)
   b. What is the opposite of $^-50$?
   c. What is the opposite of the opposite of $\frac{-1}{2}$?   (10–8)
   d. What is the additive inverse of $^-14$?
   e. Write symbolically: The opposite of negative eight is positive eight.

8. Add on the number line, using vectors: (10–9)

   a. $^+3 + {}^-7$ **c.** $^-1 + {}^+8$
   b. $^-4 + {}^-2$ **d.** $^-6 + {}^+4$

9. Add as indicated: (10–10)

   a. $^-18 + {}^+24$ **c.** $^-31 + {}^-27$
   b. $^+23 + {}^-19$ **d.** $^+42 + {}^-60$

10. Add as indicated: (10–11)

    a. $^+3\frac{1}{2} + {}^+7\frac{7}{8}$ **c.** $^-1.8 + {}^-.25$
    b. $\frac{-3}{4} + {}^+2\frac{2}{3}$ **d.** $^+.617 + {}^-.62$

11. Subtract on the number line, using vectors: (10–12)

    a. $^-7 - {^+5}$

    b. $^-8 - {^-10}$

    c. $^+3 - {^-4}$

    d. $^+6 - {^+11}$

12. Subtract as indicated: (10–13)

    a. $^-42 - {^+18}$

    b. $13 - 31$

    c. $0 - {^-12}$

    d. $^-63 - {^-100}$

13. Subtract as indicated: (10–14)

    a. $^+1\frac{1}{5} - {^-2\frac{1}{2}}$

    b. $\frac{^-5}{6} - {^-7}$

    c. $8.4 - 9$

    d. $^-.005 - {^+2.41}$

14. Multiply as indicated: (10–15)

    a. $^-15 \times {^-8}$

    b. $^+21 \times {^-43}$

    c. $(6)(^-9)(^-5)$

    d. $(^-2)(3)(^-4)(^-1)$

15. Multiply as indicated: (10–16)

    a. $\frac{^-3}{8} \times \frac{^+4}{5}$

    b. $^-3\frac{3}{4} \times {^-2\frac{2}{3}}$

    c. $.64 \times {^-1.87}$

    d. $^-80.5 \times {^-.06}$

16. Divide as indicated: (10–17)

    a. $^-30 \div {^-15}$

    b. $^+14 \div {^-14}$

    c. $^-63 \div 9$

    d. $^-28 \div {^-1}$

17. Divide as indicated: (10–18)

    a. $\frac{^-1}{2} \div \frac{^+3}{4}$

    b. $^-5\frac{1}{3} \div {^-1\frac{5}{12}}$

    c. $3.496 \div {^-.02}$

    d. $^-.1 \div {^-.001}$

18. Perform the indicated operation: (10–19)

    a. $(-7) + (-8)$

    b. $(+12) - (-9)$

    c. $(-4)(-8)$

    d. $(-21)(+3)$

19. a. Are the integers closed under the operation of addition? Subtraction? Multiplication? Division? Explain your answers. (10–10 through 10–18)

    b. Does each integer have an additive inverse? Explain your answer.

    c. Does each non-zero integer have a multiplicative inverse? Explain.

d. Do the integers have an additive identity? If so, what is it?

(10–10 through 10–18)

e. Do the integers have a multiplicative identity? If so, what is it?

f. Does the commutative property hold for the addition of integers? Subtraction of integers? Multiplication of integers? Division of integers? Explain your answers.

g. Does the associative property hold for the addition of integers? Subtraction of integers? Multiplication of integers? Division of integers? Explain your answers.

h. Does the distributive property of multiplication over addition hold for the integers? Explain your answer.

i. Are the rational numbers closed under the operation of addition? Subtraction? Multiplication? Division? Explain your answers.

j. Does each rational number have an additive inverse? Explain.

k. Does each non-zero rational number have a multiplicative inverse? Explain your answer.

l. Do the rational numbers have an additive identity? If so, what is it?

m. Do the rational numbers have a multiplicative identity? If so, what is it?

n. Does the commutative property hold for the addition of rational numbers? Subtraction of rational numbers? Multiplication of rational numbers? Division of rational numbers? Explain your answers.

o. Does the associative property hold for the addition of rational numbers? Subtraction of rational numbers? Multiplication of rational numbers? Division of rational numbers? Explain.

p. Does the distributive property of multiplication over addi-hold for the rational numbers? Explain your answer.

20. Write each of the following as an algebraic expression:

(10–21)

a. The sum of the principal (p) and the interest (i).

b. The product of c and nine.

c. The difference between the selling price (s) and the cost (c).

d. The area (A) divided by the length (l).

21. Write each of the following as an open sentence symbolically: (10–22)

    a. Some number n decreased by four is equal to twenty-one.

    b. Four times each number x increased by seven is greater than forty.

    c. Each number b divided by five is less than or equal to twelve.

    d. Each number y is less than two and greater than zero.

22. Express as a formula: The rate of discount (r) is equal to the discount (d) divided by the list price (l).   (10–23)

23. Solve and check: (10–26)

    a. $y + 26 = 57$ **d.** $\frac{n}{8} = 16$ **g.** $6t - 9 = 0$

    b. $69 = c - 81$ **e.** $3a + 11 = 38$ **h.** $\frac{3}{5}d = 30$

    c. $12x = 96$ **f.** $8y - y = 63$

24. Find the solutions of each of the following when the replacements for the variable are all the odd numbers: (10–27)

    a. $9x = 63$ **b.** $n + 4 = 6$ **c.** $\frac{a}{5} = 3$ **d.** $r - 7 = 12$

25. Find the solution of $|x| - 4 = 8$ when the replacements for the variable are all the real numbers.   (10–28)

26. Draw the graph of each of the following on the number line when the replacements for the variable are all the real numbers: (10–29)

    a. $n = 8$ **b.** $2x = 12$ **c.** $n + 5 = 10$ **d.** $3x - 2 = 10$

27. Find the solutions of: (10–30)

    a. $y - 3 < 2$ when the replacements for the variable are: 1, 4, 5, 9, and 13

    b. $3x + 5 > 5$ when the replacements for the variable are: $-2, -1, 0, 1,$ and 2

28. Graph each of the following inequalities on the number line: (10–30)

    a. $x + 1 > 6$ when the replacements for the variable are: $0, 1, 2, \ldots, 10$

    b. $2n < 4$ when the replacements for the variable are: $-3, -2, -1, \ldots, 3$

29. Find the ratio of 54 to 9. Of 6 to 21. Of 200 m to 5 km.   (10–31)

30. Solve and check: $\frac{n}{72} = \frac{17}{24}$ (10–32)

ACHIEVEMENT TEST

1. Add:

598,324 (2–9)
69,899
376,087
93,398
847,755

2. Subtract:

3,600,401 (2–10)
907,339

3. Multiply:

6,050 (2–11)
705

4. Divide:

$968\overline{)783,112}$ (2–16)

5. Add:

$3\frac{5}{6} - 4\frac{3}{4} + 1\frac{3}{8}$ (4–11)

6. Subtract:

$12 - 9\frac{11}{16}$ (4–12)

7. Multiply:

$3\frac{1}{7} \times 5\frac{7}{8}$ (4–13)

8. Divide:

$\frac{3}{5} \div 1\frac{1}{2}$ (4–15)

9. Add:

$74.8 + .859 + 6.37$ (5–7)

10. Subtract:

$4.5 - .23$ (5–8)

11. Multiply:

$.008 \times .0015$ (5–9)

12. Divide:

$.005\overline{).6}$ (5–11)

13. Find 23% of $593. (6–6)
14. What percent of $125 is $75? (6–7)
15. 9% of what number is 54? (6–8)
16. Find the square root of 82,011,136. (7–2)

17. a. Change 6.8 kilometers to meters. (8–1)
b. Change 470 milligrams to grams. (8–2)

18. 8.625 liters of water occupies a space of _____ cm³ and weighs
_____ kg. (8–5)
19. How many feet are in 7 miles? (8–1)
20. What part of a pound is 6 ounces? (8–7)
21. How many pints are in 2 gallons? (8–8)
22. What part of an hour is 18 minutes? (8–13)
23. Is a temperature of 80°C cooler than a temperature of 170°F? (8–16)
24. Express in A.M. or P.M. time: **a.** 0005 **b.** 1440 (8–17)
25. If it is midnight in Chicago, what time is it in Los Angeles?
In Boston? (8–18)

26. Which of the following numerals name integers? Which name rational numbers? Which name irrational numbers? Which name real numbers? (10–1)

$^+\frac{3}{5}$ $^-7.86$ $^+\frac{54}{3}$ $^-\sqrt{105}$ $^-9\frac{5}{12}$ $^-1$ (10–2)

27. Add as indicated: (10–10)

    a. $^-16 + {}^-21$ **c.** $^+3\frac{11}{16} + {}^-5\frac{1}{4}$ (10–11)

    b. $^-48 + {}^+75$ **d.** $^-4.82 + {}^+.594$

28. Subtract as indicated: (10–13)

    a. $39 - 72$ **c.** $^-2\frac{1}{6} - \frac{4}{5}$ (10–14)

    b. $97 - {}^-89$ **d.** $^-.095 - {}^-1.6$

29. Multiply as indicated: (10–15)

    a. $^-18 \times {}^-5$ **c.** $^+2\frac{2}{5} \times {}^-8\frac{3}{4}$ (10–16)

    b. $(3)({}^-4)(7)$ **d.** $^-.84 \times {}^-.013$

30. Divide as indicated: (10–17)

    a. $^-90 \div {}^-10$ **c.** $^-8\frac{1}{3} \div 2$ (10–18)

    b. $48 \div {}^-16$ **d.** $^-.06 \div {}^-.003$

31. Illustrate each of the following properties:

    a. Commutative property of multiplication of integers. (10–15)

    b. Associative property of addition of rational numbers. (10–11)

    c. Distributive property of multiplication over addition for the integers. (10–15)

32. Solve and check: (10–26)

    a. $c - 18 = 13$ **d.** $\frac{x}{15} = 10$ **g.** $2x + x = 42$

    b. $15n = 105$ **e.** $9y + 7 = 34$ **h.** $\frac{5}{6}d = 90$

    c. $36 = b + 21$ **f.** $8n - 6 = 0$

33. Find the solution of $|n| + 9 = 17$. (10–28)

34. Draw the graph of $5x + 3 = 13$ on the number line. (10–29)

35. Solve and check: $\frac{87}{54} = \frac{b}{36}$ (10–32)

CHAPTER 11
Informal Geometry

Geometry is the study of points, lines, planes, and space, of measurement and construction of geometric figures, and of geometric facts and relationships. The word "geometry" means "earth measure." The Egyptians developed many geometric ideas because the flooding of the Nile River destroyed land boundaries which had to be restored. Euclid, a Greek mathematician, in the third century B.C. collected and organized the geometric principles known at that time and wrote a book on geometry.

POINTS, LINES, PLANES, AND SPACE

A geometric *point* is an exact location in space. It has no size nor can it be seen. Any dot we generally use to indicate it is only a representation of a geometric point.

A geometric *line* is a collection of points. The pencil or chalk lines we draw are only representations of geometric lines. A line may be extended indefinitely in both directions because it is end-

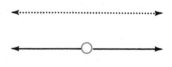

less; it has an infinite number of points but no endpoints. A definite part of a line has length but no width or thickness. We cannot see a geometric line.

A point separates a line into two *half-lines*. Each half-line extends indefinitely in one direction only and does not include the point that separates the line into two half-lines.

A geometric *plane* or flat surface is a collection of points. It is endless in extent and it has no boundaries but it has length and width which can be measured when the plane is limited. A desk

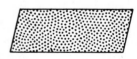

top, wall, floor, and sheet of paper are common representations of a limited plane. We cannot see a geometric plane. It extends beyond any line boundaries we use to represent it.

A line separates a plane into two half-planes.

Space is the infinite collection of all points. Its length, width, and height are endless. A limited space can be measured. A plane separates space into two half-spaces.

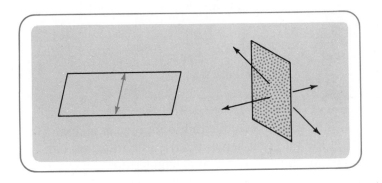

11-1 NAMING POINTS, LINES, AND PLANES

A capital letter is used to label and name a point.

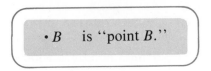

• B   is "point *B*."

A line is represented as: ⟵⟶ The arrowheads are used to show that a line is endless in both directions.

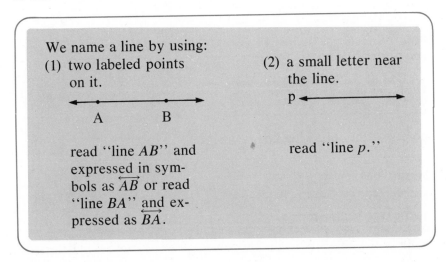

We name a line by using:
(1) two labeled points on it.

    ⟵•————•⟶
     A   B

read "line *AB*" and expressed in symbols as $\overleftrightarrow{AB}$ or read "line *BA*" and expressed as $\overleftrightarrow{BA}$.

(2) a small letter near the line.

   p ⟵————⟶

read "line *p*."

A definite part of a line including both of its endpoints is called a *line segment* or *segment*. It consists of two endpoints and all the points between. We name a line segment by its endpoints. A definite part of a line excluding its endpoints is called an *interval*.

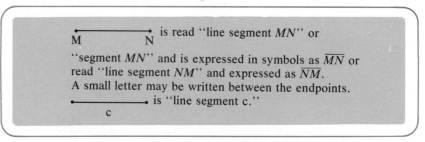

$\underset{M \qquad\qquad N}{\bullet\!\!-\!\!-\!\!-\!\!-\!\!-\!\!-\!\!\bullet}$ is read "line segment *MN*" or "segment *MN*" and is expressed in symbols as $\overline{MN}$ or read "line segment *NM*" and expressed as $\overline{NM}$.
A small letter may be written between the endpoints.
$\underset{c}{\bullet\!\!-\!\!-\!\!-\!\!-\!\!-\!\!-\!\!\bullet}$ is "line segment c."

A half-line which includes one endpoint is called a *ray*. This endpoint is the one that separates the line into two half-lines. To name a ray we use the letter first which names the endpoint and then the letter which names one other point on the ray.

$\underset{C \quad D}{\bullet\!\!-\!\!-\!\!\bullet\!\!-\!\!-\!\!\rightarrow}$ is named "ray *CD*," expressed in symbols as $\overrightarrow{CD}$. However, $\leftarrow\!\!-\!\!-\!\!\bullet\!\!-\!\!-\!\!\bullet$ $\underset{C \quad D}{}$ is named "ray *DC*," expressed in symbols as $\overrightarrow{DC}$.

A plane is named by using the letters which name three points not on the same line belonging to it, or by two capital letters at opposite corners, or by one capital letter as shown.

plane RST   plane PQ   plane M

EXERCISES

1. Name the endpoints of the following line segment: $\underset{D \qquad\qquad E}{\bullet\!\!-\!\!-\!\!-\!\!-\!\!\bullet}$

2. Name the following lines:

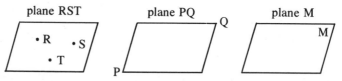

3. Name the following line segments:

4. Express the name of each of the following symbolically:

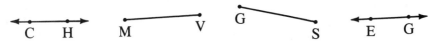

5. Name the following rays and express them symbolically:

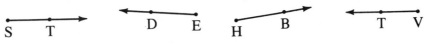

6. Name R P N M in three ways. Write the names symbolically.

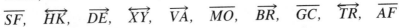

7. Read, or write in words, each of the following:

$\overline{SF}$, $\overleftrightarrow{HK}$, $\overrightarrow{DE}$, $\overrightarrow{XY}$, $\overrightarrow{VA}$, $\overline{MO}$, $\overrightarrow{BR}$, $\overleftrightarrow{GC}$, $\overrightarrow{TR}$, $\overline{AF}$

8. Name the point that is common to $\overleftrightarrow{BC}$ and $\overrightarrow{GH}$.

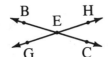

9. $\overline{XZ}$ is divided into 2 parts by point Y. Name the two segments.

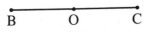

10. Point O bisects $\overline{BC}$. Name the two equal segments.

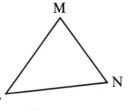

11. Points F and G separate $\overline{DE}$ into 3 parts. Name the 3 segments.

12. Name each of the following planes:

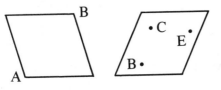
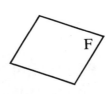

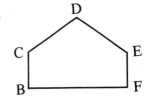

Name the line segments in each of the following figures:

13.
14.
15.

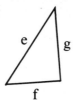

16. $\overline{PR}$ is the difference of what segments?

17. $\overline{GH}$ is the sum of what segments?

11-2 KINDS OF LINES

Lines may be *straight, curved,* or *broken*. Usually a straight line is simply called a line. All these lines are sometimes called curves.

Straight Line   Curved Line   Broken Line

What kind of line is shown by figure *a*? *b*? *c*? *d*? *e*? *f*? *g*? *h*? *i*? *j*?

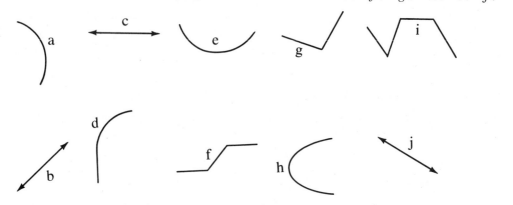

11-3 POSITION OF LINES

Lines may be in *vertical, horizontal,* or *slanting* (sometimes called *oblique*) positions.

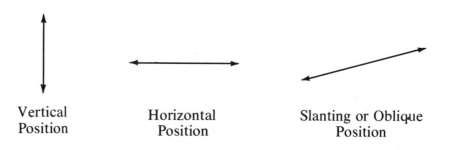

Vertical
Position

Horizontal
Position

Slanting or Oblique
Position

What position is shown by the line in figure *a*? *b*? *c*? *d*? *e*?
f? *g*? *h*? *i*? *j*?

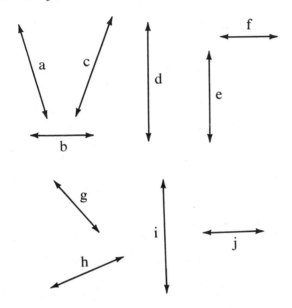

11–4 INTERSECTING, PARALLEL, AND PERPENDICULAR LINES

Lines that meet are *intersecting lines*. Since they have a common point, intersecting lines are sometimes called *concurrent lines*. Two lines in the same plane that do not meet are called *parallel lines*. Two lines not in the same plane that do not meet are called *skew lines*. Two intersecting lines or rays or segments or a line and ray or a line and segment or a ray and segment that form a right angle (see page 395) are said to be *perpendicular* to each other.

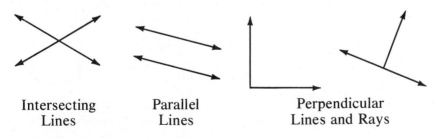

Intersecting
Lines

Parallel
Lines

Perpendicular
Lines and Rays

Informal Geometry

1. Which of the following are intersecting lines or rays? Which are parallel lines? Which are perpendicular lines or rays?

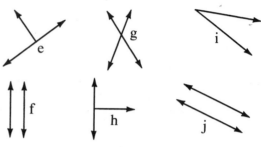

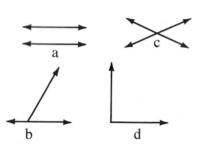

2. **a.** Which ray is perpendicular to $\overrightarrow{OB}$?

   b. Which ray is perpendicular to $\overleftrightarrow{EF}$?

3. Which line is parallel to line n?

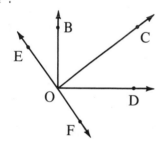

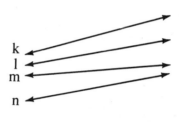

4. At what point do $\overleftrightarrow{AB}$ and $\overleftrightarrow{RS}$ intersect?

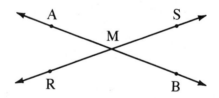

5. Find the intersection of each of the following pairs of segments:

   a. $\overline{AE}$ and $\overline{CE}$ **c.** $\overline{AC}$ and $\overline{AE}$
   b. $\overline{CE}$ and $\overline{AC}$

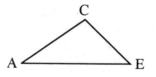

6. Find the intersection of each of the following pairs of segments:

   a. $\overline{PR}$ and $\overline{TR}$ **c.** $\overline{PS}$ and $\overline{PR}$
   b. $\overline{TS}$ and $\overline{SP}$ **d.** $\overline{ST}$ and $\overline{RT}$

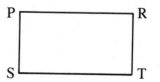

11–5 MORE FACTS ABOUT POINTS, LINES, AND PLANES

(1) Points that lie in the same straight line are called *collinear points*.

    (a) Are points *D*, *G*, and *H* collinear?

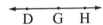

    (b) Are points *M*, *O*, and *N* collinear?
        Are points *O* and *N* collinear?
        Are points *M* and *N* collinear?
        Are points *M* and *O* collinear?

    (c) Are points *B*, *F*, and *E* collinear?
        Are points *A*, *F*, and *E* collinear?
        Are points *A*, *F*, and *C* collinear?
        Are points *C*, *F*, and *B* collinear?

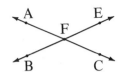

(2) Label a point on your paper as *R*. Draw a line through point *R*. Draw a different line through point *R*. Draw a third line through point *R*. Can more than one straight line be drawn through a point? How many lines can be drawn through a point? Can we say that *an infinite number of straight lines can be drawn through a point?* Since these lines have a common point, can we call them concurrent lines?

(3) Label two points on your paper as *C* and *D*. Draw a straight line through points *C* and *D*. Draw another line through points *C* and *D*. How many straight lines can be drawn through two points? Can we say that *two points determine a straight line and that one and only one straight line can pass through any two points?* Are any two points collinear?

(4) Draw a pair of intersecting lines. Draw another pair of intersecting lines. At how many points can two straight lines intersect? How many points in common does a pair of intersecting lines have? Can we say that *two straight lines can intersect in only one point?*

(5) Which of the three kinds of lines is the shortest path between points *A* and *B*? Can we say that *the shortest path between two points is along a straight line?*

Informal Geometry

(6) Select 3 points on a line. Can more than one plane pass through these 3 points? Select 3 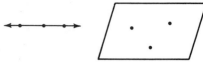 points not on the line. Can more than one plane pass through these 3 points? Can we say that *through 3 points not on the same straight line one and only one plane can pass?* Points in the same plane are called *coplanar points.*

(7) How many points does a geometric plane have? How many lines can be drawn through these points? How many lines does a geometric plane contain? Can we say that *a geometric plane contains an infinite number of points and lines?* Lines in the same plane are sometimes called *coplanar lines.*

(8) Draw two different planes that intersect as shown. What geometric figure is their intersection? Can we say that *when two different planes intersect, their intersection is a straight line?*

(9) Draw a plane and a line that is not in this plane but which intersects the plane. Can we say that their intersection is one and only one point? A plane and a line not in this plane are parallel when they have no point in common.

(10) *A line perpendicular to a plane* is a line that is perpendicular to every line in the plane that passes through its foot (the point of intersection). Can we say that a *line that is perpendicular to each of two intersecting lines at their point of intersection is perpendicular to the plane in which these lines lie?*

ANGLES

An *angle* is the figure formed by two different rays having the same endpoint. It is the union of two rays. This common endpoint is called the *vertex* of the angle and the two rays are called the *sides* of the angle. An angle may be considered as the rotation of a ray about a fixed endpoint, the angle being formed as the ray turns from one position to another. An angle is sometimes used to show direction. The symbol ∠ designates the word "angle."

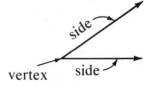

11-6 NAMING ANGLES

Angles are identified or named in the following ways:

(1) By reading the capital letter at the vertex:

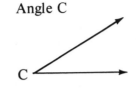

Angle C

(2) By reading the inside letter or numeral:

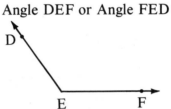

Angle a   Angle 3

(3) By reading the three letters associated with the vertex and one point on each of the sides. The middle letter always indicates the vertex.

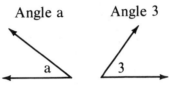

Angle DEF or Angle FED

EXERCISES

1. What is the symbol used to denote the word "angle"?

2. Name the sides and vertex of the following angle:

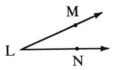

3. Name the following angle in two ways:

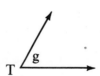

4. Name the following angle in three ways?

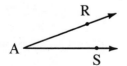

5. Name the following angle in two ways:

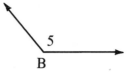

6. Name each of the following angles:

7. Name each angle of the following triangle in four ways.

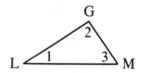

8. Name ∠1, ∠2, and ∠3 in the following figure, using three letters.

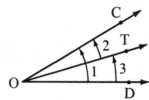

9. In the following triangle, find the angle opposite:

    a. Side *RS*   **b.** Side *RT*   **c.** Side *ST*

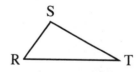

10. Name the four angles formed when $\overleftrightarrow{BD}$ intersects $\overleftrightarrow{AF}$ at point *H*, using 3 letters for each angle.

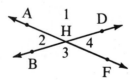

11–7 KINDS OF ANGLES

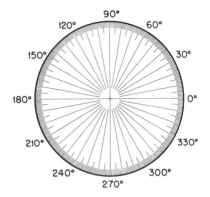

The *degree,* indicated by the symbol (°), is the unit of measure of angles and arcs. A degree is $\frac{1}{360}$ part of the entire angular measure about a point in a plane. If a circle is divided into 360 equal parts and lines are drawn from the center to these points of division, 360 equal central angles are formed each measuring 1 degree. Each of the corresponding 360 equal arcs also measures 1 degree.

The degree (°) is divided into 60 equal parts called minutes ('). The minute (') is divided into 60 equal parts called seconds (").

> To use these symbols:
>
> 360 degrees is written 360°,
> 60 minutes is written 60',
> 60 seconds is written 60".

When a ray turns from one position to another about its fixed endpoint, one complete rotation is equal to 360°.

A *right angle* is one-fourth of a complete rotation; it is an angle whose measure is 90°.

Right

An *acute angle* is an angle whose measure is greater than 0° but less than 90°.

Acute

An *obtuse angle* is an angle whose measure is greater than 90° but less than 180°.

Obtuse

A *straight angle* is one half of a complete rotation; it is an angle whose measure is 180°. The two rays that form a straight angle extend in opposite directions along a straight line that passes through the vertex.

Straight

A *reflex angle* is an angle whose measure is greater than 180° but less than 360°.

Reflex

1. What is the unit called that is used to measure angles? What symbol designates it?
2. The measure of an obtuse angle is greater than ? ° and less than ? °.
3. A right angle measures ? ° and is ? of a rotation.
4. The measure of an acute angle is greater than ? ° and less than ? °.
5. A straight angle is ? of a rotation and measures ?°.
6. One complete rotation measures ?°.
7. Which of the following are measures of an:
   a. acute angle?
   b. obtuse angle?

   93°,   37°,   90°,   175°,   196°,   64°,   0°,   119°,   1°,   180°,   89°,   101°

8. a. Draw any obtuse angle. b. Draw any acute angle.
9. Indicate by writing corresponding letters which of the following angles are:

   a. right angles   c. obtuse angles
   b. acute angles   d. straight angles

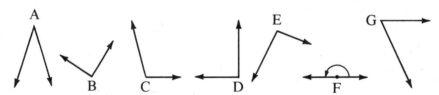

10. What kind of angle is formed by the hands of a clock at 5 o'clock? at 3 o'clock? at 1 o'clock? at 6 o'clock? In each case describe only the smaller of the two angles formed.

11–8 GEOMETRIC FIGURES

Simple Closed Plane Figures or Simple Closed Curves

Geometric figures consist of collections of points. Plane geometric figures are figures with all of their points in the same plane. A simple closed plane figure (or curve) begins at a point and returns to this point without crossing itself. It divides a plane into three collections of points, those in the interior, those in the exterior, and those on the figure.

Polygons

A *polygon* is a simple closed plane figure made up of line segments (called sides). The collection of points contained in the sides is the figure, and not the region enclosed by the figure. Each pair of adjacent sides meets in a point called a *vertex*, and forms an angle. A polygon is named by reading the letters at the vertices.

A polygon with all sides of equal length and all angles of equal measure is called a *regular polygon*.

A line segment connecting two nonadjacent vertices of a polygon is called a *diagonal*.

Some common polygons are: *triangle*, 3 sides; *quadrilateral*, 4 sides; *pentagon*, 5 sides; *hexagon*, 6 sides; *octagon*, 8 sides; *decagon*, 10 sides; *dodecagon*, 12 sides.

Triangles

When all three sides of a triangle are equal in length, the triangle is called an *equilateral triangle;* when two sides are equal, an *isosceles triangle;* when no sides are equal, a *scalene triangle*.

Triangle

When all three angles of a triangle are equal in size, the triangle is called an *equiangular triangle;* a triangle with a right angle, a *right triangle;* with an obtuse angle, an *obtuse triangle;* and with three acute angles, an *acute triangle*.

The *altitude* of a triangle is the perpendicular line segment from any vertex of a triangle to the opposite side or extension of that side.

The *median* of a triangle is the line segment connecting any vertex of a triangle to the midpoint of the opposite side.

In a right triangle the side opposite the right angle is called the *hypotenuse*. The other two sides or legs are the *altitude* and *base* of the triangle. The *base* is generally the side on which the triangle rests.

In an isosceles triangle the angle formed by the two equal sides is called the *vertex angle*. It is opposite the base. The angles opposite the equal sides are called the *base angles*.

Congruent triangles are triangles which have exactly the same shape and the same size. The corresponding sides are equal in length and the corresponding angles are equal in size. The symbol ≅ means "is congruent to."

Two triangles are congruent when any of the following combinations of three parts are known:

(1) Three sides of one triangle are equal to three sides of the second triangle.
(2) Two sides and an included angle of one triangle are equal respectively to two sides and an included angle of the other.
(3) Two angles and an included side of one triangle are equal respectively to two angles and an included side of the other.

Similar triangles are triangles which have the same shape but differ in size. Two triangles are similar when any of the following conditions are known:

(1) Two angles of one triangle are equal to two angles of the other triangle.
(2) The ratios of the corresponding sides are equivalent.
(3) Two sides of one triangle are proportional (equivalent ratios) to two corresponding sides of the other triangle and the included angles are equal.

Quadrilaterals

The following properties describe special quadrilaterals:

The *rectangle* has two pairs of opposite sides which are equal and parallel and four angles which are right angles.

The *square* has four equal sides with the opposite sides parallel and four angles which are right angles.

The *parallelogram* has two pairs of opposite sides which are parallel and equal.

The *trapezoid* has only one pair of opposite sides that are parallel.

The square is a special rectangle, and the rectangle and square are special parallelograms.

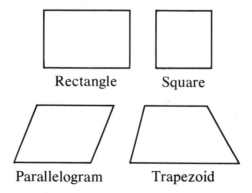

Rectangle   Square

Parallelogram   Trapezoid

Circles

A *circle* is the collection of points in a plane which are equidistant from a fixed point in the plane called the *center*. It is a simple closed curve. The *radius* of a circle is the line segment which has one endpoint at the center of the circle and the other endpoint on the circle. The *diameter* of a circle is the line segment which has both of its endpoints on the circle but passes through the center. A *chord* of a circle is the line segment which has both of its endpoints on the circle. An *arc* is a part of the circle. If the endpoints of an arc are the endpoints of a diameter, the arc is a *semi-circle*. An angle whose vertex is at the center of a circle is called a *central angle*. The *circumference* is the distance around the circle.

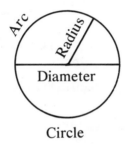

Circle

Concentric circles are circles in the same plane which have the same center but different radii.

Concentric
Circles

Solid or Space Figures

A closed geometric figure consisting of four or more polygons and their interiors, all in different planes, is called a *polyhedron*. The polygons and their interiors are called *faces*. These faces intersect in line segments called *edges*. These edges intersect in points called *vertices*.

Common polyhedra are the rectangular solid (right rectangular prism), the cube, and the pyramid.

(1)   (2)   (3)

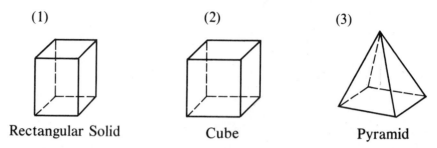

Rectangular Solid   Cube   Pyramid

(1) The *rectangular solid* has six rectangular faces.

(2) The *cube* has six squares for its faces. All the edges are equal in length.

(3) The *pyramid* has any polygon as its base and triangular faces that meet in a common vertex.

Other common solid geometric figures are the cylinder, sphere, and cone.

(4)   (5)   (6)

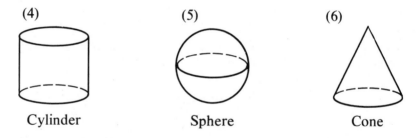

Cylinder   Sphere   Cone

(4) The *cylinder* has two equal and parallel circles as bases and a lateral curved surface.

(5) The *sphere* has a curved surface on which every point is the same distance from the center within.

(6) The *cone* has a circle for the base and a curved surface that comes to a point called the vertex.

Euler Formula

The Euler formula expresses the relationship of the faces, edges and vertices of a polyhedron. The formula $F + V - E = 2$ tells us that "the number of faces plus the number of vertices minus the number of edges is equal to two."

1. What is the name of each of the following figures?

a   b   c   d   e

f   g   h   i   j

k   l   m   n   o   p

2. What kind of triangle is each of the following?

a   b   c   d   e   f

3. Which of the following figures are parallelograms?

a   b    c    d   e

4. How many diagonals can be drawn from any one vertex in each of the following figures?

a   b   c   d   e

5. **a.** How many faces (F) does a cube have? How many vertices (V)? How many edges (E)? Does $F + V - E = 2$?
     b. How many faces (F) does a pyramid with a square base have? How many vertices (V)? How many edges (E)? Does $F + V - E = 2$?

Informal Geometry   **401**

11–9 DRAWING AND MEASURING LINE SEGMENTS

A *straightedge* is used to draw line segments. The *ruler,* which is a straightedge with calibrated measurements, is used both to draw and to measure line segments of varying lengths.

Sometimes an instrument called a *compass* is used along with the ruler to measure line segments or to draw line segments of specified lengths. Since the compass is used to draw circles and arcs of circles, the distance between the metal point and the pencil point of the compass corresponds to the radius of the circle or the radius of the arc of the circle that may be drawn.

Generally we measure the length of a line segment by using only the ruler. However when we use both a compass and a ruler to do this, we open the compass so that the metal point and the pencil point fit exactly on the endpoints of the line segment. We then transfer the compass to a ruler to determine the measurement between the metal point and the pencil point.

We reverse this operation to draw a line segment of a given length by using both a compass and a ruler. We first set the compass so that the distance between the metal point and pencil point corresponds to the given measurement on a ruler. We then apply this compass setting to a light pencil working line, using the metal point as one endpoint and the pencil point as the second endpoint.

EXERCISES

1. Using a customary ruler, draw line segments having the following dimensions:

   a. $3\frac{1}{2}$ in.   **c.** $2\frac{7}{8}$ in.   **e.** $3\frac{5}{16}$ in.

   b. $4\frac{3}{4}$ in.   **d.** $5\frac{13}{16}$ in.   **f.** $6\frac{3}{8}$ in.

2. Draw a line segment 8 inches long. Using a compass, lay off in succession on this segment lengths of $1\frac{5}{8}$ inches, $\frac{3}{4}$ inch, $2\frac{15}{16}$ inches, and $1\frac{1}{2}$ inches. Determine the length of the remaining segment by measuring it.

3. Using a metric ruler, draw line segments having the following dimensions:

a. 4 cm   **c.** 11 cm   **e.** 125 mm

b. 16 mm   **d.** 75 mm   **f.** 6.3 cm

4. The symbol $m\overline{BF}$ is read "the measure of line segment BF" and represents the length of a segment.

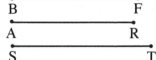

a. Find $m\overline{BF}$, $m\overline{AR}$, $m\overline{ST}$, and $m\overline{NP}$.

b. Does $m\overline{BF}$ equal $m\overline{ST}$?

c. Does $m\overline{NP}$ equal $m\overline{BF}$?

d. Does $m\overline{AR}$ equal $m\overline{NP}$?

5. a. Draw a line segment that is twice as long as $\overline{ST}$ shown in problem 4.

    b. Draw a line segment that is three times as long as $\overline{NP}$ shown in problem 4.

11–10 COPYING A LINE SEGMENT

To copy a line segment means to draw a line segment equal in length to the given line segment.

(1) *Using a ruler,* we first measure the given line segment, then we draw another line segment of the same length.

(2) *Using a compass,* we first draw a pencil working line. Then we select a point on this line where the copy of the given line segment is to begin, indicating it by a dot. We open the compass, placing the metal point on one endpoint of the given line segment and the pencil point on the other endpoint. We trans-

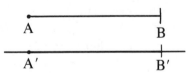

fer this fixed compass setting to the working line, placing the metal point on the marked dot. This point forms one endpoint of the copy of the given line segment. We draw an arc, cutting the working line. This intersection forms the second endpoint of the copy of the given line segment. We then draw the segment of the working line between these endpoints heavier to indicate the required line segment.

1. Make a copy of each of the following line segments, using a ruler:

   _____   _____   _____

2. Make a copy of each of the following line segments, using a compass and a straightedge. Check with ruler.

   _____   _____   _____

3. Draw any line segment and label the endpoints B and C. Label a point not on $\overline{BC}$ as D. Using a compass and a straightedge, draw a line segment $\overline{DE}$ equal in length to $\overline{BC}$.

11–11 SCALE

The scale shows the relationship between the dimensions of a drawing, plan, or map and the actual dimensions.

> A scale like 1 inch = 8 feet means that 1 scale inch represents 8 actual feet. This scale may also be written as $\frac{1}{8}$ inch = 1 foot or as the representative fraction $\frac{1}{96}$ or as the ratio 1:96. These all indicate that each scale inch represents 96 actual inches or 8 feet.

The scale ratio 1:2,000,000 indicates that 1 scale millimeter represents 2,000,000 actual millimeters which equal 2,000 meters or 2 kilometers. Therefore the ratio 1:2,000,000 could also be written as 1 mm = 2 km.

On maps we usually find a scale of miles. The scale at right indicates that each scale inch represents 100 actual miles and is equivalent to the scale: 1 inch = 100 miles.

(1) *To find the actual distance when the scale and scale distance are known,* we multiply the scale distance by the scale value of a unit (cm in the following):

If the scale is 1 cm = 40 km, what actual distance is represented by 6.8 cm?

Scale: 1 cm = 40 km

Scale distance: 6.8 cm = ? km

6.8 × 40 = 272.0 km

Answer, 272 km

(2) *To find the scale distance when the scale and the actual distance are known,* we divide the actual distance by the scale value of a unit (inch in the following):

If the scale is 1 inch = 16 feet, how many inches represent 56 feet?

Scale: 1 inch = 16 feet

? scale distance = 56 feet

$56 \div 16 = 3\frac{1}{2}$

Answer, $3\frac{1}{2}$ inches

(3) *To find the scale when the actual and scale distances are known,* we divide the actual distance by the scale distance.

Find the scale when the actual distance is 63 kilometers and the scale distance is 9 millimeters.

63 ÷ 9 = 7 Each scale millimeter represents 7 actual kilometers or 7,000,000 actual millimeters.

Thus, the scale is 1 mm = 7 km which may be written as the ratio 1:7,000,000.

Answer, 1 mm = 7 km
or scale ratio 1:7,000,000

Informal Geometry

1. If the scale is 1 mm = 10 m, what actual distance is represented by:

   a. 5 mm? **b.** 12 mm? **c.** 58 mm? **d.** 34 mm? **e.** 117 mm?

2. If the scale is 1 cm = 40 km, what actual distance is represented by:

   a. 8 cm? **b.** 19 cm? **c.** 4.5 cm? **d.** 0.7 cm? **e.** 6.4 cm?

3. If the scale is 1 inch = 32 miles, what actual distance is represented by:

   a. 5 in.? **b.** $8\frac{1}{2}$ in.? **c.** $4\frac{5}{8}$ in.? **d.** $\frac{3}{4}$ in.? **e.** $7\frac{11}{16}$ in.?

4. If the scale is $\frac{1}{4}$ inch = 1 foot, what actual distance is represented by:

   a. 1 in.? **b.** $2\frac{1}{2}$ in.? **c.** $5\frac{1}{4}$ in.? **d.** $6\frac{3}{8}$ in.? **e.** $4\frac{15}{16}$ in.?

5. If the scale is $\frac{1}{96}$, what actual distance is represented by:

   a. 2 in.? **b.** $5\frac{1}{2}$ in.? **c.** $4\frac{7}{8}$ in.? **d.** $10\frac{3}{4}$ in.? **e.** $8\frac{9}{16}$ in.?

6. The scale ratio 1:200 means:
   1 scale cm = __ actual cm = __ actual m

7. The scale ratio 1:1,000,000 means:
   1 scale mm = __ actual mm = __ m = __ km

8. The scale ratio 1:2,500,000 means:
   1 scale mm = __ actual mm = __ m = __ km

9. The scale 1 mm = 25 m means:
   1 scale mm = __ actual mm = scale ratio 1:__

10. The scale 1 cm = 50 km means:
    1 scale cm = __ actual cm = scale ratio 1:__

11. Write the scale ratio for each of the following scales:

    a. 1 mm = 9 km **b.** 1 cm = 30 m **c.** 1 mm = 6.25 km **d.** 1 cm = 55 m

12. Write in another way the scale for each of the following scale ratios:

    a. 1:4,000,000 **b.** 1:700 **c.** 1:100,000 **d.** 1:1,250,000

13. If the scale is 1:400, what actual distance is represented by:

    a. 5 m? **b.** 8.5 cm? **c.** 14.3 cm? **d.** 65 mm? **e.** 138 mm?

14. If the scale is 1:1,250,000, what actual distance is represented by:

   a. 16 mm?   **b.** 9 mm?   **c.** 75 mm?   **d.** 1 cm?   **e.** 18.6 cm?

15. If the scale is 1 inch = 48 miles, how many inches represent:

   a. 192 mi.?   **b.** 352 mi.?   **c.** 560 mi.?   **d.** 312 mi.?   **e.** 240 mi.?

16. If the scale is $\frac{1}{8}$ inch = 1 foot, how many inches represent:

   a. 64 ft.?   **b.** 76 ft.?   **c.** 42 ft.?   **d.** 25 ft.?   **e.** 127 ft.?

17. If the scale is $\frac{1}{48}$, how many inches represent:

   a. 12 ft.?   **b.** 3 ft.?   **c.** 38 ft.?   **d.** $60\frac{1}{2}$ ft.?   **e.** $27\frac{3}{4}$ ft.?

18. If the scale is 1 cm = 15 m, how many cm represent:

   a. 45 m?   **b.** 180 m?   **c.** 6 m?   **d.** 108 m?   **e.** 154.5 m?

19. If the scale is 1:4,000,000, how many millimeters represent:

   a. 20 km?   **b.** 2 km?   **c.** 112 km?   **d.** 84 km?   **e.** 39 km?

20. Find the scale when:

   a. the scale length of 9 mm represents an actual distance of 540 km
   b. the scale length of $6\frac{1}{2}$ in. represents an actual distance of 117 ft.
   c. the actual distance of 324 km is represented by the scale length of 7.2 cm
   d. the actual distance of 690 mi. is represented by the scale length of $5\frac{3}{4}$ in.
   e. the scale length of 10.8 cm represents an actual distance of 129.6 meters
   f. the scale length of $3\frac{13}{16}$ in. represents an actual distance of 61 ft.

21. Using the scale 1 cm = 100 km, draw line segments representing:

   a. 200 km   **b.** 40 km   **c.** 230 km   **d.** 380 km   **e.** 150 km

22. Using the scale $\frac{1}{8}$ inch = 1 foot, draw line segments representing:

   a. 32 ft.   **b.** 20 ft.   **c.** 3 ft.   **d.** 14 ft.   **e.** $27\frac{1}{2}$ ft.

23. What are the actual dimensions of a floor if plans drawn to the scale of $\frac{1}{4}$ inch = 1 foot show dimensions of $10\frac{1}{2}$ in. by $9\frac{3}{8}$ in.?

24. Draw a floor plan of a room 21 feet long and 17 feet wide, using the scale 1 inch = 2 feet.

25. Using the scale of miles

0 20 40 60 80

find the distance represented by each of the following line segments:

a. _____   c. _____

b. _____   d. _____

e. _____

26. Using the scale of kilometers find the distance represented

0   10   20   30   40   50

by each of the following line segments:

a. _____   c. _____

b. _____   d. _____

e. _____

27. Find the scales used to draw the following line segments representing the given distances?

a. _____120 mi._____   c. _____27 m_____
    scale: 1 inch = ?   scale: 1 : ?

b. _____90 ft._____   d. _____57 km_____
    scale: 1 inch = ?   scale: 1 : ?

28. If the distance from E to G is 36 miles, what is the distance from B to R?

_____   _____
E   G   B   R

29. If the distance from A to B is 140 kilometers, what is the distance from C to D?

_____   _____
A   B   C   D

30. Draw a plan of a living room floor 8 meters long and 5 meters wide, using the scale 1 : 200.

11–12 MEASURING ANGLES

Measuring an angle means to determine how many units of angular measure are contained in it. The protractor is an instrument used to measure an angle. Angles which have the same measure are called *equal angles*.

The size of an angle does not depend on the length of its sides. The symbol $m \angle ABC$ is read "the measure of angle *ABC*."

To measure an angle, we place the straight edge of the protractor on one side of the angle with its center mark at the vertex of the angle. We read the number of degrees at the point where the other side of the angle cuts the protractor, using the scale which has its zero on one side of the angle.

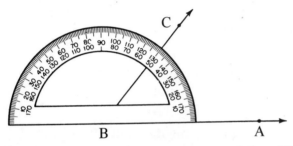

This angle measures 50° written either as $m \angle ABC = 50°$ or briefly as $\angle ABC = 50°$.

EXERCISES

1. Estimate the size of each of the following angles. Then measure each angle with a protractor.

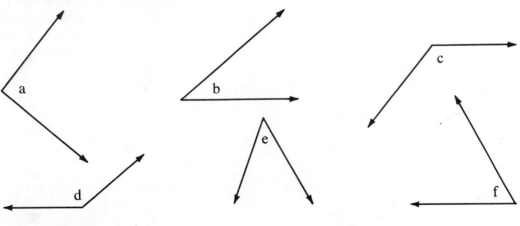

Informal Geometry

2. Write the amount of error and percent of error of each estimate you made in Exercise **1**.
3. Draw any angle. Extend the length of the two sides of the angle. Have you changed the size of the angle by doing this?
4. **a.** Which of the following angles is greater?
   b. Does the size of an angle depend upon the length of the sides?

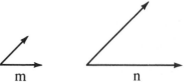

m   n

5. How many degrees are in the smaller angle formed by the hands of a clock:

   a. at 5 o'clock?   **d.** at 1 o'clock?
   b. at 2 o'clock?   **e.** at 6 o'clock?
   c. at 3 o'clock?   **f.** at 4 o'clock?

6. Through how many degrees does the minute hand of a clock turn in:

   a. 20 minutes?   **d.** 15 minutes?   **g.** 1 hour?
   b. 5 minutes?   **e.** 45 minutes?   **h.** 50 minutes?
   c. 30 minutes?   **f.** 10 minutes?   **i.** 1 minute?

11–13 DRAWING ANGLES

To draw an angle with a given measure, we draw a ray to represent one side of the angle. Sometimes this ray (or line segment which is part of a ray) is already drawn. We place the protractor so that its straight edge falls on this ray, and its center mark is on the endpoint which becomes the vertex of the angle. This vertex may also be any point on the line.

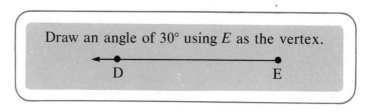

Draw an angle of 30° using *E* as the vertex.

D   E

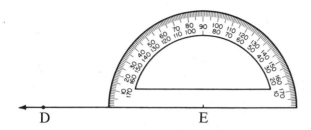

Counting on the scale which has its zero on the ray, we locate the required number of degrees and indicate its position by a dot. We remove the protractor, then we draw a ray from the vertex through this dot.

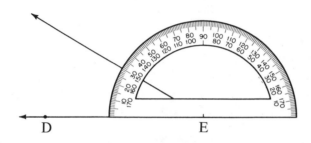

1. For each of the following first draw a ray with the endpoint either on the left or on the right as required, then with protractor draw the angle of the given measure.

   a. Left endpoint as the vertex:
   40°,   65°,   130°,   155°,   97°,   24°,   109°,   200°,   270°,   345°
   b. Right endpoint as the vertex:
   60°,   75°,   100°,   90°,   84°,   225°,   300°,   340°,   136°,   16°

2. With protractor measure each of the following angles, then draw an angle equal to it.

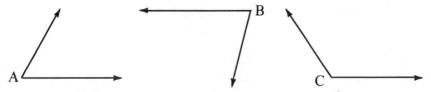

3. With protractor draw: **a.** a right angle;   **b.** a straight angle.

Informal Geometry   411

11–14 CONSTRUCTING TRIANGLES

A triangle contains three sides and three angles. A triangle may be constructed when any of the following combinations of three parts are known: (1) Three sides (2) Two sides and an included angle (3) Two angles and an included side. For example:

(1) Three Sides

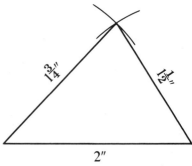

To construct a triangle whose sides measure 2 in., $1\frac{3}{4}$ in., and $1\frac{1}{2}$ in., we first use a compass to lay off a line segment 2 in. long. With one of the endpoints as the center and setting the compass so that the radius is $1\frac{3}{4}$ in., we draw an arc. With the other endpoint as the center and a radius of $1\frac{1}{2}$ in., we draw an arc crossing the first arc. From this point of intersection we draw line segments to the endpoints of the base line to form the required triangle.

EXERCISES

1. Construct triangles having sides that measure:

   a. $2\frac{1}{4}$ in., $1\frac{7}{8}$ in., $1\frac{5}{8}$ in.   **b.** 38 mm, 29 mm, 24 mm   **c.** 4.1 cm, 3.6 cm, 5.3 cm

2. Construct an equilateral triangle whose sides are 2.5 cm long. Measure the three angles. Are their measures equal?

3. Construct an isosceles triangle whose base is $1\frac{7}{8}$ in. long and each of whose two equal sides is $2\frac{3}{16}$ in. long.

4. Construct a scalene triangle. Check whether of any two:
   a. The angle opposite the greater side is greater.
   b. The side opposite the greater angle is greater.

5. Using the scale 1 in. = 40 mi., construct triangles whose sides are:

   a. 60 mi., 75 mi., 45 mi.   **b.** 100 mi., 85 mi., 110 mi.   **c.** 50 mi., $37\frac{1}{2}$ mi., 40 mi.

6. Using the scale ratio 1 : 400, construct triangles whose sides are:

   a. 8 m, 6 m, 7 m,   **b.** 10 m, 12 m, 15 m   **c.** 18 m, 14 m, 9 m

7. Construct a triangle having three sides equal in length to the following line segments. Also see 11–9 and 11–10.

_____   _____   _____

(2) Two Sides and an Included Angle

To construct a triangle with sides measuring 42 mm and 28 mm and an included angle of 90° we draw a line segment 42 mm long. Using the left endpoint as the vertex, we draw an angle of 90°. Along the ray just drawn we measure 28 mm from the vertex. We then draw a line segment connecting endpoints to form the required triangle.

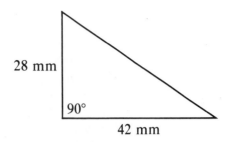

28 mm

90°

42 mm

EXERCISES

1. Construct triangles having the following sides and included angles that measure:

   a. 28 mm, 21 mm, 100°

   b. $1\frac{3}{4}$ in., $2\frac{1}{4}$ in., 75°

   c. 5 cm, 3.6 cm, 55°

2. Construct a right triangle having:

   a. An altitude of 45 mm and a base of 58 mm

   b. An altitude of $2\frac{3}{8}$ in. and a base of $1\frac{1}{2}$ in.

3. Construct an isosceles triangle in which the equal sides each measure 6.4 cm and the vertex angle formed by these sides measures 40°. Measure the angles opposite the equal sides. Are their measures equal?

4. Using the scale $\frac{1}{8}$ in. = 1 ft., construct a triangle in which two sides measure 15 ft. and 23 ft. and the included angle measures 75°.

5. Using the scale ratio 1:2,000,000, construct a triangle in which two sides measure 80 km and 60 km and the included angle measures 65°.

6. Construct a triangle having two sides and an included angle equal to the following two line segments and angle. See also sections 11–9, 11–10, and 11–18.

(3) Two Angles and an Included Side

To construct a triangle with angles measuring 37° and 27° and the included side measuring $1\frac{7}{8}$ in., we first draw a line segment $1\frac{7}{8}$ in. long. Using the left endpoint as the vertex, we draw an angle of 37°. Using the right endpoint as the vertex, we draw an angle of 27°. We extend the sides until they meet to form the required triangle.

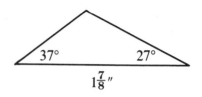

EXERCISES

1. Construct triangles having the following angles and included sides that measure:

   a. 40°, 65°, 34 mm   **b.** 105°, 30°, $1\frac{3}{4}$ in.   **c.** 90°, 45°, 2.3 cm

2. Construct a triangle having two equal angles each measuring 50° and the included side measuring $2\frac{1}{4}$ inches.

3. Construct a triangle having two equal angles each measuring 60° and the included side measuring $1\frac{5}{8}$ inches. Measure the third angle. Measure the other two sides. Is the triangle equiangular? Equilateral?

4. Construct right triangles having the following angles and included sides that measure:

   a. 90°, 30°, 45 mm   **b.** 90°, 30°, $2\frac{3}{4}$ in.   **c.** 30°, 90°, 3.7 cm

   Also select your own measurement for the included side and, using the measures of 90° and 30° for the angles, construct a right triangle. In each of these triangles measure the hypotenuse and the side opposite the 30° angle. Then compare these measurements. In each case is the hypotenuse twice as long as the side opposite the 30° angle?

5. Using the scale $\frac{1}{16}$ in. = 1 ft. construct a triangle in which two angles measure 70° and 35° and the included side measures 37 feet.

6. Using the scale 1 : 1,500, construct a triangle in which two angles measure 60° and 50° and the included side measure 120 meters.

7. Construct a triangle having two angles and an included side equal to the following two angles and line segment. Also see sections 11–9, 11–10, and 11–18.

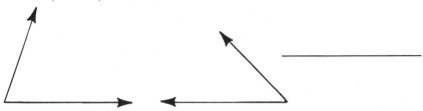

11–15   CONSTRUCTING A PERPENDICULAR TO A GIVEN LINE AT OR THROUGH A GIVEN POINT ON THE GIVEN LINE

Two lines (or rays or segments) that meet to form right angles are called *perpendicular lines* (or rays or segments). Each line is said to be perpendicular to the other. See page 389. The symbol means "is perpendicular to."

(1) *Using a protractor,* we draw a 90° angle with the given point on the line as the vertex. The ray drawn to form the angle is perpendicular to the given line.

(2) *Using a compass* (see figure):
To draw a line (or ray or segment) perpendicular to $\overleftrightarrow{AB}$ at C, we use point C as the center and with any radius we draw an arc cutting $\overleftrightarrow{AB}$ at D and E. With D and E as centers and with a radius 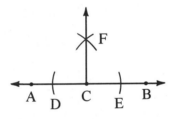 greater than $\overline{CD}$, we draw arcs crossing at F. We draw $\overrightarrow{CF}$ which is perpendicular to $\overleftrightarrow{AB}$ at point C. Or we may draw the line FC passing through point C.

EXERCISES

1. Draw any line. Select a point on this line. Construct a line perpendicular to the line you have drawn at your selected point.
2. Construct a square with each side 48 mm long.
3. Construct a rectangle $2\frac{1}{2}$ inches long and $1\frac{7}{8}$ inches wide.

4. Make a plan of a room 38 ft. by 25 ft., using the scale 1 in. = 16 ft.

5. Construct the plan of a gymnasium floor 62 meters long and 40 meters wide, using the scale 1:800.

6. Draw a circle. Draw any diameter of this circle. At the center construct another diameter perpendicular to the first diameter, dividing the circle into four arcs. Are these four arcs equal in length? Use a compass to check.

7. Draw a circle. Select any point on this circle and label it *A*. Construct a line perpendicular to the radius at point *A*. A *tangent* to a circle is a line that has one and only one point in common with the circle. Observe that a line that is perpendicular to the radius at a point on the circle is tangent to the circle.

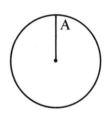

11–16 CONSTRUCTING A PERPENDICULAR TO A GIVEN LINE FROM OR THROUGH A GIVEN POINT NOT ON THE GIVEN LINE

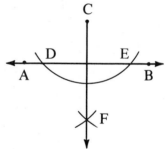

Using a compass (see figure): To draw a ray from point *C* perpendicular to $\overleftrightarrow{AB}$, we use point *C* as the center and draw an arc cutting $\overleftrightarrow{AB}$ at *D* and *E*. With *D* and *E* as centers and a radius of more than one-half the distance from *D* to *E*, we draw arcs crossing at *F*. We draw $\overrightarrow{CF}$ which is perpendicular to $\overleftrightarrow{AB}$. Or we may draw the line *FC* passing through point *C*.

1. Draw any line. Select a point not on this line. Construct a perpendicular to the line you have drawn from your selected point.

2. Construct an equilateral triangle with each side $2\frac{7}{8}$ inches long. From each vertex construct a perpendicular to the opposite side. Is each angle bisected? Is each side bisected?

3. Draw any acute triangle. From each vertex construct a perpendicular to the opposite side. What do these perpendicular line segments represent in a triangle? Are they concurrent?

4. Draw any right triangle. Construct the altitude to each side. Are they concurrent? If so, what is the common point?

5. Draw a circle. Draw any chord in this circle except the diameter. Construct a perpendicular from the center of the circle to this chord. Check whether the chord is bisected. Extend the perpendicular line segment so that it intersects the circle. Check with a compass whether the arc corresponding to the chord is also bisected. Observe that a radius of a circle that is perpendicular to a chord bisects the chord and its corresponding arc.

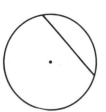

11–17 BISECTING A LINE SEGMENT

To *bisect a line segment* means to divide it into two equal parts. The point on a line segment that separates the line segment into two equal parts is called the *midpoint* of the line segment.

(1) *Using a ruler,* we first measure the line segment, then we mark off half the measurement.

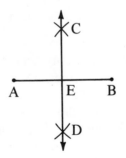

(2) *Using a compass* (see figure): To bisect $\overline{AB}$, we set the compass so that the radius is more than half the length of $\overline{AB}$. With A and B as centers we draw arcs which cross above and below the segment at C and D. Then we draw $\overleftrightarrow{CD}$ bisecting $\overline{AB}$ at E. Observe that $\overleftrightarrow{CD}$ is also perpendicular to AB. Thus a line like $\overleftrightarrow{CD}$, which both bisects a line segment and is perpendicular to it, is called the *perpendicular bisector* of the given segment.

1. Draw line segments measuring: **a.** $3\frac{1}{2}''$ **b.** 56 mm **c.** $2\frac{7}{8}''$
   Bisect each line segment using a compass. Check with a ruler.

2. Copy, then using a compass, bisect each of the following segments. Check each with a ruler.

   —_____   _____   _____

3. Copy, then using a compass, divide the following line segment into four equal parts. Check with a ruler.

   _____

4. Draw any line segment. Bisect it, using a compass. Then use a protractor to check whether each of the four angles formed is a right angle. What name do we give to a line that both bisects and is perpendicular to a line segment?

5. Draw any triangle. Bisect each side by constructing the perpendicular bisector of that side. Are these perpendicular bisectors concurrent? Do they meet in a point equidistant from the vertices of the triangle? Check by measuring. Using this common point as the center and the distance from this point to any vertex of the triangle as the radius, draw a circle through the three vertices of the triangle.

   When each side of the triangle is a chord of the circle or each vertex is a point on the circle, we say that the *circle is circumscribed about the triangle* or that the *triangle is inscribed in a circle*.

6. Draw any triangle. Find the midpoint of each side by constructing the perpendicular bisector of that side. Draw the median from each vertex to the midpoint of the opposite side. Are these medians concurrent? Along each median check whether the distance from this common point to the vertex is twice the distance from this common point to the midpoint of the opposite side.

7. Draw a right triangle. Bisect the hypotenuse of the right triangle. Draw the median from the vertex of the right angle to the hypotenuse. Check whether this median is one-half as long as the hypotenuse.

11-18 COPYING A GIVEN ANGLE

To copy a given angle means to construct an angle equal in size to the given angle.

(1) *Using a protractor,* we measure the given angle and draw another angle of the same size.

(2) *Using a compass* (see figure): To construct an angle at point C on $\overleftrightarrow{AB}$ equal to $\angle MNO$, we take point N as center and draw an arc cutting side MN at P and side NO at Q. With the same radius and point C as center, we draw an arc cutting $\overleftrightarrow{AB}$ at D. With a radius equal to PQ and point D as center, we draw an arc crossing the first arc at E. We draw $\overrightarrow{CE}$. $m\angle BCE$ is equal to $m\angle MNO$.

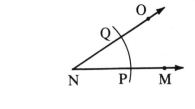

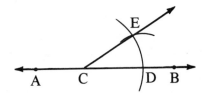

EXERCISES

1. Draw angles having the following measures, using a protractor. For each angle construct with a compass an angle of equal size. Check your copy of the angle with a protractor.

   a. 70°   **b.** 45°   **c.** 125°   **d.** 18°   **e.** 164°   **f.** 83°

2. Draw an acute angle. Construct with a compass an angle of equal size. Check both angles with a protractor.

3. Draw a right angle, using a protractor. Construct with a compass an angle of equal size. Check with a protractor.

4. Draw any obtuse angle. Construct with a compass an angle of equal size. Check both angles with a protractor.

5. Draw any angle. Construct with a compass an angle having the same measure. Check both angles with a protractor.

11–19 BISECTING AN ANGLE

To bisect an angle means to divide it into two equal angles.

(1) *Using a protractor,* we measure the given angle and mark off one-half the measurement. We then draw a ray from the vertex.

(2) *Using a compass* (see figure): To bisect $\angle ABC$ with B as the center and any radius, we draw an arc cutting side AB at D and side BC at E. With D and E as centers and a radius of more than half the distance from D to E, we draw arcs crossing at F. We then draw $\overrightarrow{BF}$ bisecting $\angle ABC$.

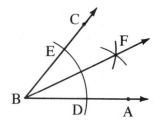

EXERCISES

1. Draw angles having the following measures. Bisect each angle using a compass. Check with a protractor.

   a. 50°   **c.** 38°   **e.** 65°
   b. 140°   **d.** 162°   **f.** 119°

2. Draw any angle. Bisect it by using a compass. Check by measuring your angle and each bisected angle.

3. Copy, then bisect each of the following angles:

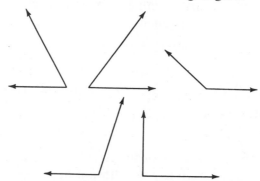

4. Draw any triangle. Bisect each angle. Do the bisectors meet at a common point? Are these bisectors concurrent? From this

common point draw a perpendicular to any side. With this common point as center and with the perpendicular distance from the common point to any side as the radius, draw a circle. Observe that each side of the triangle is tangent to the circle.

When each side of the triangle is tangent to the circle, we say that the *triangle is circumscribed about the circle* or that the *circle is inscribed in the triangle*.

5. Construct with a compass an angle measuring: **a.** 45°; **b.** 135°.

6. Draw any equilateral triangle. Select an angle and bisect it. Construct from the vertex of this selected angle the altitude (line segment that is perpendicular to the opposite side). Does this perpendicular line bisect this opposite side? From this same vertex also draw the median to the opposite side. In an equilateral triangle, are all three of these lines (angle bisector, altitude, and median) one and the same line? If this is so, will it be true if each of the other angles is selected? Check.

7. Draw any isosceles triangle. Bisect the vertex angle (angle formed by the two equal sides and opposite to the base). Then construct from the vertex of this angle the altitude (line segment that is perpendicular to the base). Does this perpendicular line bisect the base of the isosceles triangle? From this same vertex also draw the median to the base. In an isosceles triangle, are all three of these lines (bisector of the vertex angle, altitude drawn to the base, and the median drawn to the base) one and the same line?

In an isosceles triangle the angles opposite the equal sides are called *base angles*. Check whether the bisector of a base angle, the altitude and the median both drawn from the vertex of the same base angle are all one and the same line.

8. Draw any scalene triangle and do the following:

   a. Select an angle and bisect it.
   b. Construct from the vertex of this bisected angle the line segment that is perpendicular (altitude) to the opposite side.
   c. Construct the perpendicular bisector of the side opposite to the bisected angle.
   d. Draw the median from the vertex of this bisected angle to the opposite side. Are any of these four lines (angle bisector, altitude, perpendicular bisector, and median) the same line? If so, which?

Informal Geometry

11–20 CONSTRUCTING A LINE PARALLEL TO A GIVEN LINE THROUGH A GIVEN POINT NOT ON THE GIVEN LINE

Lines in the same plane which do not meet are called *parallel lines*. The symbol ∥ means "is parallel to."

To construct a line parallel to $\overleftrightarrow{AB}$ through point C (see figure), we draw any line $\overleftrightarrow{DE}$ through C meeting $\overleftrightarrow{AB}$ at F.

(1) *Using a protractor,* we measure $\angle BFC$ and draw, at point C on $\overleftrightarrow{DE}$, $\angle GCE$ equal to the corresponding $\angle BFC$. Then we extend $\overrightarrow{GC}$ through H. $\overleftrightarrow{HG}$ is parallel to $\overleftrightarrow{AB}$.

(2) *Using a compass,* we construct, at point C on $\overleftrightarrow{DE}$, $\angle GCE$ equal to the corresponding $\angle BFC$ by following the procedure explained in the preceding construction (11–18). We then extend $\overrightarrow{GC}$ through H. $\overleftrightarrow{HG}$ is parallel to $\overleftrightarrow{AB}$.

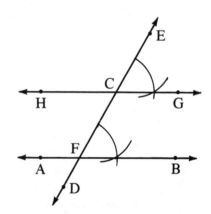

EXERCISES

1. Draw any line. Select a point that is not on this line. Through this point construct a line parallel to the line you have drawn.
2. Construct a parallelogram with a base 3 inches long, a side $2\frac{5}{8}$ inches long, and an included angle of 65°.
3. Draw any acute triangle. Bisect one of the sides. Draw a line segment from this midpoint, parallel to one of the other sides, until it intersects the third side. Does this line segment bisect the third side? Check by measuring. Also check whether this line segment is one-half as long as the side to which it is parallel. Draw other triangles and check whether the above findings are true no matter which side is used first or which side is used as the parallel side.

11–21 CONSTRUCTING REGULAR POLYGONS AND OTHER POLYGONS

A *regular polygon* is a polygon that is both equilateral (all of its sides are of equal length) and equiangular (all of its angles are of equal size). An *inscribed polygon in a circle* is a polygon whose vertices are points on the circle.

Although there are other ways to construct some of the regular polygons, in general we use a method that is based on the geometric fact that equal central angles of a circle intercept equal arcs and equal chords. A regular polygon constructed in this way is inscribed within a circle.

Therefore *to construct a regular polygon,* we first draw a circle. Then we divide this circle into the same number of equal arcs as there are sides in the required polygon by drawing a corresponding number of equal central angles. We draw line segments (chords) connecting the points of division to form the polygon.

To draw a regular octagon which is a polygon of eight equal sides, we first determine the measure of each of the eight equal central angles by dividing 360° by 8. This measure is 45°. We draw eight central angles each measuring 45°, with its sides (radii) intercepting the circle dividing it into eight equal arcs. We then draw line segments to connect the points of division to form the regular octagon.

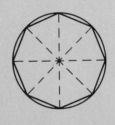

A regular hexagon (6 sides) may be drawn by the alternate way of dividing the circle into six equal arcs by using the radius of the circle as the radius of the arc. An equilateral triangle may be constructed by drawing line segments to connect alternate points of division after the circle is divided into six equal arcs.

A square may be constructed by drawing two diameters of a circle perpendicular to each other to divide the circle into four equal arcs. Line segments are then drawn to connect these points of division.

Rectangles and parallelograms of specific measurement may be constructed provided enough of these measurements are given so that basic constructions may be used.

EXERCISES

1. Construct each of the following regular polygons:

   a. Pentagon—5 sides   d. Dodecagon—12 sides
   b. Square   e. Equilateral triangle
   c. Hexagon—6 sides   f. Decagon—10 sides

2. Construct a rectangle:

   a. 4 cm long and 3 cm wide

   b. $3\frac{1}{2}$ inches long and $2\frac{5}{8}$ inches wide

   c. 43 mm long and 25 mm wide

   d. 5.4 cm long and 3.8 cm wide

3. Construct a square whose side measures:

   a. $1\frac{3}{4}$ inches   c. 1.5 cm

   b. $\frac{7}{8}$ inch   d. $3\frac{7}{16}$ inches

4. Construct a parallelogram with:

   a. A base $2\frac{3}{8}$ inches long, a side $1\frac{11}{16}$ inches long, and an included angle of 30°
   b. A base 72 mm long, a side 48 mm long, and an included angle of 75°
   c. A base $1\frac{7}{8}$ inches long, a side $2\frac{5}{16}$ inches long, and an included angle of 45°
   d. A base 4 cm long, a side 3.6 cm long, and an included angle of 100°

5. Draw a regular hexagon, each side measuring: **a.** $1\frac{1}{2}$ inches; **b.** 57 mm; **c.** $3\frac{5}{8}$ inches. In each case draw a circle whose radius has the same measure as each required side.

11–22 SUM OF ANGLES OF POLYGONS

(1) Triangle

Draw any triangle. Measure its three angles. What is the sum of the measure of these three angles? Draw a second triangle. Find the sum of the measures of its three angles. Find the sum of the measures of the three angles of a third triangle.

Do you see that *the sum of the measures of the angles of any triangle is 180°?*

(a) In each of the following, find the measure of the third angle of a triangle when the other two angles measure:

1. 67° and 41°   3. 12° and 39°   5. 72° and 72°
2. 105° and 58°   4. 81° and 75°   6. 7° and 126°

(b) Why can there be only one right angle or one obtuse angle in a triangle?

(c) In any right triangle what kind of angle must each of the other two angles be?

(d) What is the measure of each angle of an equiangular triangle?

(e) In a right triangle one of the acute angles measures 28°. What is the measure of the other acute angle?

(f) Find the measure of each of the other two angles when the vertex angle of an isosceles triangle measures 42°.

(g) If two angles of one triangle are equal respectively to two angles of another triangle, why are the third angles of the two triangles equal?

(2) Quadrilateral

Draw a parallelogram and a trapezoid. Measure the four angles in each. What is the sum of the measures of the angles of the parallelogram? Of the trapezoid?

Draw any other quadrilateral. Find the sum of the measures of the angles of the quadrilateral.

Do you see that *the sum of the measures of the angles of any quadrilateral is 360°?*

(a) What is the sum of the measures of the angles of a rectangle? Of a square?

(b) In each of the following, find the measure of the fourth angle of a quadrilateral when the other three angles are:

1. 73°, 104°, and 125°   3. 57°, 142°, and 68°
2. 90°, 90°, and 109°

(c) The opposite angles of a parallelogram are equal. If one angle measures 110°, find the measures of the other three angles.

(d) Three angles of a trapezoid measure 90°, 90°, and 121°. What is the measure of the fourth angle?

(3) Other Polygons

Draw a pentagon, a hexagon, an octagon, and a decagon. What is the sum of the measures of the angles of each of these geometric figures? Check whether your sum of measures of the angles of each of these figures matches the angular measure determined by substituting the number of sides in the polygon for n in the expression $180(n - 2)$ and performing the required operations. Is this also true for the triangle and the quadrilateral?

Do you see that *the sum of the measures of the angles of a polygon of n sides is 180(n − 2)*?

11–23 PAIRS OF ANGLES

(1) *Complementary angles* are two angles whose sum of measures is 90°.

(a) Which of the following pairs of angles are complementary?

1. $m\angle A = 30°$, $m\angle B = 60°$ 4. $m\angle c = 34°$, $m\angle d = 46°$

2. $m\angle L = 57°$, $m\angle M = 43°$ 5. $m\angle S = 80°$, $m\angle T = 100°$

3. $m\angle 1 = 72°$, $m\angle 2 = 18°$ 6. $m\angle G = 69°$, $m\angle H = 21°$

(b) Find the measure of the angle that is the complement of each of the following angles:

1. $m\angle R = 84°$ 3. $m\angle m = 75°$ 5. $m\angle N = 41°$
2. $m\angle 1 = 37°$ 4. $m\angle E = 9°$ 6. $m\angle P = 56°$

(c) Angle ABC is a right angle.

1. If $m\angle 1 = 25°$, find the measure of $\angle 2$.

2. If $m\angle 2 = 71°$, find the measure of $\angle 1$.

3. If $m\angle 1 = 82°$, find the measure of $\angle 2$.

4. If $m\angle 2 = 14°$, find the measure of $\angle 1$.

5. If $m\angle 1 = 3°$, find the measure of $\angle 2$.

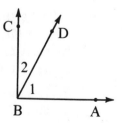

(d) The symbol $\perp$ means "is perpendicular to."
In the figure, $\overrightarrow{FB} \perp \overrightarrow{FD}$ and $\overleftrightarrow{FC} \perp \overleftrightarrow{AE}$.

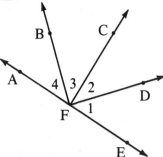

1. If $m \angle 4 = 36°$, find the measure of $\angle 1$. Of $\angle 2$. Of $\angle 3$.
2. If $m \angle 2 = 58°$, find the measure of $\angle 1$. Of $\angle 3$. Of $\angle 4$.
3. If $m \angle 3 = 79°$, find the measure of $\angle 1$. Of $\angle 2$. Of $\angle 4$.
4. If $m \angle 1 = 62°$, find the measure of $\angle 2$. Of $\angle 3$. Of $\angle 4$.

(e) Why is the complement of an acute angle also an acute angle?

(2) *Supplementary angles* are two angles whose sum of measures is 180°.

(a) Which of the following pairs of angles are supplementary?

1. $m \angle E = 70°$, $m \angle F = 110°$ 4. $m \angle m = 27°$, $m \angle n = 153°$
2. $m \angle K = 84°$, $m \angle L = 96°$ 5. $m \angle H = 48°$, $m \angle A = 42°$
3. $m \angle 4 = 108°$, $m \angle 5 = 82°$ 6. $m \angle C = 79°$, $m \angle S = 101°$

(b) Find the measure of the angle that is the supplement of each of the following angles:

1. $m \angle B = 115°$ 3. $m \angle x = 90°$ 5. $m \angle M = 167°$
2. $m \angle 3 = 74°$ 4. $m \angle D = 8°$ 6. $m \angle F = 59°$

(c) Measure $\angle MOP$ and $\angle NOP$. Is the sum of their measures 180°?

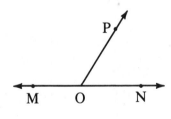

Do you see that *when one straight line meets another, the adjacent angles, which have the same vertex and a common side, are supplementary?*

1. Find the measure of $\angle NOP$ when $m \angle MOP = 135°$.
2. Find the measure of $\angle MOP$ when $m \angle NOP = 17°$.
3. What is the measure of $\angle NOP$ when $m \angle MOP = 90°$?

(3) Opposite or Vertical Angles
Draw two intersecting lines, forming four angles. Measure a pair of angles that are directly opposite to each other. Are their measures

Informal Geometry   **427**

equal? Measure the other pair of opposite angles. Are their measures equal?

Do you see that, *when two straight lines intersect, the opposite or vertical angles are equal?*

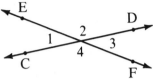

(a) In the drawing at the right, what angle is opposite to ∠2? Does ∠2 = ∠4? What angle is opposite to ∠3? Does ∠3 = ∠1?

(b) If $m\angle 3 = 43°$, what is the measure of ∠1? Of ∠2? Of ∠4?
(c) If $m\angle 4 = 98°$, what is the measure of ∠2? Of ∠1? Of ∠3?
(d) If $m\angle 1 = 69°$, what is the measure of ∠2? Of ∠3? Of ∠4?
(e) If $m\angle 2 = 135°$, what is the measure of ∠3? Of ∠4? Of ∠1?

(4) Exterior Angle of a Triangle

Draw a triangle and extend one side like the drawing at the right. Label the angles as shown in the drawing.

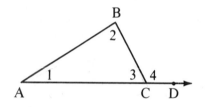

The angle formed by a side of the triangle and the adjacent side extended (see ∠4 in the drawing) is called the *exterior angle.*

Measure the three angles of the triangle and the indicated exterior angle in your drawing.

What is the sum of the measures of ∠1, ∠2, and ∠3? What is the sum of the measures of ∠4 and ∠3?

Why does the measure of ∠4 equal the sum of the measures of ∠1 and ∠2?

Do you see that *the measure of an exterior angle of a triangle is equal to the sum of the measures of the opposite two interior angles?*

(a) If $m\angle 1 = 46°$ and $m\angle 2 = 52°$, find the measure of ∠4. Of ∠3.
(b) If $m\angle 2 = 92°$ and $m\angle 3 = 68°$, find the measure of ∠1. Of ∠4.
(c) If $m\angle 1 = 33°$ and $m\angle 3 = 75°$, find the measure of ∠2. Of ∠4.
(d) If $m\angle 2 = 80°$ and $m\angle 4 = 109°$, find the measure of ∠1. Of ∠3.
(e) If $m\angle 1 = 24°$ and $m\angle 4 = 137°$, find the measure of ∠2. Of ∠3.

PROBLEM SOLVING TECHNIQUES
FOR GEOMETRIC PROBLEMS

1 Read the problem carefully to find:
   a. The facts, dimensions or values that are given.
   b. The fact, dimension or value that is to be determined.

2 Decide which formula or formulas are needed to solve the problem by selecting:

   The formula that relates the variable representing the value to be found with the variables representing the given values.

3 Solve by arranging the solution in three columns.
   a. In left column
      (1) Draw the geometric figure described in the problem.
      (2) Mark the given dimensions on the figure.
      (3) Below the figure write the variables with corresponding given values and the variable representing the unknown value.
   b. In center column, evaluate the formula.
      (1) Write the formula that relates the variables.
      (2) Substitute the known given values for the corresponding variables in the formula.
      (3) Perform the necessary operations (see step c below).
      (4) Write answer.
      (5) When necessary, solve the resulting equation.
   c. In right column
      Perform the necessary arithmetic operations.

4 Rewrite answer.

For sample solution see completely worked-out solution on page 430.

PERIMETER AND CIRCUMFERENCE

The *perimeter* of a polygon is the sum of the lengths of its sides. It is the distance around the polygon.

11–24 PERIMETER OF A RECTANGLE

We see from the figure below that the perimeter of a rectangle is equal to twice its length plus twice its width. Expressed as a formula this relationship is $p = 2l + 2w$ or $p = 2(l + w)$.

Find the perimeter of a rectangle 18 meters long and 12 meters wide:

18 m

12 m

$$p = 2l + 2w$$
$$p = 2 \times 18 + 2 \times 12$$
$$p = 36 + 24$$
$$p = 60 \text{ m}$$

$$\begin{array}{cc} 18 & 12 \\ \times 2 & \times 2 \\ \hline 36 & 24 \end{array}$$

$$\begin{array}{r} 36 \\ +24 \\ \hline 60 \end{array}$$

$l = 18$ m
$w = 12$ m
$p = ?$

Answer, 60 meters

EXERCISES

1. Find the perimeter of a rectangle:

a. 28 ft. long and 19 ft. wide

b. 96 in. long and 59 in. wide

c. 308 mm long and 465 mm wide

d. 8.3 m long and 2.7 m wide

e. 5.18 cm long and 6.59 cm wide

f. 3.875 m long and 2.375 m wide

g. $4\frac{1}{2}$ ft. long and $2\frac{3}{4}$ ft. wide

h. $6\frac{7}{8}$ in. long and $5\frac{11}{16}$ in. wide

i. 97 cm long and 63 cm wide

j. 2 m 9 cm long and 1 m 5 cm wide

k. 7 ft. long and 8 ft. 6 in. wide

l. 2 yd. 4 in. long and 1 yd. 10 in. wide

2. How many meters of hedge are needed to enclose a lot 48 m long and 33 m wide?

3. Find the total number of feet of weather stripping needed for 6 window frames, each measuring 30 in. by 62 in., 3 window frames, each measuring 36 in. by 62 in., and 2 window frames, each measuring 27 in. by 36 in.? At $.14 per foot, how much will it cost?

11–25 PERIMETER OF A SQUARE

Since the 4 sides of a square are of equal length, the perimeter of a square is 4 times the length of its side. Expressed as a formula this is $p = 4s$.

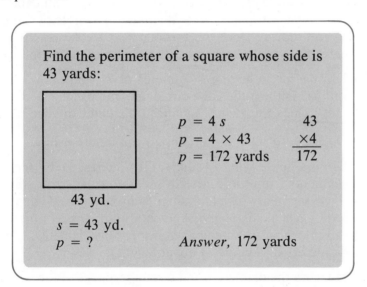

Find the perimeter of a square whose side is 43 yards:

$p = 4s$

$p = 4 \times 43$

$p = 172$ yards

$$\begin{array}{r} 43 \\ \times 4 \\ \hline 172 \end{array}$$

43 yd.

$s = 43$ yd.

$p = ?$

Answer, 172 yards

1. Find the perimeter of a square whose side measures:

a. 8 in.

b. 26 mm

c. 475 yd.

d. 5,280 ft.

e. 0.25 m

f. 2.75 km

g. 39.4 cm

h. 8.7 mm

i. $\frac{7}{8}$ in.

j. 64.25 m

k. $5\frac{9}{16}$ in.

l. $18\frac{2}{3}$ yd.

m. 2 m 8 cm

n. 1 ft. 5 in.

o. 8 ft. 11 in.

p. 4 yd. 2 ft.

2. How many meters of chrome stripping are required to finish the edge of a square table with sides each measuring 135 cm?

3. How many feet longer is the distance around a regulation baseball diamond, measuring 90 ft. between bases, than around a softball diamond, measuring 60 ft. between bases?

11–26 CIRCUMFERENCE OF A CIRCLE

The *circumference* of a circle is the length of the circle or the distance around the circle. To develop the relationship of the circumference, diameter, and radius of a circle, let us do the following:

(1) Draw a circle having a radius of 1 inch. Determine the diameter by measuring it. Is the diameter of a circle twice as long as the radius? Does the formula $d = 2r$ express this relationship when d represents the diameter, and r the radius?

(2) Draw a circle having a diameter of $2\frac{1}{2}$ inches. What is its radius? Is the radius of a circle one-half as long as the diameter? Does the radius equal the diameter divided by two?

Does the formula $r = \frac{d}{2}$ express this relationship?

(3) Draw a circle with a radius of $1\frac{1}{2}$ inches. Draw three line segments from the center to points on the circle. Measure these segments. Are all radii of a circle of equal length? Extend each of these line segments until it meets the circle, thus forming a diameter. Measure the diameters. Are all diameters of a circle of equal length?

(4) Measure the diameters and circumferences of three circular objects. Copy the following chart and tabulate your measurements. Divide the circumference of each object by its diameter, finding the quotient correct to the nearest hundredth. Find the average of these quotients.

Object	Circumference (c) of object	Diameter (d) of object	Circumference divided by diameter $(c \div d) = \pi$

The circumference is a little more than 3 times as long as the diameter. This constant ratio is represented by the Greek letter π (called pi) which equals 3.14 or $3\frac{1}{7}$ or $\frac{22}{7}$. For the greater accuracy 3.1416 is used.

Thus, the circumference of a circle is equal to pi (π) times the diameter.

Expressed as a formula it is: $c = \pi d$.

Since $d = 2r$, we may substitute $2r$ for d in the formula $c = \pi d$ to get $c = \pi 2r$ or better $c = 2\pi r$. Therefore we may say that the circumference of a circle is equal to two times pi (π) times the radius. The diameter of a circle is equal to the circumference divided by pi (π). Expressed as a formula it is $d = \frac{c}{\pi}$.

Find the circumference of a circle whose diameter is 8 centimeters:

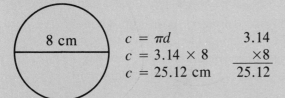

$c = \pi d$

$c = 3.14 \times 8$

$c = 25.12$ cm

$$
\begin{array}{r}
3.14 \\
\times 8 \\
\hline
25.12
\end{array}
$$

$d = 8$ cm
$\pi = 3.14$
$c = ?$ *Answer*, 25.12 centimeters

Find the circumference of a circle whose radius is 28 feet:

$c = 2\pi r$

$c = 2 \times \frac{22}{7} \times 28$

$c = 176$ feet

$$\frac{2}{1} \cdot \frac{22}{\cancel{7}} \cdot \frac{\overset{4}{\cancel{28}}}{1} = 176$$

$r = 28$ feet
$\pi = \frac{22}{7}$
$c = ?$ *Answer*, 176 feet

1. How long is the diameter of a circle if its radius is:

   a. 39 in.?   **b.** 1.25 km?   **c.** 4.8 m?   **d.** 2 ft. 11 in.?

2. How long is the radius of a circle if its diameter is:

   a. 48 mm?   **b.** 7.9 cm?   **c.** $6\frac{7}{8}$ in.?   **d.** 3 yd. 15 in.?

3. Find the circumference of a circle having a diameter of:

a. 16 m	**d.** 8.6 mi.	**g.** $1\frac{1}{2}$ ft.	**j.** 2 ft. 4 in.
b. 70 yd.	**e.** 4.7 mm	**h.** $\frac{7}{8}$ in.	**k.** 4 ft. 6 in.
c. 49 mm	**f.** 2.25 km	**i.** 5.6 cm	**l.** 1 m 5 cm

4. Find the circumference of a circle having a radius of:

a. 8 cm	**d.** 9.4 cm	**g.** $4\frac{2}{3}$ yd.	**j.** 1 ft. 2 in.
b. 21 ft.	**e.** 4.75 m	**h.** 84 mm	**k.** 3 m 1 cm
c. 105 mi.	**f.** 3.625 km	**i.** $6\frac{1}{8}$ in.	**l.** 3 ft. 11 in.

5. What distance do you ride in one turn of a merry-go-round when you sit 5.2 m from the center?

6. A bicycle has wheels measuring 26 in. in diameter. How far does the bicycle travel when its wheels make one complete turn?

AREA

The *area* of the interior (or closed region) of any plane figure is the number of units of square measure it contains. When computing the area of a geometric figure, we express all linear units in the same denomination.

11–27 AREA OF A RECTANGLE

At the right we see that one measurement indicates the number of square units in a row and the other measurement indicates how many rows there are:

Thus to find the area of the interior of a rectangle we multiply the length by the width. Expressed as a

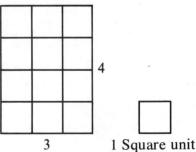

4

3   1 Square unit

formula this relationship is $A = lw$. Or, the area is equal to the altitude times the base. Formula: $A = ab$.

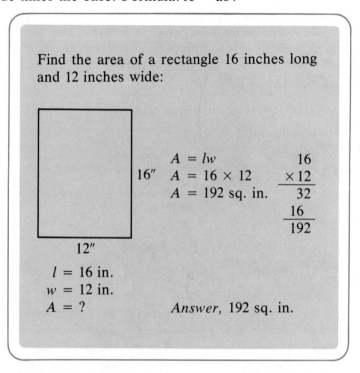

Find the area of a rectangle 16 inches long and 12 inches wide:

16″   12″

$A = lw$
$A = 16 \times 12$
$A = 192$ sq. in.

$$\begin{array}{r} 16 \\ \times\, 12 \\ \hline 32 \\ 16 \\ \hline 192 \end{array}$$

$l = 16$ in.
$w = 12$ in.
$A = ?$ *Answer,* 192 sq. in.

EXERCISES

1. Find the area of a rectangle:

   a. 17 in. long and 6 in. wide
   b. 63 m long and 80 m wide
   c. 210 yd. long and 145 yd. wide
   d. 6.7 mm long and 0.9 mm wide
   e. 7.4 m long and 5.625 m wide
   f. 9.5 km long and 10.3 km wide

   g. $8\frac{1}{2}$ in. long and 3 in. wide
   h. $3\frac{2}{3}$ yd. long and $5\frac{3}{4}$ yd. wide
   i. 8.6 cm long and 11 cm wide
   j. 7 ft. 8 in. long and 4 ft. wide
   k. 2 ft. 11 in. long and 3 ft. 6 in. wide
   l. 5 m 14 cm long and 4 m 3 cm wide

2. How many square meters of the lot are left over when a building 115 m long and 74 m wide is erected on a lot 205 m long and 168 m wide?

3. The viewing area of a rectangular TV picture tube measuring 16 in. by 20 in. is how many times as large as that of another rectangular picture tube measuring 12 in. by 15 in.?

11–28 AREA OF A SQUARE

Although we may use the formula $A = lw$ to find the area of the interior of a square, we generally use the formula $A = s^2$ where s is the length of the side of the square. Since the length and width of a square are both equal to the length of the side, s, the formula $A = lw$ becomes $A = s \times s$ or $A = s^2$.

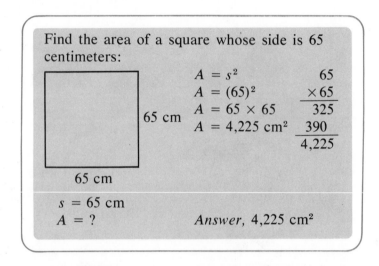

Find the area of a square whose side is 65 centimeters:

$$A = s^2$$
$$A = (65)^2$$
$$A = 65 \times 65$$
$$A = 4{,}225 \text{ cm}^2$$

```
      65
   × 65
    325
    390
  4,225
```

65 cm

65 cm

$s = 65$ cm
$A = ?$

Answer, 4,225 cm²

EXERCISES

1. Find the area of a square whose side measures:

   a. 7 cm
   b. 68 in.
   c. 880 yd.
   d. 1,000 mi.

   e. 4.7 cm
   f. 79 mm
   g. 12.8 km
   h. 1.09 m

   i. $6\frac{1}{2}$ yd.
   j. $\frac{5}{8}$ in.
   k. 0.5 km
   l. $10\frac{3}{4}$ yd.

   m. 2 ft. 6 in.
   n. 1 ft. 10 in.
   o. 6 ft. 8 in.
   p. 8 m 47 cm

2. How many square meters of sod are needed for a lawn measuring 29 m by 29 m. At $1.45 per square meter, what is the cost of the sod?

3. How many square yards of carpeting are required to cover a room measuring 13 ft. 6 in. by 13 ft. 6 in.?

4. How many square tiles, 4 in. on a side, are needed to cover half of a wall measuring 12 ft. 8 in. by 10 ft.? At $.18 each, how much will it cost?

11–29 AREA OF A PARALLELOGRAM

The *base* of a parallelogram is the side on which it rests. The *altitude* or *height* is the perpendicular segment between the base and its opposite side.

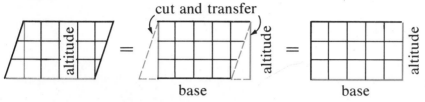

cut and transfer

The above diagrams illustrate that the area of the interior of a parallelogram is equal to the product of the altitude and the base, formula $A = ab$, or the product of the base and height, formula $A = bh$.

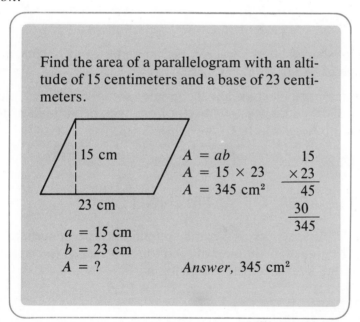

Find the area of a parallelogram with an altitude of 15 centimeters and a base of 23 centimeters.

15 cm

23 cm

$a = 15$ cm
$b = 23$ cm
$A = ?$

$A = ab$
$A = 15 \times 23$
$A = 345$ cm^2

$$\begin{array}{r} 15 \\ \times 23 \\ \hline 45 \\ 30 \\ \hline 345 \end{array}$$

Answer, 345 cm^2

EXERCISES

1. Find the area of a parallelogram with an altitude of 18 in. and a base of 31 in.
2. What is the area of a parallelogram when its base is 6.4 cm and height is 5.2 cm?

Informal Geometry

3. Find the areas of parallelograms with the following dimensions:

	Altitude	Base
a.	95 in.	103 in.
b.	172 mm	147 mm
c.	225 ft.	302 ft.
d.	4.6 m	3.8 m
e.	$5\frac{2}{3}$ yd.	$4\frac{1}{4}$ yd.

4. Find the areas of parallelograms with the following dimensions:

	Base	Height
a.	3.52 m	2.07 m
b.	6 ft.	$8\frac{3}{4}$ ft.
c.	9.9 cm	10.4 cm
d.	7 ft. 3 in.	5 ft. 6 in.
e.	8 m 15 cm	4 m 9 cm

5. A lot shaped like a parallelogram has a base of 87 m and an altitude of 68 m. What is its area?

6. Which parallelogram has the greater area, one with an altitude of 135 ft. and a base of 146 ft. or one with an altitude of 146 ft. and a base of 135 ft.?

11–30 AREA OF A TRIANGLE

A diagonal separates a parallelogram into two congruent triangles. The area of the interior of each triangle is equal to one-half the area of the interior of the parallelogram.

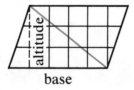

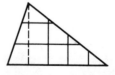

Thus the area of the interior of a triangle is equal to one-half the altitude times the base. Expressed as a formula it is $A = \frac{1}{2}ab$ or $A = \frac{ab}{2}$. Or, the area is equal to one half the base times the height. Formula: $A = \frac{1}{2}bh$.

Find the area of a triangle with an altitude of
14 meters and a base of 11 meters:

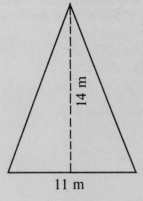

$A = \frac{1}{2}\,ab$

$A = \frac{1}{2} \times 14 \times 11$

$A = 77 \text{ m}^2$

$$\frac{1}{\underset{1}{\cancel{2}}} \times \frac{\overset{7}{\cancel{14}}}{1} \times \frac{11}{1} = 77$$

14 m

11 m

$a = 14$ m
$b = 11$ m
$A = ?$

Answer, 77 m²

EXERCISES

1. Find the area of a triangle with an altitude of 26 cm and a base of 60 cm.
2. What is the area of a triangle when its base is 125 ft. and height is 79 ft.?
3. Find the areas of triangles with the following dimensions:

Altitude	Base		Base	Height
a. 62 in.	81 in.	**f.**	7.4 cm	9.5 cm
b. 58 m	45 m	**g.**	$18\frac{3}{4}$ ft.	$13\frac{2}{3}$ ft.
c. 169 ft.	177 ft.	**h.**	5.86 m	8.67 m
d. 221 mm	193 mm	**i.**	15 ft. 4 in.	9 ft. 6 in.
e. 8 yd.	$5\frac{1}{2}$ yd.	**j.**	11 m 226 mm	7 m 69 mm

4. A triangular lot has a base of 155 ft. and an altitude of 138 ft. Find its area.
5. How many square meters of surface does each side of a triangular sail expose if its base is 5 m and its height is 7.84 m?

11–31 AREA OF A TRAPEZOID

The figure below shows that the diagonal separates the trapezoid into two triangles which have a common height but different bases. The area of one triangle is $\frac{1}{2} b_1 h$ and of the other is $\frac{1}{2} b_2 h$. The area of the interior of the trapezoid is equal to the sum of the areas of the interiors of the two triangles or $\frac{1}{2} b_1 h + \frac{1}{2} b_2 h$. Using the distributive principle, we find that the area of the interior of a trapezoid is equal to the height times the average of the two bases (parallel sides). Expressed as a formula, $A = h \times \dfrac{b_1 + b_2}{2}$ or sometimes $A = \dfrac{h}{2}(b_1 + b_2)$.

base "b_2"

base "b_1"

Find the area of a trapezoid with bases of 22 feet and 16 feet and a height of 17 feet:

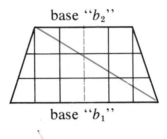

$$A = h \times \frac{b_1 + b_2}{2}$$

$$A = 17 \times \frac{22 + 16}{2}$$

$$A = 17 \times 19$$

$$A = 323 \text{ sq. ft.}$$

$$
\begin{array}{r} 22 \\ + 16 \\ \hline 38 \end{array}
\qquad
\begin{array}{r} 17 \\ \times 19 \\ \hline 153 \\ 17 \\ \hline 323 \end{array}
$$

$$
\begin{array}{r} 19 \\ 2\overline{)38} \end{array}
$$

$h = 17$ ft.
$b_1 = 22$ ft.
$b_2 = 16$ ft.
$A = ?$

Answer, 323 sq. ft.

1. What is the area of a trapezoid when its bases are 74 mm and 62 mm and its height is 57 mm?

2. Find the areas of trapezoids with the following dimensions:

Bases	Height	Bases	Height
a. 25 ft. and 19 ft.	26 ft.	**g.** 16.8 cm and 14.3 cm	21.6 cm
b. 83 cm and 42 cm	57 cm	**h.** $7\frac{5}{8}$ yd. and $9\frac{1}{3}$ yd.	$6\frac{3}{4}$ yd.
c. 95 in. and 107 in.	83 in.	**i.** 5.67 m and 6.8 m	7.4 m
d. $12\frac{1}{2}$ yd. and $8\frac{3}{4}$ yd.	$6\frac{2}{3}$ yd.	**j.** $8\frac{1}{4}$ ft. and $5\frac{1}{2}$ ft.	$2\frac{3}{4}$ ft.
e. 169 mm and 194 mm	185 mm	**k.** 10 cm and 9.4 cm	12.5 cm
f. 32 m and 18 m	19 m	**l.** 65 cm and 148 cm	1.4 m

3. A certain porch roof consists of 3 sections each shaped like a trapezoid. The bases of two sections, both alike, each measure 11 ft. and 9 ft. The bases of the third section measure 20 ft. and 18 ft. The distance between the bases in all three sections is 12 ft. Find the area of the entire roof.

11–32 AREA OF A CIRCLE

If we divide the interior of a circle into sectors and arrange them in a shape approximating a parallelogram, we see that the area of the interior of a circle equals the area of the inte-

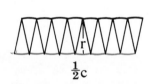

rior of the parallelogram whose base is one-half the circumference ($\frac{1}{2} c$) and that the altitude is the radius (r). The formula for this is $A = \frac{1}{2} cr$. Since $c = 2\pi r$, we may substitute $2\pi r$ for c in the formula of $A = \frac{1}{2} cr$ to obtain $A = \frac{1}{2} \cdot 2\pi r \cdot r$ which simplified is $A = \pi r^2$. The area of a circle is equal to pi (π) times the radius squared.

Or by substituting $\frac{d}{2}$ for r in the formula $A = \pi r^2$ we obtain the formula $A = \frac{1}{4} \pi d^2$ which may also be used to find the area of the interior of a circle.

Find the area of a circle having a radius of
9 inches:

$$A = \pi r^2$$
$$A = 3.14 \times (9)^2$$
$$A = 3.14 \times 81$$
$$A = 254.34 \text{ sq. in.}$$

```
  9        3.14
 ×9        ×81
 81        3 14
         251 2
         254.34
```

9″

$r = 9$ in.
$\pi = 3.14$
$A = ?$ *Answer*, 254.34 sq. in.

Find the area of a circle having a diameter of
14 millimeters:

14 mm

$$A = \tfrac{1}{4}\,\pi d^2$$
$$A = \tfrac{1}{4} \times \tfrac{22}{7} \times (14)^2$$
$$A = 154 \text{ mm}^2$$

$$\tfrac{1}{4} \times \tfrac{22}{7} \times (14)^2$$

$$\frac{1}{\cancel{4}} \times \frac{22}{\cancel{7}} \times \cancel{196}^{\,7} = 154$$

$d = 14$ mm
$\pi = \tfrac{22}{7}$ *Answer*, 154 mm²
$A = ?$

EXERCISES

1. Find the area of a circle having a radius of:

a. 5 mm

b. 56 ft.

c. 140 m

d. 69 km

e. 8.05 m

f. 0.75 cm

g. $7\tfrac{7}{8}$ in.

h. $11\tfrac{1}{2}$ ft.

i. $\tfrac{1}{4}$ in.

j. 1 ft. 9 in.

k. 9 yd. 1 ft.

l. 4 m 13 cm

2. Find the area of a circle having a diameter of:

a. 6 ft.

b. 84 km

c. 70 cm

d. 4.5 km

e. 0.4 mm

f. 10.75 m

g. $\frac{5}{8}$ in.

h. $3\frac{1}{2}$ yd.

i. $8\frac{3}{4}$ ft.

j. 6 ft. 6 in.

k. 10 ft. 8 in.

l. 1 m 57 mm

3. A revolving sprinkler sprays a lawn for a distance of 7 m in all directions. How many square meters does the sprinkler water in one revolution?

4. What is the cooking area of a circular barbecue grill having a diameter of 24 in.?

VOLUME—MEASURE OF SPACE

Space has three dimensions: length, width, and height (or depth or thickness). We live in a three-dimensional world. The volume, also called capacity or cubical contents, is the number of units of cubic measure contained in a given space. When computing the volume of a geometric solid, we express all linear units in the same denomination.

11–33 VOLUME OF A RECTANGULAR SOLID

A one-inch cube contains a volume of 1 cubic inch. The rectangular solid below has 4 cubes in each row, 3 rows of cubes and 2 layers of cubes. In one layer there are 4×3 or 12 cubes; in two layers there are $4 \times 3 \times 2$ or 24 cubes which contain a total volume of 24 cubic inches. The volume of a rectangular solid is equal to the length times the width times the height. Expressed as a formula it is $V = lwh$. Sometimes the formula $V = Bh$ is used where B is the area of the base (lw) of the rectangular solid.

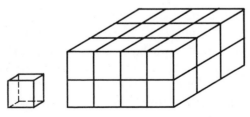

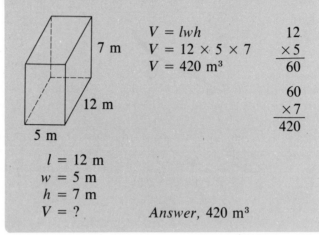

Find the volume of a rectangular solid 12 meters long, 5 meters wide, and 7 meters high:

$V = lwh$
$V = 12 \times 5 \times 7$
$V = 420 \text{ m}^3$

```
  12
 × 5
 ───
  60

  60
 × 7
 ───
 420
```

$l = 12 \text{ m}$
$w = 5 \text{ m}$
$h = 7 \text{ m}$
$V = ?$

Answer, 420 m³

EXERCISES

1. Find the volume of a rectangular solid:

   a. 8 in. long, 3 in. wide, and 7 in. high

   b. 35 ft. long, 20 ft. wide, and 15 ft. high

   c. 56 m long, 60 m wide, and 45 m high

   d. 8.25 cm long, 4.2 cm wide, and 7 cm high

   e. 4.7 m long, 3.4 m wide, and 6.5 m high

   f. $7\frac{1}{2}$ in. long, $6\frac{3}{4}$ in. wide, and 10 in. high

   g. $3\frac{1}{3}$ ft. long, $2\frac{1}{2}$ ft. wide, and $\frac{3}{4}$ ft. high

   h. 2 yd. long, 1 ft. 6 in. wide, and 2 ft. high

   i. 4 m 7 cm long, 6 m 4 cm wide, and 5 m 2 cm high

   j. 8 ft. long, 4 ft. 10 in. wide, and 1 ft. 4 in. high

2. How many cubic meters of earth must be removed to make an excavation 90 m long, 48 m wide, and 16 m deep?

3. A refrigerator-freezer unit has a freezer compartment 12 in. by 24 in. by 15 in. and a refrigerator compartment 33 in. by 24 in. by 15 in. Find the capacity in cubic feet of:
a. the freezer; **b.** the refrigerator; **c.** the total unit.

11–34 VOLUME OF A CUBE

Since the length, width and height of a cube are all equal to the length of the edge of the cube, the formula $V = lwh$ becomes $V = e \times e \times e$ or $V = e^3$. The volume of a cube is equal to the length of its edge cubed. Sometimes the formula $V = s^3$ is used.

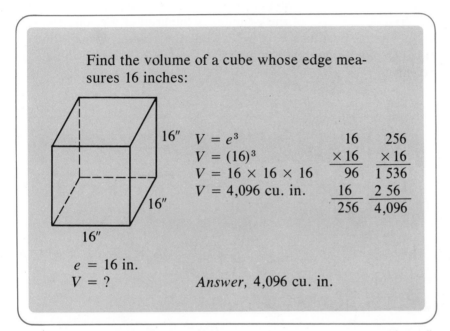

Find the volume of a cube whose edge measures 16 inches:

$e = 16$ in.
$V = ?$

$V = e^3$
$V = (16)^3$
$V = 16 \times 16 \times 16$
$V = 4{,}096$ cu. in.

```
   16        256
  ×16       ×16
   96      1 536
   16      2 56
  256      4,096
```

Answer, 4,096 cu. in.

EXERCISES

1. Find the volume of a cube whose edge measures:

   a. 15 in.

   b. 9 cm

   c. 60 ft.

   d. 128 mm

   e. 4.85 cm

   f. 0.39 m

   g. 10.5 mm

   h. 6.72 m

   i. $5\frac{1}{2}$ ft.

   j. $\frac{3}{4}$ in.

   k. $1\frac{7}{8}$ yd.

   l. 12.8 m

   m. 1 ft. 1 in.

   n. 2 ft. 9 in.

   o. 4 m 25 cm

   p. 2 yd. 8 in.

2. How many cubic feet of space does a carton occupy if it measures 3 ft. 6 in. by 3 ft. 6 in. by 3 ft. 6 in.?

3. Which has a greater volume and how much greater, a group of ten 2-centimeter cubes or two 10-centimeter cubes?

Informal Geometry

11–35 VOLUME OF A RIGHT CIRCULAR CYLINDER

To determine the formula for the volume of a right circular cylinder, we apply the principle that the volume is equal to the area of the base of the cylinder times the height ($V = Bh$). The same principle is used in determining the volume of a rectangular solid. Since the area of the base of the cylinder is the area of a circle, the formula $V = Bh$ becomes $V = \pi r^2 h$. Thus the volume of a cylinder is equal to pi (π) times the square of the radius of the base times the height.

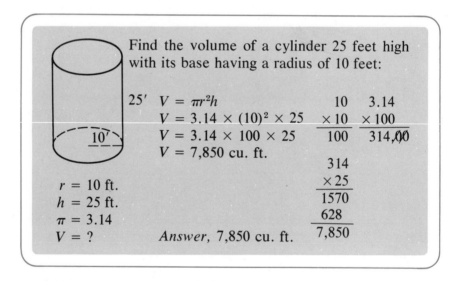

Find the volume of a cylinder 25 feet high with its base having a radius of 10 feet:

$V = \pi r^2 h$

$V = 3.14 \times (10)^2 \times 25$

$V = 3.14 \times 100 \times 25$

$V = 7,850$ cu. ft.

10	3.14
×10	×100
100	314,00

$$
\begin{array}{r}
314 \\
\times 25 \\
\hline
1570 \\
628 \\
\hline
7,850
\end{array}
$$

$r = 10$ ft.
$h = 25$ ft.
$\pi = 3.14$
$V = ?$

Answer, 7,850 cu. ft.

When the diameter is known, the formula $V = \frac{1}{4}\pi d^2 h$ may be used.

EXERCISES

1. Find the volume of a cylinder:

   a. 30 cm high with its base having a radius of 14 cm
   b. when the radius of its base is 6 in. and the height is 9 in.
   c. 8.6 m high with its base having a radius of 2.5 m
   d. when the radius of its base is $3\frac{1}{2}$ in. and the height is 10 in.
   e. 2 ft. 6 in. high with its base having a radius of 1 ft. 2 in.

2. Find the volume of a cylinder:

   a. when the diameter of its base is 42 mm and the height is 50 mm

   b. 25 ft. high with its base having a diameter of 14 ft.

   c. when the diameter of its base is 20 m and the height is 35 m

   d. 36 cm high with its base having a diameter of 15 cm

   e. when the diameter of its base is 3 ft. 6 in. and the height is 10 ft.

3. How many gallons of water are needed to fill a circular swimming pool 21 ft. in diameter to an average depth of 2 ft. 6 in.? What is the weight of the water in the pool? 1 cu. ft. holds $7\frac{1}{2}$ gallons. 1 cu. ft. of water weighs $62\frac{1}{2}$ pounds.

4. The water in a circular pond 19 meters in diameter has an average depth of 2 meters. Determine the number of liters of water and its weight in kilograms. 1 cubic meter = 1,000 liters. 1 liter of water weighs 1 kilogram.

5. Two cylindrical cans are both 20 cm high. One can has a base with a radius of 5 cm and the other a base with a radius of 15 cm. How do their volumes compare?

6. How many gallons of gasoline does a tank car hold if it is 12 ft. in diameter and 35 ft. long? 1 cubic foot holds $7\frac{1}{2}$ gallons.

7. Find the displacement of a piston (volume of an engine cylinder) whose bore (diameter) is $3\frac{1}{2}$ in. and whose stroke (height piston moves) is 5 in.

8. How many cu. yd. of earth must be removed to make a hole 6 ft. in diameter and 42 ft. deep?

9. How many liters of oil will a drum hold if its diameter is 70 centimeters and it is 1.3 meters high?

10. A water storage tank has a diameter of 4.2 meters and a height of 2.9 meters. How many liters of water will it hold? What is the weight of the water when the tank is full?

CHAPTER REVIEW

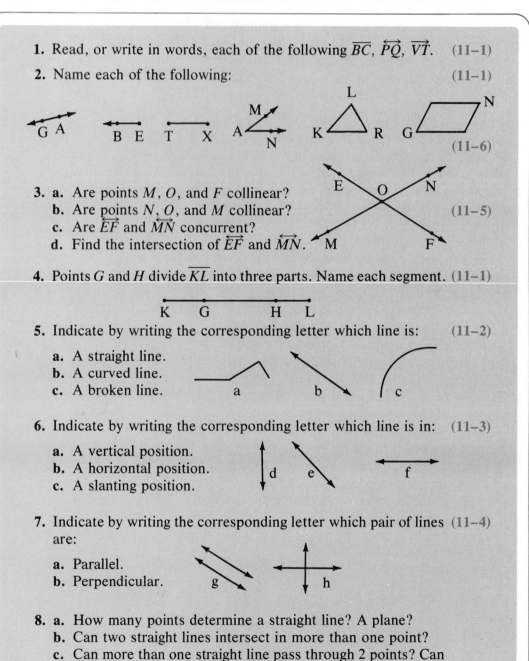

1. Read, or write in words, each of the following $\overline{BC}$, $\overleftrightarrow{PQ}$, $\overrightarrow{VT}$. (11–1)

2. Name each of the following: (11–1)

   G A   B E T X   A M N   L K R   G N (11–6)

3. a. Are points M, O, and F collinear?
   b. Are points N, O, and M collinear? (11–5)
   c. Are $\overleftrightarrow{EF}$ and $\overleftrightarrow{MN}$ concurrent?
   d. Find the intersection of $\overleftrightarrow{EF}$ and $\overleftrightarrow{MN}$.

4. Points G and H divide $\overline{KL}$ into three parts. Name each segment. (11–1)

   K G   H L

5. Indicate by writing the corresponding letter which line is: (11–2)
   a. A straight line.
   b. A curved line.
   c. A broken line.   a   b   c

6. Indicate by writing the corresponding letter which line is in: (11–3)
   a. A vertical position.
   b. A horizontal position.
   c. A slanting position.   d   e   f

7. Indicate by writing the corresponding letter which pair of lines (11–4)
   are:
   a. Parallel.
   b. Perpendicular.   g   h

8. a. How many points determine a straight line? A plane?
   b. Can two straight lines intersect in more than one point?
   c. Can more than one straight line pass through 2 points? Can

more than one plane pass through 3 points on a straight line?

    d. How many points and lines does a plane contain?

    e. What is the intersection of two planes?   (11–5)

9. a. How many diagonals can be drawn from any vertex of a hexagon?

    b. How many faces (F) does a rectangular solid have? How many vertices (V)? How many edges (E)? Does $F + V - E = 2$?   (11–8)

10. If the scale is 1 inch = 80 miles, what actual distance is represented by $5\frac{13}{16}$ inches?   (11–11)

11. If the scale is 1 : 2,000,000, how many millimeters represent 138 kilometers?   (11–11)

12. If the distance from A to T is 100 miles, what is the distance from E to D?   (11–11)

$\overline{}$ $\overline{}$

A   T   E   D

13. With protractor measure the following angle: (11–12)

14. a. With protractor draw an angle of 130°.

    b. Draw any acute angle.

    c. Draw any obtuse angle.   **d.** Draw a right angle.   (11–13)

15. a. Construct a triangle with sides $2\frac{1}{2}$ in., $1\frac{5}{8}$ in., and $2\frac{1}{16}$ in.

    b. Construct a triangle with sides measuring 43 mm and 51 mm and an included angle of 50°.

    c. Construct a triangle with angles measuring 35° and 72° and an included side measuring 3.8 cm.   (11–14)

16. Draw any line. Using a compass, construct a perpendicular to your line: (11–15)

    a. At a point on your line   **b.** From a point not on your line   (11–16)

17. Draw any line segment. Bisect this line segment, using a compass. Check with a ruler.   (11–17)

18. Draw an angle of 65°, using a protractor. Then copy this angle, using a compass. Check with a protractor.   (11–18)

19. Draw an angle. Bisect this angle, using a compass. Check with a protractor.   (11–19)

20. Draw any line. Locate a point not on this line. Through this point construct a line parallel to the line you have drawn. (11–20)

21. Draw a regular hexagon, each side measuring 1 inch. (11–21)

22. Draw a circle with a diameter of $1\frac{3}{4}$ inches. (11–26)

23. What is the complement of an angle of 66°? (11–23)

24. What is the supplement of an angle of 87°? (11–23)

25. **a.** What is the sum of measures of ∡1, 2, and 3 of triangle *ABC*? (11–22)
    b. If $m\angle 1 = 48°$ and $m\angle 4 = 125°$, find the measure of ∠2. Of ∠3. (11–23)

26. $\overleftrightarrow{AB}$ and $\overleftrightarrow{CD}$ intersect at *E*. If $m\angle 4 = 146°$, what is the measure of ∠1? Of ∠2? Of ∠3? (11–23)

Find the perimeter of:

27. A rectangle 32 meters long and 18 meters wide. (11–24)

28. A square whose side measures 47 yards. (11–25)

Find the circumference of a circle whose:

29. Diameter is 63 inches.   30. Radius is 29 millimeters. (11–26)

Find the area of: 31. A circle whose radius is 70 yards. (11–32)

32. A square whose side measures 86 centimeters. (11–28)

33. A rectangle 110 feet long and 93 feet wide. (11–27)

34. A circle whose diameter is 40 millimeters. (11–32)

35. A triangle whose altitude is 48 mm and base is 55 mm. (11–32)

36. A parallelogram with altitude $10\frac{1}{2}$ feet and base $11\frac{3}{4}$ feet. (11–29)

37. A trapezoid with bases of 37 m and 21 m and a height of 18 m. (11–31)

Find the volume of: 38. A cube whose edge measures 19 in. (11–34)

39. A rectangular solid 29 m long, 15 m wide, and 20 m high. (11–33)

40. A right circular cylinder 42 inches high with its base having a diameter of 50 inches. (11–35)

ACHIEVEMENT TEST

1. Add:

526,493
875,956
908,767
439,928
719,693   (2–9)

2. Subtract:

1,306,894
  935,968   (2–10)

3. Multiply:

5,937
8,694   (2–11)

4. Divide:

$849\overline{)3,969,075}$ (2–16)

5. Add:

$2\frac{5}{8} + \frac{13}{16} + 3\frac{2}{3}$ (4–11)

6. Subtract:

$10\frac{1}{4} - 9\frac{4}{5}$ (4–12)

7. Multiply:

$3\frac{1}{3} \times \frac{3}{4}$ (4–13)

8. Divide:

$16 \div 2\frac{1}{2}$ (4–15)

9. Add:

$8.4 + .96 + 47$ (5–7)

10. Subtract:

$.86 - .6$ (5–8)

11. Multiply:

$1.008 \times .04$ (5–9)

12. Divide:

$\$.18\overline{)\$54}$ (5–11)

13. Find $6\frac{3}{4}\%$ of $12,500.   (6–6)
14. What percent of 40 is 34?   (6–7)
15. 45% of what amount is $207?   (6–8)
16. Find the square root of 79,352,464.   (7–2)
17. Compute as indicated: (10–10) (10–13) (10–15) (10–17)

    a. $^{-}17 + {^{+}8}$ **b.** $6 - 23$ **c.** $^{-}7 \times {^{-}16}$ **d.** $^{-}54 \div {^{+}18}$

18. Solve and check: (10–26)

    a. $y + 14 = 14$ **e.** $3n + 23 = 95$

    b. $8x = 96$ **f.** $6d - 15 = 17$

    c. $52 = r - 81$ **g.** $11c - c = 110$

    d. $\frac{b}{16} = 32$ **h.** $\frac{3}{4}n = 60$

19. **a.** If the scale is 1:2,500,000, how many millimeters represent 10 km?

   b. What actual distance in kilometers is represented by 3.6 cm if the scale is 1:1,000,000?

   c. Find the scale when the scale length of $4\frac{1}{2}$ inches represents an actual distance of 54 miles. (11–11)

20. **a.** Draw a line segment measuring 4 cm. Bisect this line segment, using a compass. Check with a ruler. (11–17)

   b. Draw an angle of 56°, using a protractor. Then copy this angle, using a compass. Check with a protractor. (11–18)

   c. Draw an angle of 72°, using a protractor. Bisect this angle, using a compass. Check with a protractor. (11–19)

   d. Construct a triangle with angles measuring 90° and 34° and an included side of $3\frac{3}{4}$ inches. (11–14)

21. Find the complement and the supplement of an angle measuring 60°. (11–23)

22. What is the perimeter of a square whose side measures 57 feet? (11–25)

23. Find the perimeter of a rectangle 64 meters long and 39 meters wide. (11–24)

24. What is the circumference of a circle whose diameter is 84 centimeters? (11–26)

25. Find the area of a circle whose radius is 90 yards. (11–32)

26. Find the area of a rectangle 41 centimeters long and 29 centimeters wide. (11–27)

27. What is the area of a square whose side measures 78 inches? (11–28)

28. Find the volume of a cube whose edge measures 108 millimeters. (11–34)

29. What is the volume of a rectangular solid 23 feet long, 9 feet wide, and 17 feet high? (11–33)

30. Find the volume of a right circular cylinder 80 centimeters high with its base having a radius of 56 centimeters. (11–35)

12

CHAPTER 12
Applications of Mathematics-Problem Solving

CONSUMER SPENDING

12-1 BUYING FOOD

LEE'S FOOD MARKET

See our specials for the week

Groceries	Meats, Fish, and Dairy
Beverages, 2 bottles for 89¢	Bacon, $1.69 a pound
Grape jelly, 79¢ a jar	Margarine, $1.08 a pound
Corn, 5 cans for $1.89	Cheese, $2.56 a pound
Flour, 5 lb. for 93¢	Chicken, 80¢ a pound
Peaches, 55¢ a can	Eggs, 2 doz. for $1.59
Peas, 3 cans for 81¢	Flounder, $2.39 a pound
Soap, 4 bars for 99¢	Haddock, $1.92 a pound
Laundry detergent, $1.98	Turkey, 96¢ a pound
Soups, 3 cans for 95¢	Milk, 2 qt. for $1.29
Sugar, 5 lb. for $1.85	Rib roast, $2.88 a pound
Tomato juice, 2 cans $1.05	Sirloin, $2.40 a pound
Tuna fish, 4 cans for $5	Smoked ham, $1.60 a pound

Fruit and Produce

Apples, 39¢ a pound	Carrots, 2 bunches for 59¢
Bananas, 25¢ a pound	Celery, 49¢ a stalk
Grapefruit, 3 for 49¢	Lettuce, 2 heads for 95¢
Grapes, 89¢ a pound	Onions, 3 lb. for 75¢
Lemons, 6 for 59¢	Peppers, 3 for 39¢
Oranges, 99¢ a dozen	Potatoes, 5 lb. for 89¢
Peaches, 49¢ a pound	String beans, 32¢ a pound
Pears, 45¢ a pound	Tomatoes, 48¢ a pound

The ¢ symbol indicates cents. For easier computation you may be required to replace this symbol with the dollar mark ($) and a decimal point. For example: 49¢ may be written as $.49 and 81.7¢ as $.817. See page 460.

EXERCISES

When the result of your computation of the cost of a food item contains *any* fractional part of a cent, drop the fraction and add one cent to the cost of the item.

In each of the following problems, use the prices listed by Lee's Food Market.

1. What is the cost of:

   a. 1 lb. onions?   **f.** 1 cake?
   b. 1 bottle beverage?   **g.** 1 can corn?
   c. 1 doz. eggs?   **h.** 1 bar soap?
   d. 1 head of lettuce?   **i.** 1 can tuna fish?
   e. 1 orange?   **j.** 1 can soup?

2. What is the cost of:

   a. 2 cans peaches?   **f.** 16 cans soup?
   b. 3 lb. bananas?   **g.** 6 doz. eggs?
   c. 4 lb. flounder?   **h.** 9 lb. rib roast?
   d. 12 lemons?   **i.** 12 peppers?
   e. 5 lb. chicken?   **j.** 9 cans tuna fish?

3. What is the cost of:

   a. $\frac{1}{2}$ doz. rolls?   **e.** 3 oranges?
   b. $\frac{1}{4}$ lb. cheese?   **f.** 2 lemons?
   c. $\frac{3}{4}$ lb. cookies?   **g.** 4 cakes?
   d. $\frac{7}{8}$ lb. smoked ham?   **h.** 2 lb. onions?

Applications of Mathematics—Problem Solving

i. 3 bars soap?
j. 2 cans soup?
k. 12 oz. grapes?
l. 7 oz. cookies?
m. 8 oz. string beans?
n. 4 oz. margarine?

o. 10 oz. tomatoes?
p. 14 oz. peaches?
q. 15 oz. pears?
r. 13 oz. haddock?
s. 5 oz. cheese?
t. 14 oz. apples?

4. What is the cost of:

a. 4 cans peas?
b. 3 cans tomato juice?
c. 16 cakes?
d. 5 cans tuna fish?
e. 30 eggs?
f. 15 cans soup?
g. 10 lb. onions?
h. 7 qt. milk?
i. 8 peppers?
j. 32 rolls?

k. $2\frac{1}{2}$ lb. sirloin?
l. $4\frac{1}{4}$ lb. chicken?
m. $1\frac{3}{8}$ lb. string beans?
n. $5\frac{3}{4}$ lb. turkey?
o. $3\frac{11}{16}$ lb. pears?
p. 1 lb. 4 oz. tomatoes?
q. 3 lb. 8 oz. apples?
r. 6 lb. 14 oz. rib roast?
s. 2 lb. 9 oz. bananas?
t. 4 lb. 1 oz. flounder?

5. Find the cost of each of the following orders:

a. 2 doz. eggs, 5 lb. flour, 4 cans soup, 1 pkg. detergent.

b. 1 loaf bread, 1 qt. milk, 1 doz. cakes, $\frac{3}{4}$ lb. cheese, 4 lemons.

c. 1 jar grape jelly, 2 doz. oranges, $1\frac{1}{2}$ lb. margarine, 2 lb. bacon, 8 cans soup.

d. 12 oz. margarine, 4 lb. 8 oz. sirloin, 4 grapefruit, 1 can tuna fish, 1 bar soap.

e. 6 bottles beverage, 3 heads lettuce, $2\frac{1}{2}$ lb. tomatoes, $2\frac{3}{4}$ lb. apples, 9 rolls.

f. 5 lb. potatoes, 2 stalks celery, 5 peppers, 2 cans tomato juice, 6 cans tuna fish.

g. 1 bunch carrots, 3 loaves bread, 2 lb. 12 oz. smoked ham, 3 lb. 11 oz. haddock, 5 lb. sugar, 2 jars grape jelly, 12 oz. margarine, 4 lb. 5 oz. sirloin.

h. 6 bars soap, 10 cans corn, 2 cans peaches, 4 cans tuna fish, 1 doz. oranges, 2 lb. string beans, $1\frac{1}{2}$ lb. flounder, $9\frac{1}{2}$ lb. turkey, $5\frac{1}{4}$ lb. chicken.

i. 20 cakes, 15 rolls, 1 lb. 11 oz. tomatoes, 5 lb. potatoes, 2 lb. 14 oz. haddock, 1 doz. eggs, 1 qt. milk, 9 grapefruit, 9 oranges.

j. 2 lb. 7 oz. bananas, 3 lb. 4 oz. sirloin, 6 eggs, 1 loaf bread, 3 qt. milk, 1 lb. 5 oz. tomatoes, 2 lb. 6 oz. string beans, 1 pepper, 1 lb. 8 oz. grapes, 3 jars grape jelly.

k. 4 loaves bread, $1\frac{1}{2}$ doz. cakes, 1 head lettuce, 4 lb. onions, $2\frac{1}{2}$ doz. oranges, $4\frac{3}{4}$ lb. rib roast, 1 lb. 5 oz. pears, 2 bars soap, 3 doz. eggs, 10 cans soup.

l. 1 lb. 3 oz. cheese, 2 doz. rolls, 1 lb. 9 oz. haddock, 2 cans peas, 12 cans tuna fish, 8 oz. margarine, 1 can tomato juice, 4 lb. 3 oz. chicken, 3 cans corn, 8 bottles beverage, 3 lemons, 5 grapefruit.

6. Find the cost of each of the following weights of food:

a. (1) 2 kg (2) 750 g (3) 4.5 kg (4) 1,400 g when 1 kg of chicken costs $1.90.

b. (1) 1 kg (2) 850 g (3) 200 g (4) 1.2 kg when 500 g of cheese cost $2.55.

c. (1) 900 g (2) 2.1 kg (3) 0.8 kg (4) 1,600 g when 1 kg of onions costs 45¢.

d. (1) 460 g (2) 1 kg (3) 625 g (4) 0.4 kg when 100 g of cookies cost 60¢.

e. (1) 3 kg (2) 700 g (3) 4.9 kg (4) 2,800 g when 1 kg of shad costs $3.

f. (1) 15 kg (2) 2,400 g (3) 3.5 kg (4) 7.4 kg when 5 kg of potatoes cost $1.75.

g. (1) 125 g (2) 680 g (3) 1 kg (4) 0.6 kg when 250 g of salami cost $1.80.

h. (1) 2 kg (2) 800 g (3) 1.7 kg (4) 1,580 g when 1 kg of peas costs 65¢.

i. (1) 3 kg (2) 750 g (3) 2.1 kg (4) 975 g when 500 g of bananas cost 28¢.

j. (1) 1,500 g (2) 4 kg (3) 640 g (4) 0.7 kg when 1 kg of apples costs 75¢.

7. If gasoline costs 33.9¢ per liter, find the cost of 41.8 liters of gasoline.

8. How many 8-packs of 250 mL bottles of beverage should be purchased if you want 4 L in all? What will the total cost be if an 8-pack costs $1.99?

12–2 BUYING AT A SALE

A person buying an article at a sale expects to pay a reduced price for this article. The regular or full price of an article is generally called the *marked price* or *list price*. The reduced price is sometimes called the *sale price* or *net price*. The percent taken off is the *rate of reduction*. To find the rate of reduction, we determine what percent the reduction is of the regular price.

EXERCISES

1. How much is a basketball reduced in price at a 30% reduction sale if its regular price is $14.50? What is its sale price?
2. A dress marked $30 was sold at a reduction of 25%. What was the sale price of the dress?
3. At a clearance sale a discontinued model television set, regularly selling for $550, can now be purchased at a reduction of 18%. What is its sale price?
4. Find the sale price of each of the following articles:
   a. Football; regular price, $15.80; reduced 50%.
   b. Bicycle; regular price, $85; reduced 14%.
   c. Blanket; regular price, $14.75; reduced 22%.
   d. Rug; regular price, $375; $\frac{1}{4}$ off.
   e. Camera; regular price, $51.25; reduced 19%.

5. A department store advertises a 40% reduction on all clothing. Find the reduced price on each of the following items if the original price marked on the tag is:

   a. Coat, $95   d. Slacks, $23.75   g. Tie, $4.50
   b. Suit, $125   e. Shirt, $10.95   h. Shoes, $34.95
   c. Dress, $44.95   f. Hat, $19.75   i. Sweater, $12.99

6. A furniture and appliance store advertises a $33\frac{1}{3}$% reduction on all furniture and a 15% reduction on all appliances. Find the sale price of each of the following articles if the regular price of:

   a. A dinette set is $645.   f. A studio couch is $324.85.
   b. A bedroom set is $980.   g. An electric iron is $19.95.
   c. A refrigerator is $430.   h. A table is $113.75.
   d. A living room set is $1,095.   i. An electric heater is $21.98.
   e. An electric blender is $29.   j. A vacuum cleaner is $89.50.

7. Find the rate of reduction allowed when a typewriter that regularly sells for $300 was purchased for $250.

8. Find the rate of reduction allowed on each of the following articles:

   a. Desk; regular price, $180; sale price, $150.
   b. Freezer; regular price, $285; sale price, $228.
   c. Lawn mower; regular price, $186.75; sale price, $124.50.
   d. Automobile; regular price, $5,000; sale price, $4,200.

9. Find the regular price of a washing machine that sold for $200 at a 20% reduction sale.

10. Find the regular price of each of the following:

    a. Tire, $38 sale price when a 24% reduction was allowed.
    b. Mirror, $63 sale price when a 10% reduction was allowed.
    c. Office file, $70 sale price when a $37\frac{1}{2}$% reduction was allowed.
    d. Toaster, $17.94 sale price when a 40% reduction was allowed.

12-3 UNIT PRICING—WHICH IS THE BETTER BUY?

Generally when buying food or other commodities that are packaged and sold in two different sizes, one must consider whether the larger size will be used without waste. In the problems of this section we shall disregard this consideration.

To determine the "better buy" when two different quantities of the same item are priced at two rates, we first find the *unit price* or the cost per unit of the item at each rate and select the lower unit price as the better buy.

For example: Which is the better buy: 4 grapefruit costing 39¢ or 6 grapefruit costing 54¢?
Grapefruit at the rate of 4 for 39¢ costs 9.75¢ each, but at the rate of 6 for 54¢ costs 9¢ each. Therefore, 6 grapefruit for 54¢ is the better buy.

Not always is the larger size of an item a better buy.

For example: The 5.8-oz. tube of brand X toothpaste at a sale sells for 58¢ but the 8-oz. tube sells at the regular price of 96¢. Which is the better buy?

Toothpaste X in the 5.8-oz. tube costs 10¢ an ounce, but in the 8-oz. size costs 12¢ an ounce. Therefore, the 5.8 oz. tube is the better buy.

Observe in the above problem that the unit price is the cost per ounce. In other situations the unit of comparison may be cost per pound, cost per quart, cost per item, etc.

Sometimes in working with unit prices like cost per pound, we use parts of a cent represented by a numeral like $.238. Observe that the numeral $.238 means 23.8 cents or 23.8¢.

EXERCISES

1. Rewrite each using a dollar sign ($) and a decimal point:

   a. 24¢   **c.** 9¢   **e.** 8.6¢   **g.** $3\frac{1}{2}$¢   **i.** 64.5¢

   b. 53¢   **d.** 3¢   **f.** 19.7¢   **h.** $20\frac{1}{4}$¢   **j.** 12.48¢

2. Rewrite each of the following, using the ¢ symbol:

   a. $.61   **c.** $.05   **e.** $.029   **g.** $.656   **i.** $.8305

   b. $.08   **d.** $.93   **f.** $.542   **h.** $.075   **j.** $.0025

3. **a.** Read each of the following in terms of cents:

   (1) 47.6¢   **(2)** 2.1¢   **(3)** $.853   **(4)** $.014   **(5)** $.9875

   b. Read each of the following in terms of dollars and cents:

   (1) $1.459   **(2)** $3.842   **(3)** $1.925   **(4)** $5.607   **(5)** 1.36\frac{9}{10}$

4. Find the unit price (cost per pound) to the nearest tenth of a cent for each of the following:

   a. 2-lb. can coffee, $4.45   **b.** 2-lb. package frankfurters, $2.95

   c. 8-oz. jar peanuts, $1.39

   d. 10-oz. package yogurt, 57¢

   e. 12-oz. package bologna, $1.83

   f. $6\frac{1}{2}$-oz. can tuna fish, $1.39

   g. 1-lb. 12-oz. jar peanut butter, $2.07

   h. 10-lb. 11-oz. box detergent, $6.99

   i. 1-lb 1-oz. can peas, 41¢

   j. 2-lb. 3-oz. applesauce, $1.05

5. Find the unit price (cost per quart) to nearest tenth of a cent for each of the following:

   a. $\frac{1}{2}$-gal. package ice cream, $2.59

   b. 1-pt. bottle vinegar, 41¢

   c. 1-gal. motor oil, $4.20

   d. 16-oz. can lighter fluid, 69¢

   e. 12-oz. can soda, 35¢

   f. 18-oz. bottle mouthwash, $1.89

   g. 1-qt. 6-oz. bottle cooking oil, $1.52

   h. 11-oz. bottle shampoo, $1.98

   i. 1-pt. 8-oz. bottle syrup, $1.66

   j. 1-qt. 14-oz. can tomato juice, 95¢

6. Find the unit price (cost per ounce) to the nearest tenth of a cent for each of the following:

   a. 7-oz. can tuna fish, $1.49

   b. 12-oz. jar jelly, 89¢

   c. $10\frac{3}{4}$-oz. can soup, 42¢

   d. $5\frac{1}{2}$-oz. can fruit juice, 21¢

7. Find the unit price (cost per 50 pieces) to the nearest tenth of a cent for each of the following:

   a. Pkg. of 25 plastic bags, $1.19

   b. Pkg. of 200 facial tissues, 88¢

   c. Pkg. of 20 trash bags, $2.83

   d. Pkg. of 48 tea bags, $1.29

   e. Pkg. of 160 napkins, 96¢

   f. Roll of 120 paper towels, 79¢

8. Find the unit price (cost per pound) of each of the following packages of laundry detergent and determine the difference between the highest and lowest unit prices?

   a. 3 lb. 1 oz. at $2.10   **b.** 1 lb. 4 oz. at 88¢   **c.** 5 lb. 4 oz. at $3.50

9. Find the unit price (cost per quart) of each of the following bottles of bleach and determine the difference between the highest and lowest unit prices:

   a. 1 gal. at $1.05   **b.** $1\frac{1}{2}$ gal. at $1.55   **c.** 2 qt. at 71¢

10. Find the unit price (cost per pound) of each of the following jars of olives and determine the difference between the highest and lowest unit prices:

    a. 7 oz. at 89¢   **b.** 14 oz. at $1.69   **c.** 4 oz. at 59¢

11. Find the unit price (cost per quart) of each of the following bottles of liquid detergent and determine the difference between the highest and lowest unit prices:

    a. 12 fl. oz. at 83¢   **b.** 1 pt. 6 oz. at $1.47   **c.** 32 fl. oz. at $2.09

12. In each of the following exactly the same item is priced at two rates. Which is the better buy in each case and why?

    a. Apples; 2 for 25¢ or 3 for 40¢.

    b. Grapefruit; 5 for 80¢ or 6 for 95¢.

    c. Oranges; 1 doz. for 96¢ or 15 oranges for $1.05.

    d. Soap; 3 bars for 84¢ or 4 bars for $1.12.

    e. Pears; 4 for 39¢ or 9 for 79¢.

    f. Soup; 3 cans for 89¢ or 7 cans for $2.00.

    g. Beverage; 2 bottles for 43¢ or 5 bottles for $1.

    h. Frozen orange juice; 2 cans for 99¢ or 6 cans for $2.85.

    i. Baby food; 4 jars for $1.25 or 10 jars for $2.95.

    j. Shrimp; 2 lb. for $10.98 or 5 lb. for $24.95.

13. Find how much you save on each can when buying in quantity:

    a. 1 dozen cans of corn for $4.20 or 39¢ each.

    b. 3 cans of beans for $1 or 35¢ each.

    c. 2 cans of peas for 57¢ or 29¢ each.

    d. 24 cans of tomato juice for $9 or 41¢ each.

    e. 4 cans of cleanser for $1.65 or 43¢ each.

14. **a.** If a dozen eggs cost 75¢, how much will 20 eggs cost?

    b. If 5 dozen note books cost $14.40, what will 1 book cost?

    c. If 4 tires cost $192, how much will 7 tires cost?

    d. If 8 shirts cost $90, how much will a dozen shirts cost?

    e. If $2\frac{2}{3}$ yd. nylon fabric cost $10.40, how much will $6\frac{1}{4}$ yd. nylon fabric cost?

15. Find how much you save by buying the larger size of each of

the following items instead of an equivalent quantity in the smaller size:

a. Spaghetti; 8-oz. box at 41¢, 1-lb. box at 77¢.

b. Potato chips; 8-oz. bag at $1.29, 1-lb. bag at $2.29.

c. Peas; 2 cans each $8\frac{1}{2}$ oz., at 49¢, 1-lb. 1-oz. can at 37¢.

d. Bleach; 1-qt. bottle at 32¢, 1-gal. bottle at 75¢.

e. Vinegar; 1-gal. bottle at $2.57, 1-pt. bottle at 41¢.

f. Mayonnaise; 32-oz. jar at $1.59, 1-pt. bottle at 89¢.

g. Beverage; 2-qt. bottle at $1.19, 1-pt. bottle at 35¢.

h. Egg noodles; 8-oz. pkg. at 57¢, 1-lb. pkg. at 97¢.

i. Detergent; 1-lb. 4-oz. pkg. at 88¢, 5-lb. 4-oz. pkg. at $3.50.

j. Paint; 1-gal. can at $12.49, 1-qt. can at $4.59.

16. How much do you save per ounce by buying the larger size instead of the smaller size? Round the answers to the nearest tenth of a cent.

a. Cookies; 15-oz. pkg. at 87¢, 19-oz. pkg. at $1.05.

b. Beets; 8-oz. can at 26¢, 1-lb. can at 45¢.

c. Asparagus; $10\frac{1}{2}$-oz. can at 87¢, $14\frac{1}{2}$-oz. can at 99¢.

d. Grapefruit juice; 1-pt. 2-oz. can at 39¢, 1-qt. 14-oz. can at 73¢.

e. Salmon; $3\frac{3}{4}$-oz. can at $1.13, $7\frac{3}{4}$-oz. can at $1.79.

17. Which is the better buy and why?

a. Rolls; 8 for 75¢ or 12 for $1.

b. Shampoo; $3\frac{1}{2}$-oz. tube at $1.65 or 7-oz. tube at $2.79.

c. Bacon; 1-lb. pkg. at $1.79 or $\frac{1}{2}$-lb. pkg. at 98¢.

d. Facial tissue; 2 boxes for 87¢ or 5 boxes for $2.

e. Beverage; 6 bottles, each 1 pt., for $1.89 or 8 bottles, each 10 oz., for $1.89.

f. Aspirin; 100 tablets for $1.60 or 300 tablets for $4.27.

g. Frozen orange juice; 4 cans, each 6 oz., for $2.05 or 2 cans, each 12 oz., for $1.93.

h. Detergent; 1-lb. 4-oz. pkg. at 55¢ or 5-lb. 4-oz. pkg. at $1.98.

i. Mouthwash; 18-oz. bottle at $1.77 or 24-oz. bottle at $2.28.

j. Salmon; 1-lb. can at $3.19 or $7\frac{3}{4}$-oz. can at $1.95.

12–4 COUNT YOUR CHANGE

Usually store clerks, in making change, will add the value of the coins and bills to the amount of the purchase until the sum of the change and the amount of the purchase equals the amount offered in payment.

The symbol @ means ''at'' and indicates the unit cost. ''2 ties @ $2.50 each'' or just ''2 ties @ $2.50'' is read ''two ties at $2.50 each.''

EXERCISES

1. Find how much change you should get from $1 if your purchases cost:

   a. $.89   **b.** $.53   **c.** $.27   **d.** $.08   **e.** $.74

2. Find how much change you should get from $5 if your purchases cost:

   a. $1.42   **b.** $4.68   **c.** $3.06   **d.** $.87   **e.** $2.31

3. Find how much change you should get from $10 if your purchases cost:

   a. $5.26   **b.** $8.09   **c.** $2.44   **d.** $7.92   **e.** $9.13

4. Find how much change you should get from $20 if your purchases cost:

   a. $7.64   **b.** $15.81   **c.** $13.03   **d.** $19.18   **e.** $2.72

5. Find the cost of each of the following:

   a. 2 sweaters @ $24.95 each
   b. $1\frac{1}{2}$ lb. butter @ $1.58 per lb.
   c. 3 doz. oranges @ $1.29 per doz.
   d. $2\frac{3}{4}$ lb. chicken @ 98¢ per lb.
   e. 10 cans soup @ 39¢ each.
   f. 6 shirts @ $17.95 each

   g. 20 gal. gasoline @ $1.35\frac{9}{10}$ per gal.
   h. 75 sq. yd. broadloom @ $19.50 per sq. yd.
   i. 3.8 m linen @ $9.60 per m
   j. 5 pr. drapes @ $109.75 per pr.
   k. 9 kg potatoes @ 53¢ per kg

6. For each of the following purchases determine how much change should be given when the specified amount of money is offered in payment.

Articles Purchased	Amount Offered in Payment
a. 1 pen @ 89¢	$1.00
b. 1 book @ $3.95	$5.00
c. 2 skirts @ $15.99 each	$35.00
d. 1 pr. shoes @ $34.95, 2 shirts @ $12.95 each	$70.00
e. 1 lb. bacon @ $1.89, 1 lb. tomatoes @ 69¢	$3.00
f. 15 gal. gasoline @ $1.399 per gal., 1 qt. oil @ $1.90	$25.00
g. $\frac{1}{2}$ lb. butter @ $1.42 per lb., 2 doz. eggs @ 95¢ per doz.	$5.00
h. 6 cans soup @ 43¢ each, 5 cans fruit @ 69¢ each	$10.00
i. 4 tires @ $42.67 each	$180.00
j. 2 dresses @ $39.95 each, 1 hat @ $14.75, 3 sweaters @ $11.98 each	$150.00
k. 1 suit @ $149.50, 3 pr. slacks @ $31.95 each, 2 shirts @ $18.95 each	$300.00
l. 4 trees @ $28.50 each, 6 shrubs @ $10.75 each, 1 bag fertilizer @ $17.25	$200.00
m. 1 typewriter @ $189.75, 5 reams paper @ $8.85 each	$250.00

12–5 GAS, ELECTRICITY, WATER, HEATING, AND TELEPHONE SERVICES

People generally require all or some of the services discussed here.

In order to check bills for the gas, electricity, and water services, one must be able to read a meter measuring the consumption. To read a gas meter or an electric meter or a water meter, we select on each dial of the meter the numeral that was just passed by the dial pointer. To find the consumption during a given period, we subtract the reading at the beginning of the period from the reading at the end of the period. To find the cost, we apply the prevailing rate to the consumption.

The reading of the dials on the gas meter (see page 466) is expressed in *hundred cubic feet*. A reading such as 3692 represents 369,200 cubic feet.

The reading of the dials on the electric meter (see page 466) is expressed in *kilowatt-hours*. A reading such as 2713 represents 2,713 kilowatt-hours of electrical energy. A kilowatt is 1,000 watts. It is a unit measuring electric power. If an appliance requires the power of 1 kilowatt to be used for 1 hour, then 1 kilowatt-hour of electrical energy is furnished. Observe also that if an appliance requires the power of 200 watts but is used for 5 hours, then 1 kilowatt-hour of electricity is also used (since 200 × 5 = 1,000 watt-hours = 1 kilowatt-hour).

The reading of the dials on the water meter is expressed in *tens of gallons*. Although there is a small dial on the meter that measures from 0 to 10 gallons, it is not used as part of the reading. A reading such as 82314 represents 823,140 gallons of water.

EXERCISES

1. What is the reading of each of the following gas meters?

a. CUBIC FEET

b. CUBIC FEET

c. CUBIC FEET

2. What is the reading of each of the following electric meters?

a. KILOWATT-HOURS

b. KILOWATT-HOURS

c. KILOWATT-HOURS

3. Find the cost of the gas consumed during the months of (1) October and (2) November at the rates given below if the meters read on:

Oct. 1   Nov. 1

Dec. 1

Rates:

First 100 cu. ft. or less, $1.90

Next 900 cu. ft., 52.9¢ per 100 cu. ft.

Next 6,000 cu. ft., 40.8¢ per 100 cu. ft.

Next 63,000 cu. ft., 34.5¢ per 100 cu. ft.

Over 70,000 cu. ft., 29.9¢ per 100 cu. ft.

4. Given the reading at the beginning and at the end of the period, use the above rates in each of the following to find the cost of the gas consumed during the period.

	Reading	
	At Beginning	At End
a.	4213	4269
b.	7794	7821
c.	2155	2194
d.	0332	0400
e.	6529	6604
f.	3738	3832
g.	5624	5707
h.	9903	0008
i.	7295	7519
j.	1480	1798

5. Find the cost of the electricity consumed during the months of
(1) January and (2) February at the rates given below if the
meters read on:

KILOWATT-HOURS   Jan. 1   KILOWATT-HOURS   Feb. 1

KILOWATT-HOURS   March 1

Rates: First 10 kW·h or less, $3.60
Next 490 kW·h @ 9.8¢ each
Over 500 kW·h @ 6.9¢ each

6. Given the reading at the beginning and at the end of the period,
use the above rates in each of the following to find the cost of
the electricity used during the period.

| | Reading | | | | Reading | |
	At Beginning	At End			At Beginning	At End
a.	6895	6932		**f.**	0792	1000
b.	3414	3505		**g.**	5459	5822
c.	1325	1387		**h.**	2616	2687
d.	9962	0068		**i.**	4278	4462
e.	7289	7434		**j.**	8987	9454

7. At an average cost of 9.4¢ per kilowatt-hour, find the *hourly*
cost of operating each of the following:

a. Dryer, 5,000 watts   **f.** 100 watt light bulb
b. Heater, 1,500 watts   **g.** Percolator, 600 watts
c. Iron, 1,200 watts   **h.** Stereo set, 125 watts
d. Radio, 40 watts   **i.** Toaster, 1,000 watts
e. TV set, 250 watts   **j.** Washer, 800 watts

8. In many communities water bills are issued every 3 months.
The reading on a certain water meter on March 15th was 34765,
on June 15th it was 37024, and on September 15th it was 40009.

a. How many gallons of water were used during the 3-month
period ending June 15th? During the 3-month period ending
September 15th?

b. Find the cost of the water consumed during each of these periods using the rates:

First 2,500 gallons or less, $7.83
Over 2,500 gallons, $1.68 for every 1,000 gallons

9. Mr. Schmidt during the year bought 190 gallons of fuel oil at 98.7¢ per gallon, 175 gallons at 97.4¢ each, 210 gallons at 97.8¢ each, 225 gallons at 96.9¢ each, and 195 gallons at 98.1¢ each. How many gallons of fuel oil did he buy? What was the total cost of his fuel oil for the year?

10. The telephone message rate service for 50 calls or less per month costs $7.90 with 7.6¢ additional for each call over 50 calls. The flat rate service which allows unlimited calls costs $11.25 monthly. There is a federal tax of 2% added to the cost of telephone service. If a family expects to average no more than 100 telephone calls per month, which service is cheaper? How much cheaper?

12–6 OWNING AN AUTOMOBILE

EXERCISES

1. **a.** Mr. Fitzgerald bought a new car for $7,650. After using it for 3 years, he sold it for $2,790. What was the average yearly depreciation of the car?
   b. At the end of the first year the speedometer read 9,762 miles, at the end of the second year, 21,299 miles, and at the end of the third year 30,184 miles. How many miles did he drive during the second year? The third year?
   c. During the first year his expenses in addition to the average yearly depreciation were: gasoline, 658 gal. at $1.349 per gal; oil, 28 qt. at $1.85 per qt.; garage rent, $125 per mo.; insurance, $365 per yr.; license fees, $32 per yr.; miscellaneous expenses, $129.40. How much did it cost Mr. Fitzgerald to run his car for the year? What was the average cost per month? Per week? Per mile?

2. Mrs. Valdez bought a new car for $8,400. She insured it against fire and theft for 80% of its value. If the rate is 75¢ per $100, what is the annual premium?

3. Miss Williams insures her car costing $6,800 against fire and theft for 75% of its value. The rate is 80¢ per $100 for fire and theft insurance. If property damage insurance costs $63.50, $10,000–$20,000 liability insurance costs $76.45, and $100 deductible collision insurance costs $78, what is her total premium?

4. How far can a motorcycle go on a tankful of gasoline if it averages 85 miles on a gallon and the tank holds 2.5 gallons?

5. How long will it take a man, driving at an average speed of 45 m.p.h., to travel from New York to Cincinnati, a distance of 660 miles? If the car averages 15 miles on a gallon of gasoline, how many gallons are required to make the trip?

6. Ms. Burns had the tank of her car filled with gasoline and noted that the speedometer read 14,593. The next time she stopped for gasoline it required 14 gallons to fill the tank and the speedometer read 14,817. How many miles did the car average on a gallon of gasoline?

7. Tom's father took the family on a motor trip. How much did the trip cost if he bought 57 gallons of gasoline at $1.389 per gal. and 2 qt. of oil at $1.50 per qt., and if lodging cost $36.50 per night for 3 nights, meals $147.81, amusements $49.75, and miscellaneous expenses were $74.28?

8. Oil can be bought at $1.15 per qt. in individual cans or $22.50 for a case of 24 cans. How much do you save per quart if you buy oil by the case?

9. At a speed of 40 m.p.h., how many minutes will it take to go a distance of 18 miles?

10. If the driver's reaction time before applying the brakes is one second, how many feet will the car go in one second at each of the following speeds: **a.** 45 m.p.h.? **b.** 40 m.p.h.? **c.** 25 m.p.h.? **d.** 35 m.p.h.? **e.** 60 m.p.h.?

11. The braking distance (distance an automobile travels before coming to a stop after the brakes are applied) on a dry, level road is 30 ft. at 20 m.p.h., 67.5 ft. at 30 m.p.h., 120 ft. at 40 m.p.h., and 187.5 ft. at 50 m.p.h. If the driver's reaction time is $\frac{3}{4}$ second, find the total stopping distance (reaction time distance plus braking distance) at each of the above speeds.

12–7 HOUSEHOLD BILLS

EXERCISES

Determine the amounts of payment due in each of these bills.

1.

RATES
GENERAL SERVICE

First 200 C.F. or less $3.50
Next 1,800 C.F. @ $4.20 per M.C.F.
Next 8,000 C.F. @ $3.20 per M.C.F.
Next 70,000 C.F. @ $2.90 per M.C.F.
Additional use @ $2.70 per M.C.F.

LOCAL GAS WORKS CO.
YOUR CITY

Net Payment Period Expires Jan 2, 19__

MR. ROBERT MILLER
249 FOURTH AVE.

READING DATES		METER READINGS		CLASS	HUNDRED CU. FT. USED	AMOUNT
PREVIOUS	PRESENT	PRESENT	PREVIOUS			
Nov 15	Dec 15	404	375	DOM		

UNPAID GAS ACCOUNT______
TOTAL

#8

P. 83, #1–3
P. 91–93 #2–18
P. 95 #1–4
Pg 96–97: #1–5
Pg 98–99: #1–3

HONE COMPANY

Account No. 428-6767
Jan. 16, 19__

E JAY
Y ROAD

	Amount Due
	22.47
	8.15
	.93
.00	.63
	____
Total Amount Due	

C COMPANY
TY

Net Payment Period Expires May 1, 19__

Y
ST.

READINGS	SERVICE CODE	KILOWATT HOURS	AMOUNT OF BILL
PREVIOUS			
6068	EL		

4.

Local Department Store				
YOUR CITY				
MISS ELAINE GOMEZ			Oct. 31, 19___	
1953 WALNUT ST.				

ITEMS	CHARGES	CREDITS	DATE	LAST AMOUNT IS BALANCE DUE
Balance from Previous Bill				21.79
Dress	39.98		Oct. 3	
Coat	83.75			
Cash		21.79	5	
Shoes	34.50		10	
Chairs	96.60			
Hat	17.50		18	
Chair Returned		24.15	19	
Ties	12.67		26	

12–8 HOUSEHOLD ACCOUNTS

A *cash account* is a record of the money a person receives (receipts) and spends (expenditures). The cash on hand should equal the difference in the amounts of receipts and expenditures. Thus, by writing in the expenditure column the amount of cash on hand at the end of the period, the receipt and expenditure columns will be in balance.

EXERCISES

Make a copy, then balance the account on pg. 473 for the week of April 8. Record the following items, then balance the account for the week of April 15.

Receipts:

April 18, salary, $425

Expenditures:

April 15, rent, $470; food, $22.56

April 17, gasoline, $19.50; telephone, $13.76

April 18, insurance, $25; food, $17.82

April 20, food, $19.14; bank deposit, $20

April 21, movies, $9

RECEIPTS				EXPENDITURES			
April 8	Cash on hand	299	50	April 9	Fuel Oil	48	00
11	Salary	425	00	10	Food	27	26
					Electricity	23	68
				11	Shoes	29	90
					Movies	7	00
				12	Food	16	18
				13	Gasoline	14	50
					Bank Deposit	50	00
					Food	29	16
				14	Cash on hand		
	Total				Total		
April 15	Cash on hand						

12–9 SALES TAX

A *sales tax* is a tax on the purchase price of an article.

1. At the rate of 6% sales tax, what would the tax be on an article that sells for $12.50?

2. Find the sales tax to the nearest cent on each of the following purchases at the given tax rates:

Purchases	$15.00	$36.75	$4.98	$13.60	$59.95	$108.35
Tax Rate	5%	7%	2%	$5\frac{1}{2}\%$	4%	$3\frac{1}{2}\%$

3. Find the selling price, including tax, of each of the following articles:

a. A coat selling for $98, tax 2%.   **f.** A rug selling for $485, tax $1\frac{1}{2}\%$.

b. A radio selling for $69, tax 1%.   **g.** A dress selling for $32.98, tax 8%.

c. A football selling for $9.95, tax 3%.   **h.** A TV set selling for $369, tax $2\frac{1}{2}\%$.

d. Shoes selling for $37.75, tax 6%.   **i.** A chair selling for $179.25, tax 7%.

e. A lamp selling for $59.50, tax 4%.   **j.** A hat selling for $14.89, tax $3\frac{1}{2}\%$.

12–10 EXCISE TAX

An *excise tax* is a federal tax on certain items. The federal excise tax rate on telephone service is 1% and on fares for air travel is 5%.

1. Find the amount of tax on local telephone service costing:

   a. $5.80   **b.** $13.90   **c.** $15.95   **d.** $8.20   **e.** $11.60

2. Find the amount of tax on an air travel fare of:

   a. $72   **b.** $58.10   **c.** $141.50   **d.** $205.80   **e.** $93.25

3. Find the full amount of the bill including federal excise tax and, where given, state tax on telephone service costing:

   a. $6.65   **c.** $14.15, 5% state tax   **e.** $12.48, 2% state tax
   b. $9.40   **d.** $7.50, 3% state tax   **f.** $15.72, 4% state tax

4. Find the total cost of airplane fare including excise tax when the fare excluding excise tax is:

   a. $85   **b.** $140   **c.** $97.50   **d.** $212.75   **e.** $176.40

12–11 BANKING

There are two main kinds of banks: savings banks and commercial banks. A third type of banking institution that has grown greatly in recent years is the federal and state savings and loan association, which is very much like a savings bank. Credit unions also render both savings and loan services, but they are usually offered only to particular groups of people, like city employees, factory workers, teachers, etc.

The life of a bank depends on the use of its depositors' money as loans to business people and others at rates of interest higher than the rates of interest that the bank pays to its depositors. The difference between these rates of interest produces money for the bank both to pay its expenses and to earn a profit.

The main service offered by the savings bank is the *savings account,* on which the depositor is paid interest. Savings banks also provide other services such as passbook loans, safe deposit boxes, and money orders. We use a form called a deposit slip to deposit money and a withdrawal slip to withdraw money from our accounts.

The commercial bank provides almost similar services. However it also provides its most important service—the *checking account,* a service not furnished by the savings bank. To deposit money in a checking account, we use a *deposit slip* (see form at the right). To transfer funds from a checking account to persons or business establishments to whom we owe money, we use a form called a *check* (see form below). This method facilitates the payment of bills without any cash being handled directly. The *check stub* on the left of the check is filled out for our records.

LOCAL TRUST COMPANY
DEPOSIT

YOUR CITY _____ 19 __
ACCOUNT NO. _____
NAME _____
ADDRESS _____

CASH ➝	DOLLARS	CENTS
CHECKS BY BANK NUMBER ↓		
1		
2		
3		
4		
5		
6		
7		
TOTAL		

No._____		
_____19___		
To_____		
For_____		
	DOLLARS	CENTS
BAL. BRO'T FOR'D		
AM'T DEPOSITED		
TOTAL		
AM'T THIS CHECK		
BAL. CAR'D FOR'D		

YOUR CITY_____19____NO._____

LOCAL TRUST COMPANY

PAY TO THE ORDER OF_____ $_____

_____DOLLARS

_____

EXERCISES

Use two deposit slip forms and three check forms if available, otherwise copy them as illustrated, to record the following:

1. On June 1, you have a balance of $1,425.83. Write this balance as the balance brought forward on the first check stub.

2. On June 3, you deposit 6 $10 bills, 8 $5 bills, 17 $1 bills, and a check, numbered 1111–3, drawn on the First National Bank for $389.49. Fill in the deposit slip. Write the total amount of the deposit on the first check stub.

3. On June 6, you send a check to the Fernandez Furniture Co. in the amount of $746.95 for furniture purchased. Fill in the first check stub. Carry the balance to the second check stub. Write out the first check.

4. On June 8, you send a check to the L. & M. Television Co. in the amount of $559.50 for a television set. Fill in the second check stub. Carry the balance to the third check stub. Write out the second check.

5. On June 16, you deposit 3 $20 bills, 2 $10 bills, 4 $5 bills, 11 $1 bills, 7 quarters, 5 dimes, 9 nickels, a check, numbered 2994–3, drawn on the Bankers Trust Co. for $629.84, and a check, numbered 3004–5, drawn on the Second City Trust Co. for $287.39. Fill in the second deposit slip. Write the total amount of the deposit on the third check stub.

6. On June 17, you send a check to Todd Lieberman in the amount of $93.25 for merchandise purchased. Fill in the third check stub. Carry the balance to the fourth check stub. Write out the third check.

7. On June 22, you send a check to Peter John Rugs, Inc. in the amount of $379.60 for rugs purchased. Fill in the fourth check stub. Write out the fourth check.

MISCELLANEOUS APPLICATIONS

12–12 LATITUDE AND LONGITUDE— NAUTICAL MILE

Meridians are imaginary semicircles that extend from the North Pole to the South Pole. *Parallels of latitude* are imaginary circles that are parallel to the Equator. The meridian that passes through Greenwich near London, England, is the *prime meridian* from which longitude is calculated. West longitude (W.) extends from this prime meridian (0° longitude) westward half way around the earth to the *International Date Line* (180° longitude); east longitude (E.) extends eastward from the prime meridian to the International Date Line. The *Equator* is 0° latitude; north latitude (N.) is measured north of the Equator; and south latitude (S.) is measured south of the Equator. The *North Pole* is 90° north latitude and the *South Pole* is 90° south latitude.

The position of any point on the earth's surface is determined by the intersection of its meridian of longitude and its parallel of latitude. One minute of arc of latitude equals one nautical mile and one degree equals 60 nautical miles. To find the distance between two points on the same meridian, we find the difference in latitude in minutes of arc, then change to nautical miles. Only along the equator does one minute of arc of longitude also equal one nautical mile.

EXERCISES

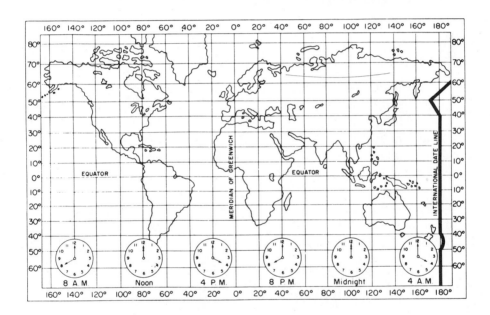

1. Locate on the above map the following points:

   a. 40° N., 60° W.   **b.** 0°, 140° W.   **c.** 30° S., 80° E.   **d.** 25° S., 90° W.

2. Locate on the map the position (approximately) of each of the following cities:

   a. New Orleans, 30° N., 90° W.   **d.** Melbourne, 38° S., 145° E.
   b. Helsinki, 60° N., 25° E.   **e.** Colon, Panama, 10° N., 80° W.
   c. Philadelphia, 40° N., 75° W.   **f.** Buenos Aires, 35° S., 58° W.

Applications of Mathematics—Problem Solving   **477**

3. Find the difference in the following latitudes:
   a. 37° N. and 22° N.
   b. 13° S. and 51° S.
   c. 24° N. and 17° S.
   d. 56° 18′ N. and 19° 45′ N.

4. Find the difference in latitudes of the following cities:
   a. Los Angeles, 34° N. **b.** Cape Horn, 56° S. **c.** Portland, Me., 43° 40′ N.
   Rio de Janeiro, 23° S.   Cape Cod, 42° N.   Portland, Ore., 45° 31′ N.

5. Find the difference in the following longitudes:
   a. 29° W. and 107° W.
   b. 18° E. and 93° E.
   c. 25° W. and 82° E.
   d. 5° 27′ E. and 73° 54′ W.

6. Find the difference in longitudes of the following cities:
   a. Savannah, 81° W.   **b.** Honolulu, 158° W.   **c.** Sydney, 151° E.
   Seattle, 122° W.   Geneva, 6° E.   Rangoon, 96° E.

7. Find how far apart in nautical miles points *A* and *B* are:

Location of Point *A*	Location of Point *B*
a. 35° N., 148° W.	21° N., 148° W.
b. 46° 30′ N., 75° 45′ W.	12° 15′ S., 75° 45′ W.

8. How many nautical miles is a ship located 35° 10′ N., 28° 20′ W. from one in distress 33° 40′ N., 28° 20′ W.? Steaming at 18 knots, how long will it take the first ship to reach the second?

9. How many nautical miles apart are St. Louis, 39° N., 90° W. and Guatemala, 15° N., 90° W.? How long should it take a plane at an average speed of 200 knots to fly from one city to the other?

10. How long should it take a plane at an average speed of 500 stat. m.p.h. to fly from Miami, 25° 47′ N., 80° W. to Pittsburgh, 40° 27′ N., 80° W.?

12–13 LONGITUDE AND TIME

The earth rotates about its axis from the west to the east, making one complete revolution each day. Thus, it takes the earth 24 hours to pass through 360° of longitude or 1 hour for 15° of longitude or 4 minutes for each degree of longitude.

The sun or solar time is the same at any given instant for all places located on any one meridian. Thus, to avoid the confusion that would arise if local sun time were used by neighboring towns, the earth is divided into time zones, each about 15° longitude in width. All places within each zone use the sun time of approximately its central meridian. The time in any zone is one hour earlier than the time in the next zone to the east and one hour later than the time in the next zone to the west.

Longitude is sometimes expressed in units of time. Both world time and longitude are calculated from the meridian of Greenwich. Thus, the longitude of any place is equal to the difference between its local sun time and Greenwich time.

To change units measuring longitude to units of time, we divide the units measuring longitude by 15. To change units of time to units of longitude, we multiply the units of time by 15. We simplify the answer when necessary.

EXERCISES

1. Express the following arcs of longitude as units of time:

a. 30°	**e.** 6°	**i.** 15° 30′	**m.** 30″
b. 75°	**f.** 58°	**j.** 4° 15′	**n.** 15′ 45″
c. 135°	**g.** 45′	**k.** 18° 10′	**o.** 90° 45′ 30″
d. 20°	**h.** 20′	**l.** 73° 18′	**p.** 105° 30′ 15″

2. Express the following units of time as arcs of longitude:

a. 3 hr.	**e.** 30 min.	**i.** 1 hr. 30 min.	**m.** 30 sec.
b. 7 hr.	**f.** 45 min.	**j.** 8 hr. 15 min.	**n.** 18 sec.
c. 19 hr.	**g.** 12 min.	**k.** 11 hr. 20 min.	**o.** 45 min. 15 sec.
d. 16 hr.	**h.** 48 min.	**l.** 6 hr. 54 min.	**p.** 4 hr. 30 min. 20 sec.

3. When it is 1200 at Greenwich, what time is it at each of the following longitudes:

    a. 45° E.?   **b.** 90° W.?   **c.** 105° W.?   **d.** 30° 45′ E.?   **e.** 120° 15′ W.?

4. If it is 0800 at 30° W. longitude, what time is it at 75° W. longitude?

5. What time is it at 42° E. longitude if it is 1530 at 28° W. longitude?

6. When it is 1500 at Greenwich, at what longitude is the time:

    a. 1200?   **b.** 0800?   **c.** 2300?   **d.** 1345?   **e.** 1630?

7. If it is 2145 at 15° W. longitude, at what longitude is the time 1715?

8. At what longitude is the time 0730 if it is 1315 at 20° E. longitude?

9. Find the difference between the standard time and the sun time at each of the following cities:

   a. New York City 73° 58′ W.
   b. Salt Lake City 111° 53′ W.
   c. Seattle 122° 19′ W.
   d. Indianapolis 86° 10′ W.

10. If the sun time at Chicago, 87° 37′ W. is 0600, what is the sun time at Baltimore, 76° 37′ W.?

11. What is the difference in standard time at Washington, 77° 04′ W. and Los Angeles, 118° 14′ W.? What is the difference in sun time at these two cities?

12. If the sun time at Oklahoma City, 97° 30′ W. is 1330, what is the sun time at each of the following cities?

   a. Boston, 71° 04′ W.
   b. San Diego, 117° 10′ W.
   c. Louisville, 85° 46′ W.
   d. Denver, 104° 57′ W.

12–14 THE WEATHER MAP

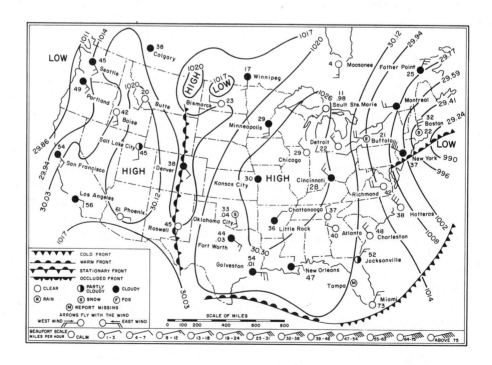

Use weather map to find answers for problems **1** through **5**.

1. At what given cities is it snowing? Partly cloudy? Clear?

2. If the figures beside the station circle indicate the Fahrenheit temperature and the decimal beneath the temperature indicates the precipitation in inches during the past six hours, what is the temperature and precipitation at Galveston? At Oklahoma City? At Fort Worth? At Salt Lake City? Winnipeg? Detroit? Jacksonville? Phoenix? San Francisco?

3. The black solid lines called *isobars* are lines of equal barometric pressure and are expressed both in inches and millibars. One inch of pressure equals 33.86 millibars.

    a. Express each of the following pressures in millibars: 30.30 in., 29.94 in., 29.41 in., 30.12 in.

    b. Express each of the following pressures in inches: 1020 mb., 1002 mb., 1011 mb., 990 mb.

    c. What is the highest pressure, expressed in millibars, shown on the map? Change pressure to inches and check with map.

    d. What is the lowest pressure, expressed in inches, shown on the map? Change pressure to millibars and check with map.

    e. What is the pressure, expressed both in millibars and inches, at Bismarck? Through what other city does the same isobar pass?

4. Winds move counter-clockwise toward the center of low-pressure areas and clockwise and outward from high-pressure areas.

    a. Check the direction of winds at Detroit, Cincinnati, Little Rock, Oklahoma City, and Minneapolis, cities in a high-pressure area.

    b. Check the direction of winds at Boston, New York, Richmond, and Hatteras, cities in a low-pressure area.

5. Using the Beaufort Scale, give the direction and velocity of winds at:

a. Boston	**d.** New Orleans	**g.** New York
b. Salt Lake City	**e.** Seattle	**h.** Minneapolis
c. Kansas City	**f.** Miami	**i.** Hatteras

Some newspapers include a table showing the existing conditions throughout the country as received in reports to the National Weather Service.

Table 1

City	Temperature in Fahrenheit ° High	Low	Precipitation in inches	Wind in m.p.h.	Weather
Atlanta	46	39	.28	27	Cloudy
Atlantic City	39	37	.45	23	Rain
Baltimore	43	33	.48	10	Rain
Bismarck	23	8	T.	12	Snow
Boston	41	29	...	5	Cloudy
Buffalo	45	32	T.	8	Rain
Charleston	56	59	1.00	12	Cloudy
Chicago	36	15	.03	19	Clear
Cincinnati	54	24	.14	19	Clear
Cleveland	53	21	.36	22	Rain
Denver	50	25	...	25	Cloudy
Des Moines	32	10	...	12	Clear
Detroit	41	19	.07	20	Cloudy
Duluth	24	−8	...	28	Clear
El Paso	56	42	...	12	Cloudy
Galveston	68	47	...	20	P. Cloudy
Honolulu	79	67	...	8	Clear
Indianapolis	49	22	.02	27	Rain
Jacksonville	71	32	.17	10	Clear
Kansas City	37	22	...	8	Clear

Use Table 1 to find answers for problems **6** through **11**:

6. Which city had the highest temperature of the day? Lowest temperature?
7. Where did the most precipitation fall? How much?
8. What was the wind velocity at Des Moines? Atlantic City?

9. If average temperature is determined by finding the average of the given high and low temperatures, find the average temperature at:

a. Baltimore
b. Cleveland
c. El Paso

d. Honolulu
e. Chicago
f. Detroit

g. Atlanta
h. Indianapolis
i. Duluth

10. Which city had the greatest range in temperature? Smallest range?

11. For each of the following cities find how many degrees the average temperature, determined from Table 1, is above or below the normal average temperature of the date:

	Normal Temperature			Normal Temperature			Normal Temperature
a. Boston	36		d. Charleston	55		g. Jacksonville	59
b. Cincinnati	37		e. Kansas City	38		h. Denver	36
c. Bismarck	21		f. Buffalo	34		i. Galveston	60

Use Table 2 to fiind answers for problems 12 through 17:

Table 2

City	Temperature in Celsius ° High	Low	Precipitation in millimeters	Wind in km/h	Weather
Los Angeles	15	9	...	Calm	Cloudy
Miami	25	18	4	16	P. Cloudy
Minneapolis	4	−18	...	18	Clear
New Orleans	19	9	...	29	Clear
New York	6	2	1	16	Rain
Norfolk	8	5	18	37	Cloudy
Philadelphia	6	0	11	13	Rain
Phoenix	21	4	...	5	Clear
Pittsburgh	13	−1	2	32	Rain
Portland, Me	6	−4	...	8	Cloudy
Portland, Ore	17	1	...	23	Clear
St. Louis	4	−7	3	23	Clear
Salt Lake City	3	−2	...	8	Cloudy

Table 2 (cont.)

| City | Temperature in Celsius ° | | Precipitation in millimeters | Wind in km/h | Weather |
	High	Low			
San Antonio	18	4	...	42	Clear
San Francisco	12	9	...	13	Cloudy
S. Ste Marie	0	−16	2	27	Snow
Savannah	14	9	12	19	Clear
Seattle	14	−1	...	8	Clear
Washington	7	1	14	13	Rain
Winnipeg	−16	−33	...	15	Clear

12. Which city had the highest temperature of the day? Lowest temperature?

13. Where did the most precipitation fall? How much?

14. What was the wind velocity at Norfolk? Portland, Ore.?

15. Find the average temperature at:

   a. Los Angeles
   b. Portland, Me.
   c. Savannah
   d. Washington
   e. San Francisco

   f. S. Ste Marie
   g. Salt Lake City
   h. Seattle
   i. Winnipeg
   j. Norfolk

16. Which city had the greatest range in temperature? Smallest range?

17. For each of the following cities find how many degrees the average temperature, determined from Table 2, is above or below the normal average temperature for the date:

	Normal Temperature			Normal Temperature
a. New York	4		f. Philadelphia	5
b. New Orleans	15		g. San Antonio	14
c. Miami	22		h. Pittsburgh	3
d. St. Louis	4		i. Minneapolis	−3
e. Phoenix	13		j. Portland, Ore.	10

12–15 SPORTS

Scoring

Find the final scores of the following games:

1. Football

    a. Jefferson   14   0   13   0 =
           Springdale   7   9   6   7 =
    b. Fernwood   0   7   12   13 =
           Washington   6   16   0   3 =

2. Basketball

    a. Kingston   13   21   17   18 =
           Bartram   18   19   16   24 =
    b. Central   15   17   14   23 =
           Jackson   12   19   18   19 =

3. Baseball

    a. North   0   1   1   3   0   2   0   4   1 =
           Greenville   2   0   4   0   1   2   1   1   0 =
    b. Wagner   1   0   2   0   1   3   0   2   0 =
           Dalton   1   1   2   0   0   4   0   0   3 =

4. Golf

Find the score of the first 9 holes, the second 9 holes, and the total.

Harrison   4   3   5   4   4   5   3   4   5 =
Santos   4   4   5   4   3   5   4   4   4 =
Harrison   5   3   4   4   4   3   5   4   4 =
Santos   4   5   4   4   5   4   5   3   4 =

5. Bowling—3-game match

Find: **a.** which player scored the most points, **b.** which team won more games, and **c.** which team had the greater total match score.

Williams	154	196	205 =	Daniels	163	150	194 =
Sonlin	148	159	165 =	Watson	188	217	163 =
Harris	206	178	157 =	Rivera	198	182	185 =

6. Track

Find the total points scored by each team if 5 points are given for each 1st place, 3 points for each 2nd place, and 1 point for each 3rd place.

	1	2	3	Total points
Team A	5	3	4 =	
Team B	4	3	3 =	
Team C	3	6	1 =	
Team D	2	1	5 =	
Team E	1	2	2 =	

7. Wrestling

Find the total points scored by each team if 5 points are given for a fall, 3 points for a decision, and 2 points for a draw.

	Team X	Team Y
Fall	2	1
Decision	2	3
Draw	1	1
Total points		

8. Cross-country

Find the scores of Teams A, B, C, D, and E by adding the numbers corresponding to the order in which the first 5 members of each team finished. The team with the lowest score (or smallest sum) is the winner. Determine which team won if the runners placed as follows:

1. B	**2.** A	**3.** D	**4.** E	**5.** C	**6.** A	**7.** D	**8.** D
9. E	**10.** B	**11.** A	**12.** C	**13.** C	**14.** A	**15.** C	**16.** B
17. D	**18.** B	**19.** E	**20.** E	**21.** E	**22.** C	**23.** A	**24.** E
25. B	**26.** D	**27.** C	**28.** A	**29.** D	**30.** E	**31.** B	**32.** A

Box Scores

9. Baseball—Find the totals:

Jefferson High

	AB	R	H	PO	A	E
Jones LF	5	1	2	1	0	0
Williams CF	4	0	1	2	0	0
Adams 1B	4	2	3	13	2	1
Harris RF	3	0	2	0	1	0
Brunner C	4	1	0	2	2	0
Wagner SS	3	0	1	0	8	0
Carter 3B	4	0	2	2	1	1
Choy 2B	4	1	3	4	5	0
Benson P	4	0	0	0	2	0
Totals						

Fernwood High

	AB	R	H	PO	A	E
Watson 1B	5	0	1	9	2	0
Thomas LF	4	2	3	4	0	0
Greene 3B	5	0	1	2	5	2
Kelley CF	4	1	2	3	0	0
Gorson SS	3	1	0	1	4	1
Hall C	4	0	1	4	3	0
Barner 2B	4	2	4	2	3	0
Jenkins RF	4	0	2	1	0	0
Morton P	3	0	1	1	0	0
Totals						

Jefferson High	0	1	0	0	2	0	1	0	1 =	
Fernwood High	0	0	3	0	1	0	0	2	x =	

Team Standing

10. Find the percent of games won by each team. Express it as a 3-place decimal numeral.

a. Baseball

	Won	Lost	Pct.
North	16	4	
Hudson	15	5	
Central	12	8	
East	10	10	
West	6	14	
South	1	19	

b. Football

	Won	Lost	Pct.
South	10	0	
East	8	2	
Hudson	4	6	
Central	4	6	
North	3	7	
West	1	9	

Averages

11. Baseball—Find the average of each player:

a. Batting

	AB	R	H	Avg.
Bevan	95	17	38	
Riley	96	19	32	
Ward	88	13	29	
Morgan	90	16	27	
Madero	84	18	24	

b. Fielding

	PO	A	E	Avg.
Hatton	108	16	1	
Chapman	60	87	3	
Souza	51	43	2	
Lee	182	34	9	
Jackson	92	26	7	

PROBLEM-SOLVING STRATEGIES—REVIEW

In each of the following problems, answer only what is asked. Do not solve the entire problem unless required.

1. **What is the question in the following problem?**
   Find how much Juanita earns per week if she works 38 hours at $7.25 per hour.

2. **Find the given facts in the following:**
   An agent sold a house for $64,900. If the rate of commission is 6%, how much commission does the agent receive?

3. **Are enough facts given to solve the problem? If not, which fact is missing?**
   A merchant sold a VCR for $589. How much profit did she make?

4. **Write a question for the following:**
   A set of golf clubs that regularly sell for $169 is now reduced 20%.

5. **Which fact is not needed to solve the following problem?**
   The school auditorium has 21 rows with 16 seats in each row. There are 1,639 students enrolled at the school. What is the total seating capacity of the auditorium?

6. **Determine the operation needed to solve the following:**
   A pipe 96 inches long is cut into 6 equal pieces. How long is each piece of pipe?

7. Express in words the relationship between the given facts and the question asked in above problem 6.

8. Write an equation that represents your plan of solution of above problem 6.

9. First estimate your answer, then perform the indicated operation: 709×87.

10. **Select the estimate that makes the answer reasonable:**
    The answer 964 is reasonable if the estimate is: **a.** 10 **b.** 100 **c.** 1,000

11. **Write the question which when answered will provide the missing fact that is needed to solve the following problem:**
    How much change should you get if you bought a shirt for $17.98 and a pair of sneakers for $29.95 and then offered a $50 bill in payment?

12. Keep guessing and testing until you find two consecutive numbers that add up to 73.

13. **Solve the following problem in two ways:**
    The regular price of a computer is $996. What is its sale price if it is reduced 25%?

14. **Work backwards to find the answer in the following:**
    If you add 2 years to 6 times my age, you get 80 years. What is my age?

15. **Use the pattern in the following to find the next 2 missing numbers:**
    1, 4, 9, 16, 25, _____, _____

COMPETENCY CHECK TEST

Select the letter corresponding to your answer. The colored numerals indicate sections where help may be found.

1. Add: 4,875 + 83,967 + 9,856
   a. 98,688 **b.** 98,598 **c.** 100,498 **d.** 99,598   (2–9)
2. Multiply: 927 × 508
   a. 927,508 **b.** 569,846 **c.** 394,696 **d.** 470,916   (2–11)
3. Subtract: $10 - 7\frac{3}{8}$ **a.** $3\frac{5}{8}$ **b.** $3\frac{3}{8}$ **c.** $2\frac{5}{8}$ **d.** $2\frac{3}{8}$ (4–12)
4. Divide: $24 \div 4\frac{1}{2}$ **a.** 108 **b.** $5\frac{1}{3}$ **c.** $6\frac{1}{2}$ **d.** $20\frac{1}{2}$ (4–15)
5. Add: 6.3 + .32 **a.** 9.5 **b.** .95 **c.** 6.62 **d.** 6.332   (5–7)
6. Multiply: .008 × 1.5 **a.** .012 **b.** .0012 **c.** .12 **d.** 9.5   (5–9)
7. Divide: $.04\overline{)\$40}$
   a. $10 **b.** $100 **c.** $1,000 **d.** answer not given   (5–11)
8. Find $13\frac{1}{2}\%$ of $10,000.
   a. $1,350 **b.** $13,500 **c.** $135 **d.** $14.50   (6–6)
9. What percent of $2,500 is $125?
   a. 4% **b.** 20% **c.** 5% **d.** 10%   (6–7)
10. 18% of what amount is $900?
    a. $2,700 **b.** $1,800 **c.** $9,000 **d.** $5,000   (6–8)
11. Which measurement is the shortest?
    a. .017 km **b.** 34 m **c.** 580 cm **d.** 7,230 mm   (8–1)
12. Which weight is the heaviest?
    a. 3,950 mg **b.** 182 cg **c.** 23 g **d.** .009 kg   (8–2)
13. Which temperature is the warmest?
    a. 42°F **b.** 7°C **c.** 43°F **d.** 6°C   (8–16)
14. Which capacity is the largest?
    a. 4 gallons **b.** 17 quarts **c.** 31 pints **d.** 480 ounces   (8–8)
15. If it is 3 P.M. in Washington, D.C., in San Francisco it is:
    a. 6 P.M. **b.** 1 P.M. **c.** 12 noon **d.** 10 A.M.   (8–18)
16. The average (arithmetic mean) of scores 83, 68, and 92 is:
    a. 78 **b.** 80 **c.** 81 **d.** 84   (9–4)
17. A negative number is named by the numeral:
    a. 0 **b.** −4 **c.** 6 **d.** +3   (10–1)
18. The absolute value of −9 is: **a.** −9 **b.** 0 **c.** 1 **d.** 9   (10–3)
19. Add: $^{+}12 + {}^{-}21$ **a.** $^{-}33$ **b.** $^{-}9$ **c.** $^{+}9$ **d.** $^{+}33$ (10–10)
20. Subtract: $^{-}8 - {}^{+}5$ **a.** $^{-}3$ **b.** $^{+}13$ **c.** $^{+}3$ **d.** $^{-}13$ (10–13)
21. Multiply: $^{-}12 \times {}^{-}5$ **a.** $^{-}17$ **b.** $^{-}60$ **c.** $^{+}60$ **d.** $^{-}7$ (10–15)
22. Divide: $^{+}54 \div {}^{-}9$ **a.** $^{-}5$ **b.** $^{-}45$ **c.** $^{+}6$ **d.** $^{-}6$ (10–17)
23. The statement "The distance (*d*) traveled at a uniform rate equals the rate (*r*) times the length of time (*t*)" expressed as a formula is:

a. $d = \dfrac{t}{r}$ **b.** $d = \dfrac{r}{t}$ **c.** $d = rt$ **d.** $d = r + t$ (10-23)

24. If $n - 6 = 3$, find n. **a.** 3 **b.** 18 **c.** 2 **d.** 9 (10-24)

25. Which of the following equations has 4 as its solution?

    a. $6 = n - 2$ **b.** $\dfrac{x}{4} = 1$ **c.** $x + 2 = 2$ **d.** $12n = 3$ (10-24)

26. The ratio of 48 minutes to 1 hour is:
    a. 4 to 5 **b.** 3 to 4 **c.** 5 to 4 **d.** 2 to 3 (10-31)

27. The position of the line $\longleftrightarrow$ is:
    a. vertical **b.** horizontal **c.** slanting **d.** answer not given (11-3)

28. An angle with a measure of 96° is:
    a. acute **b.** right **c.** obtuse **d.** straight (11-7)

29. If the scale is 1 inch = 40 miles, $3\frac{7}{8}$ inches represents:
    a. 135 miles **b.** 145 miles **c.** 155 miles **d.** 165 miles (11-11)

30. If two angles of a triangle are 63° and 59°, the third angle is:
    a. 58° **b.** 60° **c.** 65° **d.** 68° (11-22)

31. The circumference around a circular table, 21 inches in diameter, is: ($\pi = \frac{22}{7}$)
    a. 28 inches **b.** 44 inches **c.** 66 inches **d.** 1,386 inches (11-26)

32. The cost of covering a rectangular floor 15 feet long by 12 feet wide with a rug costing $17.50 per square yard is:
    a. $180 **b.** $54.50 **c.** $350 **d.** $480 (11-27)

33. Which is the best buy of oranges?
    a. 8 for $.89 **b.** 10 for $1.05 **c.** 15 for $1.57 **d.** 18 for $1.91 (12-3)

34. A radio that regularly sells for $39 is reduced 20%. Its sale price is:
    a. $19 **b.** $31.20 **c.** $7.80 **d.** answer not given (6-11, 12-2)

35. If you miss the 11:50 A.M. train and trains run every 45 minutes, the next train is scheduled to leave at:
    a. 12:35 P.M. **b.** 1:05 P.M. **c.** 1:05 A.M. **d.** 12:35 A.M. (8-13)

36. If a purchase is $5.89, the change from a $10 bill should be:
    a. $4.11 **b.** $5.11 **c.** $4.21 **d.** $5.21 (12-4)

37. The interest on $3,200 for 6 months at $14\frac{3}{4}\%$ annual rate is:
    a. $236 **b.** $320 **c.** $147.50 **d.** $1,600 (6-14)

38. If the rate is 6%, the sales tax on a camera selling for $99.50 is:
    a. $6.00 **b.** $5.50 **c.** $5.97 **d.** $.60 (12-9)

39. A real estate agent charged $3,430 commission for selling a house for $49,000. The rate of commission charged is:
    a. 5% **b.** 6% **c.** 6.5% **d.** 7% (6-12)

40. If the telephone rate is $.41 for the first minute and $.29 for each additional minute, the charges for a 9-minute call is:
    a. $1.95 **b.** $2.73 **c.** $2.80 **d.** $.70 (5-22)

TABLE OF SQUARES AND SQUARE ROOTS

No.	Square	Square Root	No.	Square	Square Root	No.	Square	Square Root
1	1	1.000	34	1,156	5.831	67	4,489	8.185
2	4	1.414	35	1,225	5.916	68	4,624	8.246
3	9	1.732	36	1,296	6.000	69	4,761	8.307
4	16	2.000	37	1,369	6.083	70	4,900	8.367
5	25	2.236	38	1,444	6.164	71	5,041	8.426
6	36	2.449	39	1,521	6.245	72	5,184	8.485
7	49	2.646	40	1,600	6.325	73	5,329	8.544
8	64	2.828	41	1,681	6.403	74	5,476	8.602
9	81	3.000	42	1,764	6.481	75	5,625	8.660
10	100	3.162	43	1,849	6.557	76	5,776	8.718
11	121	3.317	44	1,936	6.633	77	5,929	8.775
12	144	3.464	45	2,025	6.708	78	6,084	8.832
13	169	3.606	46	2,116	6.782	79	6,241	8.888
14	196	3.742	47	2,209	6.856	80	6,400	8.944
15	225	3.873	48	2,304	6.928	81	6,561	9.000
16	256	4.000	49	2,401	7.000	82	6,724	9.055
17	289	4.123	50	2,500	7.071	83	6,889	9.110
18	324	4.243	51	2,601	7.141	84	7,056	9.165
19	361	4.359	52	2,704	7.211	85	7,225	9.220
20	400	4.472	53	2,809	7.280	86	7,396	9.274
21	441	4.583	54	2,916	7.348	87	7,569	9.327
22	484	4.690	55	3,025	7.416	88	7,744	9.381
23	529	4.796	56	3,136	7.483	89	7,921	9.434
24	576	4.899	57	3,249	7.550	90	8,100	9.487
25	625	5.000	58	3,364	7.616	91	8,281	9.539
26	676	5.099	59	3,481	7.681	92	8,464	9.592
27	729	5.196	60	3,600	7.746	93	8,649	9.644
28	784	5.292	61	3,721	7.810	94	8,836	9.695
29	841	5.385	62	3,844	7.874	95	9,025	9.747
30	900	5.477	63	3,969	7.937	96	9,216	9.798
31	961	5.568	64	4,096	8.000	97	9,409	9.849
32	1,024	5.657	65	4,225	8.062	98	9,604	9.899
33	1,089	5.745	66	4,356	8.124	99	9,801	9.950

TABLES OF MEASURE

Measure of Length—Metric

10 millimeters (mm) = 1 centimeter (cm)

10 centimeters (cm) = 1 decimeter (dm)

10 decimeters (dm) = 1 meter (m)

10 meters (m) = 1 dekameter (dam)

10 dekameters (dam) = 1 hectometer (hm)

10 hectometers (hm) = 1 kilometer (km)

1 centimeter (cm) = 10 millimeters (mm)

1 meter (m) = 100 centimeters (cm) = 1,000 millimeters (mm)

1 kilometer (km) = 1,000 meters (m)

Measure of Capacity—Metric

10 milliliters (mL) = 1 centiliter (cL)
10 centiliters (cL) = 1 deciliter (dL)
10 deciliters (dL) = 1 liter (L)
10 liters (L) = 1 dekaliter (daL)
10 dekaliters (daL) = 1 hectoliter (hL)
10 hectoliters (hL) = 1 kiloliter (kL)

Measure of Weight—Metric

10 milligrams (mg) = 1 centigram (cg)
10 centigrams (cg) = 1 decigram (dg)
10 decigrams (dg) = 1 gram (g)
10 grams (g) = 1 dekagram (dag)
10 dekagrams (dag) = 1 hectogram (hg)
10 hectograms (hg) = 1 kilogram (kg)
1,000 kilograms (kg) = 1 metric ton (t)

Metric Measures of Area, Volume, and Miscellaneous Equivalents

See pages 242 and 244.

Measures of Length—Customary

1 foot (ft.) = 12 inches (in.)
1 yard (yd.) = 3 feet (ft.) = 36 inches (in.)
1 rod (rd.) = 16½ feet (ft.) = 5½ yards (yd.)
1 statute mile (stat. mi.) = 5,280 feet (ft.) = 1,760 yards (yd.) = 320 rods (rd.)
1 statute mile (stat. mi.) $\approx$ 0.87 nautical mile (0.8684 naut. mi.)
1 nautical mile (naut. mi.) $\approx$ 6,080 feet (6,080.2 ft.)
$\approx$ 1.15 statute miles (1.1515 stat. mi.)
1 fathom (fath.) $\approx$ 6 feet (ft.)

Measure of Area—Customary

1 square foot (sq. ft.) = 144 square inches (sq. in.)
1 square yard (sq. yd.) = 9 square feet (sq. ft.)
1 square rod (sq. rd.) = 30.25 square yards (sq. yd.)
1 acre = 160 square rods (sq. rd.)
= 4,840 square yards (sq. yd.)
= 43,560 square feet (sq. ft.)
1 square mile (sq. mi.) = 640 acres

Measure of Volume—Customary

1 cubic foot (cu. ft.) = 1,728 cubic inches (cu. in.)
1 cubic yard (cu. yd.) = 27 cubic feet (cu. ft.)

Liquid Measure—Customary

1 pint (pt.) = 16 ounces (oz.)
= 4 gills (gi.)
1 quart (qt.) = 2 pints (pt.)
1 gallon (gal.) = 4 quarts (qt.)

Dry Measure—Customary

1 quart (qt.) = 2 pints (pt.)
1 peck (pk.) = 8 quarts (qt.)
1 bushel (bu.) = 4 pecks (pk.)

Measure of Weight—Avoirdupois—Customary

1 pound (lb.) = 16 ounces (oz.)
1 short ton (sh. tn. or T.) = 2,000 pounds (lb.)
1 long ton (1. ton) = 2,240 pounds (lb.)

Volume, Capacity, and Weight Equivalents—Customary

1 gallon (gal.) ≈ 231 cubic inches (cu. in.)
1 cubic foot (cu. ft.) ≈ 7½ gallons (gal.)
1 bushel (bu.) ≈ 1¼ cubic feet (cu. ft.)
≈ 2,150.42 cubic inches (cu. in.)
1 cu. ft. of fresh water weighs 62½ pounds (lb.)
1 cu. ft. of sea water weighs 64 pounds (lb.)

Measure of Time

1 minute (min.) = 60 seconds (sec.)
1 hour (hr.) = 60 minutes (min.)
1 day (da.) = 24 hours (hr.)
1 week (wk.) = 7 days (da.)
1 year (yr.) = 12 months (mo.)
= 52 weeks (wk.)
= 365 days (da.)

Angles and Arcs

1 circle = 360 degrees (°)
1 degree (°) = 60 minutes (')
1 minute (') = 60 seconds (")

Measure of Speed

1 knot = 1 nautical m.p.h.

Metric—Customary Equivalents

1 meter = 39.37 inches
≈ 3.28 feet (3.2808)
≈ 1.09 yards (1.0936)
1 centimeter ≈ .39 or .4 inch (.3937)
1 millimeter ≈ .04 inch (.03937)
1 kilometer ≈ .62 mile (.6214)
1 liter ≈ 1.06 liquid quarts (1.0567)
1 liter ≈ .91 dry quart (.9081)
1 gram ≈ .04 ounce (.0353)
1 kilogram ≈ 2.2 pounds (2.2046)
1 metric ton ≈ 2,204.62 pounds
1 inch = 25.4 millimeters
1 foot ≈ .3 meter (.3048)
1 yard ≈ .91 meter (.9144)
1 mile ≈ 1.61 kilometers (1.6093)
1 liquid quart ≈ .95 liter (.9463)
1 dry quart ≈ 1.1 liters (1.1012)
1 ounce ≈ 28.35 grams (28.3495)
1 pound ≈ .45 kilogram (.4536)
1 short ton ≈ .91 metric ton (.9072)
1 square inch ≈ 6.45 square centimeters (6.4516)
1 cubic inch ≈ 16.39 cubic centimeters (16.3872)

Index

Multiplication
approximate numbers, 268
by powers of ten, 152
decimal fractions, 149–151
definition of terms, 57–58
degrees, minutes, seconds, 257
denominate numbers, 248, 250–253, 256
fractions and mixed numbers, 116–118
integers, 322–330
lattice, 62–63
positive and negative numbers, 322–334
properties, 44, 45–52, 328–330, 332–334
rational numbers, 330–334
Russian peasant, 61
whole numbers, 57–60
Multiplicative identity, 51, 95, 96, 329–330, 334
Multiplicative inverse, 118, 334, 363, 364
Multiplier, 57

Natural number, 9
Nautical mile, 477, 478
Negative number, 283
Net amount, 200
Net price, 200, 459
Net proceeds, 202
Net profit, 204
Non-metric geometry, 384–401
Non-negative integer, 284
Non-positive integer, 284
Notation
decimal, 11, 134
expanded, 24, 140
fraction, 88
scientific, 158
sigma, 279
Number, 6
approximate, 268
cardinal, 8
composite, 27
denominate, 248
directed, 283, 293
even, 26, 284

graph of, 288
integer, 284
irrational, 216, 286
mixed, 99
natural, 9
negative, 283
odd, 26, 284
ordinal, 8
positive, 283
prime, 27
rational, 88, 286
real, 286
signed, 283
whole, 9
Number line, 10, 105, 282, 283, 285, 288–291, 293–296, 298–300, 314
Number pairs, 90
Number sentences, 82
Numeral, 6
reading, 14, 138
writing, 16, 139
Numeration, systems of
decimal, 11–24, 134
Roman, 24–26
Numerator, 88
Numerical coefficient, 348
Numerical phrase or expression, 348

Obtuse angle, 395
Obtuse triangle, 397
Octagon, 397, 423
Odd number, 26, 284
One, properties of, 51
One-to-one correspondence, 7
Open sentences, 350–351
Operating (overhead) expenses, 204
Operations, 42
binary, 42
inverse, 42–43
properties, 44–52
Opposite angles, 427–428
Opposites, 283, 285, 293, 296–297
Order, dense, 105
Ordered number pair, 90
Ordinal number, 8
Owning an automobile, 469

Pairing, 7
Parallel lines, 389, 422
Parallelogram, 398, 424–426
Parentheses, 347
Partial dividend, 64
Partial product, 57, 58
Pascal's triangle, 73
Patterns, 73
Pentagon, 397
Percent, 178–213
expressed as common fractions, 182
expressed as decimal fractions, 180
finding a number when a percent of it is known, 194
finding a percent of a number, 188
finding what percent one number is of another, 191
meaning, 178
solving by equations, 197–200
solving by proportions, 196
Perfect square, 216
Perimeter, definition, 430
rectangle, 430
square, 431
Perpendicular bisector, 417
Perpendicular lines, 389, 415–417
Pi (π), 432
Place value, 11–12, 134–135
Plane, 384, 386, 392
Plane figures, 396–397
Point, 384–385, 391–392
collinear, 391
coplanar, 392
Polygon, 397–398, 423–426
inscribed, 423
regular, 397, 423
sum of angles, 425–426
Polyhedron, 399–400
Polynomial, 24, 140
Positive number, 283
Powers, 21, 22, 347
Powers of ten, 22